TROILUS AND CRISEYDE

London: Humphrey Milford
Oxford University Press

THE BOOK OF
Troilus and Criseyde

BY

GEOFFREY CHAUCER

Edited from all the Known Manuscripts by

ROBERT KILBURN ROOT

PROFESSOR OF ENGLISH IN PRINCETON UNIVERSITY

PRINCETON
PRINCETON UNIVERSITY PRESS

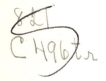
Printed in the United States of America

PREFACE

TROILUS AND CRISEYDE *is the only one of Chaucer's major undertakings which he brought to final completion. If less universal in its appeal than the varied pageant of the* Canterbury Tales, *it has, by way of compensation, the heightened power which comes from a work of creative imagination brilliantly sustained throughout a long and unified poem. It is of all Chaucer's works the most perfect expression of his art. In portrayal of character, in easy flow of dramatic action, in mastery of execution and grace of manner, it is the outstanding masterpiece of English narrative verse.*

For the integrity of its text Chaucer was deeply solicitous. The editor who has labored to purge the text of the miswritings and "mismetrings" which it underwent at the hands of the scribes and early printers, and to incorporate into it the final revisions dictated by its author's exacting taste, has thus the satisfaction of knowing that his work is in furtherance of the poet's own earnest wish. Fortunately the evidence is so full that this work of restoration can be done with a high degree of certainty. The principles on which the text has been constituted are set forth at length in the closing pages of the Introduction.

The work of an editor must always be one of many obligations. In the preparation of the text and variant readings, I have been reminded anew of the debt which all Chaucerians owe to the pioneer industry of Dr. Furnivall and his collaborators in the work of the Chaucer Society. It has materially lightened my labors to have in print literatim *copies of seven of the manuscripts of Troilus, among them the two important manuscripts, Cp and J, which have served as primary authorities for my text. I have also had in my possession a complete and careful transcript of H4 made for Dr. Furnivall but never printed. When, some years ago, I undertook to complete for the Chaucer Society a study of the textual tradition of the poem, Sir William McCormick most generously turned over to me his collations of seven of the original authorities. It is a pleasure to express anew my gratitude to him. I have myself, however, verified in large part both these collations and the Chaucer Society prints, and have gone to the original documents whenever any important question of the text was at stake.*

In my commentary I have laid under contribution the work of all the scholars who have busied themselves with the poem. Most thoroughgoing is my debt to Dr. Skeat, the only editor hitherto who has given a detailed commentary. I am under particular obligation also to the work of Professor George L. Kittredge in his Chaucer Society volume, The Date of Chaucer's Troilus, *and in his paper on "Chaucer's Lollius"; and to that of Professor Karl Young in* The Origin and Development of the Story of Troilus and Criseyde. *Other obligations I have indicated in the bibliographical list appended to the Notes.*

To my friend Professor Albert S. Cook my debt is of

a more intimate character. It was he who, years ago, first taught my feet to walk in Chaucerian ways, and who, more important still, gave me the discipline of insistent accuracy, even de minimis, which is indispensable to the work of an editor. To him I have more than once turned for advice as to the procedure to be followed in this edition, and have found him always wise in his counsel and generous in his help.

In the Introduction I have tried to present within reasonable compass the material facts upon which the literary interpretation of the poem must rest; but I have not attempted, except incidentally and by implication, an aesthetic appraisal of Chaucer's art. Nor have I tried to discuss the grammar and phonology of the poem. The essential characteristics of Chaucer's language have already been established; such matters as still remain unsettled must await for their solution a critical text of the poet's other writings. They cannot profitably be considered on the basis of a single poem.

Instead of preparing a complete glossary, I have given in the Notes my interpretation of such passages as involve obscurity, and have glossed many of the less familiar words. For quotations illustrative of such words, I have usually been content to refer the reader to the appropriate section of the New English Dictionary. *I assume that the reader of this edition will already be familiar with the common words and constructions of Chaucer's diction.*

With the ever increasing attention paid to Chaucer in schools and colleges, the number of readers to whom his language is no longer a serious barrier is large. Both in the Introduction and Notes I have had in mind the needs of this class of readers as well as those of the much smaller group of special students. To the still smaller group—though we are after all a goodly company—of professed Chaucerians, those scholars whose own studies have helped to make possible such a volume as this, I "direct" my book, begging them in the words of our kindly master,

> *To vouchensauf, ther nede is, to correcte,*
> *Of youre benignites and zeles goode.*

R. K. R.

Princeton, February 2, 1926.

CONTENTS

Chaucers Wordes Unto Adam, His Owne Scriveyn

Adam scriveyn, if ever it thee bifalle
Boece or Troilus to wryten newe,
Under thy lokkes thou most have the scalle,
But after my making thou wryte trewe.
So ofte a daye I mot thy werk renewe,
Hit to correcte and eek to rubbe and scrape;
And al is through thy negligence and rape.

INTRODUCTION

I. AUTHORSHIP AND TITLE

THAT *Troilus and Criseyde* is the work of Geoffrey Chaucer is certain beyond dispute. It is referred to as Chaucer's in the Prologue to the *Legend of Good Women* (B 332, 441, 469; A 265, 431, 459), and in the "Retractions" at the end of the *Canterbury Tales* (I 1086). It is explicitly attributed to Chaucer in three of the surviving manuscripts, R, S2, and H3, and by Lydgate in his *Sege of Troye* and in his *Fall of Princes*.[1]

By what title Chaucer wished his book to be known is not clear. Perhaps, as in the case of the *Book of the Duchess* and the *Legend of Good Women*, no single definitive title was established in his own mind. In the Prologue to the *Legend* the work is spoken of allusively rather than by title —"How that Crisseyde Troilus forsook"; though in B 441 (A 431) the name "Creseyde" is used as though it were a title. In the "Retractions" the work is called "the book of Troilus"; and the same phrase is used by Usk in his *Testament of Love* (3. 4. 258–9), and in the catalogue of John Paston's books (1482 ?).[2] Lydgate called the poem "Troilus and Cresseide"; and from Lydgate's day until our own the double title has been in general use. Recent scholars seem to prefer the shorter title "Troilus," used by Chaucer himself in the lines addressed to Adam, his own scribe.[3]

[1] See Spurgeon, 1.24, 27.
[2] Spurgeon, 1.60.
[3] The testimony of the surviving manuscripts proves only that there was a divergence of usage during the century following Chaucer's death. H4 and Cp, in the colophons, call the poem "Liber Troili"; Ph and H2 call it merely "Troylus," S1 has a colophon which echoes the opening line of the poem: "here endeth the book of Troylus of double sorowe in loving of Cri[seyde]." H1, Cl, S2, and J have the longer phrase "Liber Troili et Criseydis." R uses the English phrase "the book of Troylus and of Cresseyde." The five remaining manuscripts, of which four have lost the end of the poem, and so lack a colophon, furnish no evidence.
The colophon of Caxton's edition (*circa* 1483) reads: "Here endith

That the division into books originates with the poet himself is made clear by 3. 1818:

> My thridde book now ende ich in this wyse;

by 4. 26:

> This ilke ferthe book me helpeth fyne;

and by the formal proems which introduce the first four books.[4]

There is, however, some ground for believing that the proems to Books II, III, and IV were not present in the poet's earliest intention. Most striking is the fact that they are omitted by R. Since R is consistently a β manuscript, we must assume that these proems, which are present in all the other authorities, had already been composed before R was derived. Nor is there any reason to suppose that they were deliberately omitted by a scribe, or cancelled by the poet himself. The only plausible explanation of their absence in R is that they had been lost from the original before R was derived; and such an explanation implies that in the original they had been added later on loose leaves. It

Troylus as touchyng Creseyde." In the 1517 edition of Wynkyn de Worde the title reads: "The noble and amerous auncyent hystory of Troylus and Cresyde in the tyme of the syege of Troye"; and the colophon reads: "Thus endeth the treatyse of Troylus the hevy." Pynson's edition of 1526 has, both in title and colophon, "the boke of Troylus and Creseyde." The folio of Thynne (1532) has the title "Troylus and Creseyde"; but the colophon and the running title use the shorter form "Troylus." Stowe's edition of 1561, and Speght's editions of 1598 and 1602, follow the usage of Thynne.

[4] In the Moutier edition, *Filostrato* is divided into nine cantos, of which the last is a short envoy. In the Paris edition of 1789 the divisions are different. In the absence of a critical edition, one can have no assurance as to the exact divisions of Boccaccio's poem in the copy which Chaucer used. But they must to some extent have corresponded with those given by Moutier; for Book II of *Troilus* ends at the same point in the story as the second canto in Moutier. Book III and Proem IV correspond with Canto III. Book IV corresponds with Canto IV. Chaucer's fifth book deals with the matter found in Cantos V-VIII of Moutier's edition.

is significant also that none of the authorities has any proem to Book V.[5]

A further indication that these proems were an after-thought may be found in the fact that the γ MSS. treat the proem to Book IV as a conclusion of Book III. The last two stanzas of Book III are addressed to Venus, and constitute a sort of exordium to the book. The first stanza of the succeeding proem closely continues the thought of this exordium. In all the γ MSS., save S2 and D, the proem to Book IV is not marked off in any way from Book III. At the end of the proem, CpClH1 have the rubric: "Explicit liber Tercius. Incipit Liber Quartus," and AD begin line 29 with a special initial. In S2, Book III ends at line 1806 with the rubric: "Explicit Liber Tercius," line 1807 begins with a special initial, and before 4.29 there is a rubric: "Incipit quartus liber." In D, a contemporary hand, apparently that of the scribe, has written in the margin of 3. 1807 the word: "Prologue." The "mixed" text of H3 indicates the termination of Book III with the erroneous rubric: "Explicit Liber iiijtus"; and at the end of Proem IV writes: "Crt (Certe?) Sic explicit Liber quartus."

The proem of Book I must, however, have been present from the first. It is found regularly in all the MSS., including R.[6]

---

[5] The first two stanzas of Book V, which are based on stanzas of *Teseide*, are in the nature of a proem; but none of the authorities so mark them.

[6] It may be noted that in H1S2DigH3H4R the proem of Book I is not set off in any way from the rest of the book. In JCpClAD, line 29 of Book I has a special initial, but there is no rubric such as follows the proems of Books II and III (and, in J, Book IV also).

Though the division into books originates with the author himself, certain of the MSS. fail to indicate the division. Ph, which gives an α text throughout, originally indicated no break in the poem, save at the beginning of Book V, where there is a rubric and space for a special initial. Later the scribe himself supplied indications of books and proems in the margin, and by means of running titles. That these indications came from a γ source is shown by the fact that the proem of Book IV is treated as in the γ MSS. In the portion of H2 written by Hand 1, which is that of the same scribe who wrote Ph, there is similarly no indi-

II. DATE OF COMPOSITION

Chaucer's *Troilus* was completed and given to the public between the spring of 1385 and the end of the year 1386, or, at the very latest, the early months of 1387.

The second of these dates, the *terminus ad quem*, is established by the following facts:

(1) *Troilus* was already known to the reading public before the composition of the earlier, so-called B, version of the Prologue to the *Legend of Good Women*, in which Cupid accuses the poet of having undermined men's faith in women by saying as him list of Criseyde.[7] Fortunately we are able to date the first version of the Prologue with a good deal of certainty. Professor Lowes has shown[8] that in it Chaucer makes use of the *Lay de Franchise* of Deschamps,

cation of division into books. This portion of H2 includes the beginnings of Books II, III, and IV.

H3 indicates no break between Book I and Book II. Proem III is introduced by a special initial, and between Proem III and Book III there is an appropriate rubric. At the end of Book III is found the erroneous rubric, "Explicit Liber iiijtus," already noted above. The first stanza of Book V is treated as part of the preceding Book; and, after 5.7, is written the curious rubric: "Explicit ijda pars Vti Libri." Apparently the scribe regarded Book IV as "prima pars quinti libri"; for in H3 line 26 of Book IV reads,

Thys *fyfte and laste* boke me helpyth to dyffyne,

where the correct reading is "This ilke ferthe book." This curious aberration of H3 could be dismissed as mere scribal blundering, were it not that H4, a MS. which in this part of the text is totally unrelated to H3, reads in 4.26: "This feerde & laste book," and shows no break whatever between Book IV and Book V.

These readings of H3 and H4, taken with the absence of a proem for Book V, raise the question whether the poet may not have originally intended a division into four books only, the number of parts into which the *Knight's Tale* is divided. Such a supposition gains some support from 4.26-8.

> This ilke ferthe book me helpeth fyne,
> So that the losse of lyf and love yfeere
> Of Troilus be fully shewed here,

lines which seem to imply that the death of Troilus is to be transacted, and the poem concluded, in the fourth book.

[7] *Legend*, B 332-4. See also B 441, 469.
[8] *P.M.L.A.* 20.753-71.

a poem written about May, 1385. It seems unlikely that Chaucer should have read this poem until some months after its composition; and Professor Lowes has shown reason for believing that he did not see a copy of it before the spring or summer of 1386. But a passage of the Prologue is imitated by Thomas Usk in his *Testament of Love*,[9] a work written not later than the winter of 1387–88. The publication of the Prologue to the *Legend* falls, then, between the summer of 1385 at earliest and the autumn of 1387 at latest, with the probabilities favoring the year 1386.

(2) Thomas Usk was well acquainted also with *Troilus*. In Book III, Chapter IV, of the *Testament of Love*, the allegorical personage, Love, cites as authority "the noble philosophical poete in Englissh," and the "tretis that he made of my servant Troilus"; and the book shows throughout a detailed familiarity with the poem.[10] The *Testament of Love* was probably written in 1387. Its author was executed for treason on March 4, 1388.[11]

(3) In 1387,[12] died Ralph Strode, the London lawyer, who is probably the Strode to whom Chaucer addresses his poem.[13]

The earliest date for *Troilus*, the *terminus a quo*, is determined by the following considerations:

(1) Chaucer can hardly have been acquainted with Boccaccio's *Filostrato*, the primary source of *Troilus*, earlier than his first Italian journey of 1373.

(2) In the account of the popular tumult aroused by Hector's opposition to the exchange of Criseyde, and in the author's comment on the blindness of popular opinion (4.

---

[9] Tatlock, *Development and Chronology*, pp. 22-3.
[10] See notes to 1.217, 238; 2.807, 1335, 1380-3; 3.526, 1282; 4.460; 5.1432, and Skeat, *Oxford Chaucer* 7. xxvii.
[11] *DNB* s.v. Usk, Thomas.
[12] *DNB* s.v. Strode, Ralph.
[13] See note to 5.1857.

183–203), there seems to be, as Professor Carleton Brown has suggested,[14] a reminiscence of the great Peasants' Revolt of 1381.

(3) A date later than January 14, 1382, the date of the marriage of Richard II to Anne of Bohemia, is established, if we accept the brilliant suggestion of Professor Lowes[15] that the curious mention of the letter A in 1. 171 refers to the use of Queen Anne's initial intertwined with the initial R of her royal husband as a decorative device on courtly robes and tapestries, a use of the royal initials for which Professor Lowes cites documentary evidence.[16]

(4) In lines 624–5 of Book III, Chaucer supposes a conjunction of Jupiter, Saturn, and the crescent Moon in the sign Cancer. Conjunctions of Jupiter and Saturn take place at intervals of approximately twenty years; but the periodicity of these conjunctions is of such a nature that there are periods of approximately two hundred years during which a conjunction of Jupiter and Saturn occurs in any given sign at intervals of about sixty years, and other periods of over six hundred years during which the conjunction never occurs in that sign. Chaucer's life fell at the very end of one of these six-hundred-year periods during which Jupiter and Saturn are not conjoined in the sign Cancer; such a conjunction had not occurred since the year A.D. 769.

Now the conjunction which Chaucer supposes involves not only Jupiter and Saturn, but the crescent Moon also. In order that the Moon shall appear as a thin crescent, "with hire hornes pale," in the sign Cancer, the Sun must be in, or approaching, the next preceding sign, Gemini, and the time of year must be May or early June; for, according

---

[14] *Mod. Lang. Notes* 26.208-11 (1911).

[15] "The Date of Chaucer's *Troilus and Criseyde*," *P.M.L.A.* 23.285-306 (1908).

[16] For further discussion of this piece of evidence, see note to 1.171.

to Chaucer's calendar, the Sun entered Gemini on or about May 12. An approximate calculation, based on Newcomb's planetary tables, shows that on April 13, 1385, Jupiter and Saturn were in exact astronomical conjunction in longitude 86° 35′, i.e., near the end of the sign of Gemini, only three and a half degrees from the beginning of Cancer. But for the astrologer it is not necessary that the conjunction be exact; he would regard Jupiter and Saturn as being in "platic" conjunction when they are not more than nine degrees of longitude apart. In 1385 Jupiter entered Cancer on May 1; and Saturn entered Cancer on May 14. On the latter date both planets were in the sign of Cancer, two and a half degrees of longitude apart, and hence still in "platic" conjunction. The Moon was new on or about May 10 (within a day); and on or about May 13 the pale horns of the crescent Moon were visible very close to Jupiter and Saturn—the very disposition which Chaucer has represented in his poem, and one that previous to 1385 had not occurred for more than 600 years.

The conjunction of 1385 was remarkable enough to secure mention in Walsingham's *Historia Anglicana*:[17]

Conjunctio Jovis et Saturni

Eodem tempore Conjunctio duarum maximarum planetarum facta est, videlicet Jovis et Saturni, mense Maio; quam secuta est maxima regnorum commotio, prout patebit inferius, cum attigerit stylus locum.

It is to be noticed that Walsingham dates the conjunction as in the month of May, though the exact astronomical conjunction was on April 13. His interest in the event, as the entry shows, was astrological; and astrologically the platic conjunction in Cancer, which began on May 14, was much more significant than the exact astronomical conjunction of the preceding month, since it involved what the astrologers

[17] Rolls Series, Vol. II, p. 126. The entry appears in nearly identical language in Walsingham's *Chronicon Angliae* (Rolls Series, p. 364) and in the same author's *Ypodigma Neustriae* (Rolls Series, p. 341).

called a "permutation of triplicities," i.e., a change in the zodiacal place of major conjunctions from the "triplicity" of Gemini, Aquarius, and Libra to the "triplicity" of Cancer, Pisces, and Scorpio, where conjunctions of Jupiter and Saturn had not occurred for six hundred years. Among the astrological results of this particular change should be floods and heavy rains, precisely the influence which Chaucer has supposed in the passage under discussion.[18]

We find, then, that Chaucer has introduced into his poem an astronomical phenomenon so unusual that it had not taken place until his time for many centuries, and one which entailed important astrological consequences. By bringing into his supposed configuration the crescent Moon also in the sign of Cancer, he has made it necessary that the phenomenon should take place in May or early June. In the month of May, 1385, occurred a conjunction which strikingly agrees with that which Chaucer has supposed, and one which attracted the attention of his contemporaries. It would be hard to believe that this is mere accidental coincidence. It is more reasonable to believe that Chaucer took directly from the night's starred face these symbols which he has woven into the high romance of *Troilus*. Since the passage in question was already present in the *alpha* text of the poem, it follows that the poem was not finished earlier than the spring of 1385.

It would not be profitable to attempt to push the *terminus a quo* still later by arguing that the lines in question are found a little before the middle of the poem. We have no data by which to determine the rate at which Chaucer's literary work progressed; nor have we any assurance that he worked consecutively from episode to episode of his story, bringing one to final completion before he began the

---

[18] For a more detailed discussion of the astrological import of this conjunction, and for a full statement of the astronomical data concerned, see article by R. K. Root and H. N. Russell, "A Planetary Date for Chaucer's *Troilus*," *P.M.L.A.* 39.48-63 (1924).

next. We must be content to say that the completion of *Troilus* falls between the spring of 1385 and the early months of 1387, the latest possible date for the first version of the Prologue to the *Legend of Good Women*.

The date 1385–86 accords with all the evidence summarized above, and with the known facts of Chaucerian chronology. By a writ dated February 17, 1385, Chaucer had been granted permission to administer by a permanent deputy his duties as comptroller of customs and subsidies, and hence should have had leisure for the prosecution of literary work. By 1387 he was already engaged on the Prologue to the *Canterbury Tales*. The displeasure expressed in the Prologue to the *Legend of Good Women*, by Queen Alcestis and Cupid, at the heresy against Love's law in the story of Criseyde's falseness, takes on added significance as the echo of the sensation produced among English readers by a very recent poem.

Against this date there is but one consideration of any moment.[19] In lines 5245–56 of Gower's *Miriour de l'Omme*, an allegorical personage called Sompnolent goes to sleep in church, and dreams that he is hearing recited—

> la geste
> De Troÿlus et de la belle
> Creseide.

There is good evidence to show that this passage of the *Miriour de l'Omme* was written not later than 1377.[20] If the

---

[19] I think we may dismiss as the mistake of a not very reliable witness the statement of Lydgate in the Prologue to the *Fall of Princes* (283-7) that Chaucer wrote *Troilus* "in youthe," "longe or that he deide." In 1385-6 Chaucer was in his middle forties; but even in 1373, when he returned from his first Italian journey, he was some 33 years old, an age to which Lydgate would hardly have applied the phrase "in youthe." The date 1385-6 is sufficiently in accord with Lydgate's phrase, "longe or that he deide." It must be remembered that the very passage of Lydgate which contains these phrases says that the Italian book from which *Troilus* was "translated" bore the title "Trophe," a statement which is almost certainly a blunder (compare p. xl).

[20] See Tatlock, *Development and Chronology*, pp. 220-5.

"geste" referred to is Chaucer's poem, it would be necessary to assign *Troilus* to a date earlier than 1377. But such an interpretation of the allusion is by no means inevitable. Troilus was already a famous lover. If in the one surviving manuscript of the *Mirour* his lady's name had appeared as "Briseide" instead of "Creseide," the allusion would have been accepted by every one as a vague reference to the story as it is found in the *Roman de Troie* of Benoit. But the substitution of "Criseida" for "Briseida" seems to have been the invention of Boccaccio,[21] and there is no reason to believe that Gower read Italian. There is excellent reason, however, for supposing that, before 1377, Gower's good friend Chaucer was already acquainted with *Filostrato*, and if so, he may well have told Gower about it, and have called attention to the alteration of name.[22] In the face of the very strong evidence that *Troilus* is to be dated in 1385–86, the name "Creseide" in Gower's poem must be explained in some such way as this.[23]

III. SOURCES

As a narrative poem, Chaucer's *Troilus* is a work of great originality. One cannot exaggerate the startling sense of novelty with which its subtle blending of romance and realism, of sentiment and humor, must have impressed its earliest readers. Nothing like it existed in the literary

[21] See p. xxvii.

[22] Even Professor Tatlock (*Development and Chronology*, p. 221), who has argued at length that the reference in the *Mirour* is to Chaucer's poem, assumes that it was in conversation with Chaucer that Gower derived his slight but indisputable acquaintance with Dante.

[23] For a full presentation of the argument, based primarily on the passage in Gower, in favor of an early date for *Troilus*, see the article by Tatlock in *Mod. Phil.* 1.317-24 (1903) and the same author's *Development and Chronology* 15-33 (1907). Tatlock's argument is combatted by Lowes in *P.M.L.A.* 20.823-33 (1905) and by Kittredge in his Chaucer Society volume, *The Date of Chaucer's Troilus* (1909). It is to be remembered that Tatlock's discussions antedate the evidence offered by Lowes and by Carleton Brown for a date later than 1381, and the evidence based on the great conjunction of May, 1385.

world of the Middle Ages—English, French, or Italian. For
the reader of today it is still one of the greatest of verse
narratives, with that highest sort of originality which re-
sides in its energy, its freshness, its truth to life. But its
originality does not consist in the invention of a new story.
Like many of the world's greatest poets, Chaucer was content to breathe new life into a story already old.

Among the fruits of Chaucer's journeyings in Italy was the
acquaintance that he made with the *Filostrato* of Boccaccio,
a very lovely poetic narrative of 5704 lines in *ottava rima*,
which recounts the love of Troilo for the faithless Criseida.[24]
So far as plot and *dramatis personae* are concerned, *Troilus*
is a free reworking of *Filostrato*. The Italian poem, in its
turn, is the poetic expansion of an episode found in the
Roman de Troie of Benoit de Ste. Maure, and in the Latin
paraphrase of Benoit made by Guido delle Colonne.[25] Benoit's romance of Troy is an elaboration of the meagre epi-
tomes of Dares and Dictys. So that Chaucer's story is a
more than twice told tale.

Dares and Dictys

It will be necessary to treat only in outline the history of
the Troy story as it shaped itself through the medieval centuries. This history begins, not with Homer, but with the
De Excidio Trojae Historia of "Dares Phrygius." The events
of the *Iliad* include but an episode of the Trojan War—the
wrath of Achilles and its consequences; neither the beginnings of the conflict nor the destruction of the city concern
Homer's Muse. Moreover, as sober history the *Iliad* was
discredited among medieval critics, because its author lived

[24] The printed texts of *Filostrato* give the lady's name as *Griseida*;
and this form is found also in certain of the MSS. It is probable, however, that Boccaccio wrote *Criseida*. In any event, the substitution of
Gr for *Cr* is but a detail of Italian phonetics. See article by E. H.
Wilkins, *Mod. Lang. Notes* 24.65-7.
[25] Boccaccio seems to have used both Benoit and Guido. See the discussion of the matter by Young, *Origin and Development*, pp. 1-26.

long after the events which he describes, because he is a pronounced partisan of the Greek side, and because he has included in his narrative such impossible details as the active participation in battle of the Olympian gods. To nearly all medieval scholars and authors, also, the *Iliad* in its original language was a closed book. If they read Homer at all, it was in the *Ilias Latina* of Silius Italicus, which long went under the name of "Pindarus Thebanus," an epitome which condenses the poem into some 1100 lines of Latin hexameter, with the total loss of all the qualities which make Homer's poem great.

The *De Excidio Trojae Historia* purports to be the work of an eye-witness, Dares the Phrygian, who was himself present in the beleaguered city.[26] It survives to us in forty-four short chapters,[27] written in wretched Latin prose, which lacks not only literary charm, but the most elementary qualities of style. There is a prefatory letter, purporting to be from Cornelius Nepos to Sallust, in which Nepos declares that he found the history of Dares at Athens, and has translated it literally into Latin. But the existing text, which certainly is not by Nepos, cannot have been written earlier than the sixth century A.D.[28] The narrative begins with the Argonautic expedition, and the first destruction of Troy during the reign of King Laòmedon, gives a series of portraits of the principal Greek and Trojan leaders, recounts the various battles and intervening truces which make up the war, and describes the final destruction of the city.

Also the supposed narrative of an eye-witness is the *Ephemeris Belli Trojani* of Dictys the Cretan. The preface

---

[26] Homer, *Iliad* 5.9, mentions Dares as a rich man and blameless, a priest of Hephaestus.

[27] In the Teubner series, it fills 52 pages of text.

[28] Constans, 6.194. There is some reason to believe that there may have existed a longer Latin text of "Dares," now lost, of which the version which we possess is a condensation. For a discussion of this hypothesis see Constans 6.224-34.

of this work informs us that Dictys was a citizen of Cnossus in Crete, who, with Idomeneus and Merion, joined in the expedition against Troy. During the war he kept a journal, written in Phoenician characters, of the events which were passing before his eyes. At his death, the six books of his journal were buried with him in a tin case, which was finally brought to light by an earthquake in the thirteenth year of the reign of Nero. At the command of Nero, the document was transliterated into Greek characters; and from this Greek text was made a Latin translation by one Septimius Romanus.

This Latin version is more than twice as long as the *Historia* of Dares, and is written in excellent Latin, apparently of the fourth century A.D.[29] While the romantic story of the metal box and the earthquake need not be taken seriously, there is conclusive evidence that the Latin version is indeed a translation from a Greek original. A papyrus found at Tebtunis in 1899 contains a fragment of the Greek Dictys which corresponds with seven chapters of Book IV of the Latin version.[30] From the Greek original are derived also a number of Byzantine chronicles of the Trojan War, of which the most important is the *Chronographia* of Malalas (sixth century A.D.).[31]

The narrative of Dictys begins with the rape of Helen, and concludes with the return of the Greek heroes to their homes.

Benoit and Guido

On the basis primarily of Dares and Dictys, more particularly of the former, Benoit of Sainte Maure (near Poitiers) composed in the second half of the twelfth century his

[29] Constans, 6.196.
[30] *Tebtunis Papyri*, ed. Grenfell, Hunt, and Goodspeed, London, 1907, Vol. 2, pp. 9-18.
[31] For a list of these Byzantine writings, and for a discussion of their relation to the *Ephemeris* of Dictys, see N. E. Griffin, *Dares and Dictys*, Baltimore (Johns Hopkins Diss.), 1907, pp. 34-108, and Constans, 6.200-24.

Roman de Troie,[32] a spirited poem in rhymed octosyllabic couplets, which extends to the formidable length of 30,316 lines. Up to line 24,425 Benoit follows the outline of Dares; for the rest of the poem he draws on Dictys, with still an eye now and then on Dares. But into the dull and tedious narratives of his sources Benoit puts life and color and movement. Like many of the medieval romances, the *Roman de Troie* is unduly repetitious and prolix; but it is none the less a work of genuine literary merit.

Of the additions which Benoit made to the story, the one that concerns us is the episode of Briseida, daughter of Calchas, who, sent from Troy to her father's gorgeous tent in the Grecian camp, forgets her love for Troilus, and gives her fickle heart to Diomede. For this episode there is no hint in Dares or in Dictys—at least in the texts of which we have any knowledge. In the *Historia* of Dares there is frequent mention of Troilus, son of Priam, who is described as "magnum, pulcherrimum, pro aetate valentem, fortem, cupidum virtutis";[33] but it is always as the warrior, foremost in the field of battle, with no hint of any love-story. Among the portraits of famous personages, Dares describes also Briseida, who is "formosam, non alta statura, candidam, capillo flavo et molli, superciliis iunctis, oculis venustis, corpore aequali, blandam, affabilem, verecundam, animo simplici, piam." [34] But there is no hint of any relation of Briseida to Troilus, nor does Briseida ever figure in the narrative of Dares except for the portrait of her which has just been quoted.

So far as we know, it was Benoit who invented the story

---

[32] Of Benoit nothing is known beyond his name and residence, which he himself gives in line 132 of his poem. Other poems, *Roman de Thèbes*, *Roman d'Eneas*, formerly attributed to him, are probably the work of other poets. Constans dates the poem between 1155 and 1160. This date depends on the identification of the "Riche dame de riche rei," whom Benoit addresses in lines 13,457-70, with Eleanor, queen of Henry II of England. See Constans 6.165-91.

[33] Cap. 12.

[34] Cap. 13.

of Briseida's faithlessness in love. The story as Benoit tells it is only of the heroine's faithlessness; for it begins at the point where Briseida is to be restored to her father. Troilus is her accepted lover, but there is no account whatever of the course of their love before the separation is decreed. What we have is the portion of the story which fills Books IV and V of Chaucer's poem. The episode of Briseida occupies 1349 lines. Some 500 additional lines are devoted to the death of Troilus at the hands of Achilles. But the passages given to the episode are not consecutive; they are intercalated between accounts of the various battles. The episode begins at line 13,065 of the poem, and ends with line 20,682, or, if we continue to the death of Troilus and Hecuba's lament over her dead son, at line 21,782.[35]

In the year 1287, Guido delle Colonne, a judge of Messina in Sicily, produced in a rhetorical Latin prose a paraphrase of Benoit's poem, under the title of *Historia Trojana*. He somewhat abridged the long speeches and ornate descriptions of Benoit, and added passages of sententious moral comment and learned digressions; but he altered so little the narrative content of his original that a summary of any portion of Guido would be nearly identical with a corresponding summary of Benoit. So nearly identical are the two works in their substance, that in a majority of cases it is impossible to assert with confidence that Boccaccio, or Chaucer, is following the one rather than the other.

In accordance with the literary ethics of his day, Guido cites as authorities for his history the names of Dares and Dictys, whom he regards as the ultimate guarantors of his reliability as a sober historian, and suppresses all mention of Benoit. There is reason to believe that he had before his

---

[35] A convenient summary of the 8718 lines of Benoit's poem which include the episode is given by Professor Kittredge in his Chaucer Society volume, *The Date of Chaucer's Troilus*, pp. 62-5. (Kittredge follows the line-numbering of Joly's edition, which differs somewhat from that of Constans.)

eyes the Latin text of Dares;[36] but his overwhelming dependence on Benoit is clear beyond any doubt.[37] It seems probable that he had never read the *Ephemeris* of Dictys.[38]

Boccaccio

It was the genius of Boccaccio which seized on the episode of the faithless Briseida, as it is found in the pages of Benoit and Guido, and made of it a unified and beautiful poetic narrative. What had been an episode in a history of the Trojan War becomes the dominant substance, while the battles about the beleaguered city become only a tenuous background for the story of passionate love and sorrow, in which Boccaccio saw an analogue to his own love for Maria d'Aquino, his "Fiammetta."

Boccaccio is responsible not only for this fundamental change of emphasis. He has of his own invention devised the whole story of the falling in love of Troilo, the wooing, and the final winning of the lady—all the events, in short, which precede the decree which sends Criscida from Troy to her father's tent.[39] In Benoit, and in Guido, the episode begins with Briseida's departure, and her status as mistress of Troilus is merely taken for granted. As part of his narrative machinery, Boccaccio created the character of Pandaro, a young courtier, friend of Troilo and cousin of Criseida, to serve as confidant and go-between in the wooing.[40]

[36] Constans, 6.322-7.

[37] *Ibid.*, 6.318-22

[38] *Ibid.*, 6.326

[39] For his account of the *innamoramento* of Troilo, Boccaccio has drawn to some extent on another episode of Benoit's romance, the love of Achilles for Polyxena, on his own earlier prose romance, *Filocolo*, and on the actual events of his own relations with Maria d'Aquino. See Young, pp. 26-105.

[40] There is in Benoit a Pandarus, King of Sezile, one of the allies of Priam. He is mentioned but half a dozen times, and is in no way associated with the love of Troilus. There is a passing mention of a Pandarus, son of Lycaon, in Homer, *Iliad* 2.827, in the list of the Trojan allies; compare Virgil, *Aen.* 5.496.

Another modification in the story, for which Boccaccio is responsible, is the change of the heroine's name from Briseis or Briseida to Criseida.[41] In Homer there is Briseis, the lovely slave girl taken away from Achilles by Agamemnon, and so the occasion of Achilles' wrath, whose name appears in the accusative, Briseida, in *Iliad* I. 184, and Chryseis, daughter of the seer Chryses, whom Agamemnon relinquishes at the command of Apollo. The accusative of her name, Chryseida, occurs in *Iliad* I. 182. Dares mentions Briseida only in the portrait which he gives of her, and refers to Chryseida not at all. Dictys mentions neither name; though the two personages to whom the names apply appear as Astynome, daughter of Chryses, and Hippodamia, daughter of Brises. Benoit found in the text of Dares the portrait of a beautiful lady, Briseis, who bore no part in the story, and decided to utilize her as the heroine of one of his episodes. He seems not to have realized that the name Briseis means "daughter of Brises," and so gives her as daughter to the seer Calchas. From Dictys he later took over the Homeric story of the real Briseis, whom he knows only as Ypodamia, the daughter of Brises, and of Chryseis, who appears as Astinome, daughter of Crises.[42] When Boccaccio wrote the *Filostrato*, he was probably not acquainted with Homer; but his knowledge of Ovid was sufficient to show him that Briseis was associated, not with Troilus, but with Achilles. The third epistle of the *Heroides* is addressed by Briseis to Achilles, and conveys by implication an account of her history.[43] Of the associated story of Chryseis he could have learned something from Ovid's *Remedia Amoris* 467-84,[44] a passage which, if carelessly

---

[41] In the printed editions of *Filostrato* the name appears as Griseida; see p. xxi, n. 24.

[42] *Troie* 26,867-27,038.

[43] Boccaccio refers to Briseida's true history in the *Ameto* (p. 136) and in the *Filocolo* (1.278); see Young, p. 1, n. 1.

[44] In Ovid's *Tristia* 2.373, a majority of the MSS. read *Chryseidos*, instead of the correct reading *Briseidos*; see Wilkins, *Mod. Lang. Notes* 24.67, n. 22.

read, might suggest that Chryseis was daughter to Calchas.[45]

It would seem, then, that Boccaccio, even in his youthful days, when he composed the *Filostrato*,[46] was scholar enough to be troubled by the conflict between Benoit's story of Briseida and that found in the *Heroides* of Ovid, and to replace the name by the related name of Criseida. If this substitution involved a new conflict, at least the authentic story of Chryseis was less widely known than that of the true Briseis.

The *Filostrato* is a poem of great literary merit. If it is inferior to *Troilus* in psychological portraiture, in reality, in reflection and interpretation, it is superior to Chaucer's poem in simple directness and passionate intensity. Boccaccio has in large measure identified himself with Troilo, and has seen in the loveliness of Criseida the type of his own lady. Chaucer has told the story with a certain detachment. He is spectator rather than participant. He tells a tragic tale with the philosophic irony of great comedy. Boccaccio's narrative is sentimental, with no trace of humorous comment.

Chaucer and Boccaccio

For the main outline of his action Chaucer has been content to follow *Filostrato* faithfully; at one point only has the English poet drawn heavily on his own invention—the final surrender of Criseyde to Troilus. In stanza 131 of Boccaccio's second canto, the courtship of Troilo has progressed to the stage of an established interchange of letters, the lady's replies being sometimes *lieta*, sometimes *amara*. At the corresponding point of Chaucer's narrative his poem has reached line 1351 of Book II. Between this stanza

---

[45] Wilkins, *Mod. Lang. Notes* 24.67.
[46] The date of the *Filostrato* has not been determined with certainty. A probable conjecture places it about 1338; see H. Hauvette, *Boccace*, p. 88. In that year Boccaccio was twenty-five years old.

of *Filostrato* and the moment when Troilo reaches his final reward in his lady's arms (3. 31), there intervene 336 lines. In a scene which Chaucer has not reproduced, Pandaro pleads with Criseida to have pity on Troilo, breaks down her half-hearted reluctance, and secures the promise that she will yield as soon as time and place may serve (*Fil.* 3. 21–30). In Chaucer's narrative, 1715 lines, almost a quarter of the whole poem, are devoted to this final stage of the wooing. Chaucer has added to the story of his own invention two extended episodes: the scene laid at the house of Deiphebus, where Criseyde is brought to the feigned sick-bed of Troilus, and there promises her ultimate surrender (2. 1394—3. 231); and the even more elaborated scene of the supper at the house of Pandarus, which ends in the union of the lovers (3. 505–1309). For the first of these episodes, Chaucer found a hint in *Fil.* 7.77-85, a scene near the end of *Filostrato* not otherwise utilized by Chaucer, which is laid at the house of Deifebo. For the second, Professor Young has suggested an analogue in the episode of Boccaccio's *Filocolo* in which the lovers, Florio and Biancofiore, are secretly brought together. There is no reason why Chaucer should not have known the *Filocolo;* and there is positive reason for believing that he had read it before he wrote the *Franklin's Tale.*[47] But in the present instance Chaucer's debt to the *Filocolo*, if there be any debt at all, is but a slight one, and confined to minor details of the episode. In each case we have a secret meeting of lovers arranged by a third party; but the scene in the *Filocolo*, which has many similarities with the secret meeting of the lovers in Keats's *Eve of St. Agnes*, is in its essential and characteristic features wholly unlike that in *Troilus*. It is possible that, when Chaucer represents the impatient Troilus as watching the arrival of Criseyde "thoroughoute a litel wyndow in a stuwe" (3. 601), he is remembering that

[47] See Lowes, "The *Franklin's Tale, the Teseide,* and the *Filocolo*," *Mod. Phil.* 15.689-728.

Florio, concealed in Biancofiore's apartments, watched the merry-making "per piccolo pertugio" (*Filocolo* 2. 172).[48]

In the remainder of his narrative Chaucer follows more closely the story of the *Filostrato*. At times he translates or closely paraphrases the Italian for many stanzas together, at times he condenses, at other times expands. Throughout he frequently interpolates into the narrative passages of comment—sometimes in his own person as author, sometimes in the person of one of the characters.[49]

Up to line 1351 of Book II, the point at which begins the long addition discussed above, Chaucer follows, in the fashion just described, the first two cantos of Boccaccio's poem. The episode in which Pandarus learns from Troilus the secret of his love (1. 547–1064) is expanded to more than twice the number of lines which it occupies in the *Filostrato* (*Fil.* 2. 1–34). The episode in which Pandarus reveals the secret to Criseyde (2. 78–595) fills only 244 lines of the Italian poem (*Fil.* 2. 35–67). The striking episode in which Troilus, returning from battle, passes under Criseyde's window, and by his bearing reinforces all that Pandarus has said of him (2. 610–65) is developed from a single stanza (*Fil.* 2. 82), in which Pandaro and Troilo together ride by the lady's window. Entirely Chaucer's own is the

[48] Professor Young has enumerated several other details in which the two episodes agree—the exchange of oaths, the use of rings, etc. These resemblances may easily be explained as the inevitable coincidences growing out of the general similarity of the two situations, each a clandestine meeting of lovers. But the student should see Professor Young's statement of the case, *Origin and Development*, pp. 139-68, and the adverse criticism of Professor Cummings, *Indebtedness*, pp. 1-12. If Young tends to exaggerate the similarities, Cummings tends somewhat unduly to minimize them. Young has also pointed out a number of passages throughout the poem where Chaucer's language may be paralleled with a sentence from the *Filocolo*. Among the more striking of these passages are 1.950 and 3.1192-3 (see notes on these passages); but even in them the evidence for indebtedness is not certain.

[49] *Troilus* has a total of 8239 lines as compared with the 5704 of *Filostrato*. W. M. Rossetti, in the Prefatory Remarks to his Chaucer Society volume, *Chaucer's Troylus and Cryseyde compared with Boccaccio's Filostrato*, estimates that 2583 lines of *Troilus* are *close* adaptations of lines in *Filostrato*.

scene in Criseyde's garden where the heroine, musing on her new-found love, listens to the song of her niece Antigone, sung in praise of love.[50]

After the first night of the lovers has been brought to pass, Chaucer again follows Boccaccio's outline, though with a freedom only a little less than he has used in the first two books. In the latter part of the story, when he departs from his Italian model, it is, save for passages of interpolated reflection, chiefly because he has for this part of the narrative also before his eyes the version of the story found in Benoit and in Guido.

The Persons of the Story

The chief personages of Chaucer's poem are taken over bodily from his Italian original, but their characters have been profoundly modified by the alchemy of his art.[51]

Troilus, to be sure, remains essentially what Boccaccio made him—the brave warrior and passionate lover, valiant as a lion on the field of battle, as a lover all that the code of courtly love demands that a lover should be. Chaucer has appreciably ennobled his character, making him more the idealist. He has also heightened the trait of sentimentalism, the tendency to luxuriate in his sorrows rather than manfully to seek their practical cure. It is this trait of character which, in league with adverse fate, brings about his tragedy.

Criseyde has been more profoundly altered. Chaucer has shown in his portrayal of her character a power of subtle analysis thoroughly comparable with that of a Samuel Richardson. Her Italian original is simple and direct, a creature of sensuous instinct with a minimum of reflection, who, having once yielded her heart, moves forward to the full accomplishment of her passion with no need of elabo-

[50] The song itself seems to have been adapted from Machaut; see p. xlvi.

[51] I have elsewhere, *Poetry of Chaucer*, 2d ed., pp. 105-21, given at length my own interpretation of the chief characters of Chaucer's poem.

rate stratagem. Chaucer's heroine, with all her beauty and womanly loveliness and grace of demeanor, has from the beginning of the story a fatal weakness—the inability to make a deliberate choice. She thinks always too precisely on the event. No sooner has the love of Troilus found lodgment in her heart than she begins to reflect on the lost liberty of action which must ensue on her acceptance of it. She makes no decision, but drifts with circumstance; and the circumstances are so cleverly manipulated by her uncle that, without the need for conscious decision, her desire is accomplished. Though clearly aware whither she is drifting, she seems to herself to have been trapped, and can, without conscious hypocrisy, reproach her uncle for the perfidy that has brought her where she wished to be. In the later books of the poem, when circumstance is beyond her uncle's shrewd control, she continues to take always the easiest path. It is easier to leave Troilus, heartbroken though she be, than to defy the decree of the Trojan parliament; it is easier to remain with her father than to brave the perils of a return, though she still intends to keep her promise to her lover. Though she never quite tears the image of Troilus from her heart, it is beyond her power to resist the wooing of the "sudden" Diomede. And so she becomes the type of instability and treachery in love.

The figure of Pandarus, perhaps the finest example of Chaucer's art of portraiture, is almost wholly the creation of the English poet. Boccaccio's Pandaro is the *cousin* of Criseida (and of Troilo also), a high-spirited young gallant, not much differentiated, save in his fortunes, from the hero, Troilo. He is messenger and go-between for the lovers; but he has no need for elaborate scheming and artifice, and he is quite devoid of the ironical humor which marks his English counterpart.

In Chaucer, Pandarus is Criseyde's uncle, a relationship which suggests that he is by some years her senior. Yet he is young enough to be the inseparable companion of Troilus, and to be himself a courtly lover—though an unsuccessful one. As a friend he is untiring in his disinterested and loyal service, even when that service involves his own dishonor. For though the artificial code of courtly love blames Criseyde only for her final falseness to Troilus, it quite irrationally demands that her uncle be her jealous guardian. He is the most charming of companions—playful, witty, full of shrewd observation, never dull. He is always laughing—at himself and his own ill success in love, at the extravagances of his love-sick friend, at the irony of life which he so clearly sees. He is the dominating personage of Chaucer's poem, giving to it that pervading tone of humorous irony which is so characteristic of the poet who created him, and so foreign to the passionate intensity of Boccaccio's *Filostrato*.

The Conduct of the Action

If Chaucer has made much more subtle the characters of Boccaccio's story, he has also heightened greatly its vividness, giving to it a compelling sense of actuality.

One of the elements which contributes to this sense of the actual is the care with which Chaucer has marked the passing of his dramatic time. Boccaccio opens his poem in the springtime (*Fil.* 1. 18), but gives no further dating of his story beyond the fact that it is again springtime in *Fil.* 7.78. In Chaucer most of the important episodes are definitely placed in the calendar.

Troilus first sees Criseyde at the feast of Palladion, in the month of April (1. 156). It is on the third of May (2. 56) that Pandarus makes his first visit to Criseyde; and on the morrow of that day he persuades his niece to write Troilus a letter. An interval elapses, during which Troilus is alternately elated or depressed, according to the tenor of Criseyde's answers to his letters (2. 1338–54). Then comes the meeting at the house of Deiphebus, at which Criseyde promises full surrender. The time of year is not specified;

but a reference to "Aperil the laste" (3. 360) shows that we are still within the first year of the story. There is again an interval, in which the lovers exchange letters, and occasionally see each other (3. 435–510). Then follows the first night together, which is dated as May or early June by the presence of the crescent Moon in the sign of Cancer.[52] Apparently an entire year has passed since the beginning of the wooing. The episode of Criseyde's departure for the Grecian camp begins in late July, when the Sun is in the early degrees of Leo.[53] At the beginning of Book V (lines 8–14), we are told that there have been three spring seasons since Troilus first began to love her. If one counts as one of these springtimes that in which the story begins, Troilus has enjoyed the full love of his lady during a period of some fourteen months. How long a time elapses between Criseyde's arrival at her father's tent and her final acceptance of Diomede, Chaucer expressly refuses to say.[54]

But if the action of the story extends over at least three years, the great bulk of the narrative is devoted to the events of a few critical days. Three-quarters of the lines of Book I are given to the day on which Troilus first sees Criseyde, and to the day shortly after when he confides his secret to Pandarus. Beginning with Book II, nearly 5000 lines are devoted to the events of eight days, presented in sets of two, a day and its morrow. These four groups of two centre on Pandar's first visit to Criseyde on his friend's behalf, on the meeting at the house of Deiphebus, on the first night of the lovers, and on Criseyde's departure from Troy. Over 900 lines are given to the nine days which follow her departure. A few significant episodes are thus narrated in full detail, largely by means of dramatic dialogue, while the intervening intervals are dismissed with concise summary.

[52] See note to 3.624-6, and Introd. p. xvi.
[53] See note to 4.31-2.
[54] But see note to 5.1086-92.

Sources

Chaucer's Use of Earlier Authorities

It is characteristic of Chaucer's methods as a literary workman that, when he undertook to retell Boccaccio's tale of romantic love in Troy, he was not content to follow his Italian source alone. He certainly consulted Benoit, and probably also looked into Guido.[55] In Book IV he corrects by reference to these authorities a mistake of Boccaccio as to the circumstances of Antenor's capture in the Fifth Battle.[56] Where Boccaccio tells us that Criseyde was exchanged on even terms for Antenor, Chaucer follows the earlier authorities by bringing in the name of King Thoas, as coupled with Criseyde in the exchange of prisoners.[57] In Book V he owes to these authorities Diomede's taking of Criseyde's glove,[58] the episode of the fair bay steed, formerly the property of Troilus, which Criseyde gives to Diomede,[59] Criseyde's gift to Diomede of a "pencel of hire sleve" to be worn by him as a favor,[60] her nursing of Diomede when he was wounded,[61] and the account of Hector's death at the hands of Achilles.[62] To Benoit he owes also the lament of Criseyde as she contemplates her own infidelity.[63] More significant than any of these minor borrowings is one which affects the very conduct of the story. In Boccaccio (*Fil.* 5. 13), Diomede, after receiving Criseyde at the gates of Troy, conducts her to her father's tent without any attempt to pay court to her, deferring his love-making till a later day. Chaucer (5. 92–189) follows instead the authority of the *Roman de Troie*, where Diomede begins his courtship straightway, and receives from the lady the reply that

[55] See Young, pp. 105-39.
[56] See note to 4.50-4.
[57] See note to 4.137-8.
[58] See note to 5.1013.
[59] See note to 5.1037-9.
[60] See note to 5.1042-3.
[61] See note to 5.1044-50.
[62] See note to 5.1548-61.
[63] See note to 5.1051-85.

her heart is too sad for love, but were she to love, she would love no one sooner than Diomede.[64] This borrowing from the earlier source, like a number of those mentioned just before, tends to emphasize the heroine's faithlessness.

In Benoit, and in Guido, Chaucer found repeated appeals to the authority of Dares and Dictys. There is no evidence that Chaucer ever read the *Ephemeris* of Dictys, though he once (1. 146) echoes Benoit by appealing to Homer, Dares, and "Dite." [65] There is no evidence, either, to show that he had read the prose Dares; but for the portraits of Diomede, Criseyde, and Troilus in 5. 799–840 he has drawn heavily on a poetical paraphrase of Dares, written in Latin hexameters of considerable merit, made in the latter part of the twelfth century by an Englishman, Joseph of Exeter. This work is given by modern editors the title *De Bello Trojano*;[66] but in the three surviving manuscripts it is called "Frigii Daretis Ylias," or "Liber Frigii Daretis.[67] When he turned its pages, Chaucer may well have believed that he was reading the Latin translation of the original and ultimate source of Trojan history.[68]

Lollius

Great as is Chaucer's debt to the *Filostrato*, he never in the course of his poem, or elsewhere in his works, mentions the Italian poet by name. Nor does he ever speak of Benoit. "Guido de Columpnis" is listed among the authorities on

[64] For other instances in which Chaucer seems to have turned to Benoit or Guido, see notes to 4.18-21; 4.38-42; 4.57-8; 4.120-6; 4.203-5; 4.548; 4.813-19; 4.1401-7; 4.1411; 4.1415-21; 4.1478-82; 5.825; 5.1000-1; 5.1002-3; 5.1010-11; 5.1562-3.

[65] See note to 1.145-7. In *Fame* 1467, Dictys appears under the form *Tytus*.

[66] See Bibliography, s.v. Joseph of Exeter.

[67] The *editio princeps*, printed at Basle in 1558, bears the title, "Daretis Phrygii . . . de Bello Trojano . . . libri sex a Cornelio Nepote in Latinum conversi."

[68] See notes to 5.799-840, and my article, "Chaucer's Dares," *Mod. Phil.* 15.1-22.

the tale of Troy in *Fame* 1469, and as an authority for the story of Jason in *Legend of Good Women* 1396, 1464; but his name is not mentioned in *Troilus*. But, in suppressing the names of his actual sources, Chaucer had no desire that the reader should regard him as the inventor of the story. He assures us more than once than he is but retelling in English the history written by "myn auctour called Lollius." [69]

The name Lollius has long been one of the puzzles of Chaucerian criticism; and many attempts, some of them highly fantastic, have been made to explain it. If one begins with the testimony of Chaucer himself, one finds that "Lollius," or "myn auctour," is the writer of an "old book"[70] on the Trojan War written in Latin,[71] whose story of Troilus and Criseida Chaucer is following with scrupulous fidelity. That the name is no mere figment of Chaucer's artistic imagination, invented expressly as a supposed authority for his *Troilus*, is made certain by the fact that "Lollius" is mentioned along with other Latin and Greek writers who have treated of the Trojan War—Homer, Dares, Dictys, Guido delle Colonne, Geoffrey of Monmouth —as one of the "bearers up of Troy" in *Fame* 1468. Though the *House of Fame* has never been dated with certainty, there is strong reason for believing that it antedates *Troilus*, possibly by as much as ten years.[72] There could have been no motive for introducing into the *House of Fame* a fictitious name among the names of actual writers about

[69] 1.394. "Lollius" is named again near the end of the poem (5.1653). When, as repeatedly, Chaucer refers to "myn auctour" (2.18; 2.700; 3.502; 3.575; 3.1196; 3.1402; 3.1817) or "the storie" (5.1037; 5.1044; 5.1051; 5.1094; 5.1651), one must assume that "Lollius" is the authority invoked. The name has the fullest MS. attestation; in 1.394, ClH5 read *Lollyus*, Gg *Lollyous*, H4 *Lolkius*, W *Lellyus*, the rest *Lollius*; in 5.1653, R reads *bollius*, GgCx *lollyus*, the rest *Lollius*.

[70] 3.91; 3.1199. Compare also 2.23.

[71] 2.14. The suggestion, originating with Tyrwhitt, that "Latin" means *Latino volgare*, i.e. Italian, cannot be accepted. Unless qualified by some such adjective as "vulgar," the word Latin meant to Chaucer's readers just what it means to us.

[72] See Kittredge, *Date*, pp. 53-5.

Troy; so that we must assume that Chaucer believed in the actuality of "Lollius." For such a belief there is no foundation in fact; the most diligent search of modern scholars has discovered no author named Lollius who has written about Troy.[73]

The most probable explanation of Chaucer's mistaken belief, an explanation now generally accepted by scholars, was first offered by G. Latham in the *Athenaeum*, 1868, II, 433. According to this explanation, the idea that one Lollius was a writer about the Trojan War sprang from a misunderstanding of the opening lines of the Second Epistle of the First Book of Horace:

> Troiani belli scriptorem, Maxime Lolli,
> Dum tu declamas Romae, Praeneste relegi.

Properly these lines mean: "While you are practising oratory at Rome, Maximus Lollius, I have been rereading at Praeneste the writer of the Trojan War, i.e., Homer." Horace goes on to show his friend that useful moral teaching may be gained from the *Iliad* and the *Odyssey*.[74] If one assumes a manuscript of Horace in which scribal corruption had substituted *scriptorum* or *scriptor* for *scriptorem*, and in which the proper name Maximus was written without the initial capital, Horace might easily have been understood to be addressing Lollius as "greatest of writers of the Trojan War."[75] Whether the mistake originated with Chaucer, or with some one else from whom he took it over,

---

[73] For the attempt, which dates back to Speght's edition of 1598, to identify Chaucer's "Lollius" with Lollius Urbicus, mentioned in the *Historia Augusta* as a writer of the third century A.D. who made a history of his own time, see Kittredge, *Lollius*, pp. 82-9. See also Hammond, pp. 94-8.

[74] Maximus Lollius, to whom is addressed also *Epistle* 1.18, was a son of Marcus Lollius, consul, general, and governor of Syria, to whom Horace addresses one of his *Odes* (*Carm.* 4.9).

[75] For various ways in which this wrong understanding might have grown out of a corrupted text of Horace, see Kittredge, *Lollius*, pp. 77-80.

we cannot say;[76] but we can feel a good deal of confidence
that Chaucer had not read any Latin history of Troy which
went under the name of Lollius. When Chaucer cites Lollius, he should, according to our notions, have cited instead
Giovanni Boccaccio, who is in fact his "auctour," standing
to him in the relation which he attributes to "Lollius." [77]
But this does not mean that "Lollius" is simply another
name for Boccaccio.[78] "Lollius," it must be remembered,
wrote long ago, and in Latin.

When Chaucer read the *Filostrato*, he would inevitably
have asked himself whence Boccaccio took the story. In
Benoit and in Guido he would have found the latter part of
Boccaccio's story, though with some notable differences in
detail. For all the early part of the story, up to the time
when Criseida's exchange is decreed, he, like the modern
critic, could find no source. And yet Boccaccio, who makes
no acknowledgment of his debt to Benoit or to Guido, says
explicitly in the *Proemio* that he is following "antiche
storie." What were these "ancient histories"? It is easily
possible that Chaucer, misled by some stray bit of misin-
formation—possibly a scribal note in his own copy of *Filostrato*—actually believed that Boccaccio's source was an
ancient history written by Lollius, "Troiani belli scriptorum maximus," that in retelling the story of *Filostrato* he
was in effect following, though at second hand, the authority of the great Lollius.

Or, to vary the hypothesis a little, it may be, as Professor

---

[76] No one has yet discovered any medieval reference to Lollius as a
writer on the Trojan War save those in Chaucer. On the other hand,
there is no evidence to prove that Chaucer was acquainted with the
Epistles of Horace.

[77] Sometimes, to be sure, Chaucer cites "myn auctour" in support of a
specific statement which is not found in *Filostrato*; see Kittredge,
Lollius, pp. 92-109. In 5.1044, he expressly refers to an authority other
than "myn auctour" in support of a detail actually drawn from Benoit
or Guido. More than a single authority is implied in 5.19.

[78] For various attempts to make of "Lollius" a pseudonym for Boccaccio, see Hammond, pp. 96-8.

Kittredge has argued,[79] that, wishing to give to his story the suggestion of antiquity and authenticity, he deliberately invoked, as a piece of literary artifice, the name of Lollius, supposed author of a lost history of the Trojan War.

Further mystification has been created for Chaucerian scholars by a statement of Chaucer's disciple, Lydgate. In the Prologue to his *Fall of Princes* (lines 283–7), Lydgate says of "my maister Chaucer":

> In youthe he made a translacioun
> Off a book, which callid is Trophe,
> In Lumbard tunge, as men may reede & see,
> And in our vulgar, longe or that he deide,
> Gaff it the name off Troilus & Cresseide.

Lydgate was apparently aware that the source of *Troilus* was a book not in Latin, but in Lombard tongue, i.e., Italian;[80] but what he may have meant by saying that this Italian book was called "Trophe" no one knows; and all attempts to guess the riddle have been far from satisfactory.[81]

IV. THE RANGE OF CHAUCER'S READING AS SHOWN IN *Troilus*

In a preceding section of this Introduction we have considered those sources of *Troilus*—Boccaccio, Benoit and Guido, the paraphrase of Dares made by Joseph of Exeter —which contributed directly to the substance of the story. For the elaboration of his poem—for philosophic comment,

---

[79] *Lollius*, pp. 71-2.

[80] I take it that Lydgate means that the book was written in "Lumbard tunge," not that it was a Latin book called "Trophe" in Italian.

[81] See Hammond, p. 98, and Skeat, *Oxford Chaucer*, 2. liv-lvi. The problem is complicated by the fact that Chaucer himself cites either an author or a book which he calls "Trophee" in *Monk's Tale*, B 3307, as his authority for a statement about the pillars of Hercules. For an ingenious and plausible elucidation of this citation, see article by Kittredge, "The Pillars of Hercules and Chaucer's 'Trophee,'" *Putnam Anniversary Volume* (New York, Stechert, 1909), pp. 546-66. Professor Kittredge makes no attempt to explain Lydgate's mention of "Trophe," which he is inclined to regard as a mere blundering mistake.

for illustration, and for poetic ornament—he has drawn upon the whole range of his reading; and this reading is extensive enough to justify his contemporary, Thomas Usk, in calling him "the noble philosophical poete in Englissh."[82] *Troilus* is distinctly a "learned" poem.

Of these subsidiary sources, by all odds the most important is the *Consolation of Philosophy* of Boethius, a work which deeply influenced Chaucer's thought, and which he himself translated into English prose.[83] No less than nineteen separate passages in *Troilus* are derived directly from this treatise, passages which range in length from a single line to nineteen stanzas. In all these instances there is nothing in the corresponding portion of the *Filostrato* to suggest the Boethian philosophizing which Chaucer has introduced. Of these passages the most extended and the most significant are the discussion of Fortune in 1. 837–54, Criseyde's discussion of false felicity (3. 813–36), the hymn of Troilus sung to Love as the bond of all things (3. 1744–71), and the long soliloquy of Troilus on the conflict between God's foreknowledge and man's freedom (4. 953–1085). The ideas of Boethius are taken over not merely as poetical elaborations of Chaucer's theme; they are sum and substance of the deeper significance which he sees in the story of the tragic love of Troilus, a story which transacts itself in a world of which Destiny is the ineluctable master,[84] and in which Fortune, the principle of deceitful mutability,[85] is for ever turning into bitter vanity the hopes of man, and even the happiness which he seems to have achieved.

From the *Epistles* of Seneca [86] directly or indirectly are taken half a dozen sententious comments, of which all but

---

[82] Compare above, p. xv.

[83] For an excellent discussion of the part played in Chaucer's thought by the work of Boethius, see B. L. Jefferson, *Chaucer and the Consolation of Philosophy of Boethius*, Princeton Diss., 1917.

[84] See 2.526-8; 2.622-3; 5.3-7.

[85] See 4.1-9; 4.391-2.

[86] See article by H. M. Ayres, "Chaucer and Seneca," *Romanic Review*, 10.1-15.

one are spoken by Pandarus.[87] In one of these instances (1. 960–1), the quotation is immediately from the *Roman de la Rose;* in another (1. 964–6) it may have come from Albertano of Brescia. It is quite possible that the rest are by way of some intermediate source.

Another source of sententious wisdom is the *Liber Parabolarum* of Alanus de Insulis.[88] From the same writer's *De Planctu Naturae,* a book laid under contribution in the *Parliament of Fowls,* comes the phrase "common astrologer," applied to the cock in 3. 1415—a fact duly noted by the scribe in the margin of H4.

There are in *Troilus* only three direct quotations from the Bible,[89] and these are from the writings attributed to Solomon—two from Ecclesiastes, one from Proverbs. Indirect allusions to St. Luke's Gospel are found at 2. 1503, and 3. 1577.

From the *Metamorphoses* of Ovid is drawn the very considerable body of allusions to classic myth with which Chaucer has ornamented his poem. It is to be noted that virtually all of these allusions are of Chaucer's own addition. Though Boccaccio makes free use of Ovidian myth in the *Teseide,* he has excluded it almost entirely from the pages of the *Filostrato.* Among the myths to which Chaucer alludes are Niobe weeping for her children (1.699–700), the horses which draw the chariot of the Sun (3. 1703), the bitter tears of Myrrha metamorphosed into a myrrh tree (4. 1138–9), Ascalaphus transformed into an owl (5.319), Phaeton's disastrous handling of his father's chariot (5. 664), the hunting of the Calydonian boar (5. 1464–79), the death of Meleager (5. 1482–3), the story of Nisus and his daughter Scylla (5. 1110). Characteristic of Chaucer's attitude towards the pagan deities is a passage in the third

---

[87] See notes to 1.687-8; 1.701-7; 1.891-3; 1.960-1; 1.964-6; 4.466.
[88] See notes to 1.946-9; 1.951-2; 2.36-7; 2.1335; 3.1219-20. This debt was first pointed out by Koeppel in *Archiv für das Studium der Neueren Sprachen,* 90.150-1.
[89] See notes to 1.694-5; 3.855; 4.836.

book, in which Ovidian myth is blended with astrology.[90] Twice (4. 789–91; 4. 1543–5) there is an unmistakable echo of Ovid's language.

But Chaucer's use of Ovid is not limited to the *Metamorphoses*. The fifth epistle of the *Heroides* (Oenone to Paris) is definitely cited by Pandarus in 1. 653–5, who proceeds to paraphrase four lines of it. In 4. 1645 Criseyde translates *Her*. 1. 12. In 2. 1027 Pandarus echoes *Her*. 3. 3.[91] The *Ars Amatoria* is clearly in Chaucer's mind in 2. 1023–5; 4. 31–2; 5. 1107; and in 1. 946–7 Pandarus translates *Remedia Amoris* 45–6.[92] In 4. 1548–9 there is a clear echo of *Amores* 1. 15. 10.[93] I have found no instances of indebtedness to *Tristia* or to the *Ex Ponto*; nor is there clear evidence that Chaucer used the *Fasti*.[94]

Of Chaucer's intimate acquaintance with Virgil there can be no doubt; but he has drawn very slightly on him for the ornamentation of *Troilus*. In 3. 1495–8 there seems to be an echo of *Eclogue* 1. 60–4. In 5. 212 an allusion to Ixion, and in 5. 644 an allusion to Charybdis, may be traceable directly to the *Aeneid*.[95]

Ultimately from the *Ars Poetica* of Horace come two stanzas (2. 1030–43) in which Pandarus advises Troilus as to the literary style of his first letter to Criseyde. From the same source, apparently, are four lines (2. 22–5) in which the poet himself comments on the change which language undergoes "withinne a thousand yeer." However, the three passages of the *Ars Poetica* concerned are of the sort to be frequently quoted; so that we cannot assert that Chaucer knew Horace at first hand. Of indebtedness to other writings of Horace I have found no trace.

---

[90] See note to 3.715-32. For a similar treatment of myth in the *Knight's Tale*, see article by W. C. Curry, "Astrologising the Gods," *Anglia* 47.213-43.

[91] See also note to 4.1548-53.

[92] See also notes to 4.414-15; 4.421-4.

[93] See also notes to 3.1433-5; 4.407-12.

[94] But see note to 2.77.

[95] See also notes to 1.57-60; 5.892.

Chaucer quotes a "sentence" from the tenth Satire of Juvenal at 4. 197–201, and names Juvenal as his authority.

Of the classic poets other than Ovid, Statius seems to have been most present in Chaucer's memory at the time when he was writing *Troilus*.[96] Pandarus finds Criseyde and her ladies reading the story of Thebes (2. 100–8), and special mention is made of the catastrophic death of Amphiaraus.[97] In lines 1485–510 of Book V the *Thebais* is summarized in some detail; and in the midst of this summary all but two of the manuscripts insert a Latin argument of the poem.[98]

When Chaucer wrote *Troilus*, he was already familiar with the *Divine Comedy* of Dante.[99] It would seem, indeed, that he must have owned, or at least had easy access to, a copy of the poem. In four passages of *Troilus* (3. 1262–7; 4. 225–7; 5. 1541–5; 5. 1863–5), he is clearly writing with the page of Dante open before him.[100] Almost as striking is the debt to Dante in 3. 1419-20; 4. 1538–40; 5. 599–601. The *Divine Comedy* was probably in the poet's mind also when he wrote 2. 1–6; 3. 45; 4. 22–4; 4. 473–6; 4. 1187–8. Of the thirteen passages just cited, seven are from the *Inferno*, and three each from the *Purgatorio* and the *Paradiso*. Of the four passages which are most closely modelled on Dante, one is an address to the Blessed Virgin, which Chaucer turns to the praise of Love; one a simile which Dante in his turn owes to Virgil; one the elevated conception of Fortune as the agency of divine providence; and the

---

[96] For a general treatment of Chaucer's use of the *Thebais*, see B. A. Wise, *The Influence of Statius upon Chaucer*, Johns Hopkins Diss. 1911. Some of Dr. Wise's instances of supposed Statian influence on *Troilus* I am not able to accept.

[97] Perhaps Chaucer had in mind the old French *Roman de Thèbes* rather than the *Thebais* of Statius. See note to 2.100-8, and compare notes to 3.1600; 4.300-1.

[98] For further instances of Chaucer's debt to Statius, see notes to 1.6-9; 4.300-1; 4.762; 4.1408; 5.1789-92.

[99] For a summary and discussion of Chaucer's debt to Dante, see Lowes, "Chaucer and Dante," *Mod. Phil.* 14.705-35.

[100] In 2.967-73 and 4.239-41, Chaucer closely reproduces from the *Filostrato* lines which Boccaccio had taken almost *verbatim* from the *Divine Comedy*.

last the address to the Blessed Trinity which brings *Troilus* to its close. All of the passages where Dante's influence is manifest are of a character which adds to the tone of artistic and spiritual elevation which so markedly differentiates *Troilus* from the *Filostrato*. The influence of Dante on Chaucer's mind and art is not confined to the passages in which there is definite borrowing of a phrase or an idea. From Italy, and primarily I think from Dante, came the inspiration to tell the story of Troilus in the *bel stilo alto*, to write in the vernacular with the dignity and elevation which mark the great ancients. Particularly Dantesque is Chaucer's method of incorporating into his poem the philosophy of Boethius, and the considerable number of astrological and other scientific allusions which it contains.

Similar in character to his debt to Dante is Chaucer's debt to the *Teseide* of Boccaccio, a poem in its style as ornate and elevated as the *Filostrato* is simple and direct. Whether the *Knight's Tale*, in which Chaucer retells, though with much compression, the story of the *Teseide*, was written before *Troilus* or immediately after it, is a question to which no final answer has yet been given. But there is no question that the *Teseide* was already familiar to him.[101] Most important of the borrowings from the *Teseide* are the beautiful stanzas (5. 1807–27) which follow the soul of Troilus on its flight through the heavens—stanzas which are of prime importance in enforcing the philosophical interpretation which Chaucer has given to his story. Two other stanzas of Book V (lines 8–11 and 274–80), both of them in the grand manner, are closely imitated from the *Teseide*. Single lines are taken over in 2. 435–6 and 5. 1. Indebtedness of a more general character is found in 1. 659–65; 4. 323–9; 5. 295–322.[102]

[101] See Kittredge, *Chaucer's Lollius*, Appendix II (pp. 110-20), "Use of the *Teseide* in the *Troilus*."

[102] See also notes to 5.207-10; 5.304; 5.321-2. It is possibly worthy of remark that the debt to *Teseide* is particularly noticeable in the fifth book of *Troilus*.

To the third of the great Florentines the only case of clear indebtedness is in the song of Troilus in 1. 400–20, which is closely translated from sonnet 88 of Petrarch.

The courtly literature of thirteenth and fourteenth century France, which contributed so heavily to the *Book of the Duchess*, the *Parliament of Fowls*, and the Prologue to the *Legend of Good Women*, has little place among the influences which helped to shape *Troilus*. The only important exception to this statement is the *Roman de la Rose*, a book with which Chaucer was minutely familiar,[103] and which he had already, in part at least, translated into English verse. There are nineteen passages of *Troilus* which clearly show its influence, besides several others where the indebtedness is less certain. Of these nineteen passages, seven are from the portion of the poem written by Guillaume de Lorris, and twelve from the continuation of Jean de Meun. Sometimes [104] it is merely the turn of a phrase which shows Chaucer's debt; more often [105] a bit of sententious wisdom has been appropriated. Once (1. 638–44) a whole stanza of moralizing is taken over from the *Roman de la Rose*. In 3. 351–4 a bit of May-time landscape betrays the same inspiration. In other passages [106] it is a conceit or maxim of courtly love.

From the *Paradis d'Amour* of Guillaume de Machaut is apparently derived the general suggestion of the song in praise of love sung in 2. 827–75 by Criseyde's niece, Antigone.[107] Though there are no close verbal parallels, the general similarity of situation and ideas is striking. But with the *Roman de la Rose* and this poem of Machaut ends Chaucer's debt to the courtly literature of France, so far at

---

[103] The best treatment of Chaucer's use of the *Roman de la Rose* is by D. S. Fansler, *Chaucer and the Roman de la Rose*, Columbia Diss., New York, 1914.

[104] E.g. 1.969; 2.784; 4.519-20; 5.445.

[105] See notes to 1.449; 1.637; 1.960-1; 2.167-8; 2.716-18; 2.1564-6; 4.1305-6.

[106] See notes to 1.435-48; 1.747-8; 1.810-12; 1.927-8; 3.1634; 5.551-3.

[107] See article by Kittredge in *Mod. Lang. Notes* 25.158.

least as modern scholarship has been able to discover. It is possible that Chaucer used the twelfth-century *Roman de Thèbes*; see note to 2. 100–8.

Besides bringing to his poem the fruits of a wide reading in Latin, French, and Italian literature, Chaucer has drawn also on his very considerable knowledge of medieval science. Most striking is his acquaintance with astronomy and astrology.[108] The Sun's progress through the signs of the Zodiac marks out for the poem the seasons of the year. The passage of the Moon from Aries to the end of Leo is to measure the period of Criseyde's return to Troilus. A conjunction of Jupiter, Saturn, and the crescent Moon in the sign Cancer causes the heavy downpour of rain which makes impossible Criseyde's departure from the house of Pandarus. Without exception these references to astronomy and astrology are accurately in accord with the best scientific knowledge of Chaucer's day. Thoroughly scientific is the discussion of the significance of dreams.[109] The poem reveals also some knowledge of physiology,[110] and an acquaintance with the distinctions of scholastic dialectic.[111]

If Chaucer has enriched his poem and philosophized its story by borrowings from such wise clerks as Boethius and Seneca and Alanus de Insulis, and from such poems as the *Divine Comedy* and the *Teseide*, he has not forgotten the homelier wisdom of the popular proverb. In the notes to this edition no fewer than fifty-seven instances are pointed out in which a proverb or proverbial phrase has been utilized. Twenty-one of these instances are in speeches of Pandarus; and it would seem that the poet intended the reader to recognize a love for proverbs as one of the marks of his character.[112] Fourteen proverbs are spoken by Criseyde;

[108] For his knowledge of pure astronomy, see notes to 2.54-5; 3.3; 3.1417-20; 4.31-2; 4.1590-6; 5.652-8; 5.1016-20. For astrological references, see notes to 2.680-6; 3.22; 3.617-26; 3.715-17; 3.724; 3.1255-7.

[109] See notes to 5.360-85; 5.1275-8.

[110] See notes to 1.306-7; 3.1088-9.

[111] See notes to 3.404-6; 4.1505.

[112] See 1.756.

and sixteen occur in the comments of the author himself. Troilus invokes proverbial wisdom only three times, and Diomede once. The presence of this considerable mass of proverbial phrases contributes appreciably to the effect of the poem. If the more literary embellishments which Chaucer has added make for elevation of style, the use of proverbs makes the poem at the same time familiar, colloquial, real.

V. MORAL IMPORT

The net result of all the additions which Chaucer has super-added out of his own reading to the story which Boccaccio had told more simply is greatly to heighten its seriousness. Chaucer's narrative is not only more human, more real, more genuine in its passion; it is much wiser. In the code of courtly love which Boccaccio accepts without question, Chaucer sees inherent contradictions and fallacies, which make for a tragic issue. The poem is, in truth, as Cupid in the Prologue to the *Legend of Good Women* calls it, a "heresy" against the "law" of courtly love. But Chaucer's wise analysis goes farther than this. In the fickleness and falsehood of Criseyde, a woman so lovely, so sweet and gracious, so much to be desired, he sees the type of mutability, of the transitoriness and fallacy of earthly happiness.

Boccaccio had dedicated the *Filostrato* to Fiammetta, his own mistress, and in his envoy had warned young lovers not to put trust too lightly in every fair lady, many of whom are, like Criseida, "unstable as leaf in the wind" (*Fil.* 8. 29–33). Chaucer's poem is dedicated to "moral" Gower and to "philosophical" Strode, a poet-moralist and a learned professor of philosophy. His warning to "yonge fresshe folkes" is that this world is but a transitory Vanity Fair, that only in God is there neither variableness nor shadow of change. And then, by way of enforcing his moral, he takes over from the *Teseide*, which had in its turn taken them from the *Somnium Scipionis* of Cicero, three

noble stanzas (5. 1807–27) which follow heavenward the
soul of the slain Troilus. From his station in the eighth
heaven Troilus looks down upon the spot where he was slain,
and laughs at the woe of those who were weeping his death,
condemning our human pursuit of "blind" pleasure, which
of its very nature cannot last.

Troilus laughs. He has not laughed before in the whole
course of the poem since the very beginning of the story,
before his first sight of Criseyde, when, himself heart-free,
he made merry over the woes of foolish lovers. The ironist
Pandar, though himself a disappointed lover, laughs often
enough—a quiet, humorous laughter. He laughs even at his
own ill success in love. But Troilus has set his heart too
passionately on the things which at the very outset of the
story, and now again at its close, he recognizes as "vanitee."
He has taken life too seriously; now, like the poet who created him, he sees in life a high but comic irony.

It is in this spirit of a wise and thoughtful irony that
Chaucer has conceived and executed his poem, a spirit poles
asunder from the tender sentiment and ardent passion
which inform the *Filostrato*. He has called *Troilus* a tragedy; and it is a tragedy in the medieval sense of the term—
the story of a man cast down by adverse fortune from great
prosperity and high estate into misery and wretchedness.[113]
The five books into which he has disposed his story suggest
the five acts of tragic drama.[114] There is, moreover, a quite
tragic insistence on the idea of destiny.

It is "through his destiny" that Troilus first falls in love
with Criseyde. It is destiny again which sends him riding
"an esy pas" below Criseyde's window, at the very moment
when Pandarus has disposed the lady's thoughts to answer
love by love. Troilus, when the Trojan parliament issues its
decree for Criseyde's departure, sees the hand of destiny at
work:

[113] See note to 1.4
[114] See Horace, *Ars Poetica* 189-90.

xlix

For al that comth, comth by necessitee;
Thus to be lorn, it is my destinee.   (4. 958–9)

And so he debates the question of man's freedom and God's foreknowledge, inclining his argument to the side of predestination. The fall of fortune is made to seem inevitable and ineluctable.

And yet the story does not make on us a really tragic effect. It is rather a tragic story handled in the spirit of high comedy. Chaucer has not treated his theme with *tragic* intensity. Great tragedy leaves us with the sense of irreparable loss, of a hurt for which there is no healing. Hamlet dies with the unforgettably tragic words: "The rest is silence." The last we hear from Troilus is a peal of celestial laughter.

The poem is, of course, not written merely as an apologue, to point the moral that earthly joy is but "fals felicitee." There is full understanding and appreciation of its human values. The modern reader who dissents from this moral may disregard it, if he will, and find the story but little injured for his taste by its concluding stanzas. Yet it is no mere tacked-on moral. It is implicit in the whole poem. Of its genuineness, of the poet's complete sincerity, no one who has read Chaucer's other writings with attention can doubt. Chaucer is not so much pointing a moral, as giving us at the end his own verdict as to the permanent values of those aspects of our human life which are for the moment of such passionate importance.

For Chaucer, and for other of the finer spirits of the Middle Ages, this verdict implied no lugubrious doctrine of narrow Puritanism. Rather it made for a serene Catholic temper, which could thoroughly enjoy and understand the world, while still recognizing its "vanity," which could retain its serenity because it did not take either the joys or the sorrows of the world too seriously.

The story conceived by Benoit de Ste. Maure, and developed by Giovanni Boccaccio, has been reshaped by the

1

creative genius of Chaucer, deepened and enriched in its human values by his keen observation, interpreted in the light of much reading and wise thought, and retold with exquisite grace and beauty. Much as it owes to "olde bokes," it remains—even for an editor who has laboriously scanned its every syllable, and pursued its every allusion—something perpetually fresh and new, one of the great original and authentic poems of the English-speaking race.

VI. THE TEXT

Troilus and Criseyde is preserved in sixteen manuscript copies, of which two, H5 and Dig, are incomplete.[115] Two of the early printed copies, those of Caxton and Thynne, present texts which are independent of the existing MSS., and therefore rank with the MSS. as authorities. The 1517 edition of Wynkyn de Worde is similarly an independent authority for the first 546 lines of Book I. All the other printed editions derive either from earlier prints or from MSS. still extant, and have, therefore, no value as authorities.

I have already given, in the publications of the Chaucer Society, detailed descriptions of the manuscripts.[116] The account of them given in the following pages is, therefore, of a

---

[115] There are also three brief fragments, none of which has any critical value. Three stanzas (3.302-22), incorporated into a short poem in rhyme royal, of which they constitute stanzas 4-6, are found in the Cambridge University Library, MS. Ff 1.6, fols. 150b, 151a. (Printed in the Chaucer Society volume of *Odd Texts of Chaucer's Minor Poems*, p. xii.) One stanza (1.631-7), with the title "Pandare to Troylus," is found in Trinity College, Cambridge, MS. R. 3.20, fol. 361a, a MS. written by Shirley. (Printed in *Odd Texts*, p. x.) Two strips of vellum, found in a book-binding, which contain longitudinal sections from 5.1443-98, are described in the Appendix to the Report of the Cambridge Antiquarian Society, Vol. VI (1887), pp. 331-5. (This fragment I have not seen.) There are no variant readings in these passages which determine the affiliation of the fragments; but the last does *not* share a γ reading in 5.1449.

[116] *The Manuscripts of Chaucer's Troilus, with Collotype Facsimiles of the Various Handwritings*, Chaucer Society, First Series, No. XCVIII, 1914; and *The Textual Tradition of Chaucer's Troilus*, Chaucer Society, First Series, No. XCIX, 1916, p. 1-33.

more summary character. In the case of the printed editions, I have listed all the early prints, and identified the character of their texts; but of the more modern editions I have discussed only those which present a new text, disregarding, or at most briefly mentioning, those which are merely new printings of a text already published.

The Manuscripts

ADDITIONAL (A). British Museum, MS. Additional 12,044. A vellum manuscript, 10 x 7½ in., of 113 leaves, which contains only *Troilus*. It is written in two hands, both of the fifteenth century. The first hand has written as far as 3.1709; and the second hand has completed the volume, which has, however, lost its final leaf, and so terminates with 5. 1820. A later hand has made corrections and supplied missing lines.

A is throughout a γ manuscript, closely related to D, save for 3. 1345–414, a passage omitted by D, which the scribe of A has supplied from a source akin to GgH5. Besides the corruptions which it shares with D, it introduces many corrupt readings, frequently omitting words not necessary to the sense, but required by the metre. The readings of A, or of the AD parent, can be used to check those of ClCpH1 in reconstituting the γ original. In some instances, however, the AD parent has corrected γ errors.

CAMPSALL (Cl). The property of Mrs. Bacon-Frank, Campsall Hall, Doncaster. A vellum manuscript, 12 x 8¼ in., of 120 leaves, which contains only *Troilus*. It is beautifully written in one hand of the early fifteenth century, and was executed for Henry V while Prince of Wales, i.e. between 1399 and 1413.

Cl is consistently a γ manuscript, somewhat closer in its readings to AD than are CpH1S2Dig. Remarkably free from gross blunders, it is an authority of high value for a reconstitution of the γ original.

Cl has been printed by the Chaucer Society in *A Parallel Text Print of Chaucer's Troilus and Criseyde*, and in a separate volume.

CORPUS (Cp). Corpus Christi College, Cambridge, MS. No. 61. A vellum manuscript, 12½ x 8 7/10 in., of 151 + 2 leaves, which contains only *Troilus*. It is beautifully written in one hand of the early fifteenth century.

Cp is consistently a γ manuscript, somewhat closer in its readings to H1S2Dig than to ClAD. It presents the γ text with a high degree of purity, and is spelled with exceptional consistency. It serves as one of the basic authorities for the present edition.

Cp has been printed by the Chaucer Society in *A Parallel Text of Three More MSS. of Chaucer's Troilus.*

DIGBY (Dig). Bodleian Library, Oxford, MS. Digby 181. A paper manuscript, 11 1/8 x 8 in., of 93 + 4 leaves, which, in addition to its fragment of *Troilus*, contains a miscellaneous collection of poems by Chaucer, Lydgate, Hoccleve, etc. The *Troilus* fragment, which ends in the middle of a page with 3. 532, is written in one hand of the fifteenth century.

Dig is consistently a γ manuscript, closely related to S2, with which it shares innumerable corruptions, besides many others peculiar to itself. Its value as an authority is negligible.

DURHAM (D). Bishop Cosin's Library, Durham, MS. V. II. 13. A vellum manuscript, 11 x 7 in., of 111 + 5 leaves, which contains, besides *Troilus*, *Cupid's Letter* by Hoccleve. *Troilus* is written in one hand of the fifteenth century. Two other contemporary hands have made corrections and supplied missing lines.

D is consistently a γ manuscript closely related to A. Its text is, however, more corrupt than that of A.

CAMBRIDGE Gg 4. 27 (Gg). Cambridge University Library, MS. Gg 4. 27. A vellum manuscript, 12¾ x 7 5/8 in., of 516 leaves, which contains a miscellaneous collection of Chaucer's works, and Lydgate's *Temple of Glass*. It is written in one hand of the first half of the fifteenth century. The volume has been mutilated by the cutting out of illuminated leaves, and therefore lacks the beginning of all the books of *Troilus*, and the conclusion of all save Book II.

The text of *Troilus*, which is closely related to that of the fragmentary H5, is of composite character. In Book I, and through 2. 63, it is consistently a β manuscript, somewhat resembling the β portion of J. From 2. 64 to 2. 1209 it presents a "mixed" text, predominantly α in character but with frequent β readings. It shares, however, in none of the distinctive JRH4 readings so numerous between 2. 701 and 2. 1113. From 2. 1210 to 3. 398 it resumes its β character, with readings akin to those of J. At 3. 399 (with one earlier instance in 3. 243) Gg becomes definitely and consistently an α manuscript, and so continues to the end. As an α manuscript, it presents the text at the same stage of revision as does the α portion of J.

The text of Gg is very corrupt. Some of its corruptions are shared by H5; but many others are not. GgH5 together constitute an important witness to α, particularly in Book III, where the only other authority is H2Ph.

The *Troilus* text of Gg is printed by the Chaucer Society in *A Parallel Text Print of Chaucer's Troilus and Criseyde*.

HARLEIAN 2280 (H1). British Museum, MS. Harleian 2280. A vellum manuscript, $9\frac{1}{2}$ x 6 3/8 in., of 98 + 1 leaves, which contains only *Troilus*. It is written in one hand of the mid-fifteenth century.

H1 is consistently a γ manuscript, similar in the character of its readings to CpS2Dig. Its orthography varies but little from that of Cp. Comparatively free from corruptions of its own, it is an authority of the first importance for the reconstitution of the γ original.

H1 is printed by the Chaucer Society in *A Parallel Text Print of Chaucer's Troilus and Criseyde*.

HARLEIAN 3943 (H2). British Museum, MS. Harleian 3943. A vellum manuscript, 10¼ x 5 5/8 in., of 116 leaves, which contains only *Troilus*. It is written in four hands, all of the fifteenth century, of which the first and second seem to be earlier than the other two. Hand 1 has written 1. 71–497, 1. 568—3. 1078, 3. 1639—4. 196. Hand 2 has written 3. 1079–638 (from which lines 1289–428 are missing, because of the loss of two leaves). Hand 3 has written 1. 1–70, 1. 498–567, 4. 197–406, and has supplied missing lines in the parts written by Hands 1 and 2. Hand 4 has written from 4. 407 to the end of the poem. It would seem that the scribe of Hand 3 found an unfinished and defective volume, the work of Hands 1 and 2, which he restored and corrected, subsequently turning over the task of completing the work to Hand 4. The scribe of Hand 1 is the same as the scribe who wrote Ph.

The portions written by Hands 1 and 2 present consistently an α text, closely related to that of Ph. The portions written by Hands 3 and 4 are closely related to H4, and, like it, present α readings in Book I, and β readings in the rest of the poem. Despite many corruptions, H2 (with Ph) is an important witness to α in the first three books, and after 4. 196 (with H4) to β.

H2 is printed by the Chaucer Society in *Chaucer's Troylus and Cryseyde compared with Boccaccio's Filostrato*.

HARLEIAN 1239 (H3). British Museum, MS. Harleian 1239. A vellum manuscript, 15½ x 5¾ in., of 107 leaves, which contains, besides *Troilus*, selections from the *Canterbury Tales*. The text of *Troilus* is written by three hands. Hand 1 has written from 1.1 to 2. 1033, Hand 2 from 2. 1034 to 3. 1603, and from 3. 1758 to the end; Hand 3 has written 3. 1604–759, lines 1758, 1759 of Book III being written twice.

The text presented by H3 is both composite and "mixed." The portion written by Hand 1 is a β text of a type similar to that of the source of Cx; but there are occasional indications, more particularly in Book II, of contamination with a γ manuscript of the same type as A. H3 and Cx agree with γSI against JRH4 in the series of striking variants in 2. 701–1113. From 2. 1034 to 3. 1095, H3 is fundamentally a γ manuscript of the same type as A; but in Book III it not infrequently deserts the γ reading, and shows occasional contamination with β. From 3. 1096 to 4. 299 it is again a β manuscript, with only slight traces of contamination with γ. With 4. 300 it becomes an α manuscript, and so continues to the end of the poem, though a β reading appears in 4. 322, and in the latter part of Book V there are again indications of contamination with γ. In its α portion, H3 presents the text at a stage of revision not far removed from that found in Ph. H3Ph omit the free-choice soliloquy entire. In 4. 1301–442, H3 has a series of unique readings which seem to represent a stage more primitive than that of Ph. At the end of Book V, however, it contains the *Teseide* stanzas, derived apparently from its γ constituent.

Throughout, the text of H3 is extremely corrupt. This fact and its "mixed" character make it an unreliable authority. Its chief value lies in its testimony to an early stage of α in Book IV.

H3 is printed by the Chaucer Society in *A Parallel Text of Three More MSS. of Chaucer's Troilus.*

HARLEIAN 2392 (H4). British Museum, MS. Harleian 2392. A paper and vellum manuscript, $8\frac{1}{2}$ x $5\frac{3}{4}$ in., of $145 + 2$ leaves, which contains only *Troilus*. It is written in one hand of the middle of the fifteenth century, which has also supplied a large number of marginal notes in Latin.

H4 presents a composite text, which in certain parts of the work is also "mixed." In Book I it is definitely an α manuscript. It contains stanza 128, omitted by all other MSS. save H2Ph, and shares with H2Ph in a large number of α readings. In Book II it is a mixture of α and β, with the α element decreasing in importance as the book proceeds. In 2. 701–1113 it shares with JR in a number of striking variants, the character of which is discussed on p. lxxx. In Book III it becomes distinctively a β manuscript, and so continues to the end, sharing in virtually all the β readings of Book III, and avoiding the many α readings of Book IV. A striking instance of its "mixed" character is found in the fact that it contains stanzas 201, 202 of Book III twice over, once in the α position with α readings, and again in the β position with β readings. It omits the free-choice soliloquy of Book IV, an α characteristic not shared by the closely related H2. With H2 it omits the *Teseide* stanzas in Book V. The adhesion of H4 to the α tradition in the omission of these passages is surprising, since a contaminated text ordinarily incorporates lines found in any of its constituent authorities. With R, it omits the Latin argument of Statius in Book V.

Throughout, H4 is closely related to the portions of H2 written by Hands 3 and 4. In its β portions, the common parent of H2H4 stands somewhat nearer to R than to the other β authorities.

Though not free from corruption, H4 is purer than H2 or R. It is of the utmost importance as a witness to α in Book I; and in Book IV, after J ceases to give a β text, it is an important witness to β.

HARLEIAN 4912 (H5). British Museum, MS. Harleian 4912. A vellum manuscript, 11½ x 7 5/8 in., of 76+1 leaves, which contains only an incomplete copy of *Troilus*, ending with 4. 686. It is written in one hand of the fifteenth century.

H5 is throughout closely related to Gg; and its type of text is that already described in the account of Gg. It shares many of the corruptions of Gg, and has also many others of its own. H5 is of use chiefly for supplying deficiencies and checking errors of Gg.

St. John's (J). St. John's College, Cambridge, MS. L. 1. A vellum manuscript, 10 x 6¾ in., of 121 +8 leaves, which contains *Troilus*, and, in a sixteenth-century hand, Henryson's *Testament of Criseide*. *Troilus* is written in one hand of the fifteenth century, which has also supplied a few marginal notes in Latin.

The text of J falls into two sharply defined parts. Up to line 430 of Book IV, J is consistently a β manuscript. Between 430 and 438 it becomes an α manuscript, and so continues to the end. In its β portion, the text of J shows certain affinities with R. In 2. 701–1113 it shares with H4 and R in a series of striking variants. A connection also exists between J and the β constituent of GgH5, which is most clearly marked after 2. 1210. In its α portion, J presents the text in the same state of revision as Gg (here consistently an α MS.).

In both portions, the text of J is remarkably free from blunders. Its orthography is throughout consistent, and strikingly similar to that of Cp. It is an authority of primary importance as a witness to β in Books I–III, and to α in the last two books. In conjunction with Cp, it has been used as a basal authority for the present edition.

J is printed by the Chaucer Society in *A Parallel Text of Three More MSS. of Chaucer's Troilus*.

Phillipps (Ph.). MS. Phillipps 8250, the property of T. Fitzroy Fenwick, Esq., Cheltenham. A paper and vellum manuscript, 8¾ x 5 7/8 in., of 325 leaves, which contains, besides *Troilus*, a miscellaneous collection of pieces in prose and verse. It is written throughout in one hand of the early fifteenth century, the same hand as Hand 1 of H2.

Ph is throughout an α manuscript, except for the passages added later, on inset leaves and in the margin, which are from a γ MS. akin to H1. The scribe copied an α MS. and then, after his copy was completed, supplied its deficiencies from a γ source. The hymn to love (3. 1744–71), the free-choice soliloquy (4. 953–1085), and the *Teseide* stanzas (5. 1807–27), are on inset leaves. Ph is closely related to the portions of H2 written by Hands 1 and 2, with which it shares a great number of corrupt readings. Despite its corruptions, it is a very important witness to α. It is the only manuscript which gives an α text throughout the poem.

RAWLINSON (R). Bodleian Library, Oxford, MS. Rawlinson Poet. 163. A paper manuscript, 11½ x 8¼ in., of 115 leaves, which contains, besides *Troilus*, the unique copy of Chaucer's *Rosamund*. It is written in four hands, all of the fifteenth century. Hand 1 writes 1. 1–700; 2. 118–433, 1044–113; 3. 1373 to end of poem. Hand 2 writes 1. 701 – 2. 117; 3. 306–912. Hand 3 writes 2. 434–1043; 2. 1114 – 3. 305. Hand 4 writes 3. 913–1372. Each scribe has written marginal notes in English and in Latin. The volume seems to be the work of a group of associated scribes. The character of the text does not change significantly with the change of scribes.

R is throughout consistently a β manuscript of the same type as the β portions of J and H4, with which it shares in a series of distinctive readings, apparently authentic, in 2. 701–1113. There is no evidence of any close relationship with any of the β authorities. Moreover, R has certain unique characteristics: it omits the proems of Books II–IV, and contains after 2. 1750 a unique stanza, which seems to be genuine. With H4, it omits the Latin argument of Statius (5. 1498).

Despite manifold corruptions, R is an important witness to the text of β. It is the only manuscript which gives a β text throughout the poem.

SELDEN B 24 (S1). Bodleian Library, Oxford, MS. Selden B 24. A paper manuscript, 10¼ x 6 5/8 in., of 231 leaves, which contains, besides *Troilus*, a miscellaneous collection of English and Scottish verse of the fourteenth and fifteenth centuries, among which is the unique copy of the *Kingis Quair*. The first 209 leaves, including the whole of *Troilus*, are by one scribe, probably a Scotchman named James Graye. The MS. was executed not earlier than 1489.

S1 presents a "mixed" text, based on a γ authority akin to AD, and a β authority of the same general type as Cx and the β portions of H3. Up to 2.617 it shares virtually all γ readings, and shows only slight traces of β influence. In the remainder of Book II it shares only occasionally in distinctive γ readings; but in 2.701–1113, where JRH4 depart from the other β authorities, S1 agrees with γH3Cx. In Book III it shares in some fifteen γ readings, and in over sixty β readings, with stanzas 201, 202 in the β position. In Book IV it shares in twenty-four γ readings, but has stanza 106, which γ omits. In Book V it shares in twenty-four out of thirty-five γ readings, but has lines 60, 61 in the $\alpha\beta$ order. It would seem that the method of its scribe-editor was to take a β exemplar and "correct" it to γ readings, thoroughly at the beginning, and thereafter only spasmodically.

Despite a superficial Scottish cast, which results from the consistent writing of *qub* for *wb* and from the use of the Northern pronominal forms *thair* and·*tham*, the text of S1 is remarkably free from corruption; but its value is greatly impaired by its "mixed" and "edited" character. Its witness to the well attested text of γ is usually superfluous; as an authority for β, it can be used only with caution.

SELDEN, SUPRA 56 (S2). Bodleian Library, Oxford, MS. Selden, Supra 56. A paper manuscript, 8¾ x 5 5/8 in., of 106+1 leaves, which contains only *Troilus*. It is neatly written in one hand. The colophon gives the date of its transcription as 1441.

S2 is throughout a γ manuscript, closely related to the fragmentary Dig, with which it shares innumerable corruptions. Dialectally it is strongly marked by Northern

forms. With Dig, it is occasionally of use in determining a
γ reading where the other evidence is confused; but with
the generous attestation of γ, its evidence is seldom needed.

The Printed Editions

CAXTON'S EDITION *circa* 1483 (Cx). Caxton's edition of
Troilus, the *editio princeps* of the poem, is a small folio of
120 leaves, of which the first and the last two are blanks.
There is no title; the colophon reads: "Here endith Troylus
/as touchyng Creseyde / Explicit per Caxton." The book
was probably issued in 1483. Four copies are known to exist.
Two, one of which lacks a few leaves, are in the British Museum, one in the library of St. John's College, Oxford, and
one in the John Rylands Library at Manchester. Besides
these, there is a fragment of eight leaves in the British Museum.[117] A rotographic reproduction of the perfect British
Museum copy is deposited in the Library of Congress at
Washington.[118] This reproduction has been collated for the
present edition.

Despite its beautiful letter-press, Caxton's edition is very
carelessly edited. It must have been printed from a single
corrupt and defective manuscript. Had any attempt been
made to collate it with any other authority, Caxton would
certainly have supplied its missing passages. Twice an eight-
stanza leaf of the manuscript copy was reversed.[119] Three
times a leaf of the original was missing, with consequent
omission of eight stanzas.[120] Five stanzas are omitted at
3. 442–476. A number of lines and short passages show
unique corruptions, which may be attributed to the conjectural emendation of Caxton's editing.

Caxton's manuscript was consistently of the β type, and

---

[117] For fuller bibliographical description, see Seymour de Ricci, *A
Census of Caxtons*, Oxford, 1909, p. 30.
[118] Modern Language Association Deposit, No. 14.
[119] 1.785-812 follows 1.840, and 1.904-31 follows 1.959.
[120] 1.449-504 ; 2.246-301 ; 3.1114-69.

was similar in character to the β portions of H3. H3Cx agree with γS1, as against JRH4, in a series of striking variants in lines 701–1113 of Book II. Despite its corruptions, Cx is an important witness to the text of β. Its value is increased by the fact that it reproduces, however corruptly, a single lost manuscript.

WYNKYN DE WORDE'S EDITION 1517 (W). In 1517, Wynkyn de Worde published *Troilus* in a small quarto of 139+2 leaves, of which the first and the last are flyleaves. There are 23 quires, alternately of eight and four leaves each. Title (fol. a 1): "The noble and amerous auncyent hystory of Troylus and Cresyde, in the tyme of the syege of Troye. Compyled by Geffraye Chaucer." Below the title is a wood-cut of the hero and heroine. The text begins on fol. a 2 *ro*. A wood-cut introduces each of the succeeding books. Colophon:

> Thus endeth the treatyse / of Troylus the hevy
> By Geffraye Chaucer / compyled and done
> He prayenge the reders / this mater not deny
> Newly correcked (*sic*) / in the cyte of London
> In flete strete / at the sygne of the sonne
> Inprinted by me / Wynkyn de worde
> The .M.CCCC. and .xvii. yere of our lorde.

Wynkyn de Worde's edition is extremely rare. There is a copy in the Cambridge University Library, and one in the Henry E. Huntington Library at San Gabriel, California.[121] A rotographic reproduction of the copy in the Huntington Library is deposited in the Library of Congress at Washington.[122] After line 546 of Book I, Wynkyn de Worde's edition is a mere reprint of Caxton's, reproducing all the omissions, transpositions, and corruptions of Cx, and differing from it only in minor variations of spelling, and by the introduc-

---

[121] The leaves of this copy measure 7¼ x 5 inches.
[122] Modern Language Association Deposit, No. 31. My collations have been made from this reproduction.

tion of a few typographical errors. But, for the first 546 lines of the poem, W is entirely independent of Cx. For this portion of its text, W reproduces a lost manuscript of α type, closer to H4 than to H2Ph. Line 546 of Book I is the last line on fol. a 8 *vo.* of Caxton's edition, and is thus at the end of the first quire of eight leaves. It is clear that the copy of Cx which Wynkyn de Worde used had lost its first quire, and that this missing portion was supplied from a manuscript copy. For the first 546 lines, then, W is a valuable witness to the text of α; for the rest of the poem it has no significance.

PYNSON'S EDITION 1526. In 1526 Richard Pynson published a collection of Chaucer's works, printed in double columns, which includes *Troilus*, the *Canterbury Tales*, and certain of the minor poems.[123] It was issued in three parts, each with separate foliation, which could be bound together, or sold separately. The part containing *Troilus* has the title: "Here begynneth the boke of Troylus and Creseyde newly printed by a trewe copye." The colophon reads: "Here endeth the boke of Troylus and Creseyde / empreinted at London in Fletestrete by Rycharde Pynson / printer unto the kynges noble grace."

The "trewe copye" from which Pynson "newly printed" his text of *Troilus* was merely a copy of Caxton's edition, the omissions and transpositions of which are slavishly followed. The spelling is somewhat modernized; and there are occasional typographical errors.[124] Pynson's edition can, therefore, contribute nothing towards the establishment of Chaucer's text.

THYNNE'S EDITION 1532 (Th). In Thynne's folio edition of Chaucer's works published in 1532,[125] and reissued in

---

[123] For full contents, see Hammond, pp. 114-15.

[124] I have collated the text of Book I from rotographs of the copy in the British Museum.

[125] For my collations I have used the photographic facsimile reproduction published in 1905 by the Oxford University Press.

1542 and about 1550, the text of *Troilus* fills fols. 170–218 and part of fol. 219 a. Judged by sixteenth-century standards, and even by those of a later date, Thynne's text of the poem merits high praise. It is remarkably free from careless blunders, and preserves in a majority of the lines the integrity of Chaucer's metre. It is easily the best edition of the poem published before the nineteenth century. Unlike the prints of Caxton, Wynkyn de Worde, and Pynson, it is really edited, being based on a collation of several authorities.

These authorities were at least three: (1) Caxton's edition; (2) a γ manuscript closely akin to CpH1S2; (3) a manuscript which was of the α type, at least in Books I and II.

The use made of these authorities is not the same throughout the poem. In Book I, where γ presents the revised β text, Thynne found Cx and his γ manuscript in substantial agreement. He gave, particularly in the early part of the book, precedence to Cx, though avoiding the glaring corruptions of this authority. In Book I, Th shares very few of the distinctive γ readings. It contains, however, a considerable number of α readings, the most important of which is the inclusion of stanza 128, otherwise found only in H2PhH4. In Book II, the proportion of distinctive γ readings is much greater, and the influence of Cx is much less. In the first 800 lines are found a few α readings; but after line 800, Thynne seems to have consulted his α authority little, if at all.[126] In Books III–V, the text of Th is to all intents and purposes consistently of the γ type, save that it avoids the confusion of γ as to the proem of Book IV,[127] and contains stanza 102 of Book IV, which is omitted by γ. There are in these books no instances where an α reading has been adopted; and only rarely does one discover any trace of Cx. Th consistently avoids the dis-

[126] It is possible that this lost authority was of composite character, and ceased to present α readings after 2.800.
[127] See p. xiii.

tinctive β readings, regularly given by Cx, which are so numerous in Book III.

Despite its general excellence, the text of Th is but of slight service towards establishing a critical text. Since we possess such generous manuscript attestation for the readings of γ, there is little occasion to consult Th, save for its α readings in Book I and Book II, and then only when the α authorities are at variance. Even in these cases, the "edited" character of Th forces us to accept its readings with caution.

Stow's Edition 1561. In the edition of Chaucer's works "Imprinted at London, by Ihon Kyngston, for Ihon Wight, dwellyng in Poules Churchyarde. *Anno* 1561," which is usually referred to as Stow's edition, *Troilus* is found on fols. 151 b—194 a. The text is a mere reprint of Th, with some modernization of spelling and consequent derangement of metre, and with occasional errors of printing.

Speght's Editions of 1598 and 1602. In Speght's edition of 1598, the text of Troilus is merely an inaccurate reprint of that found in Stow's edition. Even the pagination is the same. In Speght 1598, as in Stow, it extends from fol. 151 b to fol. 194 a.[128]

In Speght's edition of 1602, *Troilus* is found on fols. 143 a —182 a. Its text of the poem varies considerably from that of the 1598 edition in minor matters of phrasing. Occasionally a printer's error of the former edition is corrected. Much more frequently, the variation is the result of editorial "improving" of the text, apparently with the idea of conforming it to the editor's notion of Chaucer's metre. I have found no evidence to suggest that the editor consulted any manuscript copies of the poem. The result is a text much more corrupt than that of its predecessors. With all its corruptions, this edition became the standard text of the poem for more than a century. It was reprinted in 1687.

[128] This leaf is erroneously numbered "Fol. 164."

SIR FRANCIS KINASTON 1635. In 1635, Sir Francis Kinaston [129] published a small quarto of 26+105+6+159 pages, the title of which reads: "Amorum / Troili / et / Creseidae / Libri duo priores / *Anglico-Latini*. / Oxoniae, / Excudebat *Iohannes Lichfield*, / Anno Domini / 1635." [130]

The volume contains on the left-hand pages a translation into accentual Latin verse, which retains the metre and rhyme-scheme of the seven-line stanza, of the first two books of *Troilus*. The translation is faithful, and not without literary quality; as an exercise in literary ingenuity it deserves high praise. On the right-hand pages, Kinaston reprinted in black-letter type the original text of Books I and II. This text is a reprint, with many new errors, of the text of Speght's edition of 1602.

It was Kinaston's desire, he tells us, to rescue the genius of Chaucer from the medium of an obsolete speech, to render him "per omnia secula (quantum in nobis est) stabilem et immotum," and to make him known beyond the limits of this too narrow island. If these two books are well received, he promises to publish the remaining books, together with a commentary on the whole poem. The promise of further publication was not carried out; but Kinaston completed both translation and commentary. His completed manuscript was preserved, and came into the hands of F. G. Waldron of Drury Lane Theatre, who in 1795 proposed to publish it, with additional notes of his own. In the following year, Waldron actually issued a thin volume of xxxii+12 pages with the title: "The Loves of Troilus and Creseid, written by Chaucer; with a Commentary, By Sir Francis Kinaston: Never Before Published. London, Printed for and Sold by F. G. Waldron, . . . M.DCCXCVI." This misleading title introduces a rambling introduction of 32 pages, the English text of the first twelve stanzas of the

---

[129] See *DNB* s.v. Kynaston, Sir Francis.

[130] On the lower margin of the title-page of my own copy of this book is written in a contemporary hand: "To be sould by James Davis in litle Brittaine."

lxvi

poem, and Kinaston's notes on these stanzas (with additions by Waldron). No further portion of the work was ever
published; and the present location of the manuscript is
not known.[131] The annotations printed, though not lacking
in intelligence, are not significant enough to make one regret the loss.

URRY'S EDITION 1721. In Urry's edition of Chaucer's
works, *Troilus* fills pages 269–333. Urry's text of the poem,
which represents the high-water mark of corruption, is,
none the less, the first since Thynne's which is based on the
collation of several authorities. Besides the earlier prints,
Urry consulted three manuscript copies of the poem: H3
(Urry's No. II), Gg (Urry's No. XI), and Ph ("MS.
Sp").[132] His method was to reproduce the text of Thynne
or of Speght, with frequent "corrections" from his other
authorities, or, when these failed him, by the free insertion
or omission of words not essential to the meaning. His sole
criterion was his belief that *"Chaucer's* Verses originally
consisted of an equal number of Feet." [133] To achieve this
metrical equality, he constantly adds inflectional syllables,
such as *-en*, in total ignorance of the true forms of Chaucer's
English.

Urry's text of *Troilus* is reproduced in John Bell's edition
of Chaucer's works 1782 (Vol. 8), and in Anderson's edition of 1793–5; but Chalmers (1810) goes back to the
"blackletter editions, which, with all their faults, are more

[131] See Hammond, p. 396.

[132] See the preface to Urry's edition, fols. k 1—l 1. Of Ph the
author of the preface (written after Urry's death by Timothy Thomas)
says: "This I found amongst Books and Papers left by Mr. *Urry*; but I
could not perceive that he had made any use of it." It seems, however,
to be the source from which Urry took a few *a* readings adopted by him
in Book I. The manuscript referred to by Thomas is easily identified as
Ph by his statement that the words "Henrici Spelman" are "written in
fair hand on the first leaf of it, and at the beginning of other Tracts
contained in that Volume"; compare *The Manuscripts of Chaucer's
Troilus*, p. 35.

[133] Preface, fol. i 4.

to be depended on than Urry's." [134] The Chiswick edition of 1822 and Moxon's edition of 1843 follow the same practice as Chalmers.[135]

ROBERT BELL'S EDITION 1854–6. In Bell's edition of the *Poetical Works of Geoffrey Chaucer*, the text of *Troilus* fills volume 5. Bell was the first editor since Thynne to base his text primarily on the manuscripts; but his choice of authorities was an unfortunate one. He used H2, H3, and H1. Up to 4. 196, at which point the first hand of H2 stops, Bell based his text on H2, with corrections from H3; after 4. 196, the text follows H1. It is curious that Bell should have preferred H2, with its manifold corruptions, to the relatively pure γ text of H1. Throughout the poem, Bell adopted readings from Speght's edition whenever they seemed to him "better" than those of his manuscripts, duly recording the fact in his foot-notes. He has, however, silently modified the spelling of his authorities. At the foot of the page are printed a few explanatory notes.

MORRIS'S EDITION 1866. In 1866 Richard Morris edited the *Poetical Works of Geoffrey Chaucer* in six volumes for a new issue of the Aldine Edition of the British Poets. *Troilus* fills volume 4 and the early pages of volume 5. In this edition, the poem is "for the first time, printed entirely from a *single* manuscript." [136] The single manuscript chosen was H1. With this, Morris collated H3, H4, H2, and A, the manuscripts available in the British Museum. His assurance that "All corrections of the original scribe . . . are printed in *italics*, so that the reader may see at a glance where the manuscript has been altered" [137] is not altogether

---

[134] Quoted by Hammond, p. 135.

[135] In all of these editions, from John Bell to Moxon, the text of the *Canterbury Tales* is that of Tyrwhitt. It is to be regretted that this great scholar did not also edit the text of *Troilus*.

[136] Preface, p. ix. But Caxton had anticipated Morris in this singleness of authority.

[137] Preface, p. vii. The edition contains no notes of any kind.

borne out by the facts. Many minor "corrections" are made without this indication.

SKEAT'S EDITION 1894. In Skeat's *Oxford Chaucer*, the text of *Troilus* fills pages 153–417 of volume 2, with explanatory notes on pages 461–506.[138] The text is based on "a close collation of Cl and Cp, taking Cl as the foundation, but correcting it by Cp throughout. . . . In a few places, as shewn by the foot-notes, the readings of other MSS. have been preferred." [139] Though Skeat examined all the extant manuscripts,[140] he collated carefully only those which had then been printed by the Chaucer Society: H1, H2, and Gg. He also collated the edition of Thynne. He recognized "two main families" of manuscripts. "The larger family is that which resembles Cl, Cp, and H [H1]. Of the smaller Cm [Gg] may be taken as the type." [141] With such authorities to guide him, it was inevitable that Skeat should have printed a γ text of the poem. His authorities, outside of the γ group, are both so corrupt that it is not strange that he failed to discriminate between scribal corruptions and authentic variants. Moreover, the composite character of both H2 and Gg served further to conceal the true relations. Only between 3. 399 and 4. 196 do both these manuscripts give consistently α readings, and, in this portion of the poem, γ also usually gives unrevised readings.

Skeat's text, then, is a print of γ, purged of its obvious errors by an eclectic adoption of readings from other authorities. Despite its deficiencies in critical method, it marks a great advance on all previous editions of the poem.

---

138 The text, without the notes, was reprinted in Skeat's single volume *Student's Chaucer*, where it fills pages 206-325.

139 *Oxford Chaucer*, 2. lxix. For Cl, Skeat relied on the Chaucer Society's reprint.

140 With the possible exception of Ph and D, about which he gives no detailed information.

141 *Oxford Chaucer* 5. lxxv. Skeat conjectured that in 4.750-6 the text of Gg "seems to represent the first draft of these lines, which were afterwards altered to the form in which they appear in the text, whilst at the same time the stanza was shifted down" (p. lxxi); but he never suspected the extent to which the poem had undergone revision.

The debt of Chaucerian scholarship to Dr. Skeat is, and must always remain, a large one.

Skeat's text was adopted by F. S. Ellis in the Kelmscott Chaucer, printed in 1896 by William Morris.

GLOBE EDITON 1898. In the Globe Edition of the *Works of Chaucer*, published by Macmillan and Company under the general editorship of Alfred W. Pollard, the text of *Troilus* was edited by Professor (now Sir) William S. McCormick. It occupies pages 438–558. In this edition, for the first time, the text of the poem rests on a thorough examination of all the MSS.;[142] but, since the Globe edition was designed by the publishers as a "popular edition," it was necessary to curtail to a minimum the bulk of critical apparatus. The "text is based upon J, and has been corrected throughout from readings of α and β types alone. But all the authorities have been examined, and all the important variations of γ type are given." [143] Since J is a composite authority, which gives a β text up to line 430 of Book IV, and thereafter an α text to the end of the poem, its choice as basal authority has had as result the printing of what is predominantly a β text for the first two-thirds of the poem, and of what is predominantly an α text for the remainder.

Textual Criticism[144]

The problem of constituting a critical text of Chaucer's *Troilus* is complicated by the fact that the existing authori-

[142] With the editor's analysis of the manuscript relations, as briefly summarized on pp. xli-xlii of the Introduction, my own conclusions are in certain respects at variance. McCormick regarded γ as representing a stage of revision later than that of β, "a later copy, either carelessly corrected by the author, or collated by some hand after Chaucer's death."

[143] Introduction, p. xlii.

[144] For an exhaustive study of the text and of the interrelations of the manuscripts, the reader is referred to the present writer's Chaucer Society volume, *The Textual Tradition of Chaucer's Troilus*. In the following pages, the conclusions of that study are restated; but it has not seemed necessary to repeat the evidence which supports the conclusions, since the publications of the Chaucer Society are accessible to all scholars.

ties present the poem in more than a single state. The editor is therefore confronted, not only with variations of reading due to scribal blundering or conscious "editing," but with other variations, some of them widely divergent, which are due to authentic revision by the poet himself.

That the poem has undergone extensive revision of a deliberate sort is clear beyond any doubt. That the reviser was the poet himself is equally clear; for the revisions, which involve the writing of new passages and the rephrasing of many individual lines, are done by a poet who understood perfectly the principles of Chaucer's metre and grammar, and who knew how to catch what we recognize as his characteristic manner.

In Book I, the earlier, "alpha" version, represented by H2PhH4, contains a stanza, number 128, which is obviously genuine, but which is not necessary to the sense. This stanza is omitted in the "beta" version.[145]

In Book III, two stanzas, numbers 201 and 202 of this edition, have been moved in the β text from a position immediately after line 1323, where they are found in α, to a position immediately before line 1415. The deliberate intention of this shift is shown by the fact that lines 1323, 1415, and the first line of the shifted passage, have been altered to suit the new relations.[146] There is also evidence that the song sung by Troilus in praise of Love (3. 1744–71), omitted by H2Ph, was not present in the earliest draft of the poem.[147]

In Book IV, the long soliloquy of Troilus on God's foreknowledge and man's freedom of choice (lines 953–1085) is not present in the α version of the poem.[148] In the earliest state of the text, represented by H3Ph and by H4, the entire passage is lacking. Before two of the α MSS., Gg and

[145] See note to 1.890-6, and *Textual Tradition*, pp. 34-5.
[146] See note to 3.1401-14.
[147] See *Textual Tradition*, pp. 155-7.
[148] For a fuller discussion of the matter, see *Textual Tradition*, pp. 216-20.

J, were derived, however, the last stanza (lines 1079–85) had been added, and lines 950–2 had been revised to suit the new context.[149]

Still another instance of revision in Book IV is the shift of stanza 108, which in the α text follows line 735. In β, this stanza has been moved to a position immediately before line 757.[150]

In the earliest version of Book V, the three stanzas (lines 1807–27) translated from Boccaccio's *Teseide*, which follow heavenward the soul of the slain Troilus, were not present.[151]

Besides these more striking instances of revision, there are many individual lines in which the phrasing of the α text has been modified. In a number of cases, the revision results in a somewhat freer rendering of the Italian source.[152] These revisions of individual lines, which are all recorded in the variant readings of this edition, are not distributed evenly through the poem. They are in large part concentrated in 1. 1–500, 2. 701–1113, and 3. 401—4. 1450. It

[149] In Gg, stanza 155 follows immediately stanza 136. In J, the whole soliloquy is found, and in the hand of the original scribe ; but after stanza 154 a blank was left of sixteen stanza-spaces. Stanza 154 is at the foot of fol. 83a. Fol. 83b, with space for five stanzas, is blank. After fol. 83, a leaf has been cancelled. The first stanza-space on fol. 84a is blank. Then comes stanza 155. With the ten stanza-spaces of the cancelled leaf, we have, then, sixteen stanza-spaces, originally blank, between stanzas 154 and 155. At the bottom of fol. 83a, after stanza 154, is written in a contemporary hand which seems to be that of the scribe : "her faileth thyng y^t is nat yt made." (See facsimile of this page in the Chaucer Society volume, *The MSS. of Chaucer's Troilus*.) We must assume that both blank and scribal note have been taken over by J from an ancestor, since the existing MS. is through more than half its extent a β MS. But there is clear indication that this ancestor of J, like the existing Gg, contained only stanza 154 of the soliloquy, and that the scribe of this ancestor knew that space was to be left for an indefinite number of stanzas "not yet made."

[150] See note to 4.750-6.

[151] They are omitted by Ph and by H2H4 ; but in Ph they are inserted by the original scribe on an inset leaf. They are, however, present in J, and were probably present in the mutilated Gg—MSS. which derive from the second stage of α. See *Textual Tradition*, pp. 245-8.

[152] For a tabulated list of such instances, see the Chaucer Society volume of *Specimen Extracts from the Nine Unprinted MSS. of Chaucer's Troilus*, pp. 61-72 (Appendix).

would seem that for some reason these portions of the poem received special attention.

What was Chaucer's motive in this extensive revision of his text one cannot say with certainty. The addition of the soliloquy on free choice, and of the stanzas from *Teseide*, enhance appreciably the serious and philosophic tone with which the poet has overcast his story. Presumably that was the effect he desired to attain. But in the other revisions no consistent tendency is discoverable. They have no bearing on plot, character, or interpretation. They are changes in words, or in arrangement of matter, rather than in ideas. In four passages (1. 9; 1. 164; 4. 300; 4. 644), the revision is in the direction of heightening the classical coloring of the poem. In 2. 115, on the other hand, the revision is in the opposite direction. Chaucer's motive seems generally to have been merely the artist's desire to improve his artistry. Sometimes the revision secures greater definiteness, or removes an awkward phrase.[153] More often the change seems to be merely capricious.

From all this it follows that the editor of a critical text must determine which variations of reading are merely scribal, and which are the result of authentic revision. Having purged the text of scribal corruption, he must next in many passages proceed to establish two authentic readings—one original, the other revised.[154] Though the problem is complicated enough, there is fortunately sufficient evidence to admit of its solution in the vast majority of cases. Considering the length of the poem, there are very few lines in which the true reading (or readings) is in serious doubt.

One MS. only, Ph, presents consistently an α text throughout the poem; and only R and Cx give β readings throughout. Unluckily these authorities are among the least reliable; they are so seriously marred by corruptions

[153] For examples, see *Textual Tradition*, p. 262.
[154] In a very few instances, it is possible to identify an intermediate reading which seems to be authentic.

that no editor could think of choosing any of them as the basis of his text. Of the remaining authorities, some are composite, i.e. derived in part from an α exemplar and in part from a β exemplar (e.g., J presents a β text through line 430 of Book IV, and an α text from that point to the end of the poem); others are derived from Chaucer's original at a time when the process of revision was not yet completed, and so present in certain parts of the poem β readings, in other parts α readings.

In this last category belongs a group of MSS., including several of very careful and beautiful execution and of early date, which are certainly derived from a lost common original, derived in its turn from Chaucer's own copy, at a time when the more important revisions had been made, but before the poet had revised certain portions of his work. This group, designated as "gamma," is made up of seven MSS.: Cp, Cl, H1, A, D, S2, Dig. *Gamma* readings are also found in the "mixed" or "contaminated" texts of S1 (particularly before 2. 617), of H3 (particularly between 2. 1033 and 3. 1095), and of the edition of Thynne. That the MSS. enumerated above are descended from a lost common original is shown by their agreement in a series of erroneous readings. They omit stanza 102 of Book IV, a stanza necessary to the sense of the context; they treat the proem of Book IV as though it were the conclusion of Book III; they share in a long list of variant readings of which a considerable number are clear cases of error, others obviously inferior, and the rest, with very few exceptions, variations of the trivial sort which normally originate with a scribe.

Within the group, certain nearer relationships are clearly discernible. S2 and Dig are late and corrupt copies of a lost γ MS., which was itself full of glaring corruptions. A and D share a long series of errors which show that they are derived from a lost γ MS, whose text, though much purer than that of the S2Dig original, is less reliable than that of

Cp, Cl, or H1. The three MSS. just named are beautifully
and carefully executed. From them alone it is usually possible to determine the reading of the γ original. In doubtful
cases the testimony of AD is generally decisive. It is seldom
necessary to consider the corrupt text of S2Dig.

The γ original must have been written at an early date;
for of the MSS. derived from it Cp is in an early fifteenth-
century hand, and Cl, which has on the lower margin of
its beautifully illuminated first page the arms of Henry V
as Prince of Wales, must have been executed between 1399
and 1413. But early though it is, there is no reason to believe that it ever passed under the poet's correcting eye.
Its errors, particularly that which concerns the proem of
Book IV, are of a sort which he could hardly have failed
to emend. Its authority, then, is that of an early, and in
the main very pure, copy of the poem, but not that which
would attach to a MS. which had undergone Chaucer's
personal "rubbing and scraping."

It was derived from Chaucer's own copy at a time when
the poet's revision of his work was not yet complete. In
Books I and IV, it gives usually revised, β, readings; in
Book II, its readings are apparently those of the final revision, though for lines 701–1113 the evidence is confused;[155]
in Book III, it gives in the main unrevised, α, readings.

I have already said that only one MS., Ph, gives consistently an α text throughout the poem. But fortunately
there is no portion of the text in which it is the sole authority for α. Several other MSS. give an α text through long
portions of the poem. These MSS. are of composite character, derived in certain parts from an α exemplar, in other
parts from a β exemplar. Often we can determine within a
few lines at what point a scribe ceased to copy one exemplar, and turned to another. Up to 3. 1078, excepting 1.
1–70 and 1. 498–567,[156] the readings of Ph can be checked

---

[155] See p. lxxx.

[156] In these two passages written by Hand 3, H2 gives an α text
closely related to that of H4.

by those of H2, which in this portion of its text is written by the same scribe who executed Ph, and copied by him from the same α exemplar. From the beginning of the poem through 2. 65, H4 also gives an α text; and for the first 546 lines of Book I we have also the independent evidence of W. From 2. 64 to 2. 1210 and from 3. 399 to the end, Gg and the closely related H5 give an α text.[157] After 4. 299, H3 becomes an α MS.; and at 4. 438, J also changes from β to α. From 1.1 to 2. 800 Th occasionally presents α readings, notably in stanza 128 of Book I.

It may be convenient to list in tabular form the authorities which attest the α text:

1. 1	— 1. 546	H2PhH4W
1. 547	— 2. 65	H2PhH4
2. 66	— 2. 1210	H2PhGgH5
2. 1211	— 3. 398	H2Ph
3. 399	— 4. 196	H2PhGgH5
4. 197	— 4. 299	GgH5Ph
4. 300	— 4. 430	GgH5H3Ph
4. 431	— 4. 686	JGgH5H3Ph
4. 687	— end	JGgH3Ph

These authorities, though associated by the fact that they present the unrevised text, do not, like the γ MSS., show any evidence of a genealogical relation. Between H2 and Ph, and between Gg and H5, there is close relationship. Each of these pairs of MSS. agrees in a long list of corrupt readings which clearly prove descent from a lost common original. But this is not true of the group as a whole. H2Ph, H4, W, GgH5, J, and H3 are derived through independent channels from Chaucer's own copy of the poem. In the few trivial instances in which they agree in readings which cannot be attributed to the poet himself, we must regard the corruption as a blunder of Chaucer's

[157] H5 is a fragment which ends with 4.686.

own scribe, which had failed to catch the poet's proof-reading eye.[158]

This original, then, was not written by Chaucer's own hand, but by the "Adam, scriveyn" to whom is addressed the well-known poetical rebuke. A study of the existing MSS. enables us to determine with a high degree of probability something of the methods of Chaucer's literary craftsmanship.[159] The poet's own draft of his poem, confused, it would seem, on many a page by erasures and interlineations, was turned over to a professional scribe, who made from it a fair copy. This copy contained not only the errors which are inevitable in the work of transcription, but others which arose from Adam's failure to understand here and there his employer's final intention, obscured as it was by a tangle of rewritings and blotted lines. When the poet had "proof-read" this copy, correcting all of Adam's errors which caught his attention, it became what we may call his own "official" text, from which new copies were made for presentation to friends and patrons. In this official text, the poet also made from time to time other alterations dictated by his own exacting poetic instinct—the addition of new passages, the rearrangement of other passages, the new turning of a phrase, the substitution of what seemed to him a happier word, the metrical revision of a halting line. These revisions were not made systematically from the beginning of the poem to the end. The revisions of Book III were made later than those of Book IV.[160] Except at the very end, Book V seems to have undergone hardly

[158] For the passage from 2.1211 to 3.398, where the α text is attested only by H2Ph, we have what is virtually the testimony of only a single authority, the lost original of H2Ph. This authority contains many corrupt readings which cannot be attributed to Chaucer's own copy. In the portions of the poem where only two independent authorities give the α text, there are a few agreements in trivial error which are to be attributed to accidental coincidence.

[159] For the general conditions which prevailed, see my article, "Publication before Printing," *P.M.L.A.* 28.417-31.

[160] The γ original was derived at a time when Book IV was already revised, but when Book III was still for the most part untouched.

any revision after the time when the α MSS. were derived. In Book II, the important revisions are confined to a passage beginning with line 701 and ending with line 1113, and in this passage, it would seem, there were two separate and conflicting revisions.

The α MSS. are derived, then, from a single authentic MS. in Chaucer's own possession, but a MS. whose text was undergoing progressive modifications. Earliest in derivation would seem to be the α portion of the text of H3. Like Ph, it omits the soliloquy on free choice entire; it contains the *Teseide* stanzas at the end of Book V, but the text of this passage indicates that it was derived from the γ authority which has contributed elsewhere to the "mixed" text of H3; between lines 1301 and 1442 of Book IV it presents a series of unique, but apparently authentic, readings which seem to represent the text in a stage more primitive than that of any other authority. Next in order of derivation is the original of H2Ph, which knows nothing of the free-choice soliloquy nor of the *Teseide* stanzas, and which omits the hymn to Love in 3. 1744–71.[161] After H3 and H2Ph were derived the originals of GgH5 and J. Gg contains the last stanza only of the soliloquy;[162] J contains the whole of the soliloquy, but there is clear evidence that it is derived from an exemplar which originally had only the last stanza.[163] J, and probably also Gg,[164] contains the *Teseide* stanzas.

After these MSS. were derived from it, the original copy was subjected to a series of revisions which affect many lines of Books I, II, and IV. It was after these revisions had been made that the γ original was written out. Subsequent to the derivation of γ, Book III underwent a thorough revision.

---

[161] Ph contains all three of these passages from a γ source as later additions on inset leaves, though in the hand of the original scribe.

[162] The fragmentary H5 ends before this passage is reached.

[163] See above, p. lxxii, n. 149.

[164] Gg has lost by mutilation the end of the poem. See p. liv.

The final, β version of the text is presented consistently by R, and by the edition of Caxton. Unluckily both these authorities are highly unreliable, so that neither of them can serve as basis for a critical text. Fortunately, however, there are other and better authorities by which the text of β can be constituted. Up to line 430 of Book IV the very accurately, carefully written J is a β authority of prime importance. After line 65 of Book II, H4, though occasionally contaminated from an α source, is an important witness to β; and after 4. 196 its readings can be checked by the closely related text of H2. For the passages 1. 1—2. 63 and 2. 1211—3. 398 GgH5 give a β text. Until 4.299 H3 gives a β text frequently contaminated from a γ source; and S1, though strongly contaminated by γ readings, is often useful as confirmatory evidence. It must be remembered also that γ was derived after most of the revisions, except those of Book III, had been completed, and that thus the text of γ is in the main a β authority.

The attestation of the β text, apart from the witness of γ, may be presented in the following table:

1. 1	— 2. 65	JGgH5H3RCx
2. 66	— 2. 1033	JRH4(H3)Cx
2. 1034	— 2. 1210	JRH4Cx
2. 1211	— 3. 398	JRH4GgH5(H3)Cx
3. 399	— 3. 1095	JRH4Cx
3. 1096	— 4. 196	JRH4(H3)Cx
4. 197	— 4. 299	JRH2H4(H3)Cx
4. 300	— 4. 430	JRH2H4Cx
4. 431	— end	H2H4RCx

The text of S1 is so seriously contaminated that I have not included it in this table. Throughout this edition the reading of S1 is separately recorded, and, after Book I, the same treatment is accorded to H3. Thus a β reading in which S1 participates is entered in the variants as "βS1," and, after

Book I, a reading in which H3 participates is entered as "βH3."

There is no evidence which establishes a genealogical relationship of these β authorities. Within the group, there is clear evidence of such relationship between Gg and H5, and between H2 and H4. With these exceptions, the β authorities seem to be derived along independent lines from Chaucer's official copy of the revised text. Though the evidence is not clear, there is some ground for believing that H2H4RCx derive from an alternative copy of the official text—a second fair copy made by "Adam scriveyn," into which had been incorporated the revisions, but which contained here and there an uncorrected slip of Adam's scribal pen.

A problem concerning the β text so baffling that I can offer no satisfactory solution is offered by a series of divergent readings found between lines 701 and 1131 of Book II. Within this passage are found over a score of variant readings, most of them of a striking sort, which point to deliberate and authentic revision. On the basis of these variations, the authorities divide sharply into three groups: H2PhGgH5, γH3CxS1, and JRH4. The first of these groups presents, presumably, the α text. We should expect that JRH4 would give the final β text, with γ occupying a middle position.[165] In certain passages this is the case; but in others JRH4 agree with H2PhGgH5, where γH3CxS1 present a revised reading. In some cases (lines 703, 721, 760–1, 813, 859, 1113), moreover, the reading of JRH4 seems to be of scribal origin rather than an authentic revision.

[165] It is to be noted that, in these instances, γ has the support of H3CxS1. Of these authorities, S1 ceases to be regularly a γ MS. after 2.617, and H3 does not become a γ MS. until 2.1034. In no part of Cx is there evidence of contamination from a γ source. Through the whole passage, then, γ has the independent support of Cx, and (barring possible contamination) of S1, and up to line 1034 of H3 as well. During this passage there are twenty-two distinctive γ readings (see *Textual Tradition*, pp. 86-8) of the sort found throughout the poem. In three of these S1 participates; Cx shares in none.

The state of things just described may perhaps have arisen in some such way as this:—From Chaucer's official archetype were derived H2Ph and GgH5. Next, certain revisions were made in this archetype, which were duly incorporated into γ and into H3, Cx, and S1. Then an accident to the archetype MS. caused the destruction or loss of five or six leaves, containing stanzas 100–59, lines 694–1113. Their place was then supplied in the archetype by reference to a copy of the poem not otherwise represented by any existing MS., which had been derived later than H2Ph and GgH5 (since it must have contained the revised reading in 734–5), but before the γH3CxS1 revisions were made. In this substituted copy new revisions were made in lines 731, 736–8, and perhaps also in 703 and 760–1; though in these two cases I suspect that we have rather scribal corruptions of the MS. from which the substituted leaves were copied. The text of JRH4 is derived from these substituted leaves.

The explanation just given is pure hypothesis. All that can be said for it is that it explains the facts, and is not inherently improbable.[166] Fortunately this is the only portion of the text about which there is serious doubt.

The Text of this Edition

It is the purpose of this edition of *Troilus* to present, so far as the evidence will permit, a text of the poem, purged from scribal corruption, which shall incorporate all the revisions which represent the poet's final preference as to the reading of his work—such a text as might have received his own final sanction.

With this end in view, I have chosen as primary bases for my text two manuscripts, wholly unrelated by any genealogical tie, each of which is clearly derived along independent lines of descent from Chaucer's own archetype.

[166] For a fuller discussion of the problem, see *Textual Tradition*, pp. 125-8.

These manuscripts are Cp and J. Each of these authorities presents a text remarkably free from scribal blunders, conscientious (though not impeccable) in its preservation of grammatical forms, and hence of Chaucer's metre, and strikingly in agreement, one with the other, in orthography.

Cp is a member of the important genealogical group designated as γ. By comparison with other γ MSS., particularly with the carefully executed Cl and H1, it is easy to purge Cp of all corruptions for which its own immediate scribe is responsible, and to bring its readings into accord with the lost γ original. Having purged its text of all idiosyncratic corruptions, the next step is to eliminate all the errors and "editings" which originate with the scribe who wrote the γ original. I have treated as of scribal origin all γ readings, even though logically and metrically possible or even acceptable, which are not confirmed by authorities independent of the γ group. This elimination of readings peculiar to γ is accomplished very easily by a substitution of the reading established on the basis of the remaining authorities, of which the most consistently reliable is J. In a majority of instances, it is sufficient to substitute for the reading peculiar to γ the reading found in J. I have found no instances of any significance in which γ and J concur in a reading not otherwise authenticated.

I have depended primarily on J, not only for the elimination of the scribal corruptions of γ, but also for the final revisions made subsequently to the derivation of γ, and hence not incorporated in its text. These revisions, unknown to the γ scribe, are most frequent in Book III. Here the corrected γ text is usually in accord with the evidence of the α MSS. (H2PhGgH5), and the revised β text is presented by JRH4Cx, with the frequent accord of S1 and of H3. Wherever J has the support of three independent β authorities, I have regarded its reading as an authentic revision, and have accordingly adopted it into the text.

It is unfortunate for the textual critic that J does not

continue to give a β text to the end of the poem. It maintains throughout its high standards of accuracy, so that it is still available for the correction of the scribal vagaries of γ; but between lines 430 and 438 of Book IV its character changes. From there until the end of the poem its text is derived from an α source, and the critic is deprived of its witness to the β text. For the latter part of the poem, then, the authorities for β are H2H4, R, Cx, and, intermittently S1. But the defection of J is less serious because after line 400 of Book IV γ has incorporated nearly all of the authentic revisions. I have, indeed, been chary of accepting as authentic revisions readings of H2H4RCx which are not found in γ, unless they have also the support of S1; but wherever I have rejected such a reading, I have recorded the fact in the notes.

I have already called attention to the fact that in the portion of Book II which falls between lines 701 and 1131 are found a series of readings the character of which cannot be satisfactorily determined.[167] Though the problem remain unsolved, it is necessary that the editor of an edition decide at least on a procedure to be followed. The question was whether to print the text of JRH4, or that of γH3CxS1, as representative of the poet's final version. After much consideration, I have decided to print the readings of γH3CxS1. The divergent readings of JRH4 are, of course, plainly indicated among the variants.

I have been very chary of adopting into the text conjectural emendations, even when a possible emendation could be taken from among the variant readings of the MSS. and early editions. Unless the MS. or edition offering such a tempting reading is in a position to speak with authority, the assumption must be that its reading, however plausible, is the happy guess of a scribal editor. In the rare cases when such a variant has been adopted, I have given my reasons for so doing in the notes. In other cases, I have been con-

---

[167] See above, p. lxxx.

tent to suggest the reading in the notes, without printing it in the text. Fortunately the authoritative attestation of *Troilus* is so complete, and the resultant text so free from difficulties, that there is but little temptation to resort to emendation. A well attested reading should be accepted as authentic, even though the variant reading of a single authority gives a smoother, perhaps a better, line. It is not to be supposed that Chaucer wrote only lines of mechanically regular metre, nor that he always succeeded in avoiding awkward constructions.

By the processes described above, it is possible to determine with a high degree of certainty the authentic text of *Troilus* so far as its essential content is concerned, to restore *verbatim* Chaucer's final version of his poem. There remains the problem of *literatim*, the determination of a satisfactory orthography. Here the critical processes already described are of small avail. In the absence of any generally accepted standard of orthography, a scribe felt no necessary obligation to conform his own spelling to that of his exemplar, nor even to follow consistently any system of his own. It is not uncommon, even in a carefully executed MS., to find the same word differently spelled within the space of two or three lines.

What may have been Chaucer's own habits of spelling we have no means of determining. No scrap of his own handwriting has survived, nor any MS. of any of his writings which we can believe that he ever saw with his own eyes. By no amount of pains can we hope to present a text spelled precisely as Chaucer wrote it. Our ambition must be confined to the attainment of an orthography which the poet and his contemporaries would have regarded as not abnormal, an orthography which above all else does not "mismetre" Chaucer's text. The modern reader, used as he is to a rigorously enforced standard of spelling, is tempted to seek a normalized spelling for a Middle English text; but among all the uncertainties this at least is certain, that in

Chaucer's day no such complete standardization existed. I have preferred to set before the modern reader a text spelled according to the practice of Chaucer's time, and the only practicable way of doing this is to accept the spelling of an early scribe.

Cp was written early in the fifteenth century; J is little if any later. Both MSS. are spelled with more consistency than most; and, what is more striking, they are spelled very much alike. Often for a whole stanza together they differ hardly at all. One is inclined to believe that each has preserved in general the orthographical character of Chaucer's "official" copy. Two other γ MSS., Cl and H1, follow in the main the same general practice, a fact which suggests that all three have kept something of the spelling of the lost γ original. It may be, however, that the orthographical similarity of these four MSS. results from the adherence of their scribes to an approximate standard established by an early fifteenth-century school of copyists. If that be the case, a modern edition may well adhere to the same practice.

I have reproduced ordinarily, therefore, the orthography of Cp; or perhaps I had better say the orthography of Cp and J conjointly. Where Cp and J are at variance, I have usually followed Cp; but I have freely substituted the spelling of J where a spelling of Cp obscures the metre, or seems otherwise to be a needless vagary.[168] These substitutions are made silently. To have recorded in the variants every such minor substitution could serve no useful purpose. When, however, I have rejected the spelling *both* of Cp and J, the fact is duly noted. The reader may be assured

---

[168] I have consistently followed J in writing *yit* instead of *yet*, the form found in Cp; since, throughout Chaucer's verse, the word rhymes only with words containing short *i* (see Wild, pp. 82, 83). I have also preferred the form *or*, found in J, to the *er* normally given by Cp for the conjunction meaning *ante*. That the form *er* of Cp is a scribal substitution is suggested by the fact that in 3.377; 3.613; 5.1334 Cp reads *er* for *or* (=*aut*). Cl makes the same error in 4.834; 5.1400. Cp reads *or* (= *ante*) in 1.1071; 4.1685.

that, unless advertised to the contrary, he has before him the spelling *either* of Cp or of J. If it should concern him to know which of these authorities has been followed in any instance, he can easily answer the question by reference to the Chaucer Society's volume, *A Parallel Text of Three More MSS. of Chaucer's Troilus*, where the texts of J and of Cp are printed *literatim* in adjoining columns.

I have rarely had occasion to reject the spellings of both Cp and J; but I have done so whenever metrical considerations have made it necessary. This has been the case when the suppression, or meaningless intrusion, of a weak *e* has affected the syllabic value of a word.[169] In such cases I have been guided by considerations of historical grammar, and by the readings of the other authorities, particularly Cl and H1. The substituted spelling is usually that of Cl or H1, and the departure from CpJ is always recorded.

Though following the spelling of the authorities scrupulously in all essentials, I have not attempted to suggest the *form* of the MS. writing. Abbreviations (which are used only sparingly by Cp and J) are expanded, without the use of italics to indicate the fact of abbreviation. An ordinary capital *F* is printed for the initial *ff* of the MSS. In Cp, the character "yogh" (ȝ) is regularly written for the palatal continuant, where J writes *y*, and occasionally at the end of a word as an abbreviation for *-es*. Cp does not use the character "thorn" (þ) at all; in J it is used only in writing the word *that* (pronoun and conjunction). Both MSS. write *gh* for the velar continuant.[170] I have had no occasion, therefore, to use either of these obsolete characters in my text. In the case of *u* and *v*, I have followed modern usage, representing the consonantal sound by *v*, and the vocalic

---

[169] I have followed Cp in writing *hire* for the personal pronoun (fem. sing., gen. and acc., and 3d plu. gen.), though the word is always a monosyllable in metrical value. The final *e* is, of course, historically justified.

[170] Very rarely Cp writes ȝ for the velar continuant. In these cases I have printed the normal *gh*.

lxxxvi

by *u*. The MSS., of course, use *v* initially, and *u* medially and finally, for both phonetic values without distinction. I have similarly printed the modern character *j*, instead of the *i* or *I* of the MSS., wherever the consonantal sound (dʒ) is intended. I cannot see that any useful purpose would be served by following the older usage in these particulars. The specialist does not need to be reminded of this usage; for the more general reader its preservation would but add an accidental detail to the substantial barriers which linguistic change has inevitably erected between him and one of the great literary masterpieces of the English tongue. We have long since abandoned the notion, current in the seventeenth century, that the text of Chaucer should be printed in black-letter type.

The punctuation has been supplied throughout the text in accordance with modern practice. The text of Cp is not pointed at all; that of J makes sparing use of the cross line (/) to indicate logical pauses, but only in the interior of a verse.[171]

It has been my purpose to record among the variants at the foot of the page every reading which could, in my judgment, be of possible significance to the student of the poem. A *complete* list of variant readings is given only in the cases where the constitution of the text or its interpretation is in doubt. In such cases the reader should have before him all the evidence, so that he may make his own text, if he is not satisfied with mine. Except in such cases, no useful purpose would be served by encumbering the page with the careless or stupid aberrations of some poor scribe, whose sins may well be forgotten, as well as forgiven.

I have not ordinarily recorded variant spellings. To have done so with any fullness would have added enormously to the bulk of variant readings. Important as some of these spellings may be for the investigation of dialect, they con-

[171] H4, R, and S1 make a more extensive use of the cross line.

cern rather the student of fifteenth-century English than the student of Chaucer; for they indicate the linguistic habits of the various scribes rather than those of the poet himself. The characteristics of Chaucer's own speech must be determined by a study of his metre and rhyme, and by comparison with documents actually written down in London during the later decades of the fourteenth century. Thanks to the work of Kittredge, Ten Brink, Wild, and others, this evidence has been so thoroughly studied that we are able to say that a given form found in the fifteenth-century MSS. is, or is not, in accord with Chaucer's linguistic usage, that a given MS., such as Cp or J, has preserved in the main the characteristics of the poet's speech. For the student who may be concerned with the dialectal peculiarities of the various MSS. of Chaucer, the *literatim* transcripts published by the Chaucer Society furnish abundant material. In the case of *Troilus*, seven MSS. have been printed entire, and copious extracts have been printed from the rest.

I have not thought it necessary to record the variants which are significant only in so far as they establish the common descent of two or more authorities from a lost common original—the blunders which serve to link together H2 and Ph, Gg and H5, A and D, S2 and Dig, H4 and the later portion of H2. Such variants are listed abundantly in my Chaucer Society volume, *The Textual Tradition of Chaucer's Troilus*. I have, however, recorded all the aberrant variants of the lost γ original. They are not, in proportion to the length of the poem, very numerous. Some of them, while not authoritative, are interesting instances of scribal "editing." In every case they serve as notice to the reader that I have rejected a reading of one of my basal authorities—Cp. There is further reason for recording them in the fact that a large number of them were adopted by Skeat.

I have recorded with absolute completeness every clearly

attested reading of the α text, and every reading, not clearly attested, which *may* have been a reading of the α text. I have also recorded every reading found in two or more independent β authorities which may possibly point to an authentic revision not sufficiently attested for adoption into the text.

Beyond the limits of these categories, the variants recorded have been selected—because they seemed to me to possess some possible interest or significance—from among the thousands of variants which I have collected in an exhaustive study of the documents.

When among the variants a reading is recorded as found in two or more authorities, it is spelled, unless otherwise noted, according to the authority first cited. A reading attributed to γ is similarly given in the spelling of Cp. A reading attributed to α is given in the spelling of that one of the authorities which present an α text for the portion of the poem in question which stands first in the following list: J, H2, Gg, H3, Ph. In consulting the variant readings, one must remember that, whereas the symbol γ represents merely a lost copy of Chaucer's original, from which have been derived certain of the existing manuscripts—a copy which presumably had never passed under the poet's eye—the symbols α and β represent Chaucer's own "official" copy of the poem in two different stages of authentic revision.

LIST OF ABBREVIATIONS

A: MS. Additional 12,044, British Museum.

Cl: Campsall MS., Doncaster.

Cp: Corpus Christi College, Cambridge, MS. 61.

Cx: Caxton's edition, *circa* 1483.

D: Bishop Cosin's Library, Durham, MS. V. II. 13.

Dig: MS. Digby 181, Bodleian Library.

F1: Fragment in Cambridge University Library, MS. Ff. 1. 6.

F2: Fragment in Trinity College, Cambridge, MS. R. 3. 20.

Fil.: Boccaccio's *Il Filostrato.*

Gg: Cambridge University Library, MS. Gg. 4. 27.

H1: MS. Harleian 2280, British Museum.

H2: MS. Harleian 3943, "   "

H3: MS. Harleian 1239, "   "

H4: MS. Harleian 2392, "   "

H5: MS. Harleian 4912, "   "

J: St. John's College, Cambridge, MS. L. 1.

NED: *A New English Dictionary on Historical Principles.*

Ph: MS. Phillipps 8250, Cheltenham.

R: MS. Rawlinson Poet. 163, Bodleian Library.

S1: MS. Selden, B. 24, Bodleian Library.

S2: MS. Selden, Supra 56, Bodleian Library.

Tes.: Boccaccio's *Teseide.*

Th: Thynne's edition of 1532.

W: Wynkyn de Worde's edition of 1517.

α: The earlier, unrevised text, and collectively the authorities (see page lxxvi) which in any given portion of the poem present this text.

β: The final, revised text, and collectively the authorities (see page lxxix) which in any given portion of the poem present this text.

γ: A lost manuscript derived from Chaucer's original before the revision of the text was completed, and collectively the existing authorities derived from this lost manuscript, *i.e.* Cp, Cl, H1, A, D, S2, Dig (see pages lxxiv-lxxv).

BOOK ONE

BOOK ONE

1

THE double sorwe of Troilus to tellen,
 That was the kyng Priamus sone of Troye,
 In lovynge how his aventures fellen
Fro wo to wele, and after out of joie,
My purpos is, or that I parte fro ye.   5
Thesiphone, thow help me for tendite
Thise woful vers, that wepen as I write.

2

To the clepe I, thow goddesse of torment,
 Thow cruel furie sorwynge evere yn peyne,
Help me that am the sorwful instrument   10
 That helpeth loveres, as I kan, to pleyne;
For wel sit it, the sothe for to seyne,
A woful wight to han a drery feere,
And to a sorwful tale a sory chere.

3

For I, that god of loves servauntes serve,   15
 Ne dar to love, for myn unliklynesse,
Preyen for speed, al sholde I therfor sterve,
 So fer am I from his help in derknesse;
But natheles, if this may don gladnesse
Unto any lovere, and his cause availle,   20
Have he my thonk, and myn be this travaille.

---

2. α(-W)H5Th *om.* the; Cx *om.* That was the.   5. H2H3S1 parte you froye: H4AW fro the, D fro you.   6. H3RPhH5W me to endite.   7. ClH1RH5W This. 9. α Thou cruel wighte that sorowist ever in peyne.   12. JH2 wel it sit, R it well syt, Cx *om.* it.   13. α Unto a wofull wighte a drery fere (H2 chere *for* fere). 15. CpClJ servaunt3, H1H4 servaunt, *rest* servauntes *or* servauntis.   16. H3CxW Ne dar not to love (Cx *om.* to).   17. α though that I shulde sterve (H2W *om.* that). 19. α myght I do yit gladnesse (H4 yit myhte I do).   20. CpH3CxThα To any (H2Ph my *for* any); H2 or my love, H4 or my book, W or elles my boke, Cx and hys lady.   21. R Hys be the thonk; H3Ph thy, H4CxS2DigW the *for* my, H2 *om.* my; ClA his, H2H4H5RCxThW the *for* this.

[3]

4

But ye loveres, that bathen in gladnesse,
If any drope of pyte in yow be,
Remembreth yow on passed hevynesse
That ye han felt, and on the adversite   25
Of other folk, and thynketh how that ye
Han felt that love dorste yow displese,
Or ye han wonne hym with to grete an ese.

5

And preieth for hem that ben in the cas
Of Troilus, as ye may after here,   30
That love hem brynge in hevene to solas;
And ek for me preieth to god so dere,
That I have myght to shewe in som manere
Swich peyne and wo as loves folk endure,
In Troilus unsely aventure.   35

6

And biddeth ek for hem that ben despeired
In love, that nevere nyl recovered be,
And ek for hem that falsly ben apeired
Thorugh wikked tonges, be it he or she;
Thus biddeth god, for his benignite,   40
So graunte hem soone out of this world to pace,
That ben despeired out of loves grace.

24-28. α *reads:*

> Remembre you of olde passid hevynesse
> For goddis love, and on adversitee
> That other suffren, thynke how somtyme þat ye
> Fownde how love durst you dispiese,
> Or ellis ye wonne hym with to grete ease.

(24. H2 for *for* of; H4 on old hevynesse, W in olde hevynesse. 25. H4 in *for* on. 26. H4 *om.* þat. 27. W Have founde; H4 *middle of line illegible.* 28. H2 it *for* hym, *om.* to). 26. ClH1 þenketh. 27. R how þat love, Cx how love. 28. H5 Or ellis ʒe have, an *over line later*; RCx *om.* an. 32. H2 þat *for* to, H4Ph *om.* to. 33. α He yeve me myghte. 34. α Some peyn or woo suche as his folke endure (H2 lovis *for* his, H4 *om.* his; Ph & *for* or). 36. CpClJ desespeired; α Praith for them that eke ben disespeyred (W Now praye you all for them that ben despayred; H4 eek that; H2H4 dispeired). 37. H3 wyll, H4Ph wil, AS1 wol, D wolde, W wel. 40. H2 Or thus, Ph And, H4 Now *for* Thus; W And praye you to god. 41. H4W let, Ph leve *for* graunte. 42. CpCl desespeired.

[4]

7

And biddeth ek for hem that ben at ese,
That god hem graunte ay good perseveraunce,
And sende hem myght hire ladies so to plese,   45
That it to love be worship and plesaunce;
For so hope I my soule best avaunce,
To preye for hem that loves servauntes be,
And write hire wo, and lyve in charite,

8

And for to have of hem compassioun,   50
As though I were hire owne brother dere.
Now herkneth with a good entencioun;
For now wol I gon streyght to my matere,
In which ye may the double sorwes here
Of Troilus in lovynge of Criseyde,   55
And how that she forsook hym or she deyde.

EXPLICIT PROHEMIUM PRIMI LIBRI.
INCIPIT LIBER PRIMUS.

9

IT is wel wist how that the Grekes stronge
In armes, with a thousand shippes, wente
To Troiewardes, and the cite longe
Assegeden, wel ten yer or they stente;   60
And, in diverse wise and oon entente,
The ravysshyng to wreken of Eleyne,
By Paris don, they wroughten al hir peyne.

44. α In love þat god them graunte perseveraunce. 45. ClADS1α loves, H1 loveres *for* ladies; ClH1S1H5Cx for *for* so, R *om.* so. 46. α That it to them be (H2H4 be to them). 47. avaunce, *so* CpClS1H5Cx, H4 tavance, *rest* to avaunce. 48. CpClJ servaunt3. H4 servant, *rest* servauntes *or* servauntis. 52. α Now herkeneth ech with goode entencion (H2 Now listenyth every wight with; Ph everych, W eche wyght *for* ech). 53. H2Ph For I will now go, H4S2Dig For I wil go, RCx For now I wole gon. 54. αH3 ye shall; H2H4RCxW sorowe. Rubric. *So* S1; Ph *in margin* Incipit liber primus; *rest omit. Line 57 begins with special capital in* Cp (*not executed*) ClADS1 JH2CxThW. 57. H4Ph Knowe thyng is, W Knowen well it is. 58. α(-H2) With armys in. 60. γS1α(-H2) neigh *for* wel. 63. α(-Ph) Full besyly *for* By Paris don; αH5 diden *for* wroughten.

10

Now fil it so that in the town ther was
Dwellynge a lord of gret auctorite,   65
A gret devyn, that cleped was Calkas,
That in science so expert was that he
Knew wel that Troie sholde destroied be,
By answere of his god, that highte thus,
Daun Phebus, or Appollo Delphicus.   70

11

So whan that Calkas knew by calkulynge,
And ek by answere of this Appollo,
That Grekes sholden swich a peple brynge,
Thorugh which that Troie moste ben fordo,
He caste anon out of the town to go;   75
For wel wiste he by sort that Troye sholde
Destroyed ben, ye, wolde who so nolde.

12

For which, for to departen softely
Took purpos ful this for-knowynge wise,
And to the Grekes oost ful pryvely   80
He stal anon; and they, in curteys wise,
Hym diden bothe worship and servyce,
In trust that he hath konnynge hem to rede
In every peril which that is to drede.

---

68. H2H4 distroied shulde be. 70. JCxTh Dann, H3A Dame, R Dam. 71. γS1α
this *for* that; Cx *om.* that. 78. αTh Wherfor to departe al softely (Th *om.* al). 82
αTh Dede hym. 83. α Hopyng in hym kunnyng hem to rede.

13

The noise up ros whan it was first aspied 85
Thorugh al the town, and generaly was spoken,
That Calkas traitour fled was, and allied
With hem of Grece, and casten to be wroken
On hym that falsly hadde his feith so broken;
And seyden he and al his kyn at ones 90
Ben worthi for to brennen, fel and bones.

14

Now hadde Calkas left in this meschaunce,
Al unwist of this fals and wikked dede,
His doughter, which that was in gret penaunce;
For of hire lif she was ful sore in drede, 95
As she that nyste what was best to rede;
For bothe a widewe was she and allone
Of any frend to whom she dorste hir mone.

15

Criseyde was this lady name al right;
As to my doom, in al Troies cite 100
Nas non so fair; for, passynge every wight,
So aungelik was hir natif beaute,
That lik a thing inmortal semed she,
As is an hevenyssh perfit creature,
That down were sent in scornynge of nature. 105

---

85. αTh Grete rumour gan (W Grete noyse began; Ph was, Th rose *for* gan).
86. H3RCxTh openly. 87. γ traitour fals fled was. 88. CxTh To hem; α With her
foos and wilned to be wrokyn (H2Ph To *for* With; H2 woldyn fayn be wrokyn).
89. H2 On hym þat had his trouþe þus falsly brokyn; Ph On hym þat falsly had his
trouþe brokyn; H4 For he was fals & his surance broken; A hadde his feith so falsly
broken; W *omits line*. 90. α And sworyn þat he (H4 They *for* And; W *om.* þat);
H1Gg þat he. 91. αCx Were worthy to be brent boþe fell and bonys (H4W Weel
worthi were; H2Ph *om.* to be; H4 brent be; W *om.* to). 93. α Unknowyng *for* Al
unwist; GgH5CxTh *om.* Al. 94. αADS1 lyvid *for* was. 95. α þerfor, H3 ful ofte,
D ofte *for* ful sore. 96. nyste, *so* JGg, CpClH1ADH5H3R nyst, S1S2Dig wist nat;
CxTh And wyst never what best was; α Ne in al þis world she nyst what to rede
(H2 nyst not; W *omits line*). 98. H2PhH4 *om.* hir. 99. CpH2RCxTh a right,
H5S2Dig ful ryght. 101. H1GgH5R Was, H3 Vas; α So fair was none for over

16

This lady, which that alday herde at ere
Hire fadres shame, his falsnesse and tresoun,
Wel neigh out of hir wit for sorwe and fere,
In widewes habit large of samyt broun,
On knees she fil biforn Ector adown;   110
With pitous vois, and tendrely wepynge,
His mercy bad, hir selven excusynge.

17

Now was this Ector pitous of nature,
And saugh that she was sorwfully bigon,
And that she was so fair a creature;   115
Of his goodnesse he gladede hire anon,
And seyde, "lat youre fadres treson gon
Forth with meschaunce, and ye youre self in joie
Dwelleth with us, whil yow good list, in Troie;

18

And al thonour that men may don yow have,   120
As ferforth as youre fader dwelled here,
Ye shul have, and youre body shal men save,
As fer as I may ought enquere or here."
And she hym thonked with ful humble chere,
And ofter wolde, and it hadde ben his wille,   125
And took hire leve, and hom and held hir stille.

---

every wight (H4 *om.* over; W *om.* for); CxTh Most fayrest lady for passyng (Th fer). 102. CxTh shone *for* was. 104. γα As doth; α a perfit hevenly; CxTh And ther wyth was she so perfyte a creature. 105. CxTh As she had be mad in; H2PhH4H5 was *for* were.
106. JGgH5H2PhW herde al day. 108. α for pure fere. 109. JGgH5H3 blak *for* large. 110. αCxTh Byfor Hector on knees she fell, GgH5 On kneis before ector sche fel. 111. α With chere & voys ful pytous & wepyng. 111, 112. CxTh *transpose lines.* 114. α how she (H4 how that she). 117. αR fadir. 118. α To sory hap and. 121. H2Ph al here, H4 ay hiere. 122. H2PhH4R shul *for* shal. 123. αR As ferforth as y may enquere & here (RW or *for* &); JH3DCxTh and *for* or. 124. H2PhH4 thonkyd oft in humble chere. 125. αGgH5 if *for* and, R *om.* and. 126. H2CxTh went home.

19

And in hire hous she abood with swich meyne
As til hire honour nede was to holde;
And whil she was dwellynge in that cite,
Kepte hir estat, and bothe of yonge and olde   130
Ful wel biloved, and wel men of hir tolde;
But wheither that she children hadde or noon,
I rede it nat, therfore I late it goon.

20

The thynges fellen, as they don of werre,
Bitwixen hem of Troie and Grekes ofte;   135
For som day boughten they of Troie it derre,
And eft the Grekes founden no thing softe
The folk of Troie; and thus Fortune on lofte
And under eft gan hem to whielen bothe,
Aftir hir cours, ay whil thei were wrothe.   140

21

But how this town com to destruccion
Ne falleth naught to purpos me to telle;
For it were here a long disgression
Fro my matere, and yow to long to dwelle;
But the Troian gestes, as they felle,   145
In Omer, or in Dares, or in Dite,
Whoso that kan may rede hem as they write.

---

127. αDS2DigCx *om.* she. 128. αGgH5ClAS1RCx to *for* til. 130. α Thurgh good
in al & eke with yong & olde (H2 Thurgh out in al with yong & eke with olde;
W Thus *for* Thurgh). 131. α & folk wele of her (W eke *for* wele). 133. α I rede
not; late, *so* CpClJH4, H1 latt, *rest* lete *or* let. 137. W *omits line*; αClAS2Dig oft,
D eke, R als *for* eft; α al unsoft (H4 as). 138. H2PhRCxW a loft, H4 o lofte.
139. Cp Now up now down gan; ClADS2DigJ And wonder ofte, H4 Right wondir
ofte, Gg And eyþer ost; whielen, *so* JH1, CpS2DigH2Ph whilen, S1 quhelen, H3
wele, ClAGg weylen, D wailen, H4 werle, R werre, Th whelmen, W whylom, H5
turne, Cx repente. 140. γ(-Cl)ThJ ay whil that thei. 143. γ(-S1)ThH5 *om.* here;
αS1 For why it were a. 144. α Of, GgH5AH3CxW For *for* Fro. 145. ClS1 Troiane,
PhR troianes, H2 troianys, D Troians. 147. αGgS2Dig *om.* that.

22

But though that Grekes hem of Troie shetten,
And hir cite bisegede al aboute,
Hire olde usage nolde they nat letten,   150
As for to honoure hir goddes ful devoute;
But aldermost in honour, out of doute,
Thei hadde a relik heet Palladion,
That was hire trust aboven everichon.

23

And so bifel, whan comen was the tyme   155
Of Aperil, whan clothed is the mede
With newe grene of lusty Veer, the pryme,
And swote smellen floures, white and rede,
In sondry wises shewed, as I rede,
The folk of Troie hire observaunces olde,   160
Palladions feste for to holde.

24

And to the temple, in al hir beste wise,
In general ther wente many a wight,
To herknen of Palladion servyce,
And namely so many a lusty knyght,   165
So many a lady fressh and mayden bright,
Ful wel arayed, bothe meste and leste,
Ye, bothe for the seson and the feste.

149. Cp biseged, J bysegede. 150. ClH1AR wolde. 150, 151. α *reads:*
The old usage nold they of troy lettyn,
As for to honour her goddis and to loute.
(H4 For al nolde thei; W Theyr olde use nolde nought them for to letten; H2Ph
her god and to loutyn; H4 & loute). 153. heet, *so* CpH1S1, J het, αGgH5ClDH3RTh
hight, Cx callid. 157. α of joly veer, H5 of forsing ver. 158. swote, *so* CpH1JD,
R soote, Cl swoot, *rest* swete; H2PhH4H5DS1CxTh smellyng. 159. α In meny
wyse (W wyses); GgH5DH3RCxTh wyse. 161. H4ADS1W Palladiones, Gg Palas
dionis, H5 Of Palidons; H2H5(*later hand*)CxTh wentyn for to holde. 162.
ClH1ADS1 yn al here goodly best wyse (A *om.* al). 164. γ the servyce. 167. CpH1
both moeste meyne and leste, Cl bothe meene meste and leste; A men bothe mest,
D bothe moste menne, S1 bothe most mene, J bothe þe meste and þe leste; H3 tho
moste; R *om.* wel. 163-167. α *reads:*
In general went every manere wight,
That thryfty was, to heryn her servise,

25

Among thise othere folk was Criseyda,
In widewes habit blak, but natheles,   170
Right as oure firste lettre is now an A,
In beaute first so stood she makeles;
Hire goodly lokyng gladede al the prees.
Nas nevere yit seyn thyng to ben preysed derre,
Nor under cloude blak so bright a sterre,   175

26

As was Criseyde, as folk seyde everichone,
That hir behelden in hir blake wede;
And yit she stood ful lowe and stille allone,
Byhynden other folk in litel brede,
And neigh the dore, ay under shames drede,   180
Simple of atire, and debonaire of chere,
With ful assured lokyng and manere.

27

This Troilus, as he was wont to gide
His yonge knyghtes, ladde hem up and down
In thilke large temple on every side,   185
Byholding ay the ladyes of the town,
Now here, now there; for no devocioun
Hadde he to non, to reven hym his reste,
But gan to preyse and lakken whom hym leste.

And þat so meny a thousand lusty knyght,
So meny a fressh mayde & lady bryght,
Ful wele byseyn, the meste meyne & leest.

(164. H4 tristi; H4W the *for* her. 166. H2 lady & maydyn. 167. H2W the moost &
eke þe leest; H4 mene). 168. H2PhH5(*corrected*)AW & eke for þe feest (W *om.* for).
169. α Among þe which was Cryseyda (H2 was this, W was than); GgH5
Cresseyde. 171. firste, *so* H4, H1 furste, H2 chef *for* firste; Ph *om.* firste, *rest* first;
H5 lettre is now and seyde; H2Ph *om.* an. 174. H1S2DigH3R Was; αAH3CxTh *om.*
yit; R thyng Ipreysed derre. 175. αH5H3R Ne. 176. α As she was as þei seydyn.
180. Cp nei3, undre; J ney, undir. 183. α Daun Troyllus. 187. CpJ devocion.

28

And in his walke ful faste he gan to wayten   190
If knyght or squyer of his compaignie
Gan for to syke, or lete his eyen baiten
On any womman that he koude espye;
He wolde smyle, and holden it folye,
And seye hym thus, "god woot, she slepeth softe   195
For love of the, whan thow tornest ful ofte.

29

"I have herd told, pardieux, of youre lyvynge,
Ye loveres, and youre lewed observaunces,
And which a labour folk han in wynnynge
Of love, and in the kepyng which doutaunces;   200
And whan youre preye is lost, woo and penaunces.
O veray fooles! nyce and blynde be ye;
Ther nys nat oon kan war by other be."

30

And with that word he gan caste up the browe,
Ascaunces, "loo! is this nat wisely spoken?"   205
At which the god of love gan loken rowe
Right for despit, and shop for to ben wroken;
He kidde anon his bowe nas nat broken;
For sodeynly he hitte hym atte fulle,
And yit as proud a pekok kan he pulle.   210

---

195. αTh O lord (H2PhW a lord) *for* god woot. 196. ClADS2DigH2PhH5 *om.*
ful. 198. γ *om.* lewed. 199. α have folk. 201. Cp prey, J praye. 202,203. α *reads:*
O verrey folys! may ye no thing se?
Kan none of yow yware by other be?
(H4W war.) 203. nys, *so* CpClJGg, *rest* is. 204. H2PhGgH5H3W his brow. 206-
209. α *reads:*
But trowe ye not þat love þo lokyd row
For þat despite, & shope to bene ywrokyn?
Yes, certein, lovis bow was not ybrokyn;
For, be myn heed, he hit hym atte fulle
(206. H4 not ye; H4W *om.* þo. 207. PhW shop how to; H4 shapid to be wrokyn.
208. H2 certis; H4 for loves bowe; H2 at þe.) 208. H3H5RDCxTh was.

31

O blynde world, O blynde entencioun!
How often falleth al the effect contraire
Of surquidrie, and foule presumpcioun;
For kaught is proud, and kaught is debonaire.
This Troilus is clomben on the staire,   215
And litel weneth that he moot descenden;
But al day faileth thing that fooles wenden.

32

As proude Bayard gynneth for to skippe
Out of the wey, so pryketh hym his corn,
Til he a lassh have of the longe whippe,   220
Than thynketh he, "though I praunce al byforn,
First in the trays, ful fat, and newe shorn,
Yit am I but an hors, and horses lawe
I moot endure, and with my feres drawe."

33

So ferde it by this fierse and proude knyght;   225
Though he a worthy kynges sone were,
And wende no thing hadde had swich myght,
Ayeyns his wil, that sholde his herte stere,
Yit with a look his herte wax a-fere,
That he, that now was moost in pride above,   230
Wax sodeynly moost subgit unto love.

---

213. H2Ph such presumpcion, H4W nyce oppynioun. 215. α Daun Troylus. 217. ClD falleth; Cl ne wenden; H2PhH4 that that folys wenden (H2 þes, Ph þe *for second* that; H2Ph wenyn; H4 fool is wende). 221. H2PhClADS1H3 thenkith. 222. newe, *so* JClAGgCxThW, *rest* new. 224. αAD as my feris. 225. αR þat *for* this. 229. GgH4A wex. 231. GgA wex, H4 wix.

34

Forthy, ensample taketh of this man,
Ye wise, proude, and worthi folkes alle,
To scornen love, which that so sone kan
The fredom of youre hertes to hym thralle;   235
For evere it was, and evere it shal byfalle,
That love is he that alle thing may bynde;
For may no man fordo the lawe of kynde.

35

That this be soth, hath preved and doth yit;
For this, trowe I, ye knowen alle or some: 240
Men reden nat that folk han gretter wit
Than they that han be most with love ynome;
And strengest folk ben therwith overcome,
The worthiest and grettest of degree;
This was, and is, and yit men shal it see.   245

36

And trewelich it sit wel to be so;
For alderwisest han therwith ben plesed;
And they that han ben aldermost in wo
With love, han ben conforted moost and esed;
And ofte it hath the cruel herte apesed,   250
And worthi folk maad worthier of name,
And causeth moost to dreden vice and shame.

232-384. *Missing in* D; *two leaves lost.* 234. CpS1S2Dig serven. 240. H2PhH5R
CxThW & some. 241. α redith. 242. Cp moste, J meste; H2Ph with love be most,
W with love moste benome, GgH5 most with love haþ ben. 244. ClAS1H4W yn
degre. 245. α may it se. 247, 248. H2PhH4H5RCx alþerwysest, althermoost. 249.
GgH5RH4W most confortid, H2 *om.* most. 252. GgH5H4R caused, Cl causen.

37

Now sith it may nat goodly ben withstonde,
And is a thing so vertuous in kynde,
Refuseth nat to love for to be bonde;   255
Syn as hym selven list he may yow bynde.
The yerde is bet that bowen wole and wynde
Than that that brest; and therfor I yow rede
To folwen love that yow so wel kan lede.

38

But for to tellen forth in special   260
As of this kynges sone, of which I tolde,
And leten other thing collateral,
Of hym thenke I my tale forth to holde,
Bothe of his joie, and of his cares colde;
And al his werk as touching this matere,   265
For I it gan, I wol therto refere.

39

Withinne the temple he wente hym forth pleyinge,
This Troilus, of every wight aboute,
On this lady, and now on that, lokynge,
Where so she were of towne or of withoute;   270
And upon cas bifel that thorugh a route
His eye percede, and so depe it wente,
Til on Criseyde it smot, and ther it stente.

---

255. α Ne grucchith not (H4 grevith). 257. α Betir is þe wand (H4 bond, W band). 258. αR *om.* and (H4 that that wil breste). 259. αTh Now folowith hym þat so wele may ȝow lede (W maye you so well; Th can), γ To folowen hym that so wele kan yow lede, GgH5 so wel can ȝow. 261. γGgH5 *om.* As; α whom *for* which. 262. αTh levyn; thing, *so* JClS1PhTh, H1 þinge, *rest* thinges. 264. JClDigGgH5W joyes. 268. H2Ph with, H4 on, ClH5 and *for* of. 271. Cp bifelle, J byfil. 272. H2PhH4 perceyvid.

40

And sodeynly he wax therwith astoned,
And gan hir bet biholde in thrifty wise.   275
"O mercy, god!" thoughte he, "wher hastow woned,
That art so fair and goodly to devise?"
Therwith his herte gan to sprede and rise,
And softe sighed, lest men myghte hym here,
And caughte ayeyn his firste pleyinge chere.   280

41

She nas nat with the leste of hire stature;
But alle hire lymes so wel answerynge
Weren to wommanhode, that creature
Nas nevere lasse mannyssh in semynge;
And ek the pure wise of hire mevynge   285
Shewed wel that men myght in hire gesse
Honour, estat, and wommanly noblesse.

42

To Troilus right wonder wel with alle
Gan for to like hire mevynge and hire chere,
Which somdel deignous was; for she let falle   290
Hire look a lite aside, in swich manere
Ascaunces, "what? may I nat stonden here?"
And after that hir lokynge gan she lighte,
That nevere thoughte hym seen so good a syghte.

274. H2 And sodenly wax wondur sore astonyd, Ph And sodenly wox for wondre astoned, H4ThW And sodenly for wondyr he wex astoyned (Th *om.* he, W was). 276. αTh O verrey god (H4 *om.* god). 279. αGgH5S2DigR And soft he (Dig hym); JH2PhGgH5AR siked. 280. H4W japyng. 281–350. *Missing in* R; *leaf lost*. 281. GgH5H4W *om.* hire. 284. γThW Was. 285. J movynge, H3 moevyng, ClS2Dig GgH5 menynge, ThW meanyng. 286. H2Ph She shewyd wele, S1 Schewed so wel; Gg my3tyn. 288. H2PhH4GgH3CxTh Tho *for* To. 289. JH3 moevynge, H5 meonynge, ClH1AS2DigGg menyng, ThW meanyng. 291. αGg lytil.

43

And of hire look in him ther gan to quyken　　　　295
So gret desir, and swiche affeccioun,
That in his hertes botme gan to stiken
Of hir his fixe and depe impressioun;
And though he erst hadde poured up and down,
He was tho glad his hornes in to shrinke;　　　　300
Unnethes wiste he how to loke or wynke.

44

Lo, he that leet hym selven so konnynge,
And scorned hem that loves peynes dryen,
Was ful unwar that love hadde his dwellynge
Withinne the subtil stremes of hire eyen;　　　　305
That sodeynly hym thoughte he felte deyen,
Right with hire look, the spirit of his herte;
Blissed be love, that kan thus folk converte.

45

She, this in blak, likynge to Troilus,
Over al thing he stood for to biholde;　　　　310
Ne his desir, ne wherfor he stood thus,
He neither chere made, ne word tolde;
But from afer, his manere for to holde,
On other thing som tyme his look he caste,
And eft on hire, while that servyse laste.　　　　315

297. CpAGgH5H4CxW herte.　305. Cp eighen, J eyne.　306. ClH4 þat he; ClAH2PhCx sholde *for* felte; ClH3H4H5W dyen.　307. γH4CxThW in *for* of. 310. H2PhH4Cl *om.* for.　312. Cl ne made ne word; CpH1H3ThW worde, *rest* word.　313. CpH1J fram; αH5Cx *om.* for.　314. CpClH1A his look som tyme.　315. CpH1Aα ofte; H5DigCx the *for* that, αClAS1S2H3Th þat þe.

46

And after this, nat fullich al awhaped,
Out of the temple al esilich he wente,
Repentynge hym that he hadde evere ijaped
Of loves folk, lest fully the descente
Of scorn fille on hym self; but what he mente,　320
Lest it were wist on ony maner syde,
His woo he gan dissimilen and hide.

47

Whan he was fro the temple thus departed,
He streyght anon unto the paleys torneth,
Right with hire look thorugh shoten and thorugh darted,
Al feyneth he in lust that he sojorneth;　326
And al his chere and speche also he borneth,
And ay of loves servantes every while,
Hym self to wrye, at hem he gan to smyle;

48

And seyde, "lord, so ye lyve al in lest,　330
Ye loveres! for the konnyngeste of yow,
That serveth most ententiflich and best,
Hym tit as often harm therof as prow;
Youre hire is quyt ayeyn, ye, god woot how,
Nought wel for wel, but scorn for good servyse;　,335
In feith, youre ordre is ruled in good wise.

---

318. GgH5H3S1W evere he hadde (Gg *om.* hadde).　322. JClCxW dissimulen.
323. H2PhGgH5W þus fro þe temple.　324. γCxTh his *for* the.　327. H2Ph he
unournith, *om.* also; H4 yit he mourned; W he kepte full well closed.　328. CpClJ
servant3, *rest* servantes *or* servantis.　329. wrye, *so* JH3W, H1Th wrie, Cp wrey,
H4H5 wreye, ClA wre, S1 wree, Gg wryþe, H2Ph were, Cx wreke.　332. Cp serven.
J servyth.　333. H2PhH5Cx þerof as oft harme, W therof harme as ofte.

49

"In noun-certeyn ben alle youre observaunces,
But it a fewe sely pointes be;
Ne no thing asketh so gret attendaunces
As doth youre lay, and that knowe alle ye;   340
But that is nat the worste, as mote I the;
But tolde I yow the worste point, I leve,.
Al seyde I soth, ye wolden at me greve.

50

"But take this: that ye loveres ofte eschuwe,
Or elles doon of good entencioun,   345
Ful ofte thi lady wol it mysconstruwe,
And deme it harm by hire opynioun;
And yit if she for other enchesoun
Be wroth, than shaltow have a groyn anon;
Lord! wel is hym that may ben of yow oon!"   350

51

But for al this, whan that he say his tyme,
He held his pees, non other boote hym gayned;
For love bigan his fetheres so to lyme,
That wel unnethe until his folk he fayned
That other besy nedes hym destrayned;   355
For wo was hym, that what to doon he nyste,
But bad his folk to gon wher that hem liste.

338. CpS2DigGgH5 But if it; CpClH1H2PhThW sely fewe, Gg *om.* sely. 341. H2GgH5CxW so, H4 also *for* as. 342. α But told y which were þe worst y leve (H4 as *for* þe worst). 345. α For good or done of good intencion (H4 with *for* of). 347. γαCxTh in *for* by. 349. α ȝet *for* than (W it). 353. H2PhH4H5Cx for *for* so. 354. αClAS1RCxTh unto.

52

And whan that he in chambre was allone,
He doun upon his beddes feet hym sette,
And first he gan to sike and eft to grone,   360
And thought ay so on hire withouten lette,
That, as he sat and wook, his spirit mette
That he hire saugh, and temple, and al the wise
Right of hire look, and gan it newe avise.

53

Thus gan he make a mirour of his mynde,   365
In which he saugh al holly hire figure;
And that he wel koude in his herte fynde,
It was to hym a right good aventure
To love swich oon, and if he dede his cure
To serven hir, yit myghte he falle in grace,   370
Or ellis for oon of hire servantes pace.

54

Imaginynge that travaille nor grame
Ne myghte for so goodly oon be lorn
As she, ne hym for his desir no shame,
Al were it wist, but in pris and up born   375
Of alle lovers wel more than biforn;
Thus argumented he in his gynnynge,
Ful unavysed of his woo comynge.

359. H4 syde *for* feet. 360. CpJ efte. 361. CpClH1AS1Th ay on hire so, Gg so ay on hire, H2Ph on her so ay, H5S2DigW *om.* so. 363. H2PhH5S2Dig in þe, Cl a, R at *for* and, Cx *om.* and; H4 He say hire ofte in temple. 367. H3H2PhH5W he cowde wel, Gg wel he coude, S1 he koude ryght. 371. CpClJ servantʒ, H3 servaunce, *rest* servauntes *or* servauntis. 372. CpH3 grace, H2PhGgH5 game. 373. CpH1JH3Th lorne; H2PhH4 borne (Ph *corrected to* lorne). 374. CpS2DigH2PhGgRCxW ne shame.

55

Thus took he purpos loves craft to suwe,
And thoughte he wolde werken pryvely,   380
First to hiden his desir in muwe
From every wight yborn, al outrely,
But he myghte ought recovered be therby,
Remembryng hym that love to wide yblowe
Yelt bittre fruyt, though swete seed be sowe.   385

56

And overe al this, muchel more he thoughte
What for to speke, and what to holden inne;
And what to arten hire to love he soughte,
And on a song anon right to bygynne,
And gan loude on his sorwe for to wynne;   390
For with good hope he gan fully assente
Criseyde for to love, and nought repente.

57

And of his song nat only the sentence,
As writ myn auctour called Lollius,
But pleinly, save oure tonges difference,   395
I dar wel seyn, in al, that Troilus
Seyde in his song, loo, every word right thus
As I shal seyn; and whoso list it here,
Loo, next this vers he may it fynden here.

379-630. *Missing in* H3; *two leaves lost.* 381. S1H5 First for to hiden, A First
he hid (*corrected to* First for to hide). 386. H4PhW *om.* al; γ this yet muchel,
H4RTh this ful moche. 390. H2Ph þo to, H4 therto *for* for to, W *omits line.* 393.
H2H4A this, GgH5 þe *for* his; H4PhRThW his, H2 þis *for* the. 394. ClH5 Lollyus,
Gg Lollyous, H4 Lolkius, W Lellyus. 395. α But eke save þat in our spech is
differens (H2 *om.* in, spechis *for* spech is; Ph þat yn our speches be difference, yn
and be *over line*; W *om.* in, *om.* be). 399. JRCxW ye *for* he.

58

"If no love is, O god! what fele I so?   CANTUS TROILI
And if love is, what thing and which is he?   401
If love be good, from whennes comth my woo?
If it be wikke, a wonder thynketh me,
Whenne every torment and adversite
That comth of hym may to me savory thinke;   405
For ay thurst I the more that ich it drynke.

59

"And if that at myn owen lust I brenne,
From whennes cometh my waillynge and my pleynte?
If harme agree me, wherto pleyne I thenne?
I noot, ne whi unwery that I feynte.   410
O quike deth! O swete harme so queynte!
How may of the in me swich quantite,
But if that I consente that it be?

60

"And if that I consente, I wrongfully
Compleyne, iwis; thus possed to and fro,   415
Al steereles withinne a boot am I
Amydde the see, bitwixen wyndes two,
That in contrarie stonden evere mo.
Allas! what is this wonder maladie?
For hete of cold, for cold of hete, I dye."   420

400. Cantus Troili, *so* H1S2DigPhH5, CpD Canticus Troili, H2RTh The Song of Troylus, Gg Cantus, *rest om.* 403. α If he be. 405. ClH4W may me so goodly þynke; R me so *for* to me. 406. H2PhH4GgRA *om.* it. 407. H2PhH4 *om.* that, in *for* at (H2Ph y yn myn owne lust brenne). 409. H4AD agreve, H5CxW angre; JGgH5H2PhH1S2DigW me I wher to pleyne I thenne (H5 ey, H2 3e *for first* I; GgW *om. second* I; H2Ph wherto þan y pleyne). 411. quike, *so* JClThW, *rest* quik. 412. H2Ph How may y se in me; H4 be, ThCxS2Dig be suche *for* swich. 413. H2PhH4S2DigCx þat hit so be. 419. Cp wondre, J wondir. 420. CpJ colde *for second* cold.

61

And to the god of love thus seyde he,
With pitous vois: "O lord, now youres is
My spirit, which that oughte youres be.
Yow thanke I, lord, that han me brought to this;
But wheither goddesse or womman, iwis,   425
She be, I not, which that ye do me serve;
But as hire man I wol ay lyve and sterve.

62

"Ye stonden in hir eyen myghtily,
As in a place unto youre vertu digne;
Wherfore, lord, if my service or I   430
May liken yow, so beth to me benigne;
For myn estat roial here I resigne
Into hire hond, and with ful humble chere
Bicome hir man, as to my lady dere."

63

In hym ne deyned spare blood roial   435
The fir of love, the wherfro god me blesse!
Ne him forbar in no degree for al
His vertu or his excellent prowesse,
But held hym as his thral, lowe in destresse,
And brende hym so in sondry wise ay newe,   440
That sexti tyme a day he loste his hewe.

421. S1 ryght thus. 423. H4W *om.* that; H4 ay aught, W ought aye, H2Ph oght
evere. 424. αGg broght me. 430. Cl my lord, S1 o lord. 433. Cp honde, J hand.
435. Cp roiale, J real. 436. the wherfro, *so* JClS1, H1H5 ye wher fro, AW fro þe
wheche, Gg (*corrected*) Cx wherfrom, *rest* wherfro; CpClH1GgH4 blisse. 440.
H2PhH4 *om.* so; H2Ph so, Cx al, R & *for* ay.

64

So muche, day fro day, his owene thought
For lust to hire gan quiken and encresse,
That every other charge he sette at nought;
Forthi ful ofte, his hote fir to cesse,   445
To sen hire goodly look he gan to presse;
For therby to ben esed wel he wende,
And ay the ner he was, the more he brende.

65

For ay the ner the fir, the hotter is, —
This, trowe I, knoweth al this compaignye;   450
But were he fer or ner, I dar sey this:
By nyght or day, for wisdom or folye,
His herte, which that is his brestes eye,
Was ay on hire, that fairer was to sene
Than evere were Eleyne or Polixene.   455

66

Ek of the day ther passed nought an houre,
That to hym self a thousand tyme he seyde:
"God goodly, to whom serve I laboure
As I best kan, now wolde god, Criseyde,
Ye wolden on me rewe, or that I deyde;   460
My dere herte, allas! myn hele and hewe
And lif is lost, but ye wol on me rewe."

442. JRS1Th mochel, H1D muchel, Gg mechil, H5 mekyll, H2Ph mych, H4ACx
moche; γ by *for* fro. 444. JADS1Th everych. 449-504. Cx. *omits eight stanzas.* 449.
αH5 it is (H2 he is). 451. C1H1 seye. 452. H2Ph by, GgH4 be, H5 be it *for* for.
453. CpGg eighe, JH4AD ye. 455. were, *so* CpH1DJGgH2, *rest* was. 457. H4 an
hundred tyme. 458. JC1S1 Good, H1 Goode *for* God; H4 Goode god; ATh to whom
I serve, D to whom to serve, C1AGgH5ThW and laboure, S2Dig in laboure. 462.
H4 My lif, A And myn lif, H2Ph Al my lyst, W And lyves lust.

67

Alle other dredes weren from him fledde,
Bothe of thassege and his savacioun;
Ne yn him desir noon other fownes bredde 465
But argumentes to his conclusioun:
That she on him wolde han compassioun,
And he to ben hire man whil he may dure,
Lo, here his lif, and from the deth his cure.

68

The sharpe shoures felle, of armes preve, 470
That Ector or his othere brethren diden,
Ne made hym only therfore ones meve;
And yit was he, where so men wente or riden,
Founde on the beste, and lengest tyme abiden
Ther peril was, and dide ek swich travaille 475
In armes, that to thynke it was mervaille.

69

But for non hate he to the Grekes hadde,
Ne also for the rescous of the town,
Ne made hym thus in armes for to madde,
But only, lo, for this conclusioun: 480
To liken hire the bet for his renoun.
Fro day to day in armes so he spedde,
That the Grekes as the deth him dredde.

465. CpGgR Nyn *for* Ne yn; JH1H2PhH4 his *for* him; Gg desyred; Cp fewnes, H4R sownes, D foules, H2Ph fantasye; D bridde; H5 Ne hym desyryd noon other brede, S2Dig No he desyred none oþer fode nor brede (Dig no nothire; S2 no brede). 466. ClH1DS1H2PhW þis *for* his. 467. γ(-Cl) of him. 469. JRH4ADW Lo here is lif; RTh hys *for* the, PhDDig *om.* the; GgH5 deþes; R the, AD is *for second* his. 470. felle, *so* JGg, H4ATh fel, W fell, CpH2Ph fil, S1 fill, ClH1 fille, D *om.*; R of armes felte. 474. CpS1DW longest, J langest. 476. CpClD thenke, H2Ph thenk; H2Ph is, H4 were *for* was; Cp merveille, J marvayle. 483. αR That al þe grekis (RH4 alle; H4 *om.* þe).

70

And fro this forth tho refte hym love his slepe,
And made his mete his foo, and ek his sorwe   485
Gan multiplie, that, whoso tok kepe,
It shewed in his hewe, on eve and morwe;
Therfor a title he gan him for to borwe
Of other siknesse, lest men of hym wende,
That the hote fir of love hym brende,   490

71

And seyde he hadde a fevere and ferde amys.
But how it was, certeyn, I kan nat seye,
If that his lady understood nat this,
Or feynede hire she nyste, on of the tweye;
But wel rede I, that by no maner weye   495
Ne semed it as that she of hym roughte,
Or of his peyne, or what so evere he thoughte.

72

But thanne felte this Troilus swich wo,
That he was wel neigh wood; for ay his drede
Was this: that she som wight hadde loved so,   500
That nevere of hym she wolde have taken hede;
For that hym thoughte he felte his herte blede,
Ne of his wo ne dorste he nat bygynne
To tellen hir, for al this world to wynne.

484-490. H2 *omits stanza.* 486. H4W gan waxe soo (W so grete). 487. γTh both *for* on. 489. H4W Of othir harm lest that. 490. DS1 so sore him brende, A hym for brende, W hym ryght soore brende. 492. CpClH1D kan I. 495. γ I rede. 496. as that, *so* JRH4H5, γThGg *om.* as, H2Ph *om.* that. 498. H2H4 *om.* this. 502. γTh For which (Cl For such); J For þat cause hym thought he; GgH5 For þat cause he þouȝte his herte blede (H5 ded blede); H4R he *for* hym. 504. CpJ worlde.

73

But whan he hadde a space from his care,   505
Thus to hym self ful ofte he gan to pleyne;
He seyde: "O fool, now artow in the snare,
That whilom japedest at loves peyne;
Now artow hent, now gnaw thin owen cheyne;
Thow were ay wont eche lovere reprehende   510
Of thing fro which thow kanst the nat defende.

74

"What wol now every lovere seyn of the,
If this be wist? but evere in thin absence
Laughen in scorne, and seyn: 'loo, ther goth he,
That is the man of so gret sapience,   515
That held us loveres leest in reverence;
Now, thanked god, he may gon in the daunce
Of hem that love list febly for to avaunce.'

75

"But, O thow woful Troilus, god wolde,
Sith thow most loven thorugh thi destine,   520
That thow beset were on swich oon that sholde
Knowe al thi wo, al lakked hir pitee;
But also cold in love towardes the
Thi ladi is, as frost in wynter moone,
And thow fordon, as snow in fir is soone.   525

507. H2H5 And *for* He; H2H4H5 *om.* O.   509. CpJ hente.   510. JH4RCx to
reprehende (R reprende). 516. CpH1S2DigH2 And *for* That. 517. ClADaGgCxTh
Now thonked be god. 518. H2PhDCx *om.* for, H4Th *om.* for to; JRH1AS1 tavaunce.
520. ClDH4H5 Syn. 522. CpH1J know. 524. H2PhH4D wyntris.

76

"God wolde I were aryved in the port
Of deth, to which my sorwe wol me lede.
A, lord, to me it were a gret confort;
Than were I quyt of languisshyng in drede;
For, be myn hidde sorwe iblowe on brede,   530
I shal byjaped ben a thousand tyme,
More than that fool of whos folie men ryme.

77

"But now, help god, and ye, swete, for whom
I pleyne, ikaught, ye, nevere wight so faste!
O mercy, dere herte, and help me from   535
The deth; for I, whil that my lyf may laste,
More than my self wol love yow to my laste;
And with som frendly look gladeth me, swete,
Though nevere no thing more ye me byhete."

78

Thise wordes, and ful many an other to,   540
He spak, and called evere in his compleynte
Hire name, for to tellen hire his wo,
Til neigh that he in salte teres dreynte.
Al was for nought, she herde nat his pleynte;
And whan that he bythought on that folie,   545
A thousand fold his wo gan multiplie.

526. CpH₁J wold. 530. CpClS₁GgCx by *for* be. 531. H4 an hundred tyme. 532.
H2 he, H4Ph on, W ony *for* that fool. 533. CpJD the, A she *for* ye. 534. CpJ the,
Cl yet *for* ye, A *om.* ye. 539. γTh more thing. 540. αH₅RTh mo *for* to. 546. H4
An hundred fold; H2H4GgH5 sorowe *for* wo. *After line 546 W becomes a mere
reprint of Cx, and its readings are no longer recorded.*

79

Bywayling in his chambre thus allone,
A frend of his, that called was Pandare,
Com oones in unwar, and herde hym groone,
And say his frende in swich destresse and care.   550
"Allas!" quod he, "who causeth al this fare?
O mercy, god! what unhap may this meene?
Han now thus soone Grekes maad yow leene?

80

"Or hastow som remors of conscience,
And art now falle in som devocioun,   555
And wailest for thi synne and thin offence,
And hast for ferde caught attricioun?
God save hem that biseged han oure town,
That so kan leye oure jolite on presse,
And bringe oure lusty folk to holynesse!"   560

81

Thise wordes seyde he for the nones alle,
That with swich thing he myght hym angry maken,
And with an angre don his sorwe falle,
As for the tyme, and his corage awaken;
But wel wist he, as fer as tonges spaken,   565
Ther nas a man of gretter hardinesse
Than he, ne more desired worthinesse.

552. Ph what may this be to mene. 557. H5Cx contricioun. 559. J konne, Gg
cunne; αH5 in, RD a *for* on. 560. H2 in to, GgH5Ph in *for* to. 562. ClGg myghte.
563. γR wo to falle *for* sorwe falle (S2Dig evelle to; Cl *om.* to). 565. γ(-S1) he
wist. 566. J nas no, H5 was no.

82

"What cas," quod Troilus, "or what aventure,
Hath gided the to sen me langwisshinge,
That am refus of every creature?   570
But for the love of god, at my preyinge,
Go hens awey; for certes my deyinge
Wol the disese, and I mot nedes deye;
Therfore go wey, ther is no more to seye.

83

"But if thow wene I be thus sik for drede,   575
It is naught so, and therfore scorne nought;
Ther is another thing I take of hede,
Wel more than aught the Grekes han yit wrought,
Which cause is of my deth for sorowe and thought;
But though that I now telle it the ne leste,   580
Be thow naught wroth, I hide it for the beste."

84

This Pandare, that neigh malt for wo and routhe,
Ful ofte seyde: "allas! what may this be?"
"Now frend," quod he, "if evere love or trouthe
Hath ben or this bitwixen the and me,   585
Ne do thow nevere swich a crueltee,
To hiden fro thi frende so gret a care;
Wostow nat wel that it am I, Pandare?

569. αGgH5ClA my *for* me; Cp lange wisshinge, J languyssynge. 572. Cp hennes, JH1 henne. 574. JGgTh nys, AD ne is. 576. H2PhAS1Cx scorne me. 580. GgH5H4 RD ne *for* now. 582. α *om*. This; JGgH5 þat wel neygh (J neyght, GgH5 ner). 585. γ(-D)αCxTh is (S1 his) *for* this.

85

"I wol parten with the al thi peyne,
If it be so I do the no comfort,   590
As it is frendes right, soth for to seyne,
To entreparten wo as glad desport.
I have and shal, for trewe or fals report,
In wrong and right, iloved the al my lyve;
Hid nat thi wo fro me, but telle it blyve."   595

86

Than gan this sorwful Troilus to syke,
And seide hym thus: "god leve it be my beste
To telle it the, for sith it may the like,
Yit wol I telle it, though **myn herte** breste;
And wel woot I, thow mayst do me no reste;   600
But lest thow deme I truste nat to the,
Now herke, frende, for thus it stant with me.

87

"Love, ayeins the which whoso defendeth
Hym selven most, hym alderlest avaylleth,
With disespeyre so sorwfulli me offendeth,   605
That streight unto the deth myn herte sailleth;
Therto desir so brennyngly me assailleth,
That to ben slayn it were a gretter joie,
To me than kyng of Grece ben, and Troye.

---

589. DS2Dig wolde. 590. Cp comforte, J dyscomforte. 592. CpJ desporte. 596.
α Tho, D And þo *for* Than. 598. H2Ph *om.* for, H4 but *for* for. 599. JH2PhGgH5
telle it the. 601. CpH1 leste, J list. 604. αGgH5DCx altherlest. 605. JGgH5AD
sorwfull. 606. CpClAJ failleth. 607. CpH1J desire; H2R massailith. 609. H2Ph
kyng to be of grece, H5RS1 kyng ben of grece, CxDig to be kyng of grece, S2 be kyng
of grece.

88

"Suffiseth this, my fulle frende Pandare,   610
That I have seyd, for now wostow my wo;
And for the love of god, my colde care
So hid it wel, I tolde it nevere to mo;
For harmes myghten folwen mo than two,
If it were wist; but be thow in gladnesse,   615
And lat me sterve, unknowe, of my destresse."

89

"How hastow, thus unkyndely and longe,
Hid this fro me, thow fool?" quod Pandarus;
"Paraunter thow mayst after swich oon longe,
That myn avys anoon may helpen us."   620
"This were a wonder thing," quod Troilus;
"Thow koudest nevere in love thi selven wisse;
How, devel, maistow brynge me to blisse?"

90

"Ye, Troilus, now herke," quod Pandare,
"Though I be nyce, it happeth often so,   625
That oon that excesse doth ful yvele fare,
By good counseil kan kepe his frende therfro;
I have my selven seyn a blynd man go,
Ther as he fel that koude loken wide;
A fool may ek a wis man ofte gide.   630

---

611. CpH₁J seyde. 612. Cp cole, GgADS₁S₂DigTh colde, *rest* cold. 614. CpS₂DigGgH₅H₄R fallen. 617. CpH₁ unkyndly, J unkyndlisch. 619. γ myght (CpD myghte, S₁ mightest), H₄ mait, Gg may₃t. 623. S₁ than maistow, H₂PhCx mayst þou þan *for* maistow; R bryng me than. 624. H₁S₂H₄Cx herke now, H₂Ph herk me, *om.* now. 628. γ I have my self ek seyn (AS₂Dig seen eek); R my selfe iseen. 629. α loke cowd. 630. CpH₁ oft, JGgH₅ *om.* ofte.

91

"A wheston is no kervyng instrument,
But yit it maketh sharpe kervyng tolis;
And there thow woost that I have aught myswent,
Eschew thow that, for swich thyng to the scole is;
Thus often wise men ben war by foolys.   635
If thow so do, thi wit is wel bewared;
By his contrarie is every thyng declared.

92

"For how myghte evere swetnesse han ben knowe
To him that nevere tasted bitternesse?
Ne no man may ben inly glad, I trowe,   640
That nevere was in sorwe or som destresse;
Eke whit by blak, by shame ek worthinesse,
Ech set by other, more for other semeth,
As men may se, and so the wyse it demeth.

93

"Sith thus of two contraries is o lore,   645
I, that have in love so ofte assayed
Grevances, oughte konne, and wel the more
Counseillen the of that thow art amayed;
And ek the ne aughte nat ben yvel apayed,
Though I desire with the for to bere   650
Thyn hevy charge; it shal the lasse dere.

---

631. DS1S2DigH5RTh whetstone. 633. F2 If þou wost ought where þat I have miswent. 636. γGgCxF2 do so. 640. αGgH5JTh Ne no man wrote what gladnes is y trow; R veryly glad. 642. Cp with, J white *for* whit. 647. αS2DigTh *om.* and. 648. H2PhCxTh dysmayed. 649. γ *om.* And; α And eke þow oghtist not; GgH5 And ek þou not; J noughte; H3R the aught not, Cx the not ought.

94

"I woot wel that it fareth thus by me
As to thi brother, Paris, an hierdesse,
Which that icleped was Oenone,
Wrot in a compleynte of hir hevynesse;   655
Ye say the lettre that she wrot, I gesse?"
"Nay, nevere yit, ywys," quod Troilus.
"Now," quod Pandare, "herkeneth, it was thus:

95

" 'Phebus, that first fond art of medicyne,'
Quod she, 'and couthe in every wightes care,   660
Remedye and reed by herbes he knew fyne,
Yit to hym self his konnyng was ful bare;
For love hadde hym so bounden in a snare,
Al for the doughter of the kyng Amete,
That al his craft ne koude his sorwes bete.'   665

96

"Right so fare I, unhappily for me;
I love oon best, and that me smerteth sore;
And yit, paraunter, kan I reden the
And nat my self; repreve me no more.
I have no cause, I woot wel, for to sore   670
As doth an hauk that listeth for to pleye;
But to thin help yit somwhat kan I seye.

---

658. CpS1 herkne, H1ADH4H5Cx herken, Cl herkene. 659. Cp fand, J fonde.
660. Cp couthe, JH2D kouth, *rest* coude. 661. JClH1AD Remede; γ(-S1) she *for*
he; Cp knewe, J knewgh. 664. GgR As, H5 Als *for* Al; H2PhGgH5JH3D *om.*
second the. 666. CpGg unhapply, J unhappely, αTh unhappy. 669. CpJ na more.
672. GgH5H3H4RCx *om.* yit.

97

"And of o thyng right siker maistow be,
That certein, for to dyen in the peyne,
That I shal nevere mo discoveren the;   675
Ne, by my trouthe, I kepe nat restreyne
The fro thi love, theigh that it were Eleyne,
That is thi brother wif, if ich it wiste;
Be what she be, and love hire as the liste.

98

"Therfore, as frende fullich in me assure,   680
And tel me plat now, what is thenchesoun,
And finaly cause of wo that ye endure;
For, douteth no thyng, myn entencioun
Nis nat to yow of reprehencioun
To speke as now; for no wight may byreve   685
A man to love, tyl that hym list to leve.

99

"And witeth wel, that bothe two ben vices,
Mistrusten alle, or elles alle leve;
But wel I woot, the mene of it no vice is,
For to trusten som wight is a preve   690
Of trouthe; and forthi wolde I fayn remeve
Thi wronge conceyte, and do the som wyght triste,
Thi wo to telle, and tel me if the liste.

675. αGgH5Cl more. 677. αGgH5Th *om.* that. 678. αGgH5ClA broþeris; α
þogh þat y wist (H4 *om.* þat). 681. γαGgH5 *om.* now; AS1Ph þe enchesoun, ClTh
þyn enchesoun, Gg þyn entencioun, H5 þy sorowe soun, H4 what is enchesoun. 682.
αRCxTh final, H5 þe fynall. 688. H2PhCx to leve, H3 beleve. 689. Cp ye menen,
JADS1 ye mene, H4 that ye meene *for* the mene; GgH5 þat *for* the mene of. 690.
JGgH1H4 For for to, Th As for to. 691. Cp wol, J wold.

100

"The wise seith: 'wo hym that is allone,
For, and he falle, he hath non helpe to ryse';   695
And sith thow hast a felawe, tel thi mone;
For this nys nat, certein, the nexte wyse
To wynnen love, as techen us the wyse,
To walwe and wepe, as Nyobe the queene,
Whos teres yit in marble ben yseene.   700

101

"Lat be thy wepyng and thi drerynesse,
And lat us lissen wo with oother speche,
So may thy woful tyme seme lesse;
Delyte nat in wo thi wo to seche,
As don thise foles that hire sorwes eche   705
With sorwe, whan thei han mysaventure,
And listen naught to seche hem other cure.

102

"Men seyn: 'to wrecche is consolacioun
To have another felawe in hys peyne';
That oughte wel ben oure opynyoun;   710
For bothen thow and I of love we pleyne.
So ful of sorwe am I, soth for to seyne,
That, certeinly, no more harde grace
May sitte on me, for why ther is no space.

---

694. H2PhGgH5 wo is hym, S1 wo to hym. 695. H4 helpe hath he non; D he
may not wel arise. 697. H2PhH3Cx is. 699. H4 Alwey to weepe. 702. αH3RAD
lessyn, H1 listen, S1 lispen, Gg wisse. 705. αH1D sorow. 712. α þe soþe; H2PhS1
CxTh. *om.* for. 714. GgH5R nys.

103

"If god wol, thow art nat agast of me,   715
Lest I wolde of thi lady the bygyle;
Thow woost thy self whom that I love, parde,
As I best kan, gon sithen longe while;
And sith thow woost I do it for no gyle,
And seist I am he that thow trustest moost,   720
Tel me somwhat, syn al my wo thow woost."

104

Yit Troilus, for al this, no worde seyde,
But longe he lay, as stylle as he ded were;
And after this with sikynge he abreyde,
And to Pandarus vois he lente his ere,   725
And up his eyen caste he, that in feere
Was Pandarus, lest that in frenesie
He sholde falle, or elles soone dye;

105

And cryde "awake," ful wonderlich and sharpe,
"What? slombrestow as in a litargie?   730
Or artow lik an asse to the harpe,
That hereth sown whan men the strenges plye;
But in his mynde of that no melodie
May sinken, hym to gladen, for that he
So dul is of his bestialite?"   735

---

715. α A god wil. 719. H4 And weel thou wost I am with oute wyle; γαCxTh
wyle. 720. γTh sith (sithen, syn) *for* seist. 723. αClADCxTh *om. first* as (D *over
line later*). 725. H2PhGg bent, H4Cx laide *for* lente. 731. α unto an harpe, Cx
unto the harp. 732. CpGgH5RH3CxTh stryngis; CpAH2PhGgRH3 pleye. 734.
ClH3R synk yn hym; H2PhCx in *for* hym. 735. αTh in *for* of.

106

And, with that, Pandare of his wordes stente;
And Troilus yit hym no thyng answerde,
For why, to tellen was nat his entente
To nevere no man, for whom that he so ferde;
For it is seyd, "men maketh ofte a yerde   740
With which the maker is hym self ybeten
In sondry manere," as thise wyse treten;

107

And, namelich, in his counseil tellynge
That toucheth love, that oughte ben secree;
For of him self it wol ynough out sprynge,   745
But if that it the bet governed be;
Ek som tyme it is a craft to seme fle
For thyng which in effect men hunte faste;
Al this gan Troilus in his herte caste.

108

But, nevertheles, whan he hadde herd hym crye   750
"Awake," he gan to syken wonder soore,
And seyde: "frende, though that I stylle lye,
I am nat deef; now pees, and crye no more,
For I have herd thi wordes and thi lore;
But suffre me my meschief to bywaille,   755
For thi proverbes may me naught availle.

---

736. αTh þis *for* that. 737. Th But Troylus to him; ClJGgH5H4 no word; R
yet nothing him, H2Ph no thing ȝet hym, H4H5 yit no word hym. 738. γ nas (ClA
nat) *for* was. 739. ClS1H3 *om.* no; H4ACx Never to no man, R Never to man,
H2Ph To no man; H5 a *for* no; H2Ph for why; H3H4H5RCx *om.* that. 740. CpH1J
seyde; CpClA man; H2H4S1H3CxTh makyn; H4 For often sithe men makyn a yerd.
742. H2Ph wise men, GgH5 clerkis *for* wyse (H5 wise *for* manere). 744. oughte, *so*
H1(ougthte)GgH5(auȝte)S1(aughten), *rest* ought; H2PhGgH5H3Cx to be. 747.
H3H4CxTh *om.* a; H2Ph Eke it is craft some tyme. 748. γ(-A) Fro thyng. 750.
γH2PhTh natheles, H5 netherlas. 751. α *om.* to. 753. JGgTh nam. 754. H3
proverbes *for* wordes. 755. α But lete me myn infortune waylyn (H4 fortune
bewaylyn), Th my fortune to bewaylen.

109

"Nor other cure kanstow non for me;
Ek I nyl nat ben cured, I wol deye.
What knowe I of the queene Nyobe?
Lat be thyne olde ensaumples, I the preye."   760
"No," quod Pandarus, "therfore I seye
Swich is delit of foles, to bywepe
Hire wo, but seken bote they ne kepe.

110

"Now knowe I that ther reson in the failleth;
But telle me, if I wiste what she were   765
For whom that the al this mysaunter ailleth,
Dorste thow that I tolde in hire ere
Thi wo, sith thow darst naught thi self for feere,
And hire bysoughte on the to han som routhe?"
"Why nay," quod he, "by god and by my trouthe." 770

111

"What? nat as bisyly," quod Pandarus,
"As though myn owene lyf lay on this nede?"
"No, certes, brother," quod this Troilus.
"And whi?"—"For that thow sholdest nevere spede."—
"Wostow that wel?"—"Ye, that is out of drede," 775
Quod Troilus; "for al that evere ye konne,
She nyl to noon swich wrecche as I ben wonne."

757. H2PhD Ne, ACx Non, JGgH5H4R For *for* Nor.   758. H3GgH5H4RDS1Cx
wil *for* nyl.   760. H4 Lat ben alle thi proverbes; H3 paroles.   761. γ(-Cp)H4 No
quod tho.   762. CpJ delite.   764. ClDH2PhH3CxTh *om.* ther.   766. mysaunter, *so* JCl,
rest mysaventure (GgH5 aventure).   767. ClH1S1R Dorstestow; GgH5H3H4 hyre in
hyre ere, H2PhAS1RCxTh it in her ere, D it þe in þin eere.   771. H5 prevely.   772.
JGg laye.   773. αTh Why no parde sir.   776. CpJ the *for* ye.

112

Quod Pandarus: "allas! what may this be,
That thow dispeired art thus causeles?
What? lyveth nat thi lady, bendiste?   780
How wostow so that thow art graceles?
Swich yvel is nat alwey booteles.
Why, put nat impossible thus thi cure;
Sith thyng to come is ofte in aventure.

113

"I graunte wel that thow endurest wo,   785
As sharp as doth he, Ticius, in helle,
Whos stomak foughles tiren evere mo,
That highten volturis, as bokes telle;
But I may nat endure that thow dwelle
In so unskilful an opynyoun,   790
That of thi wo is no curacioun.

114

"But oones nyltow, for thy coward herte,
And for thyn ire and folissh wilfulnesse,
For wantrust, tellen of thy sorwes smerte,
Ne to thyn owen help don bysynesse,   795
As muche as speke a resoun moore or lesse,
But list as he that lest of no˙thyng recche.
What womman koude loven swich a wrecche?

---

780. bendiste, *so* CpH1J, Gg benediste, *rest* benedicite. 782. Cp bootles, J
bootoles. 784. CpClH3 Syn, H2PhH5 Such, Gg Swich, R Siche. 786. αH5ClR the,
H3 tho *for* he, H1Cx *om.* he; H2 Siciphus, Ph Ciciphus, H4 Sitiphus, Th Tesiphus,
S1 Theseus, Gg which *for* Ticius. 788. Cp volturie, J voltouris. 791. H4Th nys. 794.
α And wantrowist to telle (H4 wondist). 796. αTh As mych as speke o word ye more
or lesse (H2Ph *om.* ye).

115

"What may she demen oother of thy deeth,
If thow thus deye, and she not why it is,   800
But that for feere is yolden up thy breth,
For Grekes han biseged us, iwys?
Lord, which a thonk than shaltow han of this!
Thus wol she seyn, and al the town attones:
'The wrecche is ded, the devel have his bones.'   805

116

"Thow mayst allone here wepe and crye and knele;
But, love a womman that she woot it nought,
And she wol quyte it that thow shalt nat fele;
Unknowe, unkist, and lost that is unsought.
What! many a man hath love ful deere ybought   810
Twenty wynter that his lady wiste,
That nevere yit his lady mouth he kiste.

117

"What sholde he therfore fallen in dispayre,
Or be recreant for his owne tene,
Or slen hym self, al be his lady faire?   815
Nay, nay, but evere in oon be fressh and grene
To serve and love his deere hertes queene,
And thynke it is a guerdon hire to serve,
A thousand fold moore than he kan deserve."

803. H2H4H5ACx such, H3D what *for* which; JGgH5H3H4DCx *om*. than; R
shalthow then have. Th shalt þou have. GgH5AD schuldyst þou; H2PhH5
for þis. 808. γ *om*. it (S1 so *for* it), H3 the *for* it. 811. H4S1 Ya twenti wyntir
(S1 3e). 816. Cp fresshe, J fressch. 818. CpJ thynk, H2PhCl thenk.

118

And of that word took hede Troilus,   820
And thoughte anon what folie he was inne,
And how that soth hym seyde Pandarus,
That for to slen hym self myght he nat wynne,
But bothe don unmanhod and a synne,
And of his deth his lady naught to wite;   825
For of his wo, god woot, she knew ful lite.

119

And with that thought he gan ful sore syke,
And seyde: "allas, what is me best to do?"
To whom Pandare answerde: "if the like,
The beste is that thow telle me al thi wo,   830
And have my trouthe, but thow fynde it so
I be thi boote, or that it be ful longe,
To pieces do me drawe, and sithen honge."

120

"Ye, so seystow," quod Troilus tho, "allas,
But god woot, it is naught the rather so;   835
Ful hard were it to helpen in this cas,
For wel fynde I that Fortune is my fo;
Ne alle the men that riden konne or go
May of hire cruel whiel the harm withstonde;
For, as hire list, she pleyeth with free and bonde." 840

820-822. Ph *omits*. 820. γ *om*. And; R took kepe than. 824. CpClAH2PhH5 *om*. a, S1 eke *for* a. 826. CpHI knewe, J knewgh; H2PhGgCx but lyte. 830. JGgH5 H2PhATh *om*. al. 831. αH5Th but if; γ it fynde. 834. γ thow seyst. 838. CpS1H2Ph al. 839. α wil, H3 wele *for* whiel. 840. J pleyth.

121

Quod Pandarus; "than blamestow Fortune
For thow art wroth, ye, now at erst I see;
Wostow nat wel that Fortune is comune
To everi manere wight in som degree?
And yit thow hast this comfort, lo, parde: 845
That, as hire joies moten overgone,
So mote hire sorwes passen everychone.

122

"For if hire whiel stynte any thyng to torne,
Than cessed she Fortune anon to be;
Now, sith hire whiel by no wey may sojourne, 850
What woostow if hire mutabilite,
Right as thy selven list, wol don by the,
Or that she be nat fer fro thyn helpynge?
Paraunter, thow hast cause for to synge.

123

"And therfore wostow what I the biseche?   855
Lat be thy wo and tornyng to the grounde;
For who so list have helyng of his leche,
To hym byhoveth first unwre his wownde.
To Cerberus in helle ay be I bownde,
Were it for my suster, al thy sorwe,   860
By my wil she sholde al be thyn to morwe.

857. JGgH5ClCx helpyng, R liking. 858. unwre, *so* CpClH1AS1J, Cx unkover, *rest* unwry *or* unwrie. 859. Cp *omits line, text from* J. 861. al be, *so* γ(-AD)J, Ph be al, *rest om.* al.

124

"Look up, I seye, and telle me what she is
Anon, that I may gon aboute thy nede.
Knowe ich hire ought? for my love telle me this;
Than wolde I hopen rather for to spede."   865
Tho gan the veyne of Troilus to blede,
For he was hit, and wax al reed for shame.
"A ha!" quod Pandare, "here bygynneth game."

125

And with that word, he gan hym for to shake,
And seyde: "thef, thow shalt hyre name telle."   870
But tho gan sely Troilus for to quake,
As though men sholde han led hym in to helle,
And seyde: "allas, of al my wo the welle
Than is my swete fo, called Criseyde."
And wel neigh with the word for feere he deide.   875

126

And whan that Pandare herde hire name nevene,
Lord, he was glad, and seyde: "frende so deere,
Now fare aright, for Joves name in hevene,
Love hath byset the wel; be of good cheere,
For of good name, wisdom, and manere   880
She hath ynough, and ek of gentilesse;
If she be fayre, thow woost thy self, I gesse.

---

865. ClH2PhH3H5 þe rathere.   866. α Than gan; GgH5H4R for to blede.   867.
H3 waxid, Ph wox, Th woxe, JGgH5H1DH4 wex.   871. ADS1RCx *om.* for.
872. JCl lad; αCx *om.* in.   875. H1AS1H4RH5CxTh þat *for* the.   878. ADR Jesus
(DR Ihus, A Ihs *over erasure*).   880. CpClH1DS1RTh and wisdom and manere.

127

"Ny nevere saugh a more bountevous
Of hire estat, ne gladder, ne of speche
A frendlyer, na more gracious   885
For to do wel, ne lasse hadde nede to seche
What for to don; and al this bet to eche,
In honour, to as fer as she may strecche,
A kynges herte semeth by hyrs a wrecche.

128

["And for thi loke of good comfort thow be;   890
For, certeinly, the firste poynt is this
Of noble corage, and wele ordeyne,
A man to have pees with hym self, ywis;
So oghtist thow, for noght but good it is
To loven wele, and in a worthy place;   895
The oghte not to clepe hit hap but grace.]

129

"And also thynk, and therwith glade the,
That sith thy lady vertuous is al,
So foloweth it that there is som pitee
Amonges alle thise other in general;   900
And forthi se that thow in special
Requere nat that is ayeyns hyre name,
For vertu streccheth nat hym self to shame.

---

883. Ny, *so* JH₁S₁, H₂Ph Ne y, CpClH₃Th Ne *for* Ny, H₄H₅RD Ne nevere
sauh I, Gg Ne nevere ne say, A Ne nevere man saw, Cx Never saw I none, S2 For
nevire sawe I, Dig For I nevire sawe. 884. Cp na gladder, ClTh ne a gladder, Gg
non gladere; αDRCx *om.* second ne; H₄RD of hir spech. 885. na, *so* CpClH₁J,
αH₃ ne a, Gg ne non, ADS₁H₅RCxTh ne. 889. GgH₂PhH₃A bi hire, D to hir.
890-896. *Stanza found only in* H₂PhH₄Th; *text based on H2.* 891. H2 ferst, PhTh
first. 892. H4 corage thou ordeyne the; Th and wele ordayne the; Ph ordeigne.
894. H₂Ph *om.* noght but. 895. H₂Ph love, *om.* a. 896. H4 Men ouht; H₂Ph oght,
Th ought. 897. ClAH₂Ph þenk. 900. αGgH₅Cx Among (H2 Almong), H₁
Amange.

130

"But wel is me that evere that I was born,
That thow biset art in so good a place;   905
For by my trouthe, in love, I dorste have sworn,
The sholde nevere han tid thus fayre a grace;
And wostow why? for thow were wont to chace
At love in scorn, and for despit hym calle
'Seynt Idyot, lord of thise foles alle.'   910

131

"How often hastow maad thi nyce japes,
And seyd that loves servantes everichone
Of nycete ben verray goddes apes;
And some wolde mucche hire mete allone,
Liggyng a-bedde, and make hem for to grone;   915
And som, thow seydest, hadde a blaunche fevere,
And preydest god he sholde nevere kevere.

132

"And som of hem took on hym for the colde
More than ynough, so seydestow ful ofte;
And some han feyned ofte tyme, and tolde   920
How that they waken whan thei slepen softe;
And thus they wolde han brought hem self alofte,
And natheles were under at the laste;
Thus seydestow, and japedest ful faste.

904-973. H3 *omits ten stanzas.* 904. ClDJRH5Th *om. second* that; **R was I.**
907. JGgH5 nevere in love han tid; αClDDigRCxTh so *for* thus. 912. CpH1J
seyde; €pClH1J servantz. 914. GgA meche, D mich, H2Ph monche, H4 **monchyn,**
Th monch. 915. H2PhGgH5 in bed. 917. H4H5Th thei *for* he. 918. αGgH5ACxTh
some; ClJGgH5H2PhCxTh hem, S1 tham *for* hym. 920. CpDS1JR som.

133

"Yit seydestow that, for the moore part,   925
Thise loveres wolden speke in general,
And thoughten that it was a siker art,
For faylyng, for tasayen over al.
Now may I jape of the, if that I shal;
But natheles, though that I sholde deye,   930
That thow art non of tho, I dorste seye.

134

"Now beet thi brest, and sey to god of love:
'Thy grace, lord; for now I me repente,
If I mysspak, for now my self I love';
Thus sey with al thyn herte in good entente."   935
Quod Troilus: "a lord! I me consente,
And preye to the my japes thow foryive,
And I shal nevere more whil I live."

135

"Thow seist wel," quod Pandarus, "and now I hope
That thow the goddes wrathe hast al apesed;   940
And sithen thow hast wopen many a drope,
And seyd swych thyng wherwith the god is plesed,
Now wolde nevere god but thow were esed;
And thynk wel she, of whom rist al thi wo,
Hereafter may thy comfort be also.   945

---

926. H2Ph Thes faytours. 932. CpJ bet thi breste. 937. H2PhCx to, H4 now, H5
me *for* thow. 938. α whil þat; S1 quhill I may lyve. 939. Pandarus, *so* CpClH1AJ,
Gg pandarys, *rest* Pandare *or* Pandar. 941. wopen, *so* CpClJ, H1ADGg wepen, αCx
wept, RH5 wepte, Th wepten, S1 weped; R ful many.

136

"For thilke grownde that bereth the wedes wikke
Bereth ek thise holsom herbes, as ful ofte;
Next the foule netle, rough and thikke,
The rose wexeth, swete, smothe, and softe;
And next the valeye is the hil olofte,   950
And next the derke nyght the glade morwe;
And also joie is next the fyn of sorwe.

137

"Now loke that a-tempre be thi bridel,
And, for the beste, ay suffre to the tyde;
Or elles al oure labour is on ydel;   955
He hasteth wel that wisly kan abyde.
Be diligent and trewe, and ay wel hide;
Be lusty, fre; persevere in thy servyse;
And al is wel, if thow werke in this wyse.

138

"But he that parted is in everi place   960
Is nowher hool, as writen clerkes wyse.
What wonder is, though swich oon have no grace?
Ek wostow how it fareth of som service,
As plaunte a tree or herbe in sondry wyse,
And on the morwe pulle it up as blyve,   965
No wonder is, though it may nevere thryve.

---

949. α The lilie wexith white smothe & soft; γ(-ADS1) waxeth; γ(-S2Dig)
swoote *or* sote; CpClH1DS1J and smothe and softe. 950. olofte, *so* CpH1J, GgH4
S2Dig on lofte, *rest* alofte. 957. H2PhRCx alwey *for* ay wel. 960. γTh departed
(Cp deperted).

139

"And sith that god of love hath the bistowed
In place digne unto thi worthinesse,
Stond faste, for to good port hastow rowed;
And of thi self, for any hevynesse,   970
Hope alwey wel; for but if drerinesse,
Or over haste, oure bothe labour shende,
I hope of this to maken a good ende.

140

"And wostow why I am the lasse afered
Of this matere with my nece trete?   975
For this have I herd seyd of wyse lered:
'Was nevere man nor womman yit bigete
That was unapt to suffren loves hete,
Celestial, or elles love of kynde.'
Forthy som grace I hope in hire to fynde.   980

141

"And for to speke of hire in specyal,
Hire beaute to bithynken, and hire youthe,
It sit hire naught to ben celestial
As yit, though that hire liste bothe and kowthe;
But, trewely, it sate hire wel right nowthe   985
A worthi knyght to loven and cherice,
And but she do, I holde it for a vice.

---

969. CpH1J stonde. 972. DS1 bother, H4 botheres, AGgCx bothis. 975. αH3CxD
to trete, S1 for to trete. 976. αR olde *for* wyse; Gg *om.* wyse; H3 ofte herde sey and
lerede, Cx herd sayd oft of lered. 977. nor, *so* JH3D, ClH2PhRCx ne, CpH1AS1Th
or; Gg non, H4 parfit *for* man nor.

142

"Wherfore I am, and wol ben, ay redy
To peyne me to do yow this servyse,
For bothe yow to plese this hope I   990
Herafterward; for ye ben bothe wyse,
And konne it counseil kepe in swych a wyse
That no man shal the wiser of it be;
And so we may ben gladed alle thre.

143

"And, by my trouthe, I have right now of the   995
A good conceyte in my wit, as I gesse;
And what it is, I wol now that thow se.
I thenke, sith that love of his goodnesse
Hath the converted out of wikkednesse,
That thow shalt ben the beste post, I leve,   1000
Of al his lay, and moste his foos greve.

144

"Ensample why: se now thise grete clerkes,
That erren aldermost ayeyn a lawe,
And ben converted from hire wikked werkes,   1004
Thorugh grace of god, that list hem to hym drawe,
Thanne arn they folk that han moost god in awe,
And strengest feythed ben, I undirstonde,
And konne an errour alderbest withstonde."

988. H2PhGgH3 Therefor; AD ay be; GgH3Cx al *for* ay; H2 al day be redy, Ph alwey be redy. 990. CpClH1AS1H4 thus *for* this. 993. ClH4 of it þe wiser be (H4 *om.* þe), H2Ph þerof shal the wyser be, D þerof þe wiser be, Cx the wyser therof be. 994. CpJRCxS1α al. 998. H3Th that sithe, H4 that syn, Gg to sey þat, H2Ph seth, R sithen *for* sith that. 1000. beste, *so* H1GgH4, *rest* best. 1001. moste, *so* H3Cx, *rest* moost *or* most; γ(-DS1) to greve, JRS1 ay greve. 1002. γ wise clerkes (A *om.* wise). 1003. H2PhCx are, Gg arn, D aren *for* erren. 1006. H2Ph They are the folk, H4 Than erthen folk; J ern, H1GgH5 are, H3 ar; GgH4PhCx god most.

145

Whan   Troilus had herd Pandare assented
To ben his help in lovyng of Cryseyde,   1010
Wex of his wo, as who seith, untormented;
But hotter wex his love, and thanne he seyde
With sobre chere, although his herte pleyde:
"Now blisful Venus helpe, or that I sterve,
Of the, Pandare, I mowe som thank deserve.   1015

146

"But, deere frende, how shal my wo be lesse
Til this be doon? and, good, ek telle me this:
How wiltow seyn of me and my destresse?
Lest she be wroth, this drede I moost, ywys,
Or nyl nat here, or trowen how it is.   1020
Al this drede I, and ek for the manere,
Of the, hire em, she nyl no swich thyng here."

147

Quod Pandarus: "thow hast a ful grete care
Lest that the Cherl may falle out of the moone.
Whi! lord, I hate of the thi nyce fare.   1025
Whi! entremete of that thow hast to doone.
For goddes love, I bidde the a boone,
So lat malone, and it shal be thi beste."
"Whi, frende," quod he, "now do right as the leste.

1009. CpJTh herde. 1011. CpH1 weex, JH3Cxα wax, A wix, Th wext. 1012.
CpCl weex, H2PhH3Cx wax, Th wext; γ thus, Ph þo *for* thanne. 1014. α Now
blisful Venus now help. 1015. J nowe, ClGgH3H4RCx may *for* mowe. 1018. JH1
woltow. 1026. H2Ph of þat þou hast not to done, Gg of þyng þou hast not to done.
1029. α þan *for* now.

148

"But herke, Pandare, o word, for I nolde   1030
That thow in me wendest so gret folie,
That to my lady I desiren sholde
That toucheth harm, or any vilenye;
For, dredeles, me were levere dye,
Than she of me aught elles understode   1035
But that that myghte sownen into goode."

149

Tho lough this Pandare, and anon answerde:
"And I thi borugh? fy! no wight doth but so;
I roughte nat though that she stoode and herde
How that thow seist; but farewel, I wol go.   1040
Adieu! be glad! god spede us bothe two!
Yif me this labour and this besynesse,
And of my spede be thyn al that swetnesse."

150

Tho Troilus gan doun on knees to falle,
And Pandare in his armes hente faste,   1045
And seyde: "now, fy on the Grekes alle!
Yit, parde, god shal helpe us at the laste;
And, dredeles, if that my lyf may laste,
And god to-forn, lo, som of hem shal smerte;
And yit mathinketh this avaunt masterte.   1050

1034. αH5H3A to dy. 1043. that, *so* CpClH1S1J, *rest* the. 1044-1092. *Missing in*
Gg. 1050. mathinketh, *so* JH1S1, Cp mathenketh, H2PhH5RCxTh me athinkiþ,
H4H3AD me thynkith (A *corrected to* me athenketh), Cl me of þynketh; γH3Th that
this avaunt; masterte, *so* JRS1Th, CpH2H4 me sterte, ClAPhCx me asterte,
H1DH3H5 may sterte.

151

"Now, Pandare, I kan no more seye;
But thow wis, thow woost, thow maist, thow art al;
My lif, my deth, hool in thyn honde I leye;
Help now!" Quod he: "yis, by my trowthe, I shal."
"God yelde the, frend, and this in special,"   1055
Quod Troilus, "that thow me recomaunde
To hire that may me to the deth comaunde."

152

This Pandarus tho, desirous to serve
His fulle frende, tho seyde in this manere:
"Farwel, and thenk I wol thi thank deserve,   1060
Have here my trowthe, and that thow shalt wel here";
And went his wey, thenkyng on this matere,
And how he best myghte hire biseche of grace,
And fynde a tyme therto, and a place.

153

For everi wight that hath an hous to founde   1065
Ne renneth naught the werk for to bygynne
With rakel hond; but he wol bide a stounde,
And sende his hertes line out fro withinne
Aldirfirst his purpos for to wynne.
Al this Pandare in his herte thoughte,   1070
And caste his werk ful wisly or he wroughte.

1051. JH4H3Cx Pandarus, R Now good Pandar. 1057. JH3 Til *for* To; γ(-DS1)
to the deth me may, H4DS1 to the deth may me. 1059. γ(-DS1) than, Th he *for*
tho. 1064. αH5H3R space. 1066. αH5D *om.* for. 1070. H4 Al this tho pandare, *om.*
his.

154

But Troilus lay tho no lenger down,
But up anon upon his stede bay,
And in the feld he pleyde the leoun;
Wo was that Grek that with hym mette a day.   1075
And in the town his manere tho forth ay
So goodly was, and gat hym so in grace,
That ech hym loved that loked on his face.

155

For he bicome the frendlieste wight,
The gentileste, and ek the moste fre,   1080
The thriftieste, and oon the beste knyght
That in his tyme was, or myghte be;
Dede were his japes and his cruelte,
His hye port, and his manere estraunge;
And ech of tho gan for a vertu chaunge.   1085

156

Now lat us stynte of Troilus a stounde,
That fareth lik a man that hurt is soore,
And is som deel of akyng of his wownde
Ylissed wel, but heeled no deel moore,
And, as an esy pacyent, the loore   1090
Abit of hym that gooth aboute his cure;
And thus he dryeth forth his aventure.

EXPLICIT LIBER PRIMUS.

1074. CpClH1S1H3 tho *for* the. 1075. CpClJ Who *for* Wo; CpJ Greke; H2Ph H3Cx met with hym, H4 *om.* with; a day, *so* CpH1S1J, *rest* that day. 1076. H2Ph his name sprong **for ay,** A his name sprang in fay, Cx hys manere he holdyth **ay. 1077.** H2Ph so mych, A such *for* so in. 1078. αAS1H3RCxTh in *for* on. 1079. frendlieste, *so* ClH4, *rest* frendliest. 1080. gentileste, *so* JClH4R, *rest* gentilest; moste, *so* H3H4DTh, *rest* moost *or* most. 1081. thriftieste, *so* Cl, H2PhR trustiest, *rest* thriftiest; beste, *so* ClH3H4Th, *rest* best. 1082. myghte, *so* ClH1, *rest* myght. **1084.** hye, *so* JRPhCx, CpCl heigh, H1 hieghe, H3ADS1Th high, H2 hy, H4 hih, H5 **extre** *for* hye. 1092. H2PhH5AS1CxTh driveth.

BOOK TWO

BOOK TWO

1

OWT of thise blake wawes for to saylle,
    O wynde, O wynde, the weder gynneth clere;
    For in this see the boot hath swych travaylle,
Of my konnyng that unneth I it steere.
This see clepe I the tempestous matere   5
Of desespoir that Troilus was inne;
But now of hope the kalendes bygynne.

2

O lady myn, that called art Cleo,
Thow be my speed fro this forth, and my Muse,
To ryme wel this book, til I have do;   10
Me nedeth here noon othere art to use.
Forwhi to every lovere I me excuse,
That of no sentement I this endite,
But out of Latyn in my tonge it write.

3

Wherfore I nyl have neither thank ne blame   15
Of al this werk, but prey yow mekely,
Disblameth me, if any word be lame;
For as myn auctour seyde, so sey I.
Ek though I speeke of love unfelyngly,
No wonder is, for it no thyng of newe is;   20
A blynd man kan nat juggen wel in hewis.

1-49. R *omits proem.* 1-84. *Lacking in* Gg. 4. H3H4H5S1CxTh konnyng, γJH2Ph commyng (H1 coniynge). 5. αD þis *for* the, H3 *om.* the. 11. αCl *om.* othere; α for to use. 15. αH5 neiþer have þonk. 20. α Ne wondriþ not; Cp wondre, J wondir. 21. blynd, *so* ClαH5, *rest* blynde; JH5 wight, H3 knyght *for* man; H4 deeme riht, H5 wel demyn.

4

Ye knowe ek, that in forme of speche is chaunge
Withinne a thousand yeer, and wordes tho
That hadden pris, now wonder nyce and straunge
Us thinketh hem, and yit thei spake hem so,　　　　25
And spedde as wel in love as men now do;
Ek for to wynnen love in sondry ages,
In sondry londes, sondry ben usages.

5

And forthi, if it happe in any wyse,
That here be any lovere in this place　　　　30
That herkneth, as the story wol devise,
How Troilus com to his lady grace,
And thenketh, "so nolde I nat love purchace,"
Or wondreth on his speche, or his doynge,
I noot, but it is me no wonderynge.　　　　35

6

For every wight which that to Rome went,
Halt nat o path, nor alwey o manere;
Ek in som lond were al the game shent,
If that men ferde in love as men don here,
As thus, in opyn doyng, or in chere,　　　　40
In visityng, in forme, or seyde hire sawes;
Forthi men seyn, ech contree hath his lawes.

22. JH3H5S1S2DigCxTh I knowe, A He knew; α þis *for* that. 25. CpCl thenketh.
29-42. *In* H2Ph *these stanzas follow line* 49. 31. JH5Cx can, H3 gan *for* wol. 33.
α þus *for* so. 34. α of *for* on. 35. α I note me semith it (H4 *om.* it); H3H5 it is to
me, Cx unto me it is; wonderynge, *so* ClDH3, *rest* wondrynge (Cp wondryng). 36.
CpH1J wente. 37. nor, *so* JH3, γS1 or, αH5CxTh ne. 38. α And *for* Ek; CpH1J
shente. 39. γS1Cx they *for first* men . 40. α delyng.

7

Ek scarsly ben ther in this place thre,
That have in love seid lik, and don in al;
For to thi purpos this may liken the,   45
And the right nought, yit al is seid, or shal;
Ek som men grave in tree, som in ston wal,
As it bitit; but syn I have bigonne,
Myn auctour shal I folwen, if I konne.

EXPLICIT PROHEMIUM SECUNDI LIBRI.
INCIPIT LIBER SECUNDUS.

8

I N May, that moder is of monthes glade,   50
That fresshe floures, blewe, white, and rede
Ben quike agayn, that wynter dede made,
And ful of bawme is fletyng every mede;
Whan Phebus doth his bryghte bemes sprede
Right in the white Bole, it so bitidde,   55
As I shal synge, on Mayes day the thrydde,

9

That Pandarus, for al his wise speche,
Felte ek his parte of loves shotes keene,
That koude he nevere so wel of lovyng preche,
It made his hewe a day ful ofte greene;   60
So shope it, that hym fil that day a teene
In love, for which in wo to bedde he wente,
And made, or it was day, ful many a wente.

44. CpJ seide; α or *for* and. 46. α done *for* seid. 48. α as *for* syn. 51 CpClH1ADJ
and white and rede. 54. CpH1J bryght. 55. αCl so it. 57. α This *for* That. 59.
H2Ph of love so wele, H4 so weel in love, H5 so wele of love. 63. H2PhH3Th were.

10

The swalowe, Proigne, with a sorwful lay,
Whan morwen com, gan make hire waymentynge,   65
Whi she forshapen was, and evere lay
Pandare a-bedde, half in a slomberynge,
Til she so neigh hym made hire cheterynge,
How Tereux gan forth hire suster take,
That with the noyse of hire he gan awake;   70

11

And gan to calle, and dresse hym up to ryse,
Remembryng hym his erand was to doone
From Troilus, and ek his grete emprise,
And caste and knew in good plite was the moone
To doon viage, and took his wey ful soone   75
Unto his neces paleys ther biside;
Now Janus, god of entre, thow hym gyde!

12

Whan he was come unto his neces place,
"Wher is my lady?" to hire folk quod he;
And they hym tolde, and he forth in gan pace,   80
And fond two othere ladys sete, and she,
Withinne a paved parlour, and they thre
Herden a mayden reden hem the geste
Of the sege of Thebes, whil hem leste.

---

65. CpJ come; α his *for* hire. 69. γS1 Tireux (A Cireux, H1 Tryeux), H4RCx Tereus, H3 Terous, H5 Terius, H2PhTh Thereus. 71. αRH3ACx *om.* up, D *for* for up. 74. Cp knewe, J knewgh. 78 α to *for* unto. 79. ClH2Ph seyde he. 80. Cl he yn forth, R forth in he, H5 forth he in, Th in forthe he. 81. CpJ fonde. 83. αH5 al þe geest.

13

Quod Pandarus, "madame, god yow see,   85
With al youre book, and al the compaignie."
"Ey, uncle, now welcome iwys," quod she;
And up she roos, and by the hond in hye
She took hym faste, and seyde, "this nyght thrie,
To goode mot it turne, of you I mette";   90
And with that word she doun on bench hym sette.

14

"Ye, nece, ye shal faren wel the bet,
If god wol, al this yer," quod Pandarus;
"But I am sory that I have yow let
To herken of youre book ye preysen thus.   95
For goddes love, what seith it? tel it us;
Is it of love? O, som good ye me leere!"
"Uncle," quod she, "youre maistresse is nat here."

15

With that thei gonnen laughe, and tho she seyde:
"This romaunce is of Thebes that we rede;   100
And we han herd how that king Layus deyde,
Thorugh Edippus his sone, and al that dede;
And here we stynten at thise lettres rede,
How the bisshop, as the book kan telle,
Amphiorax, fil thorugh the ground to helle."   105

---

85. αGgH5R Ma dame quod Pandare. 86. S1CxTh *om. first* al; γS1 With al
youre fayre book; Cp and al the faire compaignie. 87. γS1Th myn *for* now, H4H5
om. now; Gg Ey unkele quo sche god ȝow save & se. 94. Cp lette, J lete. 95. R to
reden on. 97. αCl *om.* O. 100. H4 This book is al of thebes. 101. CpJ herde. 103.
CpJ this. 105. H4 pit *for* ground; αA of *for* to.

16

Quod Pandarus: "al this knowe I my selve,
And al thassege of Thebes, and the care;
For herof ben ther maked bookes twelve;
But lat be this, and tel me how ye fare;
Do wey youre wympel, and shewe youre face bare; 110
Do wey youre book, rys up and lat us daunce,
And lat us don to May som observaunce."

17

"I, god forbede!", quod she, "be ye mad?
Is that a widewes lif, so god yow save?
By god, ye maken me ryght sore adrad, 115
Ye ben so wylde; it semeth as ye rave.
It satte me wel bet ay in a cave
To bidde, and rede on holy seyntes lyves;
Lat maydens gon to daunce, and yonge wyves."

18

"As evere thryve I," quod this Pandarus, 120
"Yit koude I telle a thyng to doon yow pleye."
"Now uncle deere," quod she, "telle it us,
For goddes love; is than thassege aweye?
I am of Grekes fered so that I deye."
"Nay, nay," quod he, "as evere mote I thryve, 125
It is a thing wel bet than swyche fyve."

110. γS1α youre barbe. 113. Cl A, H5Cx Ey, Th Eighe *for* I. 115. α Ye make me by Jovis. 124. γS1Cx so fered, α *om.* so.

19

"Ye, holy god!" quod she, "what thyng is that?
What! bet than swiche fyve? I, nay, ywys.
For al this world, ne kan I reden what
It sholde ben; som jape I trowe is this;   130
And but youre selven telle us what it is,
My wit is for tarede it al to leene;
As, helpe me god, I not what ye meene."

20

"And I youre borugh, ne nevere shal," quod he,
"This thyng be tolde to yow, so mote I thryve."   135
"And whi so, uncle myn, whi so?" quod she.
"By God," quod he, "that wol I telle as blyve;
For prouder womman is ther noon on lyve,
And ye it wiste, in al the town of Troye;
I jape nought, so evere have I joye!"   140

21

Tho gan she wondren moore than biforn
A thousand fold, and down hire eyen caste;
For nevere, sith the tyme that she was born,
To knowe thyng desired she so faste;
And with a sik, she seyde hym at the laste: 145
"Now, uncle myn, I nyl yow nat displese,
Nor axen moore that may do yow disese."

128. H4RH3Cx *om.* I. 133. CpClH1H3 I not nat what, S1 I wote nat quhat, A I not what it may mene, D I not what þat, GgR as I not what. 134. γ(-S2Dig)αGgH5 for me *for* quod he. 135. γS1Th as *for* so. 139. CpH1J wist; αGgH5 wist it (H4 *om.* it). 140. γS1H4 as *for* so.

22

So after this, with many wordes glade,
·And frendly tales, and with merie cheere,
Of this and that they pleide, and gonnen wade   150
In many an unkouth, gladde, and depe matere,
As frendes doon whan thei ben met yfere;
Tyl she gan axen hym how Ector ferde,
That was the townes wal, and Grekes yerde.

23

"Ful wel, I thonke it god," quod Pandarus,   155
"Save in his arme he hath a litel wownde,
And ek his fresshe brother, Troilus,
The wise, worthi Ector the secounde,
In whom that alle vertu list habounde,
As alle trouthe, and alle gentilesse,   160
Wisdom, honour, fredom, and worthinesse."

24

"In good feith, em," quod she, "that liketh me
Thei faren wel, god save hem bothe two!
For treweliche I holde it grete deynte,
A kynges sone in armes wel to do,   165
And ben of good condiciouns therto;
Fór grete power and moral vertu here
Is selde yseyn in o persone yfere."

---

151. αGgH5Cx *om.* an.   154. H3Cx wal of Troie *for* townes wal.   155. H2H4GgCl
y thonk god, PhH5 y thonkyd god; CpJ thonk.   159. αGgH5H3CxTh every, S2Dig
evere *for* alle, JClH1 al; JClH2Ph abounde.   160. CpJ trouth.   165. Cp soone,
J son.

25

"In good feith, that is soth," quod Pandarus;
"But by my trouthe, the kyng hath sones tweye,— 170
That is to meene Ector and Troilus,—
That certeynly, though that I sholde deye,
Thei ben as voide of vices, dar I seye,
As any men that lyve under the sonne;
Hire myght is wyde iknowe, and what they konne. 175

26

"Of Ector nedeth no thing for to telle;
In al this world ther nys a bettre knyght
Than he, that is of worthynesse welle;
And he wel moore vertu hath than myght;
This knoweth many a wys and worthi wight. 180
The same pris of Troilus I seye,
God helpe me so! I knowe nat swiche tweye."

27

"By god," quod she, "of Ector that is sooth;
Of Troilus the same thyng trowe I;
For, dredeles, men tellen that he doth 185
In armes day by day so worthily,
And bereth hym here at home so gentilly
To every wight, that alle pris hath he
Of hem that me were levest preysed be."

169-178 *defective and* 179-201 *lacking in* R; *leaf torn.* 176. γS1Th nedeth it no
more, GgH5H4 nediþ it nouȝt (Gg *om.* it, H5 it nediþ). 178. H2PhGgH5 As he.
184. H4 That troilus be good eek so mene I. 188. GgH5Ph al þe prys.

28

"Ye seye right sooth, ywys," quod Pandarus; 190
"For yesterday whoso hadde with hym ben
Myghte han wondred upon Troilus;
For nevere yit so thikke a swarm of ben
Ne fleigh, as Grekes fro hym gonne flen;
And thorugh the feld, in everi wightes ere, 195
Ther nas no cry but 'Troilus is there!'

29

"Now her, now ther, he hunted hem so faste,
Ther nas but Grekes blood; and Troilus,
Now hym he hurte, and hym al down he caste;
Ay wher he wente, it was arayed thus: 200
He was hire deth, and sheld and lif for us;
That, as that day, ther dorste non withstonde,
Whil that he held his blody swerd in honde.

30

"Therto he is the frendlieste man
Of gret estat that evere I saugh my lyve; 205
And wher hym list, best felawshipe kan
To swich as hym thynketh able for to thryve."
And with that word tho Pandarus as blyve,
He took his leve, and seyde, "I wol gon henne."
"Nay, blame have I, myn uncle," quod she thenne. 210

---

190. H2PhGgH5 wele *for* sooth. 192. γ(-S2Dig) He myghte. 194. CpJDS1 for
hym. 199. CpClH1H3H5 hem . . . hem; H2PhH5 a doun, Gg doun *for* al down.
204. frendlieste, *so* H1GgH4, H3S1 frendelyest, *rest* frendliest. 209. ADS1 His leve
tok, H3Cx Toke of hem leve; GgH5H3CxD he wolde gon. 209-217 *defective and*
218-247 *lacking in* R; *leaf torn.*

31

"What aileth yow to be thus wery soone?
And namelich of wommen? wol ye so?
Nay, sitteth down; by god, I have to doone
With yow to speke of wisdom or ye go."
And everi wight that was aboute hem tho,   215
That herde that, gan fer awey to stonde,
Whil they two hadde al that hem liste on honde.

32

Whan that hire tale al brought was to an ende
Of hire estat, and of hire governaunce,
Quod Pandarus: "now is tyme I wende;   220
But yit, I seye, ariseth, and lat us daunce,
And cast youre widwes habit to mischaunce.
What list yow thus youre self to disfigure,
Sith yow is tid so glad an aventure?"

33

"A, wel bithought! for love of god," quod she,   225
"Shal I nat witen what ye mene of this?"
"No, this thing axeth leyser," tho quod he;
"And ek me wolde muche greve, iwys,
If I it tolde, and ye it toke amys;
Yit were it bet my tonge for to stille,   230
Than seye a soth that were ayeyns youre wille.

---

215. ClDS1R two, GgH5 to, H3 too *for* tho. 217. J al this matere on honde;
γS1Th in honde. 220. H2Ph Now quod Pandarus; H2H3GgH5 is it tyme; S1Th
tyme is; H4H5PhS1Th that I wende. 221. CpH1S2DigS1JTh *om.* and. 224.
γ(-S2Dig) thus faire (DS1 so faire) *for* so glad; J glade. 226. αGgH5 now *for* nat.
228. α *om.* ek.

34

"For, nece, by the goddesse Mynerve,
And Jupiter, that maketh the thonder rynge,
And by the blisful Venus that I serve,
Ye ben the womman in this world lyvynge,   235
Withouten paramours, to my witynge,
That I best love, and lothest am to greve;
And that ye weten wel youre self, I leve."

35

"Iwis, myn uncle," quod she, "graunt mercy!
Youre frendshipe have I founden evere yit.   240
I am to no man holden, trewely,
So muche as yow, and have so litel quyt;
And with the grace of god, emforth my wit,
As in my gilt, I shal yow nevere offende;
And if I have or this, I wol amende.   245

36

"But, for the love of god, I yow biseche,
As ye ben he that I moost love and triste,
Lat be to me youre fremde manere speche,
And sey to me, youre nece, what yow liste."
And with that word, hire uncle anoon hire kiste,   250
And seyde: "gladly, leve nece dere,
Tak it for good, that I shal sey yow here."

---

235. αD þat in þis world. 239. γS1H3 *om.* myn; J my. 246-301. *Omitted in* Cx. 247. CpH1ADS1JTh love mooste. 248. fremde, *so* AD, Th fremed, CpH1 frende, J friende, H3 freinde, S1 fryend, H2PhH4 frend, ClGg frendly, H5 fraynyd.

37

With that she gan hire look down for to caste;
And Pandarus to coghe gan a lite,
And seyde: "nece, alwey, lo, to the laste;   255
How so it be that som men hem delite
With subtyl art hire tales for to endite,
Yit for al that, in hire entencioun,
Hire tale is al for som conclusioun.

38

"And sithen thende is every tales strengthe,   260
And this matere is so bihovely,
What sholde I peynte or drawen it on lengthe,
To yow that ben my frend so feythfully?"
And with that word, he gan right inwardly
Byholden hire, and loken on hire face,   265
And seyde: "on swiche a mirour goode grace!"

39

Than thought he thus: "if I my tale endite
Aught harde, or make a proces any whyle,
She shal no savour han therin but lite,
And trowe I wolde hire in my wil bigyle;   270
For tendre wittes wenen al be wyle,
Wher as thei kan nat pleynly understonde,
Forthi hire wit to serven wol I fonde";

---

253. *So* JH3R (β), γS1αGgH5Th hire eighen down to caste. 255. J at the laste,
R at laste. 257. αH3R *om.* for; JAS1H4Th tendite. 265. αH5H3Th in *for* on.
266. goode, *so* CpH1H3, *rest* good. 272. γ(-S2Dig)S1 There as; JTh pleynlisch.

40

And loked on hire in a bisy wyse.
And she was war that he byheld hire so,   275
And seyde: "lord! so faste ye mavise!
Sey ye me nevere or now? what sey ye? no?"
"Yis, yis," quod he, "and bet wol or I go;
But, be my trouthe, I thoughte now if ye
Be fortunat, for now men shal it se.   280

41

"For to every wight som goodly aventure
Som tyme is shape, if he kan it receyven;
And if that he wol take of it no cure,
Whan that it cometh, but wilfully it weyven,
Lo, neyther cas ne fortune hym deceyven,   285
But ryght his owne slouthe and wrecchednesse;
And swich a wight is for to blame, I gesse.

42

"Good aventure, O bele nece, have ye
Ful lightly founden, and ye konne it take;
And for the love of god, and ek of me,   290
Cache it anon, lest aventure slake.
What sholde I lenger proces of it make?
Yif me youre hond; for in this world is noon,
If that yow list, a wight so wel bygon.

275. CpH1J byhelde. 279. thoughte, *so* JGgH5H4, *rest* thought. 282. αH5H3A can hit. 283. γS1Th But *for* And. 284. Cp commeth, J comth. 286. γ(-S2Dig)S1 verray *for* owne. 288. αGgH5 *om.* O. 291. H2Ph Takiþ, Gg Tache, H5 Take *for* Cache. 292. αH3 to yow *for* of it, H5R *om.* of it.

43

"And sith I speke of good entencioun,   295
As I to yow have told wel here byforn,
And love as wel youre honour and renoun
As creature in al this world yborn,
By alle the othes that I have yow sworn,
And ye be wrooth therfore, or wene I lye,   300
Ne shal I nevere sen yow eft with eye.

44

"Beth naught agast, ne quaketh naught; wherto?
Ne chaungeth naught for feere so youre hewe;
For, hardely, the werste of this is do;
And though my tale as now be to yow newe,   305
Yit trist alwey, ye shal me fynde trewe;
And were it thyng that me thoughte unsittynge
To yow, wolde I no swiche tales brynge."

45

"Now, my good em, for goddes love I preye,"
Quod she, "come of, and telle me what it is;   310
For bothe I am agast what ye wol seye,
And ek me longeth it to wite, ywys;
For, whether it be wel or be amys,
Sey on; lat me nat in this feere dwelle."
"So wol I doon; now herkeneth, I shal telle.   315

309. γ(-S2Dig)S1 *om.* my. 315. H2Ph how y telle, R what I telle.

46

"Now, nece myn, the kynges deere sone,
The goode, wise, worthi, fresshe, and free,
Which alwey for to don wel is his wone,
The noble Troilus, so loveth the,
That, but ye helpe, it wol his bane be.   320
Lo, here is al. What sholde I moore·seye?
Do what yow list to make hym lyve or deye.

47

"But if ye late hym deye, I wol sterve,—
Have here my trouthe, nece, I nyl nat lyen,—
Al sholde I with this knyf my throte kerve."   325
With that the teris bruste out of his eyen,
And seide: "if that ye don us bothe dyen,
Thus gilteles, than have ye fisshed fayre;
What mende ye, though that we bothe apaire?

48

"Allas! he which that is my lord so deere,   330
That trewe man, that noble, gentil knyght,
That naught desireth but youre frendly cheere,
I se hym deyen, ther he goth upryght,
And hasteth hym with al his fulle myght
For to be slayn, if his fortune assente;   335
Allas! that god yow swich a beaute sente!

---

317. CpClJ good. 318. αR *om.* for. 322. CpClH1Th Doth. 323. JADS1 deyen.
326. bruste, *so* H1, J brust, Gg brostyn, Th burste, Cp breste, H3S1H2PhH5 brest,
ClH4RCx brast, A brasten; CpH1Gg eighen, JH3R eyne, H4AD yen. 328. Cp
giltles, J giltiles. 330. αH3 *om.* which. 331. αGgH5 worþi *for* gentil. 334. fulle,
so ClGg, *rest* ful. 335. ClH3GgH5 yf fortune wole assente (H3 wolde; H5 his
fortune).

49

"If it be so that ye so cruel be,
That of his deth yow liste nat to recche,
That is so trewe and worthi as we se,
No moore than of a japer, or a wrecche,— 340
If ye be swich, youre beaute may nat strecche
To make amendes of so cruel a dede;
Avysement is good, byfore the nede.

50

"Wo worth the faire gemme vertules!
Wo worth that herbe also that dooth no boote! 345
Wo worth that beaute that is routheles!
Wo worth that wight that tret ech undir foote!
And ye, that ben of beaute crop and roote,
If therwithal in yow ther be no routhe,
Than is it harm ye lyven, by my trouthe! 350

51

"And also thenk wel that this is no gaude;
For me were levere thow and I and he
Were hanged, than I sholde ben his baude,
As heigh as men myghte on us alle se;
I am thyn em, the shame were to me 355
As wel as the, if that I sholde assente,
Thorugh myn abet, that he thyn honour shente.

338. JGgH5H3H2PhCx ye *for* yow; liste, *so* H1GgH5, JTh listeth, *rest* list.
339. CpClH1AGg ye *for* we. 340. CpJH1 Na *for* No. 347. Cp eche, J ich. 349.
CpaCx *om.* ther, JGgTh ne *for* ther. 351. JGgH5S1H2 it *for* this. 354. CpClH1
S1H4Th ysee. 357. abet, *so* ClH1S1Th, Cp abbet, H3 abette, JD abit, A abite,
H4 habit, Gg abek, H2Ph abettyng, H5 advice, R doyng, Cx counsayl.

52

"Now understond, for I yow nought requere
To bynde yow to hym thorugh no byheste,
But only that ye make hym bettre cheere   360
Than ye han doon or this, and moore feste,
So that his lif be saved at the leste:
This al and som, and pleynly, oure entente;
God help me so! I nevere other mente.

53

"Lo, this requeste is nat but skile, ywys,   365
Ne doute of reson, parde, is ther noon.
I sette the worste, that ye dreden this:
Men wolde wondren sen hym come and goon;
There ayeins answere I thus, anoon,
That every wight, but he be fool of kynde,   370
Wol deme it love of frendshipe in his mynde.

54

"What! who wol demen, though he se a man
To temple go, that he thymages eteth?
Thenk ek, how wel and wisly that he kan
Governe hym self, that he no thyng foryeteth,   375
That where he cometh, he pris and thank hym geteth;
And ek, therto, he shal come here so selde,
What fors were it though al the town byhelde?

---

363. αH5DCx This is al. 366. GgCx tresoun. 367. Cp dredden, J drede. 368.
ClαGgH3CxTh to se hym, A that seen hym; γS1 or *for* and. 369. R And ther ayayn.
372. Cp wold, J wil. 373. S1 chirche. 376. Cp commeth, JH1 comth; αA þank & pris.
378. CpJTh force; αH5H3Cx if *for* though.

55

"Swych love of frendes regneth al this town,
And wry yow in that mantel evere mo; 380
And, god so wys be my savacioun,
As I have seyd, youre beste is to do soo;
But goode nece, alwey to stynte his wo,
So lat youre daunger sucred ben a lite,
That of his deth ye be nat for to wite." 385

56

Criseyde, which that herde hym in this wise,
Thoughte: "I shal felen what he mene, ywis."
"Now, em," quod she, "what wolde ye devise?
What is youre rede I sholde don of this?"
"That is wel seyd," quod he, "certein, best is 390
That ye hym love ayeyn for his lovynge;
As love for love is skilful guerdonynge.

57

"Thenk ek how elde wasteth every houre,
In eche of yow, a partie of beaute;
And therfore, or that age the devoure, 395
Go love; for olde, ther wol no wight of the;
Lat this proverbe a loore unto yow be:
'To late ywar, quod beaute, whan it paste';
And elde daunteth daunger at the laste.

382. CpH1J seyde; H3H5 ys so to doo, J is for to do, R is you to do, A *om.* soo.
383. goode, *so* GgH5H3H4, *rest* good; γS1 But alwey good nece. 384. αGgH5 *om.* so.
387. GgH5H4AS1H3Cx 3e *for* he; CpClH2PhRTh meneth, H5 woll mene. 390.
CpH1J seyde. 395. H2PhHH5ACx yow *for* the. 398. α To late y was ware (**Ph was
y**); **R** whan beaute is al paste.

58

"The kynges fool is wont to crien loude,   400
Whan that hym thinketh a womman berth hire hye,
'So longe mote ye lyve, and alle proude,
Til crowes feet be growe under youre eye,
And sende yow than a myrour in to prye,
In which that ye may se youre face a morwe,   405
I bidde wisshe yow no more sorwe'."

59

With this he stynte, and caste adown the hede;
And she began to breste a wepe anoon,
And seyde: "allas! for wo why nere I deede?
For of this world the feyth is al agoon.   410
Allas! what sholden straunge to me doon,
Whan he that for my beste frende I wende,
Ret me to love, and sholde it me defende?

60

"Allas! I wolde han trusted, douteles,
That if that I thorugh my disaventure   415
Hadde loved outher hym or Achilles,
Ector, or any mannes creature,
Ye nolde han had no mercy ne mesure
On me, but alwey had me in repreve.
This false worlde, allas! who may it leve?   420

403. αGgH5H3Cx waxen (H2PhCx wox). 405. ClH1H2PhGgH5 *om.* that. 406. γS1Th Nece I bidde wisshe. 407. H2PhGgH5AD his hede. 411. H3RCx schuld a straunger (H3 strange); H1H2Ph straunge folke (H1 folke *by later hand*), GgH5 straunge men.

61

"What! is this al the joye and al the feste?
Is this youre reed? is this my blisful cas?
Is this the verray mede of youre byheste?
Is al this peynted proces seyd, allas!
Right for this fyn? O lady myn, Pallas,   425
Thow in this dredful cas for me purveye;
For so astoned am I that I deye."

62

With that she gan ful sorwfully to syke.
"A! may it be no bet?" quod Pandarus;
"By god, I shal no more come here this wyke,   430
And god to-forn, that am mystrusted thus.
I se wel that ye sette lite of us,
Or of oure deth, allas! I woful wrecche!
Might he yit lyve, of me were nought to recche.

63

"O cruel god! O dispitouse Marte!   435
O Furies thre of helle! on yow I crye!
So lat me nevere out of this hous departe,
If that I mente harm or vilenye!
But sith I se my lord mot nedes dye,
And I with hym, here I me shryve, and seye   440
That wikkedly ye don us bothe deye.

---

432. γS1 I se ful wel that. 434. were, *so* JRH3H4 (β), *rest* is. 435. dispitouse, *so*
H1JGg, *rest* dispitous. 438. αS1 *om.* that; CpClH1AS1H2Ph or any vilenye.

64

"But sith it liketh yow that I be dede,
By Neptunus, that god is of the see,
Fro this forth shal I nevere eten brede,
Til I myn owen herte blood may see;   445
For certeyn, I wol deye as soone as he."
And up he sterte, and on his wey he raughte,
Til she agayn hym by the lappe kaughte.

65

Criseyde, which that wel neigh starf for feere,
So as she was the ferfulleste wight   450
That myghte be, and herde ek with hire ere,
And saugh the sorwful ernest of the knyght,
And in his preier ek saugh noon unryght,
And for the harm that myghte ek fallen moore,
She gan to rewe and drede hire wonder soore;   455

66

And thoughte thus: "unhappes fallen thikke
Alday for love, and in such manere cas,
As men ben cruel in hemself, and wikke;
And if this man sle here hymself, allas!
In my presence, it wol be no solas.   460
What men wolde of it deme, I kan nat seye;
It nedeth me ful sleighly for to pleie."

---

443. CpJ Neptimus. 449. α *om.* which. 454. Jα ek þat myght. 455. CpGgTh
dredde, H4S1Cx dred, Cl dradde, H5 drad, H1 dredded. 457. αH5S1RCx *om.* and.
458. αGgH5 And *for* As. 460. Jα nyl *for* wol. 462. H4Cx wisly.

67

And with a sorwful sik she seyde thrie:
"A, lord! what me is tid a sory chaunce!
For myn estat lith in a jupartie,   465
And ek myn emes lif is in balaunce;
But natheles, with goddes governaunce,
I shal so doon, myn honour shal I kepe,
And ek his lif"; and stynte for to wepe.

68

"Of harmes two the lesse is for to chese;   470
Yit have I levere maken hym good chere
In honour, than myn emes lyf to lese."
"Ye seyn, ye no thyng elles me requere?"
"No, wis," quod he, "myn owen nece dere."
"Now wel," quod she, "and I wol do my peyne;   475
I shal myn herte ayeins my lust constreyne.

69

"But that I nyl nat holden hym in honde:
Ne love a man ne kan I naught, ne may,
Ayeins my wil; but elles wol I fonde,
Myn honour sauf, plese hym fro day to day.   480
Therto nolde I nat ones have seyd nay,
But that I drede, as in my fantasye.
But cesse cause, ay cesseth maladie.

---

465. γS1 lith now in jupartie (H1 now in a jupartye); JGgH5PhCx *om.* **a.**
466. ClH4PhCxTh lyth *for* is, GgH5H2R *om.* is, H3 as *for* is; GgH5R in **a**
balaunce. 467. H2H4GgH5H3 good *for* goddes. 471. GgH5H4H3ACx hadde. 474.
ClAS1αH5H3R ywys. 478. H2PhGg no *for* a; αGgH5 þat can no wight. 479.
αGgH5Cx his *for* my. 481. CpH1J seyde.

70

"But here I make a protestacioun:
That in this proces if ye depper go,   485
That, certeynly, for no salvacioun
Of yow, though that ye sterven bothe two,
Though al the world on o day be my fo,
Ne shal I nevere of hym han other routhe."
"I graunte wel," quod Pandare, "by my trowthe." 490

71

"But may I truste wel to yow," quod he,
"That of this thyng that ye han hight me here,
Ye wole it holden trewely unto me?"
"Ye, douteles," quod she, "myn uncle deere."
"Ne that I shal han cause in this matere,"   495
Quod he, "to pleyne, or ofter yow to preche?"
"Why, no, parde; what nedeth moore speche?"

72

Tho fillen they in other tales glade,
Tyl at the laste: "O good em," quod she tho,
"For his love which that us bothe made,   500
Tel me how first ye wisten of his wo;
Woot noon of it but ye?" He seyde: "no."
"Kan he wel speke of love," quod she, "I preye?
Tel me, for I the bet me shal purveye."

---

484. γS1 And *for* But. 485. R depper if ye go, Cx or ye further go, H4 That yf ye
dispeire in this processe go. 487. H2PhGgH5D *om.* that. 489. ClH1αGgH5RTh on *for*
o'f. 491. γS1 therto *for* to yow. 493. H2PhH5 to me, Gg here *for* unto me. 498. Cp
fellen, J fille. 500. For his love, *so* γS1H3Cx, H4 For the love, JRH2PhGgH5Th
For love of god. 504. αDS1H3Cx shal me.

73

Tho Pandarus a litel gan to smyle,   505
And seyde: "by my trouthe, I shal yow telle.
This other day, nat gon ful longe while,
Within the paleis gardyn, by a welle,
Gan he and I wel half a day to dwelle,
Right for to speken of an ordinaunce,   510
How we the Grekes myghten disavaunce.

74

"Sone after that bigonne we to lepe,
And casten with oure dartes to and fro,
Tyl at the laste he seyde, he wolde slepe,
And on the gres adoun he leyde him tho;   515
And I afer gan romen to and fro,
Til that I herde, as that I welk allone,
How he bigan ful wofully to grone.

75

"Tho gan I stalke hym softely byhynde,
And sikirly, the sothe for to seyne,   520
As I kan clepe ayein now to my mynde,
Right thus to Love he gan hym for to pleyne;
He seyde: 'lord have routhe upon my peyne,
Al have I ben rebell in myn entente,
Now *mea culpa*, lord, I me repente.   525

508. γ(-S2Dig)S1 In with. 510. αGgH5 So (H4 Lo) *for* Right. 512. α So *for* Sone; αGgS1 for to lepe. 516. And I afer, *so* JR(R affer), H2Ph And yn a fere, GgH5H4H3CxTh And I aftir, γS1 And I therafter (AD And after gan I). 517. αADRCxTh *om. second* that. 521. αH5 gan *for* kan'; H2PhGgH5ARCx *om.* now.

76

" 'O god, that at thi disposicioun
Ledest the fyn, by juste purveiaunce,
Of every wight, my lowe confessioun
Accepte in gree, and sende me swich penaunce
As liketh the; but from disesperaunce,   530
That may my goost departe awey fro the,
Thow be my sheld, for thi benignite.

77

" 'For certes, lord, so soore hath she me wounded,
That stood in blak, with lokyng of hire eyen,
That to myn hertes botme it is ysounded,   535
Thorugh which I woot that I moot nedes deyen;
This is the worste, I dar me nat bywreyen;
And wel the hotter ben the gledes rede,
That men hem wrien with asshen pale and dede.'

78

"With that he smot his hed adown anon,   540
And gan to motre, I noot what, trewely.
And I with that gan stille awey to goon,
And leet therof as no thing wist hadde I,
And com ayein anon, and stood hym by,
And seyde: 'awake! ye slepen al to longe;   545
It semeth nat that love doth yow longe,

531. αDR awey departe (H2PhR alwey). 536. JH1 dyen. 537. JClH1 bywryen. 546. H3 to longe.

79

" 'That slepen so that no man may yow wake.
Who sey evere or this so dul a man?'
'Ye frend,' quod he, 'do ye youre hedes ake
For love, and lat me lyven as I kan.'   550
But though that he for wo was pale and wan,
Yit made he tho as fressh a contenaunce,
As though he sholde have led the newe daunce.

80

"This passed forth til now, this other day,
It fel that I com romynge al allone   555
Into his chaumbre, and fond how that he lay
Upon his bed; but man so soore grone
Ne herde I nevere, and what that was his mone
Ne wiste I nought; for, as I was comynge,
Al sodeynly he lefte his compleynynge.   560

81

"Of which I took somwhat suspecioun,
And ner I com, and fond he wepte soore;
And god so wys be my savacioun,
As nevere of thyng hadde I no routhe moore;
For neither with engyn, ne with no loore,   565
Unnethes myghte I fro the deth hym kepe;
That yit fele I myn herte for hym wepe.

---

551. JGgH5R love *for* wo. 555. Cp felte, J fil; αH5AD *om.* al. 564. H2PhH5RCx
om. no, Gg not *for* no. 565. Cp engyne, J eggyng.

82

"And, god woot, nevere sith that I was born,
Was I so besy no man for to preche,
Ne nevere was to wight so depe isworn,   570
Or he me tolde who myghte ben his leche.
But now to yow rehersen al his speche,
Or alle his woful wordes for to sowne,
Ne bid me naught, but ye wol se me swowne.

83

"But for to save his lif, and elles nought,   575
And to noon harm of yow, thus am I dryven;
And for the love of god that us hath wrought,
Swich cheere hym dooth, that he and I may lyven.
Now have I plat to yow myn herte shryven;
And sith ye woot that myn entent is clene,   580
Tak hede therof, for I non yvel meene.

84

"And right good thrifte, I prey to god, have ye,
That han swich oon ykaught withoute net;
And be ye wis, as ye be fair to see,
Wel in the rynge than is the ruby set.   585
Ther were nevere two so wel ymet,
Whan ye ben his al hool, as he is youre;
Ther myghty god yit graunte us see that houre."

---

574. H2Ph Bid ȝe me not.   584. JR And ye be, H5 And yf ȝe be.   588. αH3 þat,
H5Cx All *for* Ther; yit graunte, *so* ClADS1GgH5RTh, CpJ *om.* yit, H1 graunt us
þat se þat, αH3 us graunt to se, Cx graunt us to see.

85

"Nay, therof spak I nought, a ha!" quod she;
"As helpe me god, ye shenden every deel." 590
"A! mercy, dere nece," anon quod he,
"What so I spak, I mente nat but wel,
By Mars, the god that helmed is of steel;
Now beth nat wroth, my blood, my nece dere."
"Now wel," quod she, "foryeven be it here." 595

86

With this he took his leve, and home he wente;
And, lord! so he was glad and wel bygon!
Criseyde aros, no lenger she ne stente,
But streght into hire closet went anon,
And sette hire down as stylle as any ston, 600
And every word gan up and down to wynde,
That he had seyd, as it com hire to mynde.

87

And was somdel astoned in hire thought,
Right for the newe cas; but whan that she
Was ful avysed, tho fond she right nought 605
Of peril, why she ought afered be.
For man may love, of possibilite,
A womman so his herte may to-breste,
And she not love ayein, but if hire leste.

---

589. H4 Nay nay therof speke not; R Nay nay there of ne spake not I quod sche.
591. γS1 O *for* A. 596. R With that woorde he took leve. 597. H2PhGgH5Th ʒe,
H3RCx A *for* And; γ(-AD) *om.* so, GgTh how, H5 that, A *as for* so. 598. H2PhGg
H5 & nevere *for* no lenger. 603. αGgH5Th wax *for* was. 605. H4H3Cx than *for* tho.
606. αGgH5RCx to be. 607. α For a man. 608. R so til that his herte breste. 609.
CpH1S1JH3H5 liste.

88

But as she sat allone and thoughte thus, 610
Ascry aros at scarmuch al withoute,
And men criden in the strete: "se, Troilus
Hath right now put to flight the Grekes route!"
With that gan al hire meyne for to shoute:
"A! go we se, caste up the yates wyde; 615
For thorugh this strete he moot to paleys ride;

89

"For other wey is fro the yate noon
Of Dardanus, ther opyn is the cheyne."
With that com he and al his folk anoon
An esy pas rydyng, in routes tweyne, 620
Right as his happy day was, sooth to seyne;
For which men seyn, may nat distourbed be
That shal bityden of necessitee.

90

This Troilus sat on his baye steede,
Al armed, save his hede, ful richely; 625
And wownded was his hors, and gan to blede,
On which he rood a pas ful softely;
But swich a knyghtly sighte, trewely,
As was on hym, was nat, withouten faille,
To loke on Mars, that god is of bataille; 630

610. thoughte, *so* ClH4, *rest* thought (Gg seyde). 611. H4Th **Thascry, GgH5**
þe ascry (Gg acry), H2Ph In the skye. 615. H2 latis. 616. Cp thorwgh, J thorw.
617. γS1 to *for* fro. 622. JH4RTh seith.

91

So lik a man of armes, and a knyght,
He was to seen, fulfild of heigh prowesse;
For bothe he hadde a body and a myght
To don that thing, as wel as hardynesse;
And ek to seen hym in his gere hym dresse,   635
So fressh, so yong, so worthy semed he,
It was an heven upon hym for to see.

92

His helm to-hewen was in twenty places,
That by a tyssew heng, his bak byhynde;
His sheld to-dasshed was with swerdes and maces,   640
In which men myghte many an arwe fynde,
That thirled hadde horn and nerf and rynde;
And ay the peple cryde: "here cometh oure joye,
And, next his brother, holder up of Troye!"

93

For which he wex a litel reed for shame,   645
Whan he the peple upon hym herde cryen,
That to byholde it was a noble game,
How sobreliche he caste adown his eyen.
Criseyda gan al his chere aspien,
And leet it so softe in hire herte synke,   650
That to hire self she seyde: "who yaf me drynke?"

---

636. worthy, *so* JGgH5RH3Cx (β), γα weldy. 640. GgH4RCx *om.* was; GgH5R
& with macis. 641. CpH1 myght, J myghtyn. 646. αGgH5Th Whan he so herd
þe peple on hym crien (H4 herde so; Th upon). 648. γ(-AD)JCx down. 649. Criseyda,
so CpH1J; H2PhRTh Cryseyd anon gan. 650. CpAJH4 *om.* it, H1DS1GgH5R so
softe it.

94

For of hire owen thought she wex al reed,
Remembryng hire right thus: "lo, this is he
Which that myn uncle swerith he moot be deed,
But I on hym have mercy and pitee";   655
And with that thought, for pure ashamed, she
Gan in hire hed to pulle, and that as faste,
Whil he and al the peple forby paste.

95

And gan to caste and rollen up and down
Withinne hire thought his excellent prowesse,   660
And his estat, and also his renown,
His wit, his shap, and ek his gentilesse;
But moost hire favour was, for his distresse
Was al for hire, and thought it was a routhe
To sleen swich oon, if that he mente trouthe.   665

96

Now myghte som envious jangle thus:
"This was a sodeyn love; how myghte it be
That she so lightly loved Troilus
Right for the firste syghte, ye parde?"
Now whoso seith so, mot he nevere ythe;   670
For every thyng, a gynnyng hath it nede
Or al be wrought, withouten any drede.

---

656. JR worde *for* thought; RS2Dig for pure schame. 657. αS2Dig *om.* to. 664. Gg þouȝte; H2PhGgH5 it were routhe (Gg a reuthe). 667. H2PhGgH5 þis *for* it. 669. firste, *so* ClH1GgH5H4, *rest* first; syghte, *so* H4(sihte), *rest* syght. 670. α þat *for* so; αGgH5S1R nevere mote he (H5 evill *for* nevere); ythe, *so* CpH1J, *rest* the.

97

For I sey nat that she so sodeynly
Yaf hym hire love, but that she gan enclyne
To like hym first, and I have told yow whi;   675
And after that, his manhod and his pyne
Made love withinne hire for to myne;
For which, by proces and by good servyse,
He gat hire love, and in no sodeyn wyse.

98

And also blisful Venus, wel arrayed,   680
Sat in hire seventhe hous of hevene tho,
Disposed wel, and with aspectes payed,
To helpen sely Troilus of his woo;
And, soth to seyn, she nas not al a foo
To Troilus in his nativitee;   685
God woot that wel the sonner spedde he.

99

Now lat us stynte of Troilus a throwe,
That rideth forth, and lat us torne faste
Unto Criseyde, that heng hire hed ful lowe,
Ther as she sat allone, and gan to caste   690
Where on she wolde apoynte hire at the laste,
If it so were hire em ne wolde cesse,
For Troilus upon hire for to presse.

---

675. αTh þo *for* first. 676. Cp manhode, J manhed. 677. H2PhH3CxS2Dig
wiþin her hert for; R Made love in her inwardly for; Th Made that love within her
gan to myne. 679. αGgH5Th He wan. 686. Gg sonere, S1 soner, R sunder.

100

And, lord! so she gan in hire thought argue
In this matere of which I have yow tolde, 695
And what to don best were, and what eschuwe,
That plited she ful ofte in many folde.
Now was hire herte warm, now was it colde;
And what she thoughte, somwhat shal I write,
As to myn auctour listeth for tendite. 700

101

She thoughte wel, that Troilus persone
She knew by syghte, and ek his gentilesse,
And thus she seyde: "al were it nat to doone,
To graunte hym love, yit, for his worthynesse,
It were honour with pleye, and with gladnesse, 705
In honestee with swich a lord to deele,
For myn estat and also for his heele.

102

"Ek wel woot I, my kynges sone is he;
And sith he hath to se me swich delit,
If I wolde outreliche his sighte flee, 710
Paraunter he myghte have me in despit,
Thorugh which I myghte stonde in worse plit;
Now were I wis, me hate to purchace,
Withouten nede, ther I may stonde in grace?

---

694. JH4 A *for* And; JRH3H2Ph herte *for* thought, Cp thoughte. 696. GgH5Cx
to eschewe, H2Ph teschewe. 697. GgH5RH3Cx manye a fold. 701. thoughte, *so* GgH5
H4, *rest* thought; JRH4H2Ph first, GgH5 ek þis *for* wel. 703. H2PhGgH5 And seyd
þus; JRH4 And also thought it were (J nere). 709. CpH1J delite. 710. sighte, *so*
CpH1, *rest* sight. 712. myghte, *so* CpJGg, *rest* myght. 714. H2PhH4 wher.

103

"In every thyng, I woot, ther lith mesure; 715
For though a man forbede dronkenesse,
He naught forbet that every creature
Be drynkeles for alwey, as I gesse.
Ek sith I woot for me is his destresse,
I ne aughte nat for that thing hym despise, 720
Sith it is so, he meneth in good wyse.

104

"And ek I knowe, of longe tyme agon,
His thewes goode, and that he is nat nyce.
Navauntour, seith men, certein he is noon;
To wis is he to doon so gret a vice; 725
Ne als I nyl hym nevere so cherice,
That he may make avaunt, by juste cause,
He shal me nevere bynde in swich a clause.

105

"Now sette a cas: the hardest is, ywys,
Men myghten demen that he loveth me; 730
What dishonour were it unto me, this?
May ich hym lette of that? why nay, parde!
I knowe also, and alday heere and se,
Men loven wommen al biside hire leve,
And whan hem list no more, lat hem leve. 735

---

720. JRH4H3H2D *om.* ne. 721. JRH4 Yif it be so. 724. CpClH1 is he. 726.
JGgH5R Ne also, H2Ph Ne as, Cx And eke. 729. H2Ph Now set y a cas, H4 Now I
sette cas, Th Now sette I case. 731. JRH4 to myn estat is this. 734, 735. H2PhGg
H5ATh (A *late hand over erasure*):—
Men lovyn wymmen al þis toun about
Be they þe wors whi nay wiþ outyn dout
(Gg þour al; H2Ph *om.* whi). 735. CpH1 namore, J no lengere; γS1 byleve.

106

"I thenk ek how he able is for to have
Of al this noble towne the thriftieste,
To ben his love, so she hire honour save;
For out and out he is the worthieste,
Save only Ector, which that is the beste;   740
And yit his lif al lith now in my cure.
But swich is love, and ek myn aventure.

107

"Ne me to love, a wonder is it nought;
For wel wot I my self, so god me spede,
Al wolde I that no man wiste of this thought,   745
I am oon the faireste, out of drede,
And goodlieste, whoso taketh hede,
And so men seyn, in al the town of Troie.
What wonder is, though he of me have joye?

108

"I am myn owene womman, wel at ese,   750
I thank it god, as after myn estat,
Right yong, and stonde unteyd in lusty leese,
Withouten jalousie or swich debat;
Shal noon housbonde seyn to me 'chek mat.'
For either they ben ful of jalousie,   755
Or maisterful, or loven novelrye.

736. H2PhGgA able he is, H5 he is abyll; Th worthy *for* able; ClADH2PhCxTh
om. for. 736-738. JRH4:—
> Ek wot I wel he worthy is to have
> Of wommen in this world the thriftyeste
> As ferforth as she may hir honour save

(H4 Yit *for* Ek). 737. γ(-S2Dig) Of al this ilk noble. 738. H2PhGgH5Th That
woman is so she. 741. al lith now, *so* CpClH1, GgH5S1H3Cx now lyth al, JTh lith
al now, PhD lith now al, H2 lith now in al, R *om.* al, H4A *om.* al, *om.* now. 743-
749. H5 *omits stanza.* 745. γ noon *for* no man; JR my *for* this. 746. JRH4GgDS1
oon of the fayreste. 747. CpADGg who that, ThS1 who so that. 749. ClH2PhH4
of. 491. γS1 therto *for* to yow. 493. H2PhH5 to me, Gg here *for* unto me. 498. Cp.
is it, Gg ist. 753. CpJ debate. 754. H4 Ne shal; Cp housbond, J housband; CpJ
mate.

109

"What shal I doon? to what fyn lyve I thus?
Shal I nat love, in cas if that me leste?
What, pardieux! I am nat religious.
And though that I myn herte sette at reste   760
Upon this knyght, that is the worthieste,
And kepe alwey myn honour and my name,
By alle right it may do me no shame."

110

But right as whan the sonne shyneth brighte,
In March, that chaungeth ofte tyme his face,   765
And that a cloude is put with wynd to flighte,
Which oversprat the sonne as for a space,
A cloudy thought gan thorugh hire soule pace,
That overspradde hire brighte thoughtes alle,
So that for feere almost she gan to falle.   770

111

That thought was this: "allas! syn I am free,
Sholde I now love, and putte in jupartie
My sikernesse, and thrallen libertee?
Allas! how dorste I thenken that folie?
May I nat wel in other folk aspie   775
Hire dredful joye, hire constreynte, and hire peyne?
Ther loveth noon, that she nath wey to pleyne.

---

758. leste, *so* CpTh, H4S1Cx lest, *rest* liste (list).   761. JRH4 Unwist to hym
þat is (J *of for* to).   768. H3H2PhH4RS2Cx herte, Dig thought *for* soule.   772. CpJ
put.   774. Cp dorst, J durst.   775. JR by *for* in.   777. GgA why, J wex *for* wey; H2
wiþout boþe care & peyn, H4 that she noht owith to pleyne, H5 þat he have cause
to pleyne.

112

"For love is yit the moste stormy lyf,
Right of hym self, that evere was bigonne;
For evere som mystrust, or nice strif, 780
Ther is in love; som cloude is over that sonne.
Therto we wrecched wommen nothing konne,
Whan us is wo, but wepe and sitte and thinke;
Oure wreche is this, oure owen wo to drynke.

113

"Also thise wikked tonges ben so preste 785
To speke us harm; ek men ben so untrewe,
That right anon, as cessed is hire leste,
So cesseth love, and forth to love a newe;
But harm ydoon is doon, whoso it rewe;
For though thise men for love hem first to-rende, 790
Ful sharp bygynnynge breketh ofte at ende.

114

"How ofte tyme hath it yknowen be,
The tresoun that to wommen hath ben do!
To what fyn is swich love, I kan nat see,
Or wher bycometh it, whan it is ago. 795
Ther is no wight that woot, I trowe so,
Wher it bycometh; lo, no wight on it sporneth;
That erst was no thing, into nought it torneth.

781. GgH₅ADRCxTh þe *for* that. 792. JRH₄H₂PhGgH₅Th How ofte tyme may men rede and sen. 795. Cp bycommeth, JClS1 becomth; CpH1S1GgR whan that; ago, *so* CpH1JAH₅, H₂Cx gone, *rest* go. 797. Cp bycommeth, J becomth. 798. H₂PhGgH₅ no þing *for* nought.

115

"How bisy, if I love, ek moste I be
To plesen hem that jangle of love, and dremen,   800
And coye hem, that they seye noon harm of me.
For though ther be no cause, yit hem semen
Al be for harm that folk hire frendes quemen;
And who may stoppen every wikked tonge,
Or sown of belles whil that thei ben ronge?"   805

116

And after that, hire thought bygan to clere,
And seide: "he which that nothing undertaketh,
No thyng acheveth, be hym looth or deere."
And with an other thought hire herte quaketh;
Than slepeth hope, and after drede awaketh;   810
Now hoot, now cold; but thus bitwixen tweye,
She rist hire up, and wente hire for to pleye.

117

Adown the steyre anon right tho she wente
Into the gardyn, with hire neces thre,
And up and down they made many a wente,   815
Flexippe, and she, Tárbe, and Antigone,
To pleyen, that it joye was to see;
And other of hire wommen, a grete route,
Hire folwede in the gardyn al abowte.

---

800. H2PhH4GgAS1 demen. 801. CpClH1D *om.* that. 806. H3H4H5ADCx **gan to clere,** CpH1S1RTh **gan for to clere.** 808. γS1 nacheveth. 812. Cp wente here, JGgH5H4 *om. second* hire. 813. JRH4 And doun. 814. JR hir, H2Ph a *for* the. 815. γ ther, H3 the *for* they, AD ther made thei. 816. γS1 *om. first* and; CpClH1S2 Tharbe, H2Ph Tarke. 819. Cp foloweden, J folwed.

118

This yerd was large, and rayled alle thaleyes,   820
And shadwed wel with blosmy bowes grene,
And benched newe, and sonded alle the weyes,
In which she walketh arm in arm bitwene;
Til at the laste Antigone the shene
Gan on a Troian songe to singen cleere,   825
That it an hevene was hire vois to here.

119

She seyde: "O love, to whom I have and shal   CANTUS
Ben humble subgit, trewe in myn entente,   ANTIGONE
As I best kan, to yow, lord, yeve ich al,
For evere mo, myn hertes lust to rente.   830
For nevere yit thi grace no wight sente
So blisful cause as me, my lif to lede
In alle joie and seurte, out of drede.

120

"Ye, blisful god, han me so wel byset
In love, iwys, that al that bereth lif   835
Ymagynen ne koude how to be bet;
For, lord, withouten jalousie or strif,
I love oon which that is most ententif
To serven wel, unweri or unfeyned,
That evere was, and leest with harm desteyned.   840

---

822. JGgH3H2H4Cx Ibenched (*om*. And).   823. H3H4GgH5A walked, R walke.
825. JRH4H2PhGgH5 lay *for* songe (H4 say).   827. H2PhGgH5 *om*. O.   834.
JClH1GgH5CxTh The *for* Ye; H5 goddis; JACxTh hath.   838. JClH2PhH5D *om*.
that; CpH1AH4Th moost is.   840. ClH1AH2PhH3 distreyned, H4 disseynid.

121

"As he that is the welle of worthynesse,
Of trouthe ground, mirour of goodlyhede,
Of wit Appollo, stoon of sikernesse,
Of vertu roote, of lust fynder and hede,
Thorugh which is alle sorwe fro me dede,   845
Iwis, I love hym best, so doth he me;
Now good thrifte have he, wherso that he be!

122

"Whom sholde I thanken but yow, god of love,
Of al this blisse in which to bathe I gynne?
And thanked be ye, lord, for that I love!   850
This is the righte lif that I am inne,
To flemen alle manere vice and synne;
This dooth me so to vertue for tentende,
That, day by day, I in my wil amende.

123

"And whoso seith that for to love is vice,   855
Or thraldom, though he feele in it destresse,
He outher is envyous, or right nyce,
Or is unmyghty, for his shrewednesse,
To loven; for swich manere folk, I gesse,
Defamen love, as nothing of it knowe;   860
Thei speken, but thei benten nevere his bowe.

---

843. JClH₁S₁ secrenesse, H4Cx secretnesse, *rest* sikernesse. 845. alle, *so* CpH₁J, *rest* al *or* all; H3S₁Cx al my sorow. 848. Cp. shulde, JH1 shold. 850. JRH2Ph GgH5 thow *for* ye. 851. righte, *so* GgH5R, *rest* right. 855. H2PhGgH5H3CxTh þat *for* so. 859. JRH4 lo, H5 so *for* for. 860. JRH2PhH5 hym, H4 hem *for* it.

124

"What is the sonne wers, of kynde right,
Though that a man, for feblesse of his eyen,
May nat endure on it to see for bright?
Or love the wers, though wrecches on it crien?   865
No wele is worth, that may no sorwe dryen.
And, forthi, who that hath an hed of verre,
Fro caste of stones war hym in the werre!

125

"But I with al myn herte, and al my myght,
As I have seyd, wol love unto my laste   870
My deere herte, and al myn owen knyght,
In which myn herte growen is so faste,
And his in me, that it shal evere laste.
Al dredde I first to love hym to bigynne,
Now woot I wel, ther is no peril inne."   875

126

And of hir song right with that word she stente,
And therwithal, "now nece," quod Criseyde,
"Who made this songe now with so good entente?"
Antigone answerde anoon, and seyde:
"Madame, iwys, the goodlieste mayde   880
Of gret estat in al the town of Troye;
And let hire lif in most honour and joye."

864. JR hym *for* it. 868. JRH4H5ADS1 For *for* Fro. 870. CpJ. seyde. 878.
C1H2PhGgCx *om.* now.

127

"Forsothe, so it semeth by hire songe,"
Quod tho Criseyde, and gan therwith to sike,
And seyde: "lord, is ther swych blisse amonge   885
Thise loveres, as they konne faire endite?"
"Ye, wis," quod fresshe Antigone, the white,
"For al the folk that han or ben on lyve
Ne konne wel the blisse of love discryve.

128

"But wene ye that every wrecche woot   890
The parfit blisse of love? why nay, iwys;
They wenen al be love, if oon be hoot;
Do wey, do wey, they woot no thyng of this!
Men mosten axe at seyntes if it is
Aught faire in hevene; why? for they kan telle;   895
And axen fendes is it foul in helle."

129

Criseyde unto that purpos naught answerde,
But seyde: "ywys, it wol be nyght as faste."
But every word which that she of hire herde,
She gan to prenten in hire herte faste,   900
And ay gan love hire lasse for tagaste
Than it dide erst, and synken in hire herte,
That she wax somwhat able to converte.

---

887. H2PhGgH5H4H3ADS1 ywis *for* wis. 891. why nay, *so* γJTh (S1 nay nay), *rest om.* why. 893. H4 wete. 894. H2PhH4ClDTh of *for* at. 895. ClCx konne. 896. JGgH5S1 axeth, H3 askes; is it, *so* γS1JH3, *rest* if it be (H4 if ouht faile in helle). 897. *So* γS1H3CxTh (S1 lyte *for* naught), *rest* therto no thing hir answerede (JH5 no thing therto; H2Ph her no þing; H4 *om.* hir; H5 ne *for* hir). 901. CpH1 DPh lasse hire.

130

The dayes honour, and the hevenes eye,
The nyghtes foo,—al this clepe I the sonne,—   905
Gan westren faste, and downward for to wrye,
As he that hadde his dayes cours yronne;
And white thynges wexen dymme and donne
For lakke of lyght, and sterres for tapere,
That she and al hire folk in went yfeere.   910

131

So whan it liked hire to go to reste,
And voided weren tho that voiden oughte,
She seyde, that to slepen wel hire leste.
Hire wommen sone unto hire bed hire broughte.
Whan al was hust, tho lay she stille, and thoughte   915
Of al this thing the manere and the wise;
Reherce it nedeth nought, for ye ben wise.

132

A nyghtyngale, upon a cedre grene,
Under the chambre wal ther as she lay,
Ful loude song ayein the moone shene,   920
Paraunter, in his briddes wise, a lay
Of love, that made hire herte fressh and gay.
That herkened she so longe in good entente,
Til at the laste the dede slepe hire hente.

908. *So* γS1H3CxTh, H5 And wt þyng gan waxe dym and dunne, *rest gan to* waxen donne. 909. H2PhGgH5Cx and sterris to apere. 910. H2 went home, GgPhH4Cx hom wente. 912. CpClH1AH4H5Th thei *for* tho. 914. CpClH1Th til, AD to, H3H4Cx into, R in *for* unto. 915. γH3H5Th than, H2Ph þat *for* tho. 916. GgH4Cx gyse. 922. JRH4H2PhGgH5 Of love which þat made his herte gay (J weche; H2Ph her *for* his). 923. JRH4H5 Hym, Gg That *over erasure later*, H2Ph Her *for* That. 924. ClH3Cx That *for* Til.

133

And, as she slep, anon right tho hire mette,   925
How that an egle, fethered whit as bon,
Under hire brest his longe clawes sette,
And out hire herte rente, and that anon,
And dide his herte into hire brest to gon;
Of which she nought agroos, ne no thyng smerte;   930
And forth he fleigh, with herte left for herte.

134

Now lat hire slepe, and we oure tales holde
Of Troilus, that is to paleis riden,
Fro the scarmuch of the which I tolde,
And in his chambre sit, and hath abiden   935
Til two or thre of his messages yeden
For Pandarus, and soughten hym so faste,
Til they hym founde, and broughte hym at the laste.

135

This Pandarus come lepyng in at ones,
And seyde thus: "who hath ben wel ibete   940
To day with swerdes, and with slynge stones,
But Troilus that hath caught hym an hete?"
And gan to jape, and seyde: "lord, ye swete!
But ris, and lat us soupe and go to reste";
And he answerde: "do we as the leste."   945

---

925. GgH5H4RAD sche *for* hire. 928. γS1H3H5Th he rente. 937. γS1Th ful *for* so. 941. slynge, *so* H3, H1 sleynge, CpCl slyng, J slynke, Gg slynging. 943. CpClH1S2H2Ph lord so ye swete. 945. γS1H3Th answerde hym; GgH5H4RA ȝe, D you *for* the.

136

With al the haste goodly that they myghte,
They spedde hem fro the soper, and to bedde;
And every wight out at the dore hym dyghte,
And where hym liste upon his wey hym spedde;
But Troilus, that thoughte his herte bledde   950
For wo, til that he herde som tydynge,
He seyde: "frend, shal I now wepe or synge?"

137

Quod Pandarus: "ly stylle, and lat me slepe;
And don thyn hood; thy nedes spedde be;
And chese if thow wolt synge, or daunce, or lepe;   955
At shorte wordes, thow shalt truste in me.
Sire, my nece wol do wel by the,
And love the best, by god, and by my trouthe,
But lakke of pursuyt make it in thi slouthe.

138

"For thus ferforth have I thi werk bigonne,   960
Fro day to day, til this day, by the morwe,
Hire love of frendshipe have I to the wonne;
And therto hath she leyd hire feyth to borwe.
Algate a foot is hameled of thi sorwe."
What sholde I lenger sermon of it holde?   965
As ye han herd byfore, al he hym tolde.

---

947. γS1 unto *for* and to. 948. CpJ dyght. 949. CpClH1 he *for second* hym.
950. H2PhGgH5H4 *om.* But; γTh *om.* that. 953. JRH3ACxTh be *for* ly. 955.
JRS1H2PhAD daunce or synge; GgH5H3H4RAS2CxTh *om. first* or. 956. γTh
trowen me, S1 trusten me, Gg trostyn in me, RH5 trust on me, H2PhH4 trust to me.
960. CpClH1S2H3Th I have. 963. γ also, Th therfore *for* therto. 966. CpJ herde.

139

But right as floures, thorugh the cold of nyght
Iclosed, stoupen on hire stalkes lowe,
Redressen hem ayein the sonne bright,
And spreden on hire kynde cours by rowe, 970
Right so gan tho his eyen up to throwe
This Troilus, and seyde: "O Venus deere,
Thi myght, thi grace, yheried be it here!"

140

And to Pandare he held up bothe his hondes,
And seyde: "lord, al thyn be that I have; 975
For I am hool, al brosten ben my bondes;
A thousand Troyes whoso that me yave,
Ech after other, god so wys me save,
Ne myghte me so gladen; lo, myn herte,
It spredeth so for joie, it wol to-sterte. 980

141

"But, lord, how shal I doon, how shal I lyven?
Whan shal I next my deere herte see?
How shal this longe tyme awey be dryven,
Til that thow be ayein at hire fro me?
Thow maist answere: 'abid, abid'; but he 985
That hangeth by the nekke, soth to seyne,
In grete disese abideth for the peyne."

---

968. CpClH1 stalk, GgH5H3H4 stalke. 970. JRH4H2Ph in *for* on. 972. H2PhGg
H5H4R *om.* O. 976. CpH1AH3Th and *for* al, H5 all hol and. 977. CpClH1S2
Troyens. 978. JR god so my soule save, H3Cx god so me wisse and save, H5 so
wisse me and save (*om.* god). 980. H3H5Cx oute sterte. 984. H2PhH4RCx *om.* that.

142

"Al esily, now, for the love of Marte!"
Quod Pandarus, "for every thing hath tyme.
So longe abid til that the nyght departe;   990
For also siker as thow list here by me,
And god to-forn, I wol be ther at pryme;
And, forthi, werk som what as I shal seye,
Or on som other wight this charge leye.

143

"For, pardee, god woot, I have evere yit   995
Ben redy the to serve, and to this nyght
Have I nat feyned, but emforth my wit
Don al thi lust, and shal with al my myght.
Do now as I shal seyn, and fare aright;
And if thow nylt, wite al thi self thi care,   1000
On me is nought along thyn yvel fare.

144

"I woot wel that thow wiser art than I
A thousand fold, but if I were as thow,
God helpe me so, as I wolde outrely,
Right of myn owen hond, write hire right now   1005
A lettre, in which I wolde hire tellen how
I ferde amys, and hire biseche of routhe;
Now help thi self, and leve it nought for slouthe.

---

997. CpA evenforth, H3 eneforthe, RCx enforced, D forced, H2 evere for, Ph evere forþ, H4 with al, Gg evene with *for* emforth. 998. R To do, Cx For I have do (*om.* and shal). 1005. γJ *om. first* Right; H2PhH4Th write her now, H5 wryte hir as now, Cx wryte to her now. 1006. H2PhRCx telle her how. 1008. RCx let *for* leve it; H2PhH5H3RCxTh for no *for* nought for.

145

"And I my self shal therwith to hire gon;
And whan thow woost that I am with hire there,   1010
Worth upon a courser right anon,
Ye, hardily, right in thi beste gere,
And rid forth by the place, as nought ne were,
And thow shalt fynde us, if I may, sittynge
At som wyndowe, into the strete lokynge.   1015

146

"And if the list, than maistow us salue,
And upon me make thow thi contenaunce;
But, by thi lif, be war and faste eschue
To tarien ought,—god shilde us fro meschaunce!
Rid forth thi wey, and hold thi governaunce;   1020
And we shal speke of the somwhat, I trowe,
Whan thow art gon, to don thyn eris glowe.

147

"Towchyng thi lettre, thow art wys ynough,
I woot thow nylt it dygneliche endite;
As make it with thise argumentes tough,   1025
Ne scryvenliche, or craftily thow it write;
Biblotte it with thi teris ek a lite,
And if thow write a goodly word al softe,
Though it be good, reherce it nought to ofte.

1009. γS1 wol. 1010. JH2PhH4Gg *om.* that. 1011. γ(-Cl)H2PhTh Worth thow
upon, H3 Lepe thou upon. 1015. H2PhGgH5 In *for* At. 1017. JClGgH3PhCx *om.*
thow, H2R thow make. 1018. JRH4H2PhGgH5 be war þat thow eschue. 1019. H2Ph
GgH5H4 it *for* us. 1021. JR wol; Cp speek, J spek. 1024. J clerkissly, Cx clerkly,
H4 clergaly, R papally, GgH5 dyneleche ne mystileche. 1025. H2Ph Or, H4 Ne *for*
As. 1026. γS1H3Th scryvenyssh, J scryveynyssliche; JRH4GgH5Cx ne *for* or;
RCx *om.* thow; JRH4GgH5H3 *om.* it.

148

"For though the beste harpour upon lyve   1030
Wolde on the beste sowned joly harpe
That evere was, with alle his fyngres fyve,
Touche ay o streng, or ay o werbul harpe,
Were his nayles poynted nevere so sharpe,
It sholde maken every wight to dulle,   1035
To here his glee, and of his strokes fulle.

149

"Ne jompre ek no discordaunt thyng yfeere,
As thus, to usen termes of phisik
In loves termes; hold of thi matere
The forme alwey, and do that it be lik;   1040
For if a peyntour wolde peynte a pyk
With asses feet, and hedde it as an ape,
It cordeth naught; so nere it but a jape."

150

This counseil liked wel to Troilus;
But, as a dredful lovere, he seyde this: 1045
"Allas, my deere brother Pandarus,
I am ashamed for to write, ywys,
Lest of myn innocence I seyde amys,
Or that she nolde it for despit receyve;
Than were I ded, ther myght it no thyng weyve."   1050

1033. Cp stryng, JH1 strenge.   1044. CpClH1DS2H3Th unto, JH5Cx *om.* to.   1048. GgR ygnoraunce.   1050. H3RDCx nothing it, H2PhH5 no þing me (*om.* it), Gg *om.* it.

151

To that Pandare answerde: "if the lest,
Do that I seye, and lat me therwith gon;
For by that lord that formede est and west,
I hope of it to brynge answere anon
Right of hire hond, and if that thow nylt noon,   1055
Lat be, and sory mote he ben his lyve,
Ayeins thi lust that helpeth the to thryve."

152

Quod Troilus: "depardieux, ich assente;
Sith that the list, I wol arise and write;
And blisful god prey ich with good entente,   1060
The viage, and the lettre I shal endite,
So spede it; and thow, Minerva the white,
Yif thow me wit my lettre to devyse";
And sette hym down, and wrote right in this wyse:

153

First he gan hire his righte lady calle,   1065
His hertes lif, his lust, his sorwes leche,
His blisse, and ek thise other termes alle,
That in swich cas thise loveres alle seche;
And in ful humble wise, as in his speche,
He gan hym recomaunde unto hire grace;   1070
To telle al how, it axeth muchel space.

1055. γH3 *om.* Right.   1065. righte, *so* Gg (ry3te), *rest* right.   1068. GgH5H4
RCxTh ye, J the *for* thise.

154

And after this, ful lowly he hire preyde
To be nat wroth, thogh he of his folye
So hardy was to hire to write, and seyde,
That love it made, or elles moste he dye,   1075
And pitously gan mercy for to crye;
And after that he seyde, and leigh ful loude,
Hym self was litel worth, and lesse he koude;

155

And that she sholde han his konnyng excused,
That litel was, and ek he dredde hire so,   1080
And his unworthynesse he ay acused;
And after that than gan he telle his wo.;
But that was endeles, withouten ho;
And seyde, he wolde in trouth alwey hym holde;
And radde it over, and gan the lettre folde.   1085

156

And with his salte teris gan he bathe
The ruby in his signet, and it sette
Upon the wex deliverliche and rathe;
Therwith a thousand tymes, or he lette,
He kiste tho the lettre that he shette,   1090
And seyde: "lettre, a blisful destine
The shapen is, my lady shal the see."

1077. GgH5R aftyrward *for* after that, H2PhCx *om.* that.   1079. S1Cx And preyde hir have, H5 Besechyng hir have.   1081. CpAS1H3Th ay he.   1083-1085. JRH4H2PhGgH5:

> But þat was infenit for ay and o,
> And how he wolde in trowth alwey hym holde,
> And his adieux made, and gan it folde.

(1083. H2 And *for* But, *rest of line omitted but supplied later by hand* 3; Ph *omits line*, γ *reading supplied later by original scribe*; JR endles *for* infenit.   1084. H4 But how; H2Ph him alwey; H5 And he wolde ay in trowthe hym holde.   1085. J *has* γ *reading for the line*; H4 And thus an eend made; R he made; Ph to *for* it.)
1091. JR iwis *for* lettre; Gg And seyde a blysful desteny parde.

157

This Pandare tok the lettre, and that by tyme
A morwe, and to his neces paleis sterte;
And faste he swor, that it was passed prime,　　　1095
And gan to jape, and seyde: "ywys, myn herte,
So fresshe it is, although it sore smerte,
I may nat slepe nevere a Mayes morwe;
I have a joly wo, a lusty sorwe."

158

Criseyde, whan that she hire uncle herde,　　　1100
With dredful herte, and desirous to here
The cause of his comynge, thus answerde:
"Now by youre fey, myn uncle," quod she, "dere,
What maner wyndes gydeth yow now here?
Tel us youre joly wo and youre penaunce;　　　1105
How ferforth be ye put in loves daunce?"

159

"By god," quod he, "I hoppe alwey byhynde."
And she to-laugh, it thought hire herte brest.
Quod Pandarus: "lok alwey that ye fynde
Game in myn hood, but herkneth, if yow lest;　　　1110
Ther is right now come into town a gest,
A Greek espie, and telleth newe thinges,
For which I come to telle yow tydynges.

1093. CpH1J toke; Cx right *for* and that; JRH4H2PhGgH5 This Pandare up
therwith and þat bytyme. 1094. JRH4H2PhGgH5Cx On morwe. 1095. CpH1J swore;
JRH4H2PhGgH5 And seide slepe ye and it is pryme (J slepe ye yit and). 1096.
JRH4H2PhGgH5 seide thus. 1097. JRH4H2PhGgH5 So fressh is it though love do it
smerte (J it is; H5 *om.* it; H2Ph *om.* do; H4 do me sterte). 1099. CpAH2PhH4Cx
and a lusty. 1103. ClAS1H2H5H4CxTh feyth. 1104. H2PhH4RCx wynd. 1107. S1
madame *for* quod he; Cp hope, J hopp. 1108. DCx hir þought, GgH4 & þouȝte,
H2PhH5RS1 as þogh. 1109. γH2Ph *om.* that. 1113. JH4 For whi, R For thy, Cx
Wherfor; JRH4H2PhGgH5 come I; γ(-A)RTh telle yow newe tydynges (R *om.*
yow).

160

"Into the gardyn go we, and ye shal here,
Al pryvely, of this a longe sermoun."   1115
With that they wenten arm in arm yfeere
Into the gardyn, from the chaumbre down;
And whan that he so fer was that the sown
Of that he spak no man heren myghte,
He seyde hire thus, and out the lettre plighte: 1120

161

"Lo, he that is al holly youres free
Hym recomaundeth lowly to youre grace,
And sente yow this lettre here by me;
Avyseth yow on it, whan ye han space,
And of som goodly answere yow purchacc,   1125
Or, helpe me god, so pleynly for to seyne,
He may nat longe lyven for his peyne."

162

Ful dredfully tho gan she stonden stylle,
And took it naught, but al hire humble chere
Gan for to chaunge, and seyde: "scrit ne bille,   1130
For love of god, that toucheth swich matere,
Ne brynge me noon; and also, uncle deere,
To myn estat have more rewarde, I preye,
Than to his lust; what sholde I more seye?

1119. H1DDigH3Th spake, Cl þey spoke; JS1 Of þat he spak ther; H2PhGgH5H4
Of his wordis no man; R no man hit heer. 1120. H2PhGgH5H4 *om.* hire. 1122.
Cp lowely, J loughly. 1123. sente, *so* CpJRH4Th, H2Ph sent to, *rest* sent. 1125.
H2PhGgH5 *om.* of.

163

"And loketh now if this be resonable,   1135
And letteth nought, for favour ne for slouthe,
To seyn a sooth; now were it covenable
To myn estat, by god, and by youre trouthe,
To taken it, or to han of hym routhe,
In harmyng of my self, or in repreve?   1140
Ber it ayein, for hym that ye on leve!"

164

This Pandarus gan on hire for to stare,
And seyde: "now is this the moste wonder
That evere I say! lat be this nyce fare.
To dethe mot I smyten be with thonder,   1145
If, for the cite which that stondeth yonder,
Wolde I a lettre to yow brynge or take
To harm of yow; what list yow thus to make?

165

"But thus ye faren, wel neigh alle and some,
That he that most desireth yow to serve,   1150
Of hym ye recche leest wher he bycome,
Or whether that he lyve or elles sterve.
But for al that that evere I may deserve,
Refuse it nat," quod he, and hente hire faste,
And in hire bosom down the lettre he thraste,   1155

1141. H4 bi god that, R for his love *for* for hym that.   1142. H2PhGgH5H4 *om.*
This; GgH5H4 upon; H2Ph Pandare þan bygan for to stare (Ph gan þan).   1143.
γH3Th grettest; GgH4 moste, *rest* most.   1145. ClH4R be smet (R smeten with a).
1147. γH3Th unto; JR To yow a lettre wolde I.   1148. CpH1AS1H3Gg thus it make.
1152. CpClH1H3JTh And, ADS1 Ne *for* Or.   1154. JH3S1 Refuseth, H2Ph Refuse
3e.   1155. γH3GgH5Th the lettre down; H2PhH4RCx *om.* he.

166

And seyde hire: "cast it now awey anon,
That folk may seen and gauren on us tweye."
Quod she: "I kan abyde til they be gon,"
And gan to smyle, and seyde hym: "em, I preye,
Swich answere as yow list youre self purveye; 1160
For, trewely, I nyl no lettre write."
"No? than wol I," quod he, "so ye endite."

167

Therwith she lough, and seyde: "go we dyne."
And he gan at hym self to jape faste,
And seyde: "nece, I have so grete a pyne 1165
For love, that everich other day I faste,"
And gan his beste japes forth to caste,
And made hire so to laughe at his folye,
That she for laughter wende for to dye.

168

And whan that she was comen into halle, 1170
"Now, em," quod she, "we wol go dyne anon,"
And gan som of hire wommen to hire calle;
And streight into hire chaumbre gan she gon.
But of hire besynesse this was on:
Amonges othere thynges, out of drede, 1175
Ful pryvely this lettre for to rede.

1156. H2PhGgH5H4 *om.* hire; γH3Th now cast it; J *om.* now. 1159. ClGgH5
H3RCx *om.* hym; R I yow preye. 1164. JGgH5R Pandare *for* he; R at hymself gan
jape. 1172. JGg for to, H4H5 in to, Cx to *for* to hire, H2Ph *om.* to hire; R And som
of hir women gan she calle. 1174. CpS1Th besynesses.

169

Avysed word by word in every lyne,
And fond no lakke, she thoughte he koude good;
And up it putte, and wente hire in to dyne.
But Pandarus, that in a studye stood,   1180
Or he was war, she took hym by the hood,
And seyde:"ye were caught or that ye wiste."
"I vouche sauf," quod he, "do what yow liste."

170

Tho wesshen they, and sette hem down and ete;
And after noon ful sleighly Pandarus   1185
Gan drawe hym to the wyndowe next the strete,
And seyde: "nece, who hath arayed thus
The yonder hous, that stant aforyeyn us?"
"Which hous?" quod she, and gan for to byholde,
And knew it wel, and whos it was hym tolde.   1190

171

And fillen forth in speche of thynges smale,
And seten in the windowe bothe tweye,
Whan Pandarus saugh tyme unto his tale,
And saugh wel that hire folk were al aweye,
"Now, nece myn, tel on," quod he, "I seye,   1195
How liketh yow the lettre that ye woot?
Kan he theron? for, by my trouthe, I noot."

1179. H2PhH4 And put hit up. 1182. H2PhGgH5H4ClH3 *om.* that. 1184.
H2PhACx to ete, H3H5 to mete. 1189. H2PhH4Cx come *for* gan. 1190. CpH1J
knewe. 1193. JClGgH5 to *for* unto. 1195. H2PhH3 quod he tel on. 1196. H2Ph
þat he wrote.

172

Therwith al rosy hewed tho wex she,
And gan to homme, and seyde: "so I trowe."
"Aquite hym wel, for goddes love," quod he; 1200
"My self to medes wol the lettre sowe."
And held his hondes up, and fel on knowe;
"Now, goode nece, be it nevere so lite,
Yif me the labour it to sowe and plite."

173

"Ye, for I kan so writen," quod she tho, 1205
"And ek I noot what I sholde to hym seye."
"Nay, nece," quod Pandare, "sey nat so;
Yit at the leeste thonketh hym, I preye,
Of his good wil, and doth hym nat to deye.
Now for the love of me, my nece deere, 1210
Refuseth nat at this tyme my preyere."

174

"Depardieux," quod she, "god leve al be wel!
God help me so, this is the firste lettre
That evere I wroot, ye, al or any del."
And into a closet, for to avise hire bettre, 1215
She wente allone, and gan hire herte unfettre
Out of desdaynes prison but a lite,
And sette hire down, and gan a lettre write.

1201. H2PhGgH5H4 þe medis. 1202. γS1H3Th sat on knowe, H5 & knelid lowe. 1203. CpJ good. 1205. H5 Full febly can I write. 1206. H2PhGgH5JRH4 *om.* to (RPh what that). 1207. S1 Nay nece myn. 1210. JGgH5 god *for* me. 1211. JGgH2 PhH4 tid *for* tyme. 1213. firste, *so* ClH1GgH4, *rest* first. 1217. H2PhH4Cx disdeynous, H3 disdeydens, R the deinous.

175

Of which to telle in short is myn entente
Theffect, as fer as I kan understonde.   1220
She thanked hym of al that he wel mente
Towardes hire, but holden hym in honde
She nolde nought, ne make hire selven bonde
In love, but as his suster, hym to plese,
She wolde ay fayn, to doon his herte an ese.   1225

176

She shette it, and to Pandare in gan goon,
Ther as he sat and loked into the strete,
And down she sette hire by hym on a stoon
Of jaspre, upon a quysshyn gold ybete,
And seyde: "as wisly help me god the grete,   1230
I nevere dide a thing with more peyne
Than writen this, to which ye me constreyne";

177

And took it hym. He thonked hire, and seyde:
"God woot, of thyng ful ofte looth bygonne
Comth ende good; and nece myn, Criseyde,   1235
That ye to hym of hard now ben ywonne
Oughte he be glad, by god and yonder sonne.
For whi, men seith, 'impressiouns lighte
Ful lightly ben ay redy to the flighte.'

1225. γH3 *om.* ay.   1226. CpH1ADS1H3H5 and into Pandare gan goon; ClAH3Gg
Pandarus; ClCx *om.* in; H2PhTh to *for* gan.   1227. R to *for* into; CpJTh *om.* the,
Cl a *for* the.   1229. H2H4A wiþ gold ybete, PhRCxTh of gold ybete.

178

"But ye han pleyed the tirant neigh to longe,   1240
And hard was it youre herte for to grave;
Now stynt, that ye no lenger on it honge,
Al wolde ye the forme of daunger save;
But hasteth yow to doon hym joye have;
For trusteth wel, to longe ydoon hardnesse   1245
Causeth despit ful often, for destresse."

179

And right as they declamed this matere,
Lo, Troilus, right at the stretes ende,
Com rydyng with his tenthe somme yfere,
Al softely, and thiderward gan bende   1250
Ther as they sete, as was his wey to wende
To paleis-ward; and Pandarus hym aspide,
And seyde: "nece, isee who comth here ride.

180

"O fle nat in,—he seith us, I suppose,—
Lest he may thynken that ye hym eschuwe."   1255
"Nay, nay," quod she, and wex as rede as rose.
With that he gan hire humblely saluwe,
With dredful chere, and oft his hewes muwe;
And up his look debonairly he caste,
And bekked on Pandare, and forth he paste.   1260

1240. Cp played, J pleid; γ(-A)S1 *om.* the. 1247. H2PhH5H4AH3CxTh declarid, R
desputed. 1249. GgH4A tensum, H2Ph x·somme, D twelve some, R companie, H5
folk, Cx people *for* tenthe somme. 1252. γH3Gg Pandarus. 1253. JRAD se, H5 seth,
GgS1Cx lo *for* isee. 1257. γ(-AD)H3H2Ph humbly to. 1258. JR eft, GgH5 eft
gan *for* oft; R colour *for* hewes; H2PhGgH5H3AD newe, H4 mevyn *for* muwe;
Cx his hew was new.

181

God woot if he sat on his hors aright,
Or goodly was biseyn, that ilke day!
God woot wher he was lik a manly knyght!
What sholde I drecche, or telle of his aray?
Criseyde, which that alle thise thynges say,   1265
To telle in short, hire liked al in fere,
His persone, his aray, his look, his chere,

182

His goodly manere, and his gentilesse,
So wel that nevere sith that she was born
Ne hadde she swych routhe of his destresse;   1270
And how so she hath hard ben here byforn,
To god hope I, she hath now kaught a thorn;
She shal nat pulle it out this nexte wyke.
God sende mo swich thornes on to pike!

183

Pandare, which that stood hire faste by,   1275
Felte iren hoot, and he bygan to smyte,
And seyde: "nece, I pray yow hertely,
Tel me that I shal axen yow a lite:
A womman that were of his deth to wite,
Withouten his gilt, but for hire lakke of routhe, 1280
Were it wel doon?" Quod she: "nay, by my trouthe."

1271. H2PhH4H3Cx bene hard. 1272. H2PhH4ACx good, H3 gode; H2PhGgH5
H4ACx *om.* I. 1273. nexte, *so* CpGgH3H4, *rest* next. 1275. GgS1 Pandarus. 1276.
H2PhH5Cx þe iryn, Gg þe þorn. 1280. γ(-AD) for hire lakked routhe.

184

"God help me so," quod he, "ye sey me soth.
Ye felen wel youre self that I nat lye.
Lo, yond he rit!" "Ye," quod she, "so he doth."
"Wel," quod Pandare, "as I have told yow thrie, 1285
Lat be youre nyce shame **and** youre folie,
And spek with hym in **esyng** of his herte;
Lat nycete nat do yow **bothe** smerte."

185

But theron was to heven and to doone:
Considered alle thing, it may nat be;   1290
And whi for speche? and it were ek to soone
To graunten hym so grete a libertee.
For pleynly hire entente, as seyde she,
Was for to love hym unwist, if she myghte,
And guerdon hym with no thing but with sighte. 1295

186

But Pandarus thought: "it shal nat be so,
Yif that I may; this nyce opynyoun
Shal nat be holden fully yeres two."
What sholde I make of this a long sermoun?
He moste assente on that conclusioun,   1300
As for the tyme; and whan that it was eve,
And al was wel, he roos and toke his leve.

1283. H2PhGgH5H4 ne *for* nat. 1284. GgH5H4 yondir, ClH2Ph yend; CpH1Th
quod she ye, ClADH3Cx *om.* ye. 1290. alle, *so* GgD, ClH4 alle, *rest* al; H2Ph al
þing wele; Cx so be. 1291. γS1H3Th shame *for* speche. 1292. JGgH5Cx **To graunt**
hym yit. 1298. ADS1 monthes. 1299. CpH1J longe.

187

And on his wey ful faste homward he spedde,
And right for joye he felte his herte daunce;
And Troilus he fond allone abedde,   1305
That lay as don thise lovers in a traunce,
Bitwixen hope and derk desesperaunce.
But Pandarus, right at his in comynge,
He song, as who seyth, "somwhat I brynge,"

188

And seyde: "who is in his bed so soone   1310
Iburied thus?" "It am I, frende," quod he.
"Who, Troilus? nay, help me so the moone,"
Quod Pandarus, "thow shalt arise and see
A charme that was right now sent to the,
The which kan helen the of thyn accesse,   1315
So that thow do forthwith thi bisynesse."

189

"Ye, thorugh the myght of god!" quod Troilus.
And Pandarus gan hym the lettre take,
And seyde: "parde, god hath holpen us;
Have here a light, and loke on al this blake."   1320
But ofte gan the herte glade and quake
Of Troilus, whil that he gan it rede,
So as the wordes yave hym hope or drede.

1305. CpJ fonde. 1309. S1 quhoso *for* who; A se what, Th lo somwhat, S1 sumwhat now; R I þe brynge. 1310. Cp bedde, J bede. 1313. CpClADH5 rise, S1R rys up, CxTh up ryse. 1314. γ(-D)H2PhRTh sent right now (R ysent). 1316. γS1H3Th If thow do forth with al thi bisynesse, R So thow thy self do forth thi bisynesse; H2PhGg *om.* with, H4 weel *for* with; J al *over line before* thy *by early hand.* 1320. H2 se *for* loke on; H2Ph þes lettres blake (*om.* al); H1 þe, GgH5H4ATh þese, Cx thise. 1321. JH2PhGgH5H4 Lorde *for* But. 1323. JGgH5H3ARCx and *for* or.

190

But finaly he took al for the beste
That she hym wroot; for somwhat he byheld   1325
On which, hym thoughte, he myghte his herte reste,
Al covered she the wordes under sheld.
Thus to the more worthi part he held,
That, what for hope and Pandarus byheste,
His grete wo foryede he at the leste.   1330

191

But as we may alday oure selven see,
Thorugh more wode or col, the more fir;
Right so encrees of hope, of what it be,
Therwith ful ofte encresseth ek desir;
Or as an ook comth of a litel spir,   1335
So thorugh this lettre, which that she hym sente,
Encressen gan desir, of which he brente.

192

Wherfore I seye alwey, that day and nyght
This Troilus gan to desiren moore
Than he dede erst, thorugh hope, and dede his myght
To pressen on, as by Pandarus loore,   1341
And writen to hire of his sorwes soore,
Fro day to day; he leet it nat refreyde,
That by Pandare he somwhat wroot or seyde;

1326. H2PhGgH5H4RH3DCxTh he *for* hym.   1327. CpGgH5S1 tho wordes.   1333. JGgH5D encresseth hope; H4 what that, Cx what so, R or what *for* of what. 1338. H2PhS1 boþe *for* that, H4 *om.* that, H5 þat alway.   1344. γH3 he wroot somwhat, H2PhH4Gg sumwhat he wrote.

193

And dide also his other observaunces,   1345
That til a lovere longeth in this cas;
And after that his dees torned on chaunces,
So was he outher glad, or seyde "allas!"
And held after his gistes ay his pas;
And after swiche answeres as he hadde,   1350
So were his dayes sory outher gladde.

194

But to Pandare alwey was his recours,
And pitously gan ay to hym to pleyne,
And hym bisoughte of reed and som socours;
And Pandarus, that sey his woode peyne,   1355
Wex wel neigh ded for routhe, sooth to seyne,
And bisily with al his herte caste
Som of his wo to slen, and that as faste;

195

And seyde: "lord, and frend, and brother dere,
God woot that thi disese doth me wo.   1360
But wiltow stynten al this woful cheere,
And, by my trouthe, or it be dayes two,
And god to-forn, yit shal I shape it so,
That thow shalt come into a certeyn place,
There as thow mayst thi self preye hire of grace.   1365

1347. γ(-AD)H3 thise *for* his, J hise. 1349. gistes, *so* JCl, H4PhADS1Cx giftes,
H2 gyltes, H1H3GgH5RTh gestes, Cp gostes. 1352. JClGgH5 Pandarus; H2PhGg
H5AS2Dig was alwey, H4 was ay. 1353. H2Ph alwey *for* ay; CpClH1 tyl hym to,
JS1Cx unto hym, R uppon hym, H2PhGgH5H4 to hym, Th on him to, H3AD to
hym to. 1354. GgRH4S1Cx or *for* and, J *om.* and. 1358. R to fleme and þat in haste.
1364. Cp comme, J com. 1365. γ(-D)S1H4 hire preye.

196

"And certeynly I noot if thow it woost,
But tho that ben expert in love it seye,
It is oon of the thynges forthereth most
A man, to have a leyser for to preye,
And siker place his wo for to bywreye;   1370
For in good herte it mot som routhe impresse,
To here and see the giltlees in distresse.

197

"Paraunter thynkestow; though it be so,
That kynde wolde hire don for to bygynne
To han a manere routhe upon my woo,   1375
Seyth daunger: 'nay, thow shalt me nevere wynne';
So reulith hire hir hertes gost withinne,
That, though she bende, yit she stant on roote;
What in effect is this unto my boote?

198

"Thenk here ayeins: whan that the sturdy ook,   1380
On which men hakketh ofte for the nones,
Receyved hath the happy fallyng strook,
The grete sweigh doth it come al at ones,
As don thise rokkes or thise milnestones;
For swifter cours comth thyng that is of wighte,   1385
Whan it descendeth, than don thynges lighte.

1368. *So* CpH1S1JRTh, *rest* þat furþereth.   1370. H2PhH4H3 And a sykir;
H2PhGgH5 *om.* for, H4 in *for* for; H2PhH4A wrey.   1374. *So* JRH4Th, γH3Ph
don hire to bygynne, GgH5H2S1 don hire for to begynne, Cx *om.* hire.   1383. JGgH5
makith *for* doth; CpClH1 doth it to come; H2Ph þan fal, GgCx falle *for* come;
H2PhH5Cx *om.* al.

199

"But reed that boweth down for every blast,
Ful lightly, cesse wynd, it wol aryse;
But so nyl nat an ook, whan it is cast;
It nedeth me nat the longe to forbise.   1390
Men shal rejoyssen of a grete empryse
Acheved wel, and stant withouten doute,
Al han men ben the lenger ther aboute.

200

"But, Troilus, now telle me, if the lest,
A thing which that I shal now axen the: 1395
Which is thi brother that thow lovest best,
As in thi verray hertes privetee?"
"Iwis, my brother Deiphebus," quod he.
"Now," quod Pandare, "or houres twyes twelve,
He shal the ese, unwist of it hym selve.   1400

201

"Now lat malone, and werken as I may,"
Quod he; and to Deiphebus wente he tho,
Which hadde his lord and grete frend ben ay;
Save Troilus, no man he loved so.
To telle in short, withouten wordes mo,   1405
Quod Pandarus: "I prey yow that ye be
Frend to a cause which that toucheth me."

1387. γ(-S2Dig) And, S2Dig For, H4 As *for* But; H2GgH3Cx with *for* for.
1389. JGgH5H3H4RS1 wil; CpJ caste. 1390. JGgRS1Th longe the (R this *for*
the); JGgRTh *om.* to. 1394. CpClH3 yet, H1 þat *for* now, S2DigS1H2Ph *om.*
now, AD telle now me, GgH5 telle me now. 1395. γ(-D) now which that I shal;
H2PhH5H4H3 *om.* that; R the which þat, Cx the whyche *for* which that; H2PhGg
H5RCxTh *om.* now. 1399. JH2PhGgH5H4 Quod Pandarus (*om.* Now); H2PhH4
þries twelve. 1403. S1R and his gret.

202

"Yis, parde," quod Deiphebus, "wel thow woost,
In al that evere I may, and god to-fore,
Al nere it but for man I love moost,   1410
My brother Troilus; but sey wherfore
It is; for sith the day that I was bore,
I nas, ne nevere mo to ben I thynke,
Ayeins a thing, that myghte the forthynke."

203

Pandare gan hym thanke, and to hym seyde: 1415
"Lo, sire, I have a lady in this town,
That is my nece, and called is Criseyde,
Which som men wolden don oppressioun,
And wrongfully han hire possessioun;
Wherfore I of youre lordship yow biseche   1420
To ben oure frend, withouten more speche."

204

Deiphebus hym answerde: "O, is nat this,
That thow spekest of to me thus straungely,
Criseyda, my frend?" He seyde: "yis."
"Than nedeth," quod Deiphebus, "hardely,   1425
No more of this; for trusteth wel that I
Wol be hire champioun with spore and yerde;
I roughte nat though alle hire foos it herde.

1410. S1H5Cx þat I love. 1412. γPh that *for* the. 1415. GgRAS1Cx Pandarus;
J hym gan to thank; Cp thank. 1420. H3DS1Cx of your lordshippe I you, JGg I of
yowr lordshipe I yow. 1423. ClH4RCx so *for* thus. 1425. Criseyda, *so* CpClS1J,
rest Criseyde *or* Cryseyd; H3 pandare he seid sir yis, R he seyde anon right yis, S1
and he seyde ȝis, Cx he sayd she is, Th He sayd him yes; CpH1 this *for* yis. 1426.
γS1H3 No more to speke, Th No more of this to speke. 1427. H1ADH2PhGgH4H3Cx
spere; Cx swerd *for* yerde.

205

"But telle me how,—thow woost of this matere,—
It myghte best avaylen; now lat se."   1430
Quod Pandarus: "if ye, my lord so dere,
Wolden as now do this honour to me,
To preyen hire to-morwe, lo, that she
Come unto yow, hire pleyntes to devyse,
Hire adversaries wolde of it agrise.   1435

206

"And yif I more dorste preye as now,
And chargen yow to han so grete travaille,
To han som of youre bretheren here with yow,
That myghten in hire cause bet availle;
Than, wot I wel, she myghte nevere faille   1440
For to ben holpen, what at youre instaunce,
What with hire othere frendes governaunce."

207

Deiphebus, which that comen was of kynde
To alle honour and bounte to consente,
Answerde: "it shal be don; and I kan fynde   1445
Yit grettere help to this in myn entente.
What wiltow seyn, if I for Eleyne sente
To speke of this? I trowe it be the beste;
For she may leden Paris as hire leste.

1429, 1430. γ(-D)S1H3:
> But telle me, thow that woost al this matere,
> How I myght best avaylen; now lat se.

(DS1 of *for* al). 1429. H2Ph how for þou woost, R how for thow knowest this, Cx for thou wost thys; H4 *om.* of. 1430. myghte, *so* GgD, *rest* myght; R It myght her best, Cx I myght hyr best. 1433. JGgH5H4 And preyen. 1435. JGgH5 adversarie. 1436. H2PhRS1S2H3Cx if þat; H2PhRH3Cx more y durst; CpClJ prey; γ(-AD)H3 prey yow as now, Cx yow prey as now. 1439. γS1H3Th to *for* in, Cx *om.* in. 1442. CpH1 other, J oothre; H2PhRCx sustenaunce. 1447. JH4ADS1Cx yif for **Eleyne** I sente.

208

"Of Ector, which that is my lord, my brother,   1450
It nedeth naught to preye hym frend to be;
For I have herd hym, o tyme and ek oother,
Speke of Cryseyde swich honour, that he
May seyn no bet, swich hap to hym hath she.
It nedeth naught, his helpes for to crave;   1455
He shal be swich, right as we wol hym have.

209

"Speke thow thi self also to Troilus
On my byhalve, and prey hym with us dyne."
"Sire, al this shal be don," quod Pandarus;
And took his leve, and nevere gan to fyne,   1460
But to his neces hous, as streyght as lyne,
He come, and fond hire fro the mete arise,
And sette hym down, and spak right in this wise.

210

He seide: "O verray god, so have I ronne!
Lo, nece myn, se ye nat how I swete?   1465
I not whether ye the more thank me konne.
Be ye nat war how false Poliphete
Is now aboute eftsones for to plete,
And brynge on yow advocacies newe?"
"I? no," quod she, and chaunged al hire hewe.   1470

1455. H2PhCx So, H4R She *for* It; JGgH5Th hise helpis moore crave, H4 his
helpis more to crave, H2Ph us more help to crave, Cx hys help now for to crave.
1460. ClR nevere wolde he fyne. 1463. JGgH5RS1 sat, H2Ph sate. 1466. Cp
wheither, GgH5PhS1 wher, J whar; ClH3H2PhH4 ye me þe more þank, Cx the
more ye me thank.

211

"What is he more aboute, me to drecche
And don me wrong? What shal I doon, allas?
Yit of hym selve nothing wolde I recche,
Nere it for Antenor and Eneas,
That ben his frendes in swich manere cas.　　　1475
But, for the love of god, myn uncle deere,
No fors of that, lat hym han al yfeere;

212

"Withouten that, I have ynough for us."
"Nay," quod Pandare, "it shal nothing be so;
For I have ben right now at Deiphebus,　　　1480
At Ector, and myn oother lordes moo,
And shortly maked eche of hem his foo;
That, by my thrift, he shal it nevere wynne
For aught he kan, whan that so he bygynne."

213

And as thei casten what was best to doone,　　　1485
Deiphebus, of his owen curteisie,
Com hire to preye, in his propre persone,
To holde hym on the morwe compaignie
At dyner, which she nolde nat denye,
But goodly gan to his preyere obeye.　　　1490
He thonked hire, and wente upon his weye.

1473. selve, *so* AD, H3Th selfe, *rest* self; J ryght nothinge; Gg ȝit wolde I no
þyng; CpH1R ne wolde, H3Cl nolde. 1477. H2PhH4S1Cx of yt. 1480. H2Ph right
now spoke with deiphebus; Gg ryȝt now ben; Cx wyth *for* at. 1481. ClH1H3H2Ph
And *for* At. 1484. H2H5H3DS1CxTh whan so þat he, Ph whan þat he so, Gg whan
so evere he. 1489. ClH1AS1H3H4RCx wolde.

214

Whan this was don, this Pandare up anon,
To telle in short, and forth he gan to wende
To Troilus, as stille as any ston,
And al this thyng he tolde hym, worde and ende, 1495
And how that he Deiphebus gan to blende,
And seyde hym: "now is tyme, if that thow konne,
To bere the wel to-morwe, and al is wonne.

215

"Now spek, now prey, now pitously compleyne;
Lat nat for nyce shame, or drede, or slouthe.   1500
Som tyme a man mot telle his owen peyne;
Bileve it, and she shal han on the routhe;
Thow shalt be saved by thi feyth in trouthe.
But wel woot I, that thow art now in drede;
And what it is, I leye, I kan arede.   1505

216

"Thow thynkest now: 'how sholde I don al this?
For by my cheres mosten folk aspie
That for hire love is that I fare amys;
Yit hadde I levere unwist for sorwe dye.'
Now thynk nat so, for thow dost grete folie.   1510
For I right now have founden o manere
Of sleyghte, for to coveren al thi cheere.

1492. R This thing y done pandar rose up anon. 1493. γ forth gan for to wende.
1497. H2PhGgRCx *om.* hym. 1499. JGg and pitously. 1500. H2PhH4RCx Leve not.
1502. H2PhH4RCxTh wil *for* shal. 1503. H2PhH3D and *for* in. 1504. γH2PhH4
RCxTh *om.* that; H2PhH4RCxTh in a drede (H4 *om.* in). 1505. R right wel, A þe
cause *for* I leye; H2PhGgDRCx it rede, H5 rede. 1506. JH4Cx shal. 1511. ClR
right now have I, H3 ryght now I have. 1512. sleyghte, *so* CpClH4, *rest* sleight
(J slyght).

217

"Thow shalt gon over nyght, and that bylyve,
Unto Deiphebus hous, as the to pleye,
Thi maladie awey the bet to dryve,— 1515
For whi thow semest sik, soth for to seye.
Soone after that, down in thi bed the leye,
And sey, thow mayst no lenger up endure,
And lye right there, and byd thyn aventure.

218

"Sey that thi fevere is wont the for to take 1520
The same tyme, and lasten til a-morwe;
And lat se now how wel thow kanst it make,
For, parde, sik is he that is in sorwe.
Go now, farwel! and Venus here to borwe,
I hope, and thow this purpos holde ferme, 1525
Thi grace she shal fully ther conferme."

219

Quod Troilus: "iwis, thow nedeles
Conseilest me, that siklich I me feyne;
For I am sik in ernest, douteles,
So that wel neigh I sterve for the peyne." 1530
Quod Pandarus: "thou shalt the bettre pleyne,
And hast the lasse nede to countrefete,
For hym men demen hoot that men seen swete.

1513. bylyve, *so* JGgH3Th, H2PhH4S1Cx as blyve, *rest* blyve. 1516. H2PhH4RCx
the sothe to sey, D þe soth for to seye, H3 sothe to seye. 1517. CpH1S2DigH3 And,
ClADS1H2Ph So *for* Soone. 1520. H2PhGgH5H4ACx *om.* for. 1526. H2Ph fully
the, GgCx þe fulli, H5 þere þe fully, Cl þere fully, JR the fully ther. 1527.
H2PhGgH5ClA now *for* thow. 1528. H2Ph Counceilist þou me þat sike.

220

"Lo, hold the at the triste cloos, and I
Shal wel the deer unto thi bowe dryve."   1535
Therwith he took his leve al softely,
And Troilus to paleis wente blyve;
So glad ne was he nevere in al his lyve,
And to Pandarus reed gan al assente,
And to Deiphebus hous at nyght he wente.   1540

221

What nedeth yow to tellen al the cheere
That Deiphebus unto his brother made,
Or his accesse, or his siklich manere,
How men gan hym with clothes for to lade,   1544
Whan he was leyd, and how men wolde hym glade?
But al for nought; he held forth ay the wyse
That ye han herd Pandare or this devyse.

222

But certeyn is, or Troilus hym leyde,
Deiphebus had hym preied over nyght,
To ben a frend and helpyng to Criseyde.   1550
God woot, that he it graunted anon right,
To ben hire fulle frend with al his myght;
But swich a nede was to preye hym thenne,
As for to bidde a wood man for to renne.

1537. H2PhH5 as blyve. 1541. H2Ph me to telle ȝow, R it to tell you, Th it you
to tellen, JH1 *om.* to, H5 it *for* to. 1546. H2PhR alwey *for* forth ay; RCx his gyse.
1549. JGgH5H3ACxTh preyd hym (H3 yprayde). 1550. JGgH5 good frend, S1 good
lord. 1551. JGgH5H3H2PhTh *om.* it. 1552. H3AD here frynde wyth al his ful
myght. 1553. JS1Th need was it, ADCx nede it was, R nede was that, Gg nede
was for.

223

The morwen com, and neighen gan the tyme   1555
Of meltid, that the faire queene Eleyne
Shoop hire to ben, an houre after the prime,
With Deiphebus, to whom she nolde feyne;
But as his suster, homly, soth to seyne,
She com to dyner in hire pleyne entente.   1560
But god and Pandare wist al what this mente.

224

Com ek Criseyde, al innocent of this,
Antigone, hire suster Tarbe also,
But fle we now prolixitee best is,
For love of god, and lat us faste go   1565
Right to theffect, withouten tales mo,
Whi al this folk assembled in this place;
And lat us of hire saluynges pace.

225

Grete honour dide hem Deiphebus, certeyn,
And fedde hem wel with al that myghte like;   1570
But evere mo "allas!" was his refreyn,
"My goode brother, Troilus, the syke
Lith yit"; and therwithal he gan to sike;
And after that he peyned hym to glade
Hem as he myghte, and cheere good he made.   1575

1557. CpH1 shapte, Cl shapt. 1561. ClH1AS1H4 what al; H2PhRCx non *for* al; GgH5 he, R she, H2Ph it *for* this. 1563. Th nece *for* suster. 1570. RCx hem like. 1573. H2PhGgH5 gan he, *om.* to. 1575. H2PhH5H3RS1Cx good chere; H2PhGg H5RCx hem *for* he, H3D *om.* he.

226

Compleyned ek Eleyne of his siknesse
So feythfully, that pite was to here;
And every wight gan wexen for accesse
A leche anon, and seyde: "in this manere
Men curen folk; this charme I wol yow leere"; 1580
But ther sat oon, al liste hire nat to teche,
That thoughte: "best koude I yit ben his leche."

227

After compleynte, hym gonnen they to preyse,
As folk don yit, whan som wight hath bygonne
To preise a man, and up with pris hym reise 1585
A thousand fold yit hyer than the sonne:
"He is, he kan that fewe lordes konne";
And Pandarus, of that they wolde afferme,
He naught forgat hire preisynge to conferme.

228

Herde alwey this Criseyde wel inough, 1590
And every word gan for to notifie;
For which with sobre cheere hire herte lough;
For who is that nolde hire glorifie,
To mowen swich a knyght don lyve or dye?
But al passe I, lest ye to longe dwelle; 1595
For, for o fyn is al that evere I telle.

1577. J it, Th that it *for* that; GgH₅ a pete it was. 1580. JGgS₁AH₂PhH₄Th the *for* yow. 1585. γH₃H₄Th *om.* up. 1586. Cp heigher, J hiere. 1587. H₃ folkes, R knyghtes. 1589. CpJ naughte. 1590. γH₃Th Herde al this thyng, H₄ This herde alwey. 1593. JGg it that, RD that that, H₂ he þat *for* that; γ(-D)H₃Th ne wolde, Ph her nold not. 1594. JH₂PhS₁Cx to *for* don, Cl *om.* don. 1596. JGgH₅H₄Th But for.

229

The tyme com, fro dyner for to ryse,
And, as hem oughte, arisen everichon,
And gonne a while of this and that devise;
But Pandarus brak al this speche anon,   1600
And seyde to Deiphebus: "wol ye gon,
If it youre wille be, as I yow preyde,
To speke here of the nedes of Criseyde?"

230

Eleyne, which that by the hond hire helde,
Took first the tale, and seyde: "go we blyve";   1605
And goodly on Criseyde she bihelde,
And seyde: "Jovis lat hym nevere thryve,
That doth yow harm, and brynge hym soone of lyve;
And yeve me sorwe, but he shal it rewe,
If that I may, and alle folk be trewe."   1610

231

"Tel thow thi neces cas," quod Deiphebus
To Pandarus, "for thow kanst best it telle."
"My lordes and my ladyes, it stant thus;
What sholde I lenger," quod he, "do yow dwelle?"
He rong hem out a proces lik a belle   1615
Upon hire foo, that highte Poliphete,
So heynous, that men myghte on it spete.

1598. H2PhCx þei risyn; CpJ everichone. 1600. CpS1H2PhGgCx that *for* this;
Cp anone. 1601. CpC!H1 gone. 1602. γH3CxTh *om.* it. 1607. γH3S1Th Joves,
H5 Jovous. 1608. Th reve *for* brynge. 1612. H2PhH4 it best, H3 it best it. 1614.
CpDH2Cx *om.* quod he. 1615. CpJ ronge. 1616. JRH4 Unto, GgH5 Onto *for* Upon;
highte, *so* ClH1GgS1, *rest* hight.

232

Answerde of this eche worse of hem than other,
And Poliphete they gonnen thus to warien:
"Anhonged be swich oon, were he my brother;   1620
And so he shal, for it ne may nat varien."
What sholde I lenger in this tale tarien?
Pleynlich, al at ones, they hire highten
To ben hire frend in al that evere they myghten.

233

Spak thanne Eleyne, and seyde: "Pandarus,   1625
Woot ought my lord my brother this matere,
I meene Ector? or woot it Troilus?"
He seyde: "ye; but wole ye now me here?
Me thynketh this, sith that Troilus is here,
It were good, if that ye wolde assente,   1630
She tolde hire self hym al this, or she wente.

234

"For he wol have the more hir grief at herte,
By cause, lo, that she a lady is;
And, by youre leve, I wol but in right sterte,
And do yow wyte, and that anon, iwys,   1635
If that he slepe, or wol ought here of this."
And in he lepe, and seyde hym in his ere:
"God have thi soule, ibrought have I thi beere!"

1624. γH3 helpe, H2PhS1 frendis *for* frend. 1628. Cp wolle, J wol. 1629. H2Ph *om.* this; H1RCx *om.* that. 1630. R right good. 1634. ClDH3H2Ph right yn, H4Cx *om.* right. 1637. γH3S1Th lepte; R And lepe in faste.

235

To smylen of this gan tho Troilus,
And Pandarus, withouten rekenynge,   1640
Out wente anon to Eleyne and Deiphebus,
And seyde hem; "so ther be no taryinge,
Ne moore prees, he wol wel that ye brynge
Criseyda, my lady, that is here;
And as he may enduren, he wol here.   1645

236

"But wel ye woot, the chaumbre is but lite,
And fewe folk may lightly make it warm;
Now loketh ye,—for I wol have no wite,
To brynge in prees that myghte don hym harm,
Or hym disesen, for my bettre arm—   1650
Wher it be bet she bide til eft sonys;
Now loketh ye, that knowen what to doon is.

237

"I sey, for me, best is, as I kan knowe,
That no wight in ne wende, but ye tweye,
But it were I; for I kan, in a throwe,   1655
Reherce hire cas, unlik that she kan seye;
And after this, she may hym ones preye
To ben good lord, in short, and take hire leve;
This may nat muchel of his ese hym reve.

1639. H3H2PhH5 of this tho gan (H2Ph bigan), H4S1 gan of this tho (H4 the
for tho), Cx gan of thys, *om.* tho. 1644. Criseyda, *so* CpClH1D; S1RCx Criseide
anon. 1648. H2PhH4 *om.* ye. 1649. CpJ harme. 1651. Th Yet were it bet;
JGgH5H4S1Cx she abide. 1654. PhH4 yn now wend, H2 yn wend now, Cx now
wend in, H3 *om.* ne; γH3S1Gg wente. 1656. GgH5H3Cx cause.

238

"And ek for she is straunge, he wol forbere   1660
His ese, which that hym thar nat for yow;
Ek oother thing, that toucheth nought to here,
He wol yow telle, I woot it wel, right now,
That secret is, and for the townes prow."
And they, that nothyng knewe of his entente,   1665
Withouten more, to Troilus in they wente.

239

Eleyne, in al hire goodly softe wyse,
Gan hym salue, and wommanly to pleye,
And seyde: "iwys, ye moste algate arise;
Now, faire brother, be al hool, I preye."   1670
And gan hire arm right over his shulder leye,
And hym with al hire wit to reconforte;
As she best koude, she gan hym disporte.

240

So after this quod she: "we yow biseke,
My deere brother, Deiphebus, and I,   1675
For love of god, and so doth Pandare eke,
To ben good lord and frende, right hertely,
Unto Criseyde, which that certeynly
Receyveth wrong, as woot wel here Pandare,
That kan hire cas wel bet than I declare."   1680

1661. ClCx he *for* hym; GgH5CxTh dar, H2Ph oght. 1662. Gg hire. 1663.
CpClH1S2Dig me, GgH4RTh it *for* yow. 1665. JGgH5H4RS1Th knowen nothing
(RS1 knew); γS1Cx this *for* his. 1666. H4H5RCx *om.* they, Gg sche *for* they. 1669.
JGgRCxTh mote; γH3 alweies. 1670. γH3S1 beth. 1673. CpH1ADH3Th hym to
disporte. 1679. H4R weel wot.

241

This Pandarus gan newe his tonge affile,
And al hire cas reherce, and that anon.
Whan it was seyd, soone after in a while,
Quod Troilus: "as sone as I may gon,
I wol right fayn with al my myght ben oon,　　1685
Have god my trouthe, hire cause to sustene."
"Good thrift have ye," quod Eleyne, the queene.

242

Quod Pandarus: "and it youre wille be,
That she may take hire leve or that she go?"
"O, elles god forbede," tho quod he,　　1690
"If that she vouche sauf for to do so."
And with that word quod Troilus: "ye two,
Deiphebus, and my suster, lief and deere,
To yow have I to speke of o matere,

243

"To ben avysed by youre reed the bettre";　　1695
And fond, as hap was, at his beddes hed,
The copie of a tretys and a lettre,
That Ector hadde hym sent to axen reed,
If swych a man was worthi to ben ded,
Woot I nat who; but in a grisly wise　　1700
He preyede hem anon on it avyse.

1681. H2PhH5ADCx now.　1683. CpH1JRH3 seyde.　1686. ClH3H4GgH5 susteyne.
1687. ThS1 Now good thrift have ye; GgH5 quod þe quene Elyne; R heleyn tho the
queene; J Elena, H4 helena.　1688. JGgH5S1 yif *for* and.　1690. H2PhGgH5H3AD
Or, S1Cx Now *for* O, H4R *om.* O; CpH1DH3S1H2PhH4CxTh forbede it; ClH3H2Ph
om. tho.　1691. CpH5 *om.* that; JR ye, GgH5 þou *for* she; CpH1DH2Ph voucheth.
1694. H1H2PhGgH5CxTh a *for* o.　1696. H2PhH4S1Cx had *for* fond.　1699. GgH5H4
Cx were, J war *for* was.　1700. H2PhH4S1Cx Note y not who (H2Ph how); CpH1
grisely, J grislich.　1701. CpJ preyde, JGgH5 faste, Cx bothe anon *for* anon;
GgH5PhAS1 to avise, H4 tavyse.

244

Deiphebus gan this lettre to unfolde
In ernest gret; so dede Eleyne the queene;
And, romyng outward, faste it gonne byholde,
Downward a steire, and in an herber greene,   1705
This ilke thing they redden hem bitwene;
And largely, the mountaunce of an houre,
Thei gonne on it to reden and to poure.

245

Now lat hem rede, and torne we anon
To Pandarus, that gan ful faste prye   1710
That al was wel, and out he gan to gon
Into the grete chaumbre, and that in hye,
And seyde: "god save al this compaignye!
Com, nece myn, my lady, queene Eleyne,
Abideth yow, and ek my lordes tweyne.   1715

246

"Rys, take with yow youre nece, Antigone,
Or whom yow list; or no fors; hardyly
The lasse prees the bet; com forth with me,
And loke that ye thonken humblely
Hem alle thre, and, whan ye may goodly   1720
Youre tyme se, taketh of hem youre leeve,
Lest we to longe his restes hym byreeve."

1702. CpH1S1 for tonfolde, RTh for to unfolde. 1705. γH3S1H2PhTh into, Cx
and into *for* and in. 1707. JGgH5H4H3CxTh mountenaunce. 1712. S1H5Cx on hie.
1719. JH2Ph loketh.

247

Al innocent of Pandarus entente,
Quod tho Criseyde: "go we, uncle deere";
And arm in arm inward with hym she wente,   1725
Avysed wel hire wordes and hire cheere;
And Pandarus in ernestful manere,
Seyde: "alle folk, for goddes love, I preye,
Stynteth right here, and softely yow pleye.

248

"Aviseth yow what folk ben here withinne,   1730
And in what plit oon is, god hym amende!"
And inward thus: "ful softely bygynne;
Nece, I conjure, and heighly yow defende,
On his half, that soule us alle sende,
And in the vertue of corounes tweyne,   1735
Sle nat this man, that hath for yow this peyne.

249

"Fy on the devel! thynk which on he is,
And in what plit he lith; com of anon;
Thynk al swich taried tid, but lost it nys;
That wol ye bothe seyn, whan ye ben oon.   1740
Secoundely, ther yit devyneth noon
Upon yow two; com of now, if ye konne;
Whil folk is blent, lo, al the tyme is wonne.

1726. H2PhCxTh Avising.   1729. JGgH5H4Cx ye.   1730. Cp hire, J hir.   1733.
JGgH5H4 O nece; Cp heigly, J heyly.   1734. ClH3 by halve, H5 behalve, R behalf;
CpH1ADS1CxTh which that, H2Ph which *for* that; H2PhCx us soule hath sende,
Cl us alle sowle sende.   1735. JGgH5H4 *om.* the; R eke *for* in the; H1DH3Cx of þe;
H5 *om.* of; R his reignes, H5 owre goddis *for* corounes.   1739. H2PhGgH3RACx is.
1741. H4 Sekirly, Cx And sikerly, H5 Sertaynly.

250

"In titeryng, and pursuyte, and delayes,
The folk devyne at waggyng of a stree;   1745
That, though ye wolde han after merye dayes,
Than dar ye naught, and whi? for she, and she,
Spak swich a word, thus loked he, and he;
Las tyme ilost, I dar nought with yow dele;
Com of, therfore, and bryngeth hym to hele."   1750

251

But now to yow, ye loveres that ben here,
Was Troilus nat in a kankedort?
That lay, and myghte whisprynge of hem here,
And thoughte: "O lord, right now renneth my sort
Fully to deye, or han anon comfort";   1755
And was the firste tyme he shulde hire preye
Of love; O myghty god, what shal he seye?

EXPLICIT LIBER SECUNDUS.

1744. H2PhH4Cx in, R & in *for first* and, H3 *om.* 1746. γH3Th And *for* That;
Cp mirye, J myrie. 1747. H2PhH4D for why, R why for, ACx for why for *for* and
whi for. 1749. S1Ph Lasse, H4 Allas, H2H5R lest, Th Leste, H3D Last, Cx Thus;
AD is ylost, H4Ph is lost, H2RTh be lost. *After 1750 R has the following stanza:*

> For ye must outher chaungen [now?] your face,
> That is so ful of mercy and bountee,
> Or elles must ye do this man sum grace;
> For this thyng folweth of necessytee,
> As sothe as god ys in his magestee,
> That crueltee, with so benigne a chier,
> Ne may not last in o persone yfere.

1752. H2PhH4Cx kankerdorte. 1753. H4RH5CxTh the whispryng, H2Ph the
whistryng. 1754. H2PhGgH5RCx *om.* right. 1755. H2PhGgH5 dethe. 1756.
H2PhHiD shold, *rest* shulde.

BOOK THREE

BOOK THREE

1

OBLISFUL light, of which the bemes clere
Adorneth al the thridde hevene faire;
O sonnes lief, O Joves doughter deere,
Plesaunce of love, O goodly debonaire,
In gentil hertes ay redy to repaire;   5
O verray cause of heele and of gladnesse,
Iheryed be thy myght and thi goodnesse.

2

In hevene and helle, in erthe and salte see,
Is felt thi myght, if that I wel descerne;
As man, brid, best, fisshe, herbe, and grene tree   10
The fele in tymes with vapour eterne.
God loveth, and to love wol nat werne;
And in this world no lyves creature,
Withouten love, is worth, or may endure.

3

Ye Joves first to thilke effectes glade,   15
Thorugh which that thynges lyven alle and be,
Comeveden, and amoreux hem made
On mortal thyng, and as yow list, ay ye
Yeve hym in love ese or adversitee;
And in a thousand formes down hym sente   20
For love in erthe, and whom yow list, he hente.

1-49. R *omits proem.* 1-56. *Lacking in* Gg, *leaf lost.* 5. H2PhH4H3Cx *om.* ay.
8. H4H5AS1 in *for first* and; H4H5A in *for second* and. 9. wel, *so* CpAH5CxTh,
ClS1H3 wole, H1D wol, S2Dig wold, H2Ph wil, J whil, H4 myht. 11. CpAD They,
H4 Ye, H2Ph To *for* The. 12. H4PhS1Cx he wil *for* wol. 15. Cp thilk, J thikke.
17. CpH5Cx Comended, H3H4Th Comenden, ADS1 Comeved hem, H2Ph Commo-
dious, J Commoeveden, ClH1 Comeveden. 19. H2PhH4Cx Yaf; H3H4S1CxTh hem
for hym. 20. ClDS1H3H4Cx hem, H5 hath *for* hym.

4

Ye fierse Mars apaisen of his ire,
And, as yow list, ye maken hertes digne;
Algates hem that ye wol sette a-fire,
They dreden shame, and vices they resigne;   25
Ye don hem curteys be, fressh and benigne;
And heighe or lowe, after a wight entendeth,
The joies that he hath, youre myght it sendeth.

5

Ye holden regne and hous in unitee;
Ye sothfast cause of frendship ben also;   30
Ye knowe al thilke covered qualitee
Of thynges, which that folk on wondren so,
Whan they kan nought construe how it may jo,
She loveth hym, or whi he loveth here,—
As whi this fissh, and naught that, cometh to were.   35

6

Ye folk a lawe han set in universe;
And this knowe I by hem that loveres be,
That whoso stryveth with yow hath the werse.
Now lady bryght, for thi benignite,
At reverence of hem that serven the,   40
Whos clerk I am, so techeth me devyse
Som joye of that is felt in thi servyse.

---

30. CpJ sothfaste. 31. Cp thilk, J thikke. 32. JH4Cx folkes; JH5Cx wondre on
so, H4 wondren also (*om.* on), Th *om.* on. 33. H2PhAD may *for* kan. 35. H4H5D
And, J Al, Cx Or *for* As. 37. Cp lovers, J loverys.

7

Ye in my naked herte sentement
Inhielde, and do me shewe of thy swetnesse.
Caliope, thi vois be now present,   45
For now is nede; sestow nat my destresse,
How I mot telle anon right the gladnesse
Of Troilus, to Venus heryinge?
To which gladnesse, who nede hath, god hym brynge!

EXPLICIT PROHEMIUM TERCII LIBRI.
INCIPIT LIBER TERCIUS.

8

LAY al this mene while Troilus,   50
    Recordyng his lessoun in this manere:
    "Mafey," thoughte he, "thus wol I seye and
                        thus;
Thus wol I pleyne unto my lady dere;
That word is good, and this shal be my cheere;
This nyl I nat foryeten in no wise."   55
God leve hym werken as he kan devyse!

9

And, lord, so that his herte gan to quappe,
Heryng hire come, and shorte for to sike!
And Pandarus, that ledde hire by the lappe,
Com ner, and gan in at the curtyn pike,   60
And seyde: "god do boote on alle syke!
Se who is here yow comen to visite;
Lo, here is she that is youre deth to wite";

43. H2PhH4H5S1H3Cx hertis. 44. C1DH4H5 Inhelde, H2Ph Inheld, Th Inhylde.
49. γH3Th *om.* gladnesse. 52. Cp Mafay, J May fey; CpJ sey. 53. H4RH2Ph
herte *for* lady. 54. H3H4 thus, Cx that *for* this. 53, 54. JH5 *transpose lines* (Gg
missing). 56. C1H1AH2PhH4Cx gan. 58. JCx sor *for* shorte; R and often sore
sike, H4 gan ofte forto sike (*om.* and), H3 and short gan to syke.

10

Therwith it semed as he wepte almoost.
"Ha a," quod Troilus so reufully, 65
"Wher me be wo, O myghty god, thow woost;
Who is al there? I se nought, trewely."
"Sire," quod Criseyde, "it is Pandare and I."
"Ye, swete herte? allas, I may nat rise,
To knele, and do yow honour in som wyse"; 70

11

And dressed hym upward; and she right tho
Gan bothe hire hondes softe upon hym leye.
"O, for the love of god, do ye nat so
To me," quod she, "I! what is this to seye?
Sire, comen am I to yow for causes tweye: 75
First yow to thonke, and of youre lordshipe eke
Continuance I wolde yow biseke."

12

This Troilus, that herde his lady preye
Of lordshipe hym, wex neither quyk ne dede,
Ne myghte o word for shame to it seye, 80
Although men sholde smyten of his hede;
But, lord, so he wex sodeynliche rede,
And, sire, his lessoun that he wende konne,
To preyen hire, was thorugh his wit ironne.

---

65. Ha a *so* CpH1A, JGg Ha a a, S1Th A a, *rest* A ha. 66. JRAPh al *for* o. 72. RH5 softly; GgH5R on *for* upon. 74. GgH5R he *for* she; H2PhH5Th ey *for* I, RCx *om.* I. 79. H2PhRS1 Hym of lordship, H4 Lordshippe of him. 80. JRCx hir *for* it. 84. γH3Th is *for* was; H2PhCx hert *for* wit.

13

Criseyde al this aspied wel ynough,   85
For she was wis, and loved hym nevere the lasse,
Al nere he malapert, or made it tough,
Or was to bold to synge a fool a masse;
But whan his shame gan somwhat to passe,
His wordes, as I may my rymes holde,   90
I wol yow telle, as techen bokes olde.

14

In chaunged vois, right for his verray drede,
Which vois ek quook, and therto his manere
Goodly abaist, and now his hewes rede,
Now pale, unto Criseyde, his lady dere,   95
With look down cast, and humble iyolden chere,
Lo, thalderfirste word that hym asterte
Was, twyes: "mercy, mercy, swete herte!"

15

And stynte a while, and whan he myghte out brynge,
The nexte word was: "god woot, for I have,   100
As ferforthlich as I have had konnynge,
Ben youres al, god so my soule save,
And shal, til that I, woful wight, be grave;
And though I dar, ne kan, unto yow pleyne,
Iwis, I suffre nat the lasse peyne.   105

90. γH3Th resons, GgH5R werkis. 91. CpClH1 I yow wol telle. 96. CpJ caste;
iyolden, *so* CpH1H3H4Th, S2Dig humbely ȝolde, Gg & ȝoldyn, J yold, Cx lowly,
rest yolden. 101. ferforthlich, *so* JGg, H2PhRS1 ferforthly, H4H5Cx ferforth,
γH3Th feithfully. 102. H4Ph as *for* al; ClCx also god, H2 so god, R al as god *for*
al god so. 104. H2H4H3RCx ne dare ne can.

16

"Thus muche as now, O wommanliche wif,
I may out brynge, and if this yow displese,
That shal I wreke upon myn owen lif
Right soone, I trowe, and do youre herte an ese,
If with my deth youre wreththe may apese;   110
For sithen ye han herd me somwhat seye,
Now recche I nevere how soone that I deye."

17

Therwith his manly sorwe to biholde,
It myghte han made an herte of stoon to rewe;
And Pandare wep as he to water wolde,   115
And poked evere his nece newe and newe,
And seyde: "wo bigon ben hertes trewe;
For love of god, make of this thing an ende,
Or sle us bothe at ones, or ye wende."

18

"I, what?" quod she, "by god, and by my trouthe,   120
I not nat what ye wilne that I seye."
"I, what?" quod he, "that ye han on hym routhe,
For goddes love, and doth hym nat to deye."
"Now thanne thus," quod she, "I wolde hym preye
To telle me the fyn of his entente;   125
Yit wiste I nevere wel what that he mente."

---

107. H2PhS1Cx it *for* this. 110. γH3S1H2Cx herte *for* wreththe; H2 y may зour
hert; Gg I may, Ph may y, H5 *om.* may. 111. γTh But *for* For; sithen, *so* JH4S1,
αCx sith, γH3ThR syn that. 115. Cp vep, JH2PhD wepe, R weepe, GgH5S1 wepte,
H3CxTh wept, H4 wepid. 119. γThH4 er that; JH2 we, Cx we hens *for* ye. 120.
H5Cx Ey *for* I. 121. wilne, *so* CpH1JGgTh, H2H5Cx wold, *rest* wille, wil, *or* wol.
122. GgH5R on him han; H2PhH4S1Cx of *for* on. 124. S1 I wold ryt fayn hym
preye (*om.* thus).

19

"What that I mene, O swete herte deere?"
Quod Troilus, "O goodly fresshe free!
That with the stremes of youre eyen cleere,
Ye wolde frendly somtyme on me see,   130
And thanne agreen that I may ben he,
Withouten braunche of vice in any wise,
In trouthe alwey to don yow my servise,

20

"As to my lady right and chief resort,
With al my wit and al my diligence;   135
And I to han, right as yow list, comfort,
Under youre yerde, egal to myn offence,
As deth, if that I breke youre defence;
And that ye deigne me so muche honoure,
Me to comanden aught in any houre;   140

21

"And I to ben youre, verray, humble, trewe,
Secret, and in my peynes pacient;
And evere mo desiren fresshly newe
To serve, and ben ay ylike diligent;
And with good herte, al holly youre talent   145
Receyven wel, how sore that me smerte:
Lo, this mene I, myn owen swete herte."

130. γH3ThH4 somtyme frendly; H2PhH5 *om.* frendly (H2 on me rewe and se).
131. H2PhRH3Cx þat ye, H4 if that ye *for* thanne; H3Cx souffren, R vouche sauf,
H4 agreve *for* agreen; H4 thanne *for* that, R *om.* that. 133. Cx Yow for to serve lyke
as ye wyl devyse. 136. CpClH1S2Dig *om.* I. 137. Cp. omits line. 139. JGgRS1 yow
for ye, H2Ph yow *for* that ye. 143. α fresshe, R fressh & *for* fresshly. 144. GgH5
ay ben, H2PhH3Cx *om.* ay; H4 lik, R eke *for* ylike. 146. H2PhS1H3Cx Receyve in
gre.

22

Quod Pandarus: "lo, here an hard requeste,
And resonable a lady for to werne!
Now, nece myn, by Natal Joves feste,   150
Were I a god, ye sholden sterve as yerne,
That heren wel, this man wol no thing yerne
But youre honour, and sen hym almost sterve,
And ben so loth to suffren hym yow serve."

23

With that she gan hire eyen on hym caste   155
Ful esily, and ful debonairly,
Avysyng hire, and hied nat to faste
With nevere a word, but seyde hym sobrely:
"Myn honour sauf, I wol wel trewely,
And in swich forme as he gan now devyse,   160
Receyven hym fully to my servyse,

24

"Besechyng hym, for goddes love, that he
Wolde in honour of trouthe and gentilesse,
As I wel mene, ek mene wel to me,
And myn honour, with wit and bisynesse,   165
Ay kepe; and if I may don hym gladnesse,
From hennesforth, iwys, I nyl nat feyne;
Now beth al hool, no lenger ye ne pleyne.

151. H4 It were good. 154. GgH5H4PhADH3RCxTh ʒow to serve. 156. J esiliche. 157. H2PhACx hyed her. 158. γH3Th softely, Gg sekyrly. 160. JGgH5Cx ye, H2PhTh y *for* he; αH4ClS1Th can, Cx conne *for* gan. 164. GgH5 *om.* ek, H2Ph mene eke wele, R mene wel eke; Cp menene, J meene. 168. H2PhH4RCx þat ʒe pleyn.

25

"But, natheles, this warne I yow," quod she,
"A kynges sone although ye be, ywys,   170
Ye shal no more han sovereignete
Of me in love, than right in that cas is;
Ny nyl forbere, if that ye don amys,
To wreththe yow, and whil that ye me serve,
Chericen yow right after ye deserve.   175

26

"And shortly, deere herte, and al my knyght,
Beth glad, and draweth yow to lustinesse;
And I shal trewely, with al my myght,
Youre bittre tornen al into swetnesse,
If I be she that may do yow gladnesse;   180
For every wo ye shal recovere a blisse";
And hym in armes took, and gan hym kisse.

27

Fil Pandarus on knees, and up his eyen
To hevene threw, and held his hondes hye;
"Immortal god," quod he, "that mayst nat dyen, 185
Cupide I mene, of this mayst glorifie;
And Venus, thow mayst maken melodie;
Withouten hond, me semeth that in towne,
For this miracle, ich here ech belle sowne.

---

169. **H1** werne. 178. JGgH5H3Th with al my ful myghte. 180. γ(-D)S1G**g** yow
do. 183. J hise, **Cp** *om.* his. 184. Cp**J** heven; CpClH1J hise. 185. J O mortal, GgH5
O inmortal, H4 Thou mortal. 186. H2PhGgD mayst þou. 188. CpClH1S2D**ig** in the
towne. 189. CpClH1S2Dig merveille.

28

"But ho, no more as now of this matere; 190
For whi this folk wol comen up anon,
That han the lettre red; lo, I hem here;
But I conjure the, Criseyde, and oon,
And two, thow Troilus, whan thow mayst goon,
That at myn hous ye ben at my warnynge, 195
For I ful wel shal shape youre comynge;

29

"And eseth there youre hertes right ynough;
And lat se which of yow shal bere the belle
To speke of love aright,"—therwith he lough—
"For ther have ye a leiser for to telle." 200
Quod Troilus: "how longe shal I dwelle,
Or this be don?" Quod he: "whan thow mayst ryse,
This thyng shal be right as I the devyse."

30

With that Eleyne and also Deiphebus
Tho comen upward, right at the steires ende; 205
And, lord, so tho gan gronen Troilus,
His brother and his suster for to blende.
Quod Pandarus: "it tyme is that we wende;
Tak, nece myn, youre leve at alle thre,
And lat hem speke, and cometh forth with me." 210

190. αClTh *om.* as, H4 *om.* as now. 193. H4 adjure, H2Ph ajorne, Cx adjourne; GgH5H4Cx anon, Cp an oon. 194. CpAH4Ph to, GgH5H2Cx þe, H4 eek *for* two; JA the *for* thow, H2H5Cx *om.* thow. 199. GgH4RH3 and ry3t, Cx a lytel *for* aright; H1Th aright and therwith. 200. S1 may 3e have, A 3e may have *for* have ye a. 203. γH3S1 I yow, JGg thow wolt, H5 I woll, H4 thei, Th you list *for* I the. 205. H2PhS1H3Cx *om.* right. 206. γ(-AD)H3H5 thanne (H1 schame) *for* tho; H2Ph so gronith (*om.* tho gan); Cx to grone tho gan.

31

She took hire leve at hem ful thriftily,
As she wel koude, and they hire reverence
Unto the fulle deden, hardyly,
And wonder wel speken in hire absence
Of hire, in preysing of hire excellence,   215
Hire governaunce, hire wit; and hire manere
Comendeden, it joie was to here.

32

Now lat hire wende unto hire owen place,
And torne we to Troilus ayein,
That gan ful lightly of the lettre pace,   220
That Deiphebus hadde in the gardyn seyn.
And of Eleyne and hym he wolde feyn
Delivered ben, and seyde that hym leste
To slepe, and after tales have reste.

33

Eleyne hym kiste, and took hire leve blyve,   225
Deiphebus ek, and hom wente every wight;
And Pandarus, as faste as he may dryve,
To Troilus tho com as lyne right;
And on a pailet al that glade nyght
By Troilus he lay, with blisful chere,   230
To tale; and wel was hem they were yfeere.

---

211. H3 thriftfully, H5 discretly, Cx honestly. 214. JGgH5 speken wonder wel.
217. Cp Comendede, H2PhH4 Comendid, H5Cx Comendyng, S1GgR Commenden;
Cp *om.* it; R that *for* it; S1Th þat it joye was, A hit joye it was, H4 they that joie
it was, Cx it that joy it was, H2Ph it was joy, H5 hir it was joye *for* it joie was.
222. JH4RClH5 fayn. 224. H4 tc han a reste, Cx to have rest, CpH1J han reste,
H3ATh han a reste, Gg havyn rest, R hym to reste. 228. H2PhH5Cx come þo;
H2PhH4Cx as blyve, H5 anon *for* as lyne. 229. Cp paillet, J paylet. 230. γH3Th
mery *for* blisful.

34

Whan every wight was voided but they two,
And alle the dores weren faste yshette,
To telle in short, withouten wordes mo,
This Pandarus, withouten any lette,   235
Up roos, and on his beddes syde hym sette,
And gan to speken in a sobre wyse
To Troilus, as I shal yow devyse.

35

"Myn alderlevest lord, and brother deere,
God woot, and thow, that it sat me so soore,   240
When I the saugh so langwisshyng to-yere
For love, of which thi wo wax alwey moore,
That I, with al my myght and al my loore,
Have evere sithen don my bisynesse
To brynge the to joye out of distresse;   245

36

"And have it brought to swich plit as thow woost,
So that, thorugh me, thow stondest now in weye
To faren wel. I seye it for no boost;
And wostow whi? for shame it is to seye:
For the have I bigonne a gamen pleye   250
Which that I nevere don shal eft for other,
Although he were a thousand fold my brother.

---

233. H4 The dores of the chambir faste ishett. 235. H4 anon with oute lett. 236.
H4 Fro there as he was leid upright him sett. 243. α wit *for* myght. 246, 247. R
And thus trowe I that thow thyselven wost/And how that I han set the now in weye.
248. CpJ sey. 250. ClH3 a game bygonne; ClH3H2PhCx to pleye. 251. α shal
nevere do (Gg. *om.* do), R nevere shal don; H2PhGgR *om.* eft; H3 never eft shal
do. 252. H3 tymes.

37

"That is to seye, for the am I bicomen,
Bitwixen game and ernest, swich a meene
As maken wommen unto men to comen;   255
Thow woost thi selven what I wolde meene;
For the have I my nece, of vices cleene,
So fully maad thi gentilesse triste,
That al shal ben right as thi selven liste.

38

"But god, that al woot, take I to witnesse,   260
That nevere I this for coveitise wroughte,
But oonly for tabregge that distresse,
For which wel neigh thow deidest, as me thoughte.
But, goode brother, do now as the oughte,
For goddes love, and kepe hire out of blame;   265
Syn thow art wys, so save alwey hire name.

39

"For wel thow woost, the name as yit of hire
Among the peple, as who seyth, halwed is;
For nevere was ther wight, I dar wel swere,
That evere wiste that she dide amys.   270
But wo is me, that I, that cause al this,
May thenken that she is my nece deere,
And I hire em, and traitour ek yfeere.

---

256. γS1H3ThR Al sey I nought thow wost wel what I meene (R wost what I wolde mene). 262. αJDCx *om.* for; H2PhRCx thy distresse. 266. γS1Th and save, R to save, JGgH5 so kepe; H4 For thou art wis inouh to save hir name; Cx So as thou art wyse kepe hyr out of shame; H3 *omits line.* 267. H2PhGgJDig *om.* as. 268. Cp peeple, J people. 269. γH3ThH2PhR For that man is unbore. 273. H4Cx bothe *for* ek.

40

"And were it wist that I, thorugh myn engyn,
Hadde in my nece yput this fantasie,   275
To doon thi lust, and holly to ben thyn,
Whi, al the world wolde upon it crie,
And seyn that I the worste trecherie
Dide in this cas, that evere was bigonne,
And she forlost, and thow right nought ywonne.   280

41

"Wherfore, or I wol ferther gon a pas,
The preye ich eft, althogh thow sholdest deye,
That privyte go with us in this cas,
That is to seyn, that thow us nevere wreye;
And be nought wroth, though I the ofte preye   285
To holden secree swich an heigh matere;
For skilfull is, thow woost wel, my praiere.

42

"And thynk what wo ther hath bitid or this,
For makyng of avauntes, as men rede;
And what meschaunce in this world yit ther is,   290
Fro day to day, right for that wikked dede;
For which thise wise clerkes that ben dede
Han writen or this, as yit men teche us yonge,
That firste vertu is to kepe tonge.

---

277. JRCxH2Ph al þe peeple; γ upon it wolde; GgH5 wolde on it gaure & crie
(H5 þat *for* it); H4 Al this word wolde on me pleyne & cry. 280. H4 forlorn,
JRCxS1H3H2PhTh fordon. 281. Cp ferthere, J further. 282. γH3S1ThGgH5 Yet
eft I the biseche and fully seye; J preyen, shuldest. 284. H4 For no myschef thou
never us thre bewreye. 290. H2PhS1 mischef yet in þis world þer is (Ph in this
world ȝet is); Cx yit in thys world is; ClS2DigGgH5RTh *om.* ther. 293. γH3S1Thα
Han evere yet proverbed to us yonge (CpS2Dig thus, H1H3Th this *for* yet; H2Ph
proverbyd yet); H4 alwey *for* or this; J men yit. 294. firste, *so* CpClDH4, *rest*
first; H3H4H5PhTh That þe, H2Cx þe *for* That; H2Ph kepe wele þe tonge; H4H5S1
S2CxTh the tunge, RDig thy tonge, H3 his tonge.

43

"And nere it that I wilne as now tabregge   295
Diffusioun of speche, I koude almoost
A thousand olde stories the alegge
Of wommen lost thorugh fals and foles bost;
Proverbes kanst thi selve inowe, and woost,
Ayeins that vice, for to ben a labbe,   300
Though men soth seyde as often as thei gabbe.

44

"O tonge, allas, so often here byforn
Hath made ful many a lady bright of hewe
Seyd: 'weilaway! the day that I was born!'
And many a maydes sorwe for to newe;   305
And, for the more part, al is untrewe
That men of yelpe, and it were brought to preve;
Of kynde non avauntour is to leve.

45

"Avauntour and a lyere, al is on;
As thus, I pose a womman graunteth me   310
Hire love, and seith that other wol she non,
And I am sworn to holden it secree,
And after I go telle it two or thre;
Iwis, I am avauntour at the leeste,
And lyere, for I breke my biheste.   315

295-364. AD *omit.* 299. H4 And proverbis riht inowe as weel thou wost. 300. H2PhTh blabbe; H4 Declaryn that men auhte not to labbyn. 301. γS1H3Th Al seyde men soth; H4 as tonges gabbyn. 302. H4Cx For tonge, F1 O false tong. 303. γH3S1ThGgH5 Hastow made many a lady. 304. RCxH5S2Dig Sey; JH4 þat day; GgH5 þat evere I was born. 305. H3GgH5RH2S2Dig maydens, Cx mayden. 310. γH3S1ThH4 graunte, Gg grauntede. 315. CpS2DigS1H3H2PhF1Cx And a lyere.

46

"Now loke thanne, if they ben aught to blame,
Swich manere folk; what shal I clepe hem? what?
That hem avaunte of wommen, and by name,
That nevere yit bihyghte hem this ne that,
Ne knewe hem more than myn olde hat?   320
No wonder is, so god me sende hele,
Though wommen dreden with us men to dele.

47

"I sey nat this for no mystrust of yow,
Ne for no wis man, but for foles nyce,
And for the harm that in the world is now,   325
As wel for folie ofte as for malice;
For wel woot I, in wise folk that vice
No womman drat, if she be wel avised;
For wise ben by foles harm chastised.

48

"But now to purpos, leve brother deere;   330
Have al this thyng that I have seyd in mynde,
And kepe the clos, and be now of good cheere;
For at thi day thow shalt me trewe fynde.
I shal thi proces sette in swych a kynde,
And god toforn, that it shal the suffise;   335
For it shal ben right as thow wolt devyse.

316. γS1Th be nought, Cx be right nought. 319. CpH1S2DigH3Th That yet
bihyghte hem nevere. 324. γTh wise men, H4 wismen. 325. H3H4S1 this world.
328. H2PhH4CxTh dredith. 332. R right *for* now.

49

"For wel I woot, thow menest wel, parde,
Therfore I dar this fully undertake.
Thow woost ek what thi lady graunted the;
And day is set, the chartres up to make.   340
Have now good nyght; I may no lenger wake;
And bid for me, sith thow art now in blysse,
That god me sende deth or soone lisse."

50

Who myghte tellen half the joie or feste
Whiche that the soule of Troilus tho felte,   345
Heryng theffect of Pandarus byheste?
His olde wo, that made his herte swelte,
Gan tho for joie wasten and to-melte;
And al the richesse of his sikes sore
At ones fledde, he felte of hem no more.   350

51

But right so as thise holtes and thise hayis,
That han in wynter dede ben and dreye,
Revesten hem in grene, whan that May is,
Whan every lusty listeth best to pleye,
Right in that selve wise, soth to seye,   355
Wax sodeynliche his herte ful of joie,
That gladder was ther nevere man in Troie.

---

342. γH3 syn *for* sith.   349. H2Ph rehetyng, H4 tresour, Cx thoughtis *for* richesse.
352. dreye, *so* ClS1, *rest* drye.   354. γS1 liketh.   355. γS1Cx soth for to seye.

52

And gan his look on Pandarus up caste
Ful sobrely, and frendly for to se,
And seyde: "frend, in Aperil the laste,—⁣ 360
As wel thow woost, if it remembre the,—
How neigh the deth for wo thow fownde me!
And how thow dedest al thi bisynesse,
To knowe of me the cause of my destresse!

53

"Thow woost how longe ich it forbar to seye 365
To the, that art the man that I best triste;
And peril non was it to the bywreye,
That wiste I wel; but telle me, if the liste,
Sith I so loth was that thi self it wiste,
How dorste I mo tellen of this matere, 370
That quake now, and no man may us here?

54

"But natheles, by that god I the swere,
That as hym list may al this world governe,—
And if I lye, Achilles with his spere
Myn herte cleve, al were my lif eterne, 375
As I am mortal, if I late or yerne
Wolde it bywreye, or dorste, or sholde konne,
For al the good that god made under sonne;—

359. αH4H3CxTh on to *for* for to (H2PhCx un to). 360. Aperil, *so* H1, J Aperel, R Averille, GgH5H4Ph Aprille, S1 Aprile, *rest* April. 364. H4 axe. 366. H2PhH3 most *for* best. 367. ClS1H3H4 was it noon. 371. man, *so* β (JRCx), *rest* wight.

55

"But rather wolde I dye, and determyne,
As thynketh me, now stokked in prisoun,　　　　380
In wrecchednesse, in filthe, and in vermyne,
Captif to cruel kyng Agamenoun:
And this in alle the temples of this town,
Upon the goddes alle, I wol the swere
To morwe day; if that it like the here.　　　　385

56

"And that thow hast so muche idon for me,
That I ne may it nevere more deserve,
This knowe I wel, al myghte I now for the
A thousand tymes on a morwe sterve;
I kan no more but that I wol the serve　　　　390
Right as thi sclave, whider so thow wende,
For evere more unto my lyves ende.

57

"But here, with al myn herte, I the biseche,
That nevere in me thow deme swich folie
As I shal seyn: me thoughte, by thi speche,　　　　395
That this which thow me doost for compaignie,
I sholde wene it were a bauderye.
I am nat wood, al if I lewed be;
It is nat so, that woot I wel, parde.

<hr />

379-385. H5 *omits stanza.* 379. But, *so* β (H4RCxS1), Gg What, *rest* That; wolde
I dye, *so* β(JRCx), *rest* dey I wolde. 380. Cp prisone, J prison. 383. Cp all, J al.
385. like the here, *so* S1, CpH1DS1Gg liketh the here, JH4RClA liketh here, H3Th
the lyketh here, H2Cx if it lyke the to here (Cx lyketh), Ph if the it lyke to here.
391. ClGgH4R knave (Cl *corrected from* slave), A felawe, H2Ph own *for* sclave;
H5 I can *for* thi sclave. 395. H4 As thou hast seid. 396. JRS1 doost me, Cx hast
me *for* me doost. 398. H2PhH4GgD al þogh *for* al if. 399. Jα oon, Cx bawdry *for* so.

58

"But he that gooth, for gold or for richesse,   400
On swich message, calle hym what the list;
And this that thow doost, calle it gentilesse,
Compassioun, and felawship, and trist;
Departe it so; for wyde wher is wist,
How that ther is diversite requered   405
Bytwixen thynges like, as I have lered.

59

"And that thow knowe I thynke nat, ne wene,
That this servise a shame be or jape,
I have my faire suster, Polixene,
Cassandre, Eleyne, or any of the frape;   410
Be she nevere so faire or wel yshape,
Tel me which thow wilt of everychone,
To han for thyn, and lat me thanne allone.

60

"But sith thow hast idon me this servyse,
My lif to save, and for non hope of mede,   415
So, for the love of god, this grete emprise
Parforme it out; for now is most nede.
For heigh and lough, withouten any drede,
I wol alwey thyne hestes alle kepe;
Have now good nyght, and lat us bothe slepe."   420

401. αH4 *as for* what; CpH1J liste. 403. CpH1J triste. 404. CpH1J wiste. 408. H2PhH4RDS1Cx *or a jape.* 411. R Al be she. 412. γ *om.* me; H4 to whiche, S1 which þat *for* which. 413. H4 I speke for the and. 414. CpClH1Th sith that (Cl syn þat); idon, *so* JRS1H2Ph, *rest* don. 417. Th nowe is the moste (*om.* for), D moste, *rest* most. 419. H4 I wil thi lore & eek thin hestes keepe.

61

Thus held hym eche of other wel apayed,
That al the world ne myghte it bet amende;
And on the morwe, whan they were arayed,
Eche to his owen nedes gan entende.
But Troilus, though as the fir he brende   425
For sharp desir of hope and of plesaunce,
He nought forgat his wyse governaunce,

62

But in hym self with manhood gan restreyne
Eche rakel dede, and ech unbridled cheere,
That alle tho that lyven, soth to seyne,   430
Ne sholde han wist, by word or by manere,
What that he mente, as touchyng this matere.
From every wight as fer as is the cloude
He was, so wel dissimulen he koude.

63

And al this while which that I yow devyse,   435
This was his lif: with al his fulle myght
By day he was in Martes heigh servyse,
That is to seyn, in armes as a knyght;
And for the more part, the longe nyght
He lay, and thoughte how that he myght serve   440
His lady best, hire thonk for to deserve.

---

421. H4S1 *om.* hym; R eche of hem other, H2Ph eche of hem with oþir. 422. H4
So weel that no wiht myht. 425. JClH1DH3H5RCx thoght. 427. γH3S1Th gode (Cp
good) *for* wyse. 431. αH4DCx ne *for* or. 433. α From eche in that as (H5 whiche
for eche). 435. γH3Th the *for* this. 436. Cp all, J alle. 437. S1 emprise. 438.
γ(-A) This *for* That; D *omits line.* 439. αRCx most *for* more. 440. D mot, H5 myte,
R myght hir, *rest* myght.

64

I nyl nat seyn that, though he lay ful softe,
That in his thought he nas somwhat disesed;
And that he torned on his pilwes ofte,
And wolde of that he missed han ben sesed,—   445
But in swich cas men ben nought alwey plesed,
For aught I woot, no more than was he—
This kan I deme of possibilitee.

65

And certeyn is, to purpos for to go,
This mene while, as writen is in geste,   450
He say his lady som tyme, and also
She with hym spak, whan that she dorste and leste;
And by hire bothe avys, as was the beste,
Apoynteden ful warly in this nede,
In every thing how they wolden procede.   455

66

But it was spoken in so short a wise,
In swich await alwey, and in swich feere,
Lest any wight devynen or devyse
Wolde on this thing, or to it leye an ere,
That al this world so lef to hem ne were   460
As Cupido wolde hem a space sende
To maken of hire speche aright an ende.

442-476. *Cx omits five stanzas.* **442.** *So* βS1 (S1 though þat; J laye softe, *om.* ful), γH3Thα Nil I naught swere although he lay softe. **444.** γH3Thα Ne *for* And. **445.** JH4H3GgH5 esed, Cl s *of* sesed *partly erased.* **446.** CpClH1AGgH5 is *for* ben. **448.** γThα That *for* This. **449.** γH3Thα But *for* And. **450.** γH3Thα That in this while (AD That in this mene while; CpH1S2Dig which *for* while). **452.** CpH1JGgH5 or *for* and. **455.** γH3Thα So as they durste how they; H2Ph how ferre. H3DR how þat, Gg so as *for* how. **459.** on this thing, *so* βS1 (R of *for* on; H4 these thynges), α in þis speche, γH3Th of hem two. **461.** γH3S1Th As that; Cupido, *so* ClADS1 H4R, *rest* Cupide; γH3S1Thα *om.* a; γH3S1ThR grace. **462.** ADS1 of this thyng; α *om.* an.

67

But thilke litel that they spake or wroughte,
His wise goost took ay of al swych heede,
It seemed hire he wiste what she thoughte   465
Withouten word, so that it was no nede
To bidde hym ought to doon, or ought forbeede;
For which hire thoughte that love, al come it late,
Of alle joie hadde opned hire the yate.

68

And shortly of this proces for to pace,   470
So wel his werk and wordes he bisette,
That he so ful stood in his lady grace,
That twenty thousand tymes, or she lette,
She thonked god she evere with hym mette;
So koude he hym governe in swich servyse,   475
That al the world ne myghte it bet devyse.

69

For whi, she fond hym so discret in al,
So secret, and of swich obeisaunce,
That wel she felte he was to hire a wal
Of steel, and sheld from every displesaunce;   480
That to ben in his goode governaunce, —
So wis he was,—she was no more afered,
I mene, as fer as oughte ben requered.

---

464. CpJ Hise. 468. γH3S1Thα she (Cp he) *for* hire; thoughte, *so* ClGgH4R, *rest* thought. 470. H2PhH4 forth to passe. 474. CpH1H2PhR that evere she with hym. 476. myghte, *so* GgH4, *rest* myght (H3 cowde); CpH1H3 avyse. 481. S1 That for to ben; goode, *so* GgH3A, *rest* good.

70

And Pandarus, to quike alwey the fir,
Was evere ylike prest and diligent;   485
To ese his frend was set al his desir.
He shof ay on; he to and fro was sent;
He lettres bar whan Troilus was absent;
That nevere wight, as in his frendes nede,
Ne bar hym bet to don his frend to spede.   490

71

But now, paraunter, som man wayten wolde
That every word, or look, or sonde, or cheere
Of Troilus that I rehersen sholde,
In al this while unto his lady deere.
I trowe it were a long thyng for to here,   495
Or of what wight that stant in swich disjoynte,
His wordes alle, or every look, to poynte.

72

For sothe, I have nat herd it don or this,
In story non, ne no man here I wene;
And though I wolde, I koude nat, ywys;   500
For ther was som epistel hem bitwene,
That wolde, as seyth myn auctour, wel contene
An hondred vers, of which hym liste nat write;
How sholde I thanne a lyne of it endite?

484. JH4R this *for* the. 487. H2 to and fro he went, Ph he to and fro went, R
& to and fro he went. 488. CpJ bare; CpH1J absente. 489. γH3Thα man *for*
wight. 490. γH3S1Thα bet than he withouten drede. 491. H2PhH3R men. 492.
So JH4Cx, R look or every sond (*om.* word), γH3S1ThGgH5 word or sonde or look,
H2Ph sond or word or loke. 495. GgH5 tyme, R tune *for* thyng. 503. γH3S1Thα
Neigh half this book of which.

73

But to the grete effect: than seye I thus,   505
That, stondyng in concord and in quiete
Thise ilke two, Criseyde and Troilus,
As I have seyd, and in this tyme swete,—
Save only often myghte they nat mete,
Ne leiser have hire speches to fulfille—   510
That it bifel, right as I shal yow telle,

74

That Pandarus, which that alwey dide his myght
Right for the fyn that I shal speke of here,
As for to bryngen to his hous som nyght
His faire nece and Troilus yfere,   515
Where as at leiser al this heigh matere,
Touchyng hire love, were at the fulle up bounde,
Hadde, as hym thought, a tyme to it founde.

75

For he, with gret deliberacioun,
Hadde every thyng that herto myghte availle   520
Forncast, and put in execucioun,
And neither left for cost ne for travaille;
Come if hem list, hem sholde no thyng faille;
And for to ben in ought espied there,
That thoughte he wel an impossible were.   525

507. CpH1J ilk. 508. γH3Thα tolde. 510. JGgH5 speche; Th fulfell. 512. H2PhR Pandare; γH3S1Th *om.* which, JGgH5 *om.* that; γH3S1Thα evere *for* alwey. 517. Cp here *for* hire. 518. γH3Thα Hadde out of doute; RCx therto *for* to it. 520. H3ADS1CxTh therto; myghte, *so* ClGg, *rest* myght. 524. α Ne *for* And (H5 Nor). 525. γH3Thα wiste; CpJGgPhD and *for* an, H5 *om.* an; H3H4H5 it were.

76

Dredeles, it clere was in the wynd
Of every pie and every lette-game;
Thus al is wel, for al the world is blynd
In this matere, bothe wilde and tame.
This tymber is al redy up to frame;   530
Us lakketh nought but that we weten wolde
A certeyn houre, in which she comen sholde.

77

And Troilus, that al this purveiaunce
Knew at the fulle, and waited on it ay,
Hadde here upon ek made his ordinaunce,   535
And founde his cause, and therto al the aray,
That if that he were missed, nyght or day,
Ther while he was abouten this servyse,
That he was gon to don his sacrifise,

78

And moste at swich a temple allone wake,   540
Answered of Apollo for to be;
And first to sen the holy laurer quake,
Or that Apollo spake out of the tree,
To telle hym whan the Grekes sholden flee,
And forthy lette hym no man, god forbede,   545
But preye Apollo that he wolde hym spede.

---

526. H3S1CxTh And dredles; CpH1J wynde. 527. CpClS2Dig From *for* Of; JH4RGgH5D of *for* and (H4 or of). 528. γH3Thα Now *for* Thus; H2PhJRCx þis world; CpH1J blynde. 529. γThH5 fremed, H2PhGg frende *for* wilde (J wild). 531. CpH1S1H2PhCx witen. 534. Cl waytede. 535. γH3S1Th grete *for* his. 536. γ(-AD)H3Th his *for* al the. 537. γTh If that, H3 And yf that, H4 That yif *for* That if that. 538. H2GgH5Cx The while. 543. α Or þat the god ouȝt spak out of the tre (H2Ph *om.* ouȝt). 544. γH3S1Thα hym next whan; CpClH1AH3ThH4H5 *om.* the, J þat, H2Ph þat þe *for* the. 546. CpClJ prey; γH3S1Thα helpen in this nede (H2PhD help hym in his nede); H4R wil *for* wolde.

79

Now is ther litel more for to doone,
But Pandare up, and, shortly for to seyne,
Right sone upon the chaungynge of the moone,
Whan lightles is the world a nyght or tweyne,   550
And that the wolken shop hym for to reyne,
He streyght o morwe unto his nece wente;
Ye han wel herd the fyn of his entente.

80

Whan he was there, he gan anon to pleye
As he was wont, and at hym self to jape;   555
And finaly he swor and gan hire seye,
By this and that, she sholde hym nought escape,
Ne make hym lenger after hire to gape;
But certeynly she moste, by hire leve,
Come soupen in his hous with hym at eve.   560

81

At which she lough, and gan hire faste excuse,
And seyde: "it reyneth; lo, how sholde I gon?"
"Lat be," quod he, "ne stond nat thus to muse;
This moot be don, ye shal be there anon."
So at the laste, herof they fille at oon,   565
Or elles, softe he swor hire in hire ere,
He wolde nevere comen ther she were.

---

549. α Lo *for* Right. 551. wolken, *so* Cp, J wolkne, Cl walkene, H1 walken, GgA
walkyn, *rest* welkyn *or* welken. 554. γH3Thα come *for* there. 555. γ(-D)H3Thα of
for at. 558. γTh Ne lenger don hym, H3 Ne lenger hym doon, α Ne done hym
lenger; CpH1Th cape, J kape. 563. CpHl stant, J stonde. 567. CpClH1S1ThH5
nolde, H3 shulde; H3RCx ther as.

82

And she agayne gan to hym for to rowne,
And axed hym if Troilus were there.
He swor hir nay, for he was out of towne,   570
And seyde: "nece, I pose that he were,
Yow thurste nevere han the more fere;
For rather than men sholde hym ther aspie,
Me were levere a thousand fold to dye."

83

Nat list myn auctour fully to declare   575
What that she thoughte whan he seyde so,
That Troilus was out of towne yfare,
As if he seyde soth therof or no;
But that she graunted with hym for to go
Withoute await, syn that he hire bisoughte,   580
And, as his nece, obeyed as hire oughte.

84

But natheles, yit gan she hym biseche,
Although with hym to gon it was no fere,
For to be war of goosissh poeples speche,
That dremen thynges whiche that nevere were,   585
And wel avyse hym whom he broughte there;
And seyde hym: "em, syn I most on yow triste,
Loke al be wel, for I do as yow liste."

568. γH3Thα Soone after this she gan to hym to rowne (CpH1S2AH3 she to hym gan, Cl to hym she gan; H2PhH5H3D *om. second* to), S1 Soon after that she gan unto him rowne; H4Cx *om. first* to. 569. JGgH5S1 was. 571. H2Ph And seyd y suppose that he were there; Gg (*by corrector*) And seyde what I pose, H5 And he sayde what I suppose; H3Cx that he where there; H4 I suppose he ther wer; R And nyece I pose that he ther were. 572. H1Ph þow, Gg He, JH4RCxS1H5 Ye *for* Yow; CpH1 thruste, J thorste, H4 thurste, H3A thurst, D thurte, Gg þourrste, S1H5 thurft, Cl dorste, H2PhCx durst, Th durste, R aghten. 573. γH3Thα myghte. 576. CpClH2Ph whan that he. 578. H3H4RTh And *for* As; γ(-AD)Thα therof soth. 579, 580. γH3Thα :—

But that, withowten await, with hym to go
She graunted hym, sith he hire that bisoughte

(H2Ph *om.* await, H5(Ph *over line*) more *for* await; GgH5 þat he hire, it *for* hym; H2Ph *om.* that). 587. CpD moste, H2PhH5Cx must, GgH4 mot. 588. γH3S1Thα and do now as yow liste; J þat *for* as.

85

He swor hire this by stokkes and by stones,
And by the goddes that in hevene dwelle,   590
Or elles were hym levere, fel and bones,
With Pluto kyng as depe ben in helle
As Tantalus. What sholde I more telle?
Whan al was wel, he roos and took his leve;
And she to soper com, whan it was eve,   595

86

With a certein of hire owen men,
And with hire faire nece, Antigone,
And other of hire wommen nyne or ten;
But who was glad now, who, as trowe ye,
But Troilus, that stood and myght it se   600
Thorughoute a litel wyndow in a stuwe,
Ther he bishet syn mydnyght was in muwe,

87

Unwist of every wight but of Pandare?
But now to purpos: whan that she was come
With alle joie, and alle frendes fare,   605
Hire em anon in armes hath hire nome,
And after to the soper, alle and some,
Whan tyme was, ful softe they hem sette;
God woot, ther was no deynte for to fette.

589. γH3S1Th yis (Cp yes), Cx tho *for* this, H2PhH4 *om.* this. 591. γThα soule
and bones. 593. H4RCx lenger duelle, J longe telle. 594. H2 Whan þis was do,
Ph Whan tyme was. 598. α And of her wymmen wele a ix or x (H2Ph *om.* of,
GgH5 *om.* a). 599. α is glad. 601. α Thurgh out an hole wiþ yn a litil stewe (Gg
of for wiþ yn; H5 a lytyll hole of a stewe). 604. γH3Thα But to the point now;
ClH1ADH3H2PhH4 *om.* that; Cl ycome. 607. R And after ward to souper. 608.
JH4S1Cx to soper they hem sette (Cx be *for* hem); R Whan it was tyme faste
they hem sette.

88

And after soper gonnen they to rise,   610
At ese wel, with hertes fresshe and glade,
And wel was hym that koude best devyse
To liken hire, or that hire laughen made.
He song; she pleyde; he tolde tale of Wade.
But at the laste, as every thyng hath ende,   615
She took hire leve, and nedes wolde wende.

89

But O, Fortune, executrice of wyerdes,
O influences of thise hevenes hye,
Soth is that, under god, ye ben oure hierdes,
Though to us bestes ben the causes wrie.   620
This mene I now, for she gan homward hye,
But execut was al bisyde hire leve
The goddes wil, for which she moste bleve.

90

The bente moone with hire hornes pale,
Saturne, and Jove in Cancro joyned were,   625
That swych a reyn from hevene gan avale,
That every maner womman that was there
Hadde of that smoky reyn a verray feere;
At which Pandare tho lough, and seyde thenne:
"Now were it tyme a lady to gon henne!   630

612. αH3 best coude (H2Ph couþe). 614. Cl tales, H3S1H5Cx a tale, H2Ph þe tale;
R and eke he tolde of wade. 616. Cl she wolde wende, H3S1H5 wolde she wende,
Cx wold home wende. 620. α is þe cause ywrye; R be the cause. 621. α I mene it now
for she gan home to hye (H5 *om.* to). 623. γ(-AD)Th At the goddes wil. 626. α
þat madyn such a reyne fro hevyn avale. 627. RH5Cx man & womman. 629. α *om.*
tho, R that *for* tho.

91

"But, goode nece, if I myghte evere plese
Yow any thyng, than prey ich yow," quod he,
"To don myn herte as now so grete an ese
As for to dwelle here al this nyght with me,
For, nece, this is youre owen hous, parde.   635
Now, by my trouthe, I sey it nat a game,
To wende as now, it were to me a shame."

92

Criseyde, which that koude as muche good
As half a world, took hede of his preyere;
And syn it ron, and al was on a flood,   640
She thoughte, as good chepe may I dwellen here,
And graunte it gladly with a frendes chere,
And have a thonk, as grucche and thanne abide;
For hom to gon, it may nat wel bitide.

93

"I wol," quod she, "myn uncle lief and deere,   645
Syn that yow list, it skile is to be so;
I am right glad with yow to dwellen here;
I seyde but a game, I wolde go."
"Iwys, graunt mercy, nece," quod he tho,
"Were it a game or no, soth for to telle,   650
Now am I glad, syn that yow list to dwelle."

631. CpJ good. 635. γH3Thα For whi this is. 636. γTh For, H3S1 And *for* Now;
Cl for no game. 637. JH4S1GgPh to me it were, R to me were it, H3 *om.* to me. 642.
H2D frendly, Ph prevy, GgH5 frely *for* gladly. 648. H2PhH5H4Cx þat y wold
go. 650. α none; H2PhR þe soþe to tell. 651. αJ ȝe wolyn dwelle (Gg ȝe wele with
me dwelle; J wol).

94

Thus al is wel; but tho bigan aright
The newe joie, and al the feste agayn;
But Pandarus, if goodly hadde he myght,
He wolde han hyed hire to bedde fayn,   655
And seyde: "lord, this is an huge rayn!
This were a weder for to slepen inne;
And that I rede us soone to bygynne.

95

"And, nece, woot ye where I shal yow leye,
For that we shul nat liggen fer asonder,   660
And for ye neither shullen, dar I seye,
Heren noyse of reynes nor of thonder?
By god, right in my litel closet yonder.
And I wol in that outer hous allone
Be wardein of youre wommen everichone.   665

96

"And in this myddel chaumbre that ye se
Shul youre wommen slepen, wel and softe;
And al withinne shal youre selven be;
And if ye liggen wel to nyght, com ofte,
And careth nought what weder is alofte.   670
The wyn anon, and whan so that yow leste,
Than is it tyme for to gon to reste."

---

655. H2PhGg hym, H5 hem *for* hire. 659. γS1Thα wol, H3 wold *for* shal. 660. Cp
far, J for *for* fer. 661. H2Ph sholdyn neiþer, H5Cx shall neyther. 663. ClH1J lite.
665. JH4H2Ph yow (Ph *corrected later to* yower) *for* youre. 667. S1H5Cx shall all.
668. γH3Thα And there I seyde shal. 670. JH4 But *for* And. 671. H2Ph Goth yn
anone, H5 Let all alone, Cx The wyne was brought; H3 To wyn. 672. γThα So go
we slepe I trowe it be the beste (H2Ph *om.* So; Th Go we to slepe).

97

Ther was no more, but hereafter soone,
The voide dronke, and travers drawe anon,
Gan every wight, that hadde nat to done   675
More in the place, out of the chaumbre gon;
And alweye in this meene while it ron,
And blew therwith so wonderliche loude,
That wel neigh no man heren other koude.

98

Tho Pandarus, hire em, right as hym oughte,   680
With wommen swiche as were hire most aboute,
Ful glad unto hire beddes syde hire broughte,
And took his leve, and gan ful lowe loute,
And seyde: "here at this closet dore withoute,
Right overthwart, youre wommen liggen alle,   685
That whom yow list of hem ye may hire calle."

99

So whan that she was in the closet leyd,
And alle hire wommen forth by ordinaunce
Abedde weren, ther as I have seyd,
There was no more to skippen nor to traunce,   690
But boden go to bedde, with meschaunce,
If any wight was steryng any where,
And lat hem slepen that abedde were.

673. was, *so* βS1, CpClH1GgTh nys, H2PhH5AD is.   674. *So* γS1H4; JCxTh They *for* The; Gg þey voydyn dronkyn; H3 Thei dranke voyded; R Drynk voide & travers; H2Ph They voydid & drunk & curtyns drew anone; H5 Whan they had dronke than fast & þat anon.   676. αClH1 þat place.   677. γH3Thα And evere mo so sterneliche it ron.   678. Cp blewe, J blewgh.   679. H4Cx othir heer.   683. α to lout (Gg & low & gan to loute; H5 and lowe gan to lowte).   686. CpClH1 here, JH4S1D hir, H2PhA her, GgH3 *om.* hire; H5 ye may to yow calle (to *deleted*); CxTh ye may soone calle; R ye mowen calle.   687. CpJ leyde; R in closet was ileyde.   689. RS1H5Cx I have ʒow seyd.   690. JRH3H2PhGgGcx ne *for* nor.   692. αJH4Cx man *for* wight.

100

But Pandarus, that wel koude eche a del
The olde daunce, and every point therinne, 695
Whan that he sey that alle thyng was wel,
He thought he wolde upon his werk bigynne,
And gan the stuwe doore al softe unpynne,
And stille as stoon, withouten lenger lette,
By Troilus adown right he hym sette. 700

101

And, shortly to the point right for to gon,
Of al this thing he tolde hym worde and ende,
And seyde: "make the redy right anon,
For thow shalt into hevene blisse wende."
"Now seint Venus, thow me grace sende," 705
Quod Troilus, "for nevere yit no nede
Hadde ich or now, ne halvendel the drede."

102

Quod Pandarus: "ne drede the nevere a del,
For it shal be right as thow wolt desire;
So thryve I, this nyght shal I make it wel, 710
Or casten al the gruwel in the fire."
"Yit, blisful Venus, this nyght thow me enspire,"
Quod Troilus, "as wys as I the serve,
And evere bet and bet shal til I sterve.

---

694. α And *for* But. 696. α he wist (GgH5 woste); alle, *so* H1AGgH5H3, *rest al.* 699. CpH1S2Th As stille as; α more let; H4 any lett. 702. γH3S1Thα Of al this werk. 705. seint Venus, *so* JH4CxS1 (β), R Now Venus pray I þat thow, γH3Thα blisful Venus. 710. αH4Cx y shal. 712. α Now seynt Venus.

103

"And if ich hadde, O Venus ful of myrthe,   715
Aspectes badde of Mars or of Saturne,
Or thow combust or let were in my birthe,
Thy fader prey al thilke harm disturne
Of grace, and that I glad ayein may turne,
For love of hym thow lovedest in the shawe,   720
I meene Adon, that with the boor was slawe.

104

"O Jove ek, for the love of faire Europe,
The which in forme of bole awey thow fette,
Now help; O Mars, thow with thi blody cope,
For love of Cipres, thow me nought ne lette;   725
O Phebus, thynk whan Dane hire selven shette
Under the bark, and laurer wax for drede,
Yit for hire love, O help now at this nede.

105

"Mercurie, for the love of Hierse eke,
For which Pallas was with Aglauros wroth,   730
Now help; and ek Diane, I the biseke,
That this viage be nat to the looth.
O fatal sustren, which or any cloth
Me shapen was, my destine me sponne,
So helpeth to this werk that is bygonne."   735

---

715. Cp As, J An *for* And.   717. α cumbrid (H5 encumbryd).   722. CpClADS2
om. O.   724. H4R rede *for* blody.   725. JGg Cipris, H2Ph Ciphis (Ph *altered to*
Typhis), H3 Cyphres, Cx Cipac, D Cipresse, Th Cipria, H5 Venus.   726. H2Ph
CxS1 Diane, R don, Th Daphne.   729. Gg hirie, H5CxTh hir, R hyeas.   730. H1A
Aglowros, H4R Aglaures, H5 Aglours, Gg aglouros, S1Cx Aglaurus.   735. α Now
helpith.

106

Quod Pandarus: "thow wrecched mouses herte!
Artow agast so that she wol the bite?
Why, don this furred cloke upon thy sherte,
And folwe me, for I wol han the wite;
But bide, and lat me gon biforn a lite."   740
And with that word he gan undon a trappe,
And Troilus he broughte in by the lappe.

107

The sterne wynd so loude gan to route,
That no wight oother noise myghte heere;
And they that layen at the dore withoute,   745
Ful sikirly they slepten alle yfere;
And Pandarus, with a ful sobre cheere,
Goth to the dore anon withouten lette,
There as they laye, and softely it shette.

108

And as he com ayeynward pryvely,   750
His nece awook, and axed: "who goth there?"
"My dere nece," quod he, "it am I;
Ne wondreth nought, ne have of it no fere";
And ner he com, and seyde hire in hire ere:
"No word, for love of god, I yow biseche;   755
Lat no wight risen and heren of oure speche."

---

737. H2PhR lest, H4 for *for* so. 741. H2PhCx þe trappe. 751. αR seid *for* axed.
755. GgH5RCx for þe love. 756. GgH5 Let hem not rysyn.

109

"What! which wey be ye comen, benedicite?"
Quod she, "and how thus unwist of hem alle?"
"Here at this litil trappe dore," quod he.
Quod tho Criseyde: "lat me som wight calle."　　760
"I! god forbede that it sholde falle,"
Quod Pandarus, "that ye swich folye wroughte;
They myghte demen that they nevere er thoughte.

110

"It is nat good a slepyng hound to wake,
Ne yeve a wight a cause to devyne;　　765
Youre wommen slepen alle, I undertake,
So that for hem the hous men myghte myne,
And slepen wollen til the sonne shyne;
And whan my tale brought is to an ende,
Unwist, right as I com, so wol I wende.　　770

111

"Now, nece myn, ye shul wel understonde,"
Quod he, "so as ye wommen demen alle,
That for to holde longe a man in honde,
And hym hire lief and deere herte calle,
And maken hym an howve above a calle,—　　775
I meene as love another in this while,—
She doth hire self a shame, and hym a gyle.

757. J bendiste.　758. γH3ThR *om.* thus.　759. γH3Thα secre *for* litil (J lite).
761. H2PhH5 Ey, Th Eygh, Cx O *for* I; R quod he *for* that.　762. R *om.* Quod
Pandarus, folie in any maner wroughte.　763. CpClJ myght; γ(-D)Thα thyng,
H3S1D þing that *for* that.　764. CpH1J hounde.　766. H5 I dar undirtake. 766, 767.
H2Ph Your wymmen alle y dare undirtake/Slepe þat for hem men myght þis house
myne.　769. JH3DS1 ibrought is, Cl al brought is, H2PhH5H4Th is broght.　773.
γS1Thα in love *for* longe; RCx a man longe.　775. Cp in, J at, A and, αH4D a *for*
an.　776. γH3S1ThJCx in this meene while (S1 *om.* this; DCx þe *for* this).

112

"Now wherby that I telle yow al this?
Ye woot youre self, as wel as any wight,
How that youre love al fully graunted is   780
To Troilus, the worthieste knyght,
Oon of this world, and therto trouthe yplight,
That, but it were on hym alonge, ye nolde
Hym nevere falsen, while ye lyven sholde.

113

"Now stant it thus, that sith I fro yow wente,   785
This Troilus, right platly for to seyn,
Is thorugh a goter, by a pryve wente,
Into my chaumbre come in al this reyn,
Unwist of every manere wight, certeyn,
Save of my self, as wisly have I joye,   790
And by that feith I shal Priam of Troie.

114

"And he is come in swich peyne and distresse,
That, but he be al fully wood by this,
He sodeynly mot falle into woodnesse,
But if god helpe; and cause whi this is?   795
He seith hym told is of a frende of his,
How that ye sholden loven oon that hatte Horaste,
For sorwe of which this nyght shal ben his laste."

782. αH4H3Cl On, DS1CxTh One; GgH5H3Th þe *for* this. 785. S1 syn þat,
H4Cx *om*. that. 789. H2PhH5Cx eny *for* every. 791. CpH1H5Th the *for* that;
H2CxTh owe (H2 ow), H4H5 owe to *for* shal. 795. this is, *so* CpH1AS1JGg, *rest
is* this. 796. CpH1J tolde. 797. Cl loven sholde, JRH3H2Ph *om. second* that,
Cx *om*. that hatte.

115

Criseyde, which that al this wonder herde,
Gan therwith al aboute hire herte colde,   800
And with a sik she sodeynly answerde:
"Allas! I wende, who so tales tolde,
My deere herte wolde me nat holde
So lightly fals; allas! conceytes wronge,
What harm they don! for now lyve I to longe.   805

116

"Horaste, allas! and falsen Troilus!
I know hym nat, god helpe me so," quod she,
"Allas! what wikked spirit tolde hym thus?
Now certes, em, tomorwe, and I hym se,
I shal of that as ful excusen me   810
As evere dide womman, if hym like";
And with that word she gan ful soore sike.

·117

"O god!" quod she, "so worldly selynesse,
Which clerkes callen fals felicitee,
Imedled is with many a bitternesse!   815
Ful angwisshous than is, god woot," quod she,
"Condicioun of veyn prosperitee;
For either joies comen nought yfeere,
Or elles no wight hath hem alwey here.

---

799. α *of for* al.   800. γH3Thα sodeynly *for* therwith al; Cx *om.* al.   801. γH3
Thα sorwfully.   802. H4 who that, RS1 who so that *for* who so.   810. γH3S1Th
therof, H5 of þis *for* of that; ClAH2PhCx fully.   811. H2PhCx if þat hym.   813.
JH1H4RH3 wordly, GgH5 wordeli, A worthly.   819. α long *for* alwey (Gg longe
here *by corrector*).

118

"O brotel wele! O worldly joie unstable!   820
With what wight so thow be, or how thow pleye,
Either he woot that thow, joie, art muable,
Or woot it nought, it mot ben oon of tweye.
Now if he woot it nought, how may he seye
That he hath verray joie and selynesse,   825
That is of ignoraunce ay in derknesse?

119

"Now if he woot that joie is transitorie,
As every joie of worldly thyng mot flee,
Than every tyme he that hath in memorie,
The drede of lesyng maketh hym that he   830
May in no parfit selynesse be;
And if to lese his joie he sette a myte,
Than semeth it that joie is worth ful lite.

120

"Wherfore I wol deffyne in this manere:
That trewely, for aught I kan espie,   835
Ther is no verray weele in this world heere.
But O, thow wikked serpent, jalousie,
Thow mysbyleved, envyous folie,
Why hastow Troilus made to me untriste,
That nevere yit agilte hym, that I wiste?"   840

---

820. γH3Thα of mannes *for* o worldly, Cx of *for* O, JH4R wordly. 821. H2Ph *om.* so; GgH5 þat, H4Cx so that *for* so; α how so (H2 how so þat) *for* or how; R *om.* how, Cx *om.* how thow. 822. RCx art joye; α mevable (Gg movabele). 825. H4 sekirnesse. 828. H1H3GgH4R wordly. 831. H4CxTh sekirnesse. 834. CpH1DS2 H2PhTh matere. 838. γ(-AD)Th and envyous. 839. H2Ph Why hast þou þus; H1ClH3H5Cx made Troilus; H2PhAD to me made (H2 *om.* to); H4 me to, RCx *om.* to.

121

Quod Pandarus: "thus fallen is this cas."
"Why, uncle myn," quod she, "who tolde hym this?
Why doth my deere herte thus, allas?"
"Ye woot, ye nece myn," quod he, "what is.
I hope al shal be wel that is amys;   845
For ye may quenche al this, if that yow leste;
And doth right so, for I holde it the beste."

122

"So shal I do tomorwe, ywys," quod she,
"And, god to-forn, so that it shal suffise."
"Tomorwe? allas, that were a faire," quod he;   850
"Nay, nay, it may nat stonden in this wise.
For, nece myn, thus writen clerkes wise,
That peril is with drecchyng in ydrawe;
Nay, swiche abodes ben nat worth an hawe.

123

"Nece, alle thyng hath tyme, I dar avowe;   855
For whan a chaumbre afire is, or an halle,
Wel more nede is it, sodeynly rescowe
Than to dispute, and axe amonges alle
How is this candele in the straw ifalle?
A! benedicite! for al among that fare   860
The harm is don, and farewel feldefare!

---

841. H3H4H5D the *for* this. 846. H2PhH4H3Cx ye *for* yow. 847. H3H5CxTh *om.* for; H1H3H5CxTh for þe beste. 850. H2PhCxTh *om.* a; H5 all lost, S1 to ferr, A fer *for* a faire. 855. alle, *so* H1ADS1Gg, *rest* al. 857. ClR *om.* wel; α Hit nedith more sodenly (H5 the more); H3 is nede hit; ClJA to rescowe, R it rescowe, H2Ph hit to rescow. 859. γThCx How this candele in the straw is falle (CpDS2Th the *for* this; Cx dyde falle). 860. J bendiste; JRH3 this *for* that.

124

"And, nece myn, ne take it nat agrief,
If that ye suffre hym al nyght in this wo,
God helpe me so, ye hadde hym nevere lief,
That dar I seyn, now is ther but we two; 865
But wel I woot that ye wol nat do so;
Ye ben to wys to doon so grete folie,
To putte his lif al nyght in jupartie."

125

"Hadde I hym nevere lief! By god, I weene
Ye hadde nevere thyng so lief," quod she. 870
"Now, by my thrift," quod he, "that shal be seene;
For, syn ye maken this ensaumple of me,
If ich al nyght wolde hym in sorwe se,
For al the tresour in the town of Troie,
I bidde god I nevere mot have joie. 875

126

"Now loke thanne, if ye, that ben his love,
Shul putte his lif al night in jupartie
For thyng of nought, now, by that god above,
Nat oonly this delay comth of folie,
But of malice, if I shal nat lye. 880
What! platly, and ye suffre hym in destresse,
Ye neyther wisdom don ne gentilesse."

---

862. αJCl *om.* ne. 869. J ich, S1 Iche. 870. ClCx I hadde, Gg Ne hadde I, H5 Ye
ne yet ne hadde, H2Ph Yet had y. 871. H2PhH4 it *for* that. 872. GgH5H3H4 by *for*
of. 875. α I pray to god, H3 I pray gode; H2PhH5H4 y never more have joy,
GgCx neveremore have I joye. 877. GgH5DTh scholde; ClGgH5RCx al nyght his
lyf. 880. γH3S1Th if that *for* if. 882. γH3S1Thα bounte don (H2Ph Ye done hym
neiþer good; H5 bote *for* bounte), Cx wysely don.

127

Quod tho Criseyde: "wol ye don o thyng,
And ye therwith shal stynte al his disese?
Have here, and bereth hym this blewe ryng,   885
For ther is no thyng myghte hym bettre plese,
Save I my self, ne more hys herte apese;
And sey my deere herte, that his sorwe
Is causeles, that shal be sen tomorwe."

128

"A ryng!" quod he, "ye, haselwodes shaken!   890
Ye, nece myn, that ryng moste han a stoon,
That myghte dede men alyve maken;
And swich a ryng, trowe I, that ye have non.
Discrecioun out of youre hed is gon,
That fele I now," quod he, "and that is routhe;   895
O tyme ilost, wel maistow corsen slouthe!

129

"Woot ye nat wel that noble and heigh corage
Ne sorweth nat, ne stynteth ek, for lite?
But if a fool were in a jalous rage,
I nolde setten at his sorwe a myte,   900
But feffe hym with a fewe wordes white
Another day, whan that I myghte hym fynde;
But this thing stant al in another kynde.

---

884. JRCxH2PhGg stynten *for* stynte al. 885. Cp heere, J her. 889. α Is nedeles
(H5 endles); H4RACxTh he see. 890. αH4Cx hasilwode is shakyn. 892. ClR a dede
man. 898. R Ne sore oght nat be stynted for so lite. 900. H2PhR his sorow at a
myte.

130

"This is so gentil and so tendre of herte,
That with his deth he wol his sorwe wreke;   905
For trusteth wel, how sore that hym smerte,
He wol to yow no jalous wordes speke.
And forthi, nece, or that his herte breke,
So speke youre self to hym of this matere;
For with o word ye may his herte stere.   910

131

"Now have I told what peril he is inne,
And his comyng unwist is to every wight;
And, parde, harm may ther be non, ne synne;
I wol my self be with yow al this nyght.
Ye knowe ek how it is youre owen knyght,   915
And that bi right ye moste upon hym triste,
And I al prest to fecche hym whan yow liste."

132

This accident so pitous was to here,
And ek so lik a sooth at prime face,
And Troilus hire knyght to hir so deere,   920
His prive comyng, and the siker place,
That though that she dede hym as thanne a grace,
Considered alle thynges as they stoode,
No wonder is, syn she dide al for goode.

---

905. γH3S1ThGgH5 sorwes.   906. JH4 he *for* hym.   912. GgH5H4H3DCx *om.*
is; H3H4H5ACx of *for* to.   913. γH3S1Th Ne *for* And; H2PhGg here.   915. H2PhCx
wele eke, H4 weel eek how, H5 ek *for* ek how; αH4H3 he *for* it.   922. Jα tho, R
that tyme *for* thanne.   924. α for *for* syn.

133

Criseyde answerde: "as wisly god at reste   925
My soule brynge, as me is for hym wo;
And, em, iwis, fayn wolde I don the beste,
If that ich hadde grace to do so.
But whether that ye dwelle or for hym go,
I am, til god me bettre mynde sende,   930
At dulcarnon, right at my wittes ende."

134

Quod Pandarus: "ye, nece, wol ye here?
Dulcarnon called is 'flemyng of wrecches.
It semeth hard, for wrecches wol nat lere,
For verray slouthe and other wilful tecches.   935
This seyd by hem that ben nat worth two fecches;
But ye ben wis, and this matere on honde
Nis neither hard, ne skilful to withstonde."

135

"Than, em," quod she, "doth herof as yow list;
But or he come, I wol up first arise;   940
And, for the love of god, syn al my trist
Is on yow two, and ye ben bothe wise,
So werketh now in so discret a wise,
That ich honour may have and he plesaunce;
For I am here as in youre governaunce."   945

926. H4 I am. 928. CpTh a grace hadde, H1S2 grace had, JR hadde a grace;
γH3S1ThH5 for to do so. 930. H2PhH5R wit (R til god wol bettre wit me sende).
931. γS1 A *for* At (Cl *corrected from* At); CpJ dulcarnoun. 933. α clepid. 934. α
nel hit. 935. γ(-Cl)H3Th or *for* and. 936. CpAH4Th This is seyd (Cp seyde).
H5 That is seyde, H2Ph þis seid is, Cx Thys seyd he, R I sey. 937. γH3Thα and
that we han on honde (GgH3Th ȝe *for* we). 938. H2PhH4 Is; Cp noither, J
neythir. 939, 941. CpH1J liste, triste. 945. γH3S1ThH2Ph al, Cx now *for* as, H5
om. as.

136

"That is wel seyd," quod he, "my nece deere,
Ther good thrift on that wise gentil herte!
But liggeth stille, and taketh hym right here;
It nedeth nought no ferther for to sterte.
And ech of yow ese otheres sorwes smerte,   950
For love of god; and, Venus, I the herye;
For soone hope I we shul alle be merye."

137

This Troilus ful soone on knees hym sette
Ful sobrely, right by hire beddes heed,
And in his beste wyse his lady grette;   955
But, lord, so she wex sodeynliche reed!
Ne, though men sholde smyten of hire heed,
She myghte nat a word aright out brynge
So sodeynly, for his sodeyn comynge.

138

But Pandarus, that so wel koude feele   960
In every thyng, to pleye anon bigan,
And seyde: "nece, se how this lord kan knele!
Now, for youre trouthe, se this gentil man!
And with that word he for a quysshen ran,
And seyde: "kneleth now, whil that yow leste,   965
Ther god youre hertes brynge soone at reste!"

---

946. αH1Cx This *for* That; H4R was *for* is; CpH1J seyde. 950. H3H4RADCxTh
other, J oothre. 952. H2PhH4R y hope; γH3H2PhGg ben alle, S1H5Th *om.* alle.
953-959. H3 *omits stanza.* 953. α on knees sone (*om.* ful); Cp knewes, H1 knowes,
J knowe. 954. CpJ hede. 956. CpClJ sodeynlich; CpH1J rede. 957. CpJ hede; α
And þogh she shold anon have be dede (H5 anon shulde; Gg *omits line*). 958.
γH3Thα koude (Cp kouth). 962. α And seyd nece how wel lord can he knele (Ph
& seyd lord how longe wil ʒe knele). 966. RCx That *for* Ther; H2PhS1 sone
bryng; H3H4H5A to *for* at.

139

Kan I nat seyn, for she bad hym nat rise,
If sorwe it putte out of hire remembraunce,
Or elles that she took it in the wise
Of dewete, as for his observaunce; 970
But wel fynde I she dede hym this plesaunce,
That she hym kiste, although she siked sore,
And bad hym sitte adown withouten more.

140

Quod Pandarus: "now wol ye wel bigynne;
Now doth hym sitte, goode nece deere, 975
Upon youre beddes syde al ther withinne,
That eche of yow the bet may other heere."
And with that word he drow hym to the feere,
And took a light, and fond his contenaunce
As for to looke upon an old romaunce. 980

141

Criseyde, that was Troilus lady right,
And clere stood on a grounde of sikernesse,
Al thoughte she, hire servaunt and hire knyght
Ne sholde of right non untrouthe in hire gesse,
Yit natheles, considered his distresse, 985
And that love is in cause of swich folie,
Thus to hym spak she of his jalousie:

---

969. H4RCx this, H2Ph such a *for* the. 971. JH4R wot I, Cx I rede, H3 I fynde.
975. ClH2H5 sitte now, Ph sittyn doun, R thanne sitten (*om.* goode). 986. Gg *om.*
in, D *om.* in cause. 987. S1 spak she to hym.

142

"Lo, herte myn, as wolde the excellence
Of love, ayeins the which that no man may,
Ne oughte ek goodly, maken resistence,   990
And ek bycause I felte wel and say
Youre grete trouthe and servise every day,
And that youre herte al myn was, soth to seyne,
This drof me for to rewe upon youre peyne.

143

"And youre goodnesse have I founden alwey yit,   995
Of which, my deere herte and al my knyght,
I thonke it yow, as fer as I have wit,
Al kan I nought so muche as it were right;
And I emforth my connyng and my might,
Have, and ay shal, how sore that me smerte,   1000
Ben to yow trewe and hool with al myn herte;—

144

"And dredeles, this shal be founde at preve.
But, herte myn, what al this is to seyne
Shal wel be told, so that ye nat yow greve,
Though I to yow right on youre self compleyne.   1005
For therwith mene I fynaly the peyne,
That halt youre herte and myn in hevynesse,
Fully to slen, and every wrong redresse.

---

988. H4R thexcellence. **989.** αH4RCx *om.* that; α wight. **994.** H2PhGgH3Cx *om.*
for; Cl first, H1 fer *for* for. **998.** γH3S1ThH2PhCx as muche. **1002.** γH3ThαCx
that *for* this. **1004.** ClDH2PhH5Cx ye yow not. **1008.** CpH1J wronge.

145

"My goode myn, noot I for why, ne how,
That jalousie, allas, that wikked wyvere,   1010
So causeles is cropen into yow;
The harm of which I wolde fayn delyvere.
Allas, that he, al hool, or of hym slyvere,
Sholde han his refut in so digne a place,
Ther Jove hym soone out of youre herte arace!   1015

146

"But O, thow Jove, O auctour of nature,
Is this an honour to thi deyte,
That folk ungiltif suffren here injure,
And he that giltif is, al quyt goth he?
O, were it leful for to pleyne on the,   1020
That undeserved suffrest jalousie,
Of that I wolde upon the pleyne and crye.

147

"Ek al my wo is this, that folk now usen
To seyn right thus: 'ye, jalousie is love';
And wolde a busshel venym al excusen,   1025
For that o greyn of love is in it shove.
But that woot heigh god that sit above,
If it be liker love, or hate, or grame;
And after that it oughte bere his name.

1009. H2PhH3 hert myn, DCx herte, C1 *(corrected)* love *for* myn. 1011. γH3Thα Thus *for* So. 1015. H2PhH4CxTh þat *for* Ther. 1019. γ(-AD)H3Thα who *for* he. 1024. JH2PhH3Cx that, H5 þe, H4 ya *for* ye. 1025. H2Ph of jelosy, H4ACxTh of venym, H3 of women *for* venym. 1026. γS1ThH4 on *for* in. 1027. H3Th Jove. 1028. JH4H5AS1 and *for second* or.

148

"But certeyn is, som maner jalousie   1030
Is excusable more than som, iwys;
As whan cause is, and som swich fantasie
With piete so wel repressed is,
That it unnethe doth or seyth amys,
But goodly drynketh up al his distresse;   1035
And that excuse I, for the gentilesse.

149

"And som so ful of furie is and despit,
That it sourmounteth his repressioun;
But, herte myn, ye be nat in that plit,
That thonke I god, for which youre passioun   1040
I wol nat calle it but illusioun,
Of habundaunce of love and besy cure,
That doth youre herte this disese endure.

150

"Of which I am right sory, but nat wroth;
But, for my devoir and youre hertes reste,   1045
Wher so yow list, by ordal or by oth,
By sort, or in what wise so yow leste,
For love of god, lat preve it for the beste;
And if that I be giltif, do me deye.
Allas, what myghte I more don or seye?"   1050

1033. piete, *so* CpH1JS1, *res*ı pite *or* pete. 1041. α clepe. 1044. CpJ wrothe. 1046. GgH5Cx Wheþer; α ye wil (Gg wolde) *for* so yow list. 1047. GgH5 þat, H3Cx so that *for* so, H2Ph *om.* so.

151

With that a fewe brighte teris newe
Oute of hire eyen fille, and thus she seyde:
"Now god, thow woost, in thought ne dede untrewe
To Troilus was nevere yit Criseyde."
With that hire hed down in the bed she leyde, 1055
And with the sheete it wreigh, and sighte soore,
And held hire pees; nought o word spak she more.

152

But now help god to quenchen al this sorwe!
So hope I that he shal, for he best may;
For I have seyn, of a ful misty morwe 1060
Folwen ful ofte a merye someres day;
And after wynter foloweth grene May.
Men sen alday, and reden ek in stories,
That after sharpe shoures ben victories.

153

This Troilus, whan he hire wordes herde, 1065
Have ye no care, hym liste nat to slepe;
For it thoughte hym no strokes of a yerde
To heere or seen Criseyde, his lady, wepe;
But wel he felte aboute his herte crepe,
For everi tere which that Criseyde asterte, 1070
The crampe of deth, to streyne hym by the herte.

1063. α Folk, H3 For men *for* Men; H2Ph and eke men rede in story. 1064. H2Ph
is oft victory. 1067. α Eke *for* For.

154

And in his mynde he gan the tyme acorse
That he com there, or that he was born;
For now is wikke torned into worse,
And al the labour he hath don byforn,   1075
He wende it lost, he thoughte he nas but lorn.
"O Pandarus," thoughte he, "allas, thi wile
Serveth of nought, so weylaway the while!"

155

And therwithal he heng adown the hed,
And fil on knees, and sorwfully he sighte.   1080
What myghte he seyn? He felte he nas but ded;
For wroth was she that sholde his sorwes lighte.
But natheles, whan that he speken myghte,
Than seyde he thus: "god woot, that of this game,
Whan al is wist, than am I nat to blame."   1085

156

Therwith the sorwe so his herte shette,
That from his eyen fil ther nought a tere;
And every spirit his vigour in knette,
So they astoned or oppressed were.
The felyng of his sorwe, or of his fere,   1090
Or of aught elles, fled was out of towne;
And down he fil al sodeynly a-swowne.

1073. H3 That ever; CpJ come; γTh and *for* or; R yborn. 1074. JClS1H2Ph itorned. 1075. γ(-Cl)S1Thα that *for* the; GgH3S1 þat he. 1076. H2PhH5H3 it *for third* he. 1077. αH4H3AD þe while (D whyle *corrected to* wile). 1078. H2Ph þi wyle. 1079. αH3RTh his *for* the. 1080. J sorwfullisch. 1082. α daies *for* sorwes. 1083. H2 whanne he þanne, Ph þan whan he, GgH5ADCx *om.* that. 1084. α þus seide he ʒet god woot of þis game (Gg god wot ʒit). 1086. α for *for* the; H2 swelt, PhH5 swette. 1089. αClH4Cx and *for* or. 1091. CpH1ADGgTh were *for* was.

157

This was no litel sorwe for to se;
But al was hust, and Pandare up as faste,
"O nece, pes, or we be lost," quod he,   1095
"Beth nat agast"; but alwey, at the laste,
For this or that, he into bedde hym caste,
And seyde: "thef, is this a mannes herte?"
And of he rente al to his bare sherte,

158

And seyde: "nece, but ye helpe us now,   1100
Iwis, youre owen Troilus is lorn!"
"Allas, so wolde I, and I wiste how,
Ful fayn," quod she; "allas, that I was born!"
"Ye, nece, wol ye pullen out the thorn
That stiketh in his herte," quod Pandare,   1105
"Sey 'al foryeve,' and stynt is al this fare."

159

"Ye, that to me," quod she, "ful levere were
Than al the good the sonne aboute gooth";
And therwithal she swor hym in his ere:
"Iwys, my dere herte, I am nat wroth,   1110
Have here my trouthe, and many another ooth;
Now speke to me, for it am I Criseyde."
But al for nought; yit myghte he nat abreyde.

1094. H2PhH4H3Cx For *for* But; H2PhDCx but, GgH4 for *for* and, H5 *om.*
and. 1096. γThα certeyn *for* alwey. 1097. JRH3S1CxAH2 into the bedde. 1098.
γS1Thα O thef. 1101. γThα Allas *for* Iwis. 1102. γThα Iwis *for* Allas. 1106.
CpH1H3H4PhCx stynte *for* stynt is; JH4RH5 his *for* this.

160

Therwith his pous and paumes of his hondes
They gan to frote, and ek his temples tweyne;　　　1115
And to deliveren hym fro bittre bondes,
She ofte hym kiste; and shortly for to seyne,
Hym to revoken she did al hire peyne.
So, at the laste, he gan his breth to drawe,
And of his swough sone after that adawe,　　　1120

161

And gan bet mynde and reson to hym take;
But wonder soore he was abayst, iwis;
And with a sik, whan he gan bet awake,
He seyde: "O mercy, god, what thyng is this?"
"Why do ye with youre selven thus amys?"　　　1125
Quod tho Criseyde, "is this a mannes game?
What! Troilus, wol ye do thus for shame?"

162

And therwithal hire arm over hym she leyde,
And al foryaf, and ofte tyme hym keste.
He thonked hire, and to hire spak and seyde　　　1130
As fil to purpos for his hertes reste.
And she to that answerde hym as hire leste;
And with hire goodly wordes hym disporte
She gan, and ofte his sorwes to comforte.

1114-1169. **Cx** *omits eight stanzas.* 1115. γThα wete *for* ek. 1118. **H4H5** revyvyn,
Th rewaken. 1119. γTh And *for* So. 1127. α Wole Troilus do þus allas for
schame. 1129. keste, *so* CpAH4Th, H1 kyssed, *rest* kyste. 1132. **H2PhH5H3** *om.*
hym.

163

Quod Pandarus: "for aught I kan espien,   1135
I nor this candel serven here of nought;
Light is nat good for sike folkes yen;
But, for the love of god, syn ye ben brought
In thus good plit, lat now non hevy thought
Ben hangyng in the hertes of yow tweye";   1140
And bar the candel to the chymeneye.

164

Soone after this, though it no nede were,
Whan she swiche othes as hire liste devyse
Hadde of hym take, hire thoughte tho no fere,
Ne cause ek non, to bidde hym thennes rise.   1145
Yit lasse thyng than othes may suffise
In many a cas; for every wyght, I gesse,
That loveth wel meneth but gentilesse.

165

But in effect she wolde wite anon
Of what man, and ek where, and also why,   1150
He jalous was, syn ther was cause non;
And ek the signe that he took it by,
This bad she hym to telle hire bisily:
Or elles, certeyn, she bar hym on honde,
That this was don for malice, hire to fonde.   1155

1136. γH3S1 This light nor I ne serven; R Me thynk this candel serveth. 1137.
CpJ sik. 1139. H1AH3H2PhGgR þis *for* thus. 1141. CpJ bare; JH4H3Gg his *for*
first the; CpCl chymeney, J chymenaye. 1147. αA *om.* a. 1150. Cp wheer, J wher.
1151. H4 cause was ther, R ther cause was. 1153. *So* βS1, H3 Thus, α That *for*
This, γTh She bad hym that (Cp badde). 1155. γS1Thα of malice.

166

Withouten more, shortly for to seyne,
He moste obeye unto his lady heste;
And for the lasse harm, he moste feyne.
He seyde hire, whan she was at swiche a feste
She myghte on hym han loked at the leste;   1160
Noot I nat what, al deere ynough a rysshe,
As he that nedes moste a cause fisshe.

167

Criseyde answerde: "swete, al were it so,
What harm was that, syn I non yvel mene?
For, by that god that wrought us bothe two,   1165
In alle thyng is myn entente cleene.
Swiche argumentes ne ben nat worth a beene.
Wol ye the childissh jalous contrefete?
Now were it worthi that ye were ybete."

168

Tho Troilus gan sorwfully to sike;   1170
Lest she be wroth, hym thoughte his herte deyde;
And seyde: "allas, upon my sorwes sike
Have mercy, swete herte myn, Criseyde.
And if that in tho wordes that I seyde
Be any wrong, I wol no more trespace;   1175
Doth what yow list, I am al in youre grace."

1160. myghte, *so* H4GgD, *rest* myght. 1163. γTh And she answerde, α And sche answeride him. 1165. γH3Th bought *for* wrought. 1166. alle, *so* JClADH4Gg, *rest* al. 1167. H2PhGgH4RH3A *om.* ne. 1168. ClJH3H4H2Ph jalousye. 1169. R ye wurthy for to ben ibeete. 1170. R gan changen al his hewe. 1171. GgH5H3ACx were *for* be. 1172. R sorwes newe, *om.* my. 1176. Gg Seith what ʒe wil; Cx I put me in youre grace.

169

Criseyde answerde: "of gilt misericorde;
That is to seyn, that I foryeve al this;
And evere more on this nyght yow recorde,
And beth wel war ye do no more amys."   1180
"Nay, dere herte myn," quod he, "iwys."
"And now," quod she, "that I have don yow smerte,
Foryeve it me, myn owene swete herte."

170

This Troilus, with blisse of that supprised,
Putte al in goddes hond, as he that mente   1185
No thyng but wel; and, sodeynly avysed,
He hire in armes faste to hym hente.
And Pandarus, with a ful good entente,
Leyde hym to slepe, and seyde: "if ye be wise,
Swouneth nat now, lest more folk arise."   1190

171

What myghte or may the sely larke seye,
Whan that the sperhauk hath it in his foot?
I kan no more, but of thise ilke tweye,—
To whom this tale sucre be or soot,—
Though that I tarie a yer, som tyme I moot,   1195
After myn auctour, telle of hire gladnesse,
As wel as I have told hire hevynesse.

1177. γThα And she answerde. 1178. JH4H3S1H2PhGg This *for* That. 1183.
H2PhH3D dere *for* swete. 1185. Cp hand, JH1 honde, H2Ph sonde. 1194. Cl sour,
R sowre *for* sucre; H4 swete, A swoot, Cx swoote, D boote *for* soot. 1196. γS1Thα
tellen hire.

172

Criseyde, which that felte hire thus itake,
As writen clerkes in hire bookes olde,
Right as an aspes leef she gan to quake,   1200
Whan she hym felte hire in his armes folde.
And Troilus, al hool of cares colde,
Gan thanken tho the bryghte goddes sevene:
Thus sondry peynes bryngen folk to hevene.

173

This Troilus in armes gan hire streyne,   1205
And seyde: "O swete, as evere mot I gon,
Now be ye kaught, now is ther but we tweyne,
Now yeldeth yow, for other bote is non."
To that Criseyde answerde thus anon:
"Ne hadde I or now, my swete herte deere,   1210
Ben yolde, iwys, I were now nat here."

174

O sooth is seyd, that heled for to be
As of a fevere or other gret siknesse,
Men moste drynke, as men may alday se,
Ful bittre drynke; and for to han gladnesse,   1215
Men drynken ofte peyne and gret distresse;
I mene it here as for this aventure,
That thorugh a peyne hath founden al his cure.

1200. H3H4RH2PhCxTh aspen, D aspe. 1202. γTh But *for* And. 1203. γS1Th
blisful *for* bryghte. 1204. CpH1DS1J in *for* to. 1205. H2PhGg Thus. 1210.
H2PhGg Nad. 1211. H3H5R I had not now ben here (H3 nad). 1212. CpH1J
seyde. 1214. γThα(R *first copy*) ofte *for* alday. 1216. H4 suffre, Cx duren *for*
drynken. 1218. JRH3Cx now *for* al.

175

And now swetnesse semeth more swete,
That bitternesse assaied was byforn;　　　　　　1220
For out of wo in blisse now they flete,
Non swich they felten, syn they were born.
Now is this bet than bothe two be lorn.
For love of god, take every womman heede
To werken thus, whan it comth to the neede.　　　1225

176

Criseyde, al quyt from every drede and tene,
As she that juste cause hadde hym to triste,
Made hym swich feste, it joye was to sene,
Whan she his trouthe and clene entente wiste;
And as aboute a tree, with many a twiste,　　　　1230
Bytrent and writhe the swote wodebynde,
Gan eche of hem in armes other wynde.

177

And as the newe abaysed nyghtyngale,
That stynteth first whan she bygynneth to singe,
Whan that she hereth any herde tale,　　　　　　1235
Or in the hegges any wyght sterynge,
And after, siker, doth hire vois out rynge;
Right so Criseyde, whan hire drede stente,
Opned hire herte, and tolde al hire entente.

1222. ClDH3S1H5H4R(*copy* 2)Cx sith (syn) þat, H2Ph seþen, Gg sithe, Th sens, A or þat *for* syn.　1225. γThα if *for* whan (JH4 when); H4RCxH5 comyth to need.　1228. Cp *omits line*; H2Ph joye it was, H3Cx that joie it was, H5 *om.* it.　1233. ClCxThα abaysshed.　1234. αDJRTh *om.* to.　1239. γThα hym, H4 him al *for* al.

178

And right as he that seth his deth yshapen,   1240
And deyen moste in ought that he may gesse,
And sodeynly rescous doth hym escapen,
And from his deth is brought in sykernesse;
For al this world, in swych present gladnesse
Is Troilus, and hath his lady swete.   1245
With worse hap god lat us nevere mete!

179

Hire armes smale, hire streyghte bak and softe,
Hire sydes longe, flesshly, smothe, and white
He gan to stroke, and good thrift bad ful ofte
Hire snowissh throte, hire brestes rounde and lite; 1250
Thus in this hevene he gan hym to delite,
And therwithal a thousand tyme hire kiste,
That what to don for joie unnethe he wiste.

180

Than seyde he thus: "O Love, O Charite,
Thi moder ek, Citherea the swete,   1255
After thi self next heried be she,
Venus mene I, the wel-willy planete;
And next yow, Imeneus, I the grete;
For nevere man was to yow goddes holde
As I, that ye han brought fro cares colde.   1260

1240. H3R(*copy* 2)Cx saw, H4 sauh, R(*copy* 1) saght, Gg sey. 1241. γThH2PhGg mot *for* moste; H2PhS1 can, H3Cx gan *for* may; R(*copy* 2) y can *for* he may. 1245. γS1Thα Was *for* Is. 1248. Cp flesshy, JH1 flessly. 1250. αH3R snowe whit. 1252. H2PhH5H3H4S1DTh tymes, Gg siþis. 1257. H4R weel willid. 1258. γThα that (Cl þe) *for* yow, Cx *om.* yow. 1260. γS1Thα which *for* that.

181

"Benigne love, thow holy bond of thynges,
Whoso wol grace, and list the nought honouren,
Lo, his desir wol fle withouten wynges.
And noldestow of bounte hem socouren
That serven best, and most alwey labouren,   1265
Yit were al lost, that dar I wel seyn, certes,
But if thi grace passed oure desertes.

182

"And for thow me, that koude leest deserve
Of hem that noumbred ben unto thi grace,
Hast holpen, ther I likly was to sterve,   1270
And me bistowed in so heigh a place,
That thilke boundes may no blisse pace,
I kan no more; but laude and reverence
Be to thy bounte and thyn excellence!"

183

And therwithal Criseyde anon he kiste,   1275
Of which, certein, she felte no disese.
And thus seyde he: "now wolde god I wiste,
Myn herte swete, how I yow myghte plese.
What man," quod he, "was evere thus at ese,
As I, on whom the faireste and the beste   1280
That evere I say deyneth hire herte reste?

1261. H4 Hemane love. 1262. CpH1J liste. 1264. γS1Thα For *for* And. 1265.
CpDJRH3Th moste. 1268. γS1 leest koude, Th lest thonke coude. 1272. αH3CxD
ilke. 1278. H2PhDH4RCx miȝte ȝou; CpH1J myght. 1280. γThα which *for* whom.

184

"Here may men seen that mercy passeth right;
Thexperience of this is felt in me,
That am unworthi to yow, lady bright.
But, herte myn, of youre benignite,   1285
So thynketh, though that I unworthi be,
Yit mot I nede amenden in som wyse,
Right thorugh the vertu of youre heigh servyse.

185

"And, for the love of god, my lady deere,
Syn god hath wrought me for I shal yow serve,— 1290
As thus I mene, he wol ye be my steere,
To do me lyve, if that yow list, or sterve,—
So techeth me how that I may deserve
Youre thonk, so that I, thorugh myn ignoraunce,
Ne do no thing that do yow displesaunce.   1295

186

"For certes, fresshe wommanliche wif,
This dar I seyn, that trouthe and diligence,
That shal ye fynden in me al my lif;
Ne I wol nat, certein, breken youre defence;
And if I do, present or in absence,   1300
For love of god, lat sle me with the dede,
If that it like unto youre wommanhede."

1283. γS1Thα that, H4 thos *for* this; CpJ felte. 1284. γS1Thα to so swete a wight. 1287. GgH5H3H4A nedis. 1289-1428. *Missing in* H2, *two leaves lost.* 1291. JH4RCxH3 As thus he wol þat ye ben my steere (H3H4 how that ye be); CpH1S2 ye *for* he; ClPh þat ye wole 'be, GgTh wil ʒe ben *for* he wol ye be. 1295. γThα that yow be displesaunce (Gg þow 'be, H5 be to yow), R unto ʒour displesaunce. 1296. CpJ wommanlich. 1297. CpJ trouth. 1298. H4RCx *om.* That (R ʒe shullen fyndyn, Cx Ye shul in me fynden). 1299. CpH1 Ny wol, ClR Ne I wole, D Ne wol not, S1 Ne nyll, S2 Ne I nylle, H5 Nor I nyl, Cx I nyl *for* Ne I wol not.

187

"Iwys," quod she, "myn owen hertes lust,
My ground of ese, and al myn herte deere,
Gramercy, for on that is al my trust;   1305
But lat us falle awey fro this matere;
For this suffiseth, which that seyd is heere.
And at o word, withouten repentaunce,
Welcome, my knyght, my pees, my suffisaunce."

188

Of hire delit or joies oon the leeste   1310
Were impossible to my wit to seye;
But juggeth, ye that han ben at the feste
Of swiche gladnesse, if that hem liste pleye!
I kan no more, but thus thise ilke tweye
That nyght, bitwixen drede and sikernesse,   1315
They felte in love the grete worthynesse.

189

O blisful nyght, of hem so longe isought,
How blithe unto hem bothe two thow weere!
Why ne hadde I swich oon with my soule ybought,
Ye, or the leeste joie that was there?   1320
Awey, thow foule daunger and thow feere,
And lat hem in this hevene blisse dwelle,
That is so heigh that no man kan it telle.

1303. CpClH1S1Ph list, R leste. 1304. CpH1J grounde. 1305. CpClH1ADPh triste. 1307. γThα it *for* this, this (Ph þat) *for* which; CpH1J seyde. 1310. H3H4PhTh oon of the leste. 1316. γS1Thα Felten in love; R Felten the love of grete. 1317. GgH5 ful longe, D full soor. 1319. CpH1DPhRH3 nad I, Gg naddi *for* ne hadde I. 1323. γS1Thα that al ne kan I telle.

190

Thise ilke two, that ben in armes laft,
So loth to hem asonder gon it were, 1325
That ech from other wende ben biraft, (1340)
Or elles, lo, this was hir mooste feere,
Lest al this thyng but nyce dremes were;
For which ful ofte ech of hem seyde: "O swete,
Clippe ich yow thus, or elles I it meete?" 1330

191

And, lord, so he gan goodly on hire se, (1345)
That nevere his look ne blente from hire face,
And seyde: "O deere herte, may it be
That this be soth, that ye ben in this place?"
"Ye, herte myn, god thanke I of his grace," 1335
Quod tho Criseyde, and therwithal hym kiste, (1350)
That where his spirit was, for joie he nyste.

192

This Troilus ful ofte hire eyen two
Gan for to kisse, and seyde: "O eyen clere,
It weren ye that wroughte me this wo, 1340
Ye humble nettes of my lady deere. (1355)
Though ther be mercy writen in youre cheere,
God woot the text ful hard is, soth, to fynde;
How koude ye withouten bond me bynde?"

1324. *In* γThα *stanzas* 201, 202 *are found between stanzas* 189 *and* 190. *H4 has
them here with* αγ *readings and again in the later position with* β *readings. Line-
numbers in parentheses indicate the sequence of* αγ. 1324-1330. *H5 omits stanza.*
1325. H4Cx *asondir to gon,* R *to gon asonder.* 1326. Ph *have* bene, H4 *a* ben. 1328.
γS1Thα *That for* Lest; J List. 1330. PhCx *do* y, Th *do* I it *for* I it. 1331-1400. D
omits ten stanzas. 1334. γS1ThαCx it *for* this (Gg *om.* it); αA we *for* ye. 1335.
CpCl thank, J thonk. 1340. γS1Thα swiche (A *al* þe) *for* this. 1343. GgH5AH3
H4Cx þat *for* the.

193

Therwith he gan hire faste in armes take,   1345
And wel a thousand tymes gan he syke,   (1360)
Nat swiche sorwful sikes as men make
For sorwe, or elles whan that folk ben sike,
But esy sykes, swiche as ben to like,
That shewed his affeccioun withinne;   1350
Of swiche sikes koude he nat blynne.   (1365)

194

Soone after this they spake of sondry thynges,
As fil to purpos of hire aventure,
And pleyinge entrechaungeden hire rynges,
Of which I kan nat tellen no scripture;   1355
But wel I woot a broche, gold and asure,   (1370)
In which a ruby set was lik an herte,
Criseyde him yaf, and stak it on his sherte.

195

Lord, trowe ye a coveytous, or a wrecche,
That blameth love and halt of it despit,   1360
That, of tho pens that he kan mokre and crecche, (1375)
Was evere yit yyeven hym swich delit,
As is in love, in o poynt, in som plit?
Nay, douteles; for, also god me save,
So parfit joie may no nygard have.   1365

1346. γThα an hondred. 1347. CpJ swich. 1348. γS1Thα For wo. 1351. CpJ
swich; R nothyng, H5A nevere *for* nat; H1 bilynne. 1353. γS1Thα this *for* hire.
1356. GgH5ADH4RCxTh of gold & asure. 1359. H4S1PhCxTh trowe ye that a; or
a wrecche, *so* CpClH1S2J(J *by corrector*), GgS1 *om.* or, *rest om.* or a. 1361. JClAH3
PhH5Cx the *for* tho; CpH1JGg pans, H3H4H5 peynes; crecche, *so* GgH5(Gg
crache), JClCxTh kecche (J kechche), CpADH3H4 tecche, H1S1RPh theche.

196

They wol seyn "yis"; but, lord, so that they lye, (1380)
Tho besy wrecches, ful of wo and drede!
They clepen love a woodnesse or folie;
But it shal falle hem as I shal yow rede:
They shal forgon the white and ek the rede,   1370
And lyve in wo, ther god yeve hem mischaunce, (1385)
And every lovere in his trouthe avaunce!

197

As wolde god, thise wrecches that dispise
Servise of love, hadde erys also longe
As hadde Mida, ful of coveytise,   1375
And therto dronken hadde as hoot and stronge (1390)
As Crassus dide for his affectis wronge,
To techen hem that coveytise is vice,
And love is vertu, though men holde it nyce.

198

Thise ilke two, of which that I yow seye,   1380
Whan that hire hertes ful assured were,   (1395)
Tho gonne they to speken and to pleye,
And ek rehercen how, and whan, and where,
Thei knewe hem first, and every wo and feere
That passed was; but al that hevynesse,   1385
I thanke it god, was torned to gladnesse.   (1400)

1366. CpH1H3H5CxTh *om.* that. 1368. γS1Thα callen. 1371. CpJ meschaunce.
1373-1379. H3 omits *stanza.* 1373. γS1Thα tho (Cl þat, Ph þe) *for* thise. 1374. αH4
as *for* also. 1375. αA for his coveytise. 1376. αH4A & as stronge. 1378, 1379. γS1Thα
To techen hem that they ben in the vice/And loveres nought although they holde
hem nyce (S1 þough þat men *for* although they). 1380. γ(-A)Th whom *for* which.
1381. γThα wel, H3 bothe *for* ful. 1384. CpH1AS1Th or feere. 1385. γS1Thα
swiche, H3 their *for* that. 1386. Cp thank; JH3Cx Ithonked god, H5 Blessyd be
god; αH4H1Cx into.

199

And evere mo, whan that hem fil to speke
Of any wo of swich a tyme agoon,
With kissyng al that tale sholde breke,
And fallen in a newe joye anoon;   1390
And diden al hire myght, syn they were oon,   (1405)
For to recoveren blisse and ben at eise,
And passed wo with joie countrepeise.

200

Reson wol nat that I speke of slepe,
For it acordeth nought to my matere;—   1395
God woot, they took of that ful litel kepe;—   (1410)
But lest this nyght, that was to hem so deere,
Ne sholde in veyn escape in no manere,
It was byset in joie and besynesse
Of al that souneth into gentilesse.   1400

201

But how although I kan nat tellen al,
As kan myn auctour of his excellence,   (1325)
Yit have I seyd, and god toforn, and shal,
In every thing the gret of his sentence;
And if that I at loves reverence,   1405
Have any thing in eched for the beste,
Doth therwithal right as youre selven leste.   (1330)

1388. γ(-A)Th thyng *for* wo. 1392. Cp eise, ATh eyse, J esye, *rest* ese (ease).
1393. H1GgH5H3Cx countrepese. 1396. JRH5Th hit *for* that. 1397. CpH1J list.
1401-1414. *In* γThα *stanzas* 201, 202 *follow line* 1323. H4 *has them here with* β *readings*
and in the earlier position with αγ *readings*. 1401. γThα But sooth is though I, S1
But al be it þat I. 1403. and shal, *so* CpClH1S1J, GgH5DRCx I *for* and, H3H4
PhATh *om.* and. 1404. γThα al holly his sentence. 1406. γThα word *for* thing.

202

For myne wordes, heere and every part,
I speke hem alle under correccioun
Of yow that felyng han in loves art,   1410
And putte hem hool in youre discrecioun,
Tencresce or maken diminucioun   (1335)
Of my langage, and that I yow biseche;
But now to purpos of my rather speche.

203

Whan that the cok, comune astrologer,   1415
Gan on his brest to bete, and after crowe,
And Lucifer, the dayes messager,
Gan for to rise, and oute hire stremes throwe,
And estward roos, to hym that koude it knowe,
Fortuna Major, that anoon Criseyde,   1420
With herte soor, to Troilus thus seyde:

204

"Myn hertes lif, my trust and my plesaunce,
That I was born, allas, what me is wo,
That day of us moot make disseveraunce!
For tyme it is to ryse and hennes go,   1425
Or ellis I am lost for evere mo.
O nyght, allas, why nyltow overe us hove,
As longe as whan Almena lay by Jove?

1408. H4(*copy* 2)PhCx & in, H5 in, H4(*copy* 1) & on *for* and; CpH1J parte. 1410.
CpH1J arte. 1411. γThα it al, S1 tham alle *for* hem hool. 1412. αCx and *for* or.
1415. γThα But whan the cok. 1417. CpGgH5H3H4RCx messanger. 1418. Gg hese,
H5 his *for* hire; γS1Thα bemes *for* stremes, J stremyes. 1419. ClAGgH5 afterward,
D after þat *for* estward. 1422. CpH1AS1Th al, DS2 and alle *for* and.

205

"O blake nyght, as folk in bokes rede,
That shapen art by god this world to hide   1430
At certeyn tymes with thi blake wede,
That under that men myghte in rest abide,
Wel oughten bestes pleyne, and folk the chide,
That there as day with labour wolde us breste,
That thow thus fleest, and deynest us nat reste.   1435

206

"Thow doost, allas, to shortly thyn office,
Thow rakel nyght, ther god, maker of kynde,
For thow so downward hastest of malice,
The corse and to oure hemysperie bynde,
That nevere mo under the ground thow wynde!   1440
For thorugh thy rakel hying out of Troie,
Have I forgon thus hastili my joie."

207

This Troilus, that with tho wordes felte,
As thoughte hym tho, for pietous distresse
The blody teris from his herte melte,   1445
As he that nevere yit swich hevynesse
Assayed hadde, out of so gret gladnesse,
Gan therwithal Criseyde, his lady deere,
In armes streyne, and seyde in this manere :

1431. S1 termes; γThα derke *for* blake. 1433. α *om.* the (H2Ph folkis). 1435.
Cx us fleest and late us have no rest. 1436. CpH2PhH4 so shortly, A so worthy, D
full shortly. 1438. γS1Thα The for thyn haste and thyn unkynde vice; J hasteth.
1439. γS1Thα So faste ay to oure; H4Cx Thi cours. 1440. γThαCx more; CpJ
grounde. 1441. γThα For now for thow so hiest (H2Ph For now þou hiȝest so, H5 For
be cause þou so fast hiest); S1 with *for* thorugh; J lying. 1444. pietous, *so* CpS1,
H1 piteous, H2 pitouse, *rest* pitous.

208

"O cruel day, accusour of the joie 1450
That love and nyght han stole and faste iwryen,
Acorsed be thi comyng into Troye,
For every bore hath oon of thi bryghte eyen!
Envyous day, what list the so tespien?
What hastow lost? what sekist thow in this place? 1455
Ther god thi light so quenche for his grace!

209

"Allas, what han thise loveris the agilt,
Dispitous day? thyn be the pyne of helle!
For many a lovere hastow slayn, and wilt;
Thi pourynge in wol no wher late hem dwelle. 1460
What profrestow thi light here for to selle?
Go selle it hem that smale selys grave;
We wol the nought, us nedeth no day have."

210

And ek the sonne, Titan, wolde he chide,
And seyde: "O fool, wel may men the dispise, 1465
That hast al nyght the dawyng by thi syde,
And suffrest hire so soone up fro the rise,
For to disesen loveris in this wyse.
What! hold thy bed ther, thow and ek thi Morwe,
I prey to god, so yeve yow bothe sorwe!" 1470

1451. γS1Thα That nyght and love. 1454. CpClH1Th to spien, JCxα to espien,
R so aspien, H3H4ADS1 tespien. 1455. γS1Thα why sekestow this place (Cp sekes
thow); J om. in. 1458. pyne, so ClH1S1JGg, Cx pyt, H2Ph peynes, rest peyne.
1463. H2PhH5H4Cx to have. 1464. γThα gan for wolde. 1466. γS1α the dawyng al
nyght; H2Ph þe biside. 1467. H2PhGg to for so. 1469. CpJ holde; γ(-D)S1ThH5
youre bed, Gg зow, om. bed. 1470. γThα I bidde god.

211

Therwith ful soore he syghte, and thus he seyde:
"My lady right, and of my wele and wo
The verray roote, O goodly myn Criseyde,
And shal I rise, allas, and shal I so?
Now fele I that myn herte moot a-two.   1475
For how sholde I my lif an houre save,
Syn that with yow is al the lyf ich have?

212

"What shal I don? for certes I not how,
Ne whanne, allas, I may the tyme see,
That in this plit I may ben eft with yow;   1480
And of my lif, god woot how that shal be,
Syn that desir right now so streyneth me,
That I am dede anon, but I retourne.
How sholde I longe, allas, fro yow sojourne?

213

"But natheles, myn owen lady bright,   1485
Yit were it so that I wiste outrely,
That I, youre owen servant and youre knyght,
Were in youre herte iset as fermely
As ye in myn,—the which thyng, trewely,
Me levere were than thise worldes tweyne,—   1490
Yit sholde I bet enduren al my peyne."

1471. GgH5H3Cx *om. second* he. 1472. γS1Thα or *for* and. 1473. γThα The welle
and roote. 1474. Gg *om.* allas; ClD go, Gg so gọ *for* so. 1477. RH5 joye *for* lyf.
1479. γThα shal *for* may. 1480. H2PhH3Cx place. 1482. γTh biteth (Cl brenneth,
H1 bitleth). 1486. γTh *om.* Yit; Cx Yf it were so. 1487. γS1ThH2Ph humble *for*
owen. 1488. J ishet, GgH5H4Cx schet, H3 shitte; γTh so *for* as.

214

To that Criseyde answerde thus anon,
And with a sik she seyde: "O herte deere,
The game, ywys, so ferforth now is gon,
That erst shal Phebus fallen fro his spere,   1495
And everich egle ben the haukes feere,
And every roche out of his place sterte,
Or Troilus out of Criseydes herte.

215

"Ye ben so depe inwith myn herte grave,
That, though I wolde it torne out of my thought, 1500
As wisly verray god my soule save,
To dyen in the peyne, I koude nought.
And, for the love of god that us hath wrought,
Lat in youre brayn non other fantasie
So crepe, that it cause me to dye.   1505

216

"And that ye me wolde han as faste in mynde
As I have yow, that wolde I yow biseche;
And, if I wiste sothly that to fynde,
God myghte nat a poynt my joies eche.
But, herte myn, withouten more speche, 1510
Beth to me trewe, or ellis were it routhe;
For I am thyn, by god and by my trouthe.

1492. γThH2Ph right, GgH5 & þat *for* thus. 1493. H3H4Cx *om.* O. 1495. γS1Thα first *for* erst, H5 *om.* erst. 1496. γS1Thα dowves *for* haukes. 1497. H2 rock, GgH5Ph rok, ThCx rocke. 1499. inwith, *so* CpClH1JGg, H2Ph riȝt in, *rest* withinne; JH4S1Cx igrave. 1500. CpJ thoughte. 1503. GgH5R haþ us. 1506. H2Ph wolde me have, H5R wolde have me. 1512. H2Ph ȝoures, H5 youre *for* thyn.

217

"Beth glad, forthy, and lyve in sikernesse;
Thus seyde I nevere or now, ne shal to mo;
And if to yow it were a gret gladnesse   1515
To torne ayeyn soone after that ye go,
As fayn wolde I as ye that it were so,
As wisly god myn herte brynge at reste";
And hym in armes tok and ofte keste.

218

Ayein his wil, sith it mot nedes be,   1520
This Troilus up ros, and faste hym cledde,
And in his armes took his lady free
An hondred tyme, and on his wey hym spedde;
And with swich voys as though his herte bledde,
He seyde: "fare wel, dere herte swete,   1525
Ther god us graunte sownde and soone to mete."

219

To which no word for sorwe she answerde,
So soore gan his partyng hire distreyne;
And Troilus unto his paleys ferde,
As wobygon as she was, soth to seyne;   1530
So harde hym wrong of sharp desir the peyne
For to ben eft there he was in plesaunce,
That it may nevere out of his remembraunce.

1514. γS1Thα this *for* now. 1517. γThJGg *om.* that. 1518. CpH1ACxTh to *for* at. 1519. keste, *so* CpClH4S1Th, *rest* kiste (kyst). 1524. γTh swich wordes as his herte bledde; J thoght. 1525. γThH5(H5 *over erasure*) my dere herte swete. 1526. H3 sounde and sauf, D save and sounde, H5 son and sownd here to mete, Gg sone for to mete (*om.* sownde and). 1527. H2PhH5 for sorwe no word, R *om.* for sorwe.

220

Retorned to his real paleys soone,
He softe into his bed gan for to slynke,   1535
To slepe longe, as he was wont to doone;
But al for nought; he may wel ligge and wynke;
But slep ne may ther in his herte synke,
Thynkyng how she, for whom desir hym brende,
A thousand fold was worth more than he wende,   1540

221

And in his thought gan up and down to wynde
Hire wordes alle, and every contenaunce,
And fermely impressen in his mynde
The leeste point that to hym was plesaunce;
And, verraylich, of thilke remembraunce   1545
Desir al newe hym brende, and lust to brede
Gan more than erst, and yit took he non hede.

222

Criseyde also, right in the same wyse,
Of Troilus gan in hire herte shette
His worthynesse, his lust, his dedes wise,   1550
His gentilesse, and how she with hym mette,
Thonkyng love he so wel hire bisette,
Desiryng eft to han hire herte deere
In swich a plit, she dorste make hym cheere.

1538. CpH1J slepe; H4 ther may non, R ne may noon, Cx may none, S1 ne may þere non, Th may there non *for* ne may ther. 1541. H2PhGgAD wende. 1543. JH3H4 fermelisch; H2PhCx impressid, H3 impressynge, Gg in preysyng. 1548. JGgRH3 the selve wyse. 1552. H4 he gan so weel bisette. 1553. CpAH2PhH5Th ofte. 1554. H2PhGg At *for* In; Th place; H2PhH5H4S1 þat sche, Th as she.

223

Pandare, a-morwe which that comen was   1555
Unto his nece, and gan hire faire grete,
Seyde: "al this nyght so reyned it, allas,
That al my drede is that ye, nece swete,
Han litel leiser had to slepe and mete;
Al nyght," quod he, "hath reyn so do me wake,   1560
That som of us, for god, oure hede may ake."

224

And ner he com, and seyde: "how stant it now,
This brighte morwe, nece, how kan ye fare?"
Criseyde answerde: "nevere the bet for yow,
Fox that ye ben, god yeve youre herte care!   1565
God help me so, ye caused al this fare,
Trowe I," quod she; "for al youre wordes white,
O! whoso seth yow knoweth yow ful lite."

225

With that she gan hire face for to wrye
With the shete, and wax for shame al reed;   1570
And Pandarus gan under for to prie,
And seyde: "nece, if that I shal be ded,
Have here a swerd, and smyteth of myn heed."
With that his arm al sodeynly he thriste
Under hire nekke, and at the laste hire kyste.   1575

1555. CpH1 o, J of, H2PhH5H4AD on, R at *for* a. 1556. H4RCx Into. 1557.
H4Cx it reyned so, H5 reyned it so. 1561. γS1Thα I trowe hire hedes ake, Cx our
heedis ought to ake; J hir, H3 his *for* oure. 1563. γS1Thα mery (mury) *for* brighte
(βH3 bright). 1565. H2PhADJRH3 yow *for* youre; H2Ph hertis, JD herde, H3R
harde. 1567. R Traytour *for* Trowe I. 1568. ClDGgH3RCx *om.* O. 1573. CpH1J
swerde; smyteth, *so* JRS1DTh, Cp smyten, *rest* smyte. 1574. JH4GgH5A threste,
H3 thruste. 1575. ClH4 keste.

226

I passe al that which nedeth nought to seye,
What! god foryaf his deth, and she also
Foryaf, and with hire uncle gan to pleye,
For oother cause was ther non than so.
But of this thing right to theffect to go,   1580
Whan tyme was, hom to hire hous she wente,
And Pandarus hath hoolly his entente.

227

Now torne we ayeyn to Troilus,
That resteles ful longe a-bedde lay,
And pryvely sente after Pandarus,   1585
To hym to come in al the haste he may.
He com anon, nat ones seyde he "nay";
And Troilus ful sobrely he grette,
And down upon his beddes syde hym sette.

228

This Troilus, with al thaffeccioun   1590
Of frendes love that herte may devyse,
To Pandarus on knowes fil adown,
And or that he wolde of the place arise,
He gan hym thonken in his beste wise
A thousand tyme, and gan the day to blisse,   1595
That he was born to brynge hym fro destresse,

1576-1582. Cp *omits stanza; text based on* JClH1. 1576. γ(-D)Thα chargeth *for*
nedeth; R which is not goodly for to seye. 1579. ClH3H2PhH5 but, D ne *for* than.
1581. ClH1 til *for* to. 1582. γS1Thα fully *for* hoolly. 1584. H2PhH4 in bedde.
1588. J sobrelich. 1592. knowes, *so* CpH1AJ, H5 know, GgS1 kneis, *rest* knees.
1595. γThα An hondred; γ sythe, H2PhH4S1Cx tymes *for* tyme; CpH1AS2Th he *for*
and; γThα tyme *for* day to; H3 gan he day blisse, S1 þe day gan blysse; CpH2Ph
CxTh blesse.

229

And seyde: "O frend, of frendes alderbeste
That evere was, the sothe for to telle,
Thow hast in hevene ybrought my soule at reste
Fro Flegiton, the fery flood of helle;   1600
That, though I myght a thousand tymes selle,
Upon a day, my lif in thi servise,
It myghte nat a moote in that suffise.

230

"The sonne, which that al the world may se,
Saugh nevere yit, my lif that dar I leye,   1605
So inly fair and goodly as is she,
Whos I am al, and shal, tyl that I deye;
And that I thus am hires, dar I seye,
That thanked be the heighe worthynesse
Of love, and ek thi kynde bysynesse.   1610

231

"Thus hastow me no litel thing yyive,
For which to the obliged be for ay
My lif, and whi? for thorugh thyn helpe I lyve;
Or elles ded hadde I ben many a day."
And with that word down in his bed he lay,   1615
And Pandarus ful sobrely hym herde,
Til al was seyd, and thanne he thus answerde:

1597. γS₁ThGg He *for* And; CpClH₁S₁JTh the, A that alderbeste. 1599. H₃H₄D my soule brought, S₁ my soule ybrot in heven; H₂PhH₃S₁ to rest. 1600. Cp flegtoun, H₁J flagitoun (J flag- *over erasure*), H₃ conciton, H₄ contoun, R coichyton, Cx Cochita, Th Phlegeton; H₂Ph feende *for* flood. 1603. CpClH₁J myght. 1605. S₁RCx Was *for* Saugh. 1608. GgH₅H₄ may I say, H₃ may iche bodei seye, Cx I dar wel seye. 1616. J sobrelich. 1617. CpH₁J seyde; γTh hym *for* thus, H₃ thus him *for* thanne he thus.

232

"My deere frend, if I have don for the
In any cas, god wot, it is me lief;
And am as glad as man may of it be,   1620
God help me so; but—take it nat a-grief—
For love of god be war of this myschief:
That there as thow now brought art in thy blisse,
That thow thi self ne cause it nat to misse.

233

"For of fortunes sharp adversitee   1625
The worste kynde of infortune is this:
A man to han ben in prosperitee,
And it remembren whan it passed is.
Thart wis ynough, forthi do nat amys;
Be nat to rakel, though thow sitte warme,   1630
For if thow be, certeyn, it wol the harme.

234

"Thow art at ese, and holde the wel therinne;
For also seur as reed is every fir,
As gret a craft is kepe wel as wynne.
Bridle alwey wel thi speche and thi desir;   1635
For worldly joie halt nat but by a wir.
That preveth wel, it brest alday so ofte;
Forthi, nede is to werken with it softe."

1621. CpH1S2ThGg now *for* it. 1622. γThα That I shal seyn be war. 1623. CxTh *om.* thow; J now thow; H2PhGgH4 now þou art brought (Gg. *om.* þou), H3 thou art brought now, D þow art now broughte; ClGgH5 in to, H2Ph in, ThCx to thy *for* in thy. 1627. H4 felecite. 1629. Thart, *so* CpH1ADJR, *rest* Thow art. 1630. Cp theigh, J thogh. 1632. H3 and holde the nowe, RCx holde the now (R w *erased before* now), H4 now hold the *for* and holde the wel. 1633-1636. CpH1J fire, desire, wire. 1634. H2PhH4H3Cx is to kepe.

235

Quod Troilus: "I hope, and god toforn,
My deere frend, that I shal so me bere,   1640
That in my gylt ther shal no thing be lorn,
Ny nyl nat rakle as for to greven here.
It nedeth nat this matere ofte stere;
For wystestow myn herte wel, Pandare,
By god, of this thow woldest litel care."   1645

236

Tho gan he telle hym of his glade nyght,
And wherof first his herte dredde, and how,
And seyde: "frende, as I am trewe knyght,
And by that feyth I shal to god and yow,
I hadde it nevere half so hote as now;   1650
And ay the more that desir me biteth
To love hire best, the more it me deliteth.

237

"I not my self nat wisly what it is;
But now I feele a newe qualitee,
Ye, al another than I dede or this."   1655
Pandare answerde and seyde thus: that he,
That ones may in hevene blisse be,
"He feleth other weyes, dar I leye,
Than thilke tyme he first herde of it seye."

1639. JH4RH3 biforn. 1642. Ny nyl, *so* CpH1S1, ClADCxTh Ne I nyl, JH4RH3
Gg Ne I wol (R *om.* Ne); H2Ph Ne rakyl nel y be for; A be rakle; H3H4R wrathin
for greven. 1643. α al day þis þing to tere (H5 al wey; Gg þis þyng al day); stere,
so H3RS1Cx(H3Cx ofte to stere), *rest* tere. 1645. γThα God woot *for* By god. 1647.
CpH1 dred, J drede. 1649. H4H5CxTh owe *for* shal. 1657. CpH1 hevenes.

238

This is a word for al; this Troilus   1660
Was nevere ful to speke of this matere,
And for to preisen unto Pandarus
The bounte of his righte lady deere,
And Pandarus to thanke and maken cheere.
This tale was ay span newe to bygynne,   1665
Til that the nyght departed hem atwynne.

239

Soone after this, for that fortune it wolde,
Icomen was the blisful tyme swete,
That Troilus was warned that he sholde,
There he was erst, Criseyde his lady mete;   1670
For which he felte his herte in joie flete,
And feithfully gan alle the goddes herie;
And lat se now if that he kan be merie!

240

And holden was the forme and al the wise,
Of hire commyng, and ek of his also,   1675
As it was erst, which nedeth nought devyse.
But pleynly to theffect right for to go,
In joie and seurte Pandarus hem two
A-bedde brought, whan that hem bothe leste,
And thus they ben in quyete and in reste.   1680

1660. H5 And yet in trowthe for all; CpH1DS2S1Th that *for* this. 1665. CpClH1
Gg ay was, H3H5 was ever, Cx was alwey, H2Ph *om.* ay. 1671. H2PhS1Cx in joy
his hert, H3 for yoie is hert. 1675. γ(-A)H3S1Th *om.* ek. 1676. H4 what nedith it
to devyse. 1677. H2PhH4 right to þe effect, GgH5H3Cx *om.* right. 1678. CpJ suerte.
1679. J broughte; JH4GgH3ACxTh *om.* that.

241

Nat nedeth it to yow, syn they ben met,
To axe at me if that they blithe were;
For if it erst was wel, tho was it bet
A thousand fold, this nedeth nat enquere.
Agon was every sorwe and every feere;   1685
And bothe, ywys, they hadde, and so they wende,
As muche joie as herte may comprende.

242

This is no litel thyng of for to seye;
This passeth every wit for to devyse;
For eche of hem gan otheres lust obeye;   1690
Felicite, which that thise clerkes wise
Comenden so, ne may nat here suffise.
This joie may nat writen be with inke;
This passeth al that herte may bythynke.

243

But cruel day, so weylawey the stounde,   1695
Gan for taproche, as they by sygnes knewe,
For which hem thoughte feelen dethes wownde;
So wo was hem, that changen gan hire hewe,
And day they gonnen to despise al newe,
Callyng it traitour, envyous, and worse;   1700
And bitterly the dayes light thei corse.

1682. H2PhH5H4H3DCx *om.* that. 1684. αH4H3ACx to enquere. 1685. J drede,
S1R wo, H4 joie, Cx care *for* sorwe. 1687. H3 as tonge coude tell or sende; comprende, *so* CpJ, Cl complende, *rest* comprehende. 1688. JGgH1ATh nys; H2PhH5H3
om. of. 1694. H3Cx that aney hert may thynke, H5 þat hert may speke or thynke.
1696. H4 His briht hornys in every wiket gan shewe. 1697. H4 thei felten, H2PhH3
þei felt *for* feelen.

244

Quod Troilus: "allas, now am I war
That Pirous and tho swifte steedes thre,
Which that drawen forth the sonnes char,
Han gon som bipath in dispit of me;   1705
That maketh it so soone day to be;
And, for the sonne hym hasteth thus to rise,
Ne shal I nevere don hym sacrifise."

245

But nedes day departe hem moste soone,
And whan hire speche don was and hire cheere,   1710
They twynne anon as they were wont to doone,
And setten tyme of metyng eft yfeere;
And many a nyght they wroughte in this manere.
And thus Fortune a tyme ledde in joie
Criseyde and ek this kynges sone of Troie.   1715

246

In suffisaunce, in blisse, and in singynges,
This Troilus gan al his lif to lede;
He spendeth, jousteth, maketh festeyinges;
He yeveth frely ofte, and chaungeth wede,
And held aboute hym ay, withouten drede,   1720
A world of folk, as com hym wel of kynde,
The fressheste and the beste he koude fynde;

1703. Pirous, *so* H2PhATh, CpClD Piros, Gg Pirus, H5 Pyreus, H3 Pireys, H1S1R Pirors, H4 Pirers, Cx Pierers, J Pirora; JGgH2PhRH1DCx the *for* tho, H3 *om.* and tho. 1707. H2PhGgA so, H3H5 for *for* thus. 1708. γ(-A) hire *for* hym. 1711. JH2PhH3Cx ben *for* were. 1718. H2PhH3CxTh and makith, R makyth eke; festeyinges, *so* S1, ClH1 festeynynges, *rest* festynges. 1720. H2Ph holt, S1 halt, H1 hold, A holde; γS1Thα alwey out of drede.

247

That swich a vois of hym was and a stevene
Thorughout the world, of honour and largesse,
That it up rong unto the yate of hevene.   1725
And as in love he was in swich gladnesse,
That in his herte he demed, as I gesse,
That ther nys lovere in this world at ese
So wel as he; and thus gan love hym plese.

248

The goodlihede or beaute which that kynde   1730
In any other lady hadde iset
Kan nat the mountaunce of a knotte unbynde,
Aboute his herte, of al Criseydes net.
He was so narwe ymasked and iknet,
That it undon on any maner syde,   1735
That nyl nat ben, for aught that may bitide.

249

And by the hond ful ofte he wolde take
This Pandarus, and into gardyn lede,
And swich a feste and swich a proces make
Hym of Criseyde, and of hire womanhede,   1740
And of hire beaute, that, withouten drede,
It was an hevene his wordes for to here;
And thanne he wolde synge in this manere:

1723. γS1Th was of hym.   1724. CpJ worlde.   1725. ClH3 into, GgH5 ry3t to *for*
unto.   1730. JGgH5Cx bounte.   1732. Cp montance, JGgH5H4ADCxTh mountenaunce.
1736. H2PhH4 Hit *for* That.

250

"Love, that of erthe and se hath governaunce,
Love, that his hestes hath in hevenes hye,   1745
Love, that with an holsom alliaunce
Halt peples joyned, as hym list hem gye,
Love, that enditeth lawe of compaignie,
And couples doth in vertu for to dwelle,
Bynd this acord that I have told and telle.   1750

251

"That that the world, with feith which that is stable,
Diverseth so his stowndes concordynge,
That elementz that ben so discordable
Holden a bond perpetuely durynge,
That Phebus mote his rosy day forth brynge,   1755
And that the mone hath lordshipe over the nyghtes,
Al this doth Love; ay heried be his myghtes!

252

"That that the se, that gredy is to flowen,
Constreyneth to a certeyn ende so
His flodes, that so fiersly they ne growen   1760
To drenchen erthe and al for evere mo:—
And if that Love aught lete his bridel go,
Al that now loveth asonder sholde lepe;
And lost were al that Love halt now to hepe.

1744-1771. *Omitted in* H2; *on inset leaf later in* Ph. 1745. γ(-A)H3Thα hevene.
1746. JH4R which þat, H5 that whiche *for* that. 1748. γS1ThPh knetteth, H3 kennyth,
Cx endueth, H5 endith. 1751. H3RPhS2 *om. second* that; JGgH5ACx *om.* which;
H4S2 *om. third* that; JGgH5H4 unstable. 1754. JRCxGgH5 Holde in, Ph Holdyn
yn *for* Holden. 1755. H1Ph carte *for* day. 1758. R And þat. 1760. ClDH5RCx
freshly. 1764. H3R kepe.

253

"So wolde god, that auctour is of kynde,   1765
That, with his bond, Love of his vertu liste
To cerclen hertes alle, and faste bynde,
That from his bond no wight the wey out wiste;
And hertes colde, hem wolde I that he twiste
To make hem love, and that hem liste ay rewe   1770
On hertes sore, and kepe hem that ben trewe."

254

In alle nedes for the townes werre
He was, and ay, the firste in armes dyght;
And certeynly, but if that bokes erre,
Save Ector, most ydred of any wight;   1775
And this encres of hardynesse and myght
Com hym of love, his ladies thank to wynne,
That altered his spirit so withinne.

255

In tyme of trewe, on haukyng wolde he ride,
Or elles honte boor, bere, or lyoun;   1780
The smale bestes leet he gon biside.
And whan that he com ridyng into town,
Ful ofte his lady from hire wyndow down,
As fresshe as faucon comen out of muwe,
Ful redy was hym goodly to saluwe.   1785

1767. H4CxTh serchyn, ClPh cerchen, H3 cherysson. 1771. Cp Or, A Of, JGgPh
And *for* On. 1772. H1AS1H2Ph In alle the nedes. 1773. H4H5 *om.* and; CpJ
first; R He was ay first al in hys armes digh. 1777. JRH3H2PhH5Cx lady; H2Ph
grace. 1782. H2PhCx to þe, H5Th into þe *for* into. 1784. ClH2PhH3Cx cometh, H4
com, H5 cam.

256

And moost of love and vertu was his spéche,
And in despit hadde alle wrecchednesse;
And, douteles, no nede was hym biseche
To honouren hem that hadden worthynesse,
And esen hem that weren in destresse.   1790
And glad was he if any wyght wel ferde,
That lovere was, whan he it wiste or herde.

257

For soth to seyn, he lost held every wyght
But if he were in loves heigh servise,
I mene folk that oughte it ben of right.   1795
And over al this, so wel koude he devyse
Of sentement, and in so unkouth wise
Al his array, that every lovere thoughte,
That al was wel what so he seyde or wroughte.

258

And though that he be come of blood roial,   1800
Hym liste of pride at no wight for to chace;
Benigne he was to ech in general,
For which he gat hym thank in every place.
Thus wolde Love, yheried be his grace!
That pride, envye, ire, and avarice   1805
He gan to fle, and everich other vice.

1787. H3R hade he al. 1793. H2GgH5 lorn, Ph love *for* lost; H2PhGg had, H5
hald *for* held. 1795. H3H4RCx be *for* of. 1796. H3R he cowde. 1802. R alle *for*
ech. 1804. JH3 This *for* Thus. 1805. CpH1S2CxTh That pride and Ire Envye and
Avarice; JAS1 and ire and avarice. 1806. S2 (*Rubric*) Explicit Liber Tercius.

259

Thow lady bryght, the doughter to Dyone,
Thy blynde and wynged sone ek, daun Cupide,
Ye sustren nyne ek, that by Elicone,
In hil Parnaso listen for tabide,   1810
That ye thus fer han deyned me to gyde,
I kan no more, but syn that ye wol wende,
Ye heried ben for ay withouten ende.

260

Thorugh yow have I seyd fully in my song
Theffect and joie of Troilus servise,   1815
Al be that ther was som disese among,
As to myn auctour listeth to devise.
My thridde book now ende ich in this wyse;
And Troilus in lust and in quiete
Is with Criseyde, his owen herte swete.   1820

EXPLICIT LIBER TERCIUS.

1807. D *in margin* Prologus. 1807-1820. *Lacking in* Gg, *leaf lost*. 1807. JH4RH2Ph Yow, H5 Now *for* Thow; Ph 3e, R you *for* the, H5ACx *om*. the; H2PhH3ATh of *for* to. 1808. H5 Thy blynd sone eke I mene daun Cupide. 1809. Cp Yee, JRPh Yow H3H4Cx Your, ATh The *for* Ye. 1812. CpH1J namore; H5 syn this grace 3e sende. 1813. H5Cx Iheried ben 3e. 1814. Cx Now have I yow. 1818. H2Ph Me my boke, H3 My fierde boke. 1820. H3Cx lady *for* herte. *Rubric, so* JRS1A(*by later hand*)Th, H3 Explicit Liber iiijtus, H5 Explicit iij liber, Cx Here endeth the thyrde Booke And foloweth the Fourth Booke, *rest omit*.

BOOK FOUR

BOOK FOUR

INCIPIT PROHEMIUM QUARTI LIBRI.

1

BUT al to litel, weylawey the whyle,
Lasteth swich joie, ythonked be Fortune,
That semeth trewest whan she wol bygyle,
And kan to fooles so hire song entune,
That she hem hent and blent, traitour comune;   *5*
And whan a wight is from hire whiel ythrowe,
Than laugheth she, and maketh hym a mowe.

2

From Troilus she gan hire brighte face
Awey to wrythe, and took of hym non heede,
But caste hym clene oute of his lady grace,   *10*
And on hire whiel she sette up Diomede;
For which right now myn herte gynneth blede,
And now my penne, allas, with which I write,
Quaketh for drede of that I moste endite.

3

For how Criseyde Troilus forsook,   *15*
Or at the leeste how that she was unkynde,
Moot hennesforth ben matere of my book,
As writen folk thorugh which it is in mynde.
Allas! that they sholde evere cause fynde
To speke hire harm! and if they on hire lye,   *20*
Iwis, hem self sholde han the vilanye.

Rubric, so H4S1, J Prohennium quarti libri, Cx Here endeth the thyrd book of Troylus And here begynneth the prolog of the fourth book, *rest omit.* 1-112. *Lacking in* Gg; *two leaves lost.* 1-28. R *omits proem.* 3. H2Ph trusty. 7. γThα the *for* a, H3 *om.* a. 9. αH4H3Cx wrye. 12. γ(-Cl)Th myn herte right now. 19. H2PhADS1Cx evere þei shold. 21. H5DCx shall, H4 shul.

4

O ye Herynes, Nyghtes doughtren thre,
That endeles compleynen evere in pyne,
Megera, Alete, and ek Thesiphone,
Thow cruel Mars ek, fader to Quyryne,   25
This ilke ferthe book me helpeth fyne,
So that the losse of lyf and love yfeere
Of Troilus be fully shewed here.

EXPLICIT PROHEMIUM QUARTI LIBRI.
INCIPIT LIBER QUARTUS.

5

LIGGYNG in oost, as I have seyd or this,
    The Grekys stronge aboute Troie town,   30
    Byfel that, whan that Phebus shynyng is
Upon the brest of Hercules lyoun,
That Ector, with ful many a bold baroun,
Caste on a day with Grekes for to fighte,
As he was wont to greve hem what he myghte.   35

6

Not I how longe or short it was bitwene
This purpos and that day they fighten mente;
But on a day, wel armed bright and shene,
With spere in honde and bigge bowes bente,
Ector and many a worthi wight out wente;   40
And in the berd, anon withouten lette,
Hire fomen in the felde hem faste mette.

24. CxTh Allecto; H2Ph þow, H5 and þou *for* and ek.   25. αH3 god *for* Mars;
αTh of *for* to.   26. H4 This feerde & laste book, H3 Thys fyfte and laste boke.   27.
CpJ lyve. *Rubrics. so* JS1 (J prohennium). *For other variants, see Introd.*, p. xiii.   29.
CpPH1J seyde; H4H3RCx told *for* seyd.   33. αClTh *om.* ful.   35. PhCx if he, H5 as
he, D with his *for* what he.   37. JPh day thei issen mente (Ph issu), H2 day þe þus
ment, H5 day of assignemente.   39, 40. γS1ThH5 *transpose lines.*   40. DCxTh knight.
41. γTha withouten lenger lette.   42. γS1Tha anon hem mette (D *om.* anon; H2Ph
DS2 they *for* hem); R ful *for* hem; H3 faste they mette.

7

The longe day, with speres sharpe igrounde,
With arwes, dartes, swerdes, maces felle,
They fighte and bringen hors and man to grounde,   45
And with hire axes out the braynes quelle;
But in the laste shour, soth for to telle,
The folk of Troie hem selven so mysledden,
That with the wors at nyght homward they fledden.

8

At which day was taken Antenor,   50
Maugre Polydamas or Monesteo,
Santippe, Sarpedon, Polynestor,
Polite, or ek the Troian daun Rupheo,
And oothre lasse folk, as Phebuseo;
So that for harm that day the folk of Troie   55
Dredden to lese a gret part of hire joie.

9

But natheles a trewe was ther take,
At Grekes request, and tho they gonnen trete,
Of prisoners a chaunge for to make,
And for the surplus yeven sommes grete.   60
This thing anon was couth in every strete,
Bothe in thassege, in towne, and every where,
And with the firste it com to Calkas ere.

---

43. Cl faste *for* sharpe. 46. αH4 brayn. 47. H2PhR þe sothe to telle, H3 the
souþh for to telle, Cx forth for to telle, Th sothe to tell. 49. H2RH3Cx homward at
nyght. 51. H3 *om.* Maugre, Palidomas and also Menestes; H2 Penestio, Ph Polestio.
H5 Ponestes. 52. JH4R or Polynestor, D ande Polemestor. 53. H3 and *for* or; α
Or Polyte or the troian. 54. α Or *for* And. 55. H3 For al Ector so that the folk.
57-59. γH3Thα :—

                Of Priamus was yeve, at Grekes requeste,
                A tyme of trewe, and tho they gonnen trete,
                Hire prisoners to chaungen, meste and leste,
(H3H5 To pryamus; CpPh1 a greke, H5S2 a gret, H3 at his *for* at Grekes). 57. H4
nevertheles; RS1 ther was. 58. JH4 At gret, S1 At Greke; H4R gonne thei.

10

Whan Calkas knew this tretis sholde holde,
In consistorie among the Grekes soone   65
He gan in thringe forth, with lordes olde,
And sette hym there, as he was wont to doone,
And with a chaunged face hem bad a boone,
For love of god, to don that reverence,
To stynte noyse, and yeve hym audience.   70

11

Than seyde he thus: "lo, lordes myn, ich was
Troian, as it is knowen, out of drede;
And if that yow remembre, I am Calkas,
That alderfirst yaf comfort to youre nede,
And tolde wel how that ye sholden spede;   75
For dredeles, thorugh yow shal in a stownde
Ben Troie ybrend, and beten down to grownde;

12

"And in what forme, or in what manere wise,
This town to shende, and al youre lust tacheve,
Ye han or this wel herd me yow devyse;   80
This knowe ye, my lordes, as I leve.
And for the Grekis weren me so leeve,
I com my self, in my propre persone,
To teche in this how yow was best to doone,

71. ClRTh myne. 74. R counsel. 75. αCx *om.* that. 77. H2Ph Troy be brent,
Cx This Troye be brent. 78. αH4RCx and *for* or. 79. CpJ towne. 80. CpH1J herde;
γ wel herd it me; H4 me herd weel; H3 me herde or this (*om.* wel); Cx me herd wel;
RCx *om.* yow. 84. H2 what you was best, Cx what ye were best, PhH5 how hit
was best.

13

"Havyng unto my tresour ne my rente   85
Right no resport, to respect of youre ese;
Thus al my good I lefte, and to yow wente,
Wenyng in this, my lordes, yow to plese.
But al that los ne doth me no disese.
I vouchesauf, as wisly have I joie,   90
For yow to lese al that I have in Troie.

14

"Save of a doughter that I lefte, allas!
Slepyng at hom, whan out of Troie I sterte;
O sterne, O cruel fader that I was!
How myghte I have in that so harde an herte?   95
Allas! I ne hadde ibrought hire in hire sherte!
For sorwe of which I wol nat lyve to morwe,
But if ye lordes rewe upon my sorwe.

15

"For, by that cause I say no tyme or now
Hire to delivere, ich holden have my pees;   100
But now or nevere, if it like yow,
I may hire have right soone, douteles.
O help and grace! amonges al this prees,
Rewe on this olde caytyf in destresse,
Syn I thorugh yow have al this hevynesse.   105

---

85. H3H4A and, D and to *for* ne. 87. lefte, *so* JH3ADS1S2CxTh, Cp leeste, H1 leste, *rest* loste *or* lost. 88. γ(-AD)Th yow lordes for to plese. 89. Cp. tha, JH3Cx this, α my *for* that; αH4H3S2Cx *om.* ne. 93. α toun *for* Troie. 94. ClADS1JCx **and** *for second* O. 96. CpJ ibroughte. 101. γ(-H1)S1Th if that it. 102. α for þat is *for* right soone. 103. amonges, *so* CpJA, *rest* among *or* amonge. 105. α am broght in wrecchidnes.

16

"Ye have now kaught and fetered in prisoun
Troians ynowe; and, if youre willes be,
My child with oon may han redempcioun.
Now, for the love of god, and of bounte,
Oon of so fele, allas, so yeve hym me.   110
What nede were it this preiere for to werne,
Syn ye shul bothe han folk and town as yerne?

17

"On peril of my lif, I shal nat lye,
Appollo hath me told it feithfully;
I have ek founde it by astronomye,   115
By sort, and by augurye ek, trewely,
And dar wel seyn, the tyme is faste by,
That fir and flaumbe on al the town shal sprede,
And thus shal Troie torne into asshen dede.

18

"For, certein, Phebus and Neptunus bothe,   120
That makeden the walles of the town,
Ben with the folk of Troie alwey so wrothe,
They wol eft brynge it to confusioun,
Right for despit of kyng Lameadoun.
Bycause he nolde payen hem hire hire,   125
The town shal yit be set upon a fire."

107. ClDαRCx wille.   108. CpH1J childe.   110. CpH1 yif, J yive; α graunt *for* yeve (H2Ph so grauntith me).   112. H3S1Cx have bothe, H2Ph *om.* bothe; H4RCx toun & folk.   113. H2PhH5 Up, Gg Of *for* On; JH4H3AD on *for* of.   114. Cp J tolde; α hath me told sikirly.   115. ClH3H2Ph founden, H1 founde *for* founde it.   119. CpH1AS2ThH5 to, Gg tyl, ClJ in *for* into, D *om.* into.   120. CpH1J Neptimus.   121. αS1 That madyn al þe wallis.   123. γS1Thα That they wol brynge it; H3 it eft bringe.   124. γS1Thα in *for* for; H3H4H5Th Lamedon, S1 Leamydoun, Cx Laomedon.   126. γThα The town of Troie shal ben sette on fire; H4Cx on a fire.

19

Tellyng his tale alwey, this olde greye,
Humble in his speche and in his lokyng eke,
The salte teris from his eyen tweye
Ful faste ronnen down by either cheke.   130
So longe he gan of socour hem biseke,
That, for to hele hym of his sikes soore,
They yave hym Antenor withouten moore.

20

But who was glad ynough but Calkas tho?
And of this thyng ful soone his nedes leyde   135
On hem that sholden for the tretis go,
And hem for Antenor ful ofte preyde
To bryngen hom kyng Thoas and Criseyde;
And whan Priam his save garde sente,
Thembassadours to Troie streight they wente.   140

21

The cause itolde of hire comyng, the olde
Priam the kyng ful soone in general
Let her-upon his parlement to holde,
Of which theffect rehersen yow I shal.
Thembassadours ben answerd for fynal,   145
Theschaunge of prisoners and al this nede
Hem liketh wel; and forth in they procede.

130. α on *for* by. 131. α mercy *for* socour. 132. γThα sorwes *for* sikes. 135. CpClJ hise; α his nede he leyde (Gg his nede ful sone). 137. H3 And hem ful ofte specyally preyde. 138. ClAJGgCx hem *for* hom; γGg Toas, H2Ph Koas; H3 For Antenor to bringe home Creseide, H5 To bryng ffor antenor his dowter Creseyde. 139. S1 king Priam, H4Cx Priamus; H4RS1Cx saufguard (R hym sente), H3 sone gan, H5 soun garde; H2PhGg his safe conduyt hem sent (H2 her *for* his). 140. H4RH3Cx streiht to troie went (Cx ful streyghte). 143. α Gan þerupon (H2Ph *om.* on). 147. H2Ph gan *for* in.

22

This Troilus was present in the place,
Whan axed was for Antenor Criseyde;
For which ful soone chaungen gan his face,   150
As he that with tho wordes wel neigh deyde;
But, natheles, he no word to it seyde,
Lest men sholde his affeccioun espye;
With mannes herte he gan his sorwe drye,

23

And ful of angwissh and of grisly drede,   155
Abood what oother lordes wolde seye;
And if they wolde graunte, as god forbede,
Theschaunge of hire, than thoughte he thynges tweye:
First, how to save hire honour, and what weye
He myghte best theschaunge of hire withstonde;   160
Ful faste he caste how al this myghte stonde.

24

Love hym made al prest to don hire bide,
Or rather dyen than she sholde go;
But resoun seyde hym on that other syde:
"Withoute assent of hire ne do nat so,   165
If thow debate it, lest she be thy fo,
And seyn, that thorugh thy medlynge is iblowe
Youre bother love, ther it was erst unknowe."

---

151. α wel ny with þe wordis (Gg þo). 153. CpH1 List, J Liste. 154. γS1H3Th
H2PhH5 sorwes. 156. γS1α Abode what lordes wolde to it seye (CpClH1S1 unto it);
Th wolde to it sey. 159. Cp For how, H2PhH4S1S2Cx Ferst for, JGg First *for*
First how. 160. α He myght best þe grauntyng withstonde (H5 to withstonde). 161.
u þis cast he þo how. 163. γTh And *for* Or. 165. CpH1 Withouten, J Without.
166. γThα Lest for thi werk she wolde be thy fo; Cx Lest thow hyr wrath & she than
be thy foo; H4R *om.* it.

[240]

25

For which he gan deliberen for the beste,
That though the lordes wolde that she wente,   170
He wolde late hem graunte what hem leste,
And telle his lady first what that they mente;
And whan that she hadde seyd hym hire entente,
Therafter wolde he werken also blyve,
Theigh al the world ayeyn it wolde stryve.   175

26

Ector, which that wel the Grekis herde,
For Antenor how they wolde han Criseyde,
Gan it withstonde, and sobrely answerde:
"Sires, she nys no prisoner," he seyde;
"I not on yow who that this charge leyde,   180
But, on my part, ye may eftsone hem telle,
We usen here no wommen for to selle."

27

The noyse of peple up sterte thanne at ones,
As breme as blase of straw iset on fire;
For infortune it wolde, for the nones,   185
They sholden hire confusioun desire.
"Ector," quod they, "what goost may yow enspire,
This womman thus to shilde, and don us leese
Daun Antenor?—a wrong wey now ye chese,—

171. H2Ph suffre *for* late.   172. H2PhH5S2DJRCx *om*. that.   173. CpH1J seyde;
α told hym (H5 *om*. told hym).   179. αH4RH3A is.   180. ClH2PhH5H3Cx *om*. that.
181. α for *for* on.   182. JH4 We ne usen.   183. H2Ph voys; H2PhH5H3Cx of þe
peple.   185. α *om*. it.

28

"That is so wys and ek so bold baroun,   190
And we han nede of folk, as men may se.
He is ek on the grettest of this town.
O Ector, lat tho fantasies be!
O kyng Priam," quod they, "thus syggen we,
That al oure vois is to forgon Criseyde";   195
And to deliveren Antenor they preyde.

29

O Juvenal, lord! soth is thy sentence,
That litel wyten folk what is to yerne,
That they ne fynde in hire desir offence;
For cloude of errour lat hem nat discerne   200
What best is; and, lo, here ensaumple as yerne.
This folk desiren now deliveraunce
Of Antenor, that broughte hem to meschaunce.

30

For he was after traitour to the town
Of Troye; allas, they quytte hym out to rathe!   205
O nyce world, lo thy discrecioun!
Criseyde, which that nevere dide hem scathe,
Shal now no lenger in hire blisse bathe;
But Antenor, he shal come hom to towne,
And she shal out; thus seyde here and howne.   210

---

191. γ(-A)Th to *for* of.   192. α He eke is one.   193. αH4R such, DTh þi *for* tho,
H3 that fantasye.   195. H2Ph þat our wil (Ph voys *for* wil *over erasure*); GgH5 þat
oure acord.   197. H2, *with a change of hand, becomes a* β *MS., closely related to*
H4; γS1Th trewe *for* soth; H3Cx ful sothe.   200. _lat hem nat, *so* JClADS1, H1 ne
lat hem, CpH2H4Th lat hem, R lettyth hem, H3Cx let hem to.   205. quytte, *so*
H3RTh, CpH1JCx quyte, H2Ph quytt, *rest* quyt.   206. Gg But þus it fel ry3t in
conclusioun, H5 But þus to felle to conclusioun.   209. CpClH1J com; Gg in to, H5 in
to þe, Ph in *for* hom to.   210. H5 þus seyde þei up & down; Cx thus al they sayde
& sowne; R he, H2H4 her, A heer, J heere; Gg hounne, H2H3 hown, RS1 houn.

31

For which delivered was by parlement,
For Antenor to yelden out Criseyde,
And it pronounced by the president,
Altheigh that Ector "nay" ful ofte preyde;
That fynaly, what wight that it withseyde,   215
It was for nought; it moste ben, and sholde,
For substaunce of the parlement it wolde.

32

Departed out of parlement echone,
This Troilus, withouten wordes mo,
Into his chaumbre spedde hym faste allone,   220
But if it were a man of his or two,
The which he bad out faste for to go,
Bycause he wolde slepen, as he seyde,
And hastily upon his bed hym leyde.

33

And as in wynter leves ben biraft,   225
Ech after other, til the tree be bare,
So that ther nys but bark and braunche ilaft.
Lith Troilus, byraft of eche welfare,
Ibounden in the blake bark of care,
Disposed wood out of his wit to breyde,   230
So sore hym sat the chaungynge of Criseyde.

---

211. γ(-A)S₁Th delibered. 212. α To ʒilde anon for Antenore Crisseyde. 215. That. *so* H₂H₄Cx, JRH₃ What, γTh And, αS₁ But. 220. γS₁Th Unto. 222. α dede *for* bad. 224. CpJ bedde. 231. H₂RH₃ the eschaunge, H₄A the chaunge.

34

He rist hym up, and every dore he shette
And wyndow ek, and tho this sorwful man
Upon his beddes syde adown hym sette,
Ful lik a ded ymage, pale and wan;   235
And in his brest the heped wo bygan
Out breste, and he to werken in this wise
In his woodnesse, as I shal yow devyse.

35

Right as the wylde bole bygynneth sprynge
Now her, now ther, idarted to the herte,   240
And of his deth roreth in compleynynge,
Right so gan he aboute the chaumbre sterte,
Smytyng his brest ay with his fistes smerte;
His hed to the wal, his body to the grounde,
Ful ofte he swapte, hym selven to confounde.   245

36

His eyen two, for piete of herte,
Out stremeden as swifte welles tweye;
The heighe sobbes of his sorwes smerte
His speche hym refte; unnethes myghte he seye:
"O deth, allas, why nyltow do me deye?   250
Acorsed be that day which that nature
Shoop me to ben a lyves creature!"

234. H3PhRCxTh doun. 238. α distresse. 239. GgH5 gynnyth, H3Ph gynneth to,
H2H4A begynnyth to. 241. Cp dethe, J wo. 244. RS1Cx *om. first* the. 246. piete, *so*
JH2S1, *rest* pite *or* pete; ClPhRCxTh of his herte, H2H4 of the herte. 247. α So
wepyn þat þey semyn welles tweye (Gg weptyn). 248. GgH5 þerwith þe sobbis.

37

But after, whan the furie and al the rage
Which that his herte twiste and faste threste,
By lengthe of tyme somwhat gan aswage,   255
Upon his bed he leyde hym down to reste;
But tho bygonne his teeris more out breste,
That wonder is the body may suffise
To half this wo, which that I yow devyse.

38

Than seyde he thus: "Fortune, allas the while!   260
What have I don, what have I thus agilt?
How myghtestow for rowthe me bygile?
Is ther no grace, and shal I thus be spilt?
Shal thus Criseyde awey, for that thow wilt?
Allas, how maistow in thyn herte fynde   265
To ben to me thus cruel and unkynde?

39

"Have I the nought honoured al my lyve,
As thow wel woost, above the goddes alle?
Whi wiltow me fro joie thus deprive?
O Troilus, what may men now the calle   270
But wrecche of wrecches, out of honour falle
Into miserie, in which I wol bewaille
Criseyde, allas, til that the breth me faille?

---

253. CpJ alle; GgH3Ph whan al þis furye and þis rage (Gg & al þis rage); H5
whan his fury & all his rage; JH4Cx this rage. 254. R sore thresste. 258. α þat wel
oneþe þe body. 262. α How mayst þu þus for reuthe (Ph myght), H4 Hou myst thou
for reuthe thus. 266. αH4 so *for* thus. 269. α þanne of joye me deprive (Ph of þis
joy). 272. Gg Into myn deþ.

40

"Allas, Fortune, if that my lif in joie
Displesed hadde unto thi foule envye,   275
Why ne haddestow my fader, kyng of Troye,
Byraft the lif, or don my bretheren dye,
Or slayn my self, that thus compleyne and crye,
I, combre-world, that may of no thyng serve,
But alwey dye, and nevere fulli sterve.   280

41

"If that Criseyde allone were me laft,
Nought roughte I whiderward thow woldest steere;
And hire, allas, than hastow me biraft.
But evere more, lo, this is thi manere,
To reve a wight that most is to hym deere,   285
To preve in that thi gerful violence.
Thus am I lost, ther helpeth no defence.

42

"O verrey lord of love, O god, allas,
That knowest best myn herte and al my thought,
What shal my sorwful lif don in this cas,   290
If I forgo that I so deere have bought?
Syn ye Criseyde and me han fully brought
Into youre grace, and bothe oure hertes seled,
How may ye suffre, allas, it be repeled?

280. γTh evere *for* alwey. 282. γS1Thα whider thow woldest me steere; J me *inserted over line before* steere. 285. H3H4 most to hym is. 286. α gery. 288. JH1 AS1GgPhCxTh O *for* of (Gg love O lord). 289. α knowyn; CpJ thoughte. 290. α How *for* What. 291, 292. CpJ boughte, broughte. 294. αS2 þat *for* allas.

43

"What shal I don? I shal, while I may dure   295
On lyve in torment and in cruel peyne,
This infortune or this disaventure,
Allone as I was born, iwys, compleyne;
Ne nevere wol I seen it shyne or reyne;
But ende I wol, as Edippe, in derknesse   300
My sorwful lif, and dyen in distresse.

44

"O wery goost, that errest to and fro,
Why nyltow fleen out of the wofulleste
Body that evere myghte on grounde go?
O soule, lurkynge in this wo, unneste,   305
Fle forth out of myn herte, and lat it breste,
And folwe alwey Criseyde, thi lady dere;
Thi righte place is now no lenger here.

45

"O woful eyen two, syn youre disport
Was al to sen Criseydes eyen brighte,   310
What shal ye don but, for my discomfort,
Stonden for naught, and wepen out youre sighte?
Syn she is queynt, that wont was yow to lighte,
In veyn fro this forth have ich eyen tweye
Iformed, syn youre vertu is aweye.   315

---

295. γTh What I may don. 296. α In wo, RCx Ay lyve *for* On lyve. 297. α mysaventure. 298. α allas, DCxTh I wol, A I mote *for* iwys. 300. CpH1 derkenesse, J dirknesse. 300, 301. α:—
>   Ne hevenys ly3t & þus I in derknesse
>   Myn woful lyf wele endyn for distresse
(H5 No *for* Ne; Ph *om.* Ne, as *for* &); H3:—
>   Ne see no lyght And thus in derkenesse
>   My sorowful lyfe wyl enden in distresse.
301. JH2 for destresse. 302. ClH1ADPhH2H4RCx verray, J veery, CpS2H3S1H5Th wery, Gg werray. 305. H4RCxTh woful nest, Ph wo unhonest, A woo un oneste, GgH5 wonest, S2 wo unrest, H3 wrecchydnesse. 306. α Fle forþ anon & do myn herte brest (Ph to brest); Cx Flee fer oute of myn hert or it brest.

46

"O my Criseyde, O lady sovereyne
Of thilke woful soule that thus crieth,
Who shal now yeven comfort to the peyne?
Allas, no wight! but whan myn herte dieth,
My spirit, which that so unto yow hieth,   320
Receyve in gree, for that shal ay yow serve;
Forthi no fors is, though the body sterve.

47

"O ye loveris, that heyghe upon the whiel
Ben set of Fortune, in good aventure,
God leve that ye fynde ay love of stiel,   325
And longe mote youre lif in joie endure!
But whan ye comen by my sepulture,
Remembreth that youre felawe resteth there;
For I loved ek, though ich unworthi were.

48

"O olde, unholsom, and myslyved man,   330
Calkas I mene, allas, what eiled the
To ben a Grek, syn thow art born Troian?
O Calkas, which that wilt my bane be,
In corsed tyme was thow born for me!
As wolde blisful Jove, for his joie,   335
That I the hadde where I wolde in Troie!"

317. γTh this, H3Cx that *for* thilke; J thilk. 318. S1Th thy, H3 your, αH2AD
my *for* the. 322. H2H4RCxH3 For now; α whan that, J is whan *for* is though.
325. R graunte, H4H5 lende. 326. α(GgH5H3Ph) 3e *for* youre lif. (*From line 326
H3 is regularly an* α *MS.*) 327. αA And *for* But. 328. β(-H4)Ph here. 330. ClAD
GgH5H4R mysbyleved (R *om.* and), PhCx myslyvyng. 331. ClGgH3H4RCx eyleth.
334. H3H5RCx were, H4H2 art, Th waste *for* was. 336. Cl where as, H3S1 where
that.

49

A thousand sikes, hotter than the gleede,
Out of his brest ech after other wente,
Medled with pleyntes newe, his wo to feede,
For which his woful teris nevere stente;　　　　340
And shortly, so his peynes hym to-rente,
And wex so maat, that joie nor penaunce
He feleth non, but lith forth in a traunce.

50

Pandare, which that at the parlement
Hadde herd what every lord and burgeys seyde,　345
And how ful graunted was, by oon assent,
For Antenor to yelden so Criseyde,
Gan wel neigh wood out of his wit to breyde;
So that, for wo, he nyste what he mente,
But in a rees to Troilus he wente.　　　　350

51

A certeyn knyght, that for the tyme kepte
The chaumbre dore, undide it hym anon;
And Pandare, that ful tendreliche wepte,
Into his derke chaumbre, as stille as ston,
Toward the bed gan softely to gon,　　　355
So confus, that he nyste what to seye;
For verray wo his wit was neigh aweye.

337. Gg An hunderid. 340. α þerwith (Ph þat with) *for* For which. 341. αS2Th sorwis, H2 teeris *for* peynes. 342. CpH1S2Th or, H3PhH5RA ne *for* nor. 343. Ph ay lith, R lay alle, Cx lyeth thus, Th lyeth *for* lith forth. 344. γS1Thα in *for* at. 347. α chaungyn. 348. H3PhCx *om.* wood. 354. JGgCx this, γS1ThH5 the *for* his; JGgH2RA *om. first* as. 355. H2H4S1Cx softly for to gone. 357. αS1Cx was al aweye.

52

And with his chere and lokyng al totorn
For sorwe of this, and with his armes folden,
He stood this woful Troilus byforn,   360
And on his pitous face he gan byholden;
But, lord, so ofte gan his herte colden,
Seyng his frend in wo, whos hevynesse
His herte slough, as thoughte hym, for destresse.

53

This woful wight, this Troilus, that felte   365
His frend Pandare ycomen hym to se,
Gan as the snow ayeyn the sonne melte,
For which this sorwful Pandare, of pitee,
Gan for to wepe as tendreliche as he;
And specheles thus ben thise ilke tweye,   370
That neither myghte o word for sorwe seye.

54

But at the laste this woful Troilus,
Neigh ded for smert, gan bresten out to rore;
And with a sorwful noise he seyde thus,
Amonge his sobbes and his sikes sore: 375
"Lo, Pandare, I am ded withouten more.
Hastow nat herd at parlement," he seyde,
"For Antenor how lost is my Criseyde?"

358. α But *for* And; CpJ totorne.   359. α Ny dede for wo & with (H3 *omits line*)
360. α sorweful.   362. α And *for* But.   367. Cp snowe, J snowgh.   373. α For crewel
smert (H3Ph hert).   374. PhA vois.   377. CpJ herde.

55

This Pandarus, ful dede and pale of hewe,
Ful pitously answerde, and seyde: "yis;　　　　　380
As wisly were it fals as it is trewe,
That I have herd, and woot al how it is.
O mercy, god, who wolde have trowed this?
Who wolde have wend that, in so litel a throwe
Fortune oure joie wolde han overthrowe?　　　385

56

"For in this world ther is no creature,
As to my dome, that evere saw ruyne
Straunger than this, thorugh cas or aventure.
But who may al eschue, or al devyne?
Swich is this world; forthi I thus deffyne,　　　390
Ne trust no wight to fynden in Fortune
Ay propretee; hire yiftes ben comune.

57

"But tel me this, whi thow art now so mad
To sorwen thus? whi listow in this wise,
Syn thi desir al holly hastow had,　　　　　395
So that by right it oughte ynough suffise?
But I, that nevere felte in my servyse
A frendly cheere, or lokyng of an eye,
Lat me thus wepe and wailen, til I dye.

384. CpH1J wende.　386. α O *for* For; JGgH2RCx nys no.　388. αCx Strengere.
393. PhRS1 now why þou art so mad, JH2H4H5 *om.* now; H4H5Cx art thou, H3
artow.　395. CpH1J desire.　397. α fond *for* felte.　398. α castyng (Gg schaungyng) *for*
lokyng.

58

"And over al this, as thow wel woost thi selve, 400
This town is ful of ladyes al aboute;
And, to my doom, fairer than swiche twelve
As evere she was, shal I fynde in som route,
Ye, oon or two, withouten any doute.
Forthi be glad, myn owen deere brother; 405
If she be lost, we shal recovere an other.

59

"What! god forbede alwey that eche plesaunce
In o thing were, and in non other wight.
If oon kan synge, an other kan wel daunce;
If this be goodly, that is glad and light, 410
And this is faire, and that kan good aright.
Eche for his vertu holden is for deere,
Both heroner and faucoun for ryvere.

60

"And ek, as writ Zanzis, that was ful wys,
'The newe love out chaceth ofte the olde'; 415
And upon newe cas lith newe avys.
Thenk ek, thi lif to saven artow holde;
Swich fir by proces moot of kynde colde.
For syn it is but casuel plesaunce,
Som cas shal putte it out of remembraunce. 420

---

400. **RCx** wost wel, **Ph** *om.* wel. 403. α in a route. 404. αD 3a to or þre. 409. α
What *for* If. 410. γS1Th she, Cx she that, H5 the other *for* that. 410, 411. α *trans-*
poses lines. 411. α 3if þis is fayr sche þat can good ary3t (H5 *om.* þat; H5Ph hir
god; Gg & ry3t). 412. H3PhRCx full, H4 at *for second* for. 414. ATh Zansis,
C1H1Cx Zauzis, Ph Zauzius, H5 Zenes. 415. PhS1 oft chaseth out, H5 ofte owth
shettit. 417. α And þynk (Gg þyng) *for* Thenk ek; C1S2RH5Th self *for* lif, H3 selfe
erased before lyf; C1DPhCx þow art. 418. γS1ThαCx shal *for* moot; GgH5H3RCx
be (H3H5 by) *for* of.

61

"For also seur as day comth after nyght,
The newe love, labour, or oother wo,
Or elles selde seynge of a wight,
Don olde affecciouns alle over go.
And, for thi part, thow shalt have oon of tho   425
Tabregge with thi bittre peynes smerte;
Absence of hire shal dryve hire out of herte."

62

Thise wordes seyde he for the nones alle,
To helpe his frend, lest he for sorwe deyde;
For douteles to don his wo to falle   430
He roughte nat what unthrift that he seyde.
But Troilus, that neigh for sorwe deyde,
Took litel heede of al that evere he mente;
Oon ere it herde, at tother out it wente.

63

But at the laste he answerde and seyde: "frend,   435
This lechecraft, or heeled thus to be,
Were wel sittyng, if that I were a fend,
To traysen a wight that trewe is unto me!
I pray god, lat this conseil nevere the;
But do me rather sterve anon right here,   440
Or I so do, as thow me woldest leere.

---

424. CpJ overe. 429. CpJ help. 430. αH2 make *for* don. 431. roughte, *so* GgA, *rest* rought; H3PhClADH2H4Cx *om.* that. 434. CpJH2S1 at oothir, H1Ph attother, ClGgH5Th at þe oþer, H4DCx at that othir, H3AR at another. 435. JH4RH1A *om.* he; CpH1J frende. 437. CpClJ fende. 438. *With this line* J *becomes an* α *MS.*; α(JGgH5PhH3)ClAD To traysen hir þat. 439. CpH1AH4CxTh ythe *for* the. 441. γS1ThCx thus *for* so; H2H4R werke (H2 werche) *for* do.

64

"She that I serve, iwis, what so thow seye,
To whom myn herte enhabit is by right,
Shal han me holly hires til that I deye.
For, Pandarus, syn I have trouthe hire hight,   445
I wol nat ben untrewe for no wight;
But as hire man, I wol ay lyve and sterve,
And nevere other creature serve.

65

"And ther thow seist, thow shalt as faire fynde
As she, lat be, make no comparisoun   450
To creature yformed here by kynde.
O leve Pandare, in conclusioun,
I wol nat be of thyn opynyoun,
Touchyng al this; for which I the biseche,
So holde thi pees; thow sleest me with thi speche. 455

66

"Thow biddest me I sholde love an other
Al fresshly newe, and lat Criseyde go.
It lith nat in my power, leeve brother;
And though I myght, I wolde nat do so.
But kanstow pleyen raket to and fro,   460
Netle in, dokke out, now this, now that, Pandare?
Now foule falle hire, for thi wo that care!

---

443. H2H4R of, Gg þour, H5A with *for* by.   445. α What Pandarus syn I have
hir bihight; H2H4S2 plight.   454. α for thy (H3 therefore) *for* for which; Cx for
why, D wherfore.   461. Cp dok, J dookke; H2H4R now her now þer.   462. for thi wo
that care, *so* βGgPh, CpH1 for thi wo and care, J þat for thy wo þat care, A for
þi wo at care, D þat for þi woo care, ClH3 þat for þi wo hath care (Cl hath *by corrector*), S2 for þe wold wo or care, S1 þat for þi wo wold care, H5 for þi wo that
woll care.

67

"Thow farest ek by me, thow Pandarus,
As he that, whan a wight is wo bygon,
He cometh to hym a paas, and seith right thus: 465
'Thynk nat on smerte, and thow shalt fele non.'
Thow moost me first transmewen in a ston,
And reve me my passiones alle,
Or thow so lightly do my wo to falle.

68

"My deth may wel out of my brest departe   470
The lif, so longe may this sorwe myne;
But fro my soule shal Criseydes darte
Out nevere mo; but down with Proserpyne,
Whan I am dede, I wol go wone in pyne;
And ther I wol eternaly compleyne   475
My wo, and how that twynned be we tweyne.

69

"Thow hast here made an argument for fyn,
How that it sholde a lasse peyne be,
Criseyde to forgon, for she was myn,
And lyved in ese and in felicite.   480
Why gabbestow, that seydest thus to me,
That hym is wors that is fro wele ythrowe,
Than he hadde erst noon of that wele yknowe?

464. α man *for* wight. 468. CpClH1JH3H5H2R passions. 470. γS1Thα(-Gg) The deth. 474. H2 duelle, H3 lyve, H5 leve *for* wone. 476. α This wo. 477. GgH5H3 ful *for* for. 483. Ph Than if he had of wele arst none yknowe, Cx Than he that never had of wele yknow.

70

"But telle me this, syn that the thynketh so light
To chaungen so in love, ay to and fro,   485
Whi hastow nat don bisily thi myght
To chaungen hire that doth the al thi wo?
Whi nyltow lete hire fro thyn herte go?
Whi nyltow love an other lady swete,
That may thyn herte setten in quiete?   490

71

"If thow hast had in love ay yit meschaunce,
And kanst it naught out of thyn herte dryve,
I, that lyvede in lust and in plesaunce
With hire as muche as creature on lyve,
How sholde I that foryete, and that so blyve?   495
O, where hastow ben hid so longe in muwe,
That kanst so wel and formaly arguwe?

72

"Nay, nay, god wot, nought worth is al thi red,
For which, for what that evere may bifalle,
Withouten wordes mo, I wol be ded.   500
O deth, that endere art of sorwes alle,
Com now, syn I so ofte after the calle;
For sely is that deth, soth for to seyne,
That, ofte ycleped, cometh and endeth peyne.

---

484. α sey *for* telle; γS1Cx now *for* this; Cx syth ye thynk so; H2H4R *om.* so.
491-532. Cp *omits six stanzas. Text based on* JClH1.   492. α yit fro *for* out of (H3
om. yit).   496. JGgH5 Or, Cx Loo *for* O.   498. γTh Nay god wot; α Nay Pandarus
naught worth.   499. α But douteles for aught þat may bifalle.

73

"Wel wot I, whil my lif was in quyete,   505
Or thow me slowe, I wolde have yeven hire;
But now thi comyng is to me so sweete,
That in this world I no thing so desire.
O deth, syn with this sorwe I am a-fire,
Thow outher do me anon in teeris drenche,   510
Or with thi colde strok myn hete quenche.

74

"Syn that thow slest so fele in sondry wyse
Ayeins hire wil, unpreyed day and nyght,
Do me at my requeste this servyse:
Delyvere now the world, so dostow right,   515
Of me, that am the wofulleste wyght
That evere was; for tyme is that I sterve,
Syn in this world of right nought may I serve."

75

This Troilus in teris gan distille,
As licour out of a lambyc ful faste;   520
And Pandarus gan holde his tonge stille,
And to the ground his eyen down he caste.
But natheles, thus thought he at the laste:
"What! parde, rather than my felawe deye,
Yit shal I somwhat moore unto hym seye";   525

506. α deth *for* thow.   507. α his *for* thi (J is; H3 *om.* his).   509. JGgH5H2H3 on
fire.   511. hete, *so* JH4ClH1, H2 herte hete, *rest* herte.   515. α thanne *for* so.   518.
H2H3 of no þing.   519. H3PhH2H4Cx Thus.

76

And seyde: "frend, syn thow hast swich distresse,
And syn the list myn argumentz to blame,
Why nylt thy selven helpen don redresse,
And with thy manhod letten al this grame?
Go ravysshe hire; ne kanstow nat, for shame? 530
And outher lat hire out of towne fare,
Or hold hire stille, and leve this nyce care.

77

"Artow in Troie, and hast non hardyment
To take a womman which that loveth the,
And wolde hire selven ben of thyn assent? 535
Now is nat this a nyce vanitee?
Ris up anon, and lat this wepyng be,
And kith thow art a man; for in this houre
I wol ben ded, or she shal bleven oure."

78

To this answerde hym Troilus ful softe, 540
And seyde: "parde, leve brother deere,
Al this have I my self yit thought ful ofte,
And more thyng than thow devysest here.
But whi this thyng is laft, thow shalt wel here;
And whan thow hast me yeve an audience, 545
Therafter maystow telle al thi sentence.

---

527. ClRTh *om.* to. 528. JGgPhH2H4 help to don; H3AS2Cx helpe to redresse.
530. ClDJH2Cx To *for* Go. 532. γThGgCx þi, H4 al thi *for* this; γS1ThPhCx fare
for care. 533. CpH1 hardymente, J hardement, 537. α this sorwe. 539. H2H4 but she
beleve our. 540. H2GgH5PhS1 *om.* hym. 542. J my self ithought, H3PhGgH5H4Cx
my selfe thought, H2 my self ymagened. 545. PhH5H2RCxTh *om.* an, H3 an *over
line later.*

79

"First, syn thow woost this town hath al this werre
For ravysshyng of wommen so by myght,
It sholde nat be suffred me to erre,
As it stant now, ne don so gret unright.   550
I sholde han also blame of every wight,
My fadres graunt if that I so withstoode,
Syn she is chaunged for the townes goode.

80

"I have ek thought, so it were hire assent,
To axe hire at my fader of his grace;   555
Than thynke I this were hire accusement.
Syn wel I woot I may hire nought purchace;
For syn my fader, in so heigh a place
As parlement, hath hire eschaunge enseled,
He nyl for me his lettre be repeled.   560

81

"Yit drede I most hire herte to perturbe
With violence, if I do swich a game;
For if I wolde it openly disturbe,
It mooste be disclaundre to hire name.
And me were levere ded than hire defame,   565
As nolde god, but if I sholde have
Hire honour levere than my lif to save.

548. Cp myghte; JPhH1ACx nyght. 551. GgH5PhS1Cx also han; H3 I shulde
have blame as moche as any wyght. 554. GgPhR 3if *for* so. 560. α his honour. 565.
JGgH2H4 be ded, H5 to be ded, R ded be, AS1 deth, H3CxTh deye *for* ded.

82

"Thus am I lost, for aught that I kan see;
For certeyn is, syn that I am hire knyght,
I moste hire honour levere han than me   570
In every cas, as lovere ought of right.
Thus am I with desir and reson twight:
Desir for to destourben hire me redeth;
And reson nyl nat, so myn herte dredeth."

83

Thus wepyng that he koude nevere cesse,   575
He seyde: "allas, how shal I, wrecche, fare?
For wel fele I alwey my love encresse,
And hope is lasse and lasse alwey, Pandare;
Encressen ek the causes of my care.
So weylawey, whi nyl myn herte breste?   580
For as in love is ther but litel reste."

84

Pandare answerde: "frend, thow maist for me
Don as the list; but hadde ich it so hoote,
And thyn estat, she sholde go with me;
Though al this town cride on this thyng by note,   585
I nolde sette at al that noys a grote.
For whan men han wel cried, than wol they rowne;
Ek wonder last but nyne nyght nevere in towne.

---

570. α I have hir honour levere yit than me; levere han, *so* γS1Th, H4Cx levere
save, H2 save lever, R kepe levere. 571. JH3H5 And in, Gg Hadde in *for* In. 573.
H2H4R it, Cx ay *for* hire. 581. α For why in love is litel hertes reste. (H3H5 For
while I lyve); γS1Th ther is. 586. H2H4Cx I nolde nat (H4 wolde); JGgH5Cx the
for that. 587. α than lat hem rowne. 588. αD For, Cl A *for* Ek; H3PhGgH4RS1Cx
lasteth, H2AD laste; H2Ph nyghtes, GgH5CxTh dayis; nevere, *so* CpClH1DJH3,
rest om.; H2S1 in a toun, S2 in þe towne.

85

"Devyne nat in resoun ay so depe,
Ne curteisly, but help thi selve anon;　　　　　　590
Bet is that othere than thi selven wepe,
And namely, syn ye two ben al on.
Ris up, for by myn hed, she shal nat goon;
And rather be in blame a litel stounde,
Than sterve here as a gnat, withouten wounde.　　595

86

"It is no shame unto yow, ne no vice,
Hire to withholden that ye loveth moost.
Paraunter, she myghte holden the for nyce,
To late hire go thus to the Grekis oost.
Thenk ek Fortune, as wel thi selven woost,　　　　600
Helpeth hardy man to his emprise,
And weyveth wrecches for hire cowardise.

87

"And though thy lady wolde a lite hire greve,
Thow shalt thi self thi pees hereafter make;
But as for me, certeyn, I kan nat leve　　　　　605
That she wolde it as now for yvel take.
Whi sholde thanne of fered thyn herte quake?
Thenk how that Paris hath, that is thi brother,
A love; and whi shaltow nat have another?

---

590. Cp corteisly, α preciously, R preciently, Cx curyously. 594. *So* βS1, α a lite
in blame ifownde, γTh in blame a lite ifounde. 596. α It is no rape in my dom ne no
vice (GgPh jape). 597. H2H4Cx you, JH5D the, H3 thou *for* ye; CpS2R love, Gg
lovyn, JH3 lovest. 598. H2H4RCx you *for* the. 599. γThPh unto *for* to; Gg into *for*
thus to. 601. RS1Cx an hardy man. 602. αCx And fleeth fro wrechches. 604. αCl
Thow shalt thy pees ful wel hiraftir make (PhH5 *om.* ful; H5 heraftir wel); D
þiselve þi pees ful wel herafter make. 607. GgH5 for ferd, PhCxTh for fere, S1D
of fere; H2 thyne herte for drede, H4 thyn herte for feer, R thyn herte thanne **of fer**
608. γS1 ek how *for* how that, H2H4Th *om. first* that.

88

"And Troilus, o thyng I dar the swere,   610
That if Criseyde, which that is thi lief,
Now loveth the as wel as thow dost here,
God help me so, she nyl nat take a-grief,
Theigh thow do boote anon in this myschief.
And if she wilneth fro the for to passe,   615
Thanne is she fals; so love hire wel the lasse.

89

"Forthi take herte, and thynk right as a knyght;
Thorugh love is broken alday every lawe.
Kith now somwhat thi corage and thi myght;
Have mercy on thi self, for any awe.   620
Lat nat this wrecched wo thyn herte gnawe,
But manly set the world on sixe and sevene;
And if thow deye a martyr, go to hevene.

90

"I wol my self ben with the at this dede,
Theigh ich and al my kyn, upon a stownde,   625
Shulle in a strete as dogges liggen dede,
Thorough girt with many a wid and blody wownde;
In every cas I wol a frend be founde.
And if the list here sterven as a wrecche,
Adieu, the devel spede hym that recche!"   630

---

611. H2H4H5 þe *for* thi.   617. PhH5 þus as, Gg þus þat I, JH3 thus *for* right as.
622. H2H4PhCx at *for* on; CpJAS1 sex, Gg sexe.   624. ClR nede.   626. GgH5PhA
CxTh schulde.   627. H3 a depe, Ph a grete, H5 arwe *for* a wid.   628. CpJ frende.
630. α have *for* spede; H1AS1H2RH5 þat it reche.

91

This Troilus gan with tho wordes quyken,
And seyde: "frend, graunt mercy, ich assente;
But certeynly thow maist nat so me priken,
Ne peyne non ne may me so tormente,
That, for no cas, it is nat myn entente,   635
At shorte wordes, though I deyen sholde,
To ravysshe hire, but if hire self it wolde."

92

"Whi so mene I," quod Pandare, "al this day.
But telle me thanne, hastow hire wil assayed,
That sorwest thus?" And he answerde: "nay."   640
"Wherof artow," quod Pandare, "thanne amayed,
That nost nat that she wol ben yvele apayed
To ravysshe hire, syn thow hast nat ben there,
But if that Jove tolde it in thyn ere?

93

"Forthi ris up, as nought ne were, anon,   645
And wassh thi face, and to the kyng thow wende,
Or he may wondren whider thow art goon.
Thow most with wisdom hym and othere blende;
Or, upon cas, he may after the sende
Or thow be war; and, shortly, brother deere,   650
Be glad, and lat me werke in this matere."

632. JPhH4DCx gramercy. 633. H3PhGgH5 me not so, ClH2H4 not me so. 637. H3PhGgRCx *om.* it. 638. α Pandare answerde of þat be as be may (H3 be as it may, H5 be as it be may); CpClH1CxTh Pandarus. 639. ClADGgH5H2Th wel. 640. CpH1AS1H2RTh answerde hym, H4 him ansuerde. 641. H3 quod he thus amayede, Ph þan quod Pandare þus amayed, Gg quod Pandarus art þou þus amayed, H5 art þou þanne amayde (*om.* quod Pandare). 642. GgPhH4RDS1 wost, H2 knowest. 644. α But any aungel; GgH5H2H4 it þe in þyn ere, Ph þe hit in thi ere. 647. α why thow art thus gon (GgPh whedyr).

94

"For I shal shape it so, that sikerly
Thow shalt this nyght som tyme, in som manere,
Come speken with thi lady pryvely,
And by hire wordes ek, and by hire cheere,   655
Thow shalt ful sone aperceyve and wel here
Al hire entente, and of this cas the beste;
And fare now wel, for in this point I reste."

95

The swifte Fame, which that false thynges
Egal reporteth lik the thynges trewe,   660
Was thorughout Troie yfled with preste wynges
Fro man to man, and made this tale al newe,
How Calkas doughter, with hire brighte hewe,
At parlement, withouten wordes more,
Ygraunted was in chaunge of Antenore.   665

96

The whiche tale anon right as Criseyde
Hadde herd, she which that of hire fader roughte,
As in this cas, right nought, ne whan he deyde,
Ful bisily to Jupiter bisoughte
Yeve hym meschaunce that this tretis broughte.   670
But shortly, lest thise tales sothe were,
She dorste at no wight axen it for fere.

---

655. γ(-Cl)S1ThH5 as *for* and. 657. γS1Th in *for* of. 661. Ph Was þurgh the toun fled, H3 Was thurgh flede. 662. H3PhGg *om.* al; H2H4R þes tidinges new (H4 alle these; R this tydyng). 663. brighte, *so* ClGg, *rest* bright. 665. H3PhGg for *for* of. 666. CpH1J which. 667. CpH1 herde, J hard. 670. CpADH2H4RTh hem, S1 tham *for* hym. 672. H3PhH5H2H4RCx of *for* at.

97

As she that hadde hire herte and al hire mynde
On Troilus iset so wonder faste,
That al this world ne myghte hire love unbynde,   675
Ne Troilus out of hire herte caste,
She wol ben his while that hire lif may laste.
And thus she brenneth bothe in love and drede,
So that she nyste what was best to reede.

98

But as men seen in towne, and al aboute,   680
That wommen usen frendes to visite,
So to Criseyde of wommen com a route,
For pitous joie, and wenden hire delite,
And with hire tales, deere ynough a myte,
Thise wommen, which that in the cite dwelle,   685
They sette hem down, and seyde as I shal telle.

99

Quod first that oon: "I am glad, trewely,
Bycause of yow, that shal youre fader see."
Another seyde: "ywis, so nam nat I;
For al to litel hath she with us be."   690
Quod tho the thridde: "I hope, ywis, that she
Shal bryngen us the pees on every syde,
That, whan she goth, almyghty god hire gide!"

674. α biset (Ph and þat). 679. Cp beste, J beest. 680. α in townes al aboute.
686. *With this line* H5 *ends*. 688. GgCx 3e, Cl þat ye *for* that. 689. ClAS2GgH4
RCxTh am not. 691. α The thridde answerde I hope.

100

Tho wordes and tho wommanysshe thynges,
She herde hem right as though she thennes were;   695
For, god it woot, hire herte on oother thyng is,
Although the body sat among hem there.
Hire advertence is alwey elleswhere;
For Troilus ful faste hire soule soughte;
Withouten word, on hym alwey she thoughte.   700

101

Thise wommen, that thus wenden hire to plese,
Aboute naught gonne alle hire tales spende;
Swich vanyte ne kan don hire non ese,
As she that al this mene while brende
Of other passioun than that they wende;   705
So that she felte almost hire herte dye,
For wo and wery of that compaignie.

102

For which no lenger myghte she restreyne
Hire teeris, so they gonnen up to welle,
That yaven signes of the bittre peyne   710
In which hire spirit was, and moste dwelle,
Remembryng hire fro heven into which helle
She fallen was, syn she forgoth the syghte
Of Troilus; and sorwfully she sighte.

---

695. αCx *om.* hem. 696. α For al this while hir herte (Gg tyme). 697. Cp satte, JH1 sate. 698. α God wot hir advertence is elliswhere. 700. JGgH3ClH4Cx alwey on hym. 701. α so *for* thus. 702. α thus gonne hir (Ph gun her talis þus; H3 they *for* thus). 703. H3PhGgH4 *om.* ne. 706. α So þat she wende anon right for to dye. 708-714. γ *omits stanza; text based on* J. 708. H3 she myght; H2H4GgTh myght she no lenger. 712. Remembryg, whiche; H3Ph in. 713. J forgothe. 714. Gg Of Troylus hire owene hertys kny3t.

103

And thilke fooles sittynge hire aboute 715
Wenden, that she wepte and siked sore
Bycause that she sholde out of that route
Departe, and nevere pleye with hem more.
And they that hadde yknowen hire of yore,
Seigh hire so wepe, and thoughte it kyndenesse, 720
And eche of hem wepte ek for hire destresse.

104

And bisyly they gonnen hire comforten
Of thyng, god woot, on which she litel thoughte,
And with hire tales wenden hire disporten;
And to be glad they often hire bysoughte. 725
But swich an ese therwith they hire wroughte
Right as a man is esed for to feele,
For ache of hed, to clawen hym on his heele.

105

But after al this nyce vanyte
They toke hire leve; and hom they wenten alle. 730
Criseyde, ful of sorweful pite,
Into the chaumbre up wente out of the halle,
And on hire bed she gan for ded to falle,
In purpos thennes nevere for to risé;
And thus she wroughte, as I shal yow devyse. 735

---

717. α from *for* out of; H3PhH2H4Th the *for second* that.   721. GgH2H4Cx *om.*
ek.   723. H3H4 that she ful litel thoght.   724. α hir wordes.   728. Gg eche, H2H4
CxH3AS2 the *for* his.   731. CpS1 piete.   732. γTh hire chambre.   733. α for ded she
gan.   734. γS1JGg nevere thennes, H3 there never.

106

Hire ownded heer, that sonnyssh was of hewe,
She rente, and ek hire fyngeres longe and smale
She wrong ful ofte, and bad god on hire rewe,
And with the deth to doon boote on hire bale.
Hire hewe, whilom bright, that tho was pale,   740
Bar witnesse of hire wo and hire constreynte;
And thus she spak, sobbyng in hire compleynte:

107

"Allas," quod she, "out of this regioun
I, woful wrecche and infortuned wight,
And born in corsed constellacioun,   745
Moot goon, and thus departen fro my knyght.
Wo worth, allas, that ilke dayes light,
On which I saugh hym first with eyen tweyne,
That causeth me, and ich hym, al this peyne!"

108

Therwith the teris from hire eyen two   750
Down fille, as shoure in Aprille swithe;
Hire white brest she bet, and for the wo
After the deth she cryed a thousand sithe,
Syn he that wont hire wo was for to lithe,
She moot forgon; for which disaventure   755
She held hire self a forlost creature.

736. H3 clere, Cx yelowe, Ph ornyd, Gg owene, A ownne, S2 undid, H2 ougne, H4 owyn *for* ownded; Cp sonnysshe, J snowyssh. 737. H3 longe fyngres smale. 739. α *om.* to; JPh upon *for* on. 747. α Wo worth þat day and namely þat nyght. 750-756. *In* α *this stanza follows line* 735. 750. α The salte teeris from hir eyne tweyne. 751. α Out ronne as shoure; Cp falle; H4 shoures; CpJH3Cx April, Cl Aperill, H1 aperil, R Averyll; GgPhR ful swyþe, CxS1 doth swythe. 752. α for the peyne. 754. H3PhGgH4RDS2 wonte was hyr woo.

109

She seyde: "how shal he don, and ich also?
How shal I lyve, if that I from hym twynne?
O deere herte ek, that I love so,
Who shal that sorwe slen that ye ben inne?   760
O Calkas, fader, thyn be al this synne!
O moder myn, that cleped were Argyve,
Wo worth that day that thow me bere on lyve!

110

"To what fyn sholde I lyve and sorwen thus?
How sholde a fissh withouten water dure?   765
What is Criseyde worth from Troilus?
How sholde a plaunte, or lyves creature,
Lyve withoute his kynde noriture?
For which ful ofte a byword here I seye,
That 'roteles moot grene soone deye.'   770

111

"I shal doon thus: syn neither swerd ne darte
Dar I noon handle, for the crueltee,
That ilke day I moot from yow departe,
If sorwe of that nyl nat my bane be,
Than shal no mete or drynke come in me   775
Til I my soule out of my breste unshethe;
And thus my selven wol I don to dethe.

---

757. α What shal he don what shal I do also.   758. γS1ThH2H4 sholde.   762.
S1CxD art.   762, 763. α And corsed be þat day which that Argyve/Me of hir body
bar to ben on lyve.   767. α or oother creature (Ph of eny creature).   770. α ertheles;
Cp rootles.   771. CpH1J swerde.   773. I moot, *so* β, JH3Gg I shal, γS1ThPh that I
for I moot.   774. PhH4RS1S2Cx wil.   775. α Ther; CpH1 Thanne; GgPhH4RCxS1 ne,
D nor, S2 no, H2 & *for* or.

112

"And, Troilus, my clothes everychon
Shul blake ben, in tokenyng, herte swete,
That I am as out of this world agon,   780
That wont was yow to setten in quiete;
And of myn ordre, ay til deth me mete,
The observaunce evere, in youre absence,
Shal sorwe ben, compleynte, and abstinence.

113

"Myn herte, and ek the woful goost therinne,   785
Byquethe I with youre spirit to compleyne
Eternaly, for they shul nevere twynne;
For though in erthe ytwynned be we tweyne,
Yit in the feld of pite, out of peyne,
That hight Elisos, shal we be yfeere,   790
As Orpheus with Erudice his fere.

114

"Thus, herte myn, for Antenor, allas,
I soone shal be chaunged, as I wene.
But how shul ye don in this sorwful cas,
How shal youre tendre herte this sustene?   795
But, herte myn, foryete this sorwe and tene,
And me also; for, sothly for to seye,
So ye wel fare, I recche nat to deye."

780. H2H4 oute as, H1DJR *om.* as; H3PhGgR ygoon, H1S2H2 gon. 781. α
holden in (Ph þat was wont to hold ʒow). 782. α til þat *for* ay til; H2R ay till þe
dethe. 783. J observaunces. 789. Cp piete. 790. α Ther Pluto regneth shal (Ph *has*
βγ *reading written later in space left blank*); CpH1 heighte. 791. γ(-D)S1Th and
for with. 793. α yolden. 794. α woful.

115

How myghte it evere yred ben or ysonge,
The pleynte that she made in hire destresse?   800
I not; but, as for me, my litel tonge,
If I discryven wolde hire hevynesse,
It sholde make hire sorwe seme lesse
Than that it was, and childisshly deface
Hire heigh compleynte, and therfore ich it pace.   805

116

Pandare, which that sent from Troilus
Was to Criseyde,—as ye han herd devyse,
That for the best it was acorded thus,
And he ful glad to doon hym that servyse,—
Unto Criseyde, in a ful secree wise,   810
Ther as she lay in torment and in rage,
Com hire to telle al holly his message,

117

And fond that she hire selven gan to trete
Ful pitously; for with hire salte teris
Hire brest, hire face, ybathed was ful wete.   815
The myghty tresses of hire sonnyssh heeris,
Unbroiden, hangen al aboute hire eeris;
Which yaf hym verray signal of martire
Of deth, which that hire herte gan desire.

---

799. JH3 evere al red ben. 804. JPh *om.* that, Gg as *for* that. 806-826. Gg *omits four stanzas.* 807. ClCx *om.* Was; γS1ThCx unto; CpH1J herde. 809. α this (Ph his) *for* that. 817. H2 hange, H4 heeng, Cx hyng, JPhR hongynge. 818. CpJRDS1 matire, ClH1AS2H3Ph matere, CxTh matyere, H2 martir, H4 martyre. 819. α which þat for wo she gan desire.

118

Whan she hym saugh, she gan for sorwe anon   820
Hire tery face atwixe hire armes hide;
For which this Pandare is so wobygon,
That in the hous he myghte unnethe abyde,
As he that pite felte on every syde.
For if Criseyde hadde erst compleyned soore,   825
Tho gan she pleyne a thousand tymes more.

119

And in hire aspre pleynte thus she seyde:
"Pandare first of joies mo than two
Was cause causyng unto me, Criseyde,
That now transmuwed ben in cruel wo.   830
Wher shal I seye to yow 'welcome' or no,
That alderfirst me broughte into servyse
Of love, allas! that endeth in swich wise?

120

"Endeth thanne love in wo? Ye, or men lieth,
And al worldly blisse, as thynketh me.   835
The ende of blisse ay sorwe it occupieth;
And whoso troweth nat that it so be,
Lat hym upon me, woful wrecche, ysee,
That my self hate, and ay my burthe acorse,
Felyng alwey, fro wikke I go to worse.   840

820. α for shame anon. 823. α in the chambre. 828. α Myn em Pandare of joyes. 829. α first to me. 831. PhH3AH4RCxTh Wheþer, H2 Wheider *for* Wher. 834. H3H4GgCx than, D þen. 835. α And every worldly joye (JGg wordly, H3 worldes).

121

"Whoso me seeth, he seeth sorwe al at onys,
Peyne, torment, pleynte, wo, distresse.
Out of my woful body harm ther noon is,
As angwissh, langour, cruel bitternesse,
Anoy, smert, drede, fury, and ek siknesse.   845
I trowe, ywys, from hevene teeris reyne,
For pite of myn aspre and cruel peyne."

122

"And thow, my suster, ful of discomfort,"
Quod Pandarus, "what thynkestow to do?
Whi ne hastow to thy selven som resport?   850
Whi wiltow thus thi self, allas, fordo?
Leef al this werk, and take now heede to
That I shal seyn; and herkne of good entente
This which by me thi Troilus the sente."

123

Tornede hire tho Criseyde, a wo makynge   855
So gret that it a deth was for to see.
"Allas," quod she, "what wordes may ye brynge?
What wol my deere herte seyn to me,
Which that I drede nevere mo to see?
Wol he han pleynte or teris or I wende?   860
I have ynough, if he therafter sende!"

---

842. S1 Peyne and torment; ClDS2RPhCxTh and distresse, GgS1 & ek distresse.
843. α sorwful. 848. R my nyece. 851. H3H4RCx allas thyself. 852. CpJ werke.
853. JGgH3 What. 854. CpH1DS2ThH4 This message *for* This; αTh þat, S2 which
þat *for* which. 860. ClADH3 ye *for* he.

124

She was right swich to seen in hire visage
As is that wight that men on beere bynde;
Hire face, lik of Paradys the ymage,
Was al ychaunged in another kynde.   865
The pleye, the laughter, men was wont to fynde
In hire, and ek hire joies everichone,
Ben fled; and thus lieth Criseyde allone.

125

Aboute hire eyen two a purpre ryng
Bytrent, in sothfast tokenyng of hire peyne,   870
That to biholde it was a dedly thyng;
For which Pandare myghte nat restreyne
The teeris from his eyen for to reyne.
But natheles, as he best myghte, he seyde
From Troilus thise wordes to Criseyde: 875

126

"Lo, nece, I trowe ye han herd al how
The kyng, with othere lordes, for the beste,
Hath made eschaunge of Antenor and yow,
That cause is of this sorwe and this unreste.
But how this cas dooth Troilus moleste,   880
That may non erthely mannes tonge seye;—
As he that shortly shapeth hym to deye.

---

865. H3GgH4Cx into. 866. GgPhH4RCxTh were. 867. CpH1S2CxTh On *for* In;
α and oother joyes. 868. lieth, *so* H2H3S1DCx, *rest* lith; CpClH1DS1 lith now
Criseyde; α and thus for hem she lith allone. 869. CpH1J rynge. 873. Cp eighen,
J eyne. 875. Cp Fram, J For. 876. αRS1 I trowe wel ye han. 878. JR theschaunge,
H3 thys chaunge, Gg þe eschaung, H2H4 þe chaunge, Cx a chaunge, Ph chaunge.
879. α this wo. 881. α no wordly (Ph worldly). 882. γS1Th For verray wo his wit
is al aweye.

127

"For which we han so sorwed, he and I,
That into litel bothe it hadde us slawe;
But thorugh my conseyl this day, finaly,   885
He somwhat is fro wepynge now withdrawe.
And semeth me that he desireth fawe
With yow to ben al nyght, for to devyse
Remedie in this, if ther were any wyse.

128

"This, short and pleyn, theffect of my message,   890
As ferforth as my wit kan comprehende;
For ye, that ben of torment in swich rage,
May to no long prologe as now entende;
And herupon ye may answere hym sende.
And, for the love of god, my nece deere,   895
So lef this wo or Troilus be here."

129

"Gret is my wo," quod she, and sighte soore,
As she that feleth dedly sharp distresse;
"But yit to me his sorwe is muche more,
That love hym bet than he hym self, I gesse.   900
Allas, for me hath he swich hevynesse?
Kan he for me so pitously compleyne?
Iwis, this sorwe doubleth al my peyne.

---

886. α hath fro wepynge hym withdrawe. 889. H3PhS2CxTh of this. 890. GgH4
DCx þis is. 891. α And ek the beste as my wit; ClDS1H3R may *for* kan. 892.
GgPhH4 in *for* of; Gg for, Ph of, H4 & in *for* in. 903. JGgPh Now iwis (J wys)
for Iwis; αCx his *for* this.

130

"Grevous to me, god woot, is for to twynne,"
Quod she, "but yit it hardere is to me   905
To sen that sorwe which that he is inne;
For wel I wot, it wol my bane be,
And deye I wol in certeyn," tho quod she;
"But bid hym come, or deth, that thus me threteth,
Dryve out that goost which in myn herte he beteth."

131

Thise wordes seyd, she on hire armes two   911
Fil gruf, and gan to wepen pitously.
Quod Pandarus: "allas, whi do ye so,
Syn wel ye woot the tyme is faste by,
That he shal come? Aris up hastily,   915
That he yow not bywopen thus ne fynde,
But ye wol have hym wood out of his mynde.

132

"For wiste he that ye ferde in this manere,
He wolde hym selven sle; and if I wende
To han this fare, he sholde nat come here   920
For al the good that Priam may dispende.
For to what fyn he wolde anon pretende,
That knowe I wel; and forthi yit I seye,
So lef this sorwe, or platly he wol deye.

---

904. GgH3RCx for *for* to. 906. α To sen hym in þat wo þat he is inne. 907 γS1Th woot I. 910. ClADS1PhR þe *for* that; GgH3PhH4CxTh *om.* he. 911. CpH1 seyde, J seid. 914. faste, *so* ClADS1H3H4GgTh, *rest* fast. 915. α softly (Ph shortly). 916. ne fynde, *so* γS1ThR, JGg ifynde, H3PhCx fynde, H2H4 you finde. 923. α That wot I; αCx therfore. 924. α Lat be this sorwe; Cx Soo lete.

133

"And shapeth yow his sorwe for tabregge,   925
And nought encresse, leeve nece swete;
Beth rather to hym cause of flat than egge,
And with som wisdom ye his sorwe bete.
What helpeth it to wepen ful a strete,
Or though ye bothe in salte teeris dreynte?   930
Bet is a tyme of cure ay than of pleynte.

134

"I mene thus: whan ich hym hider brynge,
Syn ye ben wise, and bothe of oon assent,
So shapeth how destourbe youre goynge,
Or come ayeyn soone after ye be went.   935
Wommen ben wise in short avysement;
And lat sen how youre wit shal now availle,
And that that I may helpe, it shal nat faille."

135

"Go," quod Criseyde, "and, uncle, trewely,
I shal don al my myght me to restreyne   940
From wepyng in his sight, and bisily
Hym for to glade I shal don al my peyne,
And in myn herte seken every veyne;
If to his sore ther may be fownden salve,
It shal nat lakke, certeyn, on my halve."   945

---

926. H3PhGgH4 to encrece; α O leve nece. 928. γ(-H1)S1ThPhH2 sorwes. 933.
CpJ assente. 934. H3CxTh how to, GgR to, DS1 you to, H2 you hou to, H4 hou ye
may *for* how; αClD this *for* youre. 935. CpH1J wente. 936. αD of, H4 at *for* in.
937. ClH2H4 now how youre wit shal, H3 now how shal your wytte, Cx now youre
wyt how shal. 938. γS1Th what that, βPh þat *for* that that; α kan helpe. 944.
γ(-Cl)ThJH3Ph this *for* his. 945. GgH4RS1 lak in serteyn; H2H3Cx behalve.

136

Goth Pandarus, and Troilus he soughte,
Til in a temple he fond hym al allone,
As he that of his lif no lenger roughte;
But to the pitous goddes everichone
Ful tendrely he preyde, and made his mone,   950
To doon hym sone out of this world to pace;
For wel he thoughte ther was non other grace.

137

And shortly, al the sothe for to seye,
He was so fallen in despeir that day,
That outrely he shop hym for to deye.   955
For right thus was his argument alway:
He seyde he nas but lorn, weylaway!
"For al that comth, comth by necessitee;
Thus to be lorn, it is my destinee.

138

"For certeynly, this wot I wel," he seyde,   960
"That forsight of divine purveyaunce
Hath seyn alwey me to forgon Criseyde,
Syn god seeth every thyng, out of doutaunce,
And hem disponeth, thorugh his ordinaunce,
In hire merites sothly for to be,   965
As they shul comen by predestyne.

947. CpH1 fonde, J fownde; al allone, *so* CpS1JH3CxTh, *rest om.* al. 948. H3Ph
S1H2H4Cx no more, Gg no þyng. 950-952. H3Ph:—
       He fast made hys compleynt and hys moon,
       Besykyng hem to sende hym other grace,
       Or fro thys worlde to doon hym sone pace.
(Ph to pace). 951. CpH1J worlde. 952. JGgH2RA nas. 953-1078. *Omitted by*
GgH3H4; *later on inset leaf in* Ph. 957. JDS1Cx I am *for* he nas; JDS1S2RCx
lorn so weylaway. 964. CpJ disponyth; H2RCxADS2 disposeth.

139

"But natheles, allas, whom shal I leeve?
For ther ben grete clerkes many oon,
That destyne thorugh argumentes preve;
And som men seyn that, nedely, ther is noon,   970
But that fre chois is yeven us everychon.
O, weilawey! so sleighe arn clerkes olde,
That I not whos opynyoun I may holde.

140

"For som men seyn, if god seth al biforn,
Ne god may nat deceyved ben, parde,   975
Than moot it fallen, theigh men hadde it sworn,
That purveiaunce hath seyn byfore to be.
Wherfore I seye, that from enterne if he
Hath wist byforn oure thought ek as oure dede,
We han no fre chois, as thise clerkes rede.   980

141

"For other thought, nor other dede also,
Myghte nevere ben, but swich as purveyaunce,
Which may nat ben deceyved nevere mo,
Hath feled byforn, withouten ignoraunce.
For yf ther myghte ben a variaunce   985
To writhen out fro goddes purveyinge,
Ther nere no prescience of thyng comynge;

973.H2R whiche *for* whos.   984. RDS1Cx felt.   987. H2RS1S2Cx wer.

142

"But it were rather an opynyoun
Uncerteyn, and no stedfast forseynge;
And, certes, that were an abusioun,   990
That god sholde han no parfit cler wytynge,
More than we men that han doutous wenynge.
But swich an errour upon god to gesse
Were fals and foul, and wikked corsednesse.

143

"Ek this is an opynyoun of some   995
That han hire top ful heighe and smothe yshore:
They seyn right thus, that thyng is nat to come
For that the prescience hath seyn byfore
That it shal come; but they seyn, that therfore
That it shal come, therfore the purveyaunce   1000
Woot it byforn, withouten ignoraunce;

144

"And in this manere this necessite
Retorneth in his part contrarie agayn.
For nedfully byhoveth it nat to bee,
That thilke thynges fallen in certayn   1005
That ben purveyed; but nedly, as they seyn,
Byhoveth it that thynges whiche that falle,
That they in certayn ben purveyed alle.

989. JPhCx Unstidefast and no certein (Cx not); Cp stedfaste. 994. ClCx corsed
wykkednesse. 997. CpH2 right this. 1003. Cp agayne, J again. 1005. Cp certayne,
J certain. 1006. H2PhS2Th nedfully; Cp sayne, J seyne.

145

"I mene as though I laboured me in this,
To enqueren which thyng cause of which thyng be: 1010
As wheither that the prescience of god is
The certeyn cause of the necessite
Of thynges that to comen ben, parde;
Or if necessite of thyng comynge
Be cause certeyn of the purveyinge.   1015

146

"But now nenforce I me nat in shewynge
How the ordre of causes stant; but wel woot I,
That it byhoveth that the bifallynge
Of thynges wist byforn certeynly
Be necessarie, al seme it nat therby   1020
That prescience put fallynge necessaire
To thyng to come, al falle it foule or faire.

147

"For if ther sit a man yond on a see,
Than by necessite bihoveth it
That, certes, thyn opynyoun sooth be,   1025
That wenest, or conjectest, that he sit;
And further overe now ayeinward yit,
Lo, right so is it of the part contrarie,
As thus—nowe herkne, for I wol nat tarie—:

1019. CpH1Ph byfor, H2AS1 before.   1028. ClCx it is.

148

"I seye, that if the opynyoun of the   1030
Be soth, for that he sit, than seye I this:
That he mot sitten by necessite;
And thus necessite in eyther is.
For in hym nede of sittynge is, ywys,
And in the nede of soth; and thus, forsothe,   1035
Ther mot necessite ben in yow bothe.

149

"But thow mayst seyn, the man sit nat therfore,
That thyn opynyoun of his sittynge soth is;
But rather, for the man sit ther byfore,
Therfore is thyn opynyoun soth, ywis.   1040
And I seye, though the cause of soth of this
Comth of his sittyng, yit necessite
Is entrechaunged, bothe in hym and the.

150

"Thus in this same wise, out of doutaunce,
I may wel maken, as it semeth me,   1045
My resonyng of goddes purveyaunce,
And of the thynges that to comen be;
By which resoun men may wel yse,
That thilke thynges that in erthe falle,
That by necessite they comen alle.   1050

1031. CpJ sey. 1038. PhS2 *om.* his. 1043. H2S2Th in him & in the. 1044. ClS1 on *for* in; CpDH2CxTh the *for* this. 1047. ARCx þo *for* the.

151

"For although that, for thyng shal come, ywys,
Therfore is it purveyed, certeynly,
Nat that it comth, for it purveyed is;
Yit, natheles, bihoveth it nedfully,
That thing to come be purveyd, trewely;   1055
Or elles, thynges that purveyed be,
That they bitiden by necessite.

152

"And this suffiseth right ynough, certeyn,
For to destroye oure fre chois every del.
But now is this abusioun to seyn,   1060
That fallyng of the thynges temporel
Is cause of goddes prescience eternel.
Now, trewely, that is a fals sentence,
That thyng to come sholde cause his prescience.

153

"What myghte I wene, and I hadde swich a thought,
But that god purveyeth thyng that is to come,   1066
For that it is to come, and ellis nought?
So myghte I wene that thynges alle and some,
That whilom ben byfalle and overcome,
Ben cause of thilke sovereyn purveyaunce,   1070
That forwoot al withouten ignoraunce.

1052. ClDPh it is, JCx they ben. 1062. PhS2Th of þe goddis. 1064. Ph shul,
RCx shal. 1065-1071. Ph *omits stanza.* 1067. H1AJ *om.* it.

154

"And overe al this, yit seye I more therto,
That right as whan I wot ther is a thyng,
Iwys, that thyng moot nedfully be so;
Ek right so, whan I woot a thyng comyng,   1075
So mot it come; and thus the bifallyng
Of thynges that ben wist bifore the tyde,
They mowe nat ben eschued on no syde."

155

Thanne seyde he thus: "almyghty Jove in trone,
That woost of al this thyng the sothfastnesse,   1080
Rewe on my sorwe, and do me deyen sone,
Or bryng Criseyde and me fro this destresse."
And whil he was in al this hevynesse,
Disputyng with hym self in this matere,
Com Pandare in, and seyde as ye may here.   1085

156

"O myghty god," quod Pandarus, "in trone,
I! who say evere a wis man faren so?
Whi, Troilus, what thinkestow to doone?
Hastow swich lust to ben thyn owen fo?
What, parde, yit is nat Criseyde ago!   1090
Whi list the so thi self fordoon for drede,
That in thyn hed thyn eyen semen dede?

1072. CpH1DS1H2 herto.   1078. JS1S2Cx may.   1079-1085. *Stanza omitted in* H3H4, *added later in* Ph.   1079. Gg god, A one *for* Jove.   1080. CpClH2R *om.* this. 1081. CpClH1AS1PhR or *for* and.   1085. JCx shal, Ph shul *for* may; DR and said in þis manere.   1087. GgH2Cx Ey, Th Eygh, H4RS2 *om.* I.   1090. JH2Cx nis.   1091. GgH3Ph fordon þyn self.   1092. Cp thyne, JH1 thy.

157

"Hastow nat lyved many a yer byforn
Withouten hire, and ferd ful wel at ese?
Artow for hire and for noon other born?   1095
Hath kynde the wrought al only hire to plese?
Lat be, and thynk right thus in thi disese:
That in the dees right as ther fallen chaunces,
Right so in love ther come and gon plesaunces.

158

"And yit this is my wonder most of alle,   1100
Whi thow thus sorwest, syn thow nost nat yit,
Touchyng hire goyng, how that it shal falle,
Ne yif she kan hire self destourben it.
Thow hast nat yit assayed al hire wit.
A man may al bytyme his nekke beede   1105
Whan it shal of, and sorwen at the nede.

159

"Forthi take hede of that I shal the seye:
I have with hire yspoke and longe ybe,
So as acorded was bitwixe us tweye.
And evere mo me thynketh thus, that she   1110
Hath somwhat in hire hertes privete,
Wherwith she kan, if I shal right arede,
Destourbe al this of which thow art in drede.

1093. α lyved al thy lyf biforn (J of, Gg oftyn in *for* al). 1096. JGgPhCx iwrought the (GgCx wrouȝt); αRCx *om.* al; Cx *om.* hire, H3 hir oonly; H3Cx for to plese. 1097. α Kanstow nat thinken thus. 1098. GgPhH3RH4 on, H2 un *for* in. 1099. α(-Gg) In love also ther com. 1100. γS1Th a wonder; H2 And yet of þis I merveyle. 1101. GgPhH4CxDTh wost not, H2 knowest nat. 1106. Gg Whan þe hed schal of. 1107. JPh what þat, H3Gg what, ClA of þat þat, H1DS2Th of al þat *for* of that; γThPh *om.* the, S1 ȝow *for* the. 1113. α Stynt al this thing of which.

160

"For which my counseil is, whan it is nyght,
Thow to hire go, and make of this an ende; 1115
And blisful Juno, thorugh hire grete myght,
Shal, as I hope, hire grace unto us sende.
Myn herte seyth, certeyn, she shal nat wende;
And forthi put thyn herte a while in reste,
And hold this purpos, for it is the beste." 1120

161

This Troilus answerde, and sighte soore:
"Thow seist right wel, and I wol don right so";
And what hym liste, he seyde unto it more.
But whan that it was tyme for to go,
Ful pryvely hym self, withouten mo, 1125
Unto hire com, as he was wont to doone,
And how they wroughte, I shal yow tellen soone.

162

Soth is, that whan they gonnen first to mete,
So gan the peyne hire hertes for to twiste,
That neyther of hem other myghte grete, 1130
But hem in armes toke and after kiste.
The lasse woful of hem bothe nyste
Wher that he was, ne myghte o word out brynge,
As I seyde erst, for wo and for sobbynge.

1116. Cp Jamo, J Jono, Ph Juvo H2Gg Jove, H3 ynow, A Inne; GgPhCx his, H4H2 thi *for* hire. 1120. ClJH3H2Th þi purpos. 1123. JGgH3H2 to *for* unto; αS2H2CxTh hym *for* it. 1124. γS1ThCx And *for* But. 1127. JH3Ph he *for* they. 1129. H3 Than, Gg þey, Ph þo *for* So; α sorwe *for* peyne. 1131. α But hem in armes hente and softe kiste. 1133. αCx What for to don ne myght. 1134. GgH3Ph sorwe *for* wo; GgPh wepynge.

163

Tho woful teeris that they leten falle   1135
As bittre weren, out of teris kynde,
For peyne, as is ligne aloes or galle.
So bittre teeris weep nat, as I fynde,
The woful Mirra thorugh the bark and rynde;
That in this world ther nys so hard an herte,   1140
That nolde han rewed on hire peynes smerte.

164

But whan hire woful weri goostes tweyne
Retourned ben ther as hem oughte to dwelle,
And that somwhat to wayken gan the peyne
By lengthe of pleynte, and ebben gan the welle   1145
Of hire teeris, and the herte unswelle,
With broken vois, al hoors forshright, Criseyde
To Troilus thise ilke wordes seyde:

165

"O Jove, I deye, and mercy I beseche!
Help, Troilus!" and therwithal hire face   1150
Upon his brest she leyde, and loste speche—
Hire woful spirit from his propre place,
Right with the word, alwey o poynt to pace—
And thus she lith with hewes pale and grene,
That whilom fressh and fairest was to sene.   1155

1135. Tho, *so* CpClJGg, *rest* The. 1138, 1139. α:—
      So bittre teeris wep nat thurgh the rynde
      The woful Mirra, writen as I fynde.
(J thurght). 1143. Cp owe, H1 owen; JClH2 *om.* to. 1144. GgPh lesse, H2 makyn,
H4DS2 wake, A waylen. 1147-1153. H3 *omits seven lines.* 1151. CpClJ lost, H1
lefte. 1153. Cl up, A upon, Ph on, DS1RCxTh in, H4 is *for* o. 1155. H3 was ful
fair and fressh; GgPh were.

166

This Troilus, that on hire gan biholde,
Clepyng hire name,—and she lay as for dede,
Withoute answere, and felte hire lymes colde,
Hire eyen throwen upward to hire hede—
This sorwful man kan now no maner rede;   1160
But ofte tyme hire colde mouth he kiste.
Wher hym was wo, god and hym self it wiste!

167

He rist hym up, and long streight he hire leyde;
For signe of lif, for aught he kan or may,
Kan he non fynde in no thyng on Criseyde,   1165
For which his song ful ofte is "weylawây."
But whan he saugh that specheles she lay,
With sorweful vois, and herte of blisse al bare,
He seyde how she was fro this world yfare.

168

So after that he longe hadde hire compleyned,   1170
His hondes wrong, and seyd that was to seye,
And with his teeris salte hire brest byreyned,
He gan tho teeris wypen of ful dreye,
And pitously gan for the soule preye,
And seyde: "O lord, that set art in thi trone,   1175
Rewe ek on me, for I shal folwe hire sone!"

1160. γS1ThCx kan now noon other red (Cx *om*. now). 1162. GgH2H4A Wheþer; H4PhCx he was. 1163. H3PhAH2Cx *om*. he, D by *for* he. 1165. α in no cas; CpADS2 GgTh of, PhH4 in *for* on. 1166. GgD is ofte. Ph is oftyn, R was ofte, H2H4 is full ofte, Cx ful ofte was. 1167. α And *for* But. 1170. H3PhCx he had hir longe, Gg he longe hire hade. 1173. H2H4RCxJ þe *for* tho; JH3Gg and *for* ful. 1175. αTh *om*. O.

169

She cold was and withouten sentement,
For aught he woot, and breth ne felte he non;
And this was hym a preignant argument
That she was forth out of this world agon;　　　1180
And whan he say ther was non other woon,
He gan hire lymes dresse in swich manere
As men don hem that shul ben leyd on beere.

170

And after this, with sterne and cruel herte,
His swerd anon out of his shethe he twighte,　　　1185
Hym self to slen, how sore that hym smerte,
So that his soule hire soule folwen myghte,
Ther as the doom of Mynos wolde it dighte;
Syn Love and cruel Fortune it ne wolde,
That in this world he lenger lyven sholde.　　　1190

171

Than seyde he thus; fulfild of heigh desdayn:
"O cruel Jove, and thow Fortune adverse,
This al and som, that falsly have ye slayn
Criseyde, and syn ye may do me no werse,
Fy on youre myght and werkes so dyverse!　　　1195
Thus cowardly ye shul me nevere wynne;
Ther shal no deth me fro my lady twynne.

1178. α wiste; and breth, *so* α, γS1Th for breth, R in breth, H2H4Cx *om.* and.
1179. α And þat was. 1182. CpJ swiche. 1183. α folk *for* hem; Cp layde, JH1 layd.
1185. JGgH3H4 the *for* his. 1190. H3PhGg nomore he lyven (Gg no more leve ne
schulde). 1193. H4 This is, Ph þat is *for* This. 1194. α kan.

172

"For I this world, syn ye have slayn hire thus,
Wol lete, and folwe hire spirit lowe or hye;
Shal nevere lovere seyn that Troilus   1200
Dar nat, for fere, with his lady dye;
For certeyn, I wol beere hire compaignie.
But syn ye wol nat suffre us lyven here,
Yit suffreth that oure soules ben yfere.

173

"And thow, cite, which that I leve in wo,   1205
And thow, Priam, and bretheren al yfeere,
And thow, my moder, farwel, for I go;
And, Attropos, make redy thow my beere.
And thow, Criseyde, O swete herte deere,
Receyve now my spirit," wolde he seye,   1210
With swerd at herte, al redy for to deye.

174

But as god wolde, of swough therwith shabreyde,
And gan to sike, and "Troilus" she cride;
And he answerde: "lady myn Criseyde,
Lyve ye yit?" and leet his swerd down glide.   1215
"Ye, herte myn, that thonked be Cipride,"
Quod she; and therwithal she soore syghte;
And he bigan to glade hire as he myghte;

1199. α forth in hye (Ph now *for* forth); CpH1 low. 1203. JH3Ph nyl nat. 1205.
I leve in wo, *so* ClS1DR, H4 levest in wo, Gg I leve inne in wo, S2 which I in leve
in wo, Th in whiche I lyve in wo, *rest* I lyve in wo. 1208. Cp Atropes, ClH1 Attropes,
JS2 Attrepos, PhA Attrapes, GgH4Cx Antropos, Th Attropose, H2H3 Attropos; JGg
Thow Attrepos þat is ful redy heere (Gg art). 1209. αD *om.* O. 1211. CpJ swerde.
1214. α herte myn. 1216. αRD ithonked (Ph and thonkyd) *for* that thonked; Cipride,
so JPhH2S1, A Enpride, H4 Cupide *glossed* Venus, *rest* Cupide. 1218. CpH1 glad;
α bigan conforte hir.

175

Took hire in armes two, and kiste hire ofte,
And hire to glade he dede al his entente;   1220
For which hire goost, that flikered ay on lofte,
Into hire woful herte ayeyn it wente.
But at the laste, as that hire eye glente
Asyde, anon she gan his swerd espie,
As it lay bare, and gan for fere crye,   1225

176

And asked hym whi he it hadde out drawe;
And Troilus anon the cause hire tolde,
And how hym self therwith he wolde han slawe.
For which Criseyde upon hym gan biholde,
And gan hym in hire armes faste folde,   1230
And seyde: "O mercy, god, lo, which a dede!
Allas, how neigh we weren bothe dede!

177

"Thanne, if I nadde spoken, as grace was,
Ye wolde han slayn youre self anon?" quod she.
"Yee, douteles"; and she answerde: "allas!   1235
For by that ilke lord that made me,
I nolde a forlong wey on lyve han be
After youre deth, to han ben crowned queene
Of al the lond the sonne on shyneth sheene.

1219. H2 He toke.   1222. α Ayein into hir herte al softe wente (Gg Al softe to
hire herte aȝyn it went).   1223. α So *for* But; CpH2H4RH3Gg *om.* that, Cx ryght as
hyr; ClPhCx eyen, H3 eyne, H4 yen, Gg eyȝyn.   1226. ClGgH4RTh he hadde it,
H2 þat he hadde.   1227. αClR *om.* hire.   1228. JGg he wolde therwith aslawe.

178

"But with this selve swerd, which that here is,   1240
My selve I wolde han slayn," quod she tho;
"But hoo, for we han right ynough of this,
And lat us rise and streight to bedde go,
And there lat us speken of oure wo.
For by the morter which that I se brenne,   1245
Knowe I ful wel that day is not fer henne."

179

Whan they were in hire bed in armes folde,
Naught was it lik the nyghtes here byforn;
For pitously ech other gan byholde,
As they that hadden al hire blisse ylorn,   1250
Bywaylinge ay the day that they were born.
Til at the laste this woful wight, Criseyde,
To Troilus thise ilke wordes seyde:

180

"Lo, herte myn, wel woot ye this," quod she,
"That if a wight alwey his wo compleyne,   1255
And seketh nought how holpen for to be,
It nys but folie and encrees of peyne;
And syn that here assembled be we tweyne,
To fynde boote of wo that we ben inne,
It were al tyme soone to bygynne.   1260

1240. H3H2H4CxD the *for* this. 1241. GgR slawe. 1245. Gg percher. 1250. α hir joyes alle lorn (Ph forlorne, H3 ylorn). 1251. α Seying allas that evere they were born. 1252. γTh sorwful.

181

"I am a womman, as ful wel ye woot,
And as I am avysed sodeynly,
So wol I telle yow whil it is hoot.
Me thynketh thus, that nouther ye nor I
Oughte half this wo to maken skilfully;   1265
For ther is art ynough for to redresse
That yit is mys, and slen this hevynesse.

182

"Soth is, the wo the which that we ben inne,
For aught I woot, for nothyng ellis is
But for the cause that we shullen twynne.   1270
Considered al, ther nys no more amys.
But what is thanne a remedy unto this,
But that we shape us soone for to meete?
This al and som, my deere herte sweete.

183

"Now that I shal wel bryngen it aboute   1275
To come ayeyn, soone after that I go,
Therof am I no maner thyng in doute;
For, dredeles, withinne a wowke or two,
I shal ben here; and that it may be so,
By alle right, and in a wordes fewe,   1280
I shal yow wel an hep of weyes shewe.

1263. JGgPhS1RCx telle it yow. 1268. JGg that, Ph þat þe *for first* the, H3 *om.*
1270. γ(-A)S1ThH2 sholden. 1280. GgAH2H4RCxTh *om.* a.

184

"For which I wol nat make long sermoun,
For tyme ylost may nat recovered be;
But I wol gon to my conclusioun,
And to the beste, in aught that I kan see.   1285
But, for the love of god, foryeve it me,
If I speke aught ayeyns youre hertes reste;
For, trewely, I speke it for the beste,

185

"Makyng alwey a protestacioun,
That now thise wordes, which that I shal seye,   1290
Nis but to shewen yow my mocioun,
To fynde unto oure help the beste weye;
And taketh it non other wise, I preye.
For in effect what so ye me comaunde,
That wol I don, for that is no demaunde.   1295

186

"Now herkneth this: ye han wel understonde
My goyng graunted is by parlement
So ferforth that it may nat be withstonde,
For al this world, as by my jugement.
And syn ther helpeth non avisement   1300
To letten it, lat it passe out of mynde;
And lat us shape a bettre wey to fynde.

1282. JGgPh nyl nat.   1284. α right to conclusioun (H3 to ryght).   1286. γS1Th And *for* But.   1289. Gg here, Ph ay here *for* alwey, H3 Make here I shal.   1290. JGgPh That in effect this thing þat, H3 That doutles thys thing that in effect I sey.   1291. H4 Arn.   1292. GgH3H2H4Cx ȝoure.   1294. JGgPh For fynaly.   1295. H3Ph I wyl it doo.   1301. H3 As in thys cas lat dryve it oute of mynde.   1302. H3 fonde *for* shape.

187

"The soth is this: the twynnyng of us tweyne
Wol us disese and cruelich anoye;
But hym byhoveth som tyme han a peyne   1305
That serveth love, if that he wol have joye.
And syn I shal no ferther out of Troie
Than I may ride ayeyn on half a morwe,
It oughte lasse causen us to sorwe.

188

"So as I shal nat so ben hid in muwe,   1310
That, day by day, myn owne herte deere,—
Syn wel ye woot that it is now a trewe,—
Ye shal ful wel al myn estat yheere.
And or that trewe is doon, I shal ben heere;
And thanne have ye bothe Antenor ywonne   1315
And me also; beth glad now, if ye konne.

189

"And thenk right thus: 'Criseyde is now agon,
But, what! she shal come hastely ayeyn';
And whanne, allas? by god, lo, right anon,
Or dayes ten, this dar I saufly seyn.   1320
And thanne at erst shal we be so feyn,
So as we shul togideres evere dwelle,
That al this world ne myghte oure blisse telle.

1303. CpS2ADS1Th *om.* this, H1 *om.* is this, ClH3 þat *for* this, Gg þis is; JGgPh
that *for second* the. 1304. H3 Ful cruelly oure hertis wolde anoye. 1308. H3Ph
RS1Cx in *for* on. 1309. ClAS1H3H2H4Cx þe lasse. 1310. H3 Syn that, Cx Syth as
for So as; PhH2H4ADCx *om. second* so, Gg now, R parde *for* so. 1312, 1313. H3
Considereth now that tyme it is of trewe/Ye may not faille of myn estat to here.
1315. α And thus. 1318. CpGg hastiliche. 1320. JGgPh that, H2 þus *for* this. 1321.
CpH1 erste; JGgPh ye *for* we. 1322. JGgPh That we shul everemo to geddere dwelle
(Ph wil), H3 That I may have a liberte to dwelle. 1323. H3 cowde; α joye (H3
joyes) *for* blisse.

190

"I se that often, ther as we ben now,
That for the beste oure counseyl for to hide,   1325
Ye speke nat with me, nor I with yow,
In fourtenyght, ne se yow go ne ride.
May ye naught ten dayes thanne abide,
For myn honour, in swich an aventure?
Iwys, ye mowen ellis lite endure!   1330

191

"Ye knowe ek how that al my kyn is heere,—
But if that onliche it my fader be,—
And ek myn othere thynges alle yfeere,
And, namely, my deere herte, ye,
Whom that I nolde leven for to se   1335
For al this world, as wyde as it hath space;
Or ellis se ich nevere Joves face!

192

"Whi trowe ye my fader in this wise
Coveyteth so to se me, but for drede
Lest in this town that folkes me despise   1340
Bycause of hym, for his unhappy dede?
What woot my fader what lif that I lede?
For if he wiste in Troie how wel I fare,
Us neded for my wendyng nought to care.

1324. γS₁Th ofte tyme. 1325. H₃ Of pourviaunce our counseil. 1331. H₃ eke wele, H₂H₄Cx wel eke, Ph eke *for* ek how; CpJ kynne. 1332. JGgPh Oonly but yif it, H₃ Al holy but yf it. 1336. JGgPh muche, H₃ brode *for* wyde. 1337. H₃ And elleys come I never oute of thys place. 1338. H₃ gesse. 1341. H₃ that doon hath suche a dede. 1342. H₃ For what woote ye what lyve ys that I lyde. 1343. H₃ And yf ye wyst. 1344. CpAGgH₃Cx nedeth; GgH₃ not for myn . . . to care (H₃ for to care); JGgPhH₂H₄ going.

193

"Ye sen that every day ek, more and more,   1345
Men trete of pees; and it supposed is,
That men the queene Eleyne shal restore,
And Grekis us restoren that is mys.
So, though ther nere comfort non but this,
That men purposen pees on every syde,   1350
Ye may the bettre at ese of herte abyde.

194

"For if that it be pees, myn herte deere,
The nature of the pees moot nedes dryve
That men moste entrecomunen yfeere,
And to and fro ek ride and gon as blyve   1355
Alday, as thikke as been fleen from an hyve,
And every wight han liberte to bleve
Where as hym liste the bet, withouten leve.

195

"And though so be that pees ther may be non,
Yit hider, though ther nevere pees ne were,   1360
I moste come; for whider sholde I gon,
Or how, meschaunce, sholde I dwelle there
Among tho men of armes, evere in feere?
For which, as wisly god my soule rede,
I kan nat sen wherof ye sholden drede.   1365

1345. H3Cx eke that every day, Ph eke every day þat, Gg ek every day, *om.* that.
1348. H3 Repairen.   1350. R pursuen, H3 supposen.   1359. H3 yf it, Gg ȝif *for* though.
1363-1365. H3 :—

> In hoste amonge the grekys, ever in fere?
> Hit nyl not bee, and gode soo wysly rede
> My soule, as ye have cause noon to drede.

196

"Have here another wey, if it so be
That al this thyng ne may yow nat suffise:
My fader, as ye knowen wel, parde,
Is old; and elde is ful of coveytise.
And I right now have founden al the gise,   1370
Withouten net, wherwith I shal hym hente;
And herkeneth how, if that ye wol assente.

197

"Lo, Troilus, men seyn that hard it is
The wolf ful, and the wether hool to have;
This is to seyn, that men ful ofte, iwys,   1375
Mote spenden part, the remenaunt for to save.
For ay with gold men may the herte grave
Of hym that set is upon coveytise;
And how I mene, I shal it yow devyse.

198

"The moeble which that I have in this town   1380
Unto my fader shal I take, and seye,
That right for trust and for savacioun
It sent is from a frend of his or tweye,
The which frendes ferventliche hym preye
To senden after more, and that in hie,   1385
Whil that this town stant thus in jupartie.

1366. H3 cause *for* wey, Ph *om.* wey.   1367. H3 can not yow.   1369. CpJ olde.
1370. H3 a new gyse.   1372. CpH3GgH2H4RTh now *for* how.   1373. H3 But dere *for*
Lo; γS1Th that ful hard; CpH1J harde.   1374. CpJ whether.   1376. H3PhDS1RCx
om. for, Gg of *for* for.   1384. Cl wheche, CxTh whiche, H3 besyly hym gan preye.

199

"And that shal ben an huge quantite,—
Thus shal I seyn,—but lest it folk espide,
This may be sent by no wight but by me.
I shal ek shewen hym, if pees bitide,   1390
What frendes that I have on every side
Toward the court, to don the wrathe pace
Of Priamus, and don hym stonde in grace.

200

"So, what for o thing and for oother, sweete,
I shal hym so enchaunten with my sawes,   1395
That right in hevene his soule is, shal he meete.
For al Appollo, or his clerkes lawes,
Or calkulyng, availeth nat thre hawes;
Desir of gold shal so his soule blende,
That, as me list, I shal wel make an ende.   1400

201

"And if he wolde aught by his sort it preve,
If that I lye, in certein I shal fonde
Destourben hym, and plukke hym by the sleve,
Makynge his sort, and beren hym on honde,
He hath nat wel the goddes understonde.   1405
For goddes speken in amphibologies,
And, for a soth, they tellen twenty lyes.

1388 *middle*—1409 *middle omitted in* Cp; *text based on* JCl. 1389. H3 none, Ph
non oþer *for* no wight; H3 *om. second* by. 1390. PhS1 hym shewyn eke, H3 eke wele
shewe hym. 1392, 1393. H3 To doo the wrathe of Pryamus to passe/Towardys hym
and don. 1396. JGgH3AH2RCx *om.* is, Ph is his soule is. 1399. PhDCx hert *for*
soule. 1402. H3 Yif thys be les; H3R *om.* in. 1404. H3 In myddes hys werk; αH2H4
or *for* and; H3R bere hym fast on honde. 1405. H3 That he hath not, *om.* wel.

202

"Ek drede fond first goddes, I suppose,—
Thus shal I seyn,—and that his coward herte
Made hym amys the goddes text to glose,   1410
Whan he for fered out of Delphos sterte.
And but I make hym soone to converte,
And don my red withinne a day or tweye,
I wol to yow oblige me to deye."

203

And treweliche, as writen wel I fynde,   1415
That al this thyng was seyd of good entente;
And that hire herte trewe was and kynde
Towardes hym, and spak right as she mente;
And that she starf for wo neigh, whan she wente,
And was in purpos evere to be trewe,   1420
Thus writen they that of hire werkes knewe.

204

This Troilus, with herte and erys spradde,
Herde al this thyng devysen to and fro;
And verrayliche hym semed that he hadde
The selve wit; but yit to late hire go,   1425
His herte mysforyaf hym evere mo.
But fynaly he gan his herte wreste
To trusten hire, and took it for the beste.

1409. JGgPh ek *for* that. 1411. H3 Whan he from Delphos to the Grekys sterte. 1415. JADH2H5R is *for* as; H3Cx iwrytte as, *om.* wel (Cx ywryten). 1416. CpH1J seyde. 1421. H3 thoo that ever the jestes knewe. 1423. H2H4PhCxTh devised, R devysyng. 1424. Cp verreliche, J verraylisch; CpH1DTh it, Ph he *for* hym, H2H4 *om.* hym. 1425. ClH3 same.

205

For which the grete furie of his penaunce
Was queynt with hope; and therwith hem bitwene 1430
Bigan for joie thamorouse daunce.
And as the briddes, whan the sonne is shene,
Deliten in hire song in leves grene,
Right so the wordes that they spake yfeere
Delited hem, and made hire hertes clere.   1435

206

But natheles, the wendyng of Criseyde,
For al this world, may nat out of his mynde;
For which ful ofte he pitously hire preyde,
That of hire heste he myghte hire trewe fynde,
And seyde hire: "certes, if ye be unkynde,   1440
And but ye come at day set into Troye,
Ne shal I nevere have hele, honour, ne joye.

207

"For also soth as sonne uprist on morwe,
And, god, so wisly thow me, woful wrecche,
To reste brynge out of this cruel sorwe,   1445
I wol my selven sle, if that ye drecche.
But of my deth though litel be to recche,
Yit or that ye me causen so to smerte,
Dwelle rather here, myn owen dere herte.

1435. ClH4Th Deliten, Gg Delite, H1 Delites. 1437. JH3D ne may out. 1440. H3RCx *om.* hire. 1441. A at your day set in bone foie. 1442. H3 Shal I never as in thys worlde have joye. 1443. GgPhD rist up, Cx *om.* up; CpH1 o, J a *for* on. 1449. γTh swete *for* dere.

208

"For trewely, myn owne lady deere,   1450
Tho sleightes yit that I have herd yow stere
Ful shaply ben to faylen alle yfeere.
For thus men seyth: 'that on thenketh the beere,
But al another thenketh his ledere.'
Youre syre is wys, and seyd is, out of drede: 1455
'Men may the wise atrenne, and naught atrede.'

209

"It is ful hard to halten unespied
Byfore a crepil, for he kan the craft.
Youre fader is in sleyghte as Argus eyed;
For al be that his moeble is hym biraft,   1460
His olde sleighte is yit so with hym laft,
Ye shal nat blende hym for youre wommanhede,
Ne feyne aright, and that is al my drede.

210

"I not if pees shal evere mo bitide;
But, pees or no, for ernest ne for game,   1465
I woot, syn Calkas on the Grekis syde
Hath ones ben, and lost so foule his name,
He dar no more come here ayeyn for shame;
For which that wey, for aught I kan espie,
To trusten on, nys but a fantasie.   1470

1451. H3PhGgCxTh The *for* Tho; J þat ich yow heere stere, Gg þat I here stire;
CpH1 herde. 1453. JGgPh And *for* For; ClS1H3PhGgH2 seyn. 1454. H2H4H3Th
þe *for* his. 1455. H3PhH4Cx fadyr. 1456. H2H4 over renne, H3Th oute renne;
ClH3PhCx but *for* and; H2 over rede, Th oute rede, H3 oute ryde. 1459. Cp sleght,
J sleyght. 1461. H4Cx sleihtes ben yit with (Cx yet ben). 1465. H3PhGgGgS1R or
for ne.

211

"Ye shal ek sen, youre fader shal yow glose
To ben a wif, and as he kan wel preche,
He shal som Grek so preyse and wel alose,
That ravysshen he shal yow with his speche,
Or do yow don by force as he shal teche;　　　1475
And Troilus, of whom he nyl han routhe,
Shal causeles so sterven in his trouthe.

212

"And over al this, youre fader shal despise
Us alle, and seyn this cite nys but lorn,
And that thassege nevere shal aryse,　　　1480
For whi the Grekis han it alle sworn
Til we be slayn, and down oure walles torn.
And thus he shal yow with his wordes fere,
That ay drede I, that ye wol bleven there.

213

"Ye shal ek seen so many a lusty knyght　　　1485
Amonge the Grekis, ful of worthynesse,
And ech of hem with herte, wit, and myght
To plesen yow don al his besynesse,
That ye shul dullen of the rudenesse
Of us sely Troians, but if routhe　　　1490
Remorde yow, or vertu of youre trouthe.

1473. CpH1J Greke. 1476. H3PhS1S2Th on, H1 of on *for* of; γ(-ClA)S1ThGgPh ye *for* he. 1478. α *om.* al. 1479. H3PhGgAH4 is. 1484. GgH4 And *for* That; H3GgDH4RCx *om. second* that, Ph lest ȝe *for* that ye wol. 1490. S1 troianis.

214

"And this to me so grevous is to thynke,
That fro my brest it wol my soule rende;
Ne dredeles in me ther kan nat synke
A good opynyoun, if that ye wende;   1495
For whi youre fadres sleyghte wol us shende.
And if ye gon, as I have told yow yore,
So thenk I nam but ded, withoute more.

215

"For which with humble, trewe, and pitous herte,
A thousand tymes mercy I yow preye;   1500
So reweth on myn aspre peynes smerte,
And doth somwhat as that I shal yow seye,
And lat us stele awey bitwixe us tweye;
And thynk that folie is, whan man may chese,
For accident his substaunce ay to lese.   1505

216

"I mene thus: that syn we mowe or day
Wel stele awey, and ben togidere so,
What wit were it to putten in assay,
In cas ye sholden to youre fader go,
If that ye myghten come ayeyn or no?   1510
Thus mene I, that it were a grete folie
To putte that sikernesse in jupartie.

1493. αH2R the *for* my. 1494. J And, Gg But *for* Ne; γS1Th may. 1496. H3Ph
H2Cx sleightes. 1504. H2CxTh a man, JGgDH4R men. 1511. Cx Thus thynketh me

217

"And vulgarly to speken of substaunce
Of tresour, may we bothe with us lede
Inough to lyve in honour and plesaunce,   1515
Til into tyme that we shal ben dede;
And thus we may eschuen al this drede.
For everich other wey ye kan recorde,
Myn herte, ywys, may therwith nat acorde.

218

"And, hardily, ne dredeth no poverte,   1520
For I have kyn and frendes elleswhere,
That, though we comen in oure bare sherte,
Us sholde neyther lakken gold ne gere,
But ben honoured while we dwelten there.
And go we anon; for as in myn entente,   1525
This is the beste, if that ye wol assente."

219

Criseyde hym with a sik right in this wise
Answerde: "ywys, my deere herte trewe,
We may wel stele awey, as ye devyse,
Or fynden swich unthrifty weyes newe;   1530
But afterward ful soore it wol us rewe.
And help me god so at my mooste nede,
As causeles ye suffren al this drede.

1516. H3D Tyl unto, H2A Til unto the, Ph Unto þe (*om*. Til), H4 *om*. into. 1520.
GgPhH2H4 *om*. ne. 1524. H1DGgH2R dwellen. 1525. H3 Anon goo we forth in.
1527. γThH3Gg *om*. hym. 1529. CpJ wele. 1530. γTh And *for* Or. 1531. H3 it **wolde**
ful sore us, H4 it wil ful sore us, H2 it will us full soore, Ph it wil us sore.

220

"For thilke day that I for cherisshyng
Or drede of fader, or for other wight,   1535
Or for estat, delit, or for weddyng,
Be fals to yow, my Troilus, my knyght,
Saturnes doughter, Juno, thorugh hire myght,
As wood as Athamante do me dwelle
Eternalich in Stix, the put of helle.   1540

221

"And this on every god celestial
I swere it yow, and ek on eche goddesse,
On every Nymphe and deite infernal,
On Satiry and Fawny more and lesse,
That halve goddes ben of wildernesse;   1545
And Attropos my thred of lif to-breste
If I be fals. Now trowe me if yow leste.

222

"And thow, Symois, that as an arwe clere
Thorugh Troie rennest ay downward to the se,
Ber witnesse of this word that seyd is here,   1550
That thilke day that ich untrewe be
To Troilus, myn owene herte fre,
That thow retourne bakward to thi welle,
And I with body and soule synke in helle.

1535. CpH1S2S1ThGg any other. 1546. Cp Attrepos, JGgS1H2H4Cx Antropos.
1547. ClGg þow, H2H4RCxPhA ye *for* yow. 1549. JH3AD ay rennest, GgPhRCx
om. ay. 1550. CpH1J seyde. 1551. H3PhGgADS1H2Cx That ylke. 1554. H3PhGgH2
into, H4 doun to, ATh to *for* in.

223

"But that ye speke, awey thus for to go   1555
And leten alle youre frendes, god forbede,
For any womman, that ye sholden so,
And namely syn Troie hath now swich nede
Of help; and ek of o thyng taketh hede:
If this were wist, my lif lay in balaunce,   1560
And youre honour; god shilde us fro meschaunce!

224

"And if so be that pees hereafter take,
As alday happeth after anger game,
Whi, lord! the sorwe and wo ye wolden make,
That ye ne dorste come ayeyn for shame!   1565
And or that ye juparten so youre name,
Beth naught to hastif in this hoote fare;
For hastif man ne wanteth nevere care.

225

"What trowe ye the peple ek al aboute
Wolde of it seye? It is·ful light tarede.   1570
They wolden seye and swere it, out of doute,
That love ne drof yow naught to don that dede,
But lust voluptuous and coward drede.
Thus were al lost, ywys, myn herte deere,
Youre honour, which that now shyneth so clere.   1575

1555. ClJH3 alwey.   1557. H3PhH4 shulde doo soo.   1558. H2H4H3 *om.* now.
1564. H1H3 wo and sorwe, Gg *om.* wo and.   1566. Gg enpartyn, R in peyre, H3A
empeiren.   1568. H3PhGgH1H4Cx *om.* ne; H3PhGgDH2 wanted.   1569. H1PhH2
H4Cx ek þe peple, H3D *om.* ek.   1572. γThJ this dede.   1575. H3Ph shyneth now,
H2H4 *om.* now.

226

"And also thynketh on myn honeste,
That floureth yit, how foule I sholde it shende,
And with what filthe it spotted sholde be,
If in this forme I sholde with yow wende.
Ne though I lyvede unto the worldes ende,   1580
My name sholde I nevere ayeynward wynne;
Thus were I lost, and that were routhe and synne.

227

"And forthi sle with resoun al this hete;
Men seyn: 'the suffrant overcomth,' parde;
Ek 'whoso wol han lief, he lief moot lete';   1585
Thus maketh vertu of necessite
By pacience, and thynk that lord is he
Of Fortune ay, that naught wol of hire recche;
And she ne daunteth no wight but a wrecche.

228

"And trusteth this, that certes, herte swete,   1590
Or Phebus suster, Lucina the sheene,
The Leoun passe out of this Ariete,
I wol ben here, withouten any wene.
I mene, as help me Juno, hevenes quene,
The tenthe day, but if that deth massaile,   1595
I wol yow sen, withouten any faille."

1582. GgS1 al *for* I. 1585. lief, *so* CpH1 (H1 lief . . . lyfe), J lef, S2Cx lyef,
Th lefe, Gg leve, D life, *rest* leef. 1587. H3PhGgClAH2R Be pacient (Cl By).
1593. H3 wythoute drede or wene. 1595. H3PhGgADS1H2H4R *om.* that.

229

"And now, so this be soth," quod Troilus,
"I shal wel suffre unto the tenthe day,
Syn that I se that nede it mot be thus.
But, for the love of god, if it be may,   1600
So lat us stelen privelich away;
For evere in oon, as for to lyve in reste,
Myn herte seyth that it wol be the beste."

230

"O mercy, god, what lif is this?" quod she.
"Allas, ye sle me thus for verray tene!   1605
I se wel now that ye mystrusten me;
For by youre wordes it is wel yseene.
Now, for the love of Cinthia, the sheene,
Mistrust me nought thus causeles, for routhe;
Syn to be trewe I have yow plight my trouthe.   1610

231

"And thynketh wel that som tyme it is wit
To spende a tyme, a tyme for to wynne;
Ne, parde, lorn am I nat fro yow yit,
Though that we ben a day or two atwynne.
Drif out the fantasies yow withinne,   1615
And trusteth me, and leveth ek youre sorwe,
Or, here my trouthe, I wol nat lyve tyl morwe.

1597. H3Cx trewe. 1608. PhD Cithera, CxTh Scithya; PhDS2 the qwene. 1609.
Cp Mistrusteth. 1610. GgPhH4RCx ply3t 30w. 1611. H3PhD *om*. that. 1615. CpDS1
H4Th tho. 1617. H3PhGgADS1Cx to *for* tyl, H2H4 til to morwe.

232

"For if ye wiste how soore it doth me smerte,
Ye wolde cesse of this; for, god, thow woost,
The pure spirit wepeth in myn herte,   1620
To se yow wepen that I love moost,
And that I mot gon to the Grekis oost.
Ye, nere it that I wiste remedie
To come ayeyn, right here I wolde dye.

233

"But, certes, I am nat so nyce a wight   1625
That I ne kan ymaginen a wey
To come ayeyn that day that I have hight.
For who may holde a thing that wol awey?
My fader naught, for al his queynte pley.
And by my thrift, my wendyng out of Troie   1630
Another day shal torne us alle to joie.

234

"Forthi with al myn herte I yow biseke,
If that yow list don aught for my preyere,
And for that love which that I love yow eke,
That or that I departe fro yow here,   1635
That of so good a confort and a cheere
I may yow sen, that ye may brynge at reste
Myn herte, which that is o poynt to breste.

1623. GgPh nyste; H4CxTh a remedye. 1624. GgPhH4Cx wolde I. 1625. H4PhCx nam. 1628. ClD *om*. a, GgPh *om*. a thing. 1633. H3S1R at *for* for. 1634. ClAS1 GgH2R þe love; GgADRCx *om. second* that (D þe which). 1635. H3H4RCx *om*. that. 1638. o poynt, *so* CpClGg, J(*corrected*)H1D, a, Th at, PhAS1S2H2H4RCx in *for* o, H3, *om*. o.

235

"And over al this, I prey yow," quod she tho,
"Myn owene hertes sothfast suffisaunce,   1640
Syn I am thyn al hool, withouten mo,
That whil that I am absent, no plesaunce
Of oother do me fro youre remembraunce.
For I am evere agast; forwhy men rede,
That love is thyng ay ful of bisy drede.   1645

236

"For in this world ther lyveth lady non,
If that ye were untrewe, as god defende,
That so bitraised were or wo-bigon
As I, that alle trouthe in yow entende.
And, douteles, if that ich other wende,   1650
I nere but dede; and or ye cause fynde,
For goddes love, so beth me naught unkynde."

237

To this answerde Troilus and seyde:
"Now god, to whom ther nys no cause ywrye,
Me glad, as wys I nevere unto Criseyde,   1655
Syn thilke day I saugh hire first with eye,
Was fals, ne nevere shal til that I dye.
At shorte wordes, wel ye may me leve;
I kan no more, it shal be founde at preve."

1641. H3 yowres, H2 youre. 1642. H3DH2H4 *om.* that. 1648. GgPhAH2H4CxTh
betrayed. 1651. CpJ ner. 1652. GgPhH4R *om.* so; Gg beþ no more, Ph ne beth to
me, H4Cx be not to me (Cx beth). 1654. α thought (H3 thing) *for* cause. 1655.
H4RD as wisse as I. 1656. CpJ thilk. 1657. GgPhH2 Was nevere fals ne schal (Gg
by corrector).

238

"Graunt mercy, goode myn, iwys," quod she, 1660
"And blisful Venus lat me nevere sterve
Or I may stonde of plesaunce in degree
To quyte hym wel, that so wel kan deserve.
And whil that god my wit wol me conserve,
I shal so don; so trewe I have yow founde, 1665
That ay honour to meward shal rebounde.

239

"For trusteth wel, that youre estat roial,
Ne veyn delit, nor only worthinesse
Of yow in werre or torney marcial,
Ne pompe, array, nobleye, or ek richesse, 1670
Ne made me to rewe on youre destresse;
But moral vertu, grounded upon trouthe,
That was the cause I first hadde on yow routhe.

240

"Ek gentil herte and manhod that ye hadde,
And that ye hadde, as me thoughte, in despit 1675
Every thyng that souned into badde,
As rudenesse and poeplissh appetit,
And that youre resoun bridlede youre delit,—
This made, aboven every creature,
That I was youre, and shal, whil I may dure. 1680

1660. Cp Grant; JH4Cx Gramercy; Ph good myn hert, D my good hert, Cx good hert myn, Th good hert myne ywis *for* goode myn iwys. 1665. H3 I shal don soo I have yow trew so founde. 1667-1701. *Missing in* Gg; *leaf cut out.* 1667. Cp roiale, JH1R real, H3D ryal. 1668. CpJ delite. 1669. H2 guerre. 1670. α nor *for* or. 1680. PhDS1Th youris.

241

"And this may lengthe of yeres naught fordo,
Ne remuable Fortune deface.
But Juppiter, that of his myght may do
The sorwful to be glad, so yeve us grace,
Or nyghtes ten, to meten in this place,   1685
So that it may youre herte and myn suffise;
And fare now wel, for tyme is that ye rise."

242

But after that they longe ypleyned hadde,
And ofte ykist, and streite in armes folde,
The day gan rise, and Troilus hym cladde,   1690
And rewfullich his lady gan byholde,
As he that felte dethes cares colde.
And to hire grace he gan hym recomaunde;
Wher hym was wo, this holde I no demaunde.

243

For mannes hed ymagynen ne kan,   1695
Nentendement considere, ne tonge telle,
The cruel peynes of this woful man,
That passen every torment down in helle.
For whan he saugh that she ne myghte dwelle,
Which that his soule out of his herte rente,   1700
Withouten more, out of the chaumbre he wente.

EXPLICIT LIBER QUARTUS.

1687. CpClH1ThH2 *fareth*; R *it is tyme to rise*, S1 *tyme it is to ryse*. 1688. γS1Th
And for But. 1696. JH3 *or*, H4 *nor for* ne. 1697. γS1ThR *sorwful*. 1700. H3 *body
for* herte. H3H4A *om. rubric*, Cx *Here endyth the Fourth booke And begynneth the
Fyfthe*.

BOOK FIVE

BOOK FIVE

1

APROCHEN gan the fatal destyne
    That Joves hath in disposicioun,
    And to yow, angry Parcas, sustren thre,
Committeth to don execucioun;
For which Criseyde moste out of the town,   5
And Troilus shal dwellen forth in pyne
Til Lathesis his thred no lenger twyne.

2

The goldetressed Phebus heighe on lofte
Thries hadde al with his bemes shene
The snowes molte, and Zephirus as ofte   10
Ibrought ayeyn the tendre leves grene,
Syn that the sone of Ecuba the queene
Bigan to love hire first, for whom his sorwe
Was al, that she departe sholde a-morwe.

3

Ful redy was at prime Diomede,   15
Criseyde unto the Grekis oost to lede,
For sorwe of which she felte hire herte blede,
As she that nyste what was best to rede.
And trewely, as men in bokes rede,
Men wiste nevere womman han the care,   20
Ne was so loth, out of a town to fare.

1-35. *Missing in* Gg. 4. ClS1H3PhH2H4Cx Comytted. 7. CxTh Lachesys. 8. goldetressed, *so* H3ADTh, H2 Auricomus tressed, *rest* goldtressed. 9. Cp hise, JPh hir; shene, *so* H2H4RS1, JPh cleene, γThH3Cx clere.

4

This Troilus, withouten reed or loore,
As man that hath his joies ek forlore,
Was waytyng on his lady evere more,
As she that was the sothfast crop and more   25
Of al his lust or joies here bifore.
But, Troilus, now farewel al thi joie,
For shaltow nevere sen hire eft in Troie!

5

Soth is that whil he bood in this manere,
He gan his wo ful manly for to hide,   30
That wel unnethe it sene was in his chere;
But at the yate ther she sholde out ride,
With certeyn folk, he hoved hire tabide,
So wo-bigon, al wolde he naught hym pleyne,
That on his hors unnethe he sat for peyne.   35

6

For ire he quook, so gan his herte gnawe,
Whan Diomede on hors gan hym dresse,
And seyde unto hym self this ilke sawe:
"Allas," quod he, "thus foul a wrecchednesse,
Whi suffre ich it, whi nyl ich it redresse?   40
Were it nat bet atones for to dye
Than evere more in langour thus to drye?

23. CpJ hise. 25. CpH1DS2ThH3Ph *om.* the; H3 rote *for* crop. 26. CpH1S2Th heretofore, H3 eke byfore. 27. ClH3Ph farewel now. 29. H4 she abod. 33. Ph hir besyde. 34. H2H4RCx compleyne, *om.* hym (H2 he wolde him nat, *om.* al). 37. S1 Diomedes; J on his hors; GgH2Th horse; H3Gg (*by corrector*) hir *for* hym.

7

"Whi nyl I make atones riche and pore
To have inough to doone, or that she go?
Why nyl I brynge al Troie upon a roore?   45
Whi nyl I slen this Diomede also?
Why nyl I rather with a man or two
Stele hire awey? Whi wol I this endure?
Whi nyl I helpen to myn owen cure?"

8

But why he nolde don so fel a dede,   50
That shal I seyn, and whi hym liste it spare:
He hadde in herte alweyes a manere drede,
Lest that Criseyde in rumour of this fare
Sholde han ben slayn; lo, this was al his care.
And ellis, certeyn, as I seyde yore,   55
He hadde it don, withouten wordes more.

9

Criseyde, whan she redy was to ride,
Ful sorwfully she sighte, and seyde: "allas!"
But forth she moot, for aught that may bitide;
Ther nys non other remedie in this cas;   60
And forth she rit ful sorwfully a pas.
What wonder is though that hire sore smerte,
Whan she forgoth hire owen deere herte?

---

43. H3Gg or *for* and. 48. H3PhAH4RCx thus. 51. H4PhADCx to *for* it, H3R
om. it. 52. alweyes, *so* CpClH1S1J, *rest* alwey. 53. Cp List, JCl Liste. 57. GgH3
whan þat; JGgH3H2A was redy. 59. GgH3Ph muste. 60, 61. γTh *reverse order of
lines.* 61. H3 she went ryght sobrely; H2R soberly. 62. H3Ph she *for* hire. 63. γTh
swete herte.

10

This Troilus, in wise of curteysie,
With hauke on honde, and with an huge route   65
Of knyghtes, rood and dide hire companye,
Passyng al the valeye fer withoute,
And ferther wolde han riden, out of doute,
Ful fayn, and wo was hym to gon so sone;
But torne he moste, and it was ek to done.   70

11

And right with that was Antenor ycome
Out of the Grekis oost, and every wight
Was of it glad, and seyde he was welcome.
And Troilus, al nere his herte light,
He peyned hym with al his fulle myght   75
Hym to withholde of wepyng at the leeste;
And Antenor he kiste, and made feste.

12

And herwithal he moste his leve take,
And caste his eye upon hire pitously,
And neer he rod, his cause for to make,   80
To take hire by the honde al sobrely.
And, lord! so she gan wepen tendrely!
And he ful softe and sleighly gan hire seye:
"Now hold youre day, and do me nat to deye."

---

64. H2Th guise. 67. R wallys, H3 wey *for* valeye. 70. H3PhGgADH4Cx eke it was. 78. γS1ThJ therwithal. 82. CpGgH4 he *for* she. 84. ClJS1 doth.

13

With that his courser torned he aboute   85
With face pale; and unto Diomede
No word he spak, ne non of al his route;
Of which the sone of Tideus took hede,
As he that koude more than the Crede
In swich a craft, and by the reyne hire hente;   90
And Troilus to Troie homward he wente.

14

This Diomede, that ledde hire by the bridel,
Whan that he saugh the folk of Troie aweye,
Thoughte: "al my labour shal nat ben on ydel,
If that I may; for somwhat shal I seye.   95
For at the worste it may yit shorte oure weye.
I have herd seyd ek tymes twyes twelve:
'He is a fool that wol foryete hym selve'."

15

But natheles this thoughte he wel ynough,
That "certeynlich I am aboute nought,   100
If that I speke of love, or make it tough;
For douteles, if she have in hire thought
Hym that I gesse, he may nat ben ybrought
So soone awey; but I shal fynde a meene,
That she nat wite as yit shal what I mene."   105

89. RDCx hys *for* the. 91. RH3 homward to Troye, Gg to Troyeward hom; H3D
H4RCxTh *om.* he. 93. CpJ folke. 97. H3 And eke I have herde sey, Ph I have eke
herd sey. 99. JGgPhH2RCx thus. 105. Cl shal not as yet wete, Th nat yet wete shal,
R she shal not wite as yit what that, Cx not yet shal wyte, H4 what I shal, Gg schal
as ȝit, Ph shal yet, *om.* as.

16

This Diomede, as he that koude his good,
Whan tyme was, gan fallen forth in speche
Of this and that, and axed whi she stood
In swich disese, and gan hire ek biseche,
That if that he encresse myghte or eche   110
With any thyng hire ese, that she sholde
Comaunde it hym, and seyde he don it wolde.

17

For treweliche he swor hire, as a knyght,
That ther nas thyng with which he myghte hire plese,
That he nolde don his herte and al his myght   115
To don it, for to don hire herte an ese;
And preyde hire, she wolde hire sorwe apese,
And seyde: "iwis, we Grekis kan have joie
To honouren yow, as wel as folk of Troie."

18

He seyde ek thus: "I woot, yow thynketh straunge,—
No wonder is, for it is to yow newe, —   121
Thaqueyntaunce of thise Troians to chaunge
For folk of Grece, that ye nevere knewe.
But wolde nevere god but if as trewe
A Grek ye sholde among us alle fynde   125
As any Troian is, and ek as kynde.

---

107. γTh Whan this was don.   115. αCx nyl, H2 wil; γTh peyne *for* herte.   117. H3H4 hert *for* sorwe, Cx *om.* sorwe.   118. Cl kon, Ph kun, Cx conne.   120. H3PhD H4RCx ye thinke it (H3H4D *om.* it).   122. S1H2H4R Troianis; GgCx for to.   123. Ph which þat, H3 that yit *for* that.

19

"And by the cause I swor yow right, lo, now,
To ben youre frend, and helply to my myght,
And for that more aqueyntaunce ek of yow
Have ich had than another straunger wight,   130
So fro this forth I pray yow, day and nyght,
Comaundeth me, how soore that me smerte,
To don al that may like unto youre herte;

20

"And that ye me wolde as youre brother trete,
And taketh naught my frendshipe in despit;   135
And though youre sorwes be for thynges grete,
Not I nat whi, but out of more respit,
Myn herte hath for tamende it gret delit.
And if I may youre harmes nat redresse,
I am right sory for youre hevynesse.   140

21

"For though ye Troians with us Grekes wrothe
Han many a day ben, alwey yit, parde,
O god of love in soth we serven bothe.
And, for the love of god, my lady fre,
Whom so ye hate, as beth nat wroth with me.   145
For trewely, ther kan no wight yow serve,
That half so loth youre wratthe wolde deserve.

128. GgAH2R helpyn, H3 helping, Ph helpe ȝow. 130. H3S2H2H4RCx straunge.
133. ClGgH3R to (H3 that that may lyke). 134. GgPh woldyn me. 136. H3Ph causes
grete. 137. Cp oute of, J of on. 138. H3PhGgH4Cx *om.* for. 140. H3 Than am I
sory. 141. H3H4RCx the *for* ye. 145. H3 and, Cx ne *for* as, H2H4R *om.* as.

22

"And nere it that we ben so neigh the tente
Of Calcas, which that sen us bothe may
I wolde of this yow telle al myn entente;   150
But this enseled til another day.
Yeve me youre honde; I am, and shal ben ay,
God help me so, whil that my lyf may dure,
Youre owene aboven every creature.

23

"Thus seyde I nevere or now to womman born;   155
For, god myn herte as wisly glade so,
I lovede nevere womman here biforn
As paramours, ne nevere shal no mo.
And for the love of god, beth nat my fo;
Al kan I naught to yow, my lady deere,   160
Compleyne aright, for I am yit to leere.

24

"And wondreth nought, myn owen lady bright,
Though that I speke of love to yow thus blyve;
For I have herd or this of many a wight,
Hath loved thyng he nevere say his lyve.   165
Nor I am nat of power for to stryve
Ayeyns the god of love, but hym obeye
I wol alwey, and mercy I yow preye.

150. GgPhD telle ȝow. 151. PhA this is enseled, H4 this enselid is, Gg be þis enselyd, Cx this ensealed shal be. 152. H3 have, H4 wil *for* am. 154. H3PhD(*later hand*)Cx any. 163. GgPh *om.* that. 164. CpH1J herde. 165. GgPh saw nevere. 166. Nor, *so* JH3H4, H2Ph Ne, GgRCx For, γS1Th Ek.

25

"Ther ben so worthi knyghtes in this place,
And ye so fair, that everich of hem alle   170
Wol peynen hym to stonden in youre grace.
But myghte me so fair a grace falle,
That ye me for youre servant wolde calle,
So lowely ne so trewely yow serve
Nil non of hem, as I shal, til I sterve."   175

26

Criseyde unto that purpos lite answerde,
As she that was with sorwe oppressed so
That, in effect, she naught his tales herde,
But her and ther, now here a word or two.
Hire thoughte hire sorwful herte brast atwo;   180
For whan she gan hire fader fer espie,
Wel neigh down of hire hors she gan to sye.

27

But natheles she thonked Diomede
Of al his travaile, and his goode cheere,
And that hym liste his frendshipe hire to bede;   185
And she accepteth it in good manere,
And wol do fayn that is hym lief and dere;
And trusten hym she wolde, and wel she myghte,
As seyde she, and from hire hors shalighte.

171. JGgPhH2H4Cx hem. 172. myghte, *so* AGg, *rest* myght; S1 to me; H3Ph
H2H4 befalle. 176. ClAH3GgH2H4RCx litel. 180. H3H4R on twoo, H2PhA in
tuoo. 181. H3 hir fadres tent aspie. 184. CpJ good. 185. S1 service to hir bede.
186. H3GgAH4R accepted, H2 accepte, Cx acceptynge. 187. ClAH4Cx wold. 188.
CpJ myght.

28

Hire fader hath hire in his armes nome,   190
And twenty tyme he kiste his doughter sweete,
And seyde: "O deere doughter myn, welcome!"
She seyde ek, she was fayn with hym to mete,
And stood forth muwet, milde, and mansuete.
But here I leve hire with hire fader dwelle,   195
And forth I wol of Troilus yow telle.

29

To Troie is come this woful Troilus,
In sorwe aboven alle sorwes smerte,
With feloun look and face dispitous.
Tho sodeynly doun from his hors he sterte,   200
And thorugh his paleis, with a swollen herte,
To chaumbre he wente; of nothyng took he hede,
Ne non to hym dar speke a word for drede.

30

And ther his sorwes that he spared hadde
He yaf an issue large, and "deth!" he cride;   205
And in his throwes frenetic and madde
He corseth Jove, Appollo, and ek Cupide,
He corseth Ceres, Bacus, and Cipride,
His burthe, hym self, his fate, and ek nature,
And, save his lady, every creature.   210

---

190. CpJ hise. 192. H3S1 doughter dere. 193. H3Cx *om.* ek; H3 glade. 195. Cx
And thus I. 199. CpH1 dispitouse, J dispitus. 202. JH3PhRCx *om. first* he; α of no
wight (Gg man). 207. ClGgH2H4RCx curssed; ACxTh Juno *for* Jove; H3 *omits
line*. 208. ClGgH3H2H4RCx curssed.

31

To bedde he goth, and walwith ther and torneth
In furie, as doth he, Ixion, in helle;
And in this wise he neigh til day sojorneth.
But tho bigan his herte a lite unswelle
Thorugh teris, which that gonnen up to welle;   215
And pitously he cryde upon Criseyde,
And to hym self right thus he spak and seyde:

32

"Wher is myn owene lady lief and dere?
Wher is hire white brest, wher is it, where?
Wher ben hire armes and hire eyen cleere,   220
That yesternyght this tyme with me were?
Now may I wepe allone many a teere,
And graspe aboute I may, but in this place,
Save a pilowe, I fynde naught tenbrace.

33

"How shal I do? Whan shal she come ayeyn?   225
I not, allas! whi let ich hire to go?
As wolde god ich hadde as tho ben sleyn!
O herte myn, Criseyde, O swete fo!
O lady myn, that I love and no mo!
To whom for everemo myn herte I dowe,   230
Se how I deye; ye nyl me nat rescowe!

211. walwith, *so* GgH4Cx, R waltryth, J whieleth, Ph swellith, γS1ThH3H2 weyleth *or* waileth. 212. Cp dothe; H3H2H4R dothe the, J dostow, Ph doost þou *for* doth he; H3 Tucius; Gg (*by corrector*) as thow he leye in helle. 214. ClS1GgPhR a not fynde tenbrace. 225-231. H3 *omits stanza.* 226. CpH1 lete, J lat; H4RPh so *for* to, H2CxTh *om.* to.

34

"Who seth yow now, my righte lode sterre?
Who sit right now or stant in youre presence?
Who kan conforten now youre hertes werre?
Now I am gon, whom yeve ye audience?   235
Who speketh for me right now in myn absence?
Allas, no wight; and that is al my care;
For wel I woot as yvele as I ye fare.

35

"How sholde I thus ten dayes ful endure,
Whan I the firste nyght have al this tene?   240
How shal she don ek, sorwful creature?
For tendernesse how shal she ek sustene
Swich wo for me? O pitous, pale, and grene
Shal ben youre fresshe wommanliche face
For longynge, or ye torne into this place."   245

36

And whan he fille in any slomberynges,
Anon bygynne he sholde for to grone,
And dremen of the dredfulleste thynges
That myghte ben: as mete he were allone
In place horrible, makyng ay his mone,   250
Or meten that he was amonges alle
His enemys, and in hire hondes falle.

---

232. righte, *so* Gg (ryȝte), H3 ryghtfull, R bryght, H4 riche, *rest* right. 236.
PhH4Cx *om.* right. 238. γThS1H3 woot I. 241. H3DS1Cx ye *for* she. 242. H3S1Cx
ye *for* she; γS1Th this *for* ek. 244. H3 here *for* youre. 245. γS1Th For langour (Cp
langoure); H3 that she *for* ye; CpH1GgH2RTh unto. 247. JS1 wolde. 249. myghte,
so ClGgH4, H3A myghten, *rest* myght. 250. H4R al *for* ay. 252. H3 in hir hondes
like to falle (*om.* and).

37

And therwithal his body sholde sterte,
And with the sterte al sodeynliche awake,
And swiche a tremour fele aboute his herte,   255
That of the fere his body sholde quake;
And therwithal he sholde a noyse make,
And seme as though he sholde falle depe
From heighe olofte; and thanne he wolde wepe,

38

And rewen on hym self so pitously,   260
That wonder was to here his fantasie.
Another tyme he sholde myghtyly
Conforte hym self, and seyn it was folie,
So causeles swich drede for to drye,
And eft bygynne his aspre sorwes newe,   265
That every man myghte on his sorwes rewe.

39

Who koude telle aright or ful discryve
His wo, his pleynte, his langour, and his pyne?
Naught alle the men that han or ben on lyve!
Thow, redere, maist thi self ful wel devyne   270
That swich a wo my wit kan nat defyne.
On ydel for to write it sholde I swynke,
Whan that my wit is wery it to thynke.

255. H3AR falle, H2H4 fell, Gg fel, Ph fil. 256. H3 That wyth the drede his
hert. 264. RDCx dredes; H3 drede and woo to drye. 265. H2R peynes, H3 *om.*
sorwes. 266. H3S1 wyght *for* man; S1R peynes. 269. H3 folkis. 271. H4RD may
for kan. 273. H3 Syn that.

40

On hevene yit the sterres weren seene,
Although ful pale ywoxen was the moone;   275
And whiten gan the orisonte shene
Al estward, as it wont is to doone;
And Phebus with his rosy carte soone
Gan after that to dresse hym up to fare,
Whan Troilus hath sent after Pandare.   280

41

This Pandare, that of al the day biforn
Ne myghte han comen Troilus to se,
Although he on his hed it hadde sworn,
For with the kyng Priam alday was he,
So that it lay nat in his libertee   285
Nowher to gon,— but on the morwe he wente
To Troilus, whan that he for hym sente.

42

For in his herte he koude wel devyne
That Troilus al nyght for sorwe wook;
And that he wolde telle hym of his pyne,   290
This knew he wel ynough withoute book.
For which to chaumbre streyght the wey he took,
And Troilus tho sobreliche he grette,
And on the bed ful sone he gan hym sette.

274. PhH3H2H4Cx were ysene.   275. Gg wexen gan.   276. R the firmament ful.
277. H1 Esturwarde; Gg was wone, PhDS1R was wont, ACx is wont; JH4R for to
doone.   283. CpH1 sworne, JC1S1 isworn.   291. Cp knewe, J kneught.

43

"My Pandarus," quod Troilus, "the sorwe   295
Which that I drye, I may nat longe endure.
I trowe I shal nat lyven til to-morwe;
For which I wolde alweys, on aventure,
To the devysen of my sepulture
The forme; and of my moeble thow dispone, 300
Right as the semeth best is for to done.

44

"But of the fir and flaumbe funeral
In which my body brennen shal to glede,
And for the feste and pleyes palestral
At my vigile, I prey the, tak good hede   305
That that be wel; and offre Mars my steede,
My swerd, myn helm, and, leve brother deere,
My sheld to Pallas yef, that shyneth cleere.

45

"The poudre in which myn herte ybrend shal torne,
That preye I the thow take and it conserve 310
In a vessell, that men clepeth an urne,
Of gold, and to my lady that I serve,
For love of whom thus pitousliche I sterve,
So yeve it hire, and do me this plesaunce,
To preye hire kepe it for a remembraunce. 315

---

298. ClADH3GgH2R alwey. 306. GgAD þat it. ClH3 þat al *for* That that. 308.
CpJPh swerde *for* sheld. 310. Ph Y pray þe þow hit take. 311. H2H4PhD clepe,
H3AS1R clepen, Gg callyn. 315. γ(-H1)ThH3H4Cx to kepe it.

46

"For wel I fele, by my maladie,
And by my dremes now and yore ago,
Al certeynly that I mot nedes dye.
The owle ek, which that hette Escaphilo,
Hath after me shright al thise nyghtes two.   320
And, god Mercurye, of me now, woful wrecche,
The soule gyde, and, whan the list, it fecche!"

47

Pandare answerde and seyde: "Troilus,
My deere frende, as I have told the yore,
That it is folye for to sorwen thus,   325
And causeles, for which I kan no more.
But whoso wol nat trowen red ne loore,
I kan nat sen in hym no remedie;
But lat hym worthen with his fantasie.

48

"But, Troilus, I prey the, telle me now,   330
If that thow trowe or this that any wight
Hath loved paramours as wel as thow?
Ye, god woot; and fro many a worthi knyght
Hath his lady gon a fourtenyght,
And he nat yit made halvendel the fare.   335
What nede is the to maken al this care?

---

319. hette, *so* CpH1, Cl hatte, JH2 hete, D heet, RA hat, Ph hit, H3GgS1Th
hyght, H4 clepid is (*om*. which) ; Th Ascaphylo. 321. H3H2H4 *om*. now. 322. CpJ
liste. 329. H1CxTh worchen, Gg werchyn. 332. GgPhH2H4Cx paramour. 333. PhR
ful *for* fro; Gg & so haþ many. 334. GgPhRD forgon. 336. PhD What nediþ þe;
Gg What nediþ it þe; H3 What cause hastow.

49

"Syn day by day thow maist thi selven se
That from his love, or ellis from his wif,
A man mot twynnen of necessite,
Ye, though he love hire as his owene lif;   340
Yit nyl he with hym self thus maken strif.
For wel thow woost, my leve brother deere,
That alwey frendes may nat ben yfeere.

50

"How don this folk that seen hire loves wedded
By frendes myght, as it bitit ful ofte,   345
And sen hem in hire spouses bed ybedded?
God woot, they take it wisly, faire, and softe.
Forwhi good hope halt up hire herte o lofte,
And for they kan a tyme of sorwe endure;
As tyme hem hurt, a tyme doth hem cure.   350

51

"So sholdestow endure, and laten slide
The tyme, and fonde to ben glad and lyght.
Ten dayes nys so longe naught tabide.
And syn she the to comen hath bihight,
She nyl hire heste breken for no wight.   355
For drede the nat that she nyl fynden weye
To come ayein, my lif that dorste I leye.

---

342. Ph owne brother, Gg owene lady. 344. H4GgS1Cx these, H2 thes. 349. H3Cx
konne; H3 harde *for* sorwe. 350. H2PhCx *om.* a; Cx tyme wyl hem recure. 353.
GgPhRCx is; H3PhGgDRCxTh not so longe (R *om.* so); RS1 for tabide. 356.
H3RCx fynde a way.

52

"Thy swevenes ek and al swich fantasie
Drif out, and lat hem faren to meschaunce;
For they procede of thi malencolie,   360
That doth the fele in slepe al this penaunce.
A straw for alle swevenes signifiaunce!
God helpe me so, I counte hem nought a bene;
Ther woot no man aright what dremes mene.

53

"For prestes of the temple tellen this: 365
That dremes ben the revelaciouns
Of goddes; and as wel they telle, ywis,
That they ben infernals illusiouns.
And leches seyn that of complexiouns
Proceden they, or fast, or glotonye.   370
Who woot in soth thus what thei signifie?

54

"Ek oothre seyn that thorugh impressiouns,
As if a wight hath faste a thyng in mynde,
That therof comen swich avysiouns.
And oothre seyn, as they in bokes fynde,   375
That after tymes of the yer by kynde
Men dreme, and that theffect goth by the moone.
But leve no dreme, for it is nought to doone.

---

363. H2H4PhACx at a bene. 364. H3Ph what that they meen. 368. infernals, *so* CpClH1AS1ThJ, *rest* infernal. 373. H3H4RS1 have. 374. γS1ThH3PhGg cometh.

55

"Wel worthe of dremes ay thise olde wives,
And treweliche ek augurye of thise fowles;   380
For fere of which men wenen lese hire lyves,
As ravenes qualm, or shrichyng of thise owles.
To trowen on it bothe fals and foul is.
Allas, allas, so noble a creature
As is a man shal dreden swich ordure!   385

56

"For which with al myn herte I the biseche,
Unto thi self that al this thow foryive;
And ris now up, withowten more speche,
And lat us caste how forth may best be dryve
This tyme, and ek how fresshly we may lyve   390
Whan that she comth, the which shal be right soone;
God helpe me so, the best is thus to doone.

57

"Ris, lat us speke of lusty lif in Troie
That we han led, and forth the tyme dryve;
And ek of tyme comyng us rejoie,   395
That bryngen shal oure blisse now so blyve;
And langour of thise twyes dayes fyve
We shal therwith so foryete or oppresse,
That wel unnethe it don shal us duresse.

---

379. GgH4Cx alle *for* ay. 381. H3PhACx to lese. 382. Cp qualyn, J qualin, R
qualine; ClH3PhH2H4Cx shrykyng. 385. CxTh shold. 391. Gg Til þat sche come &
þat may ben. 392. JH1H4 thy, Ph þis *for* the, Gg. *om.* the; R as thus is best be
done, Cx this thynk me best to done. 398. or, *so* H3PhH4RTh, *rest* oure. 399.
H3GgH4RCx shal doon.

58

"This town is ful of lordes al aboute,   400
And trewes lasten al this mene while.
Go we pleye us in som lusty route
To Sarpedoun, nat hennes but a myle.
And thus thow shalt the tyme wel bygile,
And dryve it forth unto that blisful morwe,   405
That thow hire se that cause is of thi sorwe.

59

"Now ris, my deere brother Troilus;
For, certes, it non honour is to the
To wepe, and in thi bed to jouken thus.
For, trewelich, of o thyng truste me: 410
If thow thus ligge a day, or two, or thre,
The folk wol seyn that thow for cowardise
The feynest sik, and that thow darst nat rise."

60

This Troilus answerde: "O brother deere,
This knowen folk that han ysuffred peyne,   415
That though he wepe and make sorwful cheere,
That feleth harm and smert in every veyne,
No wonder is; and though ich evere pleyne,
Or alwey wepe, I am no thyng to blame,
Syn I have lost the cause of al my game.   420

---

401. H3PhGgCx lastith. 402. S1R and pleye. 403. H3 half a myle. 406. H3 That
she shal come; R causeth al thys sorowe. 407. GgPh rys up; H3 faire. 410. CpH1
DS1ThPh truste to, Cl þow trust to, H3S2Cx trust thou. 412. γS1Th wene *for* seyn.
416. H3 a sory, R sory. 419. JH1 nam.

61

"But syn of fyn force I mot arise,
I shal arise as soone as evere I may;
And god, to whom myn herte I sacrifise,
So sende us hastely the tenthe day!
For was ther nevere fowel so fayn of May,   425
As I shal ben, whan that she comth in Troie,
That cause is of my torment and my joie.

·62

"But whider is thi reed," quod Troilus,
"That we may pleye us best in al this town?"
"By god, my conseil is," quod Pandarus,   430
"To ride and pleye us with kyng Sarpedoun."
So longe of this they speken up and down,
Til Troilus gan at the laste assente
To rise, and forth to Sarpedoun they wente.

63

This Sarpedoun, as he that honourable   435
Was evere his lyve, and ful of heigh largesse,
With al that myghte yserved ben on table,
That deynte was, al coste it grete richesse,
He fedde hem day by day, that swich noblesse,
As seyden both the meste and ek the leeste,   440
Was nevere or that day wist at any feste.

421-560. *Missing in* R; *two leaves lost.* 421. H1DS1H2PhTh fyne; H4A *om.* fyn;
H4 nedis I must. 426. JGg to, PhH2 into *for* in. 432. JH3Ph spaken, Gg spoke.
436. γS1Th prowesse. 441. H3 sayn or that day. Gg or þat day sen, Cx seen or wyst
(*om.* or that day).

64

Nor in this world ther is non instrument
Delicious, thorugh wynd or touche of corde,
As fer as any wight hath evere ywent,
That tonge telle or herte may recorde,
That at the feste it nas wel herd acorde;
Ne of ladys ek so fair a compaignie
On daunce, or tho, was nevere yseyn with eye.

445

65

But what availeth this to Troilus,
That for his sorwe nothyng of it roughte?
For evere in oon his herte pietous
Ful bisyly Criseyde, his lady, soughte.
On hire was evere al that his herte thoughte,
Now this, now that, so faste ymagynynge,
That glade, iwis, kan hym no festeyinge.

450

455

66

Thise ladies ek that at this feste ben,
Syn that he saugh his lady was aweye,
It was his sorwe upon hem for to sen,
Or for to here on instrumentes so pleye.
For she that of his herte berth the keye
Was absent, lo, this was his fantasie,
That no wight sholde maken melodie.

460

---

442. H3Ph *om.* ther; H2Cx nys. 443. JGgCl or, H3H1S1Th on *for* of. 444. JGg every *for* any. 446. γ(-D)S1Th that *for* the. 447. JH1S1H3 Nof, Cx Of *for* Ne of. 448. Cp iseye, J er seyn. 451. pietous, *so* CpH1AS1J, Cx pytevous, *rest* pitous. 454. Cp ymagenynge, J ymagnynge. 455. festeyinge, *so* J, S1 festyinge, CpClCx festenynge, H2 þing, *rest* festynge. 456. JGgH3Cx the feste. 459. JGgS1H2 instrument; CpGgPhH4 to, H3 so to *for* so, DCxTh *om.* so.

67

For ther nas houre in al the day or nyght,
Whan he was there as no wight myghte hym heere,
That he ne seyde: "O lufsom lady bryght,   465
How have ye faren syn that ye were heere?
Welcome, ywis, myn owne lady deere."
But, weylaway, al this nas but a maze;
Fortune his howve entended bet to glaze.

68

The lettres ek, that she of olde tyme   470
Hadde hym ysent, he wolde allone rede
An hondred sithe atwixen noon and prime,
Refiguryng hire shap, hire wommanhede,
Withinne his herte, and every word or dede
That passed was; and thus he drof tan ende   475
The ferthe day, and seyde he wolde wende.

69

And seyde: "leve brother, Pandarus,
Intendestow that we shal here beleve
Til Sarpedoun wol forth congeyen us?
Yit were it fairer that we toke oure leve.   480
For goddes love, lat us now soone at eve
Oure leve take, and homward lat us torne;
For, treweliche, I nyl nat thus sojourne."

---

463. GgPh ne, Cx nor *for* or. 464. CpH1ADS1 nought, H3GgH2CxTh no man,
H4 non *for* no wight. 469. ClAH3PhH2H4 entendeth. 472. GgH3PhADH2Cx be-
twixe. 474. H3PhGgClH2CxTh and *for* or. 476. α and thennes wolde he wende.
478. γ(-A)S1ThJ bleve. 479. H2H4CxTh conveien. 483. Cl wol, H2H4 wil, H3 can
for nyl.

70

Pandare answerde: "be we comen hider
To fecchen fyr, and rennen hom ayein?   485
God help me so, I kan nat tellen whider
We myghte gon, if I shal sothly seyn,
Ther any wight is of us more fayn
Than Sarpedoun; and if we hennes hye
Thus sodeynly, I holde it vilanye.   490

71

"Syn that we seyden that we wolde bleve
With hym a wowke, and now thus sodeynly,
The ferthe day, to take of hym oure leve,
He wolde wondren on it, trewely.
Lat us holde oure purpos fermely;   495
And syn that ye bihighten hym to bide,
Hold forward now, and after lat us ride."

72

This Pandarus, with alle peyne and wo,
Made hym to dwelle; and at the wikes ende,
Of Sarpedoun they toke hire leve tho,   500
And on hire wey they spedden hem to wende.
Quod Troilus: "now lord me grace sende,
That I may fynden at myn hom comynge,
Criseyde comen!" and therwith gan he synge.

492. H4ACx wike, Th weke, H2 wooke, Ph while. 495. γS1Th holden forth, Cx
forth hold. 496. JGgAS1 we, H3 he *for* ye. 498. alle, *so* JAH2, *rest* al (S1 al his)
499. H3PhH1CxTh wekes, Gg woukis, H2 wookes. 500. H3 toke leve to goo. 502.
ClH3H2H4 god *for* lord. 503. CpH1J home.

73

"Ye, haselwode!" thoughte this Pandare,　　　　　505
And to hym self ful softeliche he seyde:
"God woot, refreyden may this hote fare,
Or Calkas sende Troilus Criseyde!"
But natheles he japed thus, and pleyde,
And swor, ywys, his herte hym wel bihighte,　　510
She wolde come as soone as evere she myghte.

74

Whan they unto the paleys were ycomen
Of Troilus, they doun of hors alighte,
And to the chaumbre hire wey than han they nomen;
And unto tyme that it gan to nyghte,　　　　　515
They spaken of Criseyde the brighte;
And after this, whan that hem bothe leste,
They spedde hem fro the soper unto reste.

75

On morwe, as soone as day bygan to clere,
This Troilus gan of his slepe tabreyde,　　　　520
And to Pandare, his owen brother deere,
"For love of god," ful pitously he seyde,
"As go we sen the paleys of Criseyde;
For syn we yit may have no more feste,
So lat us sen hire paleys at the leeste."　　　　525

506. ClH2 sobrelich. 509. H3 forthe *for* thus;—pleyde, *so* H3H2H4Cx (R *lacking*), *rest* seyde. 513. H3Ph tho doun of hors they lyght. 514. GgH4Cx þe *for* hire; H3GgH2H4CxTh *om.* than. 515. γS1J into. 516. J They gonne speken; Cx They speke al; S1 Criseida; Th the lady bright. 518. H3PhCx *om.* the. 521. JGgH3S1Th Pandarus. 522. GgH1AS1 preyede. 523. JGgPh *om.* As. 524. H3D non other feste.

76

And therwithal, his meyne for to blende,
A cause he fond in towne for to go,
And to Criseydes hous they gonnen wende.
But, lord! this sely Troilus was wo!
Hym thoughte his sorwful herte brast atwo.   530
For whan he saugh hire dores spered alle,
Wel neigh for sorwe adoun he gan to falle.

77

Therwith whan he was war and gan biholde
How shet was every wyndowe of the place,
As frost, hym thoughte, his herte gan to colde;   535
For which with chaunged dedlich pale face,
Withouten word, he forthby gan to pace;
And, as god wolde, he gan so faste ride,
That no wight of his contenaunce espide.

78

Than seide he thus: "O paleys desolat,   540
O hous of houses whilom best ihight,
O paleys empty and disconsolat,
O thow lanterne of which queynt is the light,
O paleys, whilom day, that now art nyght,
Wel oughtestow to falle, and I to dye,   545
Syn she is went that wont was us to gye!

530. PhH2H4Cx He *for* Hym.   533. H3 And eke whan he.   536. Cp dellich, H1 deellich, J(*over erasure*) dedlych, ClGg deedlych, H3ADS1Cx dedely, H4PhTh dedly. 538. H3 So faste he gan; H3PhCx to ryde.   541. H3 ylyght, PhCx ydight.

79

"O paleis, whilom crowne of houses alle,
Enlumyned with sonne of alle blisse,
O ryng, fro which the ruby is out falle,
O cause of wo, that cause hast ben of lisse,   550
Yit, syn I may no bet, fayn wolde I kisse
Thi colde dores, dorste I for this route;
And farewel, shryne of which the seynt is oute!"

80

Therwith he caste on Pandarus his eye
With chaunged face, and pitous to biholde;   555
And whan he myghte his tyme aright aspie,
Ay as he rod, to Pandarus he tolde
His newe sorwe, and ek his joies olde,
So pitously, and with so dede an hewe,
That every wight myghte on his sorwe rewe.   560

81

Fro thennesforth he rideth up and down,
And every thyng com hym to remembraunce,
As he rood forby places of the town
In which he whilom hadde al his plesaunce:
"Lo yonder saugh ich last my lady daunce;   565
And in that temple, with hire eyen clere,
Me kaughte first my righte lady dere.

---

550. JGg hath, Ph have; lisse, *so* CpJS1Cx, H2 hisse, *rest* blysse.   559. Gg pale.
560. H1DH3 sorwes.   563. H1S2H2H4CxTh þe places (H2 paleis, H4 paleisis);
GgPhH2H4RCx in *for* of.   564. GgH3 *om.* al.   565. γS1Th saugh ich myn owene
lady.

82

"And yonder have I herd ful lustyly
My dere herte laughe; and yonder pleye
Saugh ich hire ones ek ful blisfully;   570
And yonder ones to me gan she seye:
'Now goode swete, love me wel, I preye.'
And yond so goodly gan she me biholde,
That to the deth myn herte is to hire holde.

83

"And at that corner, in the yonder hous,   575
Herde I myn alderlevest lady deere
So wommanly, with vois melodious,
Syngen so wel, so goodly, and so cleere,
That in my soule yit me thynketh ich here
The blisful sown; and in that yonder place,   580
My lady first me took unto hire grace."

84

Than thoughte he thus: "O blisful lord Cupide,
Whan I the proces have in my memorie,
How thow me hast werreyed on every syde,
Men myghte a book make of it, lik a storie.   585
What nede is the to seke on me victorie,
Syn I am thyn, and holly at thi wille?
What joie hastow thyn owen folk to spille?

---

570. GgH3PhR busily. 573. H3PhGgH1AH2H4 yonder. 575. H2H4RCxA at the (H4 atte). 583. γS1ThPhH4 *om.* my. 584. werreyed, *so* R, J werried, H1DGgTh weryed, H3 weryede, Ph werrid, H2 weryhed, H4 werreid, A werreide, Cl waryed; H3DR *om.* on. 587. GgPh al *for* and; H3 Syn I am alwey at thin one wille. 588. Cp has thow, J(*over erasure*) hast thow.

85

"Wel hastow, lord, ywroke on me thyn ire,
Thow myghty god, and dredful for to greve. 590
Now mercy, lord; thow woost wel I desire
Thi grace moost of alle lustes leeve.
And lyve and dye I wol in thy byleve;
For which I naxe in guerdoun but a bone,
That thow Criseyde ayein me sende sone. 595

86

"Distreyne hire herte as faste to retorne
As thow doost myn to longen hire to see;
Than woot I wel that she nyl nat sojorne.
Now, blisful lord, so cruel thow ne be
Unto the blood of Troie, I preye the, 600
As Juno was unto the blood Thebane,
For which the folk of Thebes caughte hire bane."

87

And after this he to the yates wente,
Ther as Criseyde out rood, a ful good paas;
And up and down ther made he many a wente, 605
And to hym self ful ofte he seyde: "allas!
From hennes rood my blisse and my solas!
As wolde blisful god now, for his joie,
I myghte hire sen ayein come into Troie!

590. H3PhCx myghtful. 594. JAH4 o, Gg on, D one *for* a. 598. CpH1 naught,
J so, H3 not longe *for* nat. 599. JDS1 god. 601. H2Cx Jove. 608. H3H2H4RCx
And *for* As.

88

"And to the yonder hil I gan hire gyde,   610
Allas, and there I took of hire my leve!
And yond I saugh hire to hire fader ride,
For sorwe of which myn herte wol to-cleve.
And hider hom I com whan it was eve;
And here I dwelle out cast from alle joie,   615
And shal, til I may sen hire eft in Troie."

89

And of hym self ymagined he ofte
To ben defet, and pale, and waxen lesse
Than he was wont, and that men seyden softe:
"What may it be? who kan the sothe gesse   620
Whi Troilus hath al this hevynesse?"
And al this nas but his malencolie,
That he hadde of hym self swich fantasie.

90

Another tyme ymaginen he wolde,
That every wight that wente by the weye   625
Hadde of hym routhe, and that they seyn sholde:
"I am right sory Troilus wol deye."
And thus he drof a day yit forth or tweye,
As ye have herd. Swich lif right gan he lede,
As he that stood bitwixen hope and drede.   630

610-616. S1 *omits stanza*. 611. R Allas that ever y tok. 613. γTh shal. 615. CpJ
al; H4R every. 617. H3PhRCx ful ofte. 618. ClS1RTh woxen. 626. ClR seyen.
628. αR *om.* yit. 629. JGgPhCxTh *om.* right, H2H4 riȝt such lif (H2 a lif).

91

For which hym likede in his songes shewe
Thenchesoun of his wo, as he best myghte,
And made a song of wordes but a fewe,
Somwhat his woful herte for to lighte.
And whan he was from every mannes syghte,   635
With softe vois he of his lady deere,
That absent was, gan synge as ye may heere:

92

"O sterre, of which I lost have al the light,   CANTUS
With herte soore wel oughte I to biwaille,   TROILI
That evere derk in torment, nyght by nyght,   640
Toward my deth with wynd in steere I saille;
For which the tenthe nyght, if that I faille
The gydyng of thi bemes bright an houre,
Mi ship and me Caribdis wol devoure."

93

This song whan he thus songen hadde, soone   645
He fil ayeyn into his sikes olde;
And every nyght, as was his wone to doone,
He stood the brighte moone to byholde;
And al his sorwe he to the moone tolde,
And seyde: "ywis, whan thow art horned newe,   650
I shal be glad, if al the world be trewe.

631. H3Gg he *for* hym. 632. H3H2H4R Thentencion. 633. ClJ make. 637. Ph on
þis manere. 638. Cantus Troili, *so* JH1ADS1S2, Cp Canticus Troili, R the song of
Troilus, *rest omit.* 642. H3 if that the tentyth nyght. 643. Gg bryȝte. 645. H3Gg
H4Cx *om.* thus; H3GgCx hade songen. 646. CpJ hise. 647. JH3H2H4Cx as he was
wonte (H2 was he); RTh wont.

94

"I saugh thyn hornes olde ek by the morwe
Whan hennes rood my righte lady dere,
That cause is of my torment and my sorwe;
For which, O brighte Latona the clere,   655
For love of god, ren faste aboute thy spere!
For whan thyne hornes newe gynnen sprynge,
Than shal she come, that may my blisse brynge."

95

The dayes moore, and lenger every nyght,
Than they ben wont to be, hym thoughte tho;   660
And that the sonne wente his cours unright
By lenger weye than it was wont to go;
And seyde: "ywis, me dredeth evere mo,
The sonnes sone, Pheton, be on lyve,
And that his fader carte amys he dryve."   665

96

Upon the walles faste ek wolde he walke,
And on the Grekis oost he wolde se,
And to hym self right thus he wolde talke:
"Lo, yonder is myn owene lady free,
Or ellis yonder, ther the tentes be.   670
And thennes comth this eir, that is so soote,
That in my soule I fele it doth me boote.

---

652. αH2 *om.* ek, RCx ek old. 653. righte, *so* A, Gg bry3te, R rightful, *rest* right.
654. H3 That causes al my. 655. CxTh Lucyna. 658. ClH3 me *for* my, H4 *om.* my.
659. GgS2H2H4CxTh day is. 660. PhS1H2 were. 662. CpADH3RCx do *for* go. 663.
Th I drede me. 665. ClAS1GgPhH2H4 fadres, Th fathers. 666. H3ACx *om.* ek;
H3Cx he wolde. 669. H3 my lady fair and free. 670. CpClH3 tho tentes.

97

"And hardily this wynd, that more and moore
Thus stoundemele encresseth in my face,
Is of my ladis depe sikes soore.   675
I preve it thus: for in noon othere space
Of al this town, save onliche in this place,
Fele I no wynd that sowneth so lik peyne;
It seyth: 'allas, whi twynned be we tweyne?' "

98

This longe tyme he dryveth forth right thus,   680
Til fully passed was the nynthe nyght;
And ay bisyde hym was this Pandarus,
That bisily dide al his fulle myght
Hym to conforte, and make his herte light,
Yevyng hym hope alwey, the tenthe morwe   685
That she shal come, and stynten al his sorwe.

99

Upon that other syde ek was Criseyde,
With wommen fewe among the Grekis stronge;
For which ful ofte a day "allas!" she seyde,
"That I was born! Wel may myn herte longe   690
After my deth; for now lyve I to longe.
Allas! and I ne may it nat amende;
For now is wors than evere yit I wende.

---

676. γS1H3 place.   677. γ(-A)S1H3 space.   678. CpH1J like.   687. H3DH4R was eke, JCx *om.* ek (Cx was this).

100

"My fader nyl for nothyng do me grace
To gon ayeyn, for naught I kan hym queme;   695
And if so be that I my terme pace,
My Troilus shal in his herte deme
That I am fals, and so it may wel seme.
Thus shal I have unthank on every side;
That I was born, so weilaway the tide!   700

101

"And if that I me putte in jupartie,
To stele awey by nyght, and it bifalle
That I be kaught, I shal be holde a spie;
Or elles, lo, this drede I moost of alle:
If in the hondes of som wrecche I falle,   705
I nam but lost, al be myn herte trewe,
Now, myghty god, thow on my sorwe rewe!"

102

Ful pale ywaxen was hire brighte face,
Hire lymes lene, as she that al the day
Stood, whan she dorste, and lokede on the place   710
Ther she was born, and ther she dwelt hadde ay.
And al the nyght wepyng, allas, she lay.
And thus despeired out of alle cure,
She ladde hire lif, this woful creature.

694. H3GgH2H4R wyl.   695. ClS1PhH2RTh ought.   706. ClDGgPhH4Cx am.
711. γS1Th *om. second* ther.   713-719. Gg *omits seven lines.*

103

Ful ofte a day she sighte ek for destresse,   715
And in hire self she wente ay portreyinge
Of Troilus the grete worthynesse,
And alle his goodly wordes recordynge,
Syn first that day hire love bigan to springe.
And thus she sette hire woful herte afire   720
Thorugh remembraunce of that she gan desire.

104

In al this world ther nys so cruel herte
That hire hadde herd compleynen in hire sorwe,
That nolde han wepen for hire peynes smerte,
So tendrely she wepte, bothe eve and morwe.   725
Hire nedede no teris for to borwe.
And this was yit the worste of al hire peyne,
Ther was no wight to whom she dorste hire pleyne.

105

Ful rewfully she lokede upon Troie,
Biheld the toures heighe and ek the halles;   730
"Allas!" quod she, "the plesaunce and the joie,
The which that now al torned into galle is,
Have ich had ofte withinne yonder walles!
O Troilus, what dostow now?" she seyde;
"Lord! wheyther thow yit thenke upon Criseyde! 735

715. ClH3Cx *om.* ek. 716. hir sowle. 720. GgPhH4R on fyre, J in fyre.
724. wepen, *so* CpADJPh, ClH1R wopen, H2H3CxTh wepte, GgH4S1 wepid. 725.
R weep, Ph wepe. 726. nedede, *so* Cl, *rest* neded (H3 nedith, R neded nat); CpGgA
none, JH1 non. 728. GgH4 nas, J nys; PhH2RCxTh *om.* hire; GgPhH2Cx compleyne. 730. CpH1 Bihelde, J Bihold; JGgPhD walles. 732. H3PhH2H4R *om.*
al (R itorned). 733. CpH3A the yonder, ClH1S1J þo yonder. 735. GgH3H1H2H4
þou þynke ʒit, ClPh yet þou þenke, D *om.* yit.

106

"Allas, I ne hadde trowed on youre loore,
And went with yow, as ye me redde or this!
Than hadde I now nat siked half so soore.
Who myghte have seyd that I hadde don amys,
To stele awey with swich oon as he is? 740
But al to late comth the letuarie,
Whan men the cors unto the grave carie.

107

"To late is now to speke of that matere;
Prudence, allas, oon of thyn eyen thre
Me lakked alwey, or that I com here. 745
On tyme ypassed wel remembred me;
And present tyme ek koude ich wel ise;
But futur tyme, or I was in the snare,
Koude I nat sen: that causeth now my care.

108

"But natheles, bityde what bityde, 750
I shal to-morwe at nyght, by est or west,
Out of this oost stele on som maner syde,
And gon with Troilus wher as hym lest.
This purpos wol ich holde, and this is best.
No fors of wikked tonges janglerie; 755
For evere on love han wrecches had envye.

---

738. H3PhAH4 not now, Gg *om.* now. 739. CpH1J seyde. 743. ClGgPhR þis *for* that. 752. GgCx ostel *for* oost stele; JGgH3H1ADR in, H2H4 by *for* on. 754. H4R thus is, J þat is. 756. JH3 in, Gg of, Ph to, D at *for* on.

109

"For whoso wol of every word take hede,
Or reulen hym by every wightes wit,
Ne shal he nevere thryven, out of drede.
For that that som men blamen evere yit,   760
Lo, other maner folk comenden it.
And as for me, for al swich variaunce,
Felicite clepe I my suffisaunce.

110

"For which, withouten any wordes mo,
To Troie I wol, as for conclusioun."   765
But, god it wot, or fully monthes two,
She was ful fer fro that entencioun;
For bothe Troilus and Troie town
Shal knotteles thorughout hire herte slide;
For she wol take a purpos for tabyde.   770

111

This Diomede, of whom yow telle I gan,
Goth now withinne hym self ay arguynge
With al the sleighte, and al that evere he kan,
How he may best, with shortest taryinge,
Into his net Criseydes herte brynge.   775
To this entent he koude nevere fyne;
To fisshen hire, he leyde out hook and lyne.

---

757. Ph For wold a man. 764. H3PhGg *om.* any. 765. CpH1J wole. 766. H3Ph
monethes fully. 768. JH3H1A Troyes town. 769. GgPhH2H4 glyde. 770. Gg a
purpos al be syde. 771. GgPhCx I telle 30w, H3 you I telle, D I you tell, H2H4 *om.*
yow. 772. JGgPh with hymselven arguynge. 773. Cp slegthe, J sleyght.

112

But natheles, wel in his herte he thoughte,
That she nas nat withoute a love in Troie;
For nevere, sythen he hire thennes broughte,   780
Ne koude he sen hire laughe ne maken joie.
He nyste how best hire herte for tacoye.
"But for to assaye," he seyde, "it naught ne greveth;
For he that naught nasayeth, naught nacheveth."

113

Yit seide he to hym self upon a nyght: 785
"Now am I nat a fool, that woot wel how
Hire wo for love is of another wight?
And hereupon to gon assaye hire now,
I may wel wite, it nyl nat ben my prow.
For wise folk in bookes it expresse: 790
'Men shal nat wowe a wight in hevynesse.'

114

"But whoso myghte wynnen swich a flour
From hym, for whom she morneth nyght and day,
He myghte seyn, he were a conquerour."
And right anon, as he that bold was ay,   795
Thoughte in his herte: "happe how happe may,
Al sholde I deye, I wol hire herte seche;
I shal no more lesen but my speche."

---

779. Gg was. 781. γS1ThH2 or, J and *for* ne. 784. H2H4RH3 assaieþ, acheveth. 789. H3H2H4RCx wyl. 796. H3R what *for* how.

115

This Diomede, as bokes us declare,
Was in his nedes prest and corageous,   800
With sterne vois, and myghty lymes square,
Hardy, testif, strong, and chivalrous
Of dedes, lik his fader Tideus;
And som men seyn, he was of tonge large;
And heir he was of Calidoyne and Arge.   805

116

Criseyde mene was of hire stature,
Therto of shap, of face, and ek of cheere,
Ther myghte ben no fayrer creature.
And ofte tyme this was hire manere:
To gon ytressed with hire heres clere   810
Doun by hire coler at hire bak byhynde,
Which with a thred of gold she wolde bynde.

117

And save hire browes joyneden yfere,
Ther nas no lakke, in aught I kan espien.
But for to speken of hire eyen cleere,   815
Lo, trewely, they writen that hire syen,
That paradis stood formed in hire eyen.
And with hire riche beaute evere more
Strof love in hire ay, which of hem was more.

809. CpDS1H3H2 tymes. 812. GgPhR it bynde. 814. H3Cx was. 818. JH3 *om.* hire.

118

She sobre was, ek symple, and wys withal,   820
The best ynorisshed ek that myghte be,
And goodly of hire speche in general,
Charitable, estatlich, lusty, and fre;
Ne nevere mo ne lakkede hire pite;
Tendre herted, slydynge of corage;   825
But, trewely, I kan nat telle hire age.

119

And Troilus wel woxen was in highte,
And complet formed by proporcioun
So wel, that kynde it nought amenden myghte;
Yong, fressh, strong, and hardy as lyoun;   830
Trewe as steel in ech condicioun;
Oon of the beste entecched creature,
That is, or shal, whil that the world may dure.

120

And certeynly in storye it is yfounde,
That Troilus was nevere unto no wight,   835
As in his tyme, in no degree secounde
In duryng don that longeth to a knyght.
Al myghte a geant passen hym of myght,
His herte ay with the firste and with the beste
Stood paregal, to durre don that hym leste.   840

823. CpS1S2JH2 *om.* and; Ph and statly lusty fre. 827. JPhRH2 on, H4 of *for* in. 833. Ph or may be whil þe world; H4A shal be; H2H4S1Cx *om. second* that. 837. Cl In dorryng, Gg In dorynge, J Endurynge, PhRCxTh Yn daryng, H2H4 In doyng (*om.* don). 839. CpJ first. 840. Cp peregal, J parigal; H2H4PhDCx to doo, H3 to dur hir, A endeure to doo, H1 to durre to do; H3PhGgADRCxTh what, H2 what þat.

121

But for to tellen forth of Diomede:
It fil that after, on the tenthe day
Syn that Criseyde out of the citee yede,
This Diomede, as fressh as braunche in May,
Com to the tente ther as Calkas lay,   845
And feyned hym with Calkas han to doone;
But what he mente, I shal yow tellen soone.

122

Criseyde, at shorte wordes for to telle,
Welcomed hym, and down hym by hire sette;
And he was ethe ynough to maken dwelle.   850
And after this, withouten longe lette,
The spices and the wyn men forth hem fette;
And forth they speke of this and that yfeere,
As frendes don, of which som shal ye heere.

123

He gan first fallen of the werre in speche   855
Bitwixen hem and the folk of Troie town;
And of thassege he gan hire ek biseche,
To telle hym what was hire opynyoun.
Fro that demaunde he so descendeth down
To axen hire, if that hire straunge thoughte   860
The Grekis gise, and werkes that they wroughte,

843-910. *Missing in* R; *leaf torn out.* 844. Gg rose in may. 851. H3S1H2 lenger,
Cl more. 854. H4 lere. 856. H3Ph *om.* the. 859. H3H2H4 descended.

124

And whi hire fader tarieth so longe
To wedden hire unto som worthy wight.
Criseyde, that was in hire peynes stronge
For love of Troilus, hire owen knyght,   865
As ferforth as she konnyng hadde or myght,
Answerde hym tho; but, as of his entente,
It semed nat she wiste what he mente.

125

But, natheles, this ilke Diomede
Gan in hym self assure, and thus he seyde: 870
"If ich aright have taken of yow hede,
Me thynketh thus, O lady myn Criseyde:
That syn I first hond on youre bridel leyde,
Whan ye out come of Troie by the morwe,
Ne koude I nevere sen yow but in sorwe.   875

126

"Kan I nat seyn what may the cause be;
But if for love of som Troian it were,—
The which right sore wolde athynken me,
That ye, for any wight that dwelleth there,
Sholden spille a quarter of a tere,   880
Or pitously youre selven so bigile;
For, dredeles, it is nat worth the while.

862. H3H2H4 taried.   863. H3DCx knyght.   872. H1S1Gg this.   **882. GgH4A**
nys not.

127

"The folk of Troie, as who seyth, alle and some
In prison ben, as ye youre selven se;
For thennes shal nat oon on lyve come, 885
For al the gold atwixen sonne and se.
Trusteth wel, and understondeth me,
Ther shal nat oon to mercy gon on lyve,
Al were he lord of worldes twies fyve.

128

"Swich wreche on hem, for fecchynge of Eleyne, 890
Ther shal ben take, or that we hennes wende,
That Manes, whiche that goddes ben of peyne,
Shal ben agast that Grekes wol hem shende.
And men shul drede, unto the worldes ende,
From hennesforth to ravysshen any queene, 895
So cruel shal oure wreche on hem be seene.

129

"And but if Calkas lede us with ambages,
That is to seyn, with double wordes slye,
Swich as men clepe a word with two visages,
Ye shal wel knowen that I naught ne lye, 900
And al this thyng right sen it with youre eye,
And that anon; ye nyl nat trowe how sone;
Now taketh hede, for it is for to doone.

---

885. ClTh Fro, J Ne, H3GgH4 Nor, H2 Nevyr. 886. atwixen, *so* CpH1AS1JTh,
Cx bytwene, *rest* bytwixen; H3 londe *for* sonne. 887. S1Cx ryt wel. 895. Cl þe
ravesshynge of a queene. 897. H3H2H4 by *for* with. 900. H3PhGgDH2 *om*. ne.

130

"What wene ye youre wise fader wolde
Han yeven Antenor for yow anon,   905
If he ne wiste that the cite sholde
Destroied ben? Whi, nay, so mote I gon!
He knew ful wel ther shal nat scapen oon
That Troïan is; and for the grete feere,
He dorste nat ye dwelte lenger there.   910

131

"What wol ye more, lufsom lady deere?
Lat Troie and Troian fro youre herte pace!
Drif out that bittre hope, and make good cheere,
And clepe ayeyn the beaute of youre face,
That ye with salte teris so deface.   915
For Troie is brought in swich a jupartie,
That it to save is now no remedie.

132

"And thenketh wel, ye shal in Grekis fynde
A moore parfit love, or it be nyght,
Than any Troian is, and more kynde,   920
And bet to serven yow wol don his myght.
And if ye vouchesauf, my lady bright,
I wol ben he to serven yow my selve,
Ye, levere than be kyng of Greces twelve."

---

910. CpH1 dorst, J durst. 912. RCxTh Troians. 916. H3PhGgS1H2RCxTh
jupardie. 924. γS1Th lord *for* kyng.

133

And with that word he gan to waxen red,   925
And in his speche a litel wight he quook,
And caste asyde a litel wight his hed,
And stynte a while; and afterward he wook,
And sobreliche on hire he threw his look,
And seyde: "I am, al be it yow no joie,   930
As gentil man as any wight in Troie.

134

"For if my fader Tideus," he seyde,
"Ilyved hadde, ich hadde ben or this,
Of Calydoyne and Arge a kyng, Criseyde!
And so hope I that I shal yit, iwis.   935
But he was slayn; allas, the more harm is,
Unhappily at Thebes al to rathe,
Polymytes and many a man to scathe.

135

"But, herte myn, syn that I am youre man,—
And ben the firste of whom I seche grace,—   940
To serve yow as hertely as I kan,
And evere shal, whil I to lyve have space;
So, or that I departe out of this place,
That ye me graunte, that I may to-morwe
At bettre leyser tellen yow my sorwe."   945

---

927. R a doun; GgH4AS2CxTh with, R tyn *for* wight. 928. CpH1 he woke, ClJGgH3 awook *for* he wook. 931. H3PhACxTh a man. 938. γS1ThJ Polymyte, Gg Polymy3t. 940. CpJ first; H3 bethe; Ph And 3e be; Cx And ye the fyrst. 941. PhH2H4RCx And *for* To. 944. γS1Th Ye wol me graunte. 945. Gg al myn sorwe, H3S1Th of my sorowe.

136

What sholde I telle his wordes that he seyde?
He spak inough, for o day at the meeste;
It preveth wel, he spak so that Criseyde
Graunted on the morwe, at his requeste,
For to speken with hym at the leeste,   950
So that he nolde speke of swich matere;
And thus she to hym seyde as ye may here,

137

As she that hadde hire herte on Troilus
So faste, that ther may it non arace;
And straungely she spak, and seyde thus: 955
"O Diomede, I love that ilke place
Ther I was born; and Joves, for his grace,
Delyvere it soone of al that doth it care!
God, for thy myght, so leve it wel to fare!

138

"That Grekis wolde hire wraththe on Troie wreke, 960
If that they myghte, I knowe it wel, iwis.
But it shal nat byfallen as ye speke,
And god toforn; and ferther over this,
I woot my fader wys and redy is;
And that he me hath bought, as ye me tolde,   965
So deere, I am the more unto hym holde.

946. GgH3 þe wordis. 952. CpAH2H4 to hym she seyde, GgCx sche seyde to hym,
D *om.* to hym; CpH1S2 mowe, Th nowe, Gg schul *for* may. 954. H2GgH3 might;
ClH2H4Cx non it, H3 non myght it, A no man may it, Gg *om.* it. 957. GgPhH2
H4Cx Jove. 959. H3 hys *for* thy. 961. CpH1J myght. 963. CpS1 forther, J forthere,
H3RCx further, Th farther; Cp overe, J of. 966. GgPhRCx to.

139

"That Grekis ben of heigh condicioun,
I woot ek wel; but, certeyn, men shal fynde
As worthi folk withinne Troie town,
As konnyng, and as parfit, and as kynde,   970
As ben bitwixen Orcades and Inde.
And that ye koude wel yowre lady serve,
I trowe it wel, hire thank for to deserve.

140

"But as to speke of love, ywis," she seyde,
"I hadde a lord, to whom I wedded was,   975
The whos myn herte al was til that he deyde;
And other love, as help me now Pallas,
Ther in myn herte nys, ne nevere was.
And that ye ben of noble and heigh kynrede,
I have wel herd it tellen, out of drede.   980

141

"And that doth me to han so grete a wonder,
That ye wol scornen any womman so.
Ek, god woot, love and I ben fer asonder;
I am disposed bet, so mote I go,
Unto my deth to pleyne and maken wo.   985
What I shal after don, I kan nat seye;
But, trewelich, as yit me list nat pleye.

---

970. and as parfit, *so* CpH1S2S1JR, *rest om.* and (Cp perfit, J parfite). 972. R
And also wel yet can hyr lady serve. 973. γ(-A)S1Th ek *for* it. 976. GgPhAR om.
al; Cx The whiche myn hert had tyl. 978. Gg nas. 981. H3PhD *om.* a. 986.
JGgH2H4RCx can I. 987. ClH3PhH4Cx to pleye.

142

"Myn herte is now in tribulacioun,
And ye in armes bisy day by day.
Herafter, whan ye wonnen han the town,   990
Paraunter thanne so it happen may,
That whan I se that nevere yit I say,
Than wol I werke that I nevere wroughte.
This word to yow ynough suffisen oughte.

143

"To-morwe ek wol I speken with yow fayn,   995
So that ye touchen naught of this matere.
And whan yow list, ye may come here ayayn;
And, or ye gon, thus muche I seye yow here:
As help me Pallas with hire heres clere,
If that I sholde of any Grek han routhe,   1000
It sholde be youre selven, by my trouthe.

144

"I sey nat therfore that I wol yow love,
Ny sey nat nay; but in conclusioun,
I mene wel, by god that sit above."
And therwithal she caste hire eyen down,   1005
And gan to sike, and seyde: "O Troie town,
Yit bidde I god, in quiete and in reste
I may yow sen, or do myn herte breste."

---

991. GgH2H4S1ACxTh Paraventure; thanne, *so* ClAGgH4R, J then, CpPh *om.*,
rest than. 992. *So* H4PhCx, γTh that I nevere er say, S1 þat never ere I say, J þat
I nevere yit say, H3H2R that I never say, Gg þat nevere ȝit ne say. 993. H3H2S1 shal.
994. H4R inouh to you, Gg I now for ȝow suffiseþ it nouȝt, Ph *om.* ynough. 997.
H3PhGgH2 ye *for* yow. 999. H1H3Ph eres, Gg eyyn. 1000. JS1H2H4RCx on *for* of;
CpH1J Greke. 1002. CpH1 say, J seyn. 1008. JGgPhH2Cx the *for* yow.

145

But in effect, and shortly for to seye,
This Diomede al fresshly newe ayeyn   1010
Gan presen on, and faste hire mercy preye;
And after this, the sothe for to seyn,
Hire glove he took, of which he was ful fayn.
And finaly, whan it was woxen eve,
And al was wel, he roos and took his leve.   1015

146

The brighte Venus folwede and ay taughte
The wey, ther brode Phebus down alighte;
And Cynthea hire charhors overraughte
To whirle out of the Leoun, if she myghte;
And Signifer his candeles sheweth brighte;   1020
Whan that Criseyde unto hire reste wente
Inwith hire fadres faire brighte tente,

147

Retornyng in hire soule ay up and down
The wordes of this sodeyn Diomede,
His grete estat, and peril of the town,   1025
And that she was allone and hadde nede
Of frendes help. And thus bygan to brede
The cause whi, the sothe for to telle,
That she took fully purpos for to dwelle.

1013. CpJ feyn.   1020. CpJ hise; ClADGgH2H4Cx shewed; H2H4RPh light.
1021. γS1ThH3 bedde, H4 chamber.   1022. GgADH2H4RTh Withinne, Ph þerin.   1023.
GgH3RCx *om.* ay.   1024. Ph The wordis sodein of þis, R The sodeyn wordes of the.
1025. CpJ perel.   1028. JGgPhS1 causes.

148

The morwen com, and, gostly for to speke,   1030
This Diomede is come unto Criseyde;
And shortly, lest that ye my tale breke,
So wel he for hym selven spak and seyde,
That alle hire sikes soore adown he leyde.
And finaly, the sothe for to seyne,   1035
He refte hire of the grete of al hire peyne.

149

And after this the storie telleth us,
That she hym yaf the faire baye stede,
The which he ones wan of Troilus;
And ek a broche, and that was litel nede,   1040
That Troilus was, she yaf this Diomede.
And ek the bet from sorwe hym to releve,
She made hym were a pencel of hire sleve.

150

I fynde ek in stories elleswhere,
Whan thorugh the body hurt was Diomede   1045
Of Troilus, tho wepte she many a teere,
Whan that she saugh his wyde wowndes blede;
And that she took to kepen hym good hede,
And for to hele hym of his sorwes smerte
Men seyn, I not, that she yaf hym hire herte.   1050

1031. GgH4RCx is comyn to. 1032. CpJ list, H1 liste; ClDH3PhR *om.* that.
1033. Hym selven, *so* JH3ADRTh, *rest* hym self. 1037. GgH4 þus *for* us. 1038. Gg
þat he hire ȝaf. 1039. PhRCxTh she *for* he; PhCx had *for* wan; H3 The wych of
hym onys whan Troylus. 1040. H3GgRCx *om.* and; H3 ful lytel. 1044. H1S1H3RCx
in þe stories (H3Cx story). 1046. JGgPh wep, H4 wepe gan she (*om.* tho). 1047.
CpH1J hise.

151

But, trewely, the storie telleth us,
Ther made nevere woman moore wo
Than she, whan that she falsed Troilus.
She seyde: "allas! for now is clene ago
My name of trouthe in love for everemo!   1055
For I have falsed oon, the gentileste
That evere was, and oon the worthieste.

152

"Allas, of me, unto the worldes ende,
Shal neyther ben ywriten nor ysonge
No good word; for thise bokes wol me shende.   1060
O, rolled shal I ben on many a tonge;
Thorughout the world my belle shal be ronge;
And wommen moost wol haten me of alle.
Allas, that swich a cas me sholde falle!

153

"Thei wol seyn, in as muche as in me is,   1065
I have hem don dishonour, weylaway!
Al be I nat the firste that dide amys,
What helpeth that to don my blame awey?
But syn I se ther is no bettre way,
And that to late it is now for to rewe,   1070
To Diomede algate I wol be trewe.

1057. AS1Cx eke *for* oon.   1060. CpClJ wood *for* word.   1064. H3PhS1H4Cx shulde
me; H3PhGgAH2Cx byfalle.   1069. JS1Cx nys.   1070. γS1ThH3 to late is now for
me to rewe (Cl *om.* for, ADS1 me for); Ph to late is me now to repente.   1071. Ph
To this y wil be trewe in myn entente, H3 *omits line.*

154

"But, Troilus, syn I no bettre may,
And syn that thus departen ye and I,
Yit preye I god, so yeve yow right good day,
As for the gentileste, trewely,   1075
That evere I say, to serven feythfully,
And best kan ay his lady honour kepe."—
And with that word she brast anon to wepe.—

155

"And, certes, yow ne haten shal I nevere;
And frendes love, that shal ye han of me,   1080
And my good word, al myghte I lyven evere.
And, trewely, I wolde sory be
For to seen yow in adversitee.
And gilteles, I woot wel, I yow leve;
But al shal passe; and thus take I my leve."   1085

156

But, trewely, how longe it was bytwene,
That she forsook hym for this Diomede,
Ther is non auctour telleth it, I wene.
Take every man now to his bokes heede;
He shal no terme fynden, out of drede.   1090
For though that he bigan to wowe hire soone,
Or he hire wan, yit was ther more to doone.

1074. JPhH2H4 to, R he *for* so, Cx *om.* so. 1077. H2S1RTh ladies, H1Gg *om.* lady.
1080. R ye shul ay han (*om.* that). 1081. γ(-Cl)ThJH3 sholde. 1082. PhAS1RCxTh
right sory, H4 ful sory. 1088. JGg nys. 1091. H2H4DCx love *for* wowe.

157

Ne me ne list this sely womman chyde,
Forther than the storye wol devyse.
Hire name, allas, is punysshed so wide,   1095
That for hire gilt it oughte ynough suffise.
And if I myghte excuse hire any wise,
For she so sory was for hire untrouthe,
Iwis, I wolde excuse hire yit for routhe.

158

This Troilus, as I byfore have told,   1100
Thus driveth forth, as wel as he hath myght.
But often was his herte hoot and cold,
And namely that ilke nynthe nyght,
Which on the morwe she hadde hym bihight
To come ayeyn. God woot, ful litel reste   1105
Hadde he that nyght; nothyng to slepe hym leste.

159

The laurer-crowned Phebus, with his heete,
Gan, in his cours ay upward as he wente,
To warmen of the est see the wawes weete;
And Nysus doughter song with fressh entente,   1110
Whan Troilus his Pandare after sente;
And on the walles of the town they pleyde,
To loke if they kan sen aught of Criseyde.

1095. H2RCxPhTh publisshed.   1097. H2H4CxPhDTh in any wise.   1100. CpClJ
tolde.   1101. CpJ myghte.   1102. CpJ colde.   1103. Cp namly, J namelich; JGgH3
tenthe, R selven *for* nynthe.   1104. CpJ bihighte.   1108. GgH3 *om.* ay.   1109. GgCx
om. see.   1100. CxTh Cyrces *for* Nysus.   1111. GgA aftyr his pandarus, R had aftir
Pandar.

160

Tyl it was noon, they stoden for to se
Who that ther come; and every maner wight   1115
That com fro fer, they seyden it was she,
Til that thei koude knowen hym aright.
Now was his herte dul, now was it light;
And thus byjaped stonden for to stare
Aboute naught, this Troilus and Pandare.   1120

161

To Pandarus this Troilus tho seyde:
"For aught I woot, byfor noon, sikirly,
Into this town ne comth nat here Criseyde.
She hath ynough to doone, hardyly,
To wynnen from hire fader, so trowe I;   1125
Hire olde fader wol yit make hire dyne
Or that she go; god yeve his herte pyne!"

162

Pandare answerde: "it may wel be, certeyn;
And forthi lat us dyne, I the byseche;
And after noon than maystow come ayeyn."   1130
And hom they go, withoute more speche,
And comen ayeyn; but longe may they seche
Or that they fynde that they after gape;
Fortune hem bothe thenketh for to jape.

1123. αClH4R *om.* here. 1124. Cx ynough a doo there. 1125. ClDS1JH4R twynnen,
Gg wyndyn. 1132. H3Ph they may. 1133. CpClH1J cape.

163

Quod Troilus: "I se wel now that she   1135
Is taried with hire olde fader so,
That or she come, it wol neigh even be.
Com forth; I wol unto the yate go.
Thise porters ben unkonnyng evere mo;
And I wol don hem holden up the yate,   1140
As naught ne were, although she come late."

164

The day goth faste, and after that com eve,
And yit com nought to Troilus Criseyde.
He loketh forth by hegge, by tre, by greve,
And fer his hed over the wal he leyde.   1145
And at the laste he torned hym and seyde:
"By god, I woot hire menyng now, Pandare!
Almoost, ywys, al newe was my care.

165

"Now, douteles, this lady kan hire good;
I woot, she meneth riden pryvely.   1150
I comende hire wisdom, by myn hood.
She wol nat maken peple nycely
Gaure on hire, whan she comth; but softely
By nyght into the town she thenketh ride.
And, deere brother, thenk nat longe tabide.   1155

1138. CpJ wole.   1141. Gg ȝif þat sche.   1142. H1AH3PhGgH4R cometh, H2
comth.   1143. H3H2H4 cometh.   1144. GgH2H4 lokede.   1145. Cp hede, J hevede;
CpH1J walle.   1150. GgPhAH2H4 to ryde.   1152. JGgPhH2 nil; H2H4GgPh þe
people.   1153. CpClH1Th whan that.   1155. Cp thynke, J think.

166

"We han nat elles for to don, ywis.
And, Pandarus, now woltow trowen me?
Have here my trouthe, I se hire! yond she is!
Heve up thyn eyen, man! maistow nat se?"
Pandare answerde: "nay, so mote I the!   1160
Al wrong, by god; what seistow, man? where arte?
That I se yond nys but a fare-carte."

167

"Allas, thow seyst ful soth," quod Troilus;
"But, hardily, it is nat al for nought
That in myn herte I now rejoysse thus.   1165
It is ayeyns som good I have a thought.
Not I nat how, but syn that I was wrought,
Ne felte I swich a comfort, soth to seye;
She comth to-nyght, my lif that dorste I leye."

168

Pandare answerde: "it may be wel ynough,"   1170
And held with hym of al that evere he seyde;
But in his herte he thoughte, and softe lough,
And to hym self ful sobreliche he seyde:
"From haselwode, there joly Robyn pleyde,
Shal come al that that thow abidest heere;   1175
Ye, farewel al the snow of ferne yere!"

1159. R lo *for* man. 1161. Cp saistow; H2S1Th art. 1162. H1GgPh is. 1163. γ(-A)S1Th right soth. 1164. JH2 nys. 1167. JH3D But I not how. 1168. γ(-A)S1Th dar I seye. 1171. CpJ alle. 1175. CpH1H3PhGgH2CxTh *om. second* that; Cx doest abide. 1176. CpH1 snough, J snought, H3 froste; Cp farnyere, ClH1 fernyere, H2H4 feverer, DS1 feveryere, H3 fervere.

169

The wardeyn of the yates gan to calle
The folk which that withoute the yates were,
And bad hem dryven in hire bestes alle,
Or al the nyght they moste bleven there.　　1180
And fer withinne the nyght, with many a teere,
This Troilus gan homward for to ride;
For wel he seth it helpeth naught tabide.

170

But, natheles, he gladede hym in this:
He thoughte he misacounted hadde his day,　1185
And seyde: "I understonde have al amys;
For thilke nyght I last Criseyde say,
She seyde: 'I shal ben here, if that I may,
Or that the moone, O deere herte swete,
The Lyoun passe, out of this Ariete.'　　1190

171

"For which she may yit holde al hire byheste."
And on the morwe unto the yate he wente,
And up and down, by west and ek by este,
Upon the walles made he many a wente;
But al for nought; his hope alwey hym blente;　1195
For which at nyght, in sorwe and sikes sore,
He wente hym hom, withouten any more.

1185. H2H4 amys he compted had, Cx amys he had compted. 1186. JGgH3R *om.*
al. 1191. JPhCx *om.* al, R wel *for* al.

172

His hope al clene out of his herte fledde;
He nath wheron now lenger for to honge;
But for the peyne hym thoughte his herte bledde,   1200
So were his throwes sharpe and wonder stronge.
For whan he saugh that she abood so longe,
He nyste what he juggen of it myghte,
Syn she hath broken that she hym bihighte.

173

The thridde, ferthe, fifte, sixte day   1205
After tho dayes ten of which I tolde,
Bitwixen hope and drede his herte lay,
Yit somwhat trustyng on hire hestes olde.
But whan he saugh she nolde hire terme holde,
He kan now sen non other remedie,   1210
But for to shape hym soone for to dye.

174

Therwith the wikked spirit, god us blesse,
Which that men clepeth woode jalousie,
Gan in hym crepe, in al his hevynesse;
For which, by cause he wolde soone dye,   1215
He ne et ne drank, for his malencolye,
And ek from every compaignye he fledde;
This was the lif that al the tyme he ledde.

1199. GgAH4R no *for* now, H2 *om.* now; Cx no lenger now to.   1209. H4Ph termes.
1213. H3PhGgS1H2CxTh clepe; CpClDH3Ph the woode.   1214. γS1ThCx this *for* his.
1215. Gg For cause of which.   1218. JGgRCxTh this tyme.

175

He so defet was, that no maner man
Unnethe hym myghte knowen ther he wente; 1220
So was he lene, and therto pale and wan,
And feble that he walketh by potente;
And with his ire he thus hym selven shente.
But whoso axed hym wherof hym smerte,
He seyde his harm was al aboute his herte. 1225

176

Priam ful ofte, and ek his moder deere,
His bretheren and his sustren gonne hym freyne,
Whi he so sorwful was in al his cheere,
And what thyng was the cause of al his peyne.
But al for naught; he nolde his cause pleyne, 1230
But seyde he felte a grevous maladie
Aboute his herte, and fayn he wolde dye.

177

So on a day he leide hym down to slepe,
And so byfel that in his slepe hym thoughte,
That in a forest faste he welk to wepe 1235
For love of hire that hym this peyne wroughte;
And up and down as he the forest soughte,
He mette he say a boor with tuskes grete,
That slep ayein the bryghte sonnes heete;

1220. ClGgH3H4 myght hym; Cx Hym knowe mygght unnethe.   1222. H3PhGg AH2H4Cx walked.   1224. CpClJCx And *for* But; H3PhDH4RCx he *for* hym.   1228. CpH3GgH2H4 *om.* so.   1233-1274. Cp *omits six stanzas; text based on* JCl.   1234. JPhH2H4RCx he *for* hym.   1235. welk, *so* ClS1H3, JH1 welke, R wolke, PhD wente, GgAH2H4CxTh walkede.   1236. γS1ThR þese peynes.   1238. JH3PhH2H4Cx Hym mette (PhCx þoght).   1239. ClH1S1H2Th slepte, H4 slepyd.

178

And by this boor, faste in hire armes folde,   1240
Lay, kissynge ay, his lady bright, Criseyde.
For sorwe of which, whan he it gan biholde,
And for despit, out of his slep he breyde,
And loude he cried on Pandarus, and seyde:
"O Pandarus, now knowe I crop and roote.   1245
I nam but ded; ther nys non oother boote.

179

"My lady bright, Criseyde, hath me bytrayed,
In whom I trusted most of any wight;
She elliswhere hath now hire herte apayed.
The blisful goddes, thorugh hire grete myght,   1250
Han in my drem yshewed it ful right.
Thus in my drem Criseyde have I biholde:"—
And al this thing to Pandarus he tolde.

180

"O my Criseyde, allas, what subtilte,
What newe lust, what beaute, what science,   1255
What wraththe of juste cause han ye to me?
What gilt of me, what fel experience,
Hath fro me raft, allas, thyn advertence?
O trust, O feith, O depe aseurance,
Who hath me raft Criseyde, al my plesaunce?   1260

1240. ClH4 his *for* hire, H3PhH2Cx *om.* hire.   1246. GgPhDH4Cx am; H1GgH2 is.   1252. ClAH3R I have.   1253. S1 al his dreme.   1254. subtilte, *so* ClS1PhH2Th, *rest* subtilite.   1258. GgH2H4Cx 3oure, Ph myn *for* thyn.   1260. JClH1 reft.

181

"Allas, why let I yow from hennes go,
For which wel neigh out of my wit I breyde?
Who shal now trowe on any oothes mo?
God wot, I wende, O lady bright, Criseyde,
That every word was gospel that ye seyde!   1265
But who may bet bigile, if hym liste,
Than he on whom men weneth best to triste?

182

"What shal I don, my Pandarus, allas?
I fele now so sharp a newe peyne,
Syn that ther lith no remedy in this cas,   1270
That bet were it I with myn hondes tweyne
My selven slow alwey, than thus to pleyne.
For thorugh the deth my wo sholde have an ende,
Ther every day with lif my self I shende."

183

Pandare answerde and seyde: "allas, the while   1275
That I was born! Have I nat seyd or this,
That dremes many a maner man bygile?
And whi? for folk expounden hem amys.
How darstow seyn that fals thy lady is
For any drem, right for thyn owene drede?   1280
Lat be this thought; thow kanst no dremes rede.

1266. H3PhDS1 if that. 1267. GgPhS1H2H4RCxTh wenyn. 1270. γS1Th is *for*
lith. 1272. H4GgCx than thus alwey, H3Th than alwey thus. 1276. CpH1J seyde.

184

"Paraunter, ther thow dremest of this boor,
It may so be that it may signifie,
Hire fader, which that old is and ek hoor,
Ayeyn the sonne lith in poynt to dye,   1285
And she for sorwe gynneth wepe and crie,
And kisseth hym, ther he lith on the grounde;
Thus sholdestow thi dremes right expounde."

185

"How myghte I than don," quod Troilus,
"To knowe of this, ye, were it nevere so lite?"   1290
"Now seystow wisly," quod this Pandarus;
"My red is this: syn thow kanst wel endite,
That hastily a lettre thow hire write,
Thorugh which thow shalt wel bryngen it aboute,
To knowe a soth, ther thow art now in doute.   1295

186

"And se now whi: for this, I dar wel seyn,
That if so is that she untrewe be,
I kan nat trowen that she wol write ayeyn.
And if she write, thow shalt ful sone se,
As wheither she hath any liberte   1300
To come ayeyn, or ellis in som clause,
If she be let, she wol assigne a cause.

1285. CpClH1A o, GgD a, Th on, J up *for* in. 1288. CpClH1S1H3Th dreme;
γS1ThH3Gg aright. 1289. GgH4 þanne. 1295. γS1ThH3 of that thow art in doute
(H3 of wych); JCx *om.* now. 1298. JGgH3RCx *om.* that. 1299. GgDH2H4RCx
om. ful, H3 ryght, Ph wel *for* ful.

187

"Thow hast nat writen hire syn that she wente,
Nor she to the; and this I dorste leye:
Ther may swich cause ben in hire entente,   1305
That hardily thow wolt thi selven seye,
That hire abood the best is for yow tweye.
Now write hir thanne, and thow shalt feele sone
A soth of al; ther is no more to done."

188

Acorded ben to this conclusioun,   1310
And that anon, thise ilke lordes two;
And hastily sit Troilus adown,
And rolleth in his herte to and fro,
How he may best discryven hire his wo.
And to Criseyde, his owen lady deere,   1315
He wrot right thus, and seyde as ye shal here:

189

"Right fresshe flour, whos I ben have and shal,   LITERA
Withouten part of elleswhere servyse,   TROILI
With herte, body, lif, lust, thought, and al,
I, woful wyght, in everich humble wise   1320
That tonge telle or herte may devyse,
As ofte as matere occupieth place,
Me recomaunde unto youre noble grace.

1303. GgPhH2H4CxTh to hyre; H3H4RCx *om.* that.   1304. GgPhH2H4RCx Ne.
1308. GgH4 to hire.   1309. JH3H2R nys.   1316. γS1ThH3H2 may *for* shal.   1317.
GgPhDH2CxTh have ben.   1321. S1CxTh can telle, H2H4 telle can *for* telle.

190

"Liketh yow to witen, swete herte,
As ye wel knowe, how longe tyme agon   1325
That ye me lefte in aspre peynes smerte,
Whan that ye wente, of which yit boote non
Have I non had; but evere wors bigon
Fro day to day am I, and so mot dwelle,
While it yow list, of wele and wo my welle.   1330

191

"For which to yow, with dredful herte trewe,
I write, as he that sorwe drifth to write,
My wo, that everich houre encresseth newe,
Compleynyng as I dar or kan endite.
And that defaced is, that may ye wite   1335
The teris, which that fro myn eyen reyne,
That wolden speke, if that they koude, and pleyne.

192

"Yow first biseche I, that youre eyen clere
To loke on this defouled ye nat holde,
And, over al this, that ye, my lady deere,   1340
Wol vouchesauf this lettre to byholde.
And by the cause ek of my cares colde,
That sleth my wit, if aught amys masterte,
Foryeve it me, myn owen swete herte.

1324. ClGgTh Likith it yow, H4 Lyke it you, H3 And like it you, R Like hyt to
yow myn owne sweete herte. 1328. H3S1 yit *for* non; R Ne han y had; D *om.*
non had. 1329. H3Ph I am, Gg lyn *for* am I. 1334. GgH3 can or dar (H3 and).
1337. H4RCx *om. second* that; GgH2H4RCx *om.* and; Cx compleyne; Ph That if
þei couþe speke þei wold pleyne. 1340. CpJ overe; PhH2H4R *om.* al.

193

"If any servant dorste or oughte of right   1345
Upon his lady pitously compleyne,
Than wene I that ich oughte ben that wight,
Considered this, that ye thise monthes tweyne
Han taried, ther ye seyden, soth to seyne,
But dayes ten ye nolde in oost sojourne;   1350
But in two monthes yit ye nat retourne.

194

"But for as muche as me moot nedes like
Al that yow list, I dar nat pleyne moore;
But humblely, with sorwful sikes sike,
Yow write ich myn unresty sorwes soore,   1355
Fro day to day desiryng evere moore
To knowen fully, if youre wille it were,
How ye han ferd and don, whil ye be there;

195

"The whos welfare and hele ek god encresse
In honour swich, that upward in degree   1360
It growe alwey, so that it nevere cesse.
Right as youre herte ay kan, my lady free,
Devyse, I prey to god so moot it be;
And graunte it, that ye soone upon me rewe,
As wisly as in al I am yow trewe.   1365

1345-1428. *Twelve stanzas missing in* H1; *leaf lost.* 1354. humblely, *so* J, Cl humbely, GgS1 humili, *rest* humbly. 1355. ich, *so* CpClS1J, *rest* I. 1362. H3DH2 can ay, Cx best can, Ph. *om.* ay. 1364. JH4RCx *om.* it. 1365. αADH2H4 to yow (H3 unto).

196

"And if yow liketh knowen of the fare
Of me, whos wo ther may no wight discryve,
I kan no more, but, chiste of every care,
At wrytyng of this lettre I was on lyve,
Al redy out my woful gost to dryve;   1370
Which I delaye, and holde hym yit in honde,
Upon the sighte of matere of youre sonde.

197

"Myn eyen two, in veyn with which I se,
Of sorwful teris salte arn woxen welles;
My song, in pleynte of myn adversitee;   1375
My good, in harm; myn ese ek woxen helle is.
My joie, in wo; I kan sey yow naught ellis;
But torned is, for which my lif I warie,
Everich joie or ese in his contrarie.

198

"Which with youre comynge hom ayeyn to Troie   1380
Ye may redresse, and more a thousand sithe
Than evere ich hadde, encressen in me joie.
For was ther nevere herte yit so blithe
To han his lif, as I shal ben as swithe
As I yow se; and, though no maner routhe   1385
Commeve yow, yit thynketh on youre trouthe.

1366. H3 it lyke you; H3PhGgDH2H4Cx to know. 1367. CpS1J wit, H4 man *for* wight. 1368. H3GgH2H4CxTh cheste, A trist. 1380. CpJ home. 1382. H3PhDH2 my *for* me. 1386. J Commove, H3 Come in, D Comen, A Comune, CxTh Can meve, Gg Remeve, H2H4 Remorde, Ph Meve.

199

"And if so be my gilt hath deth deserved,
Or if yow list no more upon me se,
In guerdoun yit of that I have yow served,
Byseche I yow, myn hertes lady free,   1390
That hereupon ye wolden write me,
For love of god, my righte lode-sterre,
That deth may make an ende of al my werre.

200

"If other cause aught doth yow for to dwelle,
That with youre lettre ye me recomforte;   1395
For though to me youre absence is an helle,
With pacience I wol my wo comporte,
And with youre lettre of hope I wol desporte.
Now writeth, swete, and lat me thus nat pleyne;
With hope, or deth, delivereth me fro peyne.   1400

201

"Iwis, myn owene deere herte trewe,
I woot that, whan ye next upon me se,
So lost have I myn hele and ek myn hewe,
Criseyde shal nat konne knowen me.
Iwys, myn hertes day, my lady free,   1405
So thursteth ay myn herte to byholde
Youre beaute, that my lif unnethe I holde.

1390. γ(-Cl)S1ThH3 owen *for* hertes. 1391. GgH4D to me. 1392. righte, *so*
ClGg, *rest* right. 1394. JH4R do. 1396. GgRCx be. 1397. H3H4Th conforte, **Cx**
supporte. 1407. H3PhA unnethe my lyf.

202

"I sey no more, al have I for to seye
To yow wel more than I telle may;
But wheither that ye do me lyve or deye,   1410
Yit prey I god, so yeve yow right good day.
And fareth wel, goodly, faire, fresshe may,
As she that lif or'deth me may comande;
And to youre trouthe ay I me recomande

203

"With hele swich that, but ye yeven me   1415
The same hele, I shal non hele have.
In yow lith, whan yow list that it so be,
The day on which me clothen shal my grave.
In yow my lif, in yow myght for to save
Me fro disese of alle peynes smerte!   1420
And fare now wel, myn owen swete herte!
         Le vostre T."

204

This lettre forth was sent unto Criseyde,
Of which hire answere in effect was this:
Ful pitously she wroot ayeyn, and seyde,
That also sone as that she myghte, ywys,   1425
She wolde come, and mende al that was mys.
And fynaly she wroot, and seyde hym thanne,
She wolde come, ye, but she nyste whanne.

1408. CpJ namore. 1412. GgPhH4 farwel. 1413. γS1ThCx ye *for* she. 1418. γS1Th
in *for* on. 1419. Ph is might to save. 1421. Cp far, GgS1 fareþ; Le vostre T, *so*
CpJTh, S1 Le vostre Troilus, H4 Finis littere troili, *rest omit.* 1425. H3PhADH4
RTh *om.* that, Cx ever *for* that. 1426. H3PhCx *om.* al; GgH3H2RCxTh amys.

205

But in hire lettre made she swich festes,
That wonder was, and swerth she loveth hym best; 1430
Of which he fond but botmeles bihestes.
But, Troilus, thow maist now, est or west,
Pipe in an ivy lef, if that the lest.
Thus goth the world; god shilde us fro meschaunce,
And every wight that meneth trouthe avaunce! 1435

206

Encressen gan the wo fro day to nyght
Of Troilus for tarying of Criseyde;
And lessen gan his hope and ek his myght,
For which al down he in his bed hym leyde;
He ne eet, ne dronk, ne slep, ne no word seyde, 1440
Ymagynyng ay that she was unkynde;
For which wel neigh he wex out of his mynde.

207

This drem, of which I told have ek byforn,
May nevere come out of his remembraunce;
He thoughte ay wel he hadde his lady lorn, 1445
And that Joves, of his purveyaunce,
Hym shewed hadde in slep the signifiaunce
Of hire untrouthe and his disaventure,
And that this boor was shewed hym in figure.

1430. PhDRCxTh swore, Iovid. 1432. H2RS1Th & *for* or. 1438. JH3PhH2Cx lassen, R lissen. 1440. H2S1Th slepte; ne no word seyde, *so* H4RCx, H3 ne worde ne seyde, Gg He net ne drank ne no word he ne seyde, *rest om.* no. 1443. CpH1J tolde. 1445. thoughte, *so* Gg, H3 thynketh, *rest* thought. 1446. JGgPhH4F3 And þat that Joves. 1449. γS1ThH3 the *for* this.

208

For which he for Sibille his suster sente,   1450
That called was Cassandre ek al aboute;
And al his drem he tolde hire or he stente,
And hire bisoughte assoilen hym the doute
Of the stronge boor with tuskes stoute;
And fynaly, withinne a litel stounde,   1455
Cassandre hym gan right thus his drem expounde.

209

She gan first smyle, and seyde: "O brother deere,
If thow a soth of this desirest knowe,
Thow most a fewe of olde stories heere,
To purpos how that Fortune overthrowe   1460
Hath lordes olde; thorugh which, withinne a throwe,
Thow wel this boor shalt knowe, and of what kynde
He comen is, as men in bokes fynde.

210

"Diane, which that wroth was and in ire
For Grekis nolde don hire sacrifise,   1465
Ne encens upon hire auter sette afire,
She, for that Grekis gonne hire so despise,
Wrak hire in a wonder cruel wise;
For with a boor, as gret as oxe in stalle,
She made up frete hire corn and vynes alle.   1470

1453. GgA to asoylyn, H4 tassoilen. 1454. H3GgS1 with hys tuskes. 1458. GgPh
ACxTh to knowe, H4 forto knowe. 1461. H4H2RCx hie *for* olde; PhRCx *om.*
thorugh; H3 *omits line.* 1466. H1H3R Nencens.

211

"To sle this boor was al the contre reysed,
Amonges which ther com, this boor to se,
A mayde, oon of this world the best ypreysed;
And Meleagre, lord of that contree,
He loved so this fresshe mayde free,   1475
That with his manhod, or he wolde stente,
This boor he slough, and hire the hed he sente;

212

"Of which, as olde bokes tellen us,
Ther ros a contek and a gret envye;
And of this lord descended Tideus   1480
By ligne, or ellis olde bookes lye;
But how this Meleagre gan to dye
Thorugh his moder, wol I yow nat telle,
For al to longe it were for to dwelle."

213

She tolde ek how Tideus, or she stente,   1485
Unto the stronge citee of Thebes,
To cleymen kyngdom of the citee, wente,
For his felawe, daun Polymytes,
Of which the brother, daun Ethiocles,
Ful wrongfully of Thebes held the strengthe;   1490
This tolde she by proces al by lengthe.

1472. CpRTh Amonge, GgPhDH4 Among.   1475. CpHiPhRTh mayden.   1479.
H3PhGgH2R *om. second* a.   1484. Gg for us to, R for you to.   1485. PhR he *for
second* she.

214

She tolde ek how Hemonydes asterte,
Whan Tideus slough fifty knyghtes stoute.
She tolde ek alle the prophecyes by herte,
And how that seven kynges, with hire route,   1495
Bysegeden the citee al aboute;
And of the holy serpent and the welle,
And of the Furies, al she gan hym telle;

215

Of Archymoris burying and the pleyes,
And how Amphiorax fil thorugh the grounde;   1500
How Tideus was slayn, lord of Argeyes,
And how Ypomedon in litel stounde
Was dreynt, and ded Parthonope of wownde;
And also how Cappaneus, the proude,
With thonder dynt was slayn, that cride loude.   1505

216

She gan ek telle hym how that eyther brother,
Ethiocles and Polymyte also,
At a scarmuche ech of hem slough oother,
And of Argyves wepynge and hire wo;
And how the town was brent, she tolde ek tho,   1510
And so descendeth down fro gestes olde
To Diomede, and thus she spak and tolde:

1494. Gg al þe profecy. 1495. H3R knyghtes. *Between* 1498 *and* 1499 *all MSS. except* H4R *have the following verses which summarize the* Thebais *of Statius:*

    Associat profugum Tideo primus Polymytem;
    Tidea legatum docet insidiasque secundus:
    Tercius Hemoduden canit et vates latitantes;
    Quartus habet reges ineuntes prelia septem;
    Mox furie Lenne quinto narratur et anguis;   (5)
    Archimori bustum sexto ludique leguntur;
    Dat Graios Thebes et vatem septimus umbris;
    Octavo cecidit Tideus, spes, vita Pelasgis;
    Ypomedon nono moritur cum Parthenopea;
    Fulmine percussus, decimo Cappaneus superatur;   (10)
    Undecimo sese perimunt per vulnera fratres;
    Argiva flentem narrat duodenus et ignem.

(1. A (*Corrector in margin*) Polynicem. 3. A (*Corrector*) harmoniam. 5. A (*Cor-*

217

"This ilke boor bitokneth Diomede,
Tideus sone, that down descended is
Fro Meleagre, that made the boor to blede.   1515
And thy lady, wher she be, ywis,
This Diomede hire herte hath, and she his.
Wepe if thow wolt, or lef; for, out of doute,
This Diomede is inne, and thow art oute."

218

"Thow seyst nat soth," quod he, "thow sorceresse, 1520
With al thy false goost of prophecye!
Thow wenest ben a gret devyneresse;
Now sestow nat this fool of fantasie
Peyneth hire on ladys for to lye?
Awey," quod he, "ther Joves yeve the sorwe!   1525
Thow shalt be fals, paraunter, yit to-morwe!

219

"As wel thow myghtest lyen on Alceste,
That was of creatures, but men lye,
That evere weren, kyndest and the beste.
For whan hire housbonde was in jupartye   1530
To dye hym self, but if she wolde dye,
She ches for hym to dye and gon to helle,
And starf anon, as us the bokes telle."

---

rector) lemniadum furiae ; H1Th narrantur. 6. Cp Archymory, J Archemori. 7. A
(Corrector) dat Thebis vatem graiorum septimus umbris. 12. H2 *has unique addi-
tional line:* Fervidus ypomedon timidique in gurgite mersus.) 1499. ClH1J burynge,
DGg brennynge. 1502. CpTh a, H4Cx in a, Cl y *for* in; JGg with blody wownde.
1503. Cp dede; JGg And ek Parthonope in litel stownde (Gg *om.* ek). 1504. JGg
Ben slayn and how, H3 And eke how kynge, Ph She told eke how. 1507. PhTh
Polymytes. 1508. ClH1 scarmych, H3PhH2H4Th scarmyssh, R scyrmysshyng. 1510.
GgPh hym þo. 1511. H2H4RCxTh descended.
     1516. CpH1S2S1ThGgR wherso, ClCx wher þat *for* wher. 1521. false, *so* GgH2Th,
rest fals. 1522. GgPhAH2H4RCx to be. 1526. GgPh er *for* yit. 1529. GgPhH4Cx
þe kyndest. 1532. JGg She ches to dye and ek to gon (Gg deþ *for* to dye), Ph & eke
go.

220

Cassandre goth; and he with cruel herte
Foryat his wo, for angre of hire speche;   1535
And from his bed al sodeynly he sterte,
As though al hool hym hadde made a leche.
And day by day he gan enquere and seche
A sooth of this, with al his fulle cure;
And thus he drieth forth his aventure.   1540

221

Fortune, which that permutacioun
Of thynges hath, as it is hire committed
By purveyaunce and disposicioun
Of heigh Jove, as regnes shal be flitted
Fro folk in folk, or whan they shal ben smytted, 1545
Gan pulle awey the fetheres brighte of Troie
Fro day to day, til they ben bare of joie.

222

Among al this the fyn of the parodie
Of Ector gan aprochen wonder blyve;
The fate wolde his soule sholde unbodye,   1550
And shapen hadde a mene it out to dryve;
Ayeyns which fate hym helpeth nat to stryve;
But on a day to fighten gan he wende,
At which, allas, he kaughte his lyves ende.

1537. CpH1S1H2Th ymad. 1539. fulle, *so* ClS1Gg, R foule, Cx besy, *rest* ful.
1540. H3GgS1H2RCxTh dryveth, H4 dryved. 1541-1750. *Missing in* A; *three leaves
lost.* 1543. γS1Th Thorugh *for* By. 1544. H3 Juves, Ph Jovis.

223

For which me thynketh every maner wight   1555
That haunteth armes oughte to biwaille
The deth of hym that was so noble a knyght;
For as he drough a kyng by thaventaille,
Unwar of this, Achilles thorugh the maille,
And thorugh the body, gan hym for to ryve;   1560
And thus this worthi knyght was brought of lyve.

224

For whom, as olde bokes tellen us,
Was made swich wo, that tonge it may nat telle;
And namely the sorwe of Troilus,
That next hym was of worthynesse welle.   1565
And in this wo gan Troilus to dwelle,
That, what for sorwe and love, and for unreste,
Ful ofte a day he bad his herte breste.

225

But, natheles, though he gan hym dispeire,
And dradde ay that his lady was untrewe,   1570
Yit ay on hire his herte gan repeire.
And as thise loveres don, he soughte ay newe
To gete ayeyn Criseyde, bright of hewe.
And in his herte he wente hire excusynge,
That Calkas caused al hire taryinge.   1575

1561. CpH1S2H4Th the, RCx that *for* this. 1565. H3GgS1RTh the welle. 1570.
dradde, *so* CpCl, D drad, H3H4S1Th dredde, PhRCx dred, JGgH1S2H2 drede; α
om. ay.

226

And ofte tyme he was in purpos grete
Hym selven lik a pilgrym to degise,
To seen hire; but he may nat contrefete
To ben unknowen of folk that weren wise,
Ne fynde excuse aright that may suffise,   1580
If he among the Grekis knowen were;
For which he wep ful ofte and many a tere.

227

To hire he wroot yit ofte tyme al newe
Ful pitously,—he lefte it nat for slouthe,—
Bisechyng hire that, syn that he was trewe,   1585
That she wol come ayeyn and holde hire trouthe.
For which Criseyde upon a day, for routhe,—
I take it so,—touchyng al this matere
Wrot hym ayeyn, and seyde as ye may here: 1589

228

"Cupides sone, ensample of goodlihede,   LITERA
O swerd of knyghthod, sours of gentilesse!   CRISEYDIS
How myght a wight in torment and in drede,
And heleles, yow sende as yit gladnesse?
I herteles, I sik, I in destresse,
Syn ye with me, nor I with yow, may dele,   1595
Yow neyther sende ich herte may nor hele.

1582. and, *so* CpH1JH3Ph, *rest om.* 1583. H3Gg ful *for* yit. 1585. γS1Th *om.*
first that; H3H4Cx *om* *second* that (H3 sithen, H4 sithe). 1586. H3PhGgClH2H4
RCx wolde. 1591. Cp. knyghthode, J knyghthede.

229

"Youre lettres ful, the papir al ypleynted,
Conceyved hath myn hertes pietee;
I have ek seyn with teris al depeynted
Youre lettre, and how that ye requeren me   1600
To come ayeyn, which yit ne may nat be.
But whi, lest that this lettre founden were,
No mencioun ne make I now, for feere.

230

"Grevous to me, god woot, is youre unreste,
Youre haste; and that, the goddes ordinaunce,   1605
It semeth nat ye take it for the beste.
Nor other thyng nys in youre remembraunce,
As thynketh me, but only youre plesaunce.
But beth nat wroth, and that I yow biseche;
For that I tarie is al for wikked speche.   1610

231

"For I have herd wel moore than I wende,
Touchyng us two, how thynges han ystonde;
Which I shal with dissimulynge amende.
And, beth nat wroth, I have ek understonde,
How ye ne don but holden me in honde.   1615
But now no fors, I kan nat in yow gesse
But alle trouthe and alle gentilesse.

1598. pietee, *so* CpS1J, GgS2 pete, *rest* pite.   1601. CIDS2GgPhH2H4RCx *om.* ne;
GgH4 may not ȝet be.   1602. Cp list, H1 liste, J last.   1603. H3PhGgH4Cx *om.* ne.
1607. GgPhR is, Cl nys not, S2 is nought.   1617. H3 and eke all, Cx ever and al.

232

"Come I wol; but yit in swich disjoynte
I stonde as now, that what yer, or what day,
That this shal be, that kan I naught apoynte.   1620
But in effect I preye yow, as I may,
Of youre good word and of youre frendship ay;
For trewely, whil that my lif may dure,
As for a frend ye may in me assure.

233

"Yit preye ich yow, on yvel ye ne take   1625
That it is short, which that I to yow write;
I dar nat, ther I am, wel lettres make,
Ne nevere yit ne koude I wel endite.
Ek grete effect men write in place lite.
Thentente is al, and nat the lettres space;   1630
And fareth now wel, god have yow in his grace!
                    La vostre C."

234

This Troilus this lettre thoughte al straunge,
Whan he it saugh, and sorwfully he sighte;
Hym thoughte it lik a kalendes of chaunge.
But, fynaly, he ful ne trowen myghte,   1635
That she ne wolde hym holden that she hyghte;
For with ful yvel wil list hym to leve
That loveth wel, in swich cas, though hym greve.

1618. R Comen; CpClH1J wole, Gg wolde.   1628. CpDS2S1JH3H2Cx *om. second
ne.*   1629. GgPh space, H4D places.   1631. La vostre C, *so* H1DS1Th, S2 La voustre
Criseide, H4 Finis littere Cress., *rest omit.*   1636. GgDH4Cx holde hym.   1638. CpJ
swiche.

235

But, natheles, men seyn that at the laste,
For any thyng, men shal the sothe se;   1640
And swich a cas bitidde, and that as faste,
That Troilus wel understod that she
Nas nat so kynde as that hire oughte be.
And fynaly he woot now, out of doute,
That al is lost that he hath ben aboute.   1645

236

Stood on a day in his malencolie
This Troilus, and in suspecioun
Of hire for whom he wende for to dye.
And so bifel that thorughout Troye town,
As was the gise, iborn was up and down   1650
A maner cote armure, as seith the storie,
Byforn Deiphebe, in signe of his victorie;

237

The whiche cote, as telleth Lollius,
Deiphebe it hadde irent fro Diomede
The same day; and whan this Troilus   1655
It saugh, he gan to taken of it hede,
Avysyng of the lengthe and of the brede,
And al the werk; but as he gan byholde,
Ful sodeynly his herte gan to colde,

1639. Cp seyen, JH4 seith; H3Gg *om.* that. 1642. CpJ understode. 1643. PhH2
H4RCx *om.* that; H3PhGgS1H4Cx to bee. 1644. JPh now wot. 1645. ClDH3 gon *for*
ben. 1649. H3PhGgH2H4Cx thorogh (*om.* out). 1652. PhH2H4RCx *om.* his. 1653.
ClH1R which; R bollius, GgCx lollyus.

238

As he that on the coler fond withinne   1660
A broche, that he Criseyde yaf that morwe
That she from Troie moste nedes twynne,
In remembraunce of hym and of his sorwe;
And she hym leyde ayeyn hire feith to borwe
To kepe it ay; but now ful wel he wiste,   1665
His lady nas no lenger on to triste.

239

He goth hym hom, and gan ful soone sende
For Pandarus; and al this newe chaunce,
And of this broche, he tolde hym word and ende,
Compleynyng of hire hertes variaunce,   1670
His longe love, his trouthe, and his penaunce;
And after deth, withouten wordes moore,
Ful faste he cride, his reste hym to restore.

240

Than spak he thus: "O lady bright, Criseyde,
Where is youre feith, and where is youre biheste? 1675
Where is youre love, where is youre trouthe?" he seyde;
"Of Diomede have ye now al this feeste?
Allas, I wolde han trowed at the leeste,
That, syn ye nolde in trouthe to me stonde,
That ye thus nolde han holden me in honde.   1680

1666. JGgPhDH4 was, H3 vas.   1669. CpJ worde.   1674. γS1ThH3 myn *for* bright.

241

"Who shal now trowe on any othes mo?
Allas, I nevere wolde han wend or this,
That ye, Criseyde, koude han chaunged so;
Ne, but I hadde agilt and don amys,
So cruel wende I nat youre herte, ywis,   1685
To sle me thus; allas, youre name of trouthe
Is now fordon, and that is al my routhe

242

"Was ther non other broche yow liste lete
To feffe with youre newe love," quod he,
"But thilke broche that I, with teris wete,   1690
Yow yaf, as for a remembraunce of me?
Non other cause, allas, ne hadde ye
But for despit, and ek for that ye mente
Al outrely to shewen youre entente.

243

"Thorugh which I se that clene out of youre mynde
Ye han me cast; and I ne kan nor may,   1696
For al this world, withinne myn herte fynde
To unloven yow a quarter of a day!
In corsed tyme I born was, weilaway!
That yow, that doon me al this wo endure,   1700
Yit love I best of any creature.

1682. H3H2H4Cx wolde never, J noldde nevere, Ph *om*. nevere; CpH1J wende.
1684. ClDS1H2H4Cx or *for* and. 1690. CpH1J thilk broch. 1696. CpH1J caste;
GgPhH2RCx ne *for* nor. 1697. H2DS1CxTh within. 1700. ClH3PhGgH2RCx ye *for*
yow.

244

"Now god," quod he, "me sende yit the grace
That I may meten with this Diomede!
And, trewely, if I have myght and space,
Yit shal I make, I hope, his sydes blede.   1705
O god," quod he, "that oughtest taken heede
To fortheren trouthe, and wronges to punyce,
Whi nyltow don a vengeaunce of this vice?

245

"O Pandare, that in dremes for to triste
Me blamed hast, and wont art ofte upbreyde,   1710
Now maistow se thi self, if that the liste,
How trewe is now thi nece, bright Criseyde!
In sondry formes, god it woot," he seyde,
"The goddes shewen bothe joie and tene
In slep, and by my drem it is now sene.   1715

246

"And certeynly, withoute moore speche,
From hennesforth, as ferforth as I may,
Myn owen deth in armes wol I seche;
I recche nat how soohe be the day.
But, trewely, Criseyde, swete may,   1720
Whom I have ay with al my myght yserved,
That ye thus doon, I have it nat deserved."

1702-1869. *Missing in* Gg; *five leaves lost.* 1702. H4RPhCx yit sende me, H2 so
sende me yet; H4DS2Cx that, H3R thy *for* the, H2 *om.* the. 1708. ClS1PhH2H4 on
for of. 1709. γTh Pandarus.

247

This Pandarus, that al thise thynges herde,
And wiste wel he seyde a soth of this,
He nat a word ayeyn to hym answerde;   1725
For sory of his frendes sorwe he is,
And shamed for his nece hath don amys,
And stant astoned of thise causes tweye,
As stille as ston; a word ne koude he seye.

248

But at the laste thus he spak, and seyde: 1730
"My brother deere, I may do the no more.
What sholde I seyn? I hate, ywys, Criseyde!
And, god woot, I wol hate hire evere more!
And that thow me bisoughtest don of yoore,
Havyng unto myn honour ne my reste   1735
Right no reward, I dide al that the leste.

249

"If I dide aught that myghte liken the,
It is me lief; and of this tresoun now,
God woot, that it a sorwe is unto me!
And, dredeles, for hertes ese of yow,   1740
Right fayn I wolde amende it, wiste I how.
And fro this world, almyghty god I preye,
Delivere hire soone; I kan no more seye."

1729. H4R no woord ne. 1732. Cp seyen, J seye. 1736. Ph right as *for* al that;
S1 al for the beste. 1741. ClDRCx wolde I; J amende it wold I; Ph y were to
mende it. 1743. J me *for* hire.

250

Gret was the sorwe and pleynte of Troilus;
But forth hire cours Fortune ay gan to holde.　　　1745
Criseyde loveth the sone of Tideus;
And Troilus moot wepe in cares colde.
Swich is this world, whoso it kan byholde;
In ech estat is litel hertes reste;
God leve us for to take it for the beste!　　　1750

251

In many cruel bataille, out of drede,
Of Troilus, this ilke noble knyght,
As men may in thise olde bokes rede,
Was seen his kynghthod and his grete myght.
And, dredeles, his ire, day and nyght,　　　1755
Ful cruely the Grekis ay aboughte;
And alwey moost this Diomede he soughte.

252

And ofte tyme, I fynde that they mette
With blody strokes and with wordes grete,
Assayinge how hire speres weren whette;　　　1760
And, god it woot, with many a cruel hete
Gan Troilus upon his helm to bete.
But, natheles, Fortune it naught ne wolde,
Of otheres hond that eyther deyen sholde.

1745. H3PhD ay fortune.　1746. H2H4R loved.　1748. H3PhRCx the *for* this.　1749.
JPh That in ich estat, H3 That in suche thinge.　1751. S1RS2 many a.　1761. H3PhCx
om. it; JH3 *om.* a　1764. Cp oothers, J oothris.

253

And if I hadde ytaken for to write 1765
The armes of this ilke worthi man,
Than wolde ich of his batailles endite.
But for that I to writen first bigan
Of his love, I have seyd as I kan,—
His worthi dedes, whoso list hem heere, 1770
Rede Dares, he kan telle hem alle ifeere.—

254

Bysechyng every lady bright of hewe,
And every gentil womman, what she be,
That, al be that Criseyde was untrewe,
That for that gilt ye be nat wroth with me. 1775
Ye may hire gilt in other bokes se;
And gladlier I wol write, if yow leste,
Penelopes trouthe and good Alceste.

255

Ny sey nat this al oonly for thise men,
But moost for wommen that bitraised be 1780
Thorugh fals folk; god yeve hem sorwe, amen!
That with hire grete wit and subtilite
Bytraise yow! And this commeveth me
To speke, and in effect yow alle I preye,
Beth war of men, and herkneth what I seye. 1785

1769. S1 loving; CpH1J seyde; H2 that *for* as. 1775. γS1R she *for* ye. 1777.
H2H4CxS2 wolde. 1778. ClS1H2 Penelopees. 1779. Ny, *so* JH1S1R, CpD Ne, H3 Ne
sey I, *rest* Ne I sey. 1780. H3S2DH4RCxTh betrayed. 1781. ClH2R false. 1782.
ClADH3PhH2Th subtiltee. 1783. H3Cx Betrayeth, H4 Betrayes, Th Betrayen.

256

Go, litel book, go, litel myn tragedye,
Ther god thi makere yit, or that he dye,
So sende myght to make in som comedye!
But, litel book, no makyng thow nenvie,
But subgit be to alle poesie;   1790
And kis the steppes, where as thow seest space
Virgile, Ovide, Omer, Lucan, and Stace.

257

And for ther is so gret diversite
In Englissh, and in writyng of oure tonge,
So prey I god that non myswrite the,   1795
Ne the mysmetre for defaute of tonge.
And red wherso thow be, or elles songe,
That thow be understonde, god I biseche.—
But yit to purpos of my rather speche.

258

The wraththe, as I bigan yow for to seye,   1800
Of Troilus, the Grekis boughten deere;
For thousandes his hondes maden deye,
As he that was withouten any peere,
Save Ector, in his tyme, as I kan heere.
But, weilawey, save only goddes wille!   1805
Ful pitously hym slough the fierse Achille.

1789. H3PhCxTh make thow noon envie (H3 causink *for* make thow; Ph ne make
þow). 1790. RCx be thow, H4 be thou ever. 1791. ClPhH4Th pace. 1792. ADS1CxTh
Of Virgil (A O *for* Of); H2R of *for* and. 1795. αCx So prey to god, CpH1S2H2
H4Th So prey I to god, A Go praye thi god. 1798. CpClAJ *om.* I; R I god byseche.
1800. CpH1 wrath, J wrechche. 1802. CpJ hise, Cl hese. 1806. γS1ThCx Dispitously
(*om.* Ful).

259

And whan that he was slayn in this manere,
His lighte goost ful blisfully is went
Up to the holughnesse of the eighte spere,
In convers letyng everich element.   1810
And ther he saugh, with ful avysement,
The erratik sterres, herkenyng armonye
With sownes ful of hevenyssh melodie.

260

And down from thennes faste he gan avyse
This litel spot of erthe, that with the se   1815
Enbraced is, and fully gan despise
This wrecched world, and held al vanite
To respect of the pleyn felicite
That is in hevene above; and at the laste,
Ther he was slayn, his lokyng down he caste.   1820

261

And in hym self he lough right at the wo
Of hem that wepten for his deth so faste,
And dampned al oure werk that folweth so
The blynde lust, the which that may nat laste;
And sholden al oure herte on heven caste.   1825
And forth he wente, shortly for to telle,
Ther as Mercurye sorted hym to dwelle.

1807-1827. H2H4Ph *omit three stanzas*; Ph *adds them later on inset leaf.* 1809.
J holwenesse, H3ACxTh holownesse, R halghnes, Ph hynesse; J viij, R viijthe, Cx
eyght; *rest* seventhe. 1817. PhCx it *for* al. 1821-1869. *Missing in* A; *leaf lost.*
1822. JPhDCx wepen.

262

Swich fyn hath, lo, this Troilus for love!
Swich fyn hath al his grete worthynesse!
Swich fyn hath his estat real above!   1830
Swich fyn his lust! swich fyn hath his noblesse!
Swych fyn hath false worldes brotelnesse!
And thus bigan his lovyng of Criseyde,
As I have told, and in this wise he deyde.

263

O yonge fresshe folkes, he or she,   1835
In which that love up groweth with youre age,
Repeyreth hom fro worldly vanyte,
And of youre herte up casteth the visage
To thilke god that after his ymage
Yow made, and thynketh al nys but a faire   1840
This world, that passeth soone as floures faire.

264

And loveth hym which that right for love
Upon a cros, oure soules for to beye,
First starf, and roos, and sit in hevene above;
For he nyl falsen no wight, dar I seye,   1845
That wol his herte al holly on hym leye.
And syn he best to love is, and most meke,
What nedeth feyned loves for to seke?

1831. S1 hath lust; H3PhH4Cx *om.* hath; R Suche fyn hath his lust & ek hys
noblesse. 1836. JH3PhH2H4 ay *for* that. 1839. H3Cx lorde. 1840. H4S2Cx is.
1842. γS1Th the which. 1846. ClJH3 wole. 1848. H2RPh nedeþ it.

265

Lo here, of payens corsed olde rites!
Lo here, what alle hire goddes may availle!   1850
Lo here, thise wrecched worldes appetites!
Lo here, the fyn and guerdoun for travaille
Of Jove, Appollo, of Mars, of swich rascaille!
Lo here, the forme of olde clerkes speche
In poetrie, if ye hire bokes seche!   1855

266

O moral Gower, this book I directe
To the, and to the philosophical Strode,
To vouchensauf, ther nede is, to correcte,
Of youre benignites and zeles goode.
And to that sothfast Crist, that starf on rode,   1860
With al myn herte of mercy evere I preye;
And to the Lord right thus I speke and seye:

267

Thow oon, and two, and thre, eterne on lyve,
That regnest ay in thre, and two, and oon,
Uncircumscript, and al maist circumscrive,   1865
Us from visible and invisible foon
Defende; and to thy mercy everichon,
So make us, Jesus, for thi mercy digne,
For love of mayde and moder thyn benigne!   AMEN

EXPLICIT LIBER TROILI ET CRISEYDIS.

1849. H2H4H3CxTh paynymes. 1853. PhS1R *om. second of*; PhRTh and, H4 & of *for third* of, Cx *om. third* of. 1856. H3 (*rubric*) Lenvoye Du Chaucer. 1857. ClH1 S2PhR *om. second* to; CpD *om. second* the, H3H2 thy *for* the; H2R sophistical, H4 philosophie of, Ph philosophre O *for* philosophical. 1857-1862. S1 *torn; most of lines lost.* 1866. H2R Trine unite us from oure cruel foone. 1868. H2R take. 1869. Amen, *so* CpClH3Ph, H1 *after colophon, rest omit. Colophon, so* ClH1DJ (Cl Criseide, JD Criseid); S2 Explicit liber troyly et Criseide quod Chaucer. Anno domini millesimo quadringentesimo primo Anno Regni Regis Henrici Sexti post conquestum Anglie decimonono; CpH4 Explicit Liber Troily (H4 *adds* Merci dieu & grant merci quod Style); Ph Explicit Troylus; H3 Explicit; H2 Troilus adest mete/Venit explicit ergo valete; S1 here endeth the book of Troylus of double sorowe in loving of Cri . . .; R Tregentyll: Heer endith the book of Troylus and of Cresseyde: Chaucer; Cx Here endeth Troylus/as touchyng Creseyde/Explicit per Caxton; Th Thus endeth the fyfth and laste booke of Troylus.

NOTES TO BOOK ONE

NOTES TO BOOK ONE

1. The opening line of the poem contains a descriptive title. With this line, and with 1.54-5, in mind, the scribe of S1 supplies a colophon: "Here endeth the book of Troylus of double sorowe in loving of Cri. . . ."

2. "That was the son of King Priam of Troy."

4. Chaucer's poem, with its double change of fortune, is, in the medieval sense of the terms, first a comedy and then a tragedy. Dante, *Epist.* 10.10, says: "Comoedia vero inchoat asperitatem alicuius rei, sed eius materia prospere terminatur." Tragedy, on the other hand, "in principio est admirabilis et quieta, in fine sive exitu est foetida et horribilis." For Chaucer's definition of Tragedy, see *Monk's Tale*, B 3163-7. Compare also Chaucer's Boethius, 2. pr 2. 51-2: "Tragedie is to seyn, a ditee of a prosperitee for a tyme, that endeth in wrecchednesse." At 5.1786, Chaucer calls his poem a tragedy.

5. "Before I depart from you." The rhyme *Troye: fro ye* shows that *ye* is not the nominative (with long vowel), but the unemphatic form of the accusative *yow* (with the indefinite vowel). Skeat cites *Two Gentlemen of Verona* 4.1.3.

6-9. Chaucer invokes Tisiphone, one of the Furies, to help him write his sorrowful story. In *Thebais* 1.56-9 Oedipus prays:

> Di, sontes animas, angustaque Tartara poenis
> Qui regitis, tuque umbrifero Styx livida fundo,
> Quam video, multumque mihi consueta vocari
> Annue, Tisiphone, perversaque vota secunda.

In *Thebais* 1.88 Tisiphone is addressed as "crudelis Diva." Compare *Roman de Thèbes* 510: "Tesiphoné, fure d'enfer." See note to 4.22-4.

7. "These woful verses, which weep as I write them." Compare *Fil.* 1.6:

> Ciò che dirà 'l mio verso lagrimoso.

13. *Feere*, companion, i.e. Tisiphone.
15-18. Compare *Fame* 615-40.

16. *Ne dar*, dare not.

21. From *Fil.* 1.5:

> Tuo sia l'onore, e mio si sia l'affanno.

Compare 1.1042-3.

24-28. Note α reading recorded in variants. The variation is so considerable as to point clearly to authentic revision. Some of the steps of the revision can be traced. Line 24 in α is hypermetrical. In the original, *olde* had apparently been revised to read *passid*; but in H2 (Hand 3) and Ph both adjectives are retained. H4 omits *passid*. Similarly in 26, an original *somtyme* had been corrected to *that*. H4 again gives the original reading, while H2Ph are conflate. Note also the conflate reading of H5 in line 28.

28. "If you have not felt the pangs of despised love, the course of your love has been too smooth to conform to the code of courtly love."

29-46. These lines suggest the form of a "bidding prayer," when the priest exhorts the congregation to pray successively for various categories of persons. See *Catholic Encyclopaedia* s.v. Bede.

36. CpClJ read *desespeired*. The longer form is metrically necessary in the α reading, but is hypermetrical in the revised text; see variant readings. For the two forms of the word, see *NED* s.v. Despair, vb. For *despeired* in the sense of "desperate," see *NED* s.v. Despaired. Compare *Franklin's Tale*, F 943,

> He was despeyred, no thing dorste he seye,

and see line 42 below.

57-60. The number of the ships, and the ten-years' duration of the war, are not mentioned by Boccaccio; but Virgil, *Aen.* 2.198, gives both facts:

> Non anni domuere decem, non mille carinae.

Benoit gives the number of the ships as 1130; see *Troie* 5701-2, and the note by Constans, Vol. 5, p. 6. For the ten years, see *Troie* 5805-6:

> al disme an, senz nule faille,
> Iert tote fin de la bataille.

Guido gives the number of ships as 1222; but cites the statement of Homer that the number was 1186. See *Historia*, sig. e 3, b, col. 2: *Numerus navium*, and *Ilias Latina* 221.

70. Apollo's oracle was situated at Delphi. He is called "Delphicus" by Ovid, *Met.* 2.543; *Fasti* 3.856.

71-76. Calchas foresaw the destruction of Troy by several means of divination: by "calkulynge," i.e. by astrological computation; by the responses of Apollo's oracle; by "sort," i.e. by casting lots, or the chance opening of sacred books. Compare 4.114-17 and note.

81. *Stal* is the regular Chaucerian preterite sing. of *stele*, steal; see Ten Brink 142.

85. That the *a*Th reading, "Grete rumour gan," is an authentic *a* reading, is proved by *Fil.* 1.10: "Fu romor grande." Note conflate reading of W.

87. The γ reading is certainly corrupt.

88-91. Chaucer is following *Fil.* 1.10:

> Nè quasi per la più gente rimase
> Di non andargli col fuoco alle case.

Benoit, *Troie* 13107-13, says:

> Li reis Prianz jure e afie,
> S'aveir le puet en sa baillie,
> Que male fin li fera traire,
> C'iert a chevaus rompre e detraire:
> "Se por ço non que la pucele
> Est franche e proz e sage e bele,
> Por lui fust arse e desmembree."

93. *Al unwist of*, quite uninformed of. The *a* text reads *Unknowyng* for *Al unwist*. *Fil.* 1.11 reads:

> Senza niente farlene assapere.

Unwist is to be referred to the verb *wisse*, instruct, rather than to *witen*, know. Elsewhere in Chaucer, *unwist* means "unknown."

99. In the word *lady*, Chaucer regularly preserves the O.E. fem. gen. sing. without -*s*; see Ten Brink 212.

109. *Large*, ample, flowing. For *large*, JGgH5H3 read *blak*. This is inconsistent with *broun*; but compare 1.170, 177, 309.

111. The *a* reading, "With chere & voys ful pytous & wepyng," is somewhat nearer to *Fil.* 1.12.

E con voce e con vista assai pietosa.

114. In this line, H4 presents a conflate reading; see variants.

117-118. "Dismiss your father's treason from your mind, with a curse of ill luck to him." See *NED* s.v. Mischance, 3. Compare also 5.359. *Fil.* 1.13 reads:

lascia con la ria ventura
Tuo padre andar.

119. "While it is well pleasing to you."

121. "As completely as when your father dwelled here."

125. "And would have done so again, if Hector had wished."

126. "And went home and lived quietly."

132-133. Chaucer must have read the specific statement of Boccaccio, *Fil.* 1.15, that Criseida had never had either son or daughter. In Benoit, Briseida is not even a widow; in *Troie* 13111, Priam refers to her as "la pucele."

139. "Fortune wheeled them aloft, and then under again, in accordance with her revolving course." Compare Chaucer's *Fortune* 45-6,

Thou born art in my regne of variaunce,
Aboute the wheel with other most thou dryve,

and Boethius, 2. pr 2. 37-9: "I [Fortune] torne the whirlinge wheel with the torning cercle; I am glad to chaungen the lowest to the heyest, and the heyest to the lowest." See 1.837-54 and note. I adopt the reading *whielen* (*ie* representing long close *e*) as that which best explains the variants. The verb "to wheel" seems to have puzzled the scribes. H4 reads *werle*, i.e. "whirl." The reading *turne* of H5 is obviously a gloss. *Weylen* and *wailen* are certainly blunders.

145-147. Chaucer is citing the ultimate sources for the story of the Trojan war; see Introd. pp. xxi-xxiii. Benoit, in his Prologue, cites Homer and Dares as his authorities. Lines 91-2 of the critical text of *Troie* read:

L'estoire que Daire ot escrite,
En greque langue faite e dite;

but two MSS. present a variant reading:

> Et en lengue greçoise dite.

With such a MS. before him, Guido in his *Prologus* cites, after naming Homer, Virgil, and Ovid, "Ditem Graecum et Phrigium Daretem, qui tempore Troiani belli continue in eorum exercitibus fuere presentes et horum quae videre fuerunt fidelissimi relatores" (*Historia*, sig. a 1, a, col. 2 : *Prologus*). Chaucer's form of the name Dictys (*Dite*) may be due to a similar reading of this passage in Benoit; or it may be an adaptation of Benoit's regular form *Ditis* (*Dithis*), or of the Latin accusative *Ditem* of Guido (e.g. *Historia*, sig. o 7, a, col. 1). On this passage see Young, pp. 129-30, and Hamilton, pp. 69-71. Compare also *Fame* 1466-70, where Homer, Dares, "Tytus" (Dictys), "Lollius," Guido delle Colonne, and Geoffrey of Monmouth are named as "bearers up" of Troy.

152-154. Chaucer is following *Fil.* 1.17-18. The Palladium was a sacred image of Pallas; so long as it remained in the city, Troy was immune from capture. Shortly before the fall of the city, the treachery of Antenor and Aeneas removed it, and gave it to the Greeks. Compare 4.203-5 and note. According to Benoit, *Troie* 25406-8 :

> Rien en terre n'avons si chiere.
> C'est l'esperance as Troïens,
> C'est lor refuiz e toz lor biens.

See also Guido, *Historia*, sig. m 3, b, col. 2 : *Proditio Trojae*, and Virgil, *Aen.* 2.162-70.

157. *Veer, the pryme*, i.e. the Spring; compare Gower, *Conf. Am.* 7.1014: "Whan Ver his seson hath begonne."

161. The festival of the Palladion is thought of as a pagan equivalent of Easter. Chaucer places it specifically in the month of April. Boccaccio, *Fil.* 1.18, merely says that it was springtime. Boccaccio himself first saw Fiammetta in church on an Easter Even (*Filocolo* 1.5) ; the date was March 30, 1336 (Young, p. 31). *Palladions* is apparently to be stressed on first and third syllables; but see variant readings.

162-168. This stanza is expanded from two lines in *Filostrato*, 1.18 :

> Alla qual festa e donne e cavalieri
> Fur parimente, e tutti volentieri.

There is no need to seek any source for the expansion, other than Chaucer's personal experience of such occasions; but one may compare Benoit's account, *Troie* 17489-524, where knights, ladies, and townspeople throng to the tomb of Hector on the anniversary of his death. It is a time of truce; and Achilles is present, and is taken with the love of Polyxena.

171-172. In the corresponding lines of Boccaccio, *Fil.* 1.19, one reads:

> La qual, quanto la rosa la viola
> Di beltà vince, cotanto era questa
> Più ch'altra donna bella.

Chaucer has substituted for the comparison of rose to violet the curious statement that "Just as our first letter is now an A, so she stood first and matchless in beauty." In order to rhyme his line, he has in 169 given the lady's name as *Criseyda* instead of the usual *Criseyde*. Skeat cites the phrase *A-per-se*, i.e. the first of its kind, which is applied to the "fair Cresseid" by Henryson, *Testament of Cresseid* 78. But Henryson may well be echoing the present passage; he seems, at any rate, to be the first to apply *A-per-se* figuratively (see *NED* s.v. A, IV, 1, b). Professor Lowes (*P.M.L.A.* 23.285-306) has made the brilliant suggestion that Chaucer is referring to the initial of Queen Anne's name, used decoratively together with Richard's initial. *Now*, since the advent of Anne of Bohemia, an A is the first letter in *our* land of England. If this interpretation is accepted, the allusion serves to date the present passage later than January 14, 1382, the date of Richard's marriage. See Introd., p. xvi.

174. I retain *yit*, which has a preponderance of MS. authority, even though the line would be metrically more regular without it; see variant readings.

189. *Lakken*, find fault with; see *NED* s.v. Lack, vb., 5, 6.

192. *Baiten*, feed, feast; see *NED* s.v. Bait, vb., 8.

198. *Lewed*, ignorant, foolish; see *NED* s.v. Lewd, 4.

203. Compare 3.329 and note.

205. *Ascaunces*, as if to say; see *NED* s.v. Askances, conj. adv., 2.

208. *Kidde*, pret. of *kythe*, to make known; see *NED* s.v. Kithe.

210. "Love can pull out the feathers of other peacocks as proud

as Troilus." Compare *Prologue*, A 652, and the proverb: "proud as a peacock" (Hazlitt, 365).

211-213. From *Fil.* 1.25:

> O cecità delle mondane menti,
> Come ne seguon sovente gli effetti
> Tutti contrarii a'nostri intendimenti!

Compare Statius, *Theb.* 5.718-19. Lines 214-66 have no counterpart in *Filostrato*.

214-216. "Pride will have a fall" (Hazlitt, 364). See note on lines 218-24.

217. A proverb. Compare Usk, *Testament of Love* 2.8.122: "Alday fayleth thinges that fooles wende"; Barbour, *Bruce* 1.582: "Bot oft failyeis the fulis thocht."

218-224. Bayard was the name of the bay-colored magic steed given by Charlemagne to Renaud in the *chansons de gestes*, and hence a kind of mock-heroic name given to any horse (see *NED* s.v. Bayard). Compare *Canon's Yeoman's Tale*, G 1413. The spirited simile contained in this stanza is somewhat like a French proverb cited by Düringsfeld, 1. no. 741:

> Quand orgueil chevauche ou va le galoppe,
> Daim et honte le suit en croppe.

229. *A-fere*, on fire.

232-252. These lines on the power of love somewhat resemble Benoit's moralizing on the sudden and complete conquest of Achilles by the beauty of Polyxena, *Troie* 18443-59. Compare:

> Qui est qui vers Amors est sage?
> Ço n'est il pas ne ne puet estre:
> En Amors a trop grevos maistre;
> Trop par lit grevose leçon.
> Ço parut bien a Salemon.

Compare also *Filocolo* 1.96-8.

237. Compare 3.1744-71 and note.

238. "No man can undo, set at nought, the law of nature." Compare Usk, *Testament of Love* 3.1.129-30: "Trewly, lawe of kynde for goddes own lusty wil is verily to mayntene." Compare also *Knight's Tale*, A 1165-6:

> Love is a gretter lawe, by my pan,
> Than may be yeve to any erthly man.

241-247. Compare Gower, *Conf. Am.* 6.78-9:

> It falleth that the moste wise
> Ben otherwhile of love adoted.

Gower cites as examples of wise men in love: Solomon, Virgil, and Aristotle. Compare also *Wife of Bath's Prologue*, D 721-32, where Samson, Hercules, and Socrates are cited.

257-258. Compare the proverb: "Better to bow than break" (Hazlitt, 100); "Mieux vaut ployer que rompre" (Le Roux de Lincy, 2.349). Compare also 2.1387-9.

266. "I will return to it"; see *NED* s.v. Refer, 11.

270. "Whether she lived in the town of Troy, or at some country-seat in the region round about."

274. The *a* text apparently read:

> And sodeynly for wonder wax astoned.

See variant readings.

281. Boccaccio, *Fil.* 1.27, says: "Ell' era grande." Chaucer is following another authority; see 5.806 and note.

285. "And also the mere manner of her bodily movements"; see *NED* s.v. Pure, adj. 3.

292. *Ascaunces*, compare 1.205 and note.

297-298. Young (p. 169) cites a parallel from Boccaccio's *Fiammetta*, p. 9, "E già nella mia mente essendo la effige della sua figura rimasa," and Benoit, *Troie* 17555. Compare also Boethius 5. m 4.1-15, 29-32; and see 3.1499.

299-331. Compare Boccaccio's account of his own falling in love with Fiammetta, *Filocolo* 1.5: "Ma dopo alquanto spazio . . . presi ardire, e intentivamente cominciai a rimirare ne' begli occhi dell' adorna giovane, ne' quali io vidi dopo lungo guardare Amore in abito tanto pietoso, che me, cui lungamente a mia istanza avea risparmiato, fece tornare . . . subietto."

300. He was glad to "draw in his horns," i.e. to lower his pretensions, as the snail, when disturbed, draws in his horn-like tentacles; see *NED* s.v. Horn, 4 b.

306-307. The "spirit of the heart" is the "vital spirit." The "natural spirit" had its seat in the liver, the "animal spirit" in the brain. Medieval medicine supposed that these highly refined substances, or fluids, passed through the arteries, permeated the vital organs, and controlled their processes. The "vital spirit" controls pulse and breathing (Thorndike, *History of Magic*, 1.658). The phenomenon of vision was explained on the theory that a "spirit" passes from the brain to the eye through the optic nerve. From the eye it passes with marvelous celerity to the object seen, and thence back to the eye and brain (Thorndike, 2.33). Thomas of Cantimpré explains that the rays proceeding from the eye of a wolf may so dry up the *spiritus* of a man that the power of speech will be taken from him (Thorndike, 2.385). The "subtil stremes" of Criseyde's eyes produce a similar effect on Troilus. "Right with hire look," the "vital spirit" of Troilus is so affected that his heart stops beating, and his breath fails. Compare *Knight's Tale*, A 1096-7. One is tempted to believe that Chaucer wrote not *deyen* but *dreyen*, dry up; but the MSS. offer no confirmation for such a conjecture. If *deyen* is an error, it goes back to Chaucer's own scribe.

313. "In order to maintain his usual manner of behavior"—as already described in lines 183-210.

316. *Awhaped*, stupefied; see *NED* s.v. Awhaped, and Whaped.

320. *Fille*, pret. subj. of *falle*.

327. *Borneth*, polishes, brightens up; see *NED* s.v. Burn, vb. 2, H2Ph read *unournith*, of which *mourned* of H4 seems to be a corruption. It would look as though *a* had read *anorneth*, adorns; see *NED* s.v. Anorn.

333. *Hym tit*, to him betideth; see *NED* s.v. Tide, vb. 1.

336-350. "The religious order to which you belong is governed by an excellent rule of life!" Troilus ironically develops the idea in the two succeeding stanzas. All the observances of the order are uncertain—except a few unimportant points—and yet your ordinance (*lay*) demands unremitting attention. One of the articles of the "rule" is that lovers must submit patiently to the unreasonable displeasure of their ladies.

349. *Groyn*, grumbling complaint; compare *Knight's Tale*, A 2460, and see *NED* s.v. Groin, sb. 1.

353. "Love caught him as one catches birds, with bird-lime." Compare *Wife of Bath's Tale*, D 934 and see *NED* s.v. Lime, vb. 1, 3.

359. "He seated himself on the foot of his bed." For the plural *feet*, compare *Reeve's Tale*, A 4213, where *feet* is authenticated by the rhyme. See also *NED* s.v. Foot, 5 a.

363. *And temple.* Skeat, following the unique reading of Cl, prints *a temple*, i.e. in the temple. Globe, adopting the *a* reading in part only, prints *in temple*. See variant readings. *And temple* has overwhelming MS. attestation as the authentic revised reading. It was, despite Cl and S2Dig, certainly the reading of γ; it is also supported among the β MSS. by JGgH3. R substitutes *at* for *and*; Cx is noncommittal.

365. Compare Boethius, 5. m 4. 7-9 (gloss) : "Thilke Stoiciens wenden that the sowle hadde ben naked of itself, as a mirour or a clene parchemin."

384-385. Adapted from *Fil.* 1.36 :

> Pensando, che amore a molti aperto
> Noia acquistava, e non gioia per merto.

Chaucer has supplied the horticultural metaphor.

388. *Arten*, constrain ; see *NED* s.v. Art, vb. 1.

393-399. For the name "Lollius," see Introd., pp. xxxvi-xl. Chaucer declares that, whereas his author, Lollius, gives only the "sentence" of the song, i.e. its general purport, he will give every word of it fully ("pleinly"), just as Troilus said it, except for the difference in languages. Boccaccio merely says, *Fil.* 1.37 :

> E quindi lieto si diede a cantare
> Bene sperando.

(Compare line 389 above.) The song in Chaucer, which has no counterpart in Boccaccio, is from Petrarch ; see next note.

400-420. The Song of Troilus is closely translated from Petrarch, Sonnet 88 (*Rima* 133, Carducci) :

> S'amor non è, che dunque è quel ch'io sento ?
>> Ma, s'egli è Amor, per Dio che cosa e quale ?
>> Se bona, ond' è l'effetto aspro mortale ?
>> Se ria, ond' è si dolce ogni tormento ?
>
> S'a mia voglia ardo, ond' è 'l pianto e lamento ?
>> S'a mal mio grado, il lamentar che vale ?
>> O viva morte, o dilettoso male,
>> Come puoi tanto in me, s'io no'l consento ?
>
> E s'io'l consento, a gran torto mi doglio.
>> Fra si contrari venti in frale barca
>> Mi trovo in alto mar, senza governo,

Sí lieve di saver, d'error sí carca,
    Ch'i' medesmo non so quel ch'io mi voglio;
    E tremo a mezza state, ardendo il verno.

Notice that Chaucer's stanza 58 corresponds to Petrarch's first quatrain, stanza 59 to the second, and stanza 60 to the sestet, except that line 410 seems to correspond to line 13 of the sonnet. Lines 406 and 419 have no parallels in the Italian.

409. Petrarch reads: "S'a mal mio grado," which in modern Italian would be "Se malgrado mio," (French, "Si malgré moi"), i.e. "If against my will." Chaucer's phrase suggests that the text before him may have read: "Se mal mi agrada," "If evil gives me pleasure." (For English *agree* in the sense of "give pleasure" see *NED* s.v. Agree, I). Chaucer's phrase seems to have troubled the scribes, see variant readings. (In the reading of JGgH5 etc. the first *I* must be interpreted as an exclamation; note that H5 reads *ey*.)

420. The corresponding line in Petrarch ("E tremo, etc.") means, "And I shiver in midsummer, burning in the spring." Chaucer's line suggests Petrarch, *Rima* 182.5:

Trem' al più caldo, ard' al più freddo cielo.

For the antithesis of heat and cold, compare 1.523-5; 4.511; and Gower, *Conf. Am.* 6.249.

425-426. Chaucer is translating *Fil.* 1.38:

Non so s'io dico a donna, ovvero a dea
A servir dato.

Boccaccio may have been thinking of Virgil, *Aen.* 1.327-8. Troilus's doubt is echoed by Palamon, when he first sees Emily; *Knight's Tale*, A 1101-2:

I noot wher she be womman or goddesse;
But Venus is it, soothly, as I gesse.

Compare *Tes.* 3.13-14; but the passage in *K.T.* is nearer to *Troilus* than to *Teseide*.

435-448. Compare *Rose* (Langlois) 2339-57, where there is a similar playing with the idea of fire:

E saches que dou regarder
Feras ton cuer frire e larder,
Et tot adès en regardant
Aviveras le feu ardent, etc. (2341-4.)

[419]

449. Compare *Rose* (Langlois) 2358,

> Qui plus est près dou feu plus art;

and Machaut, *Jugement dou Roy de Behaingue* 1743:

> Et cils qui est plus près dou feu, plus s'art.

455. Polyxena, daughter of Priam and Hecuba, beloved of Achilles. *Fil.* 1.42 reads:

> avanza Polissena
> D'ogni bellezza, e similmente Elena.

458. "Good goodly one, to serve whom I labor." This is a nine-syllable line, unless one reads *serven*, for which there is no MS. authority. The word-order is abnormal. Skeat, without authority, reads: "to whom serve I and laboure"; Globe, equally without authority, reads: "whom to serven I laboure." The Globe reading is a tempting emendation; but I have preferred to follow the overwhelming testimony of the MSS., even though it convict Chaucer of an awkward line.

465. *Fownes*, fawns; compare *Duchess* 429. Originally *fawn* means the young of any animal; it was later specialized to mean a young deer; see *NED* s.v. Fawn, sb. 1, 1. "Desire bred in Troilus no other offspring but reasons in support of the conclusion he wished." The curious metaphor, which has no parallel in *Filostrato*, was a source of confusion to the scribes; see variant readings.

470. *Fil.* 1.45 reads:

> L'aspre battaglie e gli stormi angosciosi
> Ch'Ettore e gli altri suoi frate' faceano.

Chaucer's *felle*, cruel, dreadful, seems to translate *angosciosi*. *Shoures*, which seems to translate *stormi*, has its common M.E. sense of "attack, assault"; see *NED* s.v. Shower, sb. 1, 5. The whole line apparently means: "The sharp and dreadful assaults, of martial prowess the proof."

472. "Did not once make him move on their account," i.e. in emulation.

480-481. Chaucer's Squire also fought,

> In hope to stonden in his lady grace.

(*Prologue*, A 88.)

483. *The deth*, the pestilence; see *NED* s.v. Death, 8. Compare *Prologue*, A 605, and *Pardoner's Tale*, C 675.

517-518. Compare *Fame* 639-40:

> Although thou mayst go in the daunce
> Of hem that him [Love] list not avaunce.

523-525. From *Fil.* 1.53:

> Fredda come al sereno interza il ghiaccio,
> Ed io qual neve al fuoco mi disfaccio.

Compare 1.420; 4.511.

526-527. Chaucer's figure of the "port of death" is derived from *Fil.* 1.54. Compare 1.606.

530. "For if my hidden sorrow be blown abroad."

532. There would seem to be a specific allusion to some medieval Dunciad; but I have not been able to identify it.

557. *NED* defines Attrition, in its theological sense, as "An imperfect sorrow for sin, as if a bruising which does not amount to utter crushing (*contrition*) 'horror of sin through fear of punishment, without any loving sense, or taste of God's mercy' (Hooker), while *contrition* has its motive in the love of God."

559. Skeat glosses *leye on presse* as "compress, diminish," and cites *Prologue*, A 81. *Presse* has rather, I think, the sense of "cupboard with shelves" (*NED* s.v. Press, sb. 1, 14; compare *Miller's Tale*, A 3212). The whole phrase would mean "shut up in the closet, lay on the shelf."

560. *Holynesse*, religious piety; see article by Tatlock, *Studies in Philology* 18.422-5 (1921).

569. The Brit. Mus. MS. of *Filostrato* (Addit. 21, 246) reads in 2.2:

> Troyolo disse pandar qual fortuna
> t a qui condotto a vedermi qui languire.

This is nearer to Chaucer than Moutier's reading, "vedermi morire."

570. *Refus*, a participial adjective, "rejected, thrown aside as worthless"; see *NED* s.v. Refuse, adj., A.

617-618. In the *Roman de la Rose*, one is advised to have a friend to whom one can speak of one's love (Langlois 2686-716).

626. "That one whom excess causes to fare full evilly."

630. Compare the proverb: "A fool may give a wise man coun-

sel" (Hazlitt, 13 ; Düringsfeld 2. no. 151). See Rabelais, *Panta-gruel* 3.37 : "J'ay souvent ouy en proverbe vulguaire qu'un fol enseigne bien un saige." Compare 1.635 ; 3.329. *Fil.* 2.10 reads :

> E benchè l'uom non prenda buon consiglio,
> Donar lo puote nell' altrui periglio.

631-632. The spelling *wheston* for "whetstone" has overwhelm-ing MS. authority. Hazlitt (p. 43) records the proverb : "A whetstone, though it can't itself cut, makes tools cut."

637. Compare *Rose* (Michel) 25582-5 :

> Ainsinc va des contraires choses.
> Les unes sunt des autres gloses,
> Et qui l'une en vuet défenir,
> De l'autre li doit sovenir.

These lines from *Rose* follow closely on those quoted in the next note.

638-644. This stanza, which has no counterpart in Boccaccio, is based on *Rose* (Michel) 22562-74, where it is explained that the gourmand tries various dishes—

> Et set loer et set blasmer
> Liquex sunt dous, liquex amer,
> Car de plusors en a goustés.
> Ausinc sachiés, et n'en doutés,
> Que qui mal essaié n'aura,
> Jà du bien gaires ne saura ;
> Et qui ne set d'onor que monte,
> Jà ne saura congnoistre honte ;
> N'onc nus ne sot quel chose est aise,
> S'il n'ot avant apris mésaise, etc.

Compare 3.1212-20, and note on 3.1219-20. See also *Piers Plow-man*, C 21.209-21.

651. "It shall less injure thee" ; see *NED* s.v. Dere, vb.

653-655. The allusion is to Ovid's epistle of Oenone, *Her.* 5.

659-665. Apollo, as patron of the arts, is the inventor of medi-cine. Vincent of Beauvais, *Speculum Doctrinale*, Lib. 14, Cap. 1, says, citing "Ysidorus in libro ethy. iiij" : "Hujus artis inventor apud Grecos (ut fertur) Apollo fuit. . . . Prima methodica inventa est ab apolline." In Ovid, *Her.* 5.149-53, Oenone writes to Paris:

> Me miseram, quod amor non est medicabilis herbis!
> Deficior prudens artis ab arte mea.
> Ipse repertor opis vaccas pavisse Pheraeas
> Fertur et e nostro saucius igne fuit.

(Pherae was the capital city of King Admetus, whom Apollo served as a herdsman.) In Boccaccio, *Tes.* 4.46 we read:

> Siccome te alcuna volta Amore
> Costrinse il chiaro cielo abbandonare,
> E lungo Anfriso in forma di pastore
> Del grande Admeto gli armenti guardare;

and in *Tes.* 3.25:

> Poichè Apollo, sentita
> Cotal saetta, che i succhi mondani
> Tutti conobbe, non seppe vedere
> Medela a sè che potesse valere?

674. Compare *Knight's Tale*, A 1133,

> That never, for to dyen in the peyne;

and 3.1502.

687-688. "It is equally wrong to mistrust everyone, or to believe everyone." Compare Seneca, *Ad Lucilium, Ep.* 3.4: "Utrumque enim vitium est, et omnibus credere et nulli."

694-695. R has marginal gloss: "Salamon Ve soly"; and S1: "Ve so. . . ." The reference is to Ecclesiastes 4.10: "Vae soli; quia cum ceciderit, non habet sublevantem se."

699-700. Niobe, weeping for her seven sons and seven daughters, slain by Apollo and Diana, was turned into a stone, "et lacrimas etiam nunc marmora manant." (Ovid, *Met.* 6.312.) Compare "Etiam nunc" and "yit."

701-707. The first three lines of this stanza follow closely the first three lines of *Fil.* 2.13. The remainder of the stanza, which is not in Boccaccio, seems to reproduce Seneca, *Ep.* 99.26: "Quod enim est turpius quam captare in ipso luctu voluptatem, immo per luctum, et inter lacrimas quoque juvet, quaerere?" In the margin of line 704, R has a gloss: "Require in Metamorphosios."

After a good deal of searching, I have found no parallel in *Met.* closer than 9.142-3 (which is not very close!) :

> Indulsit primo lacrimis, flendoque dolorem
> Diffudit miseranda suum.

708-709. Compare the modern proverb: "Misery loves company," and Hazlitt 119: "Company in misery makes it light." R has marginal gloss: "Sale*mon*, Consolacio miserorum, etc." and S1 (margin trimmed): "consolacio [miserorum] habere [consor] tem in pe[na]." This Latin proverb (which is *not* in Solomon) appears in Marlowe's *Faustus* 474 as a hexameter line: "Solamen miseris socios habuisse doloris." For an inconclusive discussion of the line in Marlowe, see H. Logeman, *Faustus Notes* 55-7. Compare *Canon's Yeoman's Tale*, G 746-7. Chaucer's lines find their suggestion in *Fil.* 2.13.

713. *Harde grace*, ill luck ; see *NED* s.v. Grace, sb., 10.

714. R has marginal gloss: "Require in Ovidio." I have been unable to find any Ovidian parallel.

730. *Litargie*, lethargy. Compare Boethius, 1. pr 2. 14-15: "He is fallen into a litargie, whiche that is a comune sykenes to hertes that ben deceived." (Philosophy is applying her "medicine" to the sorrows of Boethius.)

731-735. R has marginal gloss: "Baicius de consolacione philosophie." Compare Boethius 1. pr 4.1-2: "Felestow, quod she, thise thinges, and entren they aught in thy corage? Artow lyke an asse to the harpe?" Le Roux de Lincy, 1.144, quotes a fifteenth-century proverb: "Ung asne n'entend rien en musique." Compare also Düringsfeld, 2. no. 591.

740-742. Compare the proverb: "He makes a rod for his own breech" (Hazlitt, 195) ; and Le Roux de Lincy, 2.478: "Maint homme oinst la verge dont il meismes est batu." If one tells his secret, one puts a weapon into the hands of his confidant.

747-748. Compare *Rose* (Langlois) 7557-8 :

> Or deit chacier, or deit foïr
> Qui veaut de bone amour joïr.

762-763. Compare 1.704-7 ; 4.1255-7.

780. *Bendiste*, an abbreviated pronunciation of the Latin *benedicite*, bless ye. The abbreviated form is found in CpH1J ; Gg writes *benediste*. The remaining MSS. write *benedicite* ; but the

metre clearly demands a trisyllable. It is the first word of the canticle *Benedicite omnia*, sung by the Three Children in the fiery furnace. It is used as a common exclamation, with about the force of "Lord bless me!"; see *NED* s.v. Benedicite, and compare 3.757, 860.

786-788. The fate of Tityos is told by Virgil, *Aen.* 6.595-600 (compare Ovid, *Met.* 4.457-8); but Chaucer is clearly indebted to Boethius, 3. m 12. 28, where Chaucer's translation reads: "the fowl that highte voltor, that eteth the stomak or the giser of Tityus, is so fulfild of his song that it nil eten ne tyren no more." The Latin reads: "Vultur dum satur est modis, Non traxit Tityi iecur." Similarity in phrasing suggests that Chaucer was referring to his own translation; note "stomak" as a translation of "iecur." H2PhH4, which give the *a* text, wrongly read *Siciphus*.

794. *Wantrust*, lack of confidence; see *NED* s.v.

810-812. Compare *Rose* (Michel) 21878-81:

> D'autre part, en maintes contrées
> Ont maint maintes dames amées,
> Et les servirent quanqu'il porent,
> N'onques un sol baisier n'en orent.

833. "Have me drawn by horses and then hung."

837-854. Troilus blames Fortune for his troubles; Pandarus defends the fickle goddess. So, at the beginning of the second book of the *De Consolatione*, Philosophy instructs Boethius as to the qualities of Fortune: "She, cruel Fortune, casteth adoun kinges that whylom weren ydrad; and she, deceivable, enhaunseth up the humble chere of him that is discomfited. . . . Thus she pleyeth, and thus she proeveth hir strengthes." (2. m 1. 5-11; cf. 1.839-40) "Natheles dismaye thee nat in thy thought; and thou that art put in the comune realme of alle, ne desyre nat to liven by thyn only propre right." (2. pr 2. 60-2; cf. 1.843-4.) "For if thou therfor wenest thyself nat weleful, for thinges that tho semeden joyful ben passed, ther nis nat why thou sholdest wene thyself a wrecche; for thinges that semen now sorye passen also." (2. pr 3. 52-4; cf. 1.845-7.) "Enforcest thou thee to aresten or withholden the swiftnesse and the sweigh of hir turninge whele? O thou fool of alle mortal fooles, if Fortune bigan to dwelle stable, she cesede thanne to ben Fortune!" (2. pr 1. 80-4;

cf. 1.848-50.) "What eek yif my mutabilitee yiveth thee rightful cause of hope to han yit beter thinges?" (2. pr 2. 58-60; cf. 1.851-4.) For Chaucer's conception of Fortune, see B. L. Jefferson, *Chaucer and Boethius* 49-60.

857-858. From Boethius, 1. pr 4.3-4: "Yif thou abydest after help of thy leche, thee bihoveth discovere thy wounde." *Unwre*, uncover (O.E. *wrēon*, cover). Other MSS. read *unwry* or *unwrie*, an analogical formation from *wrigen*, past participle of *wrēon* (see Wild, pp. 312-13). Le Roux de Lincy, 1.267, cites a fifteenth century proverb:

> Qui veult la garison du mire,
> Il lui convient son mal dire.

859. *Cerberus*, the canine guardian of hell. See Ovid, *Met.* 4.450; but it would be idle to seek a definite source for so familiar an allusion.

860-861. Compare 3.407-13, where Troilus, in his gratitude, makes a similar offer to Pandarus.

890-896. This stanza is found in H2PhH4(*a*) and in Th; the remaining MSS., and Cx, omit it. There is nothing to cast doubt on the genuineness of the stanza, which has the unmistakable ring of Chaucer's manner. Moreover, the first line of stanza 129 seems to echo line 890. It has no counterpart in *Filostrato*; but the same is true of the ten stanzas which follow. But, beautiful as the stanza is in itself, it breaks the continuity of the thought. Both before and after, Pandarus is speaking primarily of Criseyde, and is basing his hope for Troilus on the qualities of his niece's character. In the stanza under discussion, he turns to moralize on the strength which comes from being at peace with one's self. The excision of the stanza leaves no gap in the thought, but rather consolidates it. Its cancellation would seem to be an authentic revision.

891-893. Compare Seneca, *Ep.* 2.1; "Primum argumentum compositae mentis existimo posse consistere et secum morari"; and Boethius, 2. pr 4.96-101: "I shal shewe thee shortly the poynt of sovereyne blisfulnesse . . . yif it so be that thou art mighty over thyself, that is to seyn, by tranquillitee of thy sowle, than hast thou thing in thy power that thou noldest never lesen, ne Fortune ne may nat beneme it thee." *Ordeyne* is a trisyllable with stress on first and third syllables. It is the past participle of the Anglo-French *ordeiner*, to regulate.

897-903. Since Criseyde has all the other virtues, she must have also Pity, which is "coroune of vertues alle" (*Complaint to Pity* 58). Pity, as the active manifestation of Charity (cf. Gower, *Conf. Am.* 2.3174), is the supreme mark of Christian behavior. It was Pity that moved God to send His Son to earth for our salvation (*Conf. Am.* 7.3103 *ff.*). It is an outstanding attribute of the Blessed Virgin (*A.B.C.* 68). Among the virtues symbolized by the pentangle on Gawain's shield is "pite, þat passeȝ alle poynteȝ" (*Gawain and the Green Knight* 654). Compare *Cant. Tales*, B 660, F 479. The change of meaning which has developed the modern, and M.E., *pity* from Latin *pietatem* is an eloquent tribute to the predominance of this virtue. But Troilus must not expect that Criseyde's pity shall go so far as to lead to the blemishing of her good name; for a virtue which is stretched to the point of bringing shame on itself is no longer a virtue.

912-913. Gawin Douglas copies these lines in *Aeneis*, Prol. to Book IV, line 21 :

> And ȝour trew servandis silly goddis apis.

Ape means "fool" (cf. *Prologue*, A 706). *God's ape* seems to mean "natural born fool"; see *NED* s.v. Ape, 4.

914. *Mucche*, eat; see *NED* s.v. Mouch.

916. *Blaunche fevere*, white fever, i.e. a fever which turns its victims pale. Gower's Lover (*Conf. Am.* 6.239) also suffers from "blanche fievere." The symptoms are chills and shivers :

> And so it coldeth at myn herte,
> That wonder is hou I asterte,
> In such a point that I ne deie.
> For certes ther was nevere keie
> Ne frosen ys upon the wal
> More inly cold than I am al.

Similarly the lover in *The Cuckoo and the Nightingale*, 41, is "shaken with the fevers whyte."

918-919. *Som* here (and in 916) is singular; hence the singular reflexive *hym*. In 920 (and in 914) *some* is plural. See *NED* s.v. Some, I. The meaning of the lines is not clear. *Take on* may mean "make a fuss about" (*NED* s.v. Take, 84 j) or perhaps "put on clothing" (*Ibid.* 84 a, b). *For the colde* should mean "because of the cold," or "against the cold." The reference seems to be to the coldness which is a symptom of "blaunche fevere."

927-928. "And thought that, by trying everywhere, they would be sure to succeed in some quarter." Compare *Rose* (Michel) 22560-1:

> Qu'il fait bon de tout essaier
> Por soi miex ès biens esgaier.

946-949. A close translation of Ovid, *Remedia Amoris* 45-6:

> Terra salutares herbas eademque nocentes
> Nutrit, et urticae proxima saepe rosast.

Compare Alanus de Insulis, *Liber Parabolarum*, ed. Migne, col. 582:

> Fragrantes vicina rosas urtica perurit;

and Gower, *Mirour de l'Omme* 3721-3.

950. Compare *Filocolo* 2.276: "La tua doglia è grandissima; ma chi dubiterà che dopo gli altissimi monti non sia una profonda valle?"

951-952. Compare Alanus de Insulis, *Liber Parabolarum*, ed. Migne, col. 583 C:

> Post noctem sperare diem, post nubila solem,
> Post lacrymas risum, laetitiamque potes.

953. Compare Boethius, 5. m 1.13-15.

954. *Suffre to the tyde*, yield to the hour or season (whether favorable or unfavorable). *NED* records no instance of the phrase "suffer to."

956. Compare *Melibeus*, B 2244: "The proverbe seith: 'he hasteth wel that wysely can abyde'; and 'in wikked haste is no profit.'" See 4.1568 and note.

960-961. Compare Seneca, *Ad Lucilium, Ep.* 2.2: "Nusquam est, qui ubique est." See also Boethius, 3. pr 11.51-4. But Chaucer's lines are nearer to *Rose* (Langlois) 2245-6, where, as in Chaucer, the talk is of success in love:

> Qui en mainz leus son cuer depart,
> Par tot en a petite part.

Compare also Boethius, 3. pr 11. 46-51.

964-966. Compare Seneca, *Ad Lucilium*, *Ep.* 2.3: "Non convalescit planta, quae saepe transfertur." As Koeppel pointed out, this sentence of Seneca is quoted by Albertano of Brescia, *Liber de Amore Dei*, fol. 45 b.

969. The corresponding line in Boccaccio (*Fil.* 2. 24) reads:

> Sta' dunque fermo nell' atto proposto.

Chaucer's figure of the harbor seems to have been suggested by *Rose* (Langlois) 12760:

> A bon port estes arivez.

Compare Ovid, *Art. Am.* 2.9-10.

971-972. "For unless your dejection of spirits, or your overhaste, destroy the work of both of us"; see *NED* s.v. Dreariness, 1.

976-979. Boccaccio's Pandaro says in the corresponding context, *Fil.* 2.27:

> Io credo certo, ch'ogni donna in voglia
> Viva amorosa.

I have not been able to discover who are the "wyse lered" on whose authority the Italian lines are expanded.

985-987. In *Fil.* 2.25-6, Pandaro utters a somewhat different sentiment. He recognizes that public opinion is such that a love-affair will injure the reputation of a lady, if it is found out. What was once honorable is now, because of our folly, a matter of shame. But if a lover is discreet, he may rightly follow his high desires.

1000-1001. "Thou shalt be the best pillar of his creed." Compare *Prologue*, A 214.

1001. I read *moste* (pret. subj. 2d sing. of *mot*); but the scribes seem to have understood the superlative *most*. Both γ and JRS1 have attempted emendations for the sake of the metre.

1002-1008. St. Augustine of Hippo is a case in point.

1011. Boccaccio says, *Fil.* 2.29:

> Quasi già fuor di tutto il suo tormento.

The subject of *wex* is *Troilus*, carried over from 1009.

1014-1015. "With the help of Venus, I may, before I die, be able to do something to deserve thy thanks, Pandarus."

1021-1022. In these lines, for the first time, we learn that Pandarus is the uncle of Criseyde. *For the manere*, in accordance with the conventions of good behavior; see *NED* s.v. Manner, 3 a. *Fil.* 2.30 reads:

> per mostrarti
> D'essere onesta, non vorrà ascoltarti.

1024. The fears of Troilus are as idle as to worry lest the Man in the Moon should fall out of his orb. The idea of a Man in the Moon is at least as old as Alexander Neckam's *De Natura Rerum* (twelfth cent.); see ed. in Rolls Series, (No. 34), p. 54. The fear of his fall is found in a poem in Boeddeker's *Alteng. Dicht.*, p. 176:

> Mon in þe mone stond & strit,
>   On is bot forke is burþen he bereþ;
> Hit is muche wonder þat he nadoun slyt,
>   For doute leste he valle, he shoddreþ and shereþ.

1026. "Attend to your own business (and stop worrying about the affairs of other people)."

1038. *And I thi borugh!*, "And I thy surety!," i.e. "I'll be bound no lover has any other intentions"; see *NED* s.v. Borrow, sb., 2 b. Compare 2.134. The original meaning of *borrow* is "pledge, security"; hence the verb *borrow*, to take a thing on pledge or security given for its safe return.

1042-1043. From *Fil.* 2.32:

> Questa fatica tutta sarà mia,
> E'l dolce fine tuo voglio che sia.

Compare 1.21.

1050. "And yet I regret that this boast escaped me"; see *NED* s.v. Athink.

1052. "Thou art wise; thou knowest; thou hast power; thou art everything." *Fil.* 2.33 reads:

> Tu savio, tu amico, tu sai tutto
> Ciò che bisogni a dar fine al mio lutto.

1058. *Desirous.* The stress falls on first and last syllables; compare 2.1101, and *Squire's Tale*, F 23.

1065-1069. Compare Boethius, 4. pr 6.57-60: "For right as a werkman, that aperceyveth in his thoght the forme of the thing

that he wol make, and moeveth the effect of the werk, and ledeth
that he hadde loked biforn in his thoght simply and presently,
etc." The word *line* carries on the idea of the carpenter and his
measuring line, or plumb line; see *NED* s.v. Line, 4.

1073. The bay steed of Troilus is again mentioned in 2.624,
and 5.1038.

1074. Compare *Fil.* 7.80.

1078. The line is repeated, with change of pronoun, in *Clerk's
Tale*, E 413, where it is said of Griselda.

1092. Skeat adopts the reading *driveth* of H2PhH5AS1CxTh;
but the weight of the MS. evidence is overwhelmingly in favor of
dryeth, endures. The meaning of *dryeth forth* is "continues to
live through"; see *NED* s.v. Dree, 5.

NOTES TO BOOK TWO

NOTES TO BOOK TWO

1-6. These lines somewhat resemble Dante, *Purg.* 1.1-3:

> Per correr migliori acque alza le vele
> Omai la navicella del mio ingegno,
> Che lascia dietro a sé mar sì crudele.

As Dante's poem leaves behind the Inferno, and enters Purgatory, so Chaucer's turns from the despair of Troilus to the beginning of his hope. For the metaphor of a sea voyage, compare also Ovid, *Remedia Amoris* 811-12, and *Fil.* 9.3-4.

4. I adopt the reading *konnyng* of H3H4H5S1CxTh. Gg, which lacks the first twelve stanzas of Book II, presumably shared this reading with the closely related H5. Since R omits the Proem, its testimony is lacking. The alternative reading *commyng* has the support of γJH2Ph, but does not seem to make sense in the context. With *konnyng*, the lines means: "That with all my skill I can hardly steer my poetic bark" (so heavily does it labor in the tempestuous sea of Troilus's despair).

7. *Kalendes*, the first day of any month in the Roman calendar, and hence any beginning; see *NED* s.v. Calends, 4, and compare 5.1634. *NED* quotes *King's Quair* 177: "Gave me in hert kalendis of confort."

8-11. Clio is the Muse of history. Chaucer means that his story is sober matter of record. He needs no art of invention; it is enough if he can "ryme wel" the story as he finds it. As a matter of fact, Book II departs very widely from Boccaccio. H4 has marginal gloss: "Cleo domina eloquentie"; but the marginal notes of H4 are probably not of Chaucer's composition.

13. *Sentement*, knowledge based on my own emotional experience; see *NED* s.v. Sentiment, 1. Compare 3.43 and *Legend*, Prol. B 69. Chaucer several times assures us that he writes of love only on the authority of others; see below 2.19-20, and *Parliament* 8-11, 160-8. Compare also 1.15-18; 3.1408-13.

14. The Latin which Chaucer says he is translating is the Latin of "Lollius." One cannot accept Skeat's statement that "*Latin* seems, in this case, to mean Italian, which was called *Latino*

volgare." Apparently the "Latin" to which Chaucer refers was written a thousand years before his time; see below 2.23. See also Introd., p. xxxvii.

18. *Myn auctour*, i.e. "Lollius."

21. A proverb of wide currency. "Blind men should judge no colors" (Hazlitt, 105). See Düringsfeld 1. no. 244. Compare Dante, *De Vulg. Eloq.* 2.6.27: "quos non aliter deridemus quam caecum de coloribus distinguentem." (As Lowes points out, *Mod. Phil.* 14.710-11, the words of Dante are in a somewhat similar context.)

22-25. Derived ultimately from Horace, *Art. Poet.* 69-72:

> Nedum sermonum stet honos et gratia vivax,
> Multa renascentur quae jam cecidere, cadentque
> Quae nunc sunt in honore vocabula, si volet usus,
> Quem penes arbitriumst et jus et norma loquendi.

Compare Wace, *Roman de Rou* 77-80:

> Par lunc tens e par lungs aages,
> E par muement de langages,
> Unt perdu lur premerains nuns,
> Viles, citez e regiuns.

Compare also Seneca, *Ad Lucilium*, *Ep.* 114.13; Dante, *Convito* 1.5.55-66; 2.14.83-9 (where Horace is quoted).

28. Skeat cites *Proverbs of Hendyng* 29: "Ase fele thede, as fele thewes." Compare also Boethius, 2. pr 7.49: "Quid quod diversarum gentium mores inter se atque instituta discordant, ut quod apud alios laude apud alios supplicio dignum judicetur." See Usk, *Testament of Love* 1.5.43, and compare below 2.42.

36-37. *Went* and *halt* are present tense, wendeth, holdeth. Compare Alanus de Insulis, *Liber Parobolarum*, ed. Migne, col. 591:
> Mille viae ducunt homines per saecula Romam.

41. *Forme*, behavior according to customary rules of etiquette; see *NED* s.v. Form, sb., 15. Perhaps one should omit the comma after *visityng*, and interpret the whole phrase as "formal visiting."

42. A proverb of wide currency; see Düringsfeld 2. no. 6, and Le Roux de Lincy, 2.418: "Tant de gens tant de guise." Compare 2.28 and note.

45-46. "For in furthering thy purpose this speech may please thee (one person), and thee (another person) not at all; yet all sorts of speeches are spoken, and must be spoken."

50-55. May is the "mother of the glad months," because it initiates the most delightful months of the year. *NED* s.v. May, sb. 3, 1, cites Dunbar, *Gold. Targe* 82: "there saw I May, of myrthfull monethis quene." A thoroughly conventional spring-time passage; compare 3.351-4; *Prologue*, A 1-10; *Tes.* 3.5-6; Petrarch, *Sonn.* 42 (In morte); *Rose* (Langlois) 45-66.

54-55. In Chaucer's time the Sun entered Taurus ("the white Bole") about April 12, and passed from Taurus into the next sign, Gemini, a month later. We are told in line 50 that the month is May. Line 55 explains that it is early May; and line 56 speci-fies the date as May 3. On May 3 the Sun would be in about the 20th degree of Taurus, or a little past the middle of the sign. He would therefore spread his bright beams "right in" the sign. Compare *Nun's Priest's Tale*, B 4377-85. For the whiteness of the Bull, see Ovid, *Met.* 2.852.

56. Why Chaucer specifies the *third* of May is not clear. The day seems to have had some special significance, which has not yet been explained. It was "in May, the thridde night" that Pala-mon escaped from prison (*Knight's Tale*, A 1463); it was on May 3 that Chauntecleer was carried off by the fox (*Nun's Priest's Tale*, B 4377-85). May 3 is ecclesiastically the feast of the Invention of the Holy Cross; but this seems to offer no clue as to Chaucer's use of the date. May 3 is one of the "Egyptian days" or "dismal days" (see *NED* s.v. Dismal), on which it was unlucky to begin any new undertaking. (For Egyptian days, see Vincent of Beauvais, *Spec. Nat. Lib.* 16, Cap. 83; Salmasius, *De Annis Climacteris*, ed. 1648, pp. 815-19; Thorndike, *History of Magic*, 1.685-8.) May 3, which was also a Friday (B 4531), was an un-lucky day for Chauntecleer; but the fact that it is an Egyptian day does not seem to explain the date in *Knight's Tale*, or in *Troilus*. Possibly, however, the unlucky day brought Pandarus his "teene in love." Somewhat similar is the situation of the lover in *The Cuckoo and the Nightingale*, where (line 55) "the thridde night of May" is also specified as the date. Compare also *Duchess* 1206: "I trowe it was in the dismal," and see Skeat's note on that passage.

64-70. Progne, sister of Philomela, and wife of Tereus, was

metamorphosed into a swallow. Her sister, Philomela, attracted the desire of Tereus, who tore out her tongue. The story is told by Ovid, *Met.* 6.412-674. Compare Chaucer's *Legend of Philomela*; but, in the *Legend*, Progne is not "forshapen." The present passage seems to echo Dante, *Purg.* 9.13-15 :

> Nell' ora che comincia i tristi lai
> La rondinella presso alla mattina,
> Forse a memoria de' suoi primi guai.

See also *Tes.* 4.73.

74. Before starting a journey, or beginning any important enterprise, it was important to discover whether the time was astrologically propitious. In the matter of journeys, the "plight," or condition, of the Moon was of primary importance. A complete magician, such as Calchas, would have constructed a "figure of the heavens," with the Moon and other planets accurately disposed according to their positions in the zodiac. Pandarus was probably content to calculate the day of the lunar month, and then to consult a *Lunarium*, or "moon-book," to learn whether the day was propitious for his undertaking. See Thorndike, *History of Magic*, 1.680-2, and compare *Man of Law's Tale*, B 309-15.

77. H4 has marginal gloss: "Janus deus introit." Compare Ovid, *Fasti* 1.125-7. As god of entries, Janus gives his name to the first month of the year.

84. See note on 2.100-8.

100-108. The story of Thebes is told in the *Thebais* of Statius, and in the twelfth century *Roman de Thèbes* (ed. Constans, *Anciens Textes français*, 1890). Chaucer certainly knew the former; it is probable that he also knew the latter, or some redaction of it. The word *romaunce* (line 100) points towards the French; the mention of "bookes twelve" (line 108) towards the Latin. The death of Laius at the hands of his son Oedipus (101-2) is more fully given in the French (*Thèbes* 175-224) than in Statius, where these events are implied rather than related (1.56 *ff.*). The death of Amphiaraus, who "fil thorugh the ground to helle," is told by Statius in the closing lines of Book VII. The *Roman de Thèbes* (4711-842) gives the episode with much medieval elaboration. The Spalding MS. of *Thèbes* is particularly interesting.

Amphiaraus falls living into hell, and after passing the infernal rivers, is slain by Pluto's trident (see Constans, 2.16). Statius refers to Amphiaraus as "vates" (*Theb.* 7.815); in *Thèbes* 2026 he is called "Un arcevesque mout corteis" (cf. also 5053, 5079). Compare 5.1500, and *Anelida* 57.

103-105. *Lettres rede*, i.e. a rubric at the head of a section of the poem. Lines 104, 105 quote such a rubric. In Lydgate's *Story of Thebes*, as printed in Speght's 1598 Chaucer, we find on fol. 390 a, the heading: "How the Bishop Amphiorax fell downe into hell."

110. *Wympel.* γS1 and α read *barbe.* Either term will fit the context. The wimple was "a covering of silk, linen, or other material, laid in folds over the head and round the chin, the sides of the face, and the neck" (*Cent. Dict.*). It survives to the present day in the head-dress of nuns. The word *barbe* applies to a portion of the wimple, "consisting of a piece of white plaited linen, passed over or under the chin, and reaching midway to the waist" (*NED* s.v. Barb, sb. 2, 3). When Chaucer says of the Prioress (*Prologue*, A 151), "Ful semely hir wimpel pinched was," he is thinking of the plaited "barb." Fairholt, *Costume in England* 2.28, says the barb was "peculiar to the religious sisterhood or to widows"; but see J. H. de Hefner-Alteneck, *Costumes*, Vol. 4, Plates 222, 228, which would indicate a more general use of the barb as part of a lady's dress. *Wympel* seems to be an authentic revision. Perhaps the reason for the substitution was a desire to avoid the assonance of *barbe* and *bare*.

112. Compare *Knight's Tale*, A 1500:

And, for to doon his observaunce to May;

and Skeat's note on the passage. The proper observance of May is to go into the fields and gather flowers and greenery, rather than to sit in a "paved parlour" and listen to the tale of *Thebes*.

113. *I*, an exclamation. See variant readings, and compare 2.128.

117. *It satte.* Skeat reads *sete* and notes: "The right reading is necessarily *sete*, for A.S. *sǣte*, 3 p.s. pt. t. subj. of *sitten*." But there is no MS. authority for Skeat's form. H5Cx read *sit*; all the other authorities give *satte*, *sate*, or *sat*. *Satte* is to be explained as a new analogical subjunctive, formed from the indicative *sat*.

134. Compare 1.1038.

150-151. "They began to discuss many unfamiliar, joyous, and serious topics." Skeat interprets *unkouth* as an adverb modifying *gladde*, with the sense "exceeding"; but *NED*, s.v. Uncouth, Unco, lists no such adverbial use earlier than the eighteenth century.

154. Hector is a wall of protection for Troy, and a rod of chastisement for the Greeks.

156. In Benoit's account of the earlier battles of the war, Hector is several times wounded; but, when the nature of the wound is specified, it is always in the face. See the *Table des Noms Propres* in the edition of Constans s.v. Hector. Chaucer seems to have no specific episode in mind.

158-161. These lines, which have no counterpart in Boccaccio, seem to echo Guido, *Historia*, sig. e 2, b, col. 1: *Statura Troianorum:* "In viribus vero et strennuitate bellandi vel fuit *alius Hector, vel secundus ab ipso.* In toto etiam regno Troiae juvenis nullus fuit tantis viribus nec tanta audacia gloriosus." The corresponding passage in Benoit, *Troie* 5439-46, contains the lines:

> E li plus proz, fors que sis frere
> Hector . . .
> Flor fu cil de chevalerie,
> E cist l'en tint mout bien frarie.

Compare 3.1774-5.

167-168. Compare *Rose* (Langlois) 5660-2:

> Lucans redit, qui mout fu sages,
> Qu'onques vertu e grant poeir
> Ne pot nus ensemble voeir.

These lines follow immediately on the account of Appius and Virginia, which Chaucer used in the *Physician's Tale*. Compare Lucan, *Pharsalia* 8.494-5: "virtus et summa potestas Non coeunt."

189. "Of those that I should most like to be praised by." The phrase *of hem* is to be construed both with *alle pris*, in the preceding line, and with *preysed be.*

191-203. This account of the martial exploits of Troilus has no counterpart in Boccaccio; nor can I discover any episode of Benoit, or of Guido, which specifically corresponds to it. Nearest, perhaps, is the feat of Troilus in the Eighteenth Battle, where he drives the Myrmidons in confusion to their tents (*Troie* 21004-

24). But this battle is long after the separation of Troilus and Briseida, and shortly before the death of Troilus. Both Benoit and Guido give countless instances of the valor of Troilus. See for example *Historia* sig. k 4, b, col. 1 : *Potentia Troili.*

220. Various scribes have tried to regularize the metre of this line; see variant readings. Skeat adopts the reading *is it tyme,* found in H2H3GgH5.

236. "Apart from the question of amorous relations"; see *NED* s.v. Paramour, 2.

248. *Fremde*, distant, like a stranger; see *NED* s.v. Fremd, 3. I adopt the reading *fremde* without hesitation, though found only in AD and Th, since the context will not permit *frende* which has the authority of the MSS. One must assume that the error, a substitution of a familiar for an unfamiliar word, was present in the original of all the MSS., and that AD and Th have correctly emended.

260. Compare the proverb in MS. Douce 52.: "þe last word byndeth þe tale" (*Festschrift zum XII Allgemeinen Deutschen Neuphilologentage in Muenchen*, Erlangen, 1906, p. 47).

261. *Bihovely*, useful; compare *Parson's Tale*, I 386.

273. "Therefore I will try to adapt myself to her tender mind."

281-287. From *Fil.* 2.44:

> Sol una volta ha nel mondo ventura
> Qualunque vive, se la sa pigliare;
> Chi lei vegnente lascia, sua sciagura
> Pianga da sè senz' altrui biasimare.

Compare Shakespeare's *Julius Caesar* 4.3.218.

328. "You have had a good day's fishing."

329. "How are you to improve, though we both get worse?"

344. *Vertules*, lacking in the magic power which every gem was supposed to possess. See Thorndike's *History of Magic,* 2.387-92 *et passim* (consult index).

346-350. Compare 1.897-903 and note.

351. "It is no joke."

355-357. Compare 3.274-80.

366. *Doute of reson*, reasonable fear, or uncertainty.

384. "Let your reserve be sweetened, modified, a little."

387. *Felen*, probe.

392. Skeat cites Ovid, *Art. Am.* 2.107: "ut ameris, amabilis esto"; but Pandarus says that love for love is a reasonable reward.

393-396. Skeat cites Ovid, *Art. Am.* 2.113-14:

> Forma bonum fragilest, quantumque accedit ad annos,
> Fit minor et spatio carpitur ipsa suo;

but Chaucer is following *Fil.* 2.54:

> pensa che vecchiezza,
> O morte, torrà la tua bellezza.

398. Hazlitt (p. 501) cites a proverb: "Too late to grieve when the chance is past"; and (p. 193): "He is wise that is ware in time."

400-405. Wrinkles and gray hair are the nemesis of the proud beauty in Ovid, *Art. Am.* 2.117-18.

411-419. Compare 1.1022; 3.273.

424. *Peynted proces*, narrative or argument so colored as to conceal its real nature; see *NED* s.v. Painted, 2 b, and Process, **sb.**, 4.

425. Criseyde again invokes Pallas in 5.977, 999.

435-436. Compare *Tes.* 1.58:

> O fiero Marte, o dispettoso Iddio;

and *Tes.* 3.1:

> Marte nella sua fredda regïone
> Colle sue furie insieme s'è tornato.

See note on 4.22-4.

465. *Myn estat*, i.e. my honor as a lady.

470. "Of two ills choose the least" (Hazlitt, 343). A widely current proverb; see Düringsfeld, 2. no. 752.

507-553. This episode, which Pandarus describes to Criseyde, has not been previously narrated. It is similarly recounted by Pandaro in *Fil.* 2.56-61.

513. Throwing darts or spears, either at a mark or in competition to see who could throw farthest, was a recognized medieval game; see Strutt, *Sports and Pastimes*, ed. Cox, pp. 62-3.

516. *And I afer*, And I afar off. In this line JR alone give what must be the correct reading. *Fil.* 2.57 reads: "Io non gli era vicin."

The reading of JR gains some support from H2Ph. The reading *aftir* does violence to the metre. It is hard to see why the MSS. should have bungled so simple a line. The confusion must already have been present in the original of the existing MSS.

522-539. This confession of sin, reported by Pandarus, is a striking illustration of the medieval convention which treats of courtly love in terms of the Christian religion. It is a *confessio amantis*. Troilus confesses that he has hitherto been a rebel to Love, and uses a phrase from the *Confiteor*. He addresses Love in language suggested by words which Boethius applies to the supreme God, and prays to be defended against the mortal sin of despair. (See following notes.) On a similar principle, Gower constructs his *Confessio Amantis*.

525. *Mea culpa, mea culpa, mea maxima culpa* is part of the *Confiteor*, the Catholic formula of confession.

526-528. God so disposes events that, in accordance with impartial providence, he guides the end of all men; i.e. destiny is controlled by divine providence. The thought of these lines is in accordance with the discussion of destiny and providence given by Boethius, 4. pr 6. See in particular lines 42-56 and 149-51: "The whiche god, whan he hath biholden from the heye tour of his purveaunce, he knoweth what is covenable to every wight, and leneth hem that he wot that is covenable to hem." In Chaucer the god is Love.

530-531. The sin of "wanhope," or despairing of the mercy of God, is a branch of Accidia, "which dampnable sinne, if that it continue unto his ende, it is cleped sinning in the holy gost"; see *Parson's Tale*, I 693-704. So the lover who despairs of mercy separates his soul from Love. Compare Gower, *Conf. Am.* 4.3389-712.

538-539. *Gledes*, embers; see *NED* s.v. Gleed. Compare Ovid, *Met.* 4.64:

Quoque magis tegitur, tectus magis aestuat ignis,

where Ovid is speaking of the secret love of Pyramus and Thisbe. Chaucer uses the line again in his *Legend of Thisbe*, 735-6:

As, wry the gleed, and hotter is the fyr;
Forbede a love, and it is ten so wood.

Le Roux de Lincy cites (1.71) a fifteenth century proverb: "Le teu plus couvert est le plus ardent." Compare *Two Gentlemen of Verona* 1.2.30.

553. Compare Gower, *Conf. Am.* 6.143-5:

> Wher as I moste daunce and singe
> The hovedance and carolinge,
> Or forto go the *newefot*.

554-574. With these lines, compare 1.547 *ff*.

584-585. "Wisdom added to beauty is like a ruby set in a ring." For the comparison of wisdom to rubies, see the A.V. of Job 28.18; Proverbs 3.15; 8.11; but in the Vulgate version of these passages the ruby is not specified. Chaucer is following *Fil.* 2.43:

> Ben' è la gemma posta nell'anello,
> Se tu se' savia come tu se' bella.

610-644. This episode of the triumphal ride of Troilus through the streets of Troy has no counterpart in Boccaccio, nor any close original in Benoit or Guido. Benoit, *Troie* 10201-18, describes Hector's entry into the city after the Second Battle, in which he is seriously wounded. All the people, including ladies and "dameiseles," go out to wonder at him, and acclaim him with loud cries. Compare also *Troie* 20609-27. (For neither passage is there a parallel in Guido.) In *Troie* 10609 Troilus is pointed out among the other chiefs, as they go out to the Third Battle, by the ladies seated in the embrasures of the windows.

In *Fil.* 2.82, Troilo and Pandaro together ride by Criseida's window. From this hint, Chaucer seems to have developed this episode and that of the second ride, 2.1247-81.

611. *Ascry*, clamor, outcry; see *NED* s.v. Ascry, sb. *NED* remarks: "In many places it is impossible to tell whether we ought to read *ascrye* or *scrye*" (the aphetic form). Note that H4GgH5Th prefix the definite article.

615. One is strongly tempted to adopt the reading *latis* for *yates*; but this reading is found only in the unreliable H2, and even the closely related Ph reads ʒ*atis*. "Lattice" fits the context better than "gates," unless we may assume that the word *gate* was applied to a swinging window, an assumption for which I have found no authority. Nevertheless, I have preferred to abide by the all-but-unanimous evidence of the MSS. But see *NED* s.v. Lattice, 1.

617-618. There were six gates in the walls of Troy, of which one was called Dardanides, in honor of Dardanus, an ancient king of Troy. According to Benoit, *Troie* 3148, it was the second gate; according to Guido, *Historia* sig. c 1, b, col. 2, it was the first. By this gate the Trojans issued from the city for the Second Battle (*Troie* 7672; *Historia* sig. g 3, a, col. 2). This may suggest that it was from this battle that Troilus was returning (compare note to 2.610-44). In this battle he was in command of the second "conrei" (*Troie* 7749). Benoit describes the gate at length (*Troie* 7676-86), but says nothing of the barrier chain, which had obviously been opened to permit the egress of the troops (cf. *Troie* 7672), and left open for their return.

621. The day on which Troilus rode by Criseyde's window was one which was astrologically fortunate for him.

622-623. Compare Boethius, 5. pr 6.115-17: "And yif thou seyst heer, that thilke thing that god seeth to bityde, it ne may nat unbityde (as who seith, it mot bityde), and thilke thing that ne may nat unbityde it mot bityde by necessitee." See 4.1016-57. Le Roux de Lincy (2.259) quotes from the thirteenth century *Roman de Siperis de Vignevaux:*

> Ce qui doit advenir on ne puet nullement
> Destourner qu'il n'advienne, ce dit on bien souvent.

637. Compare *Squire's Tale*, F 558:

> His maner was an heven for to see.

644. Compare 2.158 and note.

651. "Who has given me a love-potion?"

656. *For pure ashamed*, because completely filled with shame. A similar phrase, "For pure 'abaissht," occurs in Gower, *Conf. Am.* 4.1330. On this passage Macaulay comments: "the use of the past participle with 'for' in this manner occurs several times in Lydgate, e.g. 'for unknowe,' meaning 'from ignorance,' *Temple of Glas*, 632, 'for astonied,' 934, 1366, and so with an adjective, 'for pure wood' in the English *Rom. of the Rose*, 276."

670. *ythe*, O.E. *geðēon*, prosper. The form in the text is supported by CpH1J; the remaining MSS. give the simple form *the*.

671. Compare the proverb: "Every thing has a beginning"; "En toutes choses faut-il commencement" (Düringsfeld, 1. no. 102).

677. A nine-syllable line, which various scribes have tried to regularize; see variant readings.

680-686. Venus is the most beneficent of the planets (hence "blisful"). She was well placed ("Disposed") in her "seventh house." The term "house" has two different astrological senses. It may mean the sign of the zodiac in which a given planet exerts its greatest influence. In this sense of the term, the sign Libra is the "house" of Venus. In "horary" astrology, however, a "house" denotes a one-twelfth section of the heavens, as seen from the point of observation. The whole sphere of the skies is cut in two equal portions by the circle of the horizon, half being above, half below. These hemispheres are again divided into half by a great circle, passing from the north to the south point of the horizon, and through the zenith. Each of these quarters is trisected by other great circles, passing through the north and south points of the horizon. The twelve "houses" so formed are numbered consecutively, beginning with the "house" immediately *below* the eastern horizon, and ending with the "house" immediately *above* the eastern horizon. The "seventhe hous of hevene" is, therefore, the portion of the heavens just above the *western* horizon. In the course of twenty-four hours, all the stars will pass through all twelve houses. For any question concerning love, the astrologer inquires what planets are at the moment in the seventh house, which "gives judgment of marriage and all manner of love-questions." A malefic planet—Saturn or Mars—in the seventh house causes ill fortune in love. But Venus is a benefic planet, and especially concerned with affairs of love. Venus in the seventh house marks a very propitious hour. At the time when Criseyde was making up her mind, Venus was in her seventh house, and was also "with aspectes payed," i.e. other planets stood in favorable aspects to her (see note on 3.715-17). Moreover, Venus, favorably placed at the present moment, had also been not entirely hostile ("not al a foo") to Troilus at his nativity. Compare with this passage 3.715-32 and notes.

691. "On what she would make up her mind at last"; see *NED* s.v. Appoint, 5.

700. The "auctour" whom Chaucer follows for Criseyde's cogitations is actually Boccaccio; see *Fil.* 2.69-78. But Chaucer uses his source with great freedom.

716-718. From *Rose* (Langlois) 5744-6:

> Pour ce, se je defent ivrece,
> Ne vueil je pas defendre a beivre.
> Ce ne vaudrait un grain de peivre.

724-725. Boasting of favors received is a mortal sin against the law of Love; compare Gower, *Conf. Am.* 1.2399-680. See also *Parson's Tale*, I 393.

734-735. The *alpha* text of these lines (see variant readings) is nearer than Chaucer's later text to *Fil.* 2.70:

> Io non conosco in questa terra ancora
> Veruna senza amante . . .
> E come gli altri far non è peccato,
> E non può esser da alcun biasimato.

741. See variant readings. It is plain that this line was confused in the original of all existing MSS. It is impossible to determine which word-order Chaucer intended.

752. "Untied in a pleasant pasture"; see *NED* s.v. Lease, sb. 1, and compare *Fame* 1768.

754. "Checkmate" completely ends the activities of the king in chess. Compare *Rose* (Langlois) 6652: "Eschec e mat li ala dire," where, however, the context is entirely different. See also Rutebeuf, *Le Miracle de Théophile* 6-8, and *Duchess* 659-60.

756. Compare *Squire's Tale*, F 619.

759. "I am not a 'religious,'" a member of a monastic order, and so under vows of celibacy.

767-769. *Oversprat* is a syncopated present, and *overspradde* the preterite, of *overspread* (see *NED* s.v. Spread, vb.), from O.E. *ofer* + *sprædan*. For the change of vowel, see Ten Brink, ¶ 50.

777. I retain the reading *wey*, which has overwhelming MS. attestation. It was clearly the reading of γ; so that the reading of A must be regarded as a scribal emendation. H2 has introduced a clumsy alteration of the line; but the closely related Ph reads *wey*. The impossible reading *wex* of J seems to be a corruption of *wey*. The reading *why* of Gg was, no doubt, present in the common ancestor of GgH5, H5 having substituted the gloss *cause*. Both Skeat and Globe read *why*; and it is possible that Chaucer so wrote the line. But it is clear that *wey* stood in the original of all surviving MSS. *Wey* in the sense of "way" does not seem idiomatic English. *Why* in the sense of "cause" fits the context; though it is an unusual use of the interrogative pronoun. It is possible that *wey* is a dialectal variant of *wo* (see Bradley-Stratmann, *M.E. Dict.*, s.v. Wā) ; but, if so, it can only be as an interjection (cf. *weylawey*, 3.1695), for the noun in Chaucer is regularly *wo*, as in lines 783-4 below. Perhaps the passage may be glossed : "that she does not have to say 'alas!' in her complaining" (see *NED* s.v. Complain, 1, b).

784. "Our punishment is that we must drink our own cup of sorrow." Compare *Rose* (Langlois) 11535 :

Teus genz beivent trop de mesaise.

791. S1 has marginal gloss : "Acriores in principi[o] franguntur in fine." I have not been able to trace this sentence, which seems to be a proverb. Wander (*Deutsches Sprichwörter Lexicon*, s.v. Anfang) records proverbs of similar tenor ; see nos. 32, 33, 48, 71. No. 22 reads : "Non sibi concordem spondent exordia finem."

792-793. For examples of "tresoun that to wommen hath ben do," see the *Legend of Good Women*.

797. "No man stumbles against it," i.e. it does not lie in the public way ; see *NED* s.v. Spurn, vb. 1.

798. "Ex nihilo nihil fit" (Hazlitt, 144).

802-803. "Yet all things that people do to please their friends seem to these persons harmful."

804-805. Compare 5.1062 and note.

806. This line resumes the metaphor of 764-9 above.

807-808. "Nought venture, nought have" (Hazlitt, 340). A proverb of wide currency ; see Düringsfeld, 2. no. 574. Compare Usk, *Testament of Love* 1.5.86. The same proverb appears in 5.784 in slightly different phrasing.

813-814. At the house of Deiphebus, also, one goes down stairs to the garden ; see 2.1705.

816. Criseyde's three nieces are a creation of Chaucer. The name Antigone is taken over from the tale of Thebes ; Tharbe and Flexippe seem to be names of Chaucer's invention. (I cannot accept the explanation of these names given by Hamilton, pp. 94-6.) None of the names occurs in Benoit.

825. Note the reading *lay* for *songe* found in αJRH4.

827-875. As Kittredge pointed out (*Mod. Lang. Notes* 25.158),

Antigone's song bears a general resemblance to Guillaume de Machaut's *Paradis d'Amour* (*Poésies Lyriques*, ed. Chichmaref, 2.345-51). There, as here, a lady sings her gratitude to Love for having so well bestowed her affections, and praises the power of Love, who is the source of all virtues and the enemy of vice. There are, however, no close verbal parallels; one must read Machaut's lay in its entirety to recognize the similarity. Young (pp. 174-5) points out a series of very slight resemblances between Antigone's song and *Fil.* 3.83-5; see note on 2.848-50.

841-847. Compare *Complaint of Venus* 1-24.

843. Apollo is god of intellectual illumination. *Stoon of sikernesse*, unmovable rock of security; see *NED* s.v. Stone, 3 b. It is difficult to decide on the basis of the MS. evidence whether Chaucer wrote *sikernesse* or *secrenesse*; see variant readings. Secrecy is a prime virtue of courtly love (compare Lydgate, *Temple of Glas*, 294-5: "mirrour eke was she Of secrenes"); but "stone of secrecy" seems an unnatural figure, unless, perhaps, Chaucer is thinking of some stone of magic virtue. For *sikernesse* compare *Complaint of Venus* 21, and 3.982.

848-850. These lines bear a slight resemblance to *Fil.* 3.83-5. Boccaccio's stanzas are in a song of Troilo in praise of love, the earlier part of which Chaucer has used for the Proem to Book III.

861. Hazlitt (p. 311) records the proverb: "Many talk of Robin Hood that never shot in his bow." Chaucer transfers the bow to Cupid; but the early scribes recognized the proverb. H4 reads: "Thei spekyn of robynhod but thei bente never his bowe"; and Ph has marginal gloss in a contemporary hand: "of Robyn hood."

866. "He deserves no good that cannot suffer sorrow"; compare 4.1584 and note.

867-868. "The man who has a head of glass should beware of throwing stones, when he goes to war." A variant of the familiar modern proverb: "Those who live in glass houses should not throw stones"; see Düringsfeld, 1. no. 600. Closest to Chaucer are the Italian variants cited by Düringsfeld: "Chi ha testa di vetro, non faccia a' sassi," and "Chi ha cervelliera (helmet) di vetro, non vada a battaglia di sassi."

884. *Sike* is an imperfect rhyme for *endite* and *white*. Skeat, in his notes, suggests as a conjectural emendation *site*, sorrow; see

NED s.v. Site, vb. 1 and sb. 1 ; but *site* is apparently confined to dialects more northern than Chaucer's. It represents O.N. *sýta*.

904-905. Compare *Franklin's Tale*, F 1017-18:

> For thorisonte hath reft the sonne his light;
> This is as muche to seye as it was night.

920. Compare *Knight's Tale*, A 1509:

> And loude he song ageyn the sonne shene.

Birds ordinarily sing "agayn the sonne shene" (*Squire's Tale*, F 53-5), i.e. opposite to, in full view of the sun; but the nightingale sings "against" the moon.

925-931. Criseyde's dream is not found in Boccaccio. Compare, however, *Fil.* 7.23-4. For the eagle as type of a royal lover, compare *Parliament of Fowls*.

954. *Don thyn hood*. The injunction must be metaphorical, since hoods were not ordinarily worn in the house. Only Sir Thopas was wont to "liggen in his hode" (B 2101). The whole line seems to mean: "Put on your hat (and go away); your business is attended to."

955. This line refers back to 952 above.

959. "Unless lack of pursuit, growing out of sloth, cause it (to turn out otherwise)."

964. "At any rate one foot of your sorrow has been maimed"; see *NED* s.v. Hamble.

967-973. This stanza follows closely *Fil.* 2.80. Boccaccio's lines, as Rossetti pointed out, are taken almost *verbatim* from Dante, *Inf.* 2.127-32.

1001. "Your evil faring is not chargeable to me"; see *NED* s.v. Along, adj. 1.

1017. The metrical stress, and so the logical emphasis, is on *me*.

1022. When one is being talked about, one's ears "burn" or "glow"; see quotations in *NED* s.v. Glow, vb. 1, 5.

1023-1025. Ovid, *Art. Am.* 1.455-68, advises the lover to write to his lady with caressing words. He should not address her as he would address the Senate, or a grave judge;

> Sed lateant vires, nec sis in fronte disertus.
> Effugiant voces verba molesta tuae!
> Quis, nisi mentis inops, tenerae declamat amicae?

Note variant readings to line 1024.

1026. "Do not write with the hand of a professional scrivener."

1027. Compare Ovid, *Her.* 3.3.:

> Quascumque adspicies, lacrimae fecere lituras;

and Propertius, 5.3.3-4:

> Siqua tamen tibi lecturo pars oblita derit,
> Haec erit e lacrimis facta litura meis.

1030-1036. Compare Horace, *Art. Poet.* 355-6:

> ut citharoedus
> Ridetur, chorda qui semper oberrat eadem;

and the proverbial phrase to "harp upon one string" (Hazlitt, 475).

1037-1043. Compare Horace, *Art. Poet.* 1-5:

> Humano capiti cervicem pictor equinam
> Iungere si velit et varias inducere plumas
> Undique collatis membris, ut turpiter atrum
> Desinat in piscem mulier formosa superne:
> Spectatum admissi risum teneatis, amici?

Pyk is the fish, pike.

1062. Minerva, the goddess of wisdom. Her name must be read with stress on first and last syllables.

1065-1085. Chaucer condenses into three stanzas of indirect discourse the letter given in full by Boccaccio, *Fil.* 2.96-106.

1077. *Leigh* represents O.E. *lēah*, pret. of *lēogan*, to lie. The conventions of love still demand that the lover shall think of himself as of little worth; Chaucer thought such protestations no better than lies.

1083-1085. Note variant readings. We have here a clear case of revision. The omission of 1083 by H2Ph points to a confused reading in the original of their common ancestor. In the same line, JR present a conflation of the reading of GgH5H4 and that of γ. In 1085, J leaves RH4 and gives the γ reading.

1091-1092. From *Fil.* 2.107:

> Lettera mia, dicendo, tu sarai
> Beata, in man di tal donna verrai.

Compare *Fil.* 9.5.

1093-1095. These lines show clear evidence of revision; see variant readings.

1099. Compare Gower's account of "love-drunkenness," "which cleped is the jolif wo," *Conf. Am.* 6.84.

1106-1107. Compare 1.517-18 and note.

1109-1110. "See that you always make a joke of me." Compare *Cant. Tales*, B 1630:

> The monk putte in the mannes hood an ape.

A man's face occupies his hood. To "find a joke" in his hood, or to "put an ape" in his hood, is to make him ridiculous. See *NED* s.v. Ape, sb., 4.

1119. An irregular line. Skeat, without authority, reads *speke* (pret. subj.). See variant readings.

1163. When Pandarus arrived at Criseyde's house, it was "past prime" (2.1095), i.e. past 9 a.m. Dinner would be eaten about ten or eleven (cf. 2.1557-60, and *Shipman's Tale*, B 1395-443). When dinner is finished (2.1185), it is "after noon."

1177-1178. The subject of *avysed* and *fond* is not expressed. It is understood from the preceding stanza.

1197. "Does he know anything about writing letters?"

1201. *To medes*, as a reward; see *NED* s.v. Meed, 1 c. As a reward for writing the letter, Pandarus promises to undertake the task of sewing together the leaves on which it was written. Skeat quotes Tyrwhitt, s.v. Sowe: "it was usual, and indeed necessary, formerly to *sew* letters, when they were written upon parchment; but the practice continued long after the invention of paper."

1219-1225. Boccaccio gives the letter at length, *Fil.* 2.121-7. The Italian Criseida says nothing in her letter of any sisterly relation; but, a little later (2.134), she says to Pandaro:

> Come fratel per la sua gran bontade
> L' amerò sempre.

1229. "Upon a cushion embroidered with gold thread"; see *NED* s.v. Beaten, 5 c, and compare *Knight's Tale*, A 979. See also note by O. F. Emerson in *Philological Quarterly* 2.85-9 (1923).

1238-1239. H4 has marginal gloss: "levis impressio levis recessio." The rhymed form of the phrase marks it as probably proverbial; and Chaucer's "men seith" points to the same conclusion. I have not been able to identify the proverb. Hazlitt (p.

388) records a proverb: "Soon learnt, soon forgotten." In 1238, Skeat reads *impressiounes* for the sake of the metre; but the MSS. all read *impressiouns*.

1247-1281. This episode, in which Troilus again passes under Criseyde's window, is not in Boccaccio; but see note to 2.610-44.

1249. "Together with his company of ten." For this use of the pronoun *some* preceded by a numeral, see *NED* s.v..Some, 3 and -some, suffix 2, and s.v. Thirdsome. The numeral is sometimes, as here, an ordinal, sometimes a cardinal, as in the modern Scottish *foursome*, *threesome*, etc. Note that GgH4A read *tensum* and H2Ph *x. somme*; D substitutes *twelve some*. It is not clear whether Troilus was one of the ten, or whether there were ten followers, with Troilus as an eleventh. In the passages cited by *NED*, the same doubt exists. The preposition *with* seems to suggest that Troilus rode with ten followers. Skeat leans to the other interpretation.

1272-1273. Compare 3.1104-5, where the same figure is used, and see *NED* s.v. Thorn, 2.

1274. "God grant that other ladies may similarly be pierced by thorns of love which they cannot pick out!" It is possible that *mo* should be construed with *swich thornes*; but the context suggests rather that *mo* is indirect object, and *swich thornes* direct object, of *sende*. For *mo* pronominally used in the meaning "others," see 1.613; 3.1514; 4.1125.

1276. Compare *Melibeus*, B 2226: "Whyl that iren is hoot, men sholden smyte." "Strike while the iron is hot" is a proverb of widest currency; see Düringsfeld, 1. no. 405.

1289. "But on that score there was much occasion for labor and activity."

1290. For *alle thing*, see note to 3.696.

1291. "And why do you ask me to speak with him?" The reading *for shame* (see variant readings) is a corruption of the γ original.

1309. A nine-syllable line, which the scribes have tried to emend; see variant readings.

1312. Compare 2.74 and note.

1335. *Spir*, young shoot or sprout; see *NED* s.v. Spire, 3. Compare Alanus de Insulis, *Liber Parabolarum*, ed. Migne, col. 583 A:

De nuce fit corylus: de glande fit ardua quercus.

Compare also Usk, *Testament of Love* 3.5.3-7.

1343. *Refreyde*, grow cold; compare 5.507, and *Rosemounde* 21.

1347. For the cast of dice as a metaphor of the vicissitudes of Fortune, see *Knight's Tale*, A 1238; *Monk's Tale*, B 3851; Gower, *Mirour*, 22102-3, 23399. Dice were actually used as a method of divination to foretell success in love; see Cicero, *De Divinatione* 1.13.23; 2.21.48; 2.59.121, and Macaulay's note on Gower, *Conf. Am.* 4.2792. Compare also 4.1098.

1349. *Gistes*. Skeat and Globe print *gestes*; and Skeat glosses the phrase: "according to his deeds or adventures." But a reference to the martial exploits of Troilus is not in place; and the evidence of the MSS. points strongly to *gistes* as the correct reading, though this form is found only in JCl. *Gistes* best explains the other variants. Moreover, there is no reason why the scribes should have stumbled over so familiar a word as *gestes*. I interpret *gistes* as meaning "casts" (of dice), with reference to line 1347. *Gist* is the regular Old French development of Latin *jactus*, and *jactus* is commonly used for "throw" of the dice (see Ovid, *Art. Am.* 3.353, and the passages from Cicero cited in note to line 1347). The word is used in O.F. with a variety of specialized meanings (see Godefroy, s.v. Giet); but I have found no instance in which it is used of dice, nor have I found the word in English. (*NED* enters three nouns, *gist*; but none of them is identical with that which I assume.)

1369. *Leyser*, opportunity; see *NED* s.v. Leisure, 1.

1380-1383. Imitated by Usk, *Testament of Love* 3.7.99-101: "so ofte must men on the oke smyte, til the happy dent have entred, whiche with the okes owne swaye maketh it to come al at ones." Hazlitt (p. 19) cites the proverb: "A great tree hath a great fall." Erasmus, *Adagia* 1.8.94, cites the phrase: "Multis ictibus dejicitur quercus," as applicable "de re factu quidem ardua, quae tamen assidua industria pervincatur."

1390. *Forbise*, furnish with examples. The correct form of the word should be *forbisne*, or *forbysne*, from the noun *forbysen*, example; see *NED* s.v. Forbysen.

1398. According to Benoit, *Troie* 2939, Deiphebus is the third in age of the five sons of Priam and Hecuba. In the French, the name is metrically four syllables, with stress on the second and fourth. Chaucer consistently treats it as trisyllabic, with stress sometimes on the second syllable, sometimes (2.1542, 1558, 1569, 1611, 1641, 1675) on first and last. For the affectionate relations existing between Troilo and Deifebo, see *Fil.* 7.78-85, a passage not otherwise utilized by Chaucer, which may have given the hint for the episode at the house of Deiphebus; compare Introduction, p. xxix.

1413-1414. "I have never been, and never hereafter expect to be, against a thing where my opposition might be displeasing to thee."

1427. "With spur and riding whip," i.e. "I will use every means to advance her cause"; see *NED* s.v. Yard, sb. 2, 3.

1443-1444. "Deiphebus, who by his nature was disposed to agree to all honor and goodness."

1450-1454. Compare 1.110-23; 4.176-82.

1462. "Found her just rising from the dinner table." The rhyme requires that *arise* be infinitive (with long vowel) rather than past participle (with short vowel).

1467. Chaucer seems to have invented the name of Poliphete, together with the episode of his supposed legal proceedings against Criseyde. Benoit has two personages named *Polibetes*; but they are both Greeks (see *Table des Noms Propres* in the ed. of Constans). According to Criseyde (2.1474), the "false Poliphete" can count on the friendship of Antenor and Aeneas, both of whom ultimately betrayed the city of Troy. (Compare 4.203-5 and note.) Hamilton (p. 97, n. 3) suggests that Chaucer had in mind the "Cererique sacrum Polyphoeten" of *Aen.* 6.484, "who as a Trojan priest could very properly take steps against the daughter of the renegade Calchas."

1495. *Worde and ende*, beginning and end; compare *Monk's Tale*, B 3911.

1503. Compare Luke 8.48: "Fides tua salvam te fecit"; and the almost identical phrase in Luke 18.42.

1534-1535. A metaphor from the sport of deer-hunting. The *triste* is the station taken by the hunter, armed with a bow (see *NED* s.v. Trist, sb. 2, and Tristre). Past this station the deer is driven by the trackers. This is the method of the deer-hunt in *Sir Gawain and the Green Knight*, 1146-77.

1557. Dinner is at 10 a.m.; compare note to 5.1126.

1564-1566. Compare *Rose* (Michel) 19230-3:

> Por ce les vueil ci trespasser,
> Ne si ne vueil or pas lasser
> Moi de parler, ne vous d'oïr ;
> Bon fait prolixite foïr.

Compare also *Squire's Tale*, F 401-8.

1580. Compare 2.1314-15. For the use of charms and incantations in the medical practice of the Middle Ages, see Thorndike, *History of Magic*, 2.482-3, 498, 851-2, 858.

1610. Compare 5.651.

1617. *Heynous* is apparently a trisyllable ; compare O.F. *haïneus*.

1638. "I have brought thy bier." Pandarus seems to be rallying Troilus on his feigned illness.

1644. I adopt the spelling *Criseyda* of CpClH1D, since the word is here accented on the first and third syllables ; compare 1.169.

1661. "Which he would feel no obligation to do for you."

1705. Compare 2.813-14.

1732. *And inward thus.* "And as he came into the room where Troilus lay, he said thus to Criseyde." Possibly the words *ful softely* should be taken as part of the narrative rather than of the speech. If it were possible to regard *bygynne* as a preterite, the whole line might be taken as a stage-direction.

1733. *Defende*, forbid ; see *NED* s.v. Defend, 3.

1734. "In the name of Him who sent us all our souls." *Sende*, a dialectal variant of *sente*, is used by Chaucer in *Rose* 1158 and *Reeve's Tale*, A 4136—in both instances, as here, under the rhyme. This form of the preterite, with voiced instead of breathed explosive, is listed in *NED* s.v. Send, vb. 1.

1735. I can offer no satisfactory explanation of this line. Bell suggested that the crowns were those of Priam and Hecuba, Troilus's royal parents. Skeat was inclined to see an allusion to the two crowns, of roses and of lilies, brought by an angel to St. Cecilia and her husband (*Second Nun's Tale*). Lowes has shown (*P.M.L.A.* 26.315-23 ; 29.129-33) that the crown of roses symbolizes martyrdom, and the crown of lilies virginity. In view of this, Skeat's conjecture is of no more value than is Bell's. Interpretation of the line is rendered more difficult by uncertainty as to the meaning of the words, "in the virtue of." Is Pandarus invoking a moral virtue adorned by two crowns? Or does the line mean "by the power of two crowns"? If one accepts the reading *in the vertue of*, the first of these meanings seems more probable. (But note that JGgH5H4 omit *the*, and that R presents a bungling emendation.) On this assumption, I suspect that the virtue invoked is that of pity. In *Complaint unto Pity* 58, it is called "coroune of vertues alle," and in lines 71-7 Pity is "annexed ever unto Bountee," and is "also the coroune of Beautee." In *Merchant of Venice*, 4.1.184-9, the quality of mercy "becomes the throned monarch better than his crown," and is "twice blessed." Such an interpretation gains probability from the context of the unique stanza, found in R and printed in the variants (see note to 2.1750), where cruelty is said to be incompatible with Bounty and Beauty. This unique stanza apparently was intended to follow immediately line 1736, and may have been written with the purpose of clarifying the passage. On the other assumption, that the line means "by the power of two crowns," it is possible that the crowns symbolize Justice and Mercy. In support of this suggestion, which fits the context as well as the other, see Chaucer's *A.B.C.*, 137-44. Since the Blessed Virgin received from her Son the crown of mercy, while He retained for Himself the crown of justice, it may be that Pandarus, who in the preceding line has invoked "Him who sent us all our souls," is here indirectly invoking Christ and the Blessed Virgin. But Chaucer is not elsewhere in the poem guilty of so glaring an anachronism.

1745. "People surmise at the slightest move." "Wagging of a straw" is a proverbial phrase; for illustrations see *NED* s.v. Wagging, b.

1750 (var.). Immediately after line 1750 R reads:

> Compleined ek heleyne of his siknes
> And feithfully/that pitee was to heere ;

and in the margin of these lines a contemporary hand, possibly that of the scribe, has written the word *Vacat*. After these two lines is found the unique stanza, first discovered by Sir William McCormick (*Furnivall Miscellany*, 296-300), which is printed in the variant readings. The two lines are a repetition of 2.1576-7,

.and have no possible connection with the context, nor with the unique stanza.

The stanza has every appearance of being genuine. Both grammatically and metrically it accords with Chaucer's usage, if we assume in the first line a scribal omission of some such word as *now*—and such omissions are frequent in the text of R. The manner of the lines is distinctly Chaucerian. The idea expressed—that cruelty is incompatible with beauty and bounty—is a commonplace of courtly love poetry, found also in Chaucer's *Complaint unto Pity* (see especially lines 64-77), and in 2.330-50 above. The substance of the stanza might appropriately be spoken by Pandarus to Criseyde. Its proper position, however, would seem to be after stanza 248 rather than after 250, where it is found in R. Stanza 248 contains an appeal to Criseyde not to cause her lover's death; and the unique stanza warns against the sin of cruelty. The stanza might also belong earlier in Book II, after stanza 49; but one cannot see why it should have strayed so far from its intended context.

It would look as though the stanza, which has no counterpart in *Filostrato*, was an afterthought of Chaucer, written to continue the idea of stanza 248. It may well have been written on a discarded piece of paper or parchment, at the top of which had already been written the first two lines of stanza 226. These lines he did not take the trouble to erase; nor did he indicate clearly enough the precise position of the new stanza. The copyist found this loose sheet between the leaves of his exemplar, and incorporated it bodily at the place where it appears in R. Some one, perhaps the scribe of R, troubled by the two floating lines, wrote *Vacat* beside them, by way of calling attention to an incomplete stanza.

1752. *Kankedort*, a word of unknown origin and meaning. It seems to appear, in a corrupted form, in Henry Medwall's *Nature* (*circa* 1486-1500), Tudor Facsimile Text reproduction of Brit. Mus. copy, fol. e, 1, recto:

> One thyng I am certayne
> He wyll no lengar me support
> And that were a shrewd *crank dort*
> Therfore yt ys best that I resort
> To my maysters presence.

With the form *crank dort* compare the reading *kankerdort(e)* of H2PhH4Cx. From the context here, and in Medway, the meaning seems to be "an unpleasant situation." No other instance of the word is known. For some not very profitable guesses at the etymology of the word, see Skeat's note on the passage.

NOTES TO BOOK THREE

NOTES TO BOOK THREE

1-38. These lines follow closely *Fil.* 3.74-9. Boccaccio's stanzas, which owe their suggestion to Boethius, 2. m 8, form the beginning of a song sung by Troilo after he has won the full love of Criseida. See note on 3.1744-71. In this passage, Venus is addressed sometimes as the pagan goddess, sometimes as the planet with astrological influence. She is the power of Love, both in its earthly aspect as sexual attraction, and in its Platonic aspect as the unifying principle of the universe.

1-2. From *Fil.* 3.74:

> O luce eterna, il cui lieto splendore
> Fa bello il terzo ciel.

The old astronomy assigned to each of the seven planets a sphere, or heaven, in the following order outwards from the Earth: Moon, Mercury, Venus, Sun, Mars, Jupiter, Saturn. The planet Venus, therefore, adorns the third heaven. Compare Dante, *Par.* 8.1-3.

3. From *Fil.* 3.74:

> Del sole amica, e figliuola di Giove.

Venus is the friend of the Sun astronomically, because she accompanies him through the heavens, sometimes as morning star, sometimes as evening star; compare Dante, *Par.* 8.12. Her greatest possible distance from the Sun is 45 degrees. Venus is mythologically the daughter of Jove; compare 3.718.

5. From *Fil.* 3.74:

> Benigna donna d'ogni gentil core.

Compare Dante, *Inf.* 5.100:

> Amor, che al cor gentil ratto s' apprende.

Courtly love was exclusively appropriated to those of gentle birth.

6. Boccaccio says, *Fil.* 3.74:

> Certa cagion del valor che mi muove.

Chaucer's line is more general. Venus, as a benefic planet, causes health and gladness.

8-14. Compare 3.1744-50, and note to 3.1744-71.

9. I adopt the reading *wel*, given by CpAH5CxTh (note that Gg and R lack this passage), instead of *wol*, which has better MS. authority, since *wel* is supported by the Italian source. The Moutier ed. of *Fil.* 3.75 reads: "s' io il ver discerno"; but the Paris ed. of the same passage (there numbered 4.68) reads: "se il vero *ben* discerno."

11. "Feel thee at seasons with an eternal emanation." From *Fil.* 3.75:

con eterno
Vapor ti senton nel tempo piacente.

Compare Wisdom 7.25: "[Sapientia] vapor est enim virtutis Dei, et emanatio quaedam est claritatis omnipotentis Dei sincera"; and see Dante, Purg. 11.6.

15-17. From *Fil.* 3.76:

Tu Giove prima agli alti effetti lieto,
Pe' qua' vivono e son tutte le cose,
Movesti, o bella donna.

These lines contain a curious blending of the cult of Love and of Christian theology. In the divine work of creation, the giving of life is operated through the Holy Spirit, designated in the Nicene Creed as "dominum et *vivificantem*," and the Holy Spirit impersonates the *Love* of God. Compare Thomas Aquinas, *Summa*, Pars I, Qu. 45, Art. 6: "Unde et Deus Pater operatus est creaturam per suum Verbum, quod est Filius; et per suum *amorem*, qui est Spiritus Sanctus. . . . Sed Spiritui Sancto . . . attribuitur quod dominando gubernet et *vivificet* quae sunt creata a Patre per Filium."

17. That *comeveden* is the correct reading, is shown by the Italian *movesti* (*Fil.* 3.76). The scribes found the word a stumbling block. See *NED* s.v. Commove. I retain the pronoun *hem*, since it is found in all MSS. It is probably, however, a corruption introduced by "Adam scriveyn." The context demands *hym* (i.e. Jove) and the Italian reads, *Fil.* 3.76:

e mansueto
Sovente *il* rendi all'opere noiose
Di noi mortali.

20-21. From *Fil.* 3.76:

> E in mille forme quaggiù il mandasti
> Quand' ora d' una ed or d' altra il pregasti.

(The Paris ed. reads *piagasti*, i.e. woundest.) Jove assumed the form of a swan in his pursuit of Leda, of a bull with Europa, of a golden shower with Danae, of Amphitryon to win the love of Alcmene.

22-28. This stanza follows closely *Fil.* 3.77. For the idea of love as the school of courtesy and all the virtues, compare 3.1786-806.

22. From *Fil.* 3.77:

> Tu'l fiero Marte al tuo piacer benegno
> Ed umil rendi, e cacci ciascun' ira.

Philosophically, Love, as the spirit of unity (cf. 3.29), appeases the wrath of War; astrologically, Venus, as a benefic planet, mitigates the malefic influence of Mars (see *Complaint of Mars* 36-42); mythologically, Mars became the lover of the goddess Venus (cf. 3.725).

29-30. From *Fil.* 3.78:

> Tu in unità le case e le cittadi,
> Li regni, e le provincie, e'l mondo tutto
> Tien, bella donna.

Compare Boethius 2. m 8:

> Hic sancto populos quoque
> Iunctos foedere continet.

31-34. From *Fil.* 3.78:

> Tu sola le nascose qualitadi
> Delle cose conosci, onde'l costrutto
> Vi metti tal, che fai maravigliare
> Chi tua potenza non sa riguardare.

The Paris ed. (4.71) reads:

> Delle cose viventi, e lor costrutto
> Rischiari in modo a far maravigliare.

Chaucer has made the reference of his lines more specific; Love knows why *she* loves *him*, or *he* loves *her*.

33. *Jo.* Th reads *go* and Cx *geo*; but all the MSS. have *Io* or

Ioo. Skeat suggested that *jo* represents O.F. *joer*, to play, hence to play a game, to make a move; but no other instance of the word is known in English. One is tempted to connect it with *gee*, in current colloquial use in America in the sense of "fit, suit, agree"; see *NED* s.v. Gee, vb., of doubtful etymology, of which illustrations are cited from the early eighteenth century.

35. "Why this fish, and not that, comes into the weir, where it can be caught." Compare the proverbial phrase: "There are as good fish in the sea as ever were caught," currently applied to the selection of a mate.

36-38. From *Fil.* 3.79.

39-49. In these lines, Chaucer leaves *Filostrato* and follows his own invention.

40-41. Compare 1.15.

43. Compare 2.13.

44. *Inhielde*, pour in; see *NED* s.v. Hield.

45. Calliope is the Muse of epic poetry. In 2.8, Chaucer invokes Clio, the Muse of history, as the guide of his second book, where he asserts "That of no sentement I this endite" (2.13). Here he seems to imply, he is rising to a higher level of composition. So Dante, at the beginning of the *Purgatorio* (1.7-9), says:

> Ma qui la morta poesì risurga,
> O sante Muse, poiché vostro sono,
> E qui *Calliopè* alquanto *surga.*

58. The reading of R, *and often sore sike*, since partially supported by JCx (see variant readings), may be an authentic β revision; but the evidence of the β MSS. is so confused that I have not adopted this reading into the text.

59. *Lappe*, a flap of her garment; see *NED* s.v. Lap, sb. 1, 1, and compare 2.448.

80. The reading *hir* for *it*, given by JRCx, may be an authentic β reading; but H4 reads *it.*

81. Compare *Legend* 1817:

> Men mighte smyten of her arm or heed;

and 3.957.

87. *Made it tough*, was annoyingly persistent; see *NED* s.v. Tough, 8 b, and compare 5.101.

88. "To sing a fool a mass" seems to be a proverbial expression; but I am unable to explain it. (There seems to be no connection with the ecclesiastical "Feast of Fools," though in some instances a Mass seems to have been sung as part of the Saturnalia; see Chambers, *Med. Stage* 1.287.)

91. So far as we know, Chaucer is in this episode entirely independent of "bokes olde."

110. The reading *herte* for *wreththe* (see variant readings) seems to be a γ error, accidentally shared by H2 (the closely related Ph reads *wrath*), and by Cx. *Herte* looks like a scribal repetition from 109; however, the phrase "hys herte apese" is found in 3.887. See *NED* s.v. Appease, 2 and 3.

115. Compare *Squire's Tale*, F 496:

> That other weep, as she to water wolde.

120. *I* is an exclamation; note that H5Cx write *ey*.

137-138. "Under the whip of your punishment, in proportion to my offence, even the punishment of death, if I break your prohibition." See *NED* s.v. Yard, sb. 2, 3 and *Shipman's Tale*, B 1287.

144. A slightly irregular line; *and ben ay* constitutes the second foot. Globe, following H2PhH3Cx, omits *ay*; Skeat, without warrant, reads *ylyke ay*.

145. *Talent*, inclination; see *NED* s.v. Talent, 2.

150. I interpret "Natal Joves feste" as meaning Jove's natal feast, i.e. the festival of Jove's birth. Pandarus is then invoking the pagan equivalent of Christmas. (Skeat's citation of Horace, *Ep.* 2.2.187 does not seem apposite.)

188-189. Compare the ballad of *Hugh of Lincoln*, Version A, stanza 17 (Child, 3.244):

> And a' the bells o merry Lincoln
>> Without men's hands were rung,
> And a' the books o merry Lincoln
>> Were read without man's tongue.

192. The letter is that referred to in 2.1697-708.

193-194. *And oon, and two,* both of you.

198. *Bere the belle*, take the lead, like the bell-wether of the flock. A proverbial phrase; see *NED* s.v. Bell, sb. 1, 7.

203. *As I the devyse*, as I recount to thee. The MS attestation

of this line is greatly confused; see variant readings. I adopt the reading of R, supported by H4 (where *thei* seems to be a transposition of *I the*). This reading, with *yow* for *the*, is also supported by γH3S1.

239-287. These stanzas follow closely *Fil.* 3.5-10.

241. *To-yere*, this year; see *NED* s.v. Toyear. Chaucer's phrase translates Boccaccio's *uguanno*, *Fil.* 3.5. This is an important indication of time. Criseyde accepts Troilus as her lover before the end of the year in which the story begins; compare 3.360, and see Introd., p. xxxiv.

273. Compare 2.411-19.

282. I adopt the β reading, attested by JH4RCx, although this reading is also found in H2Ph. Possibly the reading of γH3S1 + GgH5 may represent a revision which was later cancelled. It seems distinctly less apt for the context than the reading of β + H2Ph. Compare note on 3.303.

292-294. S2Dig have marginal gloss: "Cato." The reference is to Book I, Distich 3, of Dionysius Cato, a work of wide popularity:

> Virtutem primam esse puto conpescere linguam;
> Proximus ille deo est, qui scit ratione tacere.

Compare Rose (Langlois) 7055-7:

> La peuz en escrit trouver tu
> Que la prumeraine vertu
> C'est de metre a sa langue frein.

(The idea is repeated in *Rose* (Langlois) 12179-83.) Chaucer uses the distich again in *Manciple's Tale*, H 332-3:

> The firste vertu, sone, if thou wolt lere
> Is to restreyne and kepe wel thy tonge.

In his note on that passage, Skeat cites Albertano of Brescia, *De Arte Loquendi et Tacendi*, (p. xcvi), where the distich of Cato is quoted.

Note variant reading in line 293.

299-300. For a list of such proverbs, see *Manciple's Tale*, H 314-62.

302-303. In 303, γH3S1Th + GgH5 read *Hastow made many a lady*. This seems to be a γ error, shared by GgH5 (compare

note to 3.282). The error arose from the supposition that *O tonge*
is a vocative. *O* is rather to be interpreted as the numeral *one*
(note that H4Cx read *For tonge*). *O tonge* is thus the subject of
hath.

308. "In the nature of things, no boaster is to be believed."

309. Hazlitt (p. 4) cites a proverb: "A boaster and a liar are
cousin-germans"; and Le Roux de Lincy (2.282): "De grans
vanteurs petits faiseurs."

329. "For wise men are chastised, and learn, by watching the
harm that comes to a fool." Compare *Rose* (Langlois) 8003-4:

> Mout a beneüree vie
> On qui par autrui se chastie.

Langlois, in his note on the passage, cites Plautus, *Mercator*
4.4.40: "Feliciter sapit qui alieno periculo sapit." There is a
Latin proverb cited by Erasmus, *Adagia* 2.3.39: "Felix quem
faciunt aliena pericula cautum." Compare 1.203, 630, 635. See
also Nigellus Wirekus, *Speculum Stultorum*, in Wright's *Anglo-
Latin Satirical Poems*, Rolls Series, Vol. 1, p. 145.

340. "To draw up the substance of her grant in a legal document."

349. From *Fil.* 3.11:

> I sospir ch' egli aveva a gran dovizia.

Richesse is a literal translation of *dovizia.*

351-354. From *Fil.* 3.12. Compare also 2.50-5, and *Rose* (Langlois) 47-54:

> Qu'en mai estoie, ce sonjoie,
> Ou tens amoreus, plein de joie,
> Ou tens, ou toute rien s'esgaie,
> Que l'en ne voit boisson ne haie
> Qui en mai parer ne se vueille
> E covrir de novelle fueille.
> Li bois recuevrent lor verdure,
> Qui sont sec tant come ivers dure.

352. *Dreye*, though found only in ClS1, is clearly demanded by
the rhyme; compare 4.1173, and see Wild, p. 176. The other
MSS. read *drye.*

360. Compare 3.241 and note.

371. *Man* seems to be an authentic β reading, though H4 here joins the other authorities in reading *wight*.

374-375. Troilus, in the end, actually meets his death at the hands of Achilles, who cuts off his head and drags his dead body at the tail of his horse; see Benoit, *Troie* 21440-50. In the corresponding passage of *Filostrato* (3.15), Troilo says:

> E s'io non venga nelle man del duro
> Agamennon.

Chaucer transfers the reference to Agamemnon to the following stanza.

379. I adopt the reading *But* of H4RCxS1 as an authentic β reading, despite the fact that J reads *That* with the other authorities. If one reads *That*, line 379 depends for its construction on *swere* in 372; if one reads *But*, one assumes a change from indirect to direct asseveration after the long parenthesis of lines 374-8.

380. *Stokked*, set in the stocks as a punishment; see *NED* s.v. Stock, vb. 1, 1.

385. I adopt the reading of S1, as a probable representative of the original which underlay the variations presented by the MSS.; see variant readings.

404-406. *Departe it so*, make this distinction, i.e. between the man who serves in such a matter for money, and the man who acts from motives of friendship. The service in one case is superficially like that in the other; but there is a diversity in the substance, or essential nature. Troilus appeals to a common distinction ("wyde wher is wist") of scholastic philosophy between *likeness* and *identity of substance*. My colleague, Professor H. C. Longwell, refers me to the following citations: Duns Scotus, *Expositio in Metaph. Arist.*, Lib. 10, Sum. 2, Cap. 1, No. 30 (ed. Paris 1892, Vol. 6, p. 385): "Oportet ergo ad similitudinem vel aequalitatem adesse substantiae diversitatem. Et ideo bene ait Philosophus [Aristotle] quod similia dicuntur ea quae non sunt eadem simpliciter entia, scilicet secundum speciem substantiae." Thomas Aquinas, *Summa*, Pars I, Qu. 31, Art. 2, ad 1: "Diversitas requirit distinctionem substantiae, quae est essentia." Both passages rest apparently on Aristotle, *Metaphysica*. Lib. 10, cap. 3, 1054 b. Chaucer's lines bear a striking verbal similarity to the first sentence of the quotation from Scotus.

409-410. According to Benoit, *Troie* 2949-55, the three daughters of Priam and Hecuba are Andromache, Cassandra, and Polyxena. (This Andromache seems to be distinct from the wife of Hector.) *Frape*, crowd, rabble; see *NED* s.v. Frape, sb. 1.

414. I follow JRS1H2Ph in reading *idon*. Note the reading of CpClH1Th.

417. A slightly irregular line; a light syllable is omitted after the heavy caesural pause. Skeat and Globe read *moste*, a form justified neither by the MSS. nor by grammatical considerations.

442-448. This stanza shows thoroughgoing revision in its phrasing; see variant readings. Perhaps the occasion for revision was a desire to improve the metre of 442. (Skeat regards *swere* as dissylabic, despite the ensuing vowel.)

450. *As writen is in geste.* If Chaucer has a specific written authority in mind, it is probably *Fil.* 2.84:

> Griseida, la qual non men discreta,
> Gli si mostrava a' tempi vaga e lieta;

but from 3.442 to 3.1309, Chaucer's handling of the story departs far from Boccaccio's.

459. This is one of the rare instances in which *a*, *γ*, and *β* present three distinct readings. I regard the *γ* reading as a mere scribal corruption of *β*, since all MSS. read *or to it leye an ere* in the second half of the line, and in *γ* this *it* must go back for its antecedent to line 456. I take it that the *a* reading, *in his speche*, was altered to avoid the repetition of the phrase in 462. It may be of significance that, in 462, ADS1 read *of this thyng* for *of hire speche*.

490. The *β* text substitutes a significant phrase for the colorless tag of *aγ*; see variant readings.

501-504. Boccaccio, at the corresponding stage of his story, says nothing of letters. In 503, the *β* text substitutes *An hondred vers* for *Neigh half this book* of *aγ*. In *Fil.* 2.96-106, 121-7, Boccaccio gives in full letters which Chaucer (2.1065-85, 1219-25) is content to summarize. The first of these letters consists of 88 verses.

510. The MSS., without exception, read *fulfille*, and hence give a faulty rhyme. Th emends to *fulfelle*. O.E. *y* (umlaut of *u*) is regularly represented by *i* in Chaucer (Ten Brink 10, *β*); but the Kentish form with *e* sometimes appears (Ten Brink 11, *ε*).

Gower uses the form *felle* ("fill") in *Conf. Am.* 2.3448; 8.34. Compare Wild, p. 56, and in general for Chaucerian forms derived from O.E. *y*, Wild, pp. 49-70.

512. This line offers both syntactical and metrical difficulties. *That* seems to introduce a clause dependent on *bifel* in 511; but *bifel* is itself in a subordinate clause introduced by *That*. The *That* of 511, in its turn, resumes the *That* of 506. *Pandarus* is the subject of *Hadde* in 518. The whole passage, 505-18, is awkwardly involved. Metrically, *Pandarus* has the value of two syllables (note that H2PhR substitute *Pandare*). γ has attempted to improve the line by omitting *which*, and JGgH5 by omitting *that*.

526-527. The arrangements kept, like hunters, on the leeward side of chattering magpies, who might discover and reveal the secret. A *lette-game* is a "spoil-sport"; compare Usk, *Testament of Love* 1.3.124. In the *Manciple's Tale*, a crow is the spoil-sport who reveals to the injured husband his wife's secret amours. For the magpie as a tell-tale, compare *Fame* 703; *Parliament* 345.

529. βH3S1 substitute *wilde* for the less familiar synonym *fremed* (see *NED* s.v. Fremd, 2, b). Note that H2PhGg corrupt *fremed* into *frend*.

531. The MSS. favor in this line the form *weten* rather than *witen*; see Wild, p. 344.

540. According to Benoit, there was in Troy a temple of Apollo near the gate of Timbree; in this temple was erected the tomb of Hector. See *Troie* 16635-44, and compare Guido, *Historia* sig. i 6, b, col. 1: *Sepultura Hectoris*.

542-543. Skeat cites Ovid, *Met.* 1.566-7:

> factis modo laurea ramis
> Adnuit, utque caput visa est agitasse cacumen.

These lines conclude Ovid's account of Daphne, beloved of Apollo, who was metamorphosed into a laurel tree. The laurel was thus sacred ("holy") to Apollo; but I know of no authority for Chaucer's idea that Apollo speaks from out the tree. In the *Knight's Tale*, the temple doors "clatereden ful faste," and the statue of Mars made its armor ring before the response of the god (A 2422-31). So also the statue of Venus shakes after the prayer of Palamon (A 2265).

549-551. The *chaungynge of the moone* is the phase opposite

to that of full moon, when the Moon is in conjunction with the
Sun, and is hence not visible. The sky was also overcast. The
night would thus be a very dark one. So in Boccaccio, the first
night of the lovers, though very differently managed, is on a
dark and cloudy night (*Fil.* 3.24).

570. Pandarus's statement that Troilus is "out of towne" may
have been suggested by the fact that, in *Fil.* 3.21, Troilo is
actually away from the city ("alquanto di lontano"), when
Criseida first finds an opportunity to summon him to her house.

572. *Yow thurste*, it were necessary for you. Out of the confusion of forms given by the MSS., I adopt *thurste* as having the
best attestation; see variant readings. The preterite-present verb
tharf early developed a variant *thar* (see *NED* s.v. Tharf, thar).
The new preterite of *tharf* is *thurfte* (note readings of S1H5).
From the alternative form *thar* was derived the new preterite
thurte (note reading of D), and with intrusive *s* (perhaps on the
analogy of *dar*, *dorste*) the form *thurste*. The latter form, with
minor variations of orthography, is found in JH4GgH3A, and
with metathesis of *r* in CpH1. ClH2PhCxTh substitute forms of
the verb *dar*, *dorste*, with which *tharf*, *thar* was early confused;
and R incorporates a gloss *aghten*. For the present tense, Chaucer seems to have used the form *thar* (cf. 2.1661, and see Wild,
p. 348). This is the only instance in Chaucer of the preterite. (In
Rose 1089 and 1324, where Skeat prints *thurte*, the authorities
both read *durst*, though the context makes clear that a form of
thar was intended.) The MSS. are also divided on the form of the
accompanying pronoun; see variant readings. The citations in
NED show that beside the older impersonal construction, with
dative of person, there was an alternative use, with personal subject in the nominative. In 2.1661, the construction with dative
hym is clearly attested.

575. Since the whole episode of the supper at the house of
Pandarus is Chaucer's addition to the story, it is not strange that
his "auctour" should be silent on this detail. This seems to be
merely a literary device to suggest to the reader's mind a doubt
as to Criseyde's sincerity.

587. I take *triste* to be present indicative, and *most* the superlative; but it is possible that Chaucer wrote *moste* (pret. of
moot) with infinitive *triste*. See variant readings.

593. The story of Tantalus is alluded to in Boethius 3. m 12.27; compare Ovid, *Met.* 4.458. I reject the β reading *lenger duelle*, because *dwelle* is the rhyme word in 590. Note that J only partially incorporates the β reading. If an authentic revision, which I doubt, it is not a happy one.

596. For *certein* as noun, "a certain number," compare *Miller's Tale*, A 3193, and see *NED* s.v. Certain, B, 5. The men who accompanied Criseyde were doubtless servants. She is a lady of high station, attended by a numerous retinue.

601. A "stew" is a small heated room, sometimes specifically a room used for hot air or vapor baths; see *NED* s.v. Stew, sb. 2, 2 and 3. In *Fil.* 3.25, Troilo awaits Criseida's readiness "in certo luogo rimoto ed oscuro" of her house. In *Filocolo* (2.172) Florio, concealed in a neighboring room, watches the merry-making of Biancofiore and her companions "per piccolo pertugio"; see Introd., p. xxx.

608. I reject the reading of JH4S1Cx as a clear case of error. Note the emendation of R.

609. Pandarus had provided every imaginable dainty.

614. Wade is a mythical hero of Teutonic legend, to whose magic boat Chaucer alludes in *Merchant's Tale*, E 1424. His story, which was apparently current in Chaucer's time, survives to us only in scattered allusions, and in a single episode of the *Thidreks Saga* (ed. Bertelsen, Copenhagen, 1905-11, pp. 73-80), where he is represented as a giant, the father of Wayland the Smith. For a discussion of the story, see article by K. Müllenhoff in *Zeits. f. Deutsches Alterthum* 6.62-9 (1848) entitled "Wado." Speght in his Chaucer ed. of 1598, commenting on the allusion in *Merchant's Tale*, says: "Concerning *Wade* and his bote called Guingelot, as also his strange exploits in the same, because the matter is long and fabulous, I passe it over." See also Skeat's note on *Cant. Tales*, E 1424 (Skeat refers to *Thidreks Saga* under the name *Wilkina Saga*).

617-623. Fortune is the agency which, under God, executes the decrees of weird, or fate. Compare *Fortune* 65-7:

> Lo, thexecucion of the magestee
> That al purveyeth of his rightwisnesse,
> That same thing Fortune clepen ye,
> Ye blinde bestes, ful of lewednesse.

In *Knight's Tale*, A 1663-6, Destiny is the "ministre general" of divine providence. This conception of Fortune is to be traced to Dante, *Inf.* 7.78-80. Compare 5.1541-5 and note, where the lines from Dante are quoted. See also Boethius 4. pr 6.35-56; 5. m 1. 13-16. The particular astrological influences of the high heavens which, under God, brought about the tarrying of Criseyde are specified in lines 624, 625. Chaucer here accepts the orthodox opinion that astrological influences are subject to the will of God, and are, like Fortune, a means through which the divine providence is executed. We men are too dull (like beasts) to understand astrological causes clearly; compare *Man of Law's Tale*, B 194-6. See T. O. Wedel, *Mediaeval Attitude toward Astrology* (*Yale Studies in English*, 60).

624-626. *Bente moone*, the new, crescent Moon (compare 3.549, and Boethius, 1. m 5.6-7). The crescent Moon, Saturn, and Jupiter were in conjunction in the sign Cancer. If the moon is a pale crescent in the sign Cancer, the Sun must be in, or approaching, the next preceding sign, Gemini; and the time of year when Pandarus gave his supper party is clearly designated as May or early June. By Chaucer's calendar, the Sun entered Gemini on or about May 12. The conjunction supposed in these lines, a configuration of extremely rare occurrence, actually took place in May 1385. For a fuller discussion of the passage, see Introd., pp. xvi-xviii.

640. *Ron*, rained. O.E. *rīnan*, properly a weak verb, was also inflected as a strong verb of Class I, with a preterite *rān*, which regularly developed into Chaucerian *ron*, with long open *o*. The same form appears in 3.677; in 3.1557, the weak preterite *reyned* is used. See *NED* s.v. Rine, vb. 2 and Rain, vb.

648. *A game*, i.e. *on game*, in jest.

659-668. The evening's merriment presumably took place in the great hall of Pandar's house. Criseyde is to sleep in a small inner room, a "closet," opening out of the hall. By drawing the traverse (3.674), the hall is divided into two rooms. Criseyde's attending women occupy the "myddel chaumbre," the curtained off portion of the hall nearest to Criseyde's "closet"; Pandarus proposes to sleep in the "outer hous," the farther portion of the curtained hall.

671. A cup of wine was the regular preliminary to going to bed; compare *Prologue*, A 819-20:

And therupon the wyn was fet anon ;
We dronken, and to reste wente echon.

674. The *voide* was "a collation of wine accompanied by spices, comfits, or the like, partaken of before retiring to rest" ; the name is applied "with reference apparently to the withdrawing from a hall or chamber of those who were not to sleep there" (*NED* s.v. Voidee). *NED* quotes from Shirley's *Dethe of King James*, ed. 1818, p. 13 : "Withyn an owre the Kyng askid the voidee, and drank, the travers yn the chambure edraw, and every man departid and went to rist." Compare *Merchant's Tale*, E 1817 :

Men drinken and the travers drawe anon.

The *travers* was a curtain drawn across a room to partition off a portion of it for sleeping ; see *NED* s.v. Traverse, sb., 13.

694-695. Compare *Prologue*, A 476 :

For she coude of that art the olde daunce.

NED, s.v. Dance, sb., 5, quotes Cotgrave : "*Elle sçait assez de la vieille danse*, she knowes well enough what belongs to the Game." Compare also *Physician's Tale*, C 79.

696. Kittredge (*Language*, p. 109) suggests that *alle thyng*, "originally plural, became a stock phrase, of which the syntax was forgotten or obscured, so that even when a singular was used the plural form *alle* might be retained."

705. *Seint Venus*. Note that αγ read *blisful Venus*. In 712, where βγ read *blisful Venus*, α reads *seynt Venus*. For the phrase compare *Wife of Bath's Prologue*, D 604.

711. "To throw the gruel in the fire" is a proverbial phrase, meaning to end the business in failure ; compare *Richard the Redeless* 2.50-2 :

Tyl ȝe of ȝoure dulnesse · deseveraunce made,
Thoru ȝoure side signes · that shente all the browet,
And cast adoun the crokk · the colys amyd.

Compare the modern colloquial phrase, "To spill the beans."

715-732. This passage contains an interesting blending of mythology and astrology. Troilus prays first to Venus, as goddess of love, and as an astrological influence, favorable unless she was "combust or let" at his birth. He asks her to intercede with her father, Jupiter (who is astrologically benefic), to turn aside any evil planetary influence. Troilus next appeals to the gods who are identified with the several planets: Jupiter, Mars, Apollo (the Sun), Mercury, Diana (the Moon). They are named in the order of their distance from the Earth according to the old astronomy (compare note on 3.1-2). Venus, whose place is between the Sun and Mercury, has already been invoked at the beginning of the prayer. Saturn, most distant from the Earth, is not invoked, since his influence is inalterably malefic, and since there is no Ovidian myth which relates any Saturnine amour. Detailed notes on the passage follow.

715-717. Mars and Saturn are malefic planets, whereas Jupiter and Venus are benefic. The term *aspect* is used to denote the angular distance of one planet from another, as seen from the Earth, and is measured in degrees of the zodiac. Literally, it is the way in which they *look at* one another. Thus, if two planets are 30 degrees or 60 degrees apart, they are said to be in "semi-sextile" or "sextile" aspect respectively; and these are benefic aspects. The "quartile" (90 degrees) and "semi-quartile" (45 degrees) are malefic or "bad" aspects, which bring evil to the person born under them. Saturn and Mars in quartile aspect form a very powerful influence for evil. A planet is said to be *combust*, i.e. burnt up, when it is within eight and a half degrees of the Sun. Venus, if combust, loses her benefic power. This power may be *let*, i.e. hindered, by an unfavorable position, or by receiving a bad aspect of another planet. Compare *Knight's Tale*, A 1087-90.

718. H4 glosses *fader* as *iupiter*; compare 3.3.

720-721. H4 has marginal gloss: "Methomorphoseos x°, hos tu care mihi." The reference is to Ovid, *Met.* 10.705. The story of Adonis is told in *Met.* 10.503-739. Compare *Tes.* 7.43; *Knight's Tale*, A 2221-5.

722-723. H4 has marginal gloss: "Perlege methomorphoseos ij." The story of Europa is told by Ovid, *Met.* 2.833-75.

724. Mars, as god of war, is appropriately dressed in a "blody cope." The planet, as seen in the sky, has a reddish light; its astrological color is also red.

725. *Cipres*, Venus, the Cyprian; compare *Fame* 518. Th reads *Cipria*, and H5, substituting a gloss, reads *Venus*. In 5.208, Venus is called "Cipride." Troilus prays Mars, who has himself been in love with Venus, that he will not hinder him ("nought

me lette"). Since Mars is a malefic planet, he cannot help; but he may, by taking up a position in which his power is weakened, refrain from hindering.

726-728. H4 has marginal gloss: "Methomorphoseos i, Vix precatur prece finita, etc." This is an inaccurate citation of *Met.* 1.548, the line at which Daphne's metamorphosis into a laurel tree begins. The story of Daphne is told in *Met.* 1.452-567.

729-730. H4 has marginal gloss: "Methomorphoseos ij." The story of Herse, beloved of Mercury, is told by Ovid, *Met.* 2.708-832. Herse's sister, Aglauros, incurred the enmity of Pallas. Pallas caused her to envy her sister Herse; and Mercury turned her to stone. Chaucer's statement that Mercury's love for Herse was the cause of the anger of Pallas against Aglauros is not correct.

733-735. H4 has marginal gloss: "Tres sorores fatales, Cloto, Lathesis, et Attropos. Una, Cloto, colum baiulat." The three Fates are a literary commonplace for which no definite source need be sought. Clotho and her sisters had spun for Troilus the thread of his fate, before any earthly cloth had been shaped to cover his body. Compare *Legend* 2629-30:

> Sin first that day that shapen was my sherte,
> Or by the fatal sustren had my dom;

and *Knight's Tale*, A 1566:

> That shapen was my deeth erst than my sherte.

Compare also Lydgate, *Complaint of Black Knight* 489-90. For a full, though rather fanciful, discussion of these passages see L. A. Hibbard, "Chaucer's 'Shapen was my Sherte.'" *Philological Quarterly* (Univ. of Iowa) 1.222-4. Compare 4.1208, 1546; 5.3-7.

741-749. The *trappe* is a trap-door, as is explicitly stated at line 759. Ordinarily a trap-door is in floor or ceiling; but, since there is no mention of any ladder, perhaps Chaucer is thinking of a secret door (see *ay* reading in line 759) in the panelling. The trap-door seems to open directly from the "stuwe," where Troilus is concealed, into Criseyde's bedroom. By this door, Pandarus enters, leading Troilus by a flap of his cloak (742). He first softly closes the door which communicates with the room where Criseyde's women are sleeping (749). Troilus, though in the room during the whole colloquy between uncle and niece, is not seen by Criseyde till line 953.

757. *Benedicite.* See note to 1.780.

764. Hazlitt (p. 269) cites this proverb in the form: "It is evil waking of a sleeping dog." For various forms of this widely current proverb, see Düringsfeld, 2. no. 599.

775. "To give him a hood above his cap"; see *NED* s.v. Houve and s.v. Caul. The context shows that the phrase means "to deceive." Compare "sette his howve" (*Cant. Tales*, A 3911), which means "make him look ridiculous."

776. The reading of γH3S1ThJCx is hypermetrical, and clearly wrong. The introduction of a second *mene* before *while* is an easy scribal blunder; but the corruption was apparently not present in the original at the time when the *a* MSS. were derived. I suspect that what we have is an authentic revision bungled by the scribe. "As love another in this meene while" would suit metre and context perfectly. Note that H4R preserve the *a* reading.

782. *Oon of this world*, i.e. unique.

783. *On hym alonge*, chargeable to him; see note to 2.1001.

787. Hypermnestra plans to have Lino escape from her room "out at this goter" (*Legend* 2705), i.e. by help of the eaves-trough; see *NED* s.v. Gutter, sb. 1, 2.

791. *I shal*, I owe.

797. Kittredge has pointed out (*Language*, p. 347) that the name *Horaste* is a variant of *Orestes.* Gower, *Conf. Am.* 3.2176, calls Orestes "Horeste." Chaucer has invented, without any hint from his sources, this imaginary rival lover, and has chosen for him a name from classic story, just as he appropriated the name Antigone for Criseyde's niece. *Sholden loven*, are said to love.

808. The wicked spirit is that of jealousy; compare 3.837; 5.1212-14. See also *Filocolo* 1.259-60.

813-836. Criseyde's discussion of false felicity draws heavily on Boethius, 2. pr 4. 56-132: "The swetnesse of mannes weleful-nesse is sprayned with many biternesses" (86, 87). "For why ful anguissous thing is the condicioun of mannes goodes; for either it cometh nat al togider to a wight, or elles it last nat perpetuel" (56-8). "What man that this toumbling welefulnesse (caduca ista felicitas) ledeth, either he woot that it is chaungeable, or

[479]

elles he woot it nat. And yif he woot it nat, what blisful fortune may ther be in the blindnesse of ignorance? And yif he woot that it is chaungeable, he moot alwey ben adrad that he ne lese that thing that he ne doubteth nat but that he may lesen it. . . . For which, the continuel dreed that he hath ne suffreth him nat to ben weleful" (109-17). "How mighte than this present lyf maken men blisful?" (130). With this speech of Criseyde, compare Arcite's speech in *Knight's Tale*, A 1255-67, and see B. L. Jefferson, *Chaucer and Boethius* 81-93. It is an effective piece of irony that Criseyde, who utters these stanzas, should in the end become herself the type of worldly joy unstable.

837. In 3.1010, Criseyde speaks of "jalousie . . . that wikked wyvere." In Ovid, *Met.* 2.768-77, Invidia eats "vipereas carnes," and her tongue is suffused with venom. In Gower, *Mirour de l'Omme* 2641-5, Detraction, the first of the daughters of Envy, is compared to a snake in the grass. See also *Mirour de l'Omme* 3709-56.

839. *Untriste*, not trustful; see *NED* s.v. Trist, adj. 1 and Tristy, adj. 1.

850. *A faire.* Skeat glosses "a fair thing, excellent thing (sarcastically)." I think the word is rather to be referred to *Fair*, market, with some such sense as "a bad bargain"; but I have no citations in support of the conjecture. In 5.1840, "a faire" is used as type of the transitoriness of the world; see note on that passage. Note the reading of H5, *all lost*, which may be a substituted gloss.

853. H1 and H4 have marginal gloss: "Mora trahit periculum." This seems to be a proverb. Compare *Havelok the Dane* 1352: "Dwelling haveth ofte scaþe wrouht." See also Lucan, *Pharsalia* 1.281: "Tolle moras; semper nocuit differre paratis." *Drecchyng*, delaying; see *NED* s.v. Dretch, vb. 2.

855. H4 has marginal gloss: "Omnia tempus habent." The quotation is from Ecclesiastes 3.1. For the form *alle*, compare note to 3.696.

860. *Benedicite.* See note to 1.780.

861. The fieldfare is "a species of Thrush (*Turdus pilaris*), well known as a regular and common autumnal visitor throughout the British Isles" (*NED*). At the end of winter, it migrates northward. The phrase "Farewell fieldfare" seems to be a pro-

verbial expression, meaning "good-bye, I am done with you." It is so used in the Chaucerian *Romaunt of the Rose* 5510, where the French text has no corresponding phrase.

880. The final *e* of *malice*, protected by the caesura, is not elided; but note the reading of γH3S1Th.

885. Blue is the color of constancy; see *NED* s.v. Blue, 1, e.

890. "Hazel-woods shake," apparently a proverbial term of derision; compare 5.505.

891-892. For the magic properties of various stones, consult the index of Thorndike's *History of Magic* s.v. Gems. Apparently the power to bring the dead to life was beyond even the magic virtues of gems.

896. This line seems to be proverbial; but I have not been able to identify the proverb.

901. *Feffe*, present; see *NED* s.v. Feoff, and compare Boethius, 2. pr 3.44-5: "tho feffedest thou Fortune with glosinge wordes and deceivedest hir."

919. *At prime face*, prima facie.

931-938. *Dulcarnon* is a medieval Latin corruption of an Arabic term meaning "two-horned," and hence a dilemma. Criseyde says she is in a dilemma, "at my wittes ende." Pandarus takes up the word and plays on the fact that "Dulcarnon" was used as a name for the 47th proposition of the first book of Euclid (perhaps on account of the two-horned figure used in the demonstration). But he plays mistakenly; for he confuses the proposition called "Dulcarnon" with another (the 5th proposition of Book I, the "Pons Asinorum"), which was known' as "Eleufuga" or "Fuga Miserorum." (H4 has marginal gloss: "Dulcarnon: fuga miserorum.") It is this phrase which Pandarus translates as "flemyng of wrecches," a "putting to flight of wretches." He goes on to explain that the Euclidian proposition is not really so hard; it puts wretched schoolboys to flight only because of their "verray slouthe" and other wilful "tecches" (moral blemishes, vices; see *NED* s.v. Tache, sb. 1). But Criseyde is wise; and the problem of conduct before her is neither hard, nor one reasonably to be balked. This explanation of Dulcarnon was given in part by Speght in the Annotations of his edition of 1598, who cites Alexander Neckam, *De Naturis Rerum*, Cap. 173 (Rolls Series, p. 295). It was extended by Skeat in

Athenaeum, Sept. 23, 1871, p. 393, and in notes of *Oxford Chaucer*. See also *NED* s.v. Dulcarnon, where an allusion to the Chaucerian passage is cited from the works of More (1534).

936. *Fecches*, vetches, a variety of bean, used as something of little value.

957. Compare 3.81 and note. Chaucer permits himself the identical rhyme of *heed*, used figuratively of a bed (954), and *heed* in its literal sense; but see variant readings.

978. There was a fire-place in Criseyde's room; compare 3.1141.

979. *Fond his contenaunce*, made a show, pretended; see *NED* s.v. Countenance, sb., 2, b, c, d.

989-990. Compare *Knight's Tale*, A 1169.

1010. *Wyvere*, viper; see 3.837 and note.

1016-1019. Criseyde's questioning of divine justice suggests Boethius, 1. m 5 ("O stelliferi conditor orbis"), particularly lines 22-35 of the metre.

1021. "That permittest undeserved jealousy."

1035. Compare 2.784 and note.

1046-1049. Criseyde proposes to establish her innocence by one of three methods: by ordeal, i.e. by some such test as plunging her arm into molten lead; by a solemn oath, in which she should assert her innocence and call down terrible penalties on herself in case she were swearing falsely; by sortilege, i.e. a solemn drawing of lots, in the faith that divine justice would so declare her innocence. For the part played by the first two of these methods in English jurisprudence, see Pollock and Maitland, *History of English Law* 2.595-9. Proof by ordeal was abolished by the Lateran Council of 1215; and the decree became at once effective in England, except for the continuance of ordeal by battle. Purgation by oath was still a customary procedure in Chaucer's time, and even now survives half seriously in various colloquial formulas of asseveration. Proof by drawing lots plays an important part in the story of George Eliot's *Silas Marner*.

1060-1061. The merry summer day which follows on a misty morning is proverbial; see Hazlitt, p. 31: "A misty morning may have a fine day." Compare *Tale of Beryn* 3955-6:

> For aftir mysty cloudis þere comyth a clere sonne;
> So aftir bale comyth bote, whoso byde conne.

Compare also 1.951-2.

1064. "After sharp battles come victories"; see *NED* s.v. Shower, 5.

1067. To Troilus his lady's tears were no slight pain, such as being beaten with a stick.

1088-1089. *Every spirit*, i.e. the three "spirits" which, according to medieval physiology, controlled the bodily functions; see note to 1.306-7. Each of these "spirits" contracted (*in knette*) its vigor, as though stunned or oppressed. The result is a swoon.

1104-1105. Compare 2.1272-3.

1113. *Abreyde*, come out (of his swoon); see *NED* s.v. Abraid, 2, and compare *Clerk's Tale*, E 1061.

1115. In *ay*, they wet his temples.

1120. *Adawe*, wake up, literally, dawn; see *NED* s.v. Adaw, vb. 1, 1.

1154. *She bar hym on honde*, she maintained against him, i.e. accused him. *Bere on honde* seems to be a translation of the French *main-tenir*; see *NED* s.v. Bear, vb. 1, 3 e. *Hym* is dative.

1155. *Hire to fonde*, to make trial of her; see *NED* s.v. Fand, 1.

1161. What Troilus said was of so little value that it would be dear at the price of a stalk of rush. For the rush as a type of worthlessness, see *NED* s.v. Rush, sb. 1, 2. Compare 3.1167.

1184. *Supprised*, seized, violently affected, from O.F. *sousprendre*, a variant of *surprendre*; see *NED* s.v. Supprise, 2.

1189. Pandarus "laid himself down to sleep," i.e. he went to his own bedroom.

1192-1193. Compare *Filocolo* 2.165-6: "dove Filocolo timido, come la grù sotto il falcone, o la colomba sotto il rapace sparviere, dimorava." The circumstances are, however, quite different.

1194. "Regardless of whether, to a given reader, the tale may seem (sweet as) sugar or (bitter as) soot." Compare Usk, *Testament of Love* 2.9.37-9: "al sugre and hony . . . ben but soot and galle in comparison"; and *Political Songs* (Camden Society, Vol. 6), p. 195: "Hit falleth the Kyng of Fraunce bittrore then the sote." (*NED* s.v. Soot.)

1199. Chaucer's appeal to the old books of the clerks is delightfully ironic. Boccaccio's heroine (*Fil.* 3.32) does not tremble with fear.

1203. The "bryghte goddes sevene" are the seven planets,

which control our destiny. The phrase is repeated in *Envoy to Scogan* 3. The reading *blisful* for *bryghte* found in γS1Th is certainly corrupt.

1204. Troilus has passed through Purgatory into Heaven.

1212-1215. Compare the proverb: "Bitter pills may have sweet effects" (Hazlitt, p. 104).

1219-1220. Compare Alanus de Insulis, *Liber Parabolarum*, ed. Migne, col. 592:

> Dulcius haerescunt humano mella palato,
> Si malus hoc ipsum mordeat ante sapor.

See also Boethius, 3. m 1.4-5: "Hony is the more swete, yif mouthes han first tasted savoures that ben wikkid." Compare 1.638-44 and note.

1230-1232. *Bytrent* and *writhe* are both present indicative, the termination *-eth* being absorbed in the dental which ends the word. *Bytrent* means "winds about"; see *NED* s.v. Betrend. The tree and vine as a figure for a close embrace is a literary commonplace; see Ovid, *Met.* 4.365; Dante, *Inf.* 25.58-60; Petrarch, *Sonn.* 277.8; *Filocolo* 1.262.

1235. "When she hears any shepherd speak."

1241. *Moste*, pret. subj. with present meaning, indicating a weaker obligation than the present *mot*; see Wild, p. 350. Note that αγ read *mot*.

1255-1257. Venus is astrologically a benevolent ("wel-willy") planet. Note the blending of mythology and astrology. Dante, *Purg.* 27.95, applies the name "Citerea" to the planet Venus.

1258. Hymenaeus, or Hymen, patron of marriage. H4 in margin of line 1261 has gloss: "Hemaneus deus vinculorum."

1261. Compare 3.1744-71 and note.

1262-1267. Chaucer's lines are modelled on Dante, *Par.* 33. 13-18:

> Donna, sei tanto grande e tanto vali,
> Che qual vuol grazia ed a te non ricorre,
> Sua disianza vuol volar senz' ali.
> La tua benignità non pur soccorre
> A chi domanda, ma molte fïate
> Liberamente al domandar precorre.

Dante's lines are addressed to the Blessed Virgin; Chaucer trans-

fers **them** to the praise of Love. Lines 1266-7 resemble Chaucer's
A.B.C. 180:

> That, nere thy tender herte, we weren spilt.

1282. Compare *Knight's Tale*, A 3089,

> For gentil mercy oghte to passen right,

where Theseus urges Emily to show her "wommanly pitee" to
the faithful Palamon; and *Legend*, Prol. B 161-2:

> Yet Pitee, through his stronge gentil might,
> Forgaf, and made Mercy passen Right.

The language of courtly love has transferred to its own use the
theological opposition of divine mercy and strict justice. Compare Psalm 84.11: "Misericordia et veritas obviaverunt sibi:
justitia et pax osculatae sunt." See also Usk, *Testament of Love*
3.1.133-7.

1291. I retain the αγ reading in this line because the β reading,
though possibly originating in an authentic revision, is in the
existing β MSS. clearly corrupt. As found in JRCx, it is un-
metrical; and the reading *how that* of H3H4 seems to be a not
very happy scribal emendation. Note the other variant readings.

1310. From here to the end of Book III, Chaucer follows,
though freely and with numerous additions, *Fil.* 3.31-73, 90-3.

1316. Compare *Fil.* 3.32:

> D'amor sentiron l'ultimo valore;

but Chaucer has either misunderstood, or deliberately changed,
the meaning of the Italian line.

1323. Between lines 1323 and 1324, αγTh insert stanzas 201
and 202. See note on 3.1401-14. Since Skeat and Globe follow the
αγ arrangement, I have, for convenience of comparison, given in
parentheses the line-numbering of Skeat's text for the whole
passage affected by the shift.

1330. From *Fil.* 3.34:

> O t'ho io in braccio, o sogno, o se' tu desso?

1341. Compare *Fil.* 3.36:

> Voi mi tenete e sempre mi terrete,
> Occhi miei bei, nell'amorosa rete.

1346. γThα read *an hondred*. The reading *a thousand* is nearer to *Fil.* 3.37: "mille sospiri."

1352-1358. This stanza has no counterpart in *Filostrato*. In *Filocolo* (2.181) Florio solemnly espouses Biancofiore with a ring, which she had previously given to him. The lovers then leave the bed, and exchange formal vows before the image of Cupid. The gift of the ring symbolizes the fact that Florio regards the lady not as "amica," but as "inseparabile sposa." No such significance attaches to the episode in Chaucer. The interchange of rings is a commonplace of the ritual of love, for which no definite source can be assigned.

1355. *Scripture*, inscription, or motto, engraved on the rings; see *NED* s.v. Scripture, 3.

1359-1372. From *Fil.* 3.38-9.

1361. *Mokre and crecche*, hoard and scrape together; see *NED* s.v. Mucker, vb. 1, and compare Boethius, 2. pr 5. 11: "for avarice maketh alwey mokereres to ben hated." The verb is apparently derived from *Muck*, dung, contemptuously applied to accumulated wealth. I adopt the reading *crecche*, though attested only by the unreliable authority of GgH5, as best fitting the context, and serving best to explain the MS. variants. It is a dialectal variant of *cracche*; see *NED* s.v. Cratch, vb., 2, and note particularly the citation of Thomas Becon (1564), *Wks.* Pref. (1843) 26: "He that doth nothing but rake and take, *cratch* and snatch, keep and sweep all that he can get." The meaning "scrape together" continues and extends the idea of *mokre*. A scribe, unfamiliar with the form, might easily misread the initial *c* as a *t*, and so alter to *tecche* or *theche* (see variant readings). For these forms with *t*, I can see no justification. *Theche* might conceivably mean "thatch," in the sense of concealing one's gains; but I know of no such figurative use of the word. *Kecche*, the reading of JClCxTh would be a variant of *cacche*, with the significance "lay hold of" (see *NED* s.v. Catch, vb., 6 b); but it has every appearance of being a scribal emendation of *tecche*. Skeat and Globe read *kecche*. The Italian (*Fil.* 3.38) reads "a far denari," "to make money," and gives no clue to the solution of the problem. Note that *denari* is rendered by Chaucer as *pens*, pence.

1370. *The white and ek the rede* seems to mean "white silver and red gold." *Fil.* 3.39 reads: "denari perderanno." In *Par-*

doner's Tale, C 526 *whyte and rede* means "white and red wine"; compare *Nun's Priest's Tale,* B 4032. Possibly Chaucer here means that misers must forego the pleasure of drinking wine.

1373-1379. This stanza has no counterpart in *Filostrato.* The story of Midas, who was granted his wish that whatever he touched should turn to gold, and who was punished for his folly by having his ears changed into the long ears of an ass, is told by Ovid, *Met.* 11.100-93. M. Crassus, surnamed Dives, Roman general and consul, was killed in an expedition against the Parthians in 53 B.C. Florus, *Epitoma* 1.46.11, relates that his head was cut off and sent to Orodes, King of Parthia. "Aurum enim liquidum in rictum oris infusum est, ut cuius animus arserat auri cupiditate." Both Midas and Crassus are stock examples to prove that "coveytise is vice." They are so used by Dante, *Purg.* 20. 106-8, 116-17, and by Gower, *Conf. Am.* 5.141-332, 2068-224. In Gower, the potion of molten gold is administered to Crassus while still alive.

1378-1379. See variant readings. The β reading is more sharply pointed, and distinctly an improvement.

1401-1414. In the $a\gamma$ text, these two stanzas follow line 1323. In β(JRCxH3S1), they are moved to the position which they occupy in this edition. H4 (here normally a β MS.) has the two stanzas in both positions. In these stanzas, there are a number of distinctive β readings (see variants). H4 has the two stanzas in the $a\gamma$ position with $a\gamma$ readings, and then repeats them in the β position with β readings. That the shift was deliberate, is shown by the fact that β has revised 1323 to suit the new context. (S1, though transposing the stanzas, retains the $a\gamma$ reading of 1323.) That the $a\gamma$ position is more original, is shown by the echo of *telle* from 1323 to the first line of the shifted passage. Moreover, had the β position been original, there would have been no need to revise line 1415. What artistic motive may have led to the shift is not clear. The stanzas contain the author's reflections on the story, and in either position interrupt the flow of the narrative; though the β position, just before the transition to the dawn, seems a more appropriate place for comment. The passage has no counterpart in *Filostrato.*

1408-1413. Compare 2.12-35.

1415. The cock is called common astrologer, because by his

crowing he proclaims to all the approach of sunrise; compare
Nun's Priest's Tale, B 4045-8, and *Parliament* 350. S2 and S1
have marginal gloss: "Vulgaris astrologus"; and H4 glosses:
"Gallus vulgaris astrologus; Alanus de planctu nature." The
phrase is taken from Alanus de Insulis, *De Planctu Naturae*, ed.
Migne, col. 436 A: "Illic gallus tanquam vulgaris astrologus,
suae vocis horologio, horarum loquebatur discrimina."

1417-1418. S1 and S2 have marginal gloss: "Stella matutina";
and H4 glosses: "Lucifera stella matutina." The feminine pronoun *hire* indicates that the morning star was Venus. In *Knight's
Tale*, A 1491, the busy lark is called "messager of day." The
reading *bemes* for *stremes*, found in αγS1Th, gives a virtually
identical meaning. For *stremes* in the sense of "rays of light,"
compare 1.305; 3.129; *Duchess* 338; *Complaint of Mars* 83;
Knight's Tale, A 1495.

1419-1420. These lines, which have no counterpart in Boccaccio, seem to have been suggested by Dante, *Purg.* 19.4-6:

> Quando i geomanti lor maggior fortuna
> Veggiono in oriente, innanzi all'alba,
> Surger per via che poco le sta bruna.

Fortuna Major is the name of one of the sixteen "figures" of the
occult art of geomancy. Among the other figures are *Puella* and
Rubeus, referred to in *Knight's Tale*, A 2045 (see Skeat's note on
that passage, *Oxford Chaucer* 5.82-3). Geomancy is a bastard
form of "horary" astrology, by means of which one may resolve
questions without the trouble of consulting an almanach, or looking at the skies. By a process of setting down at random a series
of dots, the artist derives one or other of the sixteen figures. (See
Henry Cornelius Agrippa, *De Occulta Philosophia*, Lib. 3, *ad
fin.;* Lib. 2, Cap. 48, and the treatise of Gerardus Cremonensis
which is included in the 1531 ed. of Agrippa.) The figure so derived will refer him to one of the signs of the zodiac, and to one
of the seven planets. Thus, *Fortuna Major* refers to the Sun, and
to the sign Aquarius. By continuing the process, the geomancer
constructs an arbitrary, or fortuitous, "figure of the heavens,"
with the planets disposed among the signs, from which he can
draw astrological conclusions.

The figure of *Fortuna Major* is a disposition of points which

Skeat happily compared to a four of diamonds placed above a two of diamonds. The name, Fortuna Major, seems to have been applied to a group of six stars in the constellations of Aquarius and Pegasus, which conform roughly in disposition to the geomantic figure. For this transfer of the name, I can find no authority in the geomantic manuals which I have seen; but the fact is asserted in the fourteenth century commentary of Benvenuto da Imola on Dante, *Purg.* 19.4, and repeated thence in modern commentaries on Dante. Skeat, with the aid of Sir Robert Ball, identified the group as comprised of θ Pegasi, and α, π, γ, ζ, η Aquarii (*Academy*, November 3, 1894, p. 352). The identification may be verified from any detailed astronomical atlas. It is this group of stars, then, that was rising in the eastern sky when Lucifer appeared above the horizon. The ecliptic longitude of the centre of this group was in the latter part of the fourteenth century about 319 degrees. In the middle of May (compare note on 3.624-6) these stars should have been about 80 degrees west of the Sun. When the first light of dawn appeared in Troy, the group of stars called Fortuna Major, by "hym that koude it knowe," was about half-way between the eastern horizon and the zenith, and was still rising "estward," with the four stars properly placed above the two. (See article by R. K. Root and H. N. Russell in *P.M.L.A.* 39.56-8.)

In line 1420, the reading *that anoon Criseyde* is given in all the MSS. Skeat emends by reading *than* for *that.* I have preferred to keep the MS. reading. It would seem that Chaucer changed his mind in the middle of the sentence, and never revised the passage. For the construction, compare 4.31-3.

1423-1424. "How woful is it to me that I was ever born, now that day must divide us!"

1428. H1 has marginal gloss: "Almena mater herculis"; and H4 glosses: "Almena fuit mater herculis." When Jove lay with Alcmena to beget Hercules, he miraculously extended the duration of the night; see Hyginus, *Fab.* 29, and compare *Tes.* 4.14. According to the *Roman de Thèbes* (ed. Constans, 2.88), Alcmena lay with Jupiter "iij nuiz ensemble"; so also Boccaccio, *Gen. Deorum*, Lib. 13, who cites Lucan as his authority.

1429-1442. Criseyde's reproaching of Night has no counterpart in *Filostrato.*

1433-1435. These lines bear a general resemblance to Ovid, *Amores* 1.13.15-34.

1436-1442. The Night is thought of as circling the Earth, opposite to the Sun. But instead of keeping its proper speed, Night is doing its office too hastily (*rakel*, hasty, impetuous; see *NED* s.v. Rackle), and is maliciously hurrying below the horizon, and making way for Day. May God curse the Night, and bind it to our hemisphere, so that it may never again be able to go below the horizon. (For the use of *ther* to introduce a prayer or curse, compare 3.947, 966, 1456.) Compare *Filocolo* 1.173 for a somewhat similar address to the Night, where, however, the Night is chided for its slowness. Note αγ reading in 1438-9.

1450-1470. The only hint of this passage in Boccaccio is found in the lines (*Fil.* 3.44):

> Il giorno che venía maledicendo,
> Che lor così avaccio separava.

1453. "Every aperture (which admits the light) possesses, as it were, one of thy bright eyes."

1462. Engravers of small seals would be willing to buy additional day-light.

1464-1470. Chaucer has confused Titan, the Sun (cf. Ovid, *Met.* 1.10) with Tithonus, the mortal lover for whom Aurora, "the dawyng," the "Morwe," obtained the boon of immortality but not the gift of eternal youth. But the confusion is older than Chaucer. Servius in his comment on Virgil, *Georg.* 3.48, says: "et modo Tithonum pro Sole posuit, id est pro Titane: nam Tithonus frater Laomedontis fuit, quem proeliantem Aurora dilexit et rapuit." The same confusion occurs in Boccaccio, *Filocolo* 1.173: "O dolcissimo Apollo, il quale desideroso suoli si prestamente tornare nelle braccia della rosseggiante Aurora." (Compare also *Filocolo* 2.222.) In Dante, *Purg.* 9.1, some MSS. read *Titan*, others *Titon*, i.e. Tithonus.

1490. *Fil.* 3.47 reads:

> Più caro mi saria che'l troian regno.

In Chaucer the "Trojan kingdom" is expanded to "thise worldes tweyne," which seems to mean "two worlds such as this."

1495-1498. Skeat suggests that this passage "somewhat resembles" Virgil, *Ecl.* 1.60-4. The resemblance is entirely general, except for the last line:

Quam nostro illius labatur pectore vultus.

1495. Phoebus, the Sun, shall sooner fall out of the sphere which, in the old astronomy, carries the planet about the Earth. The sphere of the Sun is the fourth in order from the Earth.

1496. The text of αγS1Th reads *dowve*s for *haukes*. The companionship of eagle and dove seems a more striking portent than that of eagle and hawk; but eagle and night-hawk are traditional foes. Pliny, *Nat. Hist.* 10.24 says: "Nocturnus accipiter . . . bellum internecivum gerit cum aquila, cohaerentesque saepe prenduntur." The statement is repeated by Vincent of Beauvais, *Spec. Nat.* Lib. 17, Cap. 20.

1499. Compare Boethius, 5. m 4.1-15: "That wenden that images and sensibilitees . . . weren empreinted into sowles fro bodies withoute-forth; . . . right as we ben wont som tyme, by a swifte pointel, to ficchen lettres empreinted in the smothenesse or in the pleinnesse of the table of wex." Compare also 1.297-8.

1502. Compare 1.674 and note.

1546. Compare *Legend* 1156-7:

Of which ther gan to breden swich a fyr,
That sely Dido hath now swich desyr.

1577. Perhaps an echo of Luke 23.34: "Iesus autem dicebat: Pater, dimitte illis; non enim sciunt quod faciunt"; but *his* may refer to Pandarus (compare line 1572).

1595. The evidence of the MSS. is overwhelmingly in favor of *blisse*.

1600. Phlegethon is the infernal river of fire (Virgil, *Aen.* 6.551). Note variant readings. H4RH3Cx (and probably J before erasure) contain forms which are intended for Cocytus, the river of lamentation. It is interesting to note that MS. S of *Roman de Thèbes* makes "Cochiton" a river "ardanz a toutes leis Assez plus qe nuls fous grezeis" (ed. Constans, 2.17). It is possible that the β MSS. represent a mistaken alteration on the part of Chaucer himself. This is the only passage in Chaucer in which either river is mentioned. Compare Gower, *Conf. Am.* 5.1109-10.

1622-1624. *Filostrato* 3.60 reads:

che dove'l tormento
Hai tolto via con dilettosa gioia,
Per favellar non ti ritorni in noia.

1625-1628. A free rendering of Boethius, 2. pr 4.4-7: "Sed hoc est quod recolentem vehementius coquit. Nam in omni adversitate fortunae infelicissimum est genus infortunii fuisse felicem." Chaucer here follows the Latin more closely than in his translation of Boethius: "But this is a thing that greetly smerteth me whan it remembreth me. For in alle adversitee of fortune, the most unsely kinde of contrarious fortune is to han ben weleful." Compare Dante, *Inf*. 5.121-3:

Nessun maggior dolore
Che ricordarsi del tempo felice
Nella miseria.

Compare also Thomas Aquinas, *Summa* 2.2.36.1, and Tennyson, *Locksley Hall* 76: "That a sorrow's crown of sorrow is remembering happier things."

1634. Compare Ovid, *Art. Am.* 2.11-13:

Non satis est venisse tibi me vate puellam:
Arte mea captast, arte tenenda meast.
Nec minor est virtus, quam quaerere, parta tueri.

Chaucer's line is perhaps a little closer to the paraphrase of Ovid in *Rose* (Langlois) 8261-3:

Car la vertu n'est mie mendre
De bien garder e de defendre
Les choses, quant eus sont aquises.

1636. Compare 3.813-15, 820, 836.

1642. It seems clear that *rakle*, ordinarily an adjective meaning "hasty, rash," is here used as a verb; see *NED* s.v. Rackle. The readings of H2Ph and A seem to be scribal attempts at emendation.

1643. I adopt the reading *stere* on the authority of H3RS1Cx, since it so perfectly fits the context. To "stir a matter," or "stir a question," is a common locution in the sense of "bring into notice or debate"; see *NED* s.v. Stir, vb., 10, and compare Boethius, 3. pr 12.148. I can find no justification for "tearing a matter." The reading *tere* must be explained as a scribal corruption in the original MS. which long escaped correction. (Note that J reads *of to tere*, with *to* written over erasure.)

1685. The β MSS. are confused in their reading. In the β original, the word *sorwe* was either omitted or illegible; and various scribes have tried to emend.

1687. *Comprende*, a shortened form of *comprehende*, is clearly demanded by the metre; see *NED* s.v. Comprend.

1691-1692. Compare Boethius, 3. pr 2. 6-9: "And blisfulnesse is swiche a good, that whoso that hath geten it, he ne may, over that, nothing more desyre. And this thing is forsothe the sovereyn good that conteyneth in himself alle maner goodes."

1693. Compare Dante, *Par.* 19.8:

> Non portò voce mai, *né scrisse inchiostro.*

1703. The chariot of the Sun is drawn by four horses: Pyrois, Eous, Aethon, and Phlegon; see Ovid, *Met.* 2.153-4. Note variant readings.

1705-1706. The horses of the Sun have taken a short cut, which has brought day in ahead of its due time.

1707-1708. Troilus was apparently in the habit of doing sacrifice to Apollo; compare 3.539-41.

1716-1719. Chaucer's lines are a composite of two widely separated passages in Boccaccio. *Fil.* 3.72 reads:

> Era contento Troilo, ed in canti
> Menava la sua vita e in allegrezza;

and *Fil.* 2.84:

> Troilo canta e fa mirabil festa,
> Armeggia, spende, e dona lietamente,
> E spesso si rinnuova e cangia vesta.

Compare also *Tes.* 4.62.

1718. I read *festeyinges* on the authority of S1 alone, since the metre clearly demands the four syllables. The reading gains support from the *festeynynges* of ClH1. Compare 5.455 and the variant readings of that line. *Festeyinges* must be referred to O.F. *festeier*, to make a feast, give an entertainment.

1744-1771. Troilus's hymn to Love is a close paraphrase of Boethius, 2. m 8 (though with some rearrangement in the order of the ideas): "That the world with stable feith varieth acord-

able chaunginges; that the contrarious qualitee of elements
holden among hemself aliaunce perdurable; that Phebus the
sonne with his goldene chariet bringeth forth the rosene day;
that the mone hath commaundement over the nightes, which
nightes Hesperus the eve-sterre hath brought; that the see, greedy
to flowen, constreyneth with a certein ende hise flodes, so that it
is nat leveful to strecche his brode termes or boundes upon the
erthes, that is to seyn, to covere al the erthe :—al this acordaunce
of thinges is bounden with Love, that governeth erthe and see,
and hath also commaundementes to the hevenes. And yif this Love
slakede the brydeles, alle thinges that now loven hem togederes
wolden maken a bataile continuely, and stryven to fordoon the
fasoun of this worlde, the whiche they now leden in acordable
feith by faire moevinges. This Love halt togideres poeples
joigned with an holy bond, and knitteth sacrement of mariages
of chaste loves; and Love endyteth lawes to trewe felawes. O!
weleful were mankinde, yif thilke Love that governeth hevene
governed youre corages!"

At this point in *Filostrato*, Troilo sings to Love a hymn (3.74-9)
which is also based in part on this Metre of Boethius. These stanzas of *Filostrato* Chaucer has used as Proem (lines 1-38) to his
third book. Having so used them, it was necessary to find new
material for the song of Troilus; and Chaucer turned back to
the passage in Boethius from which Boccaccio had received his
inspiration. The four stanzas of Troilus's hymn are omitted by
H2; in the closely related Ph they have been added later, though
by the original scribe, on an inset leaf. Since in this part of the
poem H2Ph represent the earliest state of Chaucer's text, it
would seem that the poet did not in his first draft provide a song
for Troilus to sing. In GgH5, however, which also give an *a*
text, the stanzas are already present. For further discussion of
the matter, see Introd., p. lxxi.

1748. *Enditeth.* Note the variant reading *knetteth* found in
γS1Th and in Ph. (H3 reads *kennyth*.) H2 omits the entire passage; Ph has the passage on inset leaf, and its text is apparently
derived from a γ source. The original of line 1748 is the "Hic
fidis etiam sua *Dictat* iura sodalibus" of Boethius, 2. m 8; but
line 1749 reproduces "Hic et coniugii sacrum Castis *nectit* amori-
bus," which in the Latin immediately precedes. (For Chaucer's

translation of the passage, see preceding note.) If *enditeth* translates *dictat, knetteth* is a literal rendering of *nectit*. The γ reading
cannot, therefore, be dismissed as a scribal corruption. Apparently
Chaucer first wrote *knetteth* and then changed to *enditeth*, which
is the proper word in the context. If so, GgH5 must have derived
their text of the hymn from a β source.

1754. That the reading of JRCxGgH5, *Holde in*, is a scribal
corruption of *Holden* is proved by the Latin, "Foedus perpetuum
tenen·" of Boethius, 2. m 8.

1774-1775. The corresponding lines of *Filostrato* (3.90) read:

> Che ciascun ne dottava, se non erra
> La storia.

The comparison with Hector has the authority of Benoit, *Troie*
3990-2:

> Mais ço nos retrait bien l'Autor,
> Poi ert meins forz en son endreit
> Ne meins hardiz qu'Hector esteit.

Compare 2.158-61 and note. See also Guido, *Historia* sig. k 6, a,
col. 2: *Potentia Troili.*

1779-1781. From *Fil.* 3.91.

1782-1785. *Fil.* 3.91 reads:

> Ed a'suoi tempi Griseida vedendo
> Si rifaceva grazioso e bello
> Come falcon ch'uscisse di cappello.

In the Italian it is Troilo who is compared to the falcon.

1805. Chaucer specifies four of the Seven Deadly Sins.

1807-1810. The Proem to Book III is a hymn to Love, and an
appeal to the Muse Calliope; and at the close of the book, Chaucer again addresses Venus and the Muses. That Venus was daughter to Dione, Chaucer might have learned from Virgil, *Aen.* 3.19,
or from Claudian, *De Rapt. Pros.* 3.433. It is possible that the
suggestion of lines 1807-8 came from Dante, *Par.* 8.7-8:

> Ma Dione onoravano e Cupido,
> Quella par madre sua, questo per figlio.

Compare also *Tes.* 1.3. Lines 1809-10 are certainly inspired by
the *Teseide*. At the very beginning of that poem we read:

> O *sorelle* Castalie, che nel monte
> Elicona *contente dimorate*
> D'intorno al sacro gorgoneo fonte.

And in *Tes.* 11.63:

> E quindi sotto l'ombre graziose
> Sopra Parnaso presso all'Elicone
> Fonte seder con le nove amorose
> Muse, e cantar maestrevol canzone.

Helicon was *not* near Parnassus; but Chaucer places them to-gether also in *Anelida* 16-17; and in *Fame* 518-22 we find:

> Now faire blisful, O Cipris,
> So be my favour at this tyme!
> And ye, me to endyte and ryme
> Helpeth, that on Parnaso dwelle
> By Elicon, the clere welle.

Actually Helicon is a mountain in Boeotia, on whose slopes was the fount of Hippocrene. In *Fame* Helicon becomes a "clere welle"; and in the present passage also it is probable that Chaucer thought of it as a fountain. Boccaccio, in *Tes.* 1.1, calls Elicona a mountain; but in *Tes.* 11.63 it is a fountain. Compare Dante, *Purg.* 29.40, and Virgil, *Aen.* 7.641, which might suggest that Helicon was a fountain. Compare also Guido, *Historia*, sig. a 5, a, col. 1: "Sic totum cordis aviditate scientiae *imbibens* Elicona." For the proximity of Helicon and Parnassus, there is abundance of post-classical authority, e.g. Servius in his commentary on *Aen.* 7.641. For further references on this point, and for an illuminating discussion of Chaucer's use of Dante and Boccaccio in the present passage, see article by Lowes, *Mod. Phil.* 14.705-35.

NOTES TO BOOK FOUR

NOTES TO BOOK FOUR

1-9. Lines 1 and 2 are from *Fil.* 3.94:

> Ma poco tempo durò cotal bene,
> Mercè della fortuna invidiosa.

The remainder of the stanza is made up out of memories of Boethius. With lines 3-5, compare Boethius, 2. pr 1. 12-15: "Fortune . . . useth ful flateringe familiaritee with hem that she enforceth to bigyle; so longe, til that she confounde with unsufferable sorwe hem that she hath left in despeyr unpurveyed." With lines 6 and 7, compare 2. m 1.8-10: "She is so hard that she laugheth and scorneth the wepinges of hem, the whiche she hath maked wepe." With these lines, compare also *Rose* (Langlois) 8039-41:

> E me firent trestuit la moe
> Quant il me virent souz la roe
> De Fortune.

Lines 8 and 9 return to *Fil.* 3.94:

> Ella li volse la faccia crucciosa.

With the whole passage, compare 1.139, 837-54 and notes.

18-21. No specific allusion seems to be intended. Boccaccio, Benoit, and Guido all find cause to speak harm of the heroine. Young (p. 127) refers particularly to *Troie* 13429-94, 13859-66 and *Historia* sig. i 2, a, col. 2; sig. i 3, a, col. 2. In these passages the authors take occasion from the falseness of Briseida to point the essential fickleness of woman.

22-24. H4 has marginal gloss: "Herine furie infernales; unde lucanus: me pronuba ducit herinis." The reference is to *Pharsalia* 8.90; but the passage in Lucan has no bearing on Chaucer's lines. The idea that the Furies are daughters of Night may have been derived from Ovid, *Met.* 4.451-2: "illa sorores Nocte vocat genitas." (Compare Aeschylus, *Eumen.* 323, 419; Sophocles, *Oed. Col.* 40, 106; Boccaccio, *Gen. Deorum.* 3.6-9.) Chaucer's lines suggest Dante's picture of the "Tre furie infernal," *Inf.* 9 37-51:

"Guarda," mi disse, "le feroci Erine.
Questa è Megera dal sinistro canto;
Quella che *piange* dal destro è Aletto:
Tesifone è nel mezzo."

But Chaucer might have learned of the Furies from many sources; see Wise, *Statius*, pp. 12-13; Fansler, *Rose*, pp. 50-1; Lowes, *Mod. Phil.* 14.718-20, and compare 1.9; *Franklin's Tale*, F 950.

25. Quirinus is a name given to Romulus, the mythical founder of Rome (Ovid, *Fasti* 2.475-6). He was a son of Mars according to Virgil, *Aen.* 1.274-6. 292; Ovid. *Met.* 15.863, *Fasti* 2.419. Compare Dante, *Par.* 8.131-2. For the epithet "cruel," compare Statius, *Theb.* 7.703. Astrologically, Mars is a malefic planet.

29-35. Chaucer is following closely *Fil.* 4.1. This battle, in which Antenor is captured, is the Fifth Battle of Benoit (*Troie* 11995-2682) and Guido (*Historia* sig. h 5, b, col. 1, *Bellum quintum*).

31-32. The Sun was in the early part of the sign Leo. In Chaucer's time, the Sun entered Leo on or about July 12. Since the figure of the Lion, which gives its name to the constellation, faces towards the west, the breast of the Lion would be the portion which the Sun first enters. But even in Chaucer's time the constellation Leo had, as a result of the precession of the equinoxes, long ceased to coincide with the zodiacal sign Leo. Since Chaucer's intention is to indicate the season of the year, one may assume that he is thinking of the *sign* rather than of the *constellation*. (Compare note to 4.1590-6.) I believe, therefore, that Skeat's reference to the star Regulus, also known as Cor Leonis, is beside the point. The phrase *Hercules lyoun* alludes to the labor of Hercules in killing the Nemaean lion. The Chaucerian passage is an adaptation of Ovid, *Art. Am.* 1.68:

Cum sol Herculei terga Leonis adit.

37. Note the readings of JH2PhH5 (Gg lacking), which point to an authentic *a* reading *issen* (retained also by J, which does not become an *a* MS. till after 4.430). The verb *issen* (O.F. *issir*), to issue forth, is used by Chaucer in the second sing. *issest* in Boethius, 3. pr 12.119. The reading is supported by *Fil.* 4.1: "Ettor . . . Incontro a' Greci *uscì* negli ampi piani."

38-42. These lines, which have no counterpart in Boccaccio,

suggest the opening lines of Benoit's account of the Fifth Battle
(*Troie* 11996-2006) :

> E senz nule autre demoree
> Se rarmerent tost e isnel,
> Quar venir veient tel cembel
> Ou a dis mile chevaliers
> Trestoz armez sor lor destriers ;
> N'i a cel n'ait heaume lacié,
> Escu e lance e bon espié
> Cler e trenchant d'acier molu.
> Cil de Troie s'en sont eissu
> Volenterif e desiros
> De Grezeis faire coroços.

There is no parallel passage in Guido.

39-40. Note that γS1Th and H5 (Gg lacking) transpose the
order of these lines. Either order is possible ; but the arrangement
of γ separates *armed bright and shene* of line 38 from *with spere
in honde* of line 39.

47. *Shour.* Compare 3.1064 and note.

50-54. The corresponding lines in Boccaccio (*Fil.* 4.2-3) read :

> Ed assai ve ne furon per prigioni,
> Nobili re, ed altri gran baroni.
>
> Tra' quali fu il magnifico Antenorre,
> Polidamas suo figlio, e Menesteo,
> Santippo, Serpedon, Polinestorre,
> Polite ancora, ed il troian Rifeo,
> E molti più.

For this heaping up of prisoners, Boccaccio has no authority
either in Benoit or in Guido. According to these authorities, Polidamas, who was not with his father Antenor at the moment of his
capture, tried to deliver him, and vainly urged the Trojans to
continue the battle. Santippo seems to be Antipus, King of Frisia,
and ally of Priam, who was killed in the same battle (the Fifth)
in which Antenor was captured. Even in Boccaccio, Sarpedon is
in Troy to entertain Troilo and Pandaro shortly after this battle.
Polimestor, king of Thrace, is mentioned by Benoit (*Troie*

26723 *ff.*), but not in connection with this battle. Boccaccio seems to have taken the other names from Virgil—Polites, *Aen.* 2.526; Rhipeus, *Aen.* 2.339; Mnestheus, *Aen.* 5.116, 184, 194, etc. (Benoit's Menesteus, Duke of Athens, is a Greek).

Chaucer has kept the list of names, to which he has added, apparently from his own invention, that of "Phebuseo"; but he has brought the passage into accord with Benoit and Guido by the word "maugre." Antenor was taken "in spite of" the efforts of Polydamas and the rest. According to Guido, the Trojans retired from the field, leaving Antenor prisoner, "*non obstante quod Polidamas, Anthenoris filius, qui sui patris non interfuit captioni, pro recuperatione ipsius multa commisisset in bello*" (*Historia* sig. i 1, a, col. 1: *Bellum quintum*). Compare Benoit, *Troie* 12551-65. H3 in line 51 reads *Palidomas and also Menestes*, omitting *maugre*, and in line 53 reads *and* for *or*. This brings its reading into conformity with Boccaccio. After line 299 of Book IV, H3 becomes an *a* MS.; and between line 1301 and line 1442 gives a number of unique readings, some of which appear to represent Chaucer's text in its earliest state. One is tempted to regard the H3 reading in this passage as Chaucer's earliest draft, subsequently revised to bring it into accord with Guido; but it may be only a scribal revision of what is, after all, a somewhat confused stanza.

57-58. *Fil.* 4.4 reads:

Chiese Priamo triegua, e fugli data.

Both the final *β* text, given in this edition, and the *αγ* text definitely contradict Boccaccio's statement. Chaucer, however, is in agreement with Benoit and Guido, where Ulysses and Diomede are sent by the Greeks to ask for a truce, which is granted by Priam and his council, though against the advice of Hector. See *Troie* 12853-3008; *Historia* sig. i 1, a: *Bellum sextum*. H3 here, as in the preceding stanza, has a reading which accords with Boccaccio (see variant readings).

66. *Thringe*, press, push forward; see *NED* s.v. Thring, vb., 2.

86. *Resport*, regard; see *NED* s.v. Resport. The word is used again in 4.850; *NED* records no other instances of its use.

87. I adopt the reading *lefte*, since it is supported by *Fil.* 4.7:

Ma ciò che aveva tutto vi *lasciai*.

The γ original apparently read *lefte* (altered by Cl to *loste*); *leeste*, the reading of CpH1, seems to be a miswriting of *lefte*, since *leste* is not a correct preterite of the verb *lose*. Chaucer uses either *lees* (O.E. lēas), or *loste* (from O.E. weak verb *losian*). The reading *loste* of aH4R may be due to *los* of line 89, and *lese* of 91. In 92, all authorities read *lefte*.

96. *In hire sherte*, i.e. without any of her belongings. The shirt is the irreducible minimum of clothing; compare 3.1099; 4.1522; *Legend*, B 405; *Wife of Bath's Tale*, D 1186.

104. In *Fil.* 4.10, Calchas refers to himself as "questo vecchio cattivo, Che d'ogni altro sollazzo è voto e privo."

106-107. *Fil.* 4.10 reads:

> Qui son con voi di nobili baroni
> Troiani, ed altri assai, cui voi cambiate
> Con gli avversarii, pe' vostri prigioni.

According to Boccaccio, *Fil.* 4.2-3, many prisoners were taken along with Antenor; but see note to 4.50-4.

114-117. Calchas is an accomplished magician (cf. 1.71-6), who practises various arts of divination. He interprets the oracular responses of Apollo; he is an astrologer; he practises casting of lots ("sort"); he understands augury, i.e. divination from the flight and chirping of birds. For a succinct account of the various branches of magic, see Isidore of Seville, *Etymol.*, Lib. 8, Cap. 9. One may further consult the index of Thorndike, *History of Magic*.

120-126. According to Benoit, *Troie* 25920-3, Neptune built the walls of Troy, and Apollo consecrated them. (Guido omits this statement.) Benoit says nothing of the withheld wages. Homer, *Iliad* 21.441-57, tells how Apollo and Neptune were forced by Jupiter to serve King Laomedon (father of Priam) for a year in return for promised hire. Neptune built the walls of the city; Apollo tended the king's cattle. At the end of the year, Laomedon refused to pay their hire; and they departed angry against the king and against Troy. In Hyginus, *Fab.* 89, the story is briefly told with the statement: "Neptunus et Apollo dicuntur Trojam muro cinxisse." See also Servius, *Comm. in Aen.* 2.610: "Neptunus cum Apolline Troiae fabricati sunt muros"; and compare Boccaccio, *Gen. Deorum*, Lib. 6, Cap. 6.

137-138. Calchas asks that an exchange be made of King Thoas and Criseyde for the Trojan Antenor, held by the Greeks. In *Fil.* 4.12-17, there is no mention of Thoas; Criseida is exchanged on even terms for Antenor. Chaucer has supplemented his Italian source by an appeal to more ultimate authority. In Benoit, *Troie* 13079-120, an exchange is made of Thoas and Antenor; and at the same time Priam freely grants that Briseida be sent to her father. Guido says, *Historia* sig. i 1, b, col. 1: *Bellum sextum:* "Sed rex Priamus ad petitionem Graecorum inter commutationem Anthenoris et regis Thoas Breseidam Graecis voluntarie relaxavit."

143. Chaucer is translating *Fil.* 4.13:

> onde un parlamento
> Di ciò si tenne.

In Benoit, Priam and the Greek princes both assemble "a parlement." Guido uses the word "consilium." Perhaps, as Skeat suggested, the phrase *"his* parlement" gives to Chaucer's line the more specific idea of a legislative body. Compare 4.217.

167. *Iblowe*, published, proclaimed; see *NED* s.v. Blow, vb., 1, 13, and compare 1.384.

176-196. This interposition of Hector has no counterpart in *Filostrato*. The suggestion for it probably came from 1.106-26, which is based on *Fil.* 1.12-14.

186. Compare 4.203 and note.

197-201. Compare Juvenal, *Sat.* 10.2-4:

> pauci dignoscere possunt
> Vera bona atque illis multum diversa, remota
> Erroris nebula.

200. Globe adopts the reading of R, *lettyth hem*, hinders them; compare *Merchant's Tale*, E 1573. Note the reading of H3Cx. Neither the MS. testimony, nor the passage of Juvenal which Chaucer is paraphrasing, permits us to decide whether we have a form *leten, laten* (O.E. *lǣtan*) or of *letten* (O.E. *lettan*). I have followed the authority of Jγ in reading *lat hem nat*, permits them not.

203-205. Antenor and Aeneas persuaded Priam to treat with the Greeks for peace, and, having entered into treasonable negotiations with the Greeks, delivered to them the Palladium. The loss of this sacred relic led the way to the destruction of Troy. See Benoit, *Troie* 24397-5713, and Guido, *Historia* sig. m 1, a, col. 1—sig. m 4, a, col. 1 : *Proditio Troiae*. Compare also *Duchess* 1119-20.

210. *Here and howne*. This phrase, though the reading is clearly attested by the MSS., remains an unsolved problem of Chaucerian lexicography. The context suggests that it means something like "one and all," "persons of high estate and low"; but neither the phrase nor its constituent words can be identified. Skeat's very cautious suggestion that *here* is O.E. *hēore*, gentle (see *NED* s.v. Here, adj.) and *howne* a development of "an A.S. *Hūna*, which may mean a Hun, a savage" is not satisfactory. There is an O.N. *hūn*, which means a "young bear," and hence metaphorically "urchin, boy"; and one might conceivably refer *here* to O.N. *herra*, lord, master. But this suggestion is as unconvincing as Skeat's. H5 and Cx present bungling attempts at emendation.

215. Note variant readings. The reading *But* of *a* was apparently revised to *That*; but the alteration in the MS. seems to have resulted in illegibility. *And* is a substitution of the γ original. *What* of JRH3 is a misreading influenced by the succeeding *what*.

217. *Substaunce*, majority ; see *NED* s.v. Substance, 15.

225-227. These lines are imitated from Dante, *Inf.* 3.112-14 :

> Come d'autunno si levan le foglie
> L'una appresso dell'altra, infin che il ramo
> Vede alla terra tutte le sue spoglie.

Dante uses the simile to describe the damned on the shores of Acheron. His lines are modelled on Virgil, *Aen.* 6.309-12.

229. A rather violent extension of the preceding simile. Troilus, bereft of the leaves of happiness, is like the naked tree in winter, his life closed in by the black bark of care.

239-241. Chaucer's simile follows closely *Fil.* 4.27. Boccaccio, in his turn, is imitating Dante, *Inf.* 12.22-4 :

> Qual è quel toro che si slaccia in quella
> Che ha ricevuto già il colpo mortale,
> Che gir non sa, ma qua e là saltella.

Dante is in turn indebted to Virgil, *Aen.* 2.222-4.

246. From *Fil.* 4.28:

> I miseri occhi per pietà del core,

i.e. his eyes wept out of compassion for his broken heart. The form *piete* (three syllables), though found only in JH2S1, seems clearly right. The reading *of his herte* I take to be a scribal attempt to repair the metre broken by the corruption of *piete* into *pite*.

247. The *a* reading is closer to the Italian "*parean* due fontane," *Fil.* 4.28.

251-252. Compare *Clerk's Tale*, E 902-3:

> Curseth the day and tyme that nature
> Shoop him to been a lyves creature.

Lyves is gen. sing. of *life* used attributively as equivalent to *living*; see *NED* s.v. Life, 15, b. Compare *Merchant's Tale*, E 1864, and Gower, *Conf. Am.* 4.382.

263. H1 has marginal gloss: "Sine causa."

260-287. The references to Fortune in this passage are found also in the corresponding stanzas of *Filostrato* (4.30-2). They are Boethian commonplaces. Compare 1.837-54; 4.1-9.

271-272. Compare the Monk's definition of tragedy (B 3165-7) as the story—

> Of him that stood in greet prosperitee
> And is yfallen out of heigh degree
> Into miserie, and endeth wrecchedly.

(Compare Boethius, 2. pr 2. 51-2.) Troilus recognizes that he is a tragic figure; compare 5.1786; 1.4 and note. The present passage looks like an echo of the lines of the *Monk's Prologue*. Scholars are inclined to believe that the *Monk's Tale* was written earlier than *Troilus*. Perhaps the definition of the *Monk's Prologue* was taken over from the pre-Canterbury form of the work.

279. *Combre-world*, one who uselessly encumbers the earth; see *NED* s.v. Cumber-world.

300-301. Oedipus, horror-stricken at the discovery that he had killed his father and married his mother, tore out his eyes. Compare Statius, *Thebais* 1.46-52, and *Roman de Thèbes* 497-500.

See also note on 2.100-8. The reference to Oedipus is not present in the *a* text; see variant readings.

302. I adopt the reading *wery*, in spite of the fact that *verray* has somewhat better MS. attestation; see variant readings. *Wery* is much better suited to the context, and has the support of *Fil.* 4.34:

> O anima tapina ed ismarrita,

where *tapina*, wretched, corresponds to *wery*. *Wery* is also supported by 4.1142. I regard *verray* as a scribal substitution under the influence of line 288; the corruption, however, was probably present in the original of all the MSS., since Ph reads *verrey*. Note the reading *werray* of Gg, which looks like a conflation of the two rival readings.

316. Compare *Legend*, B 94, where Chaucer applies to the daisy the phrase "lady sovereyne," and B 275, where it is applied to Alcestis. In the corresponding passage of *Filostrato* (4.36), Troilo addresses Criseida as "o dolce bene."

323-329. This stanza bears a general resemblance to *Tes.* 11.91.

356-357. Compare *Man of Law's Tale*, B 608-9:

> allas! what mighte she seye?
> For verray wo hir wit was al aweye.

Note that *a*S1Cx read *was al aweye* in line 357.

381. "If it only were as certainly false as it is (actually) true."

392-393. Compare Boethius, 2. pr 2. 7-9: "And yif thou mayst shewen me [Fortune] that ever any mortal man hath received any of tho thinges to ben hise in propre, than wol I graunte frely that alle thilke thinges weren thyne whiche that thou axest." (Fortune is speaking of riches and dignities.) Compare also 1.843.

407-412. These lines suggest Ovid, *Amores* 2.4.9-48.

413. The *heroner* is a falcon specially trained to fly at the heron; see *NED* s.v. Heroner. *For ryvere* means "for the sport of hawking," the banks of a river being a particularly favorable place for the sport; see *NED* s.v. River, sb. 1, 2, and compare *Sir Thopas*, B 1927:

> And ryde an hauking for riveer.

414-415. The quotation assigned to "Zanzis" is from Ovid, *Remedia Amoris* 462:

> Successore novo vincitur omnis amor.

Chaucer is following *Fil.* 4.49:

> E come io udii già sovente dire,
> Il nuovo amor sempre caccia l'antico.

Boccaccio gives no definite authority for the quotation. Ovid's line introduces a passage in which it is explained that Atrides consoled himself for the loss of Chryseis by accepting Briseis, slave of Achilles, as a substitute; so that it has a particular (though perhaps fortuitous) appropriateness. Compare also *Remedia Amoris* 484, the line which ends the exemplum:

> Et positast cura cura repulsa nova.

Neither Boccaccio nor Chaucer would have gone so far on the path of anachronism as to let Pandarus mention the name of Ovid. But why Chaucer chose the name "Zanzis" (compare various readings) as his imaginary authority, has never been explained. In *Physician's Tale*, C 16, "Zanzis" (variant reading: *Zephirus*) is referred to as a painter, along with Apelles. There Chaucer presumably meant Zeuxis. Kittredge notes (*Chaucer's Lollius* 70, n. 3) that in the Alexander story there is a Zeuxis (not the painter) who was one of Philip's courtiers, and who wrote to Philip to inform him of Alexander's extravagance. Rossetti conjectured that "Zansis" resulted from a corrupt reading of Boccaccio's "già sovente" in the lines quoted above.

418. Compare *Fil.* 4.59:

> ma puonne ben cadere
> In processo di tempo.

421-424. Compare *Fil.* 4.59, and Ovid, *Remedia Amoris* 139-44, 149-50, 205-6, 214-40.

431. *Unthrift*, folly, wickedness; compare *Purity* 516, 1728. The Man of Law's tale of Constance is a "thrifty tale" (B 1165).

432-434. Compare *Rose* (Langlois) 4639-42:

> Quant au sarmon seiant m'aguiete,
> Par l'une des oreilles giete
> Quanque Raison en l'autre boute,
> Si qu'ele i pert sa peine toute.

435. A slightly irregular line; *he answerde* constitutes the third foot. Note that JH4RH1A omit *he*, a possible reading if line 434 is regarded as parenthetical.

443. *Enhabit*, a syncopated form of the past participle, *enhabited*, in the sense of "established in"; see *NED* s.v. Inhabit, 4. *NED* cites *Act* 12 *Hen. VII*, c. 6: "The Merchauntes Adventurers inhabite and dwelling in divers parties of this Realme of England." Chaucer's line corresponds to *Fil.* 4.50:

A cui son dato, e tutto son di lei.

460-461. These lines are imitated by Usk, *Testament of Love* 1.2.166-7: " 'Ye wete wel, lady, eke,' quod I, 'that I have not played raket, nettil in, docke out, and with the wethercocke waved.' " In the game of racket, two players "strike the ball alternately with their rackets and endeavour to keep it rebounding from a wall" (*NED*). Line 461 alludes to a "charm uttered to aid the cure of nettle-stings by dock leaves; hence . . . a proverbial expression for changeableness and inconstancy. The charm to be repeated during the rubbing process is: 'Nettle in, dock out, Dock in, nettle out, Nettle in, dock out. Dock rub nettle out' "; see *NED* s.v. Dock, sb. 1, 3, where several examples of the proverbial phrase are cited. Compare *Notes and Queries*, (Ser. 1) 3.133.

462. *Care* is present subjunctive. The failure so to understand it has led the scribes into many vain attempts at emendation; see variant readings.

466. Compare Seneca, *Ad Lucilium Ep.* 78.13: "Levis est dolor, si nihil illi opinio adiecerit; contra, si exhortari te coeperis ac dicere: 'Nihil est aut certe exiguum est. Duremus; iam desinet'; levem illum, dum putas, facies." See also Boethius, 2. pr 4. 79-82.

468. "Make me into a Stoic," like Seneca, from whom is derived the quotation of line 466.

473-476. Chaucer is here following freely *Fil.* 4.54. Boccaccio, however, does not mention Proserpine. Compare *Fame* 1511, where Chaucer cites Claudian's *De Raptu Prosperpinae*. Dante, *Inf.* 9.44, refers to Proserpine as "regina dell' eterno pianto." With 475-6, compare 4.786-7.

481-483. *Why gabbestow*, "Why do you talk idly, you who

formerly said to me:". Troilus reminds Pandarus of the words which he had spoken in 3.1625-8.

503-504. *Sely*, happy, blessed; see *NED* s.v. Seely. Mod. Eng. *silly* is the same word with modified meaning. These lines are from Boethius, 1. m 1.12-14: "Thilke deeth of men is weleful that ne cometh not in yeres that ben swete, but cometh to wrecches, often ycleped."

505-511. A free adaptation of *Fil.* 4.61.

506. "I would have paid thee money not to slay me."

511. H4 glosses "cold: mors; hete: vita." Compare 1.420.

519-520. Compare *Rose* (Langlois) 6382-3:

> Je vei maintes feiz que tu pleures
> Come alambic seur alutel.

An alembic is an apparatus formerly used in distilling; its modern equivalent is a retort. All the MSS. give the aphetized form *lambyc* or *lambek*; H2H3 omit the indefinite article *a*.

548. After the first destruction of Troy, Hesione, sister of Priam, was forcibly carried away to Greece by Telamon (Benoit, *Troie* 2793-804). Priam sent Antenor as ambassador to the Greeks to demand her return (*Troie* 3187 *ff.*); but the Greeks refused to surrender her. The rape of Helen by Paris is done as a reprisal for the refusal to give up Hesione (*Troie* 4059-68). The "ravysshyng" of these two women led to the Trojan war.

556. Were Troilus to ask Criseyde openly from his father, the request would be an accusation of her, in that it would reveal the fact that she was his mistress. *Fil.* 4.69 reads:

> Poi penso questo fora un accusarla,
> E far palese le cose commesse.

557. *Syn*, a reduced form of *sithen*, is here used adverbially in the sense of "in the next place, furthermore"; see *NED* s.v. Sith, 1 b, and Sithen, 1. *Purchace*, get possession of, acquire (with no implication of money payment); see *NED* s.v. Purchase, vb., 4. The whole line corresponds to *Fil.* 4.69:

> Nè spero *ancora* ch'el dovesse *darla*.

560. In *Fil.* 4.69, Troilo adds as a further reason for Priam's refusal—

> E perchè la direbbe diseguale
> A me, al qual vuol dar donna reale.

585. *By note*, i.e. in musical accord; see. *NED* s.v. Note, sb. 2, 3 c.

588. A proverb; see *NED* s.v. Nine, 3 a and 4 b, for examples.

594. The γα reading *ifounde* is somewhat closer to *Fil.* 4.72: "innanzi esser ripreso alquanto."

595. A *gnat* is a recognized type of little value; see *NED* s.v. Gnat, 1 b. The whole phrase is equivalent to "here sterven as a wrecche" of line 629, below.

600-602. H4 has marginal gloss: "Audaces fortuna juvat etc." Erasmus, *Adagia* 1.2.45, cites Cicero, *Tuscul. Quaest.*, Lib. 2: "Fortes enim non modo fortuna adjuvat, ut est in veteri proverbio, etc." Compare Virgil, *Aen.* 10.284: "Audentes Fortuna iuvat." The proverb appears in slightly different form in *Legend* 1773, and *Reeve's Tale*, A 4210. *Fil.* 4.73 reads:

> la fortuna aiuta
> Chiunque è ardito, e' timidi rifiuta.

607. *Of fered*, frightened off (or "because of being frightened"); see *NED* s.v. Fear, vb., 2. But see variant readings.

608-609. In *Fil.* 4.74, Pandaro gives a different turn to the idea:

> Passisene ella come fa Elèna;

i.e. "let her put up with the publicity of her love, just as Helen does."

618. Chaucer is reproducing *Fil.* 4.75:

> Amor promessa non cura, nè fede;

but his language is an echo of that in *Knight's Tale*, A 1163-8:

> Wostow nat wel the olde clerkes sawe,
> That "who shal yeve a lover any lawe?"
> Love is a gretter lawe, by my pan,
> Than may be yeve to any erthly man.
> And therefore positif lawe and swich decree
> Is broke al-day for love, in ech degree.

The passage in *Knight's Tale* is a development of Boethius, 4. m 6. 37-9. Boccaccio's line may have been suggested by Ovid, *Art. Am.* 1.631-6.

622. "Bravely venture everything on a single play, even though the odds are against you." The reference is to the game of hazard,

of which the American craps is a simplified form. A player throws two dice, and the sum of the numbers which fall is the "main." If the "main" is six, the caster may win by throwing at the next cast either six or twelve. If he throws 2, 3, or 11, he loses. If his second throw is a number other than these, that number becomes his "chance." He continues to throw until he wins by throwing again the "chance," or loses by throwing the "main." If six is the "main" and seven the "chance," probability favors the "caster" at the odds of six to five. The chances are correspondingly *against* the "setter," who bets against him. To "set" one's all on six and seven is, therefore, to venture with the odds against one. The phrase therefore became a proverbial expression for taking a long chance. Cotgrave, in his Dictionary (1611), s.v. Desesperade, glosses: "*Iouër à la desesperade*, to set his whole rest, or set all on sixes, and sevens" (*NED*). For the later development of the phrase, which is responsible for the modern "To be at sixes and sevens," see *NED* s.v. Six, B 5. (I cannot agree with the explanation of the origin of the phrase there given.) For other references to the game of hazard, see *Cant. Tales*, B 125, C 653. Compare also 2.1347.

627. In *Knight's Tale*, A 1010, Palamon and Arcite are found lying on the field of Thebes,

> Thurgh-girt with many a grevous blody wounde.

630. *Spede* must be read as two syllables, though we should expect elision. Skeat and Globe read *that it recche*; but *recche* does not elsewhere govern a direct object—compare 1.496, 797; 2.338, 434; 4.1447, 1588.

644. Note the *a* reading *But any aungel* for *But if that Jove*. The revision heightens the classical coloring.

659-661. Chaucer is translating closely *Fil.* 4.78. Boccaccio is in turn imitating Virgil's account of Fame, *Aen.* 4.188:

> Tam ficti pravique tenax quam nuntia veri.

683. *For pitous joie* translates "tutte piene Di pietosa allegrezza" of *Fil.* 4.80.

684. "Dear enough, even if one paid only a mite." The same phrase is found in *Legend* 741. Compare 3.900.

708-714. This stanza is omitted by γ. The omission must be due to a scribal lapse; for the stanza is present in all the other authorities, and corresponds to the first four lines of *Fil.* 4.84. The remainder of this stanza of the Italian is represented by Chaucer's lines 715-21.

727-728. "As much relief as a man feels if one scratches his heel to cure his headache." The figure is taken over from *Fil.* 4.85:

> e non era altro che grattarla
> Nelle calcagne, ove'l capo prudea;

but in the Italian it is an *itching* head rather than an *aching* head. Perhaps Chaucer wrote *icche* instead of *ache*; but the MSS. all read *ach*, *ache*, or *ake*, except Gg which reads *eche*.

736. *Ownded*, waved, wavy, from O.F. *ondé*, ultimately derived from Lat. *unda*, wave; see *NED* s.v. Oundy, and compare *Fame* 1386.

745. Criseyde, overwhelmed with sorrow, concludes that she must have been born "in an evil constellation," i.e. at a time when the planets were in unfavorable "houses" and in unfavorable "aspects" one to another. See notes to 2.680-6, and 3.715-17. This meaning of *constellation* is its older meaning; the modern meaning, a permanent grouping of fixed stars, is first recorded by *NED* under date of 1551.

750-756. In *a*(JGgPhH3) this stanza follows immediately line 735; in *βγ* it is moved down to the position which it occupies in this edition. Moreover, *βγ* has revised the first line of the stanza to accommodate it to its new position, and has similarly revised line 757, which in *βγ* immediately follows the stanza. There can be no doubt that the transposition is deliberate; nor can there be any doubt which position was the original one. In Boccaccio a single stanza, *Fil.* 4.87, serves as source for the last three lines of stanza 105, for the transposed stanza, and for stanza 106; and the details are found in the same sequence as in the *a* text of Chaucer. Stanza 88 of *Filostrato* corresponds to stanza 107 of *Troilus*. The *βγ* position of stanza 108 disturbs the order of Boccaccio, by inserting a stanza of Criseyde's words between two stanzas which describe her conduct. It succeeds somewhat better in coordinating words and deeds.

762. Boccaccio does not mention Criseyde's mother, and Benoit is equally silent. Chaucer seems to have taken the name from the

story of Thebes, where Argia (*Thebais* 2.297, and 12. *passim*) is the wife of Polynices. This Theban "Argyve" is mentioned by Chaucer in 5.1509. Boccaccio's Criseida merely says, *Fil.* 4.88:

> Deh or fuss'io nel nascere affogata.

765. Compare *Prologue*, A 179-80:

> a monk, whan he is cloisterlees,
> Is lykned to a fish that is waterlees.

767-768. Compare Boethius, 3. pr 11.75-90.

770. Criseyde says that the phrase "roteles moot grene soone deye" is a "byword," i.e. a proverb. Le Roux de Lincy, 1.83, cites the phrase: "Seiche racine de l'arbre la ruyne."

776. Boccaccio says, *Fil.* 4.89: "sen va la smarrita Anima fuor del corpo." Chaucer's curious metaphor suggests Dante, *Par.* 1.20-1:

> Si come quando Marsia traesti
> Della *vagina* delle membra sue.

But Dante is referring to the *flaying* of Marsyas.

778-784. Criseyde will wear the black habit of a nun, who has renounced the world; and the observances of her religious "order" shall be sorrow, lamentation, and abstinence. According to *Fil.* 4.90 her "vestimento nero" is to be testimony that she is in effect a widow, now that she must be separated from Troilo.

789-791. Compare Ovid, *Met.* 11.61-6:

> Umbra subit terras, et quae loca viderat ante,
> Cuncta recognoscit: quaerensque per arva piorum
> Invenit Eurydicen, cupidisque amplectitur ulnis.
> Hic modo coniunctis spatiantur passibus ambo,
> Nunc praecedentem sequitur, nunc praevius anteit,
> Eurydicenque suam iam tuto respicit Orpheus.

Lines 61-64 of this passage are quoted by the scribe in the margin of H4. See also *Met.* 10.1-85; Virgil, *Georg.* 4.453-527. Chaucer's "feld of pite" seems to be an adaptation of Ovid's "arva piorum." Perhaps, also, he had run across some etymology which connected *Elysium* with the Greek 'ελεέω, to have pity (cf. *Kyrie eleison* of the Mass). The word *Elysium* is not, however, etymologized by Isidore of Seville. Note that *a* reads *Ther Pluto regneth* for *That hight Elisos.*

813-819. This stanza follows closely *Fil.* 4.96. For lines 816-17, however, the Italian has only the single word "scapigliata," dishevelled. In 4.87, occurs the line:

> E i biondi crin tirandosi rompea;

compare above 4.736-7. Guido, in his account of Briseida's grief at her departure from Troy, *Historia*, sig. i 2, a, col. 2: *Bellum sextum*, says: "aureos crines suos a lege ligaminis absolutos a lactea sui capitis cute divellit." There is no corresponding phrase in Benoit (see *Troie* 13261-322). But dishevelled hair is a commonplace of grief; compare *Filocolo* 1.188.

818. That *martire*, though attested only by H2H4, is the correct reading is established by *Fil.* 4.96:

> Dar vero segno degli aspri martiri.

Boccaccio rhymes *martiri* with *disiri*; so that Chaucer has taken over not only the word but the rhyme. The reading *matere* fits neither sense nor rhyme. Note, however, that CpJRDS1 give the form *matire*. For *matire* as a variant of the normal *matere* see *Canon's Yeoman's Tale*, G 770.

829. *Cause causyng.* Criseyde is translating the logical term "causa causans," i.e. primary, original, cause, as opposed to "causa causata," a secondary cause.

836. H4 has marginal gloss: "Extrema gaudij luctus." The quotation is from Proverbs 14.13: "Risus dolore miscebitur, et extrema gaudii luctus occupat." The same text is quoted by Chaucer in *Man of Law's Tale*, B 424, and *Nun's Priest's Tale*, B 4395.

841-847. Cummings (p. 73) points out that this stanza is based on *Fil.* 4.97. In Boccaccio these lines are spoken by Pandaro to Criseida.

850. *Resport*, regard; see note to 4.86.

865. Compare *Knight's Tale*, A 1400-1:

> And saugh that chaunged was al his colour,
> And saugh his visage al in another kinde.

Chaucer is there speaking of the love-lorn Arcite.

868. A slightly irregular line; note variant readings.

870. *Bytrent*, winds around; see 3.1231 and note.

880. *Fil.* 4.102 reads:

> E quanto questo sia cosa molesta
> A Troilo.

This suggests that *moleste* is a noun (see *NED* s.v. Molest, sb.), the direct object of *dooth*, causes, with *Troilus* as indirect object.

884. *Into litel*, within a little, very nearly; see *NED* s.v. Little, B 8.

887. *Fawe*, dialectal variant of *fayn*; see *NED* s.v. Fain. *Fawe* is found in *Wife of Bath's Prologue*, D 220, there also under the rhyme.

910. "Before death completely drive out that spirit which he is assailing in my heart." The *goost* is apparently the "vital spirit," whose seat is the heart; compare note to 1.306-7. I follow the preponderance of MS. authority, and read *he beteth*; but see variant readings.

922. "For to what end (death) he would straightway direct his course"; see *NED* s.v. Pretend, 12.

927. The "flat" of a sword is its broad surface, as opposed to the edge; see *NED* s.v. Flat, C. 1, b. In *Squire's Tale*, F 156-65, there is a magic sword which will heal the wounds it has given, if one strokes them with the "platte" of the sword. Chaucer's line clearly means "be to him a cause of healing rather than of injury"; and it is probable that he is alluding to some such magic as that of the *Squire's Tale*. Achilles had a spear, the wounds given by which could be cured only by applying rust scraped from the spear itself; see *Met.* 13.171-2. In *Remedia Amoris* 44-8 Ovid applies the idea to the wounds and healing of the lover. Compare Dante, *Inf.* 31.4-6:

> Così od'io che soleva la lancia
> D'Achille e del suo padre esser cagione
> Prima di trista e poi di buona mancia.

Scartazzini, in his note on this passage, says that the conceit is much used by "nostri poeti antichi." Dante's "esser cagione" suggests Chaucer's "Beth . . . cause." Compare *Squire's Tale*, F 239-40.

936. Compare 4.1261-3.

947. I follow CpS1JH3CxTh in reading *al allone*; scribal omission of the *al* is a highly probable error.

953-1085. The long discussion of God's foreknowledge in its relation to man's freedom is a close paraphrase of Boethius, 5. pr 3.7-71. In Prose 2, Philosophy has asserted both the doctrine of the liberty of free will and that of God's providence. In Prose 3, Boethius, speaking as a character in the dialogue, replies with a long argument to prove that if God foreknows our actions, these actions cannot proceed from our own free choice, and insists that "the bitydinge of the thing ywist biforn ne may nat ben eschued." This argument Troilus reproduces point by point. In the remainder of Prose 3, Boethius points out certain conclusions which must follow on the denial of free will. The reply of Philosophy is contained in Proses 4-6. She resolves the conflict by declaring that necessity is of two sorts: simple necessity, which cannot be avoided, and conditional necessity. The necessity which derives from God's foreknowledge is of the second sort. *If* God foreknows that a man will do a certain thing, he will necessarily do it; but the man's action is free, and is not constrained by God's foreknowledge of the choice that he will freely make. It is this reply of Philosophy (in Prose 4) that underlies the playful discussion of the same problem in *Nun's Priest's Tale*, B 4424-40. On the whole question of Chaucer's interest in this much disputed question, see B. L. Jefferson, *Chaucer and Boethius*, 71-80.

This long soliloquy was not present in Chaucer's earliest draft of the poem. For a full discussion of the matter, see Introd., pp. lxxi-lxxii.

958-959. These lines state the thesis which Troilus sets out to prove. Compare Boethius, 5. pr 4.47-8: "It bihoveth first to shewen, that nothing ne bitydeth that it ne bitydeth by necessitee." It was the destiny of Troilus to be lost.

960-966. Boethius, 5. pr 3.7-10: 'For yif so be that god loketh alle thinges biforn, ne god ne may nat ben desseived in no manere, than mot it nedes been, that alle thinges bityden the whiche that the purviaunce of god hath seyn biforn to comen." Troilus makes a specific application to his own case.

967-973. The argument is interrupted while Troilus bewails the fact that doctors disagree. Compare *Nun's Priest's Tale*, B 4424-9:

> But what that god forwoot mot nedes be,
> After the opinioun of certeyn clerkis.

Witnesse on him, that any perfit clerk is,
That in scole is gret altercacioun
In this matere, and greet disputisoun
And hath ben of an hundred thousand men.

Among the great clerks who assert the power of destiny, are
Cicero in his *De Divinatione*, and Bishop Bradwardine (1290?-
1349) in his *De Causa Dei* (cf. *N.P.T.*, B 4432). The orthodox
doctrine of "fre chois" is upheld by St. Augustine in *De Civitate
Dei*, Lib. 5, Cap. 8-12 (cf. *N.P.T.*, B 4431) and by Boethius. Pandarus cites a similar disagreement of authorities in support of
his conviction (5.360-85) that no reliance is to be placed on
dreams.

974-980. Boethius, 5. pr 3. 10-12: "For which, yif that god
knoweth biforn nat only the werkes of men, but also hir conseiles
and hir willes, thanne ne shal ther be no libertee of arbitre."
Chaucer expands freely.

981-987. Boethius, 5. pr 3. 12-17: "ne, certes, ther ne may be
noon other dede, ne no wil, but thilke which that the divyne purviaunce, that may nat ben desseived, hath feled biforn. For yif
that they mighten wrythen awey in othre manere than they ben
purveyed, than sholde ther be no stedefast prescience of thing
to comen."

988-994. Boethius, 5. pr 3. 17-19: "but rather an uncertein
opinioun; the whiche thing to trowen of god, I deme it felonye
and unleveful."

995-1001. Boethius, 5. pr 3. 22-6: "For, certes, they seyn that
thing nis nat to comen for that the purviaunce of god hath seyn
it biforn that is to comen, but rather the contrarye: . . . that,
for that the thing is to comen, therfore ne may it nat ben hid fro
the purviaunce of god." In 996, the reference is to the tonsure
of clerks.

1002-1008. Boethius, 5. pr 3. 26-9: "and in this manere this
necessitee slydeth ayein into the contrarye partye: ne it ne bihoveth nat, nedes, that thinges bityden that ben purvyed, but it
bihoveth, nedes, that thinges that ben to comen ben yporveyed."

1009-1015. Boethius, 5. pr 3. 30-4: "but as it were ytravailed,
as who seyth, that thilke answere procedeth right as thogh men
travaileden, or weren bisy to enqueren, the whiche thing is cause
of the whiche thing:—as, whether the prescience is cause of the

necessitee of thinges to comen, or elles that the necessitee of thinges to comen is cause of the purviaunce."

1016-1022. Boethius, 5. pr 3.35-9: "But I ne enforce me nat now to shewen it, that the bitydinge of thinges ywist biforn is necessarie, how so or in what manere that the ordre of causes hath itself; althogh that it ne seme nat that the prescience bringe in necessitee of bitydinge to thinges to comen."

1019. *Byforn* is to be read as three syllables with syllabic *r*.

1023-1029. Boethius, 5. pr 3.39-41: "For certes, yif that any wight sitteth, it bihoveth by necessitee that the opinioun be sooth of him that coniecteth that he sitteth; and ayeinward also is it of the contrarye." *See*, seat; see *NED* s.v. See, sb. 1. *Conjectest* translates the Latin: "quae eum sedere coniectat veram esse." Line 1027 is probably the least poetical line that Chaucer ever wrote.

1030-1036. Boethius, 5. pr 3.41-5: "Yif the opinioun be sooth of any wight for that he sitteth, it bihoveth by necessitee that he sitte. Thanne is heer necessitee in that oon and in that other: for in that oon is necessitee of sittinge, and, certes, in that other is necessitee of sooth."

1037-1043. Boethius, 5. pr 3.45-51: "But therfore ne sitteth nat a wight, for that the opinioun of the sittinge is sooth; but the opinioun is rather sooth, for that a wight sitteth biforn. And thus, althogh that the cause of the sooth cometh of that other syde (as who seyth, that althogh the cause of sooth comth of the sitting, and nat of the trewe opinioun), algates yit is ther comune necessitee in that oon and in that other." Troilus, alone in the temple, imagines himself as engaged in a discussion with an opponent. Note that line 1038 is hypermetrical.

1044-1050. Boethius, 5. pr 3.51-3: "Thus sheweth it, that I may make semblable skiles of the purviaunce of god and of thinges to comen."

1051-1057. Boethius, 5. pr 3.53-8: "For althogh that, for that thinges ben to comen, therfore ben they purveyed, nat, certes, for that they ben purveyed, therfore ne bityde they nat. Yit natheles, bihoveth it by necessitee, that either the thinges to comen ben ypurveyed of god, or elles that the thinges that ben purveyed of god bityden."

1058-1064. Boethius, 5. pr 3.58-62: "And this thing only suffiseth ynough to destroyen the freedom of oure arbitre, that is to seyn, of oure free wil. But now, certes, sheweth it wel, how fer fro the sothe and how up-so-doun is this thing that we seyn, that the bitydinge of temporel thinges is cause of the eterne prescience."

1065-1071. Boethius, 5. pr 3.62-5: "But for to wenen that god purvyeth the thinges to comen for they ben to comen, what other thing is it but for to wene that thilke thinges that bitidden whylom ben causes of thilke soverein purvyaunce that is in god ?"

1072-1078. Boethius, 5. pr 3.66-71: "And herto I adde yit this thing: that, right as whan that I wot that a thing is, it bihoveth by necessitee that thilke selve thing be; and eek, whan I have knowe that any thing shal bityden, so byhoveth it by necessitee that thilke thing bityde:—so folweth it thanne, that the bitydinge of the thing ywist biforn ne may nat ben eschued."

1078. After stanza 154, is found in J, written in a contemporary hand, probably that of the scribe: "her faileth thyng y^t/is nat yt made." See further, Introd., p. lxxii, n. 149.

1079-1085. Troilus has completed his argument; but he is not sure of his conclusion, that all things come by necessity. Jove alone knows the truth of the matter. May Jove save him and Criseyde from distress! Chaucer has utilized only the first half of the long Prose 3 of Book V. Boethius gives one more argument to prove that things betide by necessity—the impiety of supposing that there can be any uncertainty in God's foreknowledge, an argument already implied in what has gone before—and then considers certain logical consequences, such as the absurdity of prayer, which proceed from the conclusion. With these consequences Troilus has no immediate concern. With lines 1079-80, compare Gower, *Conf. Am.* Prol. 534: "God wot of bothe which is soth."

1086. The first line of Pandar's speech echoes line 1079, spoken by Troilus. Since stanza 156 was apparently written before stanza 155 (see Introd., p. lxxii), the echo is actually the other way around. For the rhyme of *trone*, which should normally have open *o* with *doone*, and in the preceding stanza with *sone*, see Wild, p. 215.

1088. With this line, Chaucer turns back to *Fil.* 4.109, a stanza the first line of which is reproduced by Chaucer in 4.946. From here to the end of Book IV, Chaucer follows, with a few additions, the remaining stanzas of Boccaccio's fourth canto.

1094. *Ferd* is past participle of the weak verb *feren* (O.E. *fēran*). O.E. *fēran* is a secondary derivative of the strong verb *faran*, which appears as *faren* in 4.1087. For the confusion and ultimate coalescence of these two verbs in modern English, see *NED* s.v. Fare, vb. 1.

1098. Compare 2.1347 and note.

1105-1106. "It is time enough to offer one's neck to the executioner, when one's head must really come off."

1116. The invocation of Juno is not found in *Filostrato*.

1137. *Ligne aloes* is an adaptation of Latin *lignum aloes*, where *aloes* is gen. sing. of *aloe*; see *NED* s.v. Lign-aloes. The aloe is a drug proverbial for its bitterness; see *NED* s.v. Aloe, 4.

1138-1139. The story of Myrrha, who, metamorphosed into a myrrh tree, wept tears of precious gum, which distilled through its bark, is told by Ovid, *Met.* 10.298-502. The scribe of H4 quotes in the margin lines 500-1:

> Flet tamen, et tepide manant ex arbore gutte.
> Est honor et lacrimis stillataque cortice mirra.

(*Et* in the second of these lines is a corruption of the preposition *e*.)

1142-1143. *Fil.* 4.116 reads:

> Ma poscia che gli spiriti affannati,
> Per l'angoscia del pianto e de'sospiri,
> Furon nelli lor luoghi ritornati.

By *spiriti*, Boccaccio seems to mean the *spiritus* which control the various functions of the body (see notes to 1.306-7; 4.910). Recovering from the weariness caused by anguish, each of the three *spiritus* returned to its proper place: the "vital spirit" to the heart, the "natural spirit" to the liver, the "animal spirit" to the brain. Chaucer, though familiar with these physiological ideas, interprets Boccaccio's *spiriti* as meaning the *souls* of the two grief-stricken lovers. Compare 4.1152 and note; the line of Boccaccio quoted there seems to have determined Chaucer's understanding of the present passage.

1152. *Woful spirit* is equivalent to *woful weri goost* of line 1142. *Fil.* 4.117 reads:

> Ed ingegnossi l'alma di fuggirsi.

His propre place echoes line 1143. Compare note to 4.1142-3.

1159. *Fil.* 4.117 reads: "E gli occhi suoi velati," "and her eyes veiled, i.e. closed." Chaucer's line seems to mean that in her swoon Criseyde's eyes were rolled upwards, so that only the whites were visible. I suspect that Chaucer's copy of *Filostrato* read *levati* for *velati*. (In the Paris ed. this stanza, 6.9, is so different from the Moutier text that there is no equivalent for the words here quoted.)

1174. Compare *Prologue*, A 301:

> And bisily gan for the soules preye.

Chaucer's line has no counterpart in Boccaccio.

1179. *Preignant*, urgent, compelling, from O.F. *preignant*, ultimately Latin *premere*, press; see *NED* s.v. Pregnant, adj. 1. The word was early confused with *pregnant*, with child. *Fil.* 4.119 reads: "vero argomento."

1181. *Woon*, hope, resource; see Bradley-Stratmann s.v. Wān.

1187-1188. *Fil.* 4.120 reads:

> Acciocchè il suo spirto seguitasse
> Quel della donna con sì trista sorte,
> E nell'inferno con lei abitasse.

Rossetti explains that *inferno* means only Hades; but Chaucer has preferred to soften the idea. Minos is the judge who passes judgment on the souls of the dead; see Virgil, *Aen.* 6.431-3, and Dante, *Inf.* 5.4-6. In *Inf.* 13.94-6, Minos judges the souls of suicides.

1192. From *Fil.* 4.121:

> O crudel Giove, e tu fortuna ria.

1205. The reading *I leve in wo*, I leave behind me in wo, though given only by ClS1DR, is established as correct by *Fil.* 4.123:

> E tu città, la qual'io *lascio* in guerra.

The corrupt substitution of *lyve* for *leve* must have been present in the original MS.

1208. Atropos is the third of the three Fates. She cuts the thread of life (cf. 4.1546), and so makes ready the funeral bier. H4 glosses: "Antropos: mors."

1216. I adopt the reading *Cipride*, though found only in JPhH2S1 (but note *Enpride* of A), because transcriptional probability is on the side of the less familiar name. Note also that H4, which reads *Cupide*, glosses the name "Venus." *Cipride* is the Cyprian Venus; compare 3.725; 5.208.

1221-1222. From *Fil.* 4.124:

> e l'anima smarrita
> Tornò al core, onde s'era fuggita.

1237. *A forlong wey*, as long a time as it takes one to walk a furlong (an eighth of a mile); compare *Miller's Tale*, A 3637.

1241. An irregular line; perhaps the diphthong of *Slayn* is to be stretched into two syllables. GgR read *slawe*.

1245. *Morter*, "a bowl of wax or oil with a floating wick, and later a kind of thick candle, used especially as a night-light" (*NED* s.v. Mortar, sb. 1, 2). Gg substitutes the word *percher*, a tall candle; see *NED* s.v. Percher, sb. 2.

1255-1257. Compare 1.704-7, 762-3.

1261-1263. "As a woman, I speak without delay what comes suddenly to my mind"; compare 4.936.

1291. *Mocioun*, inclination, desire; see *NED* s.v. Motion, sb. 9. (But *NED* cites this passage, wrongly I think, under meaning 7.)

1305-1306. These lines bear a certain resemblance to *Rose* (Langlois) 2601-2, where Amors is comforting the lover:

> E plus en gré sont receü
> Li bien don l'en a mal eü.

1321. The MSS. strongly favor *erst;* only CpH1H2 read *erste*. Perhaps the *r* of *erst* is to be given syllabic value.

1345-1349. From *Fil.* 4.131.

1356. The simile of the bees is found also in *Summoner's Prologue*, D 1693, and in 2.193.

1373-1374. "People say that it is hard to have the wolf full and the sheep whole." This seems to be a proverb; but I have not been able to find any other instance of it. Its purport is similar to "You cannot have your cake and eat it." Its application seems to be that Calchas, in order to satiate his own wolvish greed, will let Criseyde go back to Troy, and so will lose her.

1377. *Grave*, engrave, make an impression on; compare 2.1241.

1401-1407. This passage, which has no counterpart in Boccaccio, somewhat resembles words actually spoken by Briseida to her father in Benoit and Guido. Briseida is reproaching him for his treachery to the city. In *Troie* 13768-9 she says:

> Trop i mesfist dant Apollin,
> Se il tel respons vos dona.

In *Historia*, sig. i 3, a, col. 1: *Bellum sextum*, this becomes: "Sane deceperunt te Appollinis falsa responsa."

1406. *Amphibologies*, ambiguous sentences; see *NED* s.v. Amphibology. *NED* records no other instance of the word in English earlier than 1552. Chaucer has adapted a late Latin word. Cicero, *De Div.* 2.56.116, uses *amphibolia* in speaking of an oracular response.

1408. H4 has marginal gloss: "Timor invenit deos." Statius, *Theb.* 3.661, says: "Primus in orbe deos fecit timor." Statius took the phrase from Petronius (*Fragm.* 27). It was doubtless already a commonplace.

1411. According to Benoit, *Troie* 5817-927, Calchas had been sent by the Trojans to consult the oracle at "Delfos." He there met Achilles, who with Patroclus was consulting the oracle on behalf of the Greeks. Warned by the oracle of the fall of Troy, Calchas returned with Achilles to Athens, and threw in his lot with the Greeks. See also Guido, *Historia*, sig. e 6, a, cols. 1, 2: *Principium Idolatriae*.

1415-1421. Chaucer has abundant authority for his statement. See *Fil.* 5.7. With line 1419 compare Benoit, *Troie* 13495-7:

> La danzele cuide morir,
> Quant de celui deit departir
> Qu'ele tant aime e tant a chier.

See also Guido, *Historia*, sig. i 2, a, col. 2: *Bellum sextum*.

1429-1435. This stanza follows closely *Fil.* 4.138.

1450-1454. *Deere* from O.E. *dēore*, and *yfeere* from O.E. *gefēre*, have long close *e*; the rhyme words in 1451, 1453, 1454 have open *e*.

1453-1454. "The trained bear thinks one thing, but the bear-leader has other plans." I have not been able to identify this proverb, which is equivalent, on a lower scale, to "Man proposes, God disposes."

1457-1458. "It is hard to sham lameness before a cripple, without being detected; for he knows the art of limping." Le Roux de Lincy, 1.211, cites a fifteenth century proverb: "Clochier ne faut devant boiteux." Compare Düringsfeld, 1. no. 736.

1459. Compare Ovid, *Met.* 1.625:

> Centum luminibus cinctum caput Argus habebat.

1473. *Alose*, praise; see *NED* s.v. Alose, vb.

1478-1482. Chaucer is expanding *Fil.* 4.142:

> E mostreratti che stare assediata
> È dubbio di venire a rio partito.

It is possible that he turned also, as Hamilton (p. 111) thinks, to Benoit, *Troie* 13803-9, or to Guido, *Historia*, sig. i 3, a, col. 1: *Bellum sextum*.

1505. In the Aristotelian philosophy of the schoolmen, the "substance" is the essential nature of a thing, which underlies the appearances or "accidents" by which we perceive it. Compare *Pardoner's Tale*, C 539. In the sacrament of the altar, the "substance" bread becomes the "substance" *corpus Christi*; but the "accidents," such as color, taste, texture, remain unchanged. "It is folly to lose the essential for the non-essential." But, as the next stanza shows, Troilus is playing also with the more popular meaning of *accident*. "It is folly to give up certainty (*sikernesse*) for uncertainty."

1522. Compare 4.96 and note.

1538-1540. Athamas, king of Thebes, was driven mad by Juno, who brings Tisiphone from hell to haunt him. In his madness, he brutally murdered his own son. See Ovid, *Met.* 4.416-562, and compare in particular "Saturnia Iuno" of line 448. But Chaucer's mention of Athamas was probably suggested by Dante, *Inf.* 30.1-12, where "Atamante," driven mad by Juno, is a type of the "falsitori" who dwell in the tenth "bolgia" of the eighth circle. Criseyde prays that Juno may condemn her to hell, mad as Athamas, if she is ever *false* to Troilus.

Styx is properly a river, not a pit; but Dante, *Inf.* 7.106, calls it "una palude." H4 has marginal gloss: "Stix puteus infernalis."

1543-1545. Compare Ovid, *Met.* 1.192-3:

> Sunt mihi semidei, sunt rustica numina, nymphae
> Faunique satyrique et monticolae Silvani.

See also *Met.* 6.392-4, and Statius, *Theb.* 4.683-4.

1546. Atropos breaks the fatal thread of life; compare 4.1208; 3.733-5, and see *Rose* (Michel) 20702-3:

> Mes Atropos ront et descire
> Quanque ces deus puéent filer.

H4 has marginal gloss: "Parcas, Cloto, Lathesis, Antropos."

1548-1553. Criseyde's promise that, when she is false to Troilus, the river Simois will flow backward to its source, is a blending of two passages of Ovid. Compare *Amores* 1.15.10:

> Dum rapidas Simois in mare volvet aquas;

and *Her.* 5.29-30:

> Cum Paris Oenone poterit spirare relicta,
> Ad fontem Xanthi versa recurret aqua.

The passage from *Heroides* is reproduced in *Rose* (Langlois) 13225-8. Both Xanthus and Simois are mentioned in *Her.* 13.53. Simois is mentioned by Virgil, *Aen.* 1.100. Neither river is mentioned by Benoit.

1568. Compare *Proverbs of Hending*, st. 33: "Oft rap reweth," and Gower, *Conf. Am.* 3.1625:

> Men sen alday that rape reweth.

Hazlitt, p. 20, cites the proverb: "A hasty man never wants woe." See 1.956 and note.

1584. Compare *Franklin's Tale*, F 773-5:

> Pacience is a heigh vertu, certeyn;
> For it venquisseth, as thise clerkes seyn,
> Thinges that rigour sholde never atteyne.

Compare also *Piers Plowman*, B 13.135: "Pacientes vincunt," and *ibid.*, C 14.202-6. In his note on *Franklin's Tale*, Skeat quotes the proverb: "Vincit qui patitur," and cites Dionysius Cato, *Distich.* 1.38, Virgil, *Aen.* 5.710. Le Roux de Lincy, 2.407, cites a fifteenth century proverb: "Qui seufre, Il vainct." The proverb is quoted and elaborated by Machaut, *Dit dou Lyon* 2040-76. (Line 2071 reads: "Et se dit on: 'Qui sueffre, il veint.' ")

1585. "Whoever wishes to have a dear thing must give up a dear thing." Hazlitt, p. 340, cites a proverb from Heywood: "Nought lay down, nought take up." Compare 4.1611-12.

1586. This familiar proverb appears also in *Knight's Tale*, A 3042, and *Squire's Tale*, F 593. See Düringsfeld, 1. no. 139. The proverb is at least as old as St. Jerome (*In Rufinum* 3.2), See also Boccaccio, *Tes.* 12.11, and *Rose* (Langlois) 14015-16.

1587-1589. From *Fil.* 4.154:

> Dunque prendi conforto, e la fortuna
> Col dare il dosso vinci e rendi stanca;
> Non soggiacette a lei giammai nessuna
> Persona in cui trovasse anima franca.

Compare also *Fortune* 8, 16, 24:

> For fynally, Fortune, I thee defye.

1590-1596. Criseyde promises that, before the Moon has passed from Aries, where it now is, through Taurus, Gemini, and Cancer to the end of Leo, she will return. As the Moon completes the circuit of the twelve signs in about twenty-eight days, it would travel from about the twentieth degree of Aries to the end of Leo in ten days. Chaucer has already placed the season of Criseyde's departure at the time of year when the Sun is "upon the brest of Hercules lyoun" (4.32). It follows that as soon as the Moon has passed out of Leo, it will be visible as a crescent. Criseyde's promise implies, then, that she will return before the next new Moon; and Troilus so understands it (5.652-8). In Boccaccio, there is at this point no mention of the Moon; Criseida merely promises: "al decimo giorno Senza alcun fallo qui farò ritorno" (*Fil.* 4.154). Later (*Fil.* 5.69), Troilo translates the promise into terms of lunar progress, though without specifying which zodiacal signs are concerned.

1591. Compare *Franklin's Tale*, F 1045:

> Your blisful suster, Lucina the shene.

The relation of Diana and Apollo is a commonplace.

1594. Chaucer has given to Juno the title, "Regina caeli," applied to the Blessed Virgin.

1608. Cinthia is the Moon; compare 5.1018, and Ovid, *Met.* 2.465. Criseyde has already (4.1591-3) made the Moon surety for her return. Compare *Romeo and Juliet* 2.2.109-11.

1611-1612. From *Fil.* 4.159:

> L'aspettar tempo è utile talvolta
> Per tempo guadagnare.

1620. From *Fil.* 4.158:

> Ch'el me ne piange l'anima nel core.

1628. Compare Hazlitt, p. 540: "Who may hold that will away?," and Le Roux de Lincy, 2.336: "L'on doit laisser aller ce que l'en ne peut tenir."

1645. Compare Ovid, *Her.* 1.12:

> Res est solliciti plena timoris amor.

1667-1682. These lines follow closely *Fil.* 4.164-6; but in Boccaccio these stanzas are spoken by Troilo to Criseida.

1682. *Remuable Fortune* translates "mobile fortuna" of *Fil.* 4.166.

NOTES TO BOOK FIVE

NOTES TO BOOK FIVE

1. Compare *Tes.* 9.1:

> Già s'appressava il doloroso fato.

3-7. H4 has marginal gloss: "Parkas, Cloto, Lathesis, Antropos." The idea that the Fates are ministers for the execution of Jove's decrees is to be traced to Boethius, 4. pr 6. 29-56. Lachesis is the second of the Fates, who presides over the continuance of man's life, as Clotho over its beginning, and Atropos over its end. Compare *Rose* (Michel) 20701:

> E Lachesis qui les filz tire.

See note on 3.733-5. The form *Lathesis* is found in all the MSS.; Cx and Th emend to *Lachesys*. MS. confusion of *c* and *t* is of frequent occurrence.

8-11. Closely imitated from *Tes.* 2.1:

> Il sole avea due volte dissolute
> Le nevi agli alti poggi, ed alᵗrettante
> Zefiro aveva le frondi rendute
> Ed i be'fiori alle spogliate piante,
> Poichè. . . .

In H4, *goldetressed* is glossed "auricomus"; and the closely related H2 reads: *The Auricomus tressed Phebus.* Compare Valerius Flaccus, *Argonauticon* 4.92: "Sol auricomus, cingentibus Horis." (Other MSS. of *Argonauticon* read *auricomis*.) There had been three spring seasons since Troilus first loved Criseyde. See Introd., p. xxxiv.

9. I adopt *shene*, on the attestation of H2H4RS1, as an authentic β reading, though with some misgiving, since the substitution of so obvious a word for the less obvious *cleene* may be a scribal emendation. *Cleene* is found only in JPh; but Gg is missing, and the corrupt *clere* of γThH3Cx is apparently derived from *cleene*. *Cleene* in the sense of "pure" is a possible reading; and though *cleene* should normally have open *e*, whereas *grene*

and *queene* have close *e*, we find the rhyme *clene: ysene* in *Franklin's Tale*, F 995.

15-88. These lines follow closely *Fil.* 5.1-13.

15-19. *Diomede* and *blede* have long close *e*; *lede* and *rede* (the latter used in two different meanings, "advise" and "read") have long open *e*.

22-26. In *loore* (line 22) and *more* (line 24) the vowel goes back to O.E. *ā*, and is therefore a long open *o*. In *forlore*, *more* ("root," line 25), and *bifore* the tonic vowel goes back to O.E. short open *o*; but this vowel, in an open syllable, was regularly lengthened. It would seem that in Chaucer's pronunciation some distinction in the quality of these two sets of vowels still persisted. Compare the rhymes of the preceding stanza, and of stanza 32, below.

25. *Crop and more*, topmost branch and root; see *NED* s.v. Crop, sb., 4, 5, and More, sb. 1.

37. *Hors* is apparently to be read with syllabic *r*.

67. *Fil.* 5.10 reads:

> e compagnia
> Le fece infino fuor di tutto il vallo,

"and bore her company till they were entirely outside the wall." Chaucer seems to have misread *vallo* as *valle*, valley. R reads *wallys* for *valeye*; but this agreement with the Italian on the part of a MS. so corrupt in its readings as R is presumably only coincidence. That *valeye* is the correct reading is corroborated by 5.610.

71. Antenor was the Trojan who was to be exchanged for King Thoas and Criseyde; compare 4.137.

89. Creed, Pater Noster, and Hail Mary are the first rudiments of an education. Diomede is no school-boy.

90. As Rossetti pointed out, Chaucer's statement that Diomede caught hold of Criseyde's bridle rein seems to rest on a misunderstanding of Boccaccio's "di colei si piglia" (*Fil.* 5.13), which actually means "he is taken with her, he takes a fancy to her."

92-189. In Boccaccio (*Fil.* 5.13), Diomede conducts Criseida to her father's tent without any attempt to pay court to her, deferring his love-making till a later day. Chaucer follows the version of the story given by Benoit (*Troie* 13529-712). See detailed parallels in following notes. Guido (*Historia*, sig. i 2, b, col. 1 : *Bellum sextum*) follows Benoit, but condenses the episode into a few short sentences.

98. Le Roux de Lincy, 1.237, quotes a thirteenth century proverb : "Fouz est qui se oblie." See *ibid*. 1.241, and 2.464 : "Mal ovre ki se obblie."

101. Compare 3.87 and note.

106. Compare 5.1149.

115. *Herte* is the reading of all the authorities except γTh, which read *peyne*. But I have found no other examples of the phrase *don his herte*. *Herte* may be a scribal anticipation from the next line ; but if so, it must have been present in the original of all the manuscripts. The reading of γ seems to be an emendation.

113-116. These lines somewhat resemble Benoit, *Troie* 13596-610.

122. A nine-syllable line ; *thaqueyntaunce* is to be stressed on first and third syllables. But see variant readings.

124-126. Compare 5.918-21.

151. *This*, a contraction of *this is*.

155-158. Compare Benoit, *Troie* 13591-6 :

> Mainte pucele avrai veüe
> E mainte dame coneüe :
> Onc mais a rien ne fis preiere
> De mei amer en tel maniere.
> Vos en estes la premeraine,
> Si sereiz vos la dereraine.

Compare also *Troie* 13556-8.

164-165. Compare Benoit, *Troie* 13552-5 :

> Mais j'ai oï assez parler
> Que gent qu'onc ne s'erent veü
> Ne acointié ne coneü
> S'amoënt mout, ç'avient adès.

176-189. Criseyde's reply to Diomede reproduces the general tenor of the reply of Briseida in Benoit, *Troie* 13617-80. Briseida answers discreetly that she is in no mood for love ; her heart is too sad ; but if she were to love, she would love no one sooner than Diomede. Compare Guido, *Historia*, sig. i 2, b, col. 1 : *Bellum sextum*. Some of the material in this passage of Benoit is utilized by Chaucer in a later speech of Criseyde (5.953-1008).

207-210. *Fil.* 5.17 reads:

> El bestemmiava il giorno che fu nato,
> E gli dei e le dee e la natura
> E'l padre, e chi parola conceduta
> Avea che fosse Griseida renduta.

Why Chaucer has introduced precisely the deities mentioned is not clear. Cipride (Venus) is associated with Bacchus and Ceres in *Tes.* 7.66, a passage used by Chaucer in *Parliament* 274-7. Bacchus and Ceres, as deities of wine and food, are appropriate servitors of Venus. Apollo had been responsible for the treachery of Calchas, and so ultimately for the present grief of Troilus.

211. I adopt the reading *walwith*, wallows, of GgH4Cx, supported by *waltryth* of R, as the form which will best explain the various readings. It is corroborated by *Fil.* 5.19 :

> E sè in qua ed ora in là *volgendo*.

212. See Virgil, *Aen.* 6.601, and *Georg.* 3.38; but Ixion and his "immanem rotam" are a commonplace. Compare Boethius, 3. m 12.26.

218-222. For the rhymes, compare 5.15-19 and note. *Dere* and *cleere* have long close *e*; the vowel in the other rhyme-words is long open *e*.

218-245. This complaint of Troilus is adapted, with some rearrangement in order, from *Fil.* 5. 19-25.

223-224. Compare *Legend* 2186, and Ovid, *Her.* 10.12; but Chaucer is following *Fil.* 5.20 :

> ora abbracciando
> Vado il piumaccio.

230. *Dowe*, give as an endowment; see *NED* s.v. Dow, vb. 2.

246-259. The terrifying dreams of Troilus are identical with those of Boccaccio's Troilo (*Fil.* 5.26-7). Troilus believes (5.317) that they portend his death.

274-280. Closely imitated from *Tes.* 7.94:

> Il ciel tuttè le stelle ancor mostrava,
> Benchè Febea già palida fosse;
> E l'orizzonte tutto biancheggiava
> Nell'oriente, ed eransi già mosse
> L'Ore, e col carro, in cui la luce stava,
> Giungevano i cavai, vedendo rosse
> Le membra del celeste bue levato,
> Dall'amica Titonia accompagnato.

Compare also Boethius, 2. m 3.1-4. Chaucer has suppressed Boccaccio's reference to the sign Taurus; at this point in the English poem, the Sun is in Leo (4.32).

277. Perhaps *for to doone* of JH4R should be regarded as an authentic β reading; it would improve an awkward line.

295-322. These directions of Troilus for the conduct of his own funeral rites have no counterpart in *Filostrato*. Certain details seem to have been suggested by the death of Arcita in Boccaccio's *Teseide*. Compare *Tes.* 10.89, where the dying Arcita asks his friends to provide "vittime, legni, ed olocausti," so that Mercury may lead his spirit "in luogo ameno"; and *Tes.* 10.93-8. In *Tes.* 11.58, Egeo takes the ashes of Arcita, and places them "in un' urna d' oro"; compare also *Tes.* 11.69, 90. For other parallels, none of them very striking, see *Tes.* 11.13, 14, 35, 52, 55, 56, 59, 60. Compare also *Knight's Tale*, A 2889-966.

304. *Pleyes palestral*, i.e. games of wrestling. The *palaestra* was the wrestling school. Compare *Tes.* 7.27: "mio palestral giuoco."

319. Ascalaphus, son of Acheron and Orphne, was metamorphosed into an owl, "venturi nuntia luctus"; see Ovid, *Met.* 5.533-50. H4 in margin mistakenly cites "Methomorphoseos ij."

321-322. Mercury is the guide of souls on their way to the lower world; compare 5.1827, and *Tes.* 10.89, 93-8, where Arcita prays Mercury to conduct his soul to Elysium. See also Virgil, *Aen.* 4.243.

360-385. In Boccaccio, Pandaro merely asserts that dreams "procedon da malinconia" (*Fil.* 5.32). Chaucer's Pandarus discusses the question of dreams more fully. His conviction that dreams are not worth a bean is based on the fact that so many different explanations have been given of the cause of dreams. He enumerates four explanations: (1) Priests say that they are sometimes divine revelations, sometimes infernal illusions; (2) doctors say they are the result of our physical condition, e.g. the humor of melancholy; (3) some say that they result from an idea deeply impressed on the mind; (4) others say that the significance of dreams is determined by the season of the year, and by the phase of the Moon. Dame Partlet in *Nun's Priest's Tale*, B 4112-29, gives only the second of these explanations in defense of her assertion that dreams are nothing but vanity. The explanations of Pandarus are commonplaces of the medieval discussion of dreams; see Thorndike, *History of Magic* 2.290-302. The curious reader may consult Albertus Magnus, *De Somno et Vigilia*. Tract II of Book III is entitled "De causis somniorum in nobis." Albert, though admitting that many dreams have a purely physiological cause, and are therefore without significance, believes that some dreams are significant. Compare the following passages: "Dicunt autem isti somnia animarum esse per substantias quae daemones ab eis vocantur: visiones autem per deos corporeos" (3.1.8). "Sic igitur quaedam somnia ab his quae in corpore sunt passionibus et dispositionibus causantur, et ipsa nihil aliud quam talia in corpore existentia significant" (3.2.1). "Actiones ante factae vel pertractatae sunt aliquando causae phantasmatum quae postea apparent in somniis" (3.2.2). See also John of Salisbury, *Polycraticus*, Lib. 2, Cap. 14-17, and Vincent of Beauvais, *Spec. Nat.*, Lib. 27, Cap. 52-61.

365-368. Compare *Rose* (Langlois) 18509-12:

> Ou se Deus par teus visions
> Enveie revelacions,
> Ou li malignes esperiz,
> Pour metre les genz es periz.
> De tout ce ne m'entremetrai.

379. "May good come to old women from dreams"; i.e. let old women concern themselves with dreams. Compare *Fame* 53:

> Wel worthe of this thing grete clerkes.

There also the discussion is about the significance of dreams.

382. *Qualm*, croaking; see *NED* s.v. Qualm, sb. 2.

387. *Fil.* 5.33 reads: "a te stesso perdona."

403. The visit to Sarpedon follows closely *Fil.* 5.38-49. Chaucer places his residence "nat hennes but a myle"; in *Fil.* 5.40, the distance is "forse quattromila passi." Sarpedon was king of Licia. With his father, Glaucon, he brought more than 3000 knights to the aid of Priam, to whom he was related by blood. See Benoit, *Troie* 6685-90; Guido, Historia, sig. f 5, b, col. 2. He was killed by Palamedes in the Twelfth Battle (*Troie* 18784-818).

409. *Jouken*, lie at rest like a falcon on its perch; see *NED* s.v. Jouk, vb. 1.

421. *Of fyn force*, by absolute necessity; see *NED* s.v. Fine, adj., 3. A nine-syllable line. The reading *fyne* is but poorly attested, and seems to have no grammatical justification. Perhaps Chaucer wrote *sithen* for *syn*.

445. This line is repeated, with substitution of *devyse* for *recorde*, at 5.1321, and, with slight variation, in *Merchant's Tale*, E 1341. Compare *Rose* (Langlois) 2965-6:

> Cuers ne porroit mie penser
> Ne bouche d'ome recenser.

The couplet of *Rose* is repeated with slight variation in lines (Michel) 21307-8.

455. For the form *festeyinge*, compare note to 3.1718, and see variant readings.

460. *For*, because. The conceit of the key which locks the lover's heart is a commonplace. See *Rose* (Langlois) 2009-10:

> E ferma mon cuer si soef
> Qu'a grant poine senti la clef.

Langlois in his note on this passage cites *Ivain* 4632-4, and *Perceval* 3810. Compare *Anelida* 323. Chaucer is following *Fil.* 5.43:

> Nelle cui mani amor posto la chiave
> Avea della sua vita tapinella.

469. "Fortune intended to glaze his head-covering still better," i.e. to provide him with a hood or cap (see *NED* s.v. Houve) of glass—a delusive protection. In *Piers Plowman*, B 20.171 (C 23.172) we read: "And thei gyven hym agayne a glasen houve,"

where the context suggests that *glasen houve* is equivalent to a "delusive hope." Compare also *Debate of Body and Soul* 245:

> That thou lovedest me thou lete,
> And madest me an houve of glas.

NED cites *Adrian* 228 (*Legends of the Saints in the Scottish Dialect*. Scottish Text Soc.):

> þu did nocht ellis, I se now,
> Bot to god mad a clasine [= glasine] how.

It is possible that the phrase is associated with the proverb quoted in 2.867-8. Compare also Skeat's note on *Monk's Tale*, B 3562.

478. *Congeyen*, dismiss, give leave to go; see *NED* s.v. Congee, vb. The reading *conveien* of H2H4, taken over by Cx and Th, is certainly corrupt.

484-485. From *Fil.* 5.47:

> Pandaro allora: Or siam noi per lo fuoco
> Venuti qui?

If one goes to borrow fire from a neighbor, one will hurry home before the live coals are extinguished. Hazlitt, p. 468, records the proverbial phrase: "To come to fetch fire."

492. *Wowke*, see note on 5.499.

497. *Forward*, agreement; see *NED* s.v. Foreward, sb. 1.

499. *Wikes*. Beside the O.E. (West Saxon) *wucu*, week, which is represented by *wowke* of line 492, there is the Anglian *wicu*, which results in *wike*. Why the two dialectal forms should occur only seven lines apart in Chaucer's text it is hard to say; but the evidence of the MSS. strongly supports the two readings. In 4.1278, the form *wowke* is clearly attested; in 2.430, 1273, the form *wyke* occurs under the rhyme. For discussion of the forms, see Wild, p. 144.

505. "Hazle-wood" is a term of scornful incredulity; compare 3.890; 5.1174.

507. *Refreyden*, compare 2.1343 and note.

516. *Criseyde* is apparently to be read as four syllables; but see variant readings.

531. *Spered*, shut up, closed; see *NED* s.v. Spear, vb. 1. The MSS. unanimously support *spered* rather than *sperred* (see *NED* s.v. Spar, vb. 1), the form printed by Skeat.

540-550. This apostrophe to the empty house of Criseyde is elaborated from *Fil.* 5.53:

> Lasso, quanto luminoso
> Era il luogo e piacevol, quando stava
> In te quella beltà, che'l mio riposo
> Dentro dagli occhi suoi tutto portava;
> Or se' rimaso oscuro senza lei,
> Nè so se mai riaver la ti dei.

The conceit of the ring which has lost its ruby seems to be Chaucer's own.

551-553. Compare *Rose* (Langlois) 2535-8:

> Si te dirai que tu doiz faire
> Por l'amor dou haut *saintuaire*
> De quoi tu ne puez avoir aise:
> Au revenir *la porte baise*.

Compare also *Filocolo* 1.124.

580. The "yonder place" is the palace of Deiphebus.

582-595. These lines are adapted from *Fil.* 5.56-7.

584. *Werreyed*, made war upon (O.F. *werreier*); compare *Knight's Tale*, A 1544.

599-601. Compare Dante, *Inf.* 30.1-2:

> Nel tempo che Giunone era crucciata
> Per Semele contra il sangue tebano.

See also Statius, *Theb.* 1.11-16, *Tes.* 3.1; 4.16, and *Knight's Tale*, A 1329-31.

618. *Defet*, disfigured, from O.F. *defeit*, past participle of *defaire* or *desfaire*; see *NED* s.v. Defeit, and compare 5.1219.

626. The final syllable of *routhe*, protected by caesura, is not elided; but note reading of ClR.

638-644. As Rossetti pointed out, the metaphor of a sea-voyage seems to have been suggested by a false reading of *Fil.* 5.62, "disii porto di morte," I carry desires of death, which Chaucer apparently translated, "I desire the harbor of death."

641. *With wynd in steere*, with wind astern; see *NED* s.v. Steer, sb. 2, 2 d.

644. Charybdis, the whirlpool between Italy and Sicily, which threatened the ship of Aeneas; Virgil, *Aen.* 3.420-3.

648. This line must mean that every night Troilus looked to see whether the new Moon was yet visible; compare note on 5.652-8.

652-658. This stanza follows closely *Fil.* 5.69. When Criseyde left Troy, the Moon was, according to Chaucer, in Aries (4.1592) and the Sun in Leo (4.32). The Moon was, therefore, in the phase of last quarter, when its waning horns are visible only in the late night and early morning. When it should have passed beyond Leo, its new horns would begin to spring. Compare note on 4.1590-6. It is to be noted that, at the time of Criseyde's expected return, the Moon did *not* shine bright, as Shakespeare declares that it did (*Merchant of Venice* 5.1.1).

655. H4 glosses "Latona: luna." Thynne, following Caxton, emends to *Lucyna*; and Skeat adopts the emendation, comparing 4.1591. But *Latona* has overwhelming MS. authority. Diana is called "Latonia" in *Aen.* 9.405; 11.534; *Met.* 1.696; 8.394. Properly Latona is the mother of Diana and Apollo.

664. H4 has marginal gloss: "Pheton filius solis, methomorphoseos 2°." The story of Phaeton, who drove amiss the cart of his father the Sun, is told by Ovid, *Met.* 2.1-328.

671-672. Similarly Arcita, standing on the shore of Aegina, and looking towards Athens, fancies that the wind which comes thence is peculiarly soft—*Tes.* 4.32:

> E quasi il vento ch' indi era spirato,
> Più ch'altro gli pareva mite e pio,
> Ei ricevendol, dicea seco stesso:
> Questo fu ad Emilia molto presso.

So, also, Boccaccio himself, addressing Fiammetta in the proem to *Filostrato*, says: "Quindi ogni aura, ogni soave vento che di colà viene, così nel viso ricevo, quasi il vostro senza niuno fallo abbia tocco: nè è perciò troppo lungo questo mitigamento." Compare also *Fil.* 5.70.

724. *Wepen*, past participle of *wepen*, weep. The historically correct form *wopen* is found in ClH1R. In *wepen*, the vowel is analogically levelled to that of the present, and of the strong preterite *weep*. But side by side with the strong forms, one finds a weak preterite and past participle. In line 725, the MSS. strongly

favor the form *wepte*. See variant readings, and compare Wild, p. 310.

741-742. An electuary is "a medicinal conserve or paste, consisting of a powder or other ingredient mixed with honey, preserve, or syrup or some kind" (*NED*). Compare *Cant. Tales*, A 426, C 307, E 1809. "It is too late to give medicine when one is carrying the corpse to the grave." Düringfeld, 2. no. 122, cites many versions of this proverb, of which the nearest to Chaucer is the Italian: "Dopo la morte non val medicina."

745-749. According to Cicero, *De Inventione* 2.53 (160), Prudence has three parts: "Memoria, intellegentia, providentia. Memoria est, per quam animus repetit illa, quae fuerunt; intellegentia, per quam ea perspicit, quae sunt; providentia, per quam futurum aliquid videtur ante quam factum est." Compare Thomas Aquinas, *Summa* I 2.57.6. Prudence hence is said to have three eyes. Compare Dante, *Purg.* 29.132, where the Cardinal Virtues follow—

> dietro al modo
> D'una di lor ch'aveva tre occhi in testa.

The fourteenth century commentary of Benvenuto da Imola reads: "prudentia, *ch'avea tre occhi in testa*, quia respicit praeterita, praesentia, et futura." The same explanation is given by the *Ottimo Commento*.

757-761. These lines, which have no counterpart in Boccaccio, resemble somewhat a proverb recorded by Düringsfeld, 2. no. 235. The French version of the proverb runs: "Tous se mêlent de donner des avis, un sot est celui qui les tous suit."

763. *Suffisaunce*, satisfaction, contentment; see *NED* s.v. Suffisance, 5. Compare Boethius, 2. pr 4.96-101. See also 1.891-3 and note.

769. "Shall slip through her heart like a string without knots."

782. *Acoye*, soothe, coax; see *NED* s.v. Accoy.

784. See 2.807-8 and note.

790-791. I have not been able to identify this quotation.

799-840. Chaucer interrupts his narrative, which in this part of Book V follows closely the early part of Canto VI of *Filostrato*, to draw portraits of Diomede, Criseyde, and Troilus. These portraits are primarily indebted to the *Frigii Daretis Ylias* of Joseph of Exeter, a poem in six books of Latin hexameters, written near the end of the twelfth century, and based apparently on the prose Dares. A text of this poem, marred by many corrupt readings, is available in the Delphin Classics, where it is given the title: *De Bello Trojano*. The first book, edited from the Paris MS., is printed by J. J. Jusserand in his thesis, *De Josepho Exoniensi vel Iscano*, Paris, 1877. The quotations from the poem in the following notes are from my own transcript of the MS. in the Chapter Library of Westminster Abbey. With the matter derived from Joseph, Chaucer has combined details from Benoit and stray hints from *Filostrato*. For further discussion of the matter, see Introd., p. xxxvi, and my article, "Chaucer's Dares," *Mod. Phil.* 15.1-22.

799-805. Compare Joseph of Exeter, 4.124-7:

> Voce ferox, animo preceps, fervente cerebro,
> Audentique ira, validos quadratur in artus
> Titides, plenisque meretur Tidea factis;
> Sic animo, sic ore fero, sic fulminat armis.

(The Bodleian MS. reads *Ardentique*.) In J, a corrupt copy of these lines, by the original scribe, is given in the margin of stanza 115: "Voce ferox a*n*imo *p*receps/audentiq*u*e ira. Validos/ quadrat*ur* in art*us* tetides/pleni*u*sque meret*ur* tidea f*ac*tis/sic a*n*imo sic ore fero *sic et cetera*." Joseph is expanding the portrait of the prose Dares (Cap. 13): "Diomedem fortem, quadratum, corpore honesto, vultu austero, in bello acerrimum, clamosum, cerebro calido, inpatientem, audacem." Compare Benoit, *Troie* 5211-24, and Guido, *Historia*, sig. e 2, a, col. 1. Line 804 is based on *Fil.* 6.33:

> Egli era grande e bel della persona,
> Giovane fresco e piacevole assai,
> E forte e fier *siccome si ragiona,*
> E *parlante quant'altro Greco mai.*

In the margin of line 805, immediately following the lines from Joseph, the scribe of J has written: "Calidonius heres." In Joseph's poem, 4.349, Diomede is referred to as "Calydonius heros"; perhaps *heres* is a misreading of *heros*. Chaucer's line seems, however, to be derived from *Fil.* 6.24; compare 5.932-5 and note.

806-826. Compare Joseph of Exeter's portrait of Briseis (4. 156-62):

> In medium librata statum Briseis heriles
> Promit in aspectum vultus, nodatur in equos
> Flavicies crinita sinus, umbreque minoris
> Delicias oculus iunctos suspendit in arcus.
> Diviciis forme certant insignia morum:
> Sobria simplicitas, comis pudor, arida numquam
> Poscenti pietas, et fandi gracia lenis.

(In line 157, the Westminster MS. reads *affectum*; the reading *aspectum* is from the Bodleian MS.) The intricacies of Joseph's rhetoric may be translated thus: "Balanced in medium stature, Briseis sets forth to view her lordly features. Her hairy yellowness is knotted into equal folds, and her eye lifts into joined arches the delights of lesser shadow [i.e. her eyebrows]. With the riches of her form, strive the marks of character: sober simplicity, a pleasing modesty, a pity never arid for him who asks, and gentle grace of speech."

The scribe of J has quoted these lines, with a few corrupt readings. In the margin of stanza 116: "In medium librata/statum Criseis he/riles promit in affec/tum vultus nodatur/in equos flavicies/crinata"; in the margin of stanza 117: "Umbraque minoris/delicias oculus iunc/tos suspendit in/arcus/divicijs forme cer/tant insignea amorum"; in the margin of stanza 118: "Sobria simplicitas/comis pudor ari/da numquam/poscenti/pietas gracia fandi lenis." In Gg, between lines 819 and 820, the scribe has written:

> *Versus* Sobria simplicitas sonus pudor arida numquam
> *Versus* Poscente poetas gracia fandi lenis.

It is to be noted that J reads *Criseis* for *Briseis*. The reading *amorum* for *morum* is responsible for Chaucer's *love* in line 819.

Joseph's portrait is expanded from the portrait of Briseis in the prose Dares (Cap. 13): "Briseidam formosam, non alta statura, candidam, capillo flavo et molli, superciliis junctis, oculis venustis, corpore aequali, blandam, affabilem, verecundam, animo simplici, piam." Benoit reproduces this portrait of Dares in *Troie* 5275-88; Guido paraphrases Benoit in *Historia*, sig. e 2, a, col. 2.

806. Boccaccio says of Criseida, *Fil.* 1.27: "Ell' era grande"; and Chaucer in 1.281, following Boccaccio, says:

> She nas nat with the leste of hire stature.

In the present passage, Chaucer is following Joseph's "In medium librata statum." Benoit says, *Troie* 5276:

> Ne fu petite ne trop grant;

and Guido, *Historia*, sig. e 2, a, col. 2: "Nec longa nec brevis."

809-812. In *Tes.* 7.65, Boccaccio says of the goddess Venus:

> Ella avea d'oro i crini, e rilegati
> Intorno al capo senza treccia alcuna.

In Joseph's portrait of Briseis, her hair is knotted into equal folds. Benoit and Guido do not mention the lady's coiffure.

813-814. The trait of the joined brows is recorded by Dares, Joseph, Benoit, and Guido; but only Benoit and Guido suggest that this was a defect ("lak"). Benoit says, *Troie* 5279-80:

> Mais les sorcilles li joigneient,
> Que auques li mesaveneient.

Antiquity regarded joined eyebrows as beautiful; see articles by G. P. Krapp in *Mod. Lang. Notes* 19.235, and by G. L. Hamilton, *ibid.* 20.80.

815-817. Compare *Fil.* 1.27:

> Il viso aveva adorno di bellezza
> Celestiale.

Compare also *Fil.* 4.100. Dryden seems to have remembered this passage of Chaucer in *Absalom and Achitophel* 30.

825. Chaucer's *slydynge of corage* echoes Benoit, *Troie* 5286:

> Mais sis corages li chanjot,

and Guido, *Historia*, sig. e 2, a, col. 2: "animi constantiam non servasset." In Dares and in Joseph, who know nothing of the loves of Briseis, there is no mention of her fickleness.

827-840. Chaucer's portrait of Troilus is less dependent on sources than are the portraits of Diomede and Criseyde; but

Joseph of Exeter's description (4.60-3) has contributed several details:

> Troilus in spacium surgentes explicat artus,
> Mente gigas, etate puer, nullique secundus
> Audendo virtutis opus; mixtoque vigore
> Gratior illustres insignit gloria vultus.

In the margin of stanza 119, the scribe of J has written: "Troilus in spacium/surgentes expli/cat arcus/Mente gigas eta/te puer, mixtoque/vigore"; and in the margin of stanza 120: "Nullique secundus/virtutis opis." In Gg, between lines 826 and 827, the scribe has written:

> *Versus* Troilus in spacium surgentes explicat artus
> *Versus* Mente gigas etate puer mixtoque vigore
> *Versus* Nullique secundus audendo virtutis opis.

It is to be noted that, both in J and Gg, the words *mixtoque vigore* are transposed from their proper place.

In the prose Dares (Cap. 12), the portrait of Troilus is very brief: "Troilum magnum, pulcherrimum, pro aetate valentem, fortem, cupidum virtutis." Benoit, *Troie* 5393-446, expands these hints without adding any significant details. See also Guido, *Historia*, sig. e 2, b, col. 1-2.

832. *Beste entecched*, imbued with best qualities; see *NED* s.v. Entach.

835-837. Chaucer is here following Joseph; see preceding note. In 2.158, however, Troilus is "The wise, worthi Ector the secounde"; see note on that passage. *Duryng don*, daring to do (see *NED* s.v. Dare, vb. 1, 6), translates Joseph's *audendo*. S1 has marginal gloss: "audendo." The phrase proved puzzling to some of the scribes; see variant readings of lines 837, 840.

842. Boccaccio, *Fil.* 6.9, puts this episode on the *fourth* day after Criseida's departure from Troy. Chaucer gains in irony by making the scene synchronous with the eager waiting of Troilus.

850. *Ethe*, easy; see *NED* s.v. Eath.

852. Spiced wine, served as a light entertainment offered to guests between meals, or at the very end of the evening; compare *Squire's Tale*, F 291-5, where it is served between dinner and supper, and see 3.674 and note. Compare also *Gawain and the Green Knight* 979-80.

883-884. From *Fil.* 6.15:

> Li Troian son, si può dire, in prigione.

892. Chaucer uses *Manes* as equivalent to "infernal deities." Compare Virgil, *Georg.* 1.243; *Aen.* 6.743; Statius, *Theb.* 8.84, where *Manes* is used as a metaphor for *poenae* or *supplicia*. The Greeks will strike terror even to the deities of hell.

897. *Ambages*, equivocations, ambiguities; see *NED* s.v. Ambage. Chaucer has taken over the word from *Fil.* 6.17:

> Se Calcas per *ambage* e per errori.

He thinks it necessary to explain the word in line 898.

932-938. Tydeus, Diomede's father, King of Calydon, led the expedition of the seven against Thebes. He was killed in battle, and his death was a severe blow to Polynices, whose cause Tydeus was supporting. Compare 5.1501. Chaucer is translating *Fil.* 6.24:

> Se'l padre mio Tideo fosse vissuto,
> Com'el fu morto a Tebe combattendo,
> Di Calidonia e d'Argo saria suto
> Re, siccom'io ancora essere intendo.

938. *Polymytes*, Polynices; compare 5.1488, 1507.

940. The subject of *ben* is implied in the pronoun *youre* of the preceding line. Note the scribal emendations of Ph and Cx.

953-1008. Criseyde's reply to Diomede follows closely *Fil.* 6.26-31. Lines 1000-3, however, are from Benoit; see note below.

971. The Orkney Islands, off the north coast of Scotland, are the most northwesterly, and India the most southeasterly regions of the habitable globe, according to medieval geography. Dante thought of the mouths of the Ganges as ninety degrees east from Jerusalem (*Purg.* 2.5); and medieval maps show India as extending south and east from China. In *Wife of Bath's Prologue*, D 824, Denmark and India are mentioned as extreme limits; compare also *Pardoner's Tale*, C 722; *Duchess* 889; Boethius, 3. m 5. The Orcades are mentioned as a remote region by Juvenal, *Sat.* 2.161.

975. Compare 1.97.

977. Criseyde invokes Pallas (Minerva) as a female deity, and as patroness of Troy. The invocation is repeated in 5.999. Compare also 2.425.

992-993. "When I see what I have never yet seen, then I will do what I have never done." Should the Greeks win the town of Troy, Criseyde may relent.

1000-1001. Compare Benoit, *Troie* 13677-9:

> Si poëz bien estre certains,
> S'a ço me voleie aproismier,
> Nul plus de vos n'avreie chier.

These lines are spoken by Briseida to Diomede, as he accompanies her on her ride from Troy to the Grecian camp. There is no corresponding speech in Guido.

1002-1003. Compare Benoit, *Troie* 13673-5:

> Ne jo nos refus autrement.
> Mais n'ai corage ne talent
> Que vos ne autre aim aparmains.

Chaucer's lines are nearer to Guido, *Historia*, sig. i 2, b, col. 1: "Amoris tui oblationem ad presens nec repudio nec admitto."

1010-1011. Compare Benoit, *Troie* 15053-6.

1013. This detail is not found in *Filostrato*. Benoit says, *Troie* 13709-11:

> Un de ses guanz li a toleit,
> Que nus nel set ne aparceit:
> Mout s'en fait liez.

Guido, *Historia*, sig. i 2, b, col. 1-2: *Bellum sextum*, says: "unam de cirothecis quam Briseida gerebat in manu ab ea, nullo percipiente, furtive subtraxit." Both in Benoit and in Guido, this taking of the glove is at the end of Briseida's ride from Troy to her father's tent.

1016-1020. Venus was evening star. As such, she followed the Sun in her setting, and by her bright shining in the western sky pointed to the place where he had gone down. Cynthia, the Moon, was urging the horses of her chariot to reach the end of the sign Leo—so that the ten days are nearly ended (cf. 4.1590-6). Since the Moon and the Sun (4.32) are both in Leo, the Moon is not visible; and Signifer's candles would therefore shine brightly. Signifer is the zodiacal belt which "carries" the twelve signs. For the word *Signifer*, see Claudian, *In Rufinum* 1.365, and Pliny, *Nat. Hist.* 2.10.7. ¶ 48.

1023-1024. Compare 2.601-2 ; 3.1541-2.

1030. *Gostly* should mean "spiritually, devoutly." In the present context, it seems to mean "with the certitude which pertains to things of the spirit."

1037-1039. The episode of the "faire baye stede," which is found neither in Boccaccio nor in Guido, is taken from Benoit, *Troie* 15079-172. Diomede had captured the steed of Troilus, and had presented it to Briseida. When Diomede loses his own charger, he asks Briseida to give him the horse of Troilus. Briseida says she will lend it to him. Compare 1.1073, where Troilus mounts his "stede bay," and 2.624. Benoit does not specify the color of the horse.

1040-1041. The episode of the brooch is from *Fil.* 8.8-10, where Troilo discovers it on a cloak which Deiphebus has captured from Diomede. Compare 5.1646-66.

1042-1043. From Benoit, *Troie* 15176-9 :

> La destre manche de son braz
> Nueve e fresche d'un ciglaton
> Li baille en lieu de confanon.
> Joie a cil qui por li se peine.

The episode is not found in Boccaccio nor in Guido.

1044-1050. Chaucer found the material for this stanza, which has no counterpart in *Filostrato*, in Benoit, *Troie* 20131-46, 20202-28. He might also have found it in Guido, *Historia*, sig. k 6, b, col. 2—sig. l 1, a, col. 1 : *Bellum undecimum*. With line 1045, compare also *Troie* 555-8 (from the introductory *resumé*).

1051-1085. This passage, which has no counterpart in Boccaccio, is based on a long speech of Briseida in *Troie* 20237-340. Compare in particular the following lines :

> De mei n'iert ja fait bon escrit
> Ne chantee bone chançon. (20237-8)
>
> · · ·   · · ·   · · ·
>
> Lor paroles de mei tendront
> Les dames que a Troie sont.
> Honte i ai fait as dameiseles
> Trop lait e as riches puceles. (20257-60)
>
> · · ·   · · ·   · · ·

E que me vaut, se m'en repent?
En ço n'a mais recovrement.
Serai donc a cestui leiaus,
Qui mout est proz e bons vassaus. (20275-8)

. . .   .

Trop poüsse ore consirer
E plaindre e mei desconforter
E endurer jusqu'a la mort:
N'eüsse ja de la confort. (20291-4)

. . .   .

Ensi est or, jo n'en sai plus.
Deus donge bien a Troïlus!
Quant nel puis aveir, ne il mei,
A cestui me doing e otrei. (20317-20)

In Guido, *Historia*, sig. l 1, a, col. 1: *Bellum undecimum,* the final surrender of Briseida to Diomede is treated only in a brief summary.

1062. *My belle shal be ronge,* my infamy will be proclaimed; compare 2.804-5. This is apparently a proverbial phrase; compare Gower, *Conf. Am.* 2.1727-9:

How Perse after his false tunge
Hath so thenvious belle runge,
That he hath slain his oghne brother.

(i.e. Perseus spread abroad lying stories that Demetrius had slain his own brother.) Compare also Lydgate, *Compl. of Black Knight* 262:

And Fals-Report so loude rong the belle.

1084. "I leave you through no fault of yours."

1086-1092. It is true, as Chaucer says, that his authors do not say in so many words how long a time elapses before Criseyde surrenders to Diomede; but if one takes careful heed of the time-indications in the book of Benoit, one finds that between the arrival of Briseida at the Grecian camp and her final acceptance of Diomede there is an interval of *at least* twenty-one months. Briseida arrives in the truce between the Seventh and Eighth Battles. The Eighth Battle lasts a month (*Troie* 14516), and is followed by a truce of six months (15187). The short Ninth Battle is followed by a truce of one month (15221). It is in the

Tenth Battle that Hector is killed. At the end of the Eleventh Battle a year has passed since his death (17489). Between the Thirteenth and Fourteenth Battles there is a truce of two months (19384). Between the Fourteenth and Fifteenth there is a week's truce (20060). It is in the Fifteenth Battle that Diomede is severely wounded. Shortly thereafter Briseida surrenders. The total elapsed time can hardly be less than two full years.

1095. I adopt the reading *punysshed*, which has a preponderance of MS. authority. I regard *publisshed* of H2RCxPhTh as a scribal substitution of a more familiar for a less familiar phrase. It is to be noted that, though H2 reads *publisshed*, the closely related H4 reads *punysshid*. Criseyde's name, her reputation, has been so widely punished, that her guilt needs no other penalty.

1107. H4 glosses "laurigerus"; and the closely related H2 reads: "The Laurer Laurgerus crouned Phebus." Compare Ovid, *Art. Am.* 3.389: "Visite laurigero sacrata Palatia Phoebo."

1110. H4 glosses: "nisus: rex; douhter: allauda." Scylla, daughter of King Nisus, was metamorphosed into the bird "ciris" (Ovid, *Met.* 8.11-151), which is identified with the lark. Compare Virgil, *Georg.* 1.405-9.

1115. *Come*, preterite subjunctive.

1124. *Doone* represents the O.E. gerundive *dōnne*, and is here dissyllabic.

1126. The hour of dinner was about 10 a.m.; see 2.1557, and *Shipman's Tale*, B 1394-444. Criseyde could not remain to dinner with her father, and have time to reach Troy before noon. Troilus and Pandarus go to a late dinner at noon (line 1129).

1134. "Fortune intends to beguile them both." Compare 4.3.

1140. Troilus will see that the city gate is kept open longer than usual; compare 5.1177-80.

1162. Just what sort of a vehicle a *fare-carte* may be is not clear. I have found no other instance of the phrase. It would seem to mean a cart used for merchandise, and not, therefore, the sort of vehicle in which a lady would travel. *Fil.* 7.8 has merely *carro*. H2H4 substitute *a soory carte*.

1174-1175. "From the hazel-wood, where jolly Robin played," i.e. from the land of fancy. It will never come at all. Robin and Marion were hero and heroine of many thirteenth century *pas-*

tourelles, and were taken over by Adam de la Halle into his *Gieus de Robin et de Marion* (end of thirteenth century) a pastoral comedy which continued its popularity into the fifteenth century. See Monmerqué et Michel, *Théatre Français au Moyen Age* 26-8, 102-35, and compare *Twelfth Night* 4.2.78.

1176. "Good-bye to the snow of last year"; see *NED* s.v. Fernyear. Some of the scribes, misunderstanding the word, changed it to *feverer,* February; see variant readings. This proverbial phrase, which means "It is all done and finished," appears in Villon's famous *Ballade des Dames du Temps Jadis:* "Mais où sont les neiges d'antan !".

1177-1180. These lines follow closely *Fil.* 7.11.

1185. The grounds on which Troilus believed that he had miscounted his day are clearer in Boccaccio. Troilo decides that Criseida had meant to say that she would remain ten days with her father, and then return. He should have expected her, then, on the eleventh day *(Fil.* 7.12-13). The promise of the Italian Criseida was not couched in terms of the Moon's progress. Chaucer's Troilus thinks he has misunderstood the precise position of the Moon which was to mark her return; or perhaps he thinks that he has miscalculated the Moon's position.

1187-1190. Compare 4.1590-6.

1212-1214. From *Fil.* 7.18: "e 'l nemico Spirto di gelosia"; compare 3.808, 837, 1010.

1219. *Defet,* see note to 5.618.

1222. *Potente,* a staff with a cross-piece to lean upon; see *NED* s.v. Potent, sb. and compare *Summoner's Tale,* D 1776.

1233-1243. The dream of Troilus is taken from *Fil.* 7.23-4. In the Italian, however, the boar is tearing out Criseida's heart with his claws—but Criseida "quasi piacere Prendea di ciò che fece l' animale."

1275-1278. Pandarus, who had previously (5.360-85) denied the significance of dreams, now takes the more orthodox position that dreams deceive us because we wrongly interpret them. On the difficulty of interpretation, see Albertus Magnus, *De Somno et Vigilia* 3.2.9. Chaucer is following closely *Fil.* 7.40.

1317-1421. The letter of Troilus is freely adapted from *Fil.* 7.52-75.

1321. Compare 5.445 and note.

1322. Since "Nature abhors a vacuum," space is always occupied by matter.

1348. *Fil.* 7.54 gives the time as forty days.

1368. "Receptacle of every sorrow."

1375-1379. These lines, which have no counterpart in Boccaccio, resemble *Duchess* 599-616. Compare *Rose* (Langlois) 4293-330.

1431. "Bottomless promises," i.e. without foundation; see *NED* s.v. Bottomless, 1 b.

1432-1433. Troilus may spend his time blowing on an ivy leaf to make a squeaking noise. He will have no more amusing occupation; for Criseyde will not return. So Theseus, explaining to Palamon and Arcite that one or the other of them must be disappointed in his love for Emily, says, *Knight's Tale*, A 1837-8:

> That oon of yow, al be him looth or leef,
> He moot go pypen in an ivy leef.

Compare Usk, *Testament of Love* 3.7.50: "He may pype with an yve-lefe; his frute is fayled." See Hazlitt, p. 486: "To pipe with an ivy leaf, to go and engage in any sterile or idle occupation."

1440. I adopt the reading *ne no word* of H4RCx, which receives additional support from H3Gg. *No* is necessary to the metre, unless *word* be pronounced as a dissyllable with vocalic *r*.

1443-1449. Compare 5.1233-43. Troilus adopts the belief that dreams are divine revelations. Compare note on 5.360-85, and see 5.1714-15.

1450. The term sibyl is used generically for a female prophet. Isidore of Seville says, *Etymol.* Lib. 8, Cap. 8: "Sicut enim omnis vir prophetans, vel *vates* dicitur, vel *propheta*, ita omnis femina prophetans *Sibylla* vocatur. Quod nomen ex officio, non ex proprietate vocabuli est." Cassandra is called "Sibille" in Gower, *Conf. Am.* 5.7451-5. G. C. Macaulay in his note on that passage cites Godfrey of Viterbo, *Pantheon* (ed. 1584), p. 214. Hamilton, p. 158, quotes the passage from Pistorius, *Scriptores de Rebus Germanicis* 2.157: "Fuit igitur haec Sibylla Priami regis filia, et ex matre Hecuba procreata. Vocata est autem in Graeco Tiburtina; Latine vero Albunea nomine, vel Cassandra." Chaucer, following some such authority, clearly regards the names *Sibille* and *Cassandre* as alternative names of the same person.

1451. Cassandra was the second of the three daughters of Priam and Hecuba, and so own sister to Troilus (*Troie* 2953). She predicted the ruin of Troy if Paris should wed a Greek wife. Her prophecies are disregarded; and on two occasions she is locked in her room so that people may not have to listen to her. See the *Table des Noms Propres* in Constans' edition of *Troie*. In *Filostrato* (7.77-102), Deiphebus overhears a lament of Troilo from which he discovers that his brother is pining away for love of Criseida. He communicates the fact to his other brothers. They send their sisters to comfort Troilo; but Cassandra taunts him with his love for the daughter of a wicked priest, a lady below his princely rank. Troilo rebukes her for talking too much, and for prying into secrets. It is Chaucer who makes her the interpreter of Troilus' dream. In Boccaccio (*Fil.* 7.25-8), Troilo interprets the dream himself.

1459-1461. The "fewe of olde stories" may be found in the *Thebais* of Statius and the *Metamorphoses* of Ovid.

1464-1479. The story of the Calydonian boar is told by Ovid, *Met.* 8.270-444.

1472. *A mayde*, Atalanta.

1480-1481. Chaucer's authority for the statement that Tydeus was descended from Meleager is found in *Fil.* 7.27:

> Questo cinghiar ch'io vidi è Diomede,
> Perocchè l'avolo uccise il cinghiaro
> Di Calidonia, se si può dar fede
> A'nostri antichi.

As a matter of fact, "olde bookes" and "nostri antichi" report that Tydeus was *brother* to Meleager. It was the *uncle* of Diomede who killed the boar, and not the grandfather (avolo). In *Gen. Deorum*, Lib. 9, Boccaccio gives the family relationships correctly.

1482-1483. The story of Meleager's death is told by Ovid, *Met.* 8.445-525. His mother, Althaea, incensed at Meleager's killing of her two brothers, threw into the fire the fatal brand. As it consumed in the flames, Meleager died.

1485-1491. This stanza summarizes the first two books of the *Thebais* of Statius. The form *Polymytes* (or *Polymite*) for *Poly-*

nices is used consistently by Chaucer (cf. 5.938), and is found in the Latin summary which follows 5.1498. For this form, see *Roman de Thèbes*, ed. Constans, Vol. 2, p. clix, n. 1.

1492-1494. Hemonydes, i.e. Maeon, son of Haemon, was one of fifty Thebans sent by Eteocles to waylay Tydeus. The latter, single-handed, slew forty-nine of the company, but spared Maeon that he might return to Thebes and tell the story. His return is told near the beginning of the third book of the *Thebais*. The latter part of the book contains the prophecies of Amphiaraus.

1495-1498. These lines summarize books IV and V of the *Thebais*. The "holy serpent," sent by Jupiter, kills Archemorus, infant son of King Lycurgus.

1498. After line 1498, all the authorities, except H4R, contain in the body of the text twelve lines of Latin verse, which summarize the twelve books of the *Thebais* of Statius. This summary is expanded by Chaucer in lines 1485-510. The Latin verses are inserted in the middle of the passage, apparently by way of justification for the English summary. Their presence is probably due to Chaucer himself; but, since they are omitted by H4 and R, which in Book V represent the poem in its final state, and since they are in the nature of a gloss, I have relegated them to the bottom of the page. This argument of the *Thebais* is printed in the Delphin edition, 2.592, and in the edition of Lemaire. M. Manitius, in *Rheinisches Museum für Philologie* 57.397-8 (1902), prints the summary from a thirteenth century MS. of Statius in the Royal Library at Dresden. See also article by G. L. Hamilton in *Mod. Lang. Notes* 23.127.

The summary is found in H2 (though here a MS. closely related to H4) with a unique additional line: "Fervidus ypomedon timidique in gurgite mersus." *Timidique* is a corrupt reading of *tumidoque*. The line is taken from a twelve-line argument to the ninth book of the *Thebais* found in certain MSS.; see Delphin ed. 3.1251, and compare 5.1502-3. The phrase "holy serpent" in line 1497 echoes (as Dr. F. P. Magoun has pointed out to me) the "sacro serpente" of the twelve-line argument to Book V. Chaucer clearly knew these arguments; but his summary contains details which they do not mention.

1499. The sixth book of Statius is devoted to the funeral of

Archemorus. His body is burned on a splendid pyre, and the ashes are placed in a magnificent tomb. Elaborate games are instituted in his honor. In *Roman de Thèbes* 2621-30, the child is buried, unburned, in a marble tomb. Though the Latin summary reads "Archemori *bustum*," the reading *Archymoris burying* seems to be authentic. *Brennynge* of Gg and D is probably a scribal emendation introduced independently by these unrelated MSS. Note, however, the reading *burynge* of ClH1J.

1500. See note on 2.100-8. The death of Amphiaraus is told at the end of the seventh book of the *Thebais*.

1501. See *Thebais* VIII.

1502-1503. See *Thebais* IX. Hippomedon is drowned in the river Ismenus. Parthenopaeus died of wounds received at the hands of Dryas.

1504-1505. See *Thebais* X. Capaneus scaled the walls of Thebes, and from their height hurled rocks into the city. In his pride he shouted blasphemous defiance against the gods. Jupiter struck him dead with a thunderbolt.

1506-1508. See *Thebais* XI.

1509. See *Thebais* XII. Argyve, i.e. Argia, wife of Polynices, bewails her slain husband. Compare note to 4.762.

1510. After the repulse of the Greek assault on Thebes, Creon refuses to permit the burial of the slain Greeks. The widows appeal to Theseus, who marches against Thebes, captures the city, slays Creon, and gives funeral honors to the fallen Greeks. Compare *Knight's Tale*, A 893-1004. Neither in the *Thebais* nor in the *Knight's Tale* does Theseus *burn* the city. In *Roman de Thèbes* 10131 he hurls fire into the city. The Latin summary contains the word "ignem" (for which one should probably read *ignes*); but the reference is to funeral fires.

1527-1533. This brief summary of the story of Alcestis, who died that her husband Admetus might live, resembles that in *Legend*, B 510-16, A 498-504. In what book Chaucer read the story has not been determined; but, as Skeat has shown (*Oxford Chaucer* 3. xxix), all the details which Chaucer mentions are contained in the short account given by Boccaccio in *De Genealogia Deorum*, Lib. 13, Cap. 1. In the *Legend*, Chaucer adds, apparently out of his own fancy, that Alcestis was changed into a daisy. Gower tells the story, with some modifications and elaborations, in *Conf. Am.* 7.1917-49, as an example of woman's truth and love.

1540. *Drieth*, endures, suffers; see *NED* s.v. Dree, vb. The variant reading *dryveth* is certainly a scribal corruption.

1541-1545. For the conception of Fortune as the agency of divine providence, see 3.617 and note. The present passage is clearly influenced by Dante, *Inf.* 7.78-82:

> Ordinò general ministra e duce [Fortuna]
> Che permutasse a tempo li ben' vani
> Di gente in gente e d'uno in altro sangue,
> Oltre la difension de'senni umani.
> Perché una gente impera e l'altra langue.

1545. *Smytted*, tarnished, sullied, brought to disgrace; see *NED* s.v. Smit, vb., 1 c.

1546. For the metaphor, see *NED* s.v. Feather, sb., 1 b.

1548. *Parodie* seems to be a mistaken adaptation of the French *periode*. CpH1H4 gloss the word "duracioun." Lydgate has taken over the word from Chaucer; see citations of *NED* s.v. Parody, sb. 2. The word appears as *paryode* in Caxton's edition of the *Pilgrimage of the Sowle* (*NED* s.v. Period). *NED* cites no instance of *period*, correctly spelled, earlier than 1530.

1548-1561. The episode of Hector's death, which is not in *Filostrato*, is told at length by Benoit, *Troie* 16007-316. That Chaucer is following Benoit is shown by the following passage (16215-28).

> Li cri i sont grant e li hu,
> Qu'*Ector ot un rei abatu*;
> Prendre le vout e retenir
> E as lor par force tolir:
> *Par la ventaille* le teneit,
> *Fors de la presse le traeit*,
> De son escu ert descoverz.
> E quant l'aparceit li coilverz,—
> C'est Achillès qui le haeit,—
> Cele part est alez tot dreit.
> Dreit a lui broche le destrier:
> *Nel pot quarir l'auberc doblier*
> *Que tot le feie e le poumon*
> *Ne li espande* sor l'arçon.

The corresponding passage in Guido (*Historia*, sig. i 6, a, col. 1 : *Bellum octavum*) is less detailed. Compare, however: "Quod Achilles, dum persensit Hectorem ante pectus scuti sui subsidium non habere, accepta quadam lancea valde forti, *non advertente Hectore*, velociter in Hectorem irruit," which suggests Chaucer's "Unwar of this."

1558. The aventail is the "movable front or mouthpiece of a helmet, which may be raised to admit fresh air"; see *NED* s.v. Aventail, Ventail.

1562-1563. The lamentations of the Trojans at the death of Hector are recounted by Benoit, *Troie* 16317-502. See in particular lines 16357-9:

> La est li dueus si angoissos,
> Si pesmes e si doloros
> Que nus nel porreit reconter.

The corresponding account in Guido is found in *Historia*, sig. i 6, col. 1-2 : *Sepultura Hectoris*. But Chaucer is following *Fil.* 8.1 :

> L' alto dolor, da non poter mai dire.

1564-1589. From *Fil.* 8.1-5.

1590-1631. This letter of Criseyde has no counterpart in *Filostrato*.

1634. *Kalendes of chaunge*, the beginning of a change; compare 2.7 and note. Chaucer seems here to be playing on a phrase, "calends of exchange," which is cited by *NED* s.v. Calends, 3 a.

1646-1666. This episode follows closely *Fil.* 8.8-10; it is not found in Benoit or in Guido. Compare 5.1040-1. Neither Chaucer nor Boccaccio mentions the giving of this brooch in his account of the final parting of Troilus and Criseyde. Compare, however, 3.1356-8, where Criseyde gives Troilus a brooch of gold and azure.

1653. *Lollius*, compare 1.394, and see Introd., pp. xxxvi-xl.

1709-1715. Troilus insists that it is now proved that dreams are divine revelations; compare 5.360-85, 1443-9 and notes.

1748-1750. These lines point briefly the same moral given later at more length in lines 1835-48. Compare 3.836.

1751-1764. Chaucer is following *Fil.* 8.25-6. The martial exploits of Troilus are recounted at length by Benoit, *Troie* 19955-20156, 20462-600, 20832-7, 21005-189.

1771. *Dares*, see Introd., pp. xxi-xxii.

1777-1785. These lines foreshadow the *Legend of Good Women*, which was written shortly after *Troilus*. See in paritcular *Legend*, B 485-9, 2387, 2546.

1778. *Penelope* is apparently to be accented on the first and third syllables; compare *Cant. Tales*, B 75.

1786-1799. These stanzas constitute an envoy to the poem; but at line 1800 the narrative is resumed, and at line 1856 we find a second envoy. With lines 1786-8, compare *Fil.* 9.8 :

> Or va' : ch'io prego Apollo che ti presti
> Tanto di grazia ch'ascoltata sii,
> E con lieta risposta a me t'invii.

These lines conclude *Filostrato*. For further examples of the "Go little book" conceit, which goes back to the

> Parve, nec invideo, sine me, liber ibis in Urbem

of Ovid, *Tristia* 1.1.1, see Tatlock, "The Epilog of Chaucer's *Troilus*," *Mod. Phil.* 18.627-30.

1786. See note to 1.4, and Introd., pp. xlix-l.

1788. Having brought to conclusion the "tragedy" of Troilus, Chaucer naturally prays that he may now write a "comedy." (For the definition of "comedy," see note to 1.4.) It is not necessary to assume that Chaucer had any specific work in mind. The modern reader is tempted to think of the *comédie humaine* of the *Canterbury Tales*, certainly begun as early as 1387, and perhaps already in the poet's mind; but it is doubtful whether that work would have been designated as *comedia* by a medieval critic.

1789-1792. Statius concludes his *Thebais* with a prayer (12. 816-17) that the poem may live; but he warns his book not to emulate the *Aeneid* ;

> nec tu divinam Aeneida tempta,
> Sed longe sequere, et vestigia semper adora.

With these lines in mind, Chaucer bids his poem not to be emulous, but to be subject to all great poetry, and to kiss the footsteps, wherever his book may see Virgil, Ovid, Homer, Lucan, and Statius walking by. Boccaccio, in ending *Filocolo*, addresses "piccolo mio libretto" in a long envoy, which may well have been modelled on Statius, in which, among many other injunctions, he bids it to leave to great geniuses the great verses of Virgil, to leave to soldiers the verses of Lucan and of Statius. Let successful lovers follow Ovid. Seek not to be present where the measured verses of Dante are read, "il quale tu, siccome piccolo servidore, molto dei reverente seguire." Too much weight must not be attached to the fact that Boccaccio here names four of the five poets mentioned by Chaucer; they are the great names of narrative verse. Nothing else in *Filocolo* furnishes so close a parallel to Chaucer as the "*vestigia* semper adora" of Statius.

1791. *Space*, to walk (Latin *spatiari*); see *NED* s.v. Space, vb. 6. ClPhH4Th read *pace*; but of these authorities Ph and H4 are not reliable, and Th presents an edited text. The MS. authority is overwhelmingly in favor of *space*.

1793-1796. This passage suggests Chaucer's lines addressed to Adam, his own scrivener; see Introd., p. x. One of the causes which actually contributed to the corruption of Chaucer's text was the "gret diversite" of English dialects. MS. S1, for example, is colored by the native speech of its Scottish scribe. Diversity of dialect, and the changes in the spoken speech which were already under way in the poet's life-time, resulted in much "mismetring" of his text. See further Tatlock, "The Epilog to Chaucer's *Troilus*." *Mod. Phil.* 18.626, n. 1.

1797. One can hardly suppose that such a poem as *Troilus* was ever sung. Skeat suggested that *songe* means "read aloud, recited in an intoned voice." There is evidence in the poem itself that Chaucer had in mind a public reading of his poem. I suspect that the use of *sing* in connection with a poem is a conventional survival; compare Gower, *Conf. Am.* 3.330-1:

> Ha, who herde evere singe or rede
> Of such a thing as that was do?

1800-1806. This stanza is adapted from *Fil.* 8.27, which ends with the line:

> Miseramente un dì l'uccise Achille.

Benoit, *Troie* 21190-450, relates how, in the Nineteenth Battle, Achilles slew Troilus, and dragged his dead body at the tail of his horse; compare note to 3.374-5.

1807-1827. These stanzas are closely imitated from *Tes.* 11. 1-3 where Boccaccio is describing the death of Arcita:

Finito Arcita colei nominando,
La qual nel mondo più che altro amava,
L'anima lieve se ne gì volando
Ver la concavità del cielo ottava;
Degli elementi i convessi lasciando,
Quivi le stelle erratiche ammirava,
L'ordine loro e la somma bellezza,
Suoni ascoltando pien d'ogni dolcezza.

Quindi si volse in giù a rimirare
Le cose abbandonate, e vide il poco
Globo terreno, a cui d'intorno il mare
Girava e l'aere, e di sopra il foco,
Ed ogni cosa da nulla stimare
A rispetto del ciel; ma poi al loco
Là dove aveva il suo corpo lasciato
Gli occhi fermò alquanto rivoltato.

E seco rise de'pianti dolenti
Della turba lernea; la vanitate
Forte dannando delle umane genti,
Li qua' da tenebrosa cechitate,
Mattamente oscurata nelle menti,
Seguon del mondo la falsa biltate,
Lasciando il cielo; e quindi se ne gío
Nel loco a cui Mercurio la sortio.

It will be noticed that Chaucer's lines correspond, stanza by stanza, with Boccaccio's. The passage in *Teseide* finds its suggestion in the *Somnium Scipionis* of Cicero (*De Re Publica*, Lib. 6). One may consult Chaucer's summary of the passage in *Parliament* 29-84. For further discussion of this passage, which was not in Chaucer's first draft of *Troilus*, see Introd., p. lxxii.

1809-1813. *Teseide* 11.1 reads:

> Ver la concavità del cielo *ottava*.

This strongly supports the reading *eighte*, which I adopt on the authority of JRCx, as against *seventhe*, the reading of γS1Th+ H3Ph (on inset leaf), which I regard as a γ error introduced into H3 and Ph (see Introd., p. lxxviii). It is to be noted that the evidence of Gg is lost through mutilation of the volume. Scribal substitution of *vij* for *viij* is an easy corruption.

If we accept *eighte* as correct, (and we must accept Boccaccio's *ottava*, which falls under the rhyme), it remains to determine which of the spheres is meant. The old astronomy assumes eight star-bearing spheres, concentric with the Earth, of which seven carry, each, one of the planets, and the last contains the fixed stars. These spheres are numbered sometimes from the Earth outwards, as in Dante's *Paradiso*, sometimes in the reverse order, beginning with the planet Saturn, as in Chaucer's *Complaint of Mars* (where in line 29 Mars is lord of the third heaven). So also Gower, *Conf. Am.* 7.721-946, begins with the Moon and ends with Saturn. By this numbering, the eighth sphere is the sphere of the fixed stars, beyond the spheres of the planets. In *Franklin's Tale*, F 1280, and *Astrolabe* 1.21.55, the "eighte spere" is that of the fixed stars. But Boccaccio's stanzas are derived from the *Somnium Scipionis* of Cicero; and there the spheres ("globi") are numbered "a summo in imum," the Earth itself being "media et *nona*" (Cap. 17). It is in this order that Chaucer names the planetary gods in 3. 715-32. On this principle, the eighth sphere is that of the Moon, the nearest to the Earth. In support of this interpretation it may be noted (1) that Troilus, though able to see the planets "with ful avysement," is near enough to Earth to distinguish the spot "ther he was slayn," which he could hardly do from the eminence of the outermost sphere. (2) The line "In convers letyng everich element" refers clearly to terrestrial regions. According to the old cosmogony, the four elements are arranged, according to their lightness, in four layers: earth, water, air, fire (see Macrobius, *Comm. in Somn. Scip.* 1.22). Troilus, in his flight upwards, leaves behind him "in convers." (Is this an error for *in convess*, i.e. "in convex"? Boccaccio says "Degli elementi i *convessi* lasciando"; see *NED* s.v. Convers.) the elements of air and fire, and approaches the sphere of the Moon. So Dante and Beatrice mount upwards from the summit of the Mount of Purgatory, through the heaven of fire, to the sphere of the Moon. While passing through the heaven of fire, they first hear the harmony of the spheres (*Par.* 1.77-81), as Troilus hears it from his station in the "eighte spere." It is possible that Boccaccio, following the *Somnium Scipionis*, meant the sphere of the Moon, but that Chaucer understood it to be that of the fixed stars. It must be remembered, on the other hand, that, in Cicero, Scipio takes his stand in the Milky Way (Cap. 16.) Compare note to 3.1-2.

1812-1813. The allusion to the harmony of the spheres is from *Teseide*. Boccaccio found it in *Somnium Scipionis*, Cap. 18. Compare *Parliament* 59-63.

1814-1819. Compare *Somnium Scipionis*, Cap. 19-20: "te sedem etiam nunc hominum ac domum contemplari; quae si tibi parva, ut est, ita videtur, haec caelestia semper spectato, illa humana contemnito. . . . Omnis enim terra, quae colitur a vobis . . . parva quaedam insula est circumfusa illo mari, quod Atlanticum, quod magnum, quem Oceanum appellatis in terris." (See also *Parliament* 57-8.) Chaucer's "pleyn felicite" is his own Boethian addition to the passage of *Teseide*.

1827. Compare 5.321-2 and note.

1828-1834. This stanza returns to *Fil.* 8.28, which repeats four times the words "Cotal fine." Chaucer's line 1832 is a more generalized moral than Boccaccio's—

> Cotal fin' ebbe la speranza vana
> Di Troilo in Griseida villana.

1835-1848. In the corresponding passage of *Filostrato* (8.29), Boccaccio addresses "yonge freshe folkes"—

> O giovanetti, ne' quai coll'etate
> Surgendo vien l'amoroso disio—

and urges them to restrain evil appetite. They must take example from Troilo, and not lightly place faith in every beautiful lady, many of whom are vain and fickle. There is no hint of the high moral pointed by Chaucer. See Introd., pp. xlviii-l.

1837-1841. Compare Chaucer's *Balade de Bon Conseyl* ("Truth") 17-20:

> Her nis non hoom, her nis but wildernesse:
> Forth, pilgrim, forth! Forth, beste, out of thy stal!
> Know thy contree, look up, thank God of al;
> Hold the hye wey, and lat thy gost thee lede.

Compare also Hoccleve, *Regement of Princes* 1289:

> This lyf, my sone, is but a chirie-faire;

and Gower, *Conf. Am.* Prol. 454-5:

> For al is bot a chirie feire
> This worldes good, so as thei telle.

1849-1855. In this stanza, which has no counterpart in Boccaccio, Professor Tatlock sees a sort of antidote to the acceptance of the pagan gods and to the general pagan atmosphere of the poem; see "The Epilog of Chaucer's *Troilus*," *Mod. Phil.* 18. 635-59.

1853. Wise, p. 129, cites *Roman de Thèbes*, MS. S, 4341-2:

> Cil dui [Mars et Pallas] vailent en la bataille
> Plus qe toute l'autre *raschaille*.

1854. The context suggests that *forme* is here used in the sense given to *forma* by scholastic philosophy, i.e. "the essential principle of a thing which makes it what it is"; see *NED* s.v. Form, sb., 4 a. Chaucer uses the word in this sense in *Legend* 1582:

> As matere appetyteth forme alwey.

Compare also *Legend* 2228. The meaning of the sentence would then be: "See what is the essential principle which informs ancient pagan poetry!", i.e. a set of false gods, and "thise wrecched worldes appetites."

1856-1859. There is nothing in *Filostrato* which corresponds to these lines. The poem is "directed" only to Boccaccio's lady. But in other works of Boccaccio—*Ameto*, *Life of Dante*, *De Casibus*, *De Genealogia*—the book is addressed to a patron, with the request for revision and correction. For these and other parallels to Chaucer's lines, see Tatlock, "The Epilog to Chaucer's *Troilus*," *Mod. Phil.* 18.631-5. Compare 3.1405-12, and *Second Nun's Tale*, G 78-84.

1856. There can be no doubt that "moral Gower" is the poet, John Gower. He had already written his French poem, *Mirour de l'Omme* (about 1376-79), and his Latin poem, *Vox Clamantis* (soon after 1381). Each of these poems contains a moral analysis of human life and existing institutions which justifies Chaucer's epithet "moral," i.e. a writer of moral precepts" (see *NED* s.v. Moral, adj., 3 a). In *Confessio Amantis* (first version apparently published 1390), Gower returns the compliment of Chaucer's dedication by a graceful address to his brother poet (*Conf. Am.* 8.2941*-57*. The fact that this address is omitted in the later version of *Conf. Am.*, along with the praise of King Richard, may possibly, though not necessarily, imply that, when Gower turned from the king's party, his relations with Chaucer became less friendly. (See Macaulay's ed. of Gower, 2. xxvi-xxviii.) The friendship of the two poets dates at least from 1378, when, on the occasion of his second journey to Italy, Chaucer named John Gower as one of his attorneys to act for him in his absence.

1857. The epithet "philosophical" makes it fairly certain that the person intended is Ralph Strode, who was before 1360 a fellow of Merton College, Oxford, and who was the author of important writings on logic and philosophy. "His tendencies seem to have been realistic, but he followed in the footsteps of Albert the Great, Thomas Aquinas, and Bonaventura, the inaugurators of that 'school of the middle' whose members were called nominalists by extreme realists, and realists by extreme nominalists." (*DNB*.) At Oxford he was an opponent of Wiclif, but seems, none the less, to have been on friendly terms with him. Apparently Strode was a poet as well as a philosopher. A fifteenth century catalogue of the fellows of Merton College says: "Nobilis poeta fuit et versificavit librum elegiacum vocatum Phantasma Radulphi" (*DNB*). This poem has not been identified.

In 1373, soon after the last mention of Strode in the records of Merton College, a Ralph Strode was elected Common Pleader of the City of London. He was subsequently Standing Counsel for the City and a sergeant-at-arms. He died in 1387. From 1373 to 1382, while Chaucer was living in the dwelling over Aldgate, the lawyer Strode occupied a similar mansion over the neighboring Aldersgate. There is good ground for believing that the Oxford philosopher and the London lawyer are one and the same person. For a fuller account of Strode, see the article by Sir Israel Gollancz in *DNB* s.v. Strode, Ralph, and an article by E. P. Kuhl, "Some Friends of Chaucer," in *P.M.L.A.* 29.272-5.

1863-1865. These lines are closely modeled on Dante, *Par.* 14.28-30:

Quell' Uno e Due e Tre che sempre vive,
E regna sempre in Tre e Due e Uno,
Non circonscritto, e tutte circonscrive.

Dante and Beatrice are in the Fourth Heaven (of the Sun) among the doctors of philosophy and theology.

1866. The reading of H2R has every appearance of being a genuine β reading; but, since H4, closely related to H2, and Cx do not support it, I have not adopted it into the text.

1868. The reading *take* of H2R fits the context better than *make* of the other authorities. I have, however, been unwilling to adopt it into the text on the basis of such slight attestation. Compare preceding note.

BIBLIOGRAPHICAL LIST
Of Certain Books and Articles Frequently Cited in this Edition

AYRES, H. M., "Chaucer and Seneca," *Romanic Review* 10. 1-15 (1919).

I am indebted to this article for the Senecan parallels given in the notes.

BENOIT DE SAINTE-MAURE, *Le Roman de Troie*, ed. L. Constans, Société des Anciens Textes Français, 6 vols., Paris, 1904-1912.

BOCCACCIO, G., *Il Filostrato*, ed. P. Savj-Lopez, (Bibliotheca Romanica, Nos. 146-148), Strasburg, n.d.

The text of this convenient edition is a reprint of that given by I. Moutier, *Opere Volgari di Giovanni Boccaccio*, Florence, 1827-1834, Vol. 12. Citations are by canto and stanza. I have occasionally quoted from the Paris edition of 1789, where its reading differs significantly from that of the Moutier text. In this edition the numbering of cantos and stanzas is at variance with that of Moutier. Despite many omissions and obvious corruptions, this text sometimes presents a reading closer than that of Moutier to Chaucer's copy of the poem. A critical edition of *Il Filostrato* is greatly to be desired.

A very readable translation is that of Hubertis Cummings, Princeton, 1924. The prose translation by W. M. Rossetti, published in the Chaucer Society volume, *Chaucer's Troylus and Cryseyde compared with Boccaccio's Filostrato*, is convenient for purposes of comparison with the English poem, but is too fragmentary to give any adequate idea of Boccaccio's poem as a whole.

BOCCACCIO, G., *Filocolo, Opere Volgari*, ed. I. Moutier, Florence, 1827-1834, Vols. 7 and 8.

Citations are by volume and page. For the parallels from *Filocolo* given in the notes, I am usually indebted to Young, *Origin and Development*.

BOCCACCIO, G., *La Teseide, Opere Volgari*, ed. Moutier, Vol. 9. Citations are by book and stanza.

BRUSENDORFF, A., *The Chaucer Tradition*, Copenhagen and London, [1925]. On pages 166-74, the author discusses briefly, but with a somewhat facile assurance, the textual tradition of *Troilus*, and dissents from the conclusions of my

Chaucer Society study of the text. Much of the pertinent evidence is disregarded. The book came to my hands after this edition was in final page-proof; but, even if it had appeared earlier, I should have found no occasion to modify my position.

CHAUCER, G., *Works*, ed. W. W. Skeat, 6 vols., Oxford, 1894. A supplementary volume contains works formerly attributed to Chaucer, including Usk's *Testament of Love*. My citations of Chaucer, other than those from *Troilus*, are from Skeat's text.

CONSTANS, L. See Benoit de Sainte-Maure, and *Roman de Thèbes*.

CUMMINGS, H. M., *The Indebtedness of Chaucer's Works to the Italian Works of Boccaccio*, (Princeton Diss.), Cincinnati, 1916.

DÜRINGSFELD, IDA VON, UND OTTO FREIHERR VON REINSBERG-DÜRINGSFELD, *Sprichwörter der Germanischen und Romanischen Sprachen*. 2 vols., Leipzig, 1872-1875. References are to volume and serial number.

FANSLER, D. S., *Chaucer and the Roman de la Rose*, (Columbia Diss.), New York, 1914.
This volume contains the fullest treatment of Chaucer's debt to the *Roman de la Rose*, superseding earlier studies by Koeppel, Skeat, and Cipriani. I am frequently indebted to it in my notes.

GUIDO DELLE COLONNE, *Historia Trojana*, Strasburg, 1489. Citations are by signature, folio, and column.

HAMILTON, G. L., *The Indebtedness of Chaucer's Troilus and Criseyde to Guido delle Colonne's Historia Trojana*, (Columbia Diss.), New York, 1903.

HAMMOND, E. P., *Chaucer, a Bibliographical Manual*, New York, 1908.

HAZLITT, W. C., *English Proverbs and Proverbial Phrases*, London, 1907.

JEFFERSON, B. L., *Chaucer and the Consolation of Philosophy of Boethius*, (Princeton Diss.), 1917.

JOSEPH OF EXETER, *Frigii Daretis Ilias*. The most available edition is in Valpy's reissue of the Delphin Classics, London, 1825, where it is included in one volume with the texts of Dares and Dictys under the title, "Josephi Iscani de Bello Trojano Libri Sex."

KITTREDGE, G. L., "Chaucer's Lollius," *Harvard Studies in Classical Philology* 28. 47-133 (1917).

KITTREDGE, G. L., *The Date of Chaucer's Troilus and other*

Chaucer Matters, Chaucer Society, Second Series, No. 42, 1909.

KITTREDGE, G. L., *Observations on the Language of Chaucer's Troilus*, Chaucer Society, Second Series, No. 28, 1891.

LE ROUX DE LINCY, A. J. V., *Le Livre des Proverbes Français*, 2d ed., 2 vols., Paris, 1859. References are to volume and page.

LOWES, J. L., "Chaucer and Dante," *Modern Philology* 14. 705-35 (1917). This article speaks the final word hitherto on Chaucer's use of Dante. I am frequently indebted to it in my notes.

Roman de la Rose, par Guillaume de Lorris et Jean de Meun, ed. E. Langlois, Société des Anciens Textes Français, Paris, 1914— (4 vols. hitherto published). I have cited this edition up to line 19438, the point reached by Vol. 4 (1922). After that point, I have cited the edition of F. Michel, Paris, 1864.

Roman de Thèbes, ed. L. Constans, Société des Anciens Textes Français, 2 vols, Paris, 1890.

ROOT, R. K., *The Manuscripts of Chaucer's Troilus*, Chaucer Society, First Series, No. 98, 1914.

ROOT, R. K., *The Textual Tradition of Chaucer's Troilus*, Chaucer Society, First Series, No. 99, 1916.

SKEAT, W. W., *Early English Proverbs*, Oxford, 1910.

SPURGEON, CAROLINE F. E., *Five Hundred Years of Chaucer Criticism and Allusion*, Chaucer Society, Second Series, Nos. 48, 49, 50, 52, 1914-1921.

TATLOCK, J. S. P., *The Development and Chronology of Chaucer's Works*, Chaucer Society, Second Series, No. 37, 1907.

TEN BRINK, B., *The Language and Metre of Chaucer*, trans. M. Bentinck Smith, London, 1901.

THORNDIKE, L., *A History of Magic and Experimental Science during the First Thirteen Centuries of our Era*, 2 vols., New York, 1923.

WILD, F., *Die Sprachlichen Eigentümlichkeiten der wichtigeren Chaucer-Handschriften, Wiener Beiträge zur Englischen Philologie*, Band 44, 1915.

WISE, B. A., *The Influence of Statius upon Chaucer*, (Johns Hopkins Diss.), Baltimore, 1911.

YOUNG, K., *The Origin and Development of the Story of Troilus and Criseyde*, Chaucer Society, Second Series, No., 41, 1908.

YOUNG, K., "Aspects of the Story of Troilus and Criseyde," *University of Wisconsin Studies in Language and Literature* 2. 367-94.

INDEX OF PROPER NAMES

[571]